The Theory
and Practice of
INTERNATIONAL RELATIONS

The Theory and

Practice of

PRENTICE-HALL, INC.

Englewood Cliffs, N. J.

INTERNATIONAL RELATIONS

David S. McLellan

Assistant Professor of Political Science
University of California at Riverside

William C. Olson

Associate Professor of Political Science
Pomona College
Chairman of the Committee
on International Relations

Fred A. Sondermann

Associate Professor of Political Science
The Colorado College

THE THEORY AND PRACTICE OF
INTERNATIONAL RELATIONS

McLellan, Olson, Sondermann

Library of Congress Catalog Card No.: 60–12289

First printing ....July, 1960

Second printing ....June, 1961

Third printing ....June, 1962

Fourth printing ....June, 1965

Printed in the United States of America

91320—C

To
Ann, Betsy, and Marion

• Preface

This book is addressed to two groups of readers: the college student of international relations, and the interested lay reader who—by himself or as a member of a study-group—searches for a concise introduction to the complex field of international relations. We hope that the combination of exposition, theory, and practice will meet the needs of a growing number of persons who wish to exercise their responsibilities as informed and aware citizens. It has been the purpose of the authors/editors to present more than just another book of readings. Rather, it has been our hope that we might compile selected writings of some of the best contemporary students of international relations, accompanied by introductory textual material, within a conceptual framework which enhances understanding.

The organization of the book does not depart radically from the type of "actor-capacities-goals-methods" analysis which seems to prevail in the study of international relations. However, certain portions (for example, Part IV: "Tension, Conflict, and Violence" and Part V: "The Reduction of Tension") deal with various underlying patterns in a way not usually encountered in existing works on international relations. In addition, the book contains some case studies of certain outstanding problems which characterize the present era of international relations. Two additional considerations should be noted: (1) No student of international relations has as yet succeeded in sharply separating the various ingredients of the subject for purposes of analysis. Certain common themes, such as the existence of great-power conflict, cannot be confined to a single chapter. (2) We have attempted to include some contributions which reflect newer tendencies in the study of international relations, by drawing on the work of sociologists, psychologists, and anthropologists. Some of the work in these fields is still in an early stage, but we look to other disciplines for further enlightenment about our own subject and wish to alert the reader to the relevance of work going on in related fields.

It is perhaps important to note also what this book is *not* designed to do: It is not a text on foreign policies of states, except insofar as foreign policies fall into recognizable patterns of international relationships. It is not a "current affairs" text. What statesman X said to statesman Y on date Z is not the type of material to be looked for, except for purposes of exemplifying some general pattern of international relations. The authors believe that true understanding of international relations depends first of all upon an adequate conceptual framework within which to view these most complex patterns of human relationships. Nor is the book meant to convey the impression that there is an easily available key—a "short-cut"—to the understanding of the subject. We are dealing with one of the most difficult, and certainly one of the most dangerous, areas of human relations; and no approach short of serious application and dedication will yield meaningful results. Furthermore, it is necessary to admit that there are many aspects of the topic that no one has as yet fully explored or understood; to define the area of ignorance is no less important than to ratify the area of achievement.

In the task of selecting appropriate readings, it is inevitable that tastes will differ. We have undoubtedly included some selections which will seem inappropriate to some students of the subject, just as we have certainly excluded some writings which others would wish to see in this volume. In part such problems relate to the need for brevity. In some areas there is so much good material that a book three times this size could have easily been written. We can only hope that our selections will, in general, meet the needs of our readers and provide stimulus for meaningful thought and discussion and that the book will contribute to a better understanding of the subject it is designed to cover.

David McLellan
William C. Olson
Fred H. Sondermann

• Acknowledgments

So many people have aided us in writing and compiling this book that we are tempted to paraphrase Winston Churchill by saying that seldom have so few owed so much to so many.

First, we wish to thank those authors and publishers who granted us permission to reprint articles and other materials which first appeared elsewhere. Without exception, permissions were given readily and generously, and we are duly grateful.

To the Social Science Research Committee of Pomona College and the Research Committee of The Colorado College we extend our thanks for grants which helped in the reproduction of materials and in obtaining clerical help to complete the manuscript.

Libraries and librarians at The University of California at Riverside, The Colorado College, and Pomona College, as well as the Libraries of St. Antony's College, Oxford; The Social Science Foundation, Denver; and the Bureau of International Relations at Berkeley cooperated generously in facilitating the search for suitable materials. We single out for special thanks, Dr. Ellsworth G. Mason and Miss Joan L. Shinew of The Colorado College Library, Mrs. Platt Lawton of the Social Science Foundation Library, and Gordon Martin and Dorothea Berry of the Library at the University of California at Riverside.

All three of us made use of student-assistants in the search for and reproduction of materials which went into the book. Our thanks go to Garry Mertz and Joan Kretschmer of The Colorado College, Kenneth Lee Brown (now at Yale) and Ralph Bolton of Pomona College, Edward Levy and Judy Millman of The University of California at Riverside.

One of the present authors wishes to express his special gratitude to Professor Clifford P. Ketzel of The University of Kansas, with whom he was previously associated in an effort to produce a book of this kind. In correspondence and discussions about the problems and potentialities of such a book, Professor Ketzel was unfailingly helpful, constructive, and understanding.

ix

A number of our professional colleagues whose helpful criticism encouraged us to proceed with our task read and commented upon outlines and early versions of the present book. These include Barbara Ward, Lady Jackson (formerly Foreign Affairs Editor of the London *Economist*); Dr. Kenneth Thompson (The Rockefeller Foundation); Dr. Bernard C. Cohen (Princeton University); Dr. R. Barry Farrell (Northwestern University); Dr. Ernst B. Haas (University of California); Dr. Warner Schilling (Columbia University); Dr. Vernon V. Aspaturian (Pennsylvania State University); Dr. Vernon van Dyke (State University of Iowa); Dr. Andrew Gyorgy (Boston University); Dr. H. Field Haviland Jr. (The Brookings Institution); Dr. Harold K. Jacobson (University of Michigan); and Dr. James R. Roach (University of Texas).

Three personal acknowledgements seem appropriate. The first is to our former teachers at Yale University. Their names, Arnold Wolfers, Hajo Holborn, Gabriel Almond, Nathan Leites, Wm. T. R. Fox, Frederick S. Dunn, Klaus Knorr, Samuel F. Bemis, Walter R. Sharp, Bernard Brodie provide a roster of some of the most distinguished students of foreign policy and international relations.

The second acknowledgment should be made to each other. We started the enterprise as friends of long standing. We completed it and still remained friends. Anyone who has ever engaged in a cooperative effort of this kind will appreciate that this is no mean achievement.

Finally we thank our wives—Ann McLellan, Betsy Olson, and Marion Sondermann—to whom this book is affectionately dedicated.

With so much help, who is responsible for infelicities of thought and style and for such errors of fact and judgment as may be found in this book? The answer is simple and depressing: we are.

D. McL.
W. C. O.
F. A. S.

• Contents

II · Capacities and Qualities of States

III · Objectives and Methods of States

IV · Tension, Conflict, and Violence

V · The Reduction of Tension: Understanding and Collaboration

VI · Organizing International Society

VII · Nation and World in the Space Age: A Problem in Faith and Rationality

The Theory

and Practice of

INTERNATIONAL RELATIONS

THE STUDY OF INTERNATIONAL RELATIONS: INTRODUCTION

Every one is naturally reluctant to classify his own field of study as *the* most important. This reluctance is appropriate: given our present state of knowledge, none of us know enough to claim with confidence that one subject is more significant than another, except in terms of our personal preferences.

Yet it is also true that most people manage to overcome their reluctance —and soon! The authors are no exception, and therefore advance, none too modestly, the proposition that if there is any truly crucial set of problems which confronts our society (and, indeed, other societies as well), it is the set of problems generally spoken of under the heading "international relations." A glance at any morning's headlines will readily convince anyone of the accuracy of this statement. It is not too much to say that the solution (or lack of solution) of problems in this area of human relationships will shape the design of our future. As a matter of fact, such solutions may well determine whether there is to be a future at all. For an increasing number of states, the United States included, wise and skillful participation in world affairs is a precondition for continued existence. In a recent article, this point was well expressed: "...I would argue that the architectonic role Aristotle attributed to the science of the Polis might well belong today to international relations, which have become the very condition of our daily life." [1]

The fact that this particular segment of human relationships is of such crucial significance and extraordinary difficulty can best be understood if we briefly survey the nature of international relations and the environment in which these relations take place.

Our own national society exists in a world in which there are a constantly growing number of other national societies, politically organized as states. Some of these are not very powerful in an overall context, although they

[1] Stanley H. Hoffmann, "International Relations: The Long Road to Theory," *World Politics,* XI (1959), 347.

may be quite strong and effective within their regions. Others, however, are possessed of might great enough to implement their purposes on a larger, indeed a world-wide, scale. Each organized human group has certain goals. The goals of various groups are not necessarily complementary, nor are they easily reconciled with those of other groups. In the present stage of world affairs, for example, certain extremely powerful states strive for what seem to be basically antagonistic goals.

Although relations between nations in many ways resemble relations of groups within societies, there are important ways in which they differ. In contrast to the situation *within* states, there is no natural consensus *among* the various groups which participate in international relations. The groups lack a universal, or even a widely shared, common cultural, social, or historical background; hence they lack similar values for the present and common goals for the future. The late Secretary of State Dulles, in an address to the American Society of International Law in 1956, pointed out that within a state, order is maintained and violence is prevented due to the presence of six conditions or institutions: 1) laws—written or unwritten—which reflect the moral judgment of the community; 2) political machinery to change these laws when change is needed; 3) an executive body to administer the laws; 4) courts to settle disputes in accordance with law; 5) superior public force which deters acts of individual or sub-group violence; and 6) "a state of public well-being sufficient that people are reasonable and prudent and are not driven by a sense of desperation to follow ways of violence."[2]

As one considers these preconditions for order and stability within a society, one finds that they are either completely absent from the international scene (2, 3, 5, 6), or else exist only in very rudimentary form (1, 4). International relations, thus, take place in a special type of environment, to which Professor Dunn, in the selection reprinted in this chapter, refers as "one made up of autonomous units without a central authority having a monopoly of power." A good, brief term for this is "anarchy."

Given the nature of this environment, the compulsions which operate on participants in international relations are extraordinarily complex and demanding. The basic goal of security for a given country, for example, can almost never be perfectly attained. Indeed, it is one of the many paradoxes of international relations that in the pursuit of many goals, countries are forced to adopt policies which, however effective they may seem in the short run, will almost certainly defeat the long-range achievement of the desired objectives.

The problem of effective behavior in international relations, thus, is intrinsically difficult enough. In addition, a number of significant changes have taken place during the past half-century (some within the past two decades),

---

2 "The Institutionalizing of Peace," *Department of State Bulletin*, XXXIV, #880 (May 7, 1956).

which have fundamentally altered the traditional bases of international relations. One such change is the shift of power from western Europe to the peripheral areas. In the immediate post-World War II period, this trend was reflected in the bi-polarization of power, centering upon the Soviet Union and the United States. In the more recent past, other states and groups of states have assumed considerable importance. There are continuing fluctuations in the power distribution, and it would be preposterous to assume that the process of change has come to an end. We also witness continuing changes in the nature of technology (especially in the weapons field), and it is by no means clear whether the precise impact of these technological developments is as yet fully understood. (See, for example, the article by Herz in Chapter II.) The recent past has witnessed the downfall of long-established colonial empires and the emergence, at a bewildering pace, of new states which insist upon independence of action and freedom from entanglement in the conflicts between the Communist and the non-Communist blocs. (See the article by Scalapino in Chapter XVI.) In the areas where the new nationalism is expressing itself, we also witness a "revolution of rising expectations"—an unwillingness of peoples constituting more than half of the world's rapidly growing population to continue their long-established patterns of misery and deprivation. These people want improvements, they want them fast, and they may be prepared to subordinate certain preferences as to means to the overriding purpose of achieving their goal. Finally, the fairly recent past has witnessed the emergence of the Soviet Union as an immensely powerful nation, with thrust and purpose provided by history, leadership, and ideology. Our era is marked by the efforts of that country to play an influential—and, where possible, dominant—part in the affairs of other countries, especially in Eastern and Central Europe, Asia, and Africa. This goal is opposed by a coalition of states of which the United States is the most powerful member. The contest is referred to as the "cold war," and is discussed in more detail in Chapter XV.

All of these events and trends have profoundly changed the international environment. Change is the law of human life; but change with such speed (one is reminded of Stuart Chase's phrase "an express-train out of control") poses most serious problems of understanding and adaptation.

With this understanding of the environment in which international relationships occur, the problem of defining a particular country's part in that process should now also be clearer. A country's goals may be "reasonable" —by its own standards, though not necessarily those of others. Its capacities may be considerable, but there are always limits on what can be done. These limits are a function of the international system, or lack of system, itself. It is unrealistic for any country to expect that it can impose solutions which reflect only gain for its own position. Indeed, the task of statesmanship is often to "cut one's losses" and accept the least of several evils.[3]

---

[3] The best exposition of this point can be found in Charles Burton Marshall, *The Limits of Foreign Policy* (New York: Henry Holt & Co., 1954).

Within an environment tending toward anarchy, it is necessary for countries to coalesce with other countries in the pursuit of common goals. Such cooperation between legal equals imposes strains and tensions, just as does the opposition between contending states or groups of states.

There are only limited alternatives to the solution of international conflict: the ability to arrive at compromise settlements; the willingness to live with unresolved, ambiguous situations; or the employment of force. The first two alternatives are neither heroic nor glamorous, but the last is outdated by the destructiveness of modern weapons if used in a total war.

Having thus set the stage with this brief description of the nature of international relations and the limitations imposed upon state action by the environment in which those relations take place, it becomes appropriate to proceed to a more specific introduction of international relations as a subject of study, to indicate the richness and variety of its material, and to acknowledge some of the many points of view from which the subject can be approached.

One faces, first of all, the problem of definition—not because a definition *solves* problems, but rather because it delineates the territory to be covered and hopefully gives impetus to important questions that must be asked and answered. There are almost as many definitions of international relations as there are writers and teachers of the subject. Yet certain uniformities are apparent in the way in which the subject is viewed by most of its students. All definitions of international relations include relations other than purely political ones, such as cultural and economic relations. All definitions speak, explicitly or implicitly, in terms of individuals or groups (most frequently states and their governments) acting in pursuit of certain goals. And finally, all definitions stress the significance of locale: the study relates to activities *transcending national boundaries*. (A congressional decision to impose tariffs on imports is, from one point of view, a purely domestic decision; but surely it affects the country's international relationships, though indirectly, in important ways.)

While it is true, as Thompson points out in the article reprinted in this chapter, that the study of international relations has become closely linked to the study of *internal* aspects of participating states (a point reiterated by Dunn, who identifies the study of international relations with that of decision-making), this formulation does not appear to be fully comprehensive. Any social activity can be studied not only in terms of the behavior of participants in it, but also in terms of the larger context within which it takes place and which affects the behavior of participants.

"Many theories (and texts) look at (international) relations from one angle only: the foreign policies of the units; the perspective is from below (the units), looking up. This is indispensable, but it is not enough. The situations created by the interaction of the units, whether their occurrence was expected by the units or not, have a logic of their own; the types of power configurations that result not only from the conflict, or convergence, of foreign policies, but also from the very structure of the world and from the operation of transnational forces, in turn reshape, condition, and often command foreign policies. Thus we also need another kind of perspective: from the top, looking down." [4]

Since it is obviously impossible to study everything that goes on across national boundaries (the teaching of French cooking or the incidence of seasickness might be included under such a broad definition), a widely accepted limiting concept is the use of "political" relations, or *international politics*. The most commonly accepted point of view is that, in order for an action to qualify as "political," it must at some point involve the governmental organization of a country. This is no longer as limiting a factor as it may once have been. Many relationships which were formerly private in character have become linked with government activities, and this trend seems to be continuing.

A question that has given rise to some disputation is whether or not the study of international relations is a branch of another discipline, or whether it can be considered a discipline in itself. To most people in the field this is not a terribly important question. Both Kennan and Thompson (in the selections presented) doubt whether the study of international relations is a discipline in its own right, although the latter at least does not exclude the possibility that it may become one in the future. Other students contend that questions arising in the field do have an internal coherence and differ from questions which arise in any other single field of inquiry. Dunn's article suggests a useful way of looking at this problem. Perhaps the best position is one advanced by another writer, who believes that the study of international relations is "a point of view, an outlook, a search for answers to questions in a way not now being utilized by the long-established disciplines." [5]

Thompson's article presents the evolution of the study of international relations in the United States. To his discussion it need only be added that the more recent trends have been away from purely political analysis (especially if that term is narrowly defined as the study of institutions and structures), and in the direction of utilizing materials from the so-called behavioral sciences, especially sociology, psychology (social psychology), and anthropology. The article by Wright is an example of one of the newer approaches. The student of international relations transcends traditional disciplinary boundary lines which have in the past linked him most closely with history and political science—subjects which remain important to him. He learns from sociologists about the group context of human behavior and from psychologists about the behavior-patterns of individuals. The anthropologist informs him of the variety of cultural systems and the need for comparative studies of men and societies. If one adds to all this

---

[4] Hoffmann, *op. cit.*, p. 372.

[5] C. Dale Fuller, *Training of Specialists in International Relations* (Washington, D.C.: American Council on Education, 1957), p. 26.

the obvious contributions of such fields as economics, geography, demography, technology, and even strategy, one begins to have a sense of the richness of the enterprise. No one can expect to know all there is to know in all of these fields. It is important, however, to know what questions to ask and where to go for the answers.

Finally, let it be repeated that while the student of international relations draws freely on other disciplines, he performs a task which differs from that of specialists in other fields. In his avowedly inter-disciplinary endeavor, he studies the relations between units—individuals, groups, state, and governments—within the particular context of anarchy.

1 • Training for Statesmanship *

George F. Kennan

Mr. Kennan, former high-ranking Foreign Service official, was U.S. Ambassador to the Soviet Union in the early 1950's. After his expulsion from Moscow in 1952, he joined the staff of the Institute of Advanced Studies at Princeton. Among his publications are American Diplomacy, 1900–1950 *(1951) and* Russia, the Atom and the West *(1958). Mr. Kennan is credited with being the author of the "containment" policy, and has written extensively for journals in the field of foreign policy.*

One can hardly complain today about the time and effort devoted in American colleges and universities to instruction in foreign affairs. I doubt whether there is a liberal arts curriculum in the country which does not offer courses or activities in this field, and many of the technical institutions also are beginning to include such courses.

There are people, I am sure, who would feel that the high volume of instruction in this field is in itself the guarantee of a fairly respectable measure of achievement. These people would argue that some instruction in international affairs is obviously better than none at all, and that therefore this impressive volume of activity must produce useful results, regardless of the content of the courses.

About this I have my doubts. I am not certain that there is any virtue in teaching people about international affairs—aside from such virtue as may reside in the tenor of the teaching itself. Since the amount of relevant factual material is infinite, embracing in the last analysis practically everything there is to know about the human family, international affairs is a field in which the pursuit of knowledge without understanding is peculiarly pointless and useless. This being the case, mere volume

---

* *The Princeton Alumni Weekly*, March 6, 1953, pp. 10–12. Reprinted by permission.

of instruction does not guarantee anything at all in the way of desirable results. In fact, if instruction does not proceed from a realistic understanding of the subject, it can be worse than useless. I think anyone who has lectured extensively about foreign affairs will have had the same experience I have had—of noting that the questions asked by simple and relatively uneducated people are often more sensible and penetrating than those asked by people who have had a good deal of teaching on these subjects but have been taught the wrong way.

Instruction in international affairs can be given for two different purposes. The first is to instill into the student the type of understanding of the subject needed by the man who is not going to make participation in international affairs his business in life but who wants to acquit himself creditably of his duties of citizenship. A man who wants to be a good citizen needs to be able to judge men and issues in national life. But there are few important issues of national policy that can be understood today except in relation to our international position. And even the quality of the statesmanship of our national leaders often becomes manifest primarily in their reactions to problems that are at least partly problems of international life. The conscientious citizen therefore obviously requires as broad and enlightened an understanding of this subject as he can get.

The second purpose, which instruction in international affairs can serve, is to prepare men for service in the foreign field, either in governmental or in other positions.

It is a mistake to think of international affairs as anything outside the regular context of life—as anything which a man could hope to understand without having to understand things much more basic. There is no such thing as foreign affairs in the abstract. The relations between nations are part of the whole great problem of politics—of the behavior of man as a political animal. They are inseparably connected with the fundamental human problem of power that lies at the heart of all politics: the problem of how the freedom of choice of the individual, or of the organized society, is to be limited in order to repress chaos and ensure the good order necessary to the continuation of civilization.

We Americans have a strange—and to me disturbing—attitude toward the subject of power. We don't like the word. We don't like the concept. We are suspicious of people who talk about it. We like to feel that the adjustment of conflicting interests is something that can be taken care of by juridical norms and institutional devices, voluntarily accepted and not involving violence to the feelings or interests of anyone. We like to feel that this is the way our own life is arranged. We like to feel that if this principle were to be understood and observed by others as it is by us, it would put an end to many of the misunderstandings and conflicts that have marked our time.

But we ignore the fact that power underlies our own society as it underlies every other order of human affairs distinguishable from chaos. Order and civilization are not self-engendering. They do not flow from themselves or even from any universal and enlightened understanding of political institutions in the abstract.

In our country, the element of power is peculiarly diffused. It is not concentrated, as it is in other countries, in what we might call the "pure form" of a national uniformed police establishment functioning as the vehicle of a central political will. Power with us does exist to some extent in courts of law and in police establishments, but it also exists in many other American institutions. It exists in our economic system, though not nearly to the degree the Marxists claim. Sometimes, unfortunately, it exists in irregular forces—in underworld groups, criminal gangs, or informal associations of a vigilante nature—capable of terrorizing their fellow citizens in one degree or another. Above all, it exists in the delicate compulsions of our social life, the force of community opinion within our country—in the respect we have for the good opinion of our neighbors. For reasons highly complex, we Americans place upon ourselves quite extraordinary obligations of conformity to the group in utterance and behavior, and this feature of our national life seems to be growing rather than declining. All these things can bring us to put restraints upon ourselves which in other parts of the world would be imposed upon people only by the straightforward exercise of the central police authority.

Now I am not taking exception to this curious diffusion, within American life, of the power to make men conform to given patterns of behavior. It has both advantages and dangers. It represents unquestionably a manner of protecting the interests of the individual against the more dangerous and humiliating forms of tyranny and oppression in normal times. But we must not permit this advantage to blind us to the fact that such a thing as power does exist and is, indeed, a necessity of civilization, flowing from certain facts about human nature—certain imperfections if you will —that are basic and that are not going to be corrected by any man-made device, whether institutional or educational. These basic facts provide one of the main keys to the understanding of history. They lie at the heart of our problem of living together as human beings within the borders of this land. And they also lie at the heart of our problem of living side by side with other human societies within the broader framework of this planet.

Whoever would understand foreign affairs, therefore, cannot and will not do it solely by understanding the intricacies of tariffs or the various classifications of treaties or the ways in which the United Nations Charter differs from the Covenant of the League of Nations or the techniques of sampling mass opinion. International affairs are primarily a matter of the behavior of governments. But the behavior of governments is in turn a matter of the behavior of individual man in the political context, and of the workings of all those basic impulses— national feeling, charity, ambition, fear, jealousy, egotism, and group attachment —which are the stuff of his behavior in the community of other men.

Whoever does not understand these things will never understand what is taking place in the interrelationships of nations. And he will not learn them from courses that purport to deal with international affairs alone. He will learn them, rather, from those things which have been recognized for thousands of years as the essentials of humanistic study; from history and from the more subtle and revealing expressions of man's nature that go by the names of art and literature.

I would say, therefore: Let the international affairs course stand as an addendum to basic instruction in the humanities. Let it stand as an exercise in which the student is told to take what he has already learned about the characteristics of the human animal and to note in what curious and marvelous ways they find their ultimate expression in the behavior of governments. Let foreign relations be viewed as one area—an extremely important one—in which these laws of nature work themselves out. But let the teaching of the subject not be permitted to obscure its basic components. Let no one be permitted to think that he is learned in something called a "science" of international relations unless he is learned in the essentials of the political process from the grass roots up and has been taught to look soberly and unsparingly, but also with charity and sympathy, at his fellow human beings. International affairs is not a science. And there is no understanding of international affairs that does not embrace understanding of the human individual.

Only if these principles are observed will we be able to free ourselves from the strain of utopianism that has been present in the teaching of international affairs in our country in recent decades. By this I mean teaching that portrays incorrectly the nature of our world environment and our relation to it and encourages students to disregard the urgent real requirements of international life in favor of the cultivation of artificial and impractical visions of world betterment. This argument about the philosophy of our approach to our problems of foreign relations is one that has been agitating our academic communities intensely in recent months. I am myself a partisan in the dispute. I shall only say here that further exposure to the bitter realities of the practice of international relations, in a place where these realities are about as bitter as they can conceivably be, has strengthened my conviction that the shortcomings in the teaching of international affairs, and primarily the leanings toward shallow and

utopian interpretations, represent, in their ultimate effect, an important limitation of our ability to handle ourselves effectively in world affairs. Admittedly this is largely a question of general educational level, and not just of the philosophical tenor of courses on foreign affairs; but that is precisely my point. Until we can achieve a deeper and more realistic understanding generally, among the influential strata of this country, as to what is really involved in the process of international relations, I fear we shall not succeed in reducing appreciably the number of bewildering and painful surprises our people derive from the unfolding of international events.

If the young men of this day are to be trained to look clearly and intelligently on America's foreign relations, the teaching to which they are subjected must be stern and uncompromising. It must be founded in humility and renunciation of easy effects. It must exclude all that is Pollyannaish and superficial. It must reject utopianism and every form of idealism not rooted in an honest and unsparing recognition of the nature of man. It must free itself from the tyranny of slogans, fashionable words, and semantic taboos. It must proceed from a recognition that the understanding of this subject can never be more simply acquired than the understanding of its basic component, which is man himself.

. . . .

2 • The Study of International Politics: A Survey of Trends and Developments *

Kenneth W. Thompson

The author, a graduate of Augustana College, received his Ph.D. at the University of Chicago. Prior to becoming the Associate Director, Division of Social Sciences, the Rockefeller Foundation, he taught at the University of Chicago and Northwestern University. He is co-author of Principles and Problems of International Politics *(1950), and a frequent contributor to scholarly journals.*

The question was raised at the end of World War II as to whether or not international relations could stand as a separate field of study. Views were expressed by scholars and teachers in history and political science to the effect that in substance there was nothing peculiar to the subject matter of international relations which did not fall under other separate fields of social studies. At some universities and colleges there were dissenters to this prevailing viewpoint. Their particular philosophy manifested itself in attempts to create and establish integrated curricula under academic committees or departments dedicated to the broad generalized study of the subject matter of the field. It is still too early to pass judgment with any finality on the merits of these two points of view, the one viewing international relations as a mere duplication of the subject matter of many fields; the other insisting that there must be an ordering and integrative approach to the field. No serious student would presume to claim that the study of international relations had arrived at the stage of an independent academic discipline. How-

ever, there have been three significant developments within no more than a single generation which illuminate certain aspects of this problem. First we have witnessed the evolution and development of a point of focus or core in the field. Secondly, there have been the first faint and feeble beginnings of attempts to create a methodology appropriate for the field, or at least to determine those related methodologies in the social sciences whose methods and techniques could most usefully be appropriated for the study of persistent international issues. Thirdly, inventories have been drawn up by individual scholars, universities and institutes, of topics and concrete projects which would best serve in the development of general principles in the field and the validation of them through systematic inquiry.

1. THE CORE SUBJECT OF INTERNATIONAL RELATIONS

The movement in the direction of a focus or point of reference has its origin

* *Review of Politics,* XIV (1952), 433–43. Reprinted by permission.

in time primarily in the years immediately preceding and following World War II. To understand this development it is necessary to consider the four general stages through which the study of international relations has passed. While sometimes paralleling and supporting one another in time, these phases can be separated because of their particular implications. The first phase was the period in which the study of diplomatic history was prevalent. At this point the significant treatises and monographs, especially in England, dealt with concrete diplomatic events which had taken place over the past several centuries. For example, the studies of the conduct of British foreign policy by noted statesmen and diplomatists covering limited historical periods as, for example, the foreign policies of Palmerston, Castlereagh and Canning, represent the best and most fruitful studies in this period. Perhaps what most distinguishes this period is the high level of historical accuracy and the faithful attention to the canons of historiography and historical method by which it was characterized. Indeed, it is plain from the words and deeds of historians that they conceived their first duty to have been the foreswearing of every temptation to generalize about their observations.... Professor Samuel Elliot Morison in his address as retiring president of the American Historical Association in 1950 declared that the sole aim of any objective and scientific historian ought to be the full and complete reconstructing of a selected incident in history. The historian should avoid every temptation to generalize or dabble in universal principles in recording a story which it was his duty to portray in all its essential simplicity. Every effort to connect an event with what had gone before or to draw up lofty and ambitious principles could only weaken this first paramount undertaking. Indeed, we are given in capsule form in Professor Morison's address the prevailing philosophy which influenced most early studies in diplomatic history. In all fairness, the participants in this approach must be praised for their faithful adherence to principles of historical research and documentation.

The price which was paid for this rigorous, objective and nongeneralized approach to the field was the absence of anything corresponding to a theory of international relations. Because of the poverty of available documentary material on recent events, historians have shown themselves reluctant to face instant problems or to offer propositions about others in the recent past. Moreover, the criticism was voiced that this approach left public opinion and the general citizenry without leadership and without guides for understanding and action. As a consequence there grew up during the truce between the two wars an overriding concern for some means of exploring and studying the immediate present. In place of the detached and highly specialized techniques of history in general and diplomatic history in particular there developed an approach that we may designate the current events point of view. The "bible" for the study of international relations became *The New York Times,* and the role and function of the teacher of international affairs became one of interpreting and explaining the immediate significance of current events. This occasioned a flurry of popular interest in the field which, however, proved premature in that it rested on weak and unstable foundations. For this version of teaching and scholarship in international affairs, requiring as it did qualities on the part of the individual for performing the dual functions of pundit and advocate, made of specialists in the field little more than "special pleaders." In this sense, the areas which might have been exploited from the earlier study of diplomatic history were left essentially untouched. Since the study of the present was pursued without any reference to history, there were no ordering principles drawn from past experience. Instead each scholar became a spokesman for his own brand of international legislation or reform. Some discussed off the cuff free trade *versus* protectionism, others international monetary reforms, and others new ways and means of transforming international organization. But none attempted to relate the post-war political problems with comparable problems that might have existed at particular times in the past. To do so would have been antiquarian and proved that the scholar was at odds with his times.

President Wilson inveighed against the use of studies on the Congress of Vienna which the British proposed at the time of the Paris Peace Conference. From him any lesson or enlightenment which the methods of Talleryrand and Metternich might have thrown on the methods of Clemenceau or Lloyd George was ruled out of order. Therefore, the viewpoint of current events became a day-by-day exercise in proposing and disposing of each minor world problem as it presented itself. Furthermore, the absence of any firm methodological foundation for the study of these events led to a grand and extravagant conception of what international studies should encompass. It was said that all experiences and events which involved peoples of many lands should constitute the core of the field. Everything from the anthropology of the most primitive and pre-modern tribes to xenophobia was considered equally important. In these terms an informed discussion of the Olympic Games was as appropriate as an analysis of the latest move in German diplomacy. However engaging this appeared in theory and however appropriate for group discussion, it scarcely led to any carefully conceived approach to the most relevant international problems upon which war and peace might hinge. Someone has said, facetiously to be sure, that this was an era of letters to Congressmen, to editors, and to the public without more than a line or two of scholarly political or diplomatic monographs.

A third phase was inaugurated immediately following World War I. Coming at this time, it paralleled and strengthened and indeed gave its own emphasis and meaning to the current events that students were discussing. The dominant viewpoint in international relations between the two wars was the viewpoint of international law and organization. Here again, the conception of scholarship which underlay this method of study was two-fold in nature. The mission of students in the field had been to discover the goals and objectives toward which international society ought to be tending. Once this step had been taken and the goal of an ideal world commonwealth accepted, the first explicit task of those engaged in this field of study was to bring about the necessary transformation of institutions and societies whereby these goals could be attained. In this way, the scholar became a crusader and reformer so that it was said by critics of this mode of thinking that in no other field had scholars become to such a degree captive of their own emotions and visions of the future.

...What inspired most of the thinking and a great deal of the writing in this period was a single belief. It was widely imagined that once an international organization had been established, all of the baffling and perplexing issues of international politics would disappear. International relations was defined as "the study of those related problems of law and ... of ethics which were raised by the project of a League of Nations." Hence, the moral obligation of the scholar required that he preach and teach the urgent need for those actions by which an international organization could be established and made acceptable to all the world's peoples.

There are three characteristics of this period in international studies which are essential for considering its successes and failures. First, it was dominated by a spirit of unbounded optimism. Secondly, the research and academic interests, as well as the special competence and qualifications of men in the field, was concentrated primarily in the sphere of international law and organizations. Thirdly, a tendency to draw moral judgments in favor of all international ventures and developments at the expense of any national experience or action which might have its own peculiar international implication was always apparent....

Secondly, the research of specialists in the field indicates the degree to which the study of international law and organization prevailed. The scholarship of individuals like Professors Berdahl, Colegrove, Fenwick, Garner, Hershey, Hyde, Potter, Shotwell, Wilson, and Wright was characterized in a positive way by great technical competence and a remarkable absence of parochialism and chauvinism. It is notable, however, that of the twenty-four scholars in the field who held the rank of professor by 1930, eighteen had devoted themselves exclusively to the study of international law and organization. Moreover a tendency persisted throughout these years of equating peace with government on the one hand, and war with power politics, and the balance of power on the other. When international politics and its enduring practices and techniques was studied at all, it was studied by the diplomatic historian, but within the limits of his orientation. The experiences of the nineteenth century in the easing of international tensions were considered irrelevant as subjects deserving serious inquiry. Instead, technical

and procedural problems and organizational reforms and improvements of international government preoccupied almost every scholar.

Thirdly, there was an implicit if unstated assumption which underlay the selection of almost every subject of inquiry. It was widely believed that everything international was good, and everything national was bad. Hence, those forms of international practice selected for study included such good and constructive international experiments as the League of Nations, and such questionable and dubious national issues and problems as imperialism and nationalism. The so-called bad or morally ambiguous international activities involved in the operations of the Third International were not discussed nor were examples of good national activities, such as the quest for national security by this country. Indeed, one of the illnesses from which the study of international relations still suffers is the cult of internationalism which places its own moral evaluations on the field of study in terms of the dichotomy of good internationalism and bad nationalism.

Following World War II, however, a tendency which has its inception in a period antedating World War II came to the forefront. The study of international politics replaced the study of international organization as the guiding concern and fundamental point of reference in international relations. An approach was made to recurrent world issues not with a view to praise or condemn but to understand them. Professor Grayson Kirk, ... [now President] of Columbia University, in a survey of courses and students in the field immediately following the war found that international politics had become the basic introductory field of study almost everywhere throughout the country. In place of the examination of structure and organization in international society, students had turned to the study of underlying forces and trends which shape and mold the behavior of all nation-states. It became the objective of international politics to study the field in much the same terms that domestic politics had been studied for almost a generation. In the same way that American government has proceeded from the study of the American Constitution and the basic law to the examination of practical politics and pressure groups, so international studies became concerned with the study of trends in the foreign policies of separate nation-states and the forms and techniques through which the various national policies of states could be compromised and adjusted on the international plane. Instead of beginning with the *international* structure and society, the new line of inquiry has emphasized the urgency of examining *national* goals and objectives as a logical point of departure. Just as no one would imagine for a moment that national policy on the domestic scene is a quantity that is given at the outset but instead would expect that national policy derived from compromise and adjustment among the major political parties and pressure groups, so it has been argued that international policy, say, within the United Nations, must be studied as the resultant policy of the pressures and claims of many nations on the international scene. The practices and policies of international organization are from this viewpoint no longer comprehended as abstract considerations. Instead they are conceived in the framework of national aims and aspirations, the points of conflict of these aspirations and their areas of compatibility and incompatibility. In this way, the historic policies of England, the United States, or the Soviet Union become subjects of more vital interest than isolated studies of international government divorced from

international politics as such. The international organization finds its proper and appropriate place if conceived of as a forum within which national rivalries are compromised and adjusted through novel political processes.

What this has done in practice has been to tie the study of international relations to political science as a primary unifying and integrating core. Without this core international relations had tended to ride off in all directions. With it the chances of discovering some relevant and general principles by which statesmen and citizens might be guided have become for the first time a reality. For political science assumes that the rivalry among groups and individuals for political power and the ways in which power and authority are exercised can be made a proper subject of inquiry and study. In the same way, international politics assumes that the struggle for power and influence on the international scene can be tested and examined on its own terms....

In summary, then, the development of the study of international affairs has progressed through four relatively distinct stages or phases. Prior to and including World War I, diplomatic historians enjoyed what amounted to a virtual monopoly over this area. However, the imprint they made on the field by techniques of historical research still left crucial areas of inquiry outside of the range of international studies. Specifically, the analysis of recent events was hardly amenable to scientific history with its two-fold requirement of abundant documentation and the perspective of time. So the period between World War I and II found two distinct viewpoints vying for influence among teachers and scholars. There emerged, on the one hand, an energetic movement which aspired to examine the areas from which diplomatic history had excluded itself. Popularizers of international studies leaped boldly into the breach and a high-falutin' approach to everyday garden-variety current events grew up. The skills and techniques of the social sciences were used indifferently or not at all in this enterprise. Since the standard for embarking on research was the contribution a project would make to universal understanding and cooperation or to the encouragement of the aims and purposes of the League of Nations, it was hardly to be expected that any system for analysis could emerge at this time. Nor did the second viewpoint which prevailed during much of the interwar period mitigate these problems. Alongside the modish conception of international studies as the equivalent of current events, the prevailing point of reference was international law and organization. International relations were construed as moving along two different planes. One plane was the legal sphere in which nations were told how to act. The other was the sphere of actual conduct among states which had to be judged and evaluated in terms of conformity or divergence from the rules of international law. So exclusive an emphasis on law and organization had three consequences in practice. It led to research that was generally devoid of social and political analysis in so far as it stressed the form instead of the functions of international affairs. It invited the acceptance of a line of least resistance in the choice of areas of research. That is to say, official reports and publications in the field of law and organization poured across the desks of teachers in the field in streams that overpowered even those whose natural bent might have guided their studies along other lines of inquiry. It insured that the model for analysis would be a universal world state characterized by perpetual peace. The present tragic order of power politics among states was studied and assessed not by attempting to understand the underlying conditions which were responsible for its persistence among nation-states but through establishing the sharp deviation of this situation from the model of one world commonwealth.

The failure of this point of view to conform even accidentally with the facts of the inter-war period ushered in the final stage in contemporary international studies. International politics has become the focal point of present-day research and teaching partly because of the march of events in the 1930's. For the crises which have followed one another in rapid succession from Mukden Bridge in 1931 to the present have found both teachers and students emotionally and intellectually unprepared for meeting each new challenge. The widespread belief which was engendered by claims that the new formal institutions would soon modify international behavior bore little resemblance to the events which followed. The relations of civilized nations which were to be modified by the operations of the League of Nations progressively deteriorated as the European balance of power was threatened by Germany and Italy. No minor constitutional defect of the League of Nations but the political conditions under which it operated was the primary factor which led to its breakdown. Yet only a realistic assessment of international phenomena could have anticipated and accounted for its decline and fall. The troublesome problem of assessing circumstances and conditions under which national interests could have been harmonized was subordinated to the study of form and structure of the novel international organization. The clue to the basic point of departure of international politics as distinguished from international organization may be found in the way that the current United Nations is evaluated. Formerly, the League had been at the center of the majority of recognized studies; now world politics is the milieu or setting in which every other subject is studied including the functions of the United Nations. International organization, law, trade and finance are studied in a political instead of a constitutional context. And political scientists are accorded the task of asking questions covering problems which continue to vex our society. Inasmuch as the rivalries which occasion international tensions are now generally assumed to be political in character, this movement of the political scientist to the center of international studies is rooted in the facts of the situation. Today the threefold concern of international politics is with the forces and influences which bear on the conduct of foreign policy everywhere, the techniques and machinery by which foreign policy is executed, and both the novel institutions and traditional practices whereby the conflicts among nations are adjusted and accommodated. The fundamental and persistent forces of world politics such as nationalism, imperialism and the balance of power, however, have only belatedly become an appropriate subject for inquiry. The basic drives which determine the foreign policies of states, their desire for security and power, are the elemental facts with which international politics is fundamentally concerned. International politics is the study of rivalry among nations and the conditions and institutions which ameliorate or exacerbate these relationships.

. . . .

3 • The Scope of International Relations *

Frederick S. Dunn

Frederick S. Dunn is Albert G. Milbank Professor of International Law and Practice and Director of the Center of International Studies at Princeton University. His publications include War and the Minds of Men *(1950).*

Four able and penetrating writers have recently given us their considered views on the nature and scope of international relations as a branch of higher learning.[1] While each of them starts from a somewhat different intellectual viewpoint, they display a striking similarity of conception of the general place of international relations (hereafter referred to as IR) in the spectrum of human knowledge. I propose here, not

---

[1] Grayson Kirk, *The Study of International Relations in American Colleges and Universities* (New York, Council on Foreign Relations, 1947); Klaus Knorr, "Economics and International Relations: A Problem in Teaching," *Political Science Quarterly,* Vol. LXII, no. 4, December, 1947, pp. 552–68; E. L. Woodward, *The Study of International Relations at a*

* *World Politics,* I (1949), 142–46. Reprinted by permission.

University (Oxford, Clarendon Press, 1945); Waldemar Gurian, "On the Study of International Relations," *Review of Politics,* Vol. VIII, no. 3, July, 1946, pp. 275–82.

to subject these writings to critical scrutiny, but to use them as a starting point for a brief inspection of the scope of international relations as it now seems to be taking form in the work of the leading scholars in the field.

It is necessary to note in the beginning that "scope" is a dangerously ambiguous word. It suggests that the subject matter under inquiry has clearly discernible limits, and that all one has to do in defining its scope is to trace out these boundaries in much the manner of a surveyor marking out the bounds of a piece of real property. Actually, it is nothing of the sort. A field of knowledge does not possess a fixed extension in space but is a constantly changing focus of data and methods that happen at the moment to be useful in answering an identifiable set of questions. It presents at any given time different aspects to different observers, depending on their point of view and purpose. The boundaries that supposedly divide one field of knowledge from another are not fixed walls between separate cells of truth but are convenient devices for arranging known facts and methods in manageable segments for instruction and practice. But the foci of interest are constantly shifting and these divisions tend to change with them, although more slowly because mental habits alter slowly and the vested interests of the intellectual world are as resistant to change as those of the social world.

If one keeps this in mind, it is not difficult to answer the hotly debated question whether IR should be regarded as a separate branch of learning or as just a miscellany of materials and methods drawn from existing subjects. The answer seems to depend entirely on considerations of utility. New subjects of learning have always in the past grown out of new bodies of questions that have insistently called for answers by some means other than consulting the stars or tossing coins. Invariably, such subjects were originally attached to existing divisions of knowledge and appeared as mere extensions of them. Eventually, as the complexities of the newly observed body of questions began to mount and the inadequacies of offhand answers became apparent, some adventurous minds put in a good deal of time and effort finding aids to better solutions. Their labors led to the building up of a special body of knowledge which everyone who wanted to become expert in answering questions in the field had to master. As soon as this became a full-time occupation and a proper label was found, a new branch of knowledge was born.

The questions which arise out of the relations among nations are certainly important and difficult. They likewise possess their own coherence and uniqueness since they arise out of relations in a special kind of community, namely, one made up of autonomous units without a central authority having a monopoly of power. Pulling together the scattered fragments of knowledge about them obviously serves to focus attention on them and to encourage the development of more intelligent ways of handling them. Recent events have reinforced the growing conviction that the questions of international relations are too complex and dangerous to be dealt with any longer as sidelines of existing disciplines.

. . . .

What I shall do here is merely to state certain propositions about the nature and scope of IR which seem to represent the present views of some mature scholars in the field. In setting these forth I do not mean to imply that they incorporate the correct or final form of the subject. In my own view, the present basic divisions of the field are far from satisfactory from the standpoint of creative scholarship and the next few years are apt to witness the development of more imaginative classifications. But in the early stages of any subject it is the wisest course to make use of existing terms and categories. To try to invent a set of new ones at the start usually results in an inability to communicate with anyone else.

The following statements are dogmatically phrased for the reason that sufficient space is not available to express all the possible qualifications. For the same reason, no attempt has been made to squeeze out the last drop of ambiguity from them.

1. IR may be looked upon as the actual relations that take place across national boundaries, or as the body of knowledge which we have of those relations at any given time.

The latter is always more restricted in extent than the former, and its contents will depend, among other things, upon the intellectual trends of the times and the point of view and purpose of the observer.

2. As a branch of learning, IR consists of both a subject-matter and a set of techniques and methods of analysis for dealing with new questions.

The subject-matter consists of whatever knowledge, from any sources, may be of assistance in meeting new international problems or understanding old ones. It includes both general knowledge about the behavior of political groups or individuals and particular information about events or policy questions.

In the case of questions of general knowledge, the techniques and methods of analysis include the logical devices for arriving at hypotheses and for testing and verifying or rejecting them. In the case of practical questions they include the devices for revealing the issues involved, classifying the value •objectives, indicating the alternative courses of action available and their probable consequences, and selecting the one

most likely to lead to the desired end.

3. The distinguishing characteristic of IR as a separate branch of learning is found in the nature of the questions with which it deals.

IR is concerned with the questions that arise in the relations between autonomous political groups in a world system in which power is not centered at one point.

4. An IR analyst is one who purports to have some skill in dealing with the questions that arise out of the relations of nations.

The core of his interest lies in the conflict, adjustment and agreement of national policies. When he concerns himself with related subjects, such as demography, anthropology and sociology, it is to the extent that these throw light on international questions. This distinguishes his interest in these fields from that of the professional demographer, anthropologist or sociologist.

5. The technical knowledge of IR is not merely the extension to a wider geographical scale of knowledge of social relations inside the national community, but has unique elements of its own.

Thus international politics is concerned with the special kind of power relationships that exist in a community lacking an overriding authority; international economics deals with trade relations across national boundaries that are complicated by the uncontrolled actions of sovereign states; and international law is law that is based on voluntary acceptance by independent nations.

6. Since the questions with which IR deals arise primarily out of social conflicts and adjustments, its approach is in large part instrumental and normative in character.

IR is concerned primarily with knowledge that is relevant to the control and improvement of a particular set of social conditions. Its goal is not merely knowledge for its own sake but knowledge for the purpose of molding practical events in desired directions. In this sense it is a policy science. As such it does not differ from traditional politics, economics, jurisprudence, and similar social disciplines, all of which had their origin in a desire to improve a particular segment of social relations.

7. The normative character of IR refers to the kinds of questions dealt with and does not imply that the subject-matter is associated with any particular ideal conception of the international community.

The study of IR has been inspired from the beginning by a deep interest in how wars may be avoided. The early students of IR tended to conceive of ideal social systems in which wars did not exist and then to evaluate existing practices in the light of these ideal conceptions. The present tendency among scholars is to give primary attention to the ascertainable facts of international life and the forces and conditions that influence behavior among nations, as well as the ways in which these can be used for desired ends.

8. Foreign policies can only be understood in the light of knowledge of internal conditions of the states involved.

For many purposes it is possible to talk about the relations of states as if they were relations between solid bodies with wills of their own apart from human wills. Thus it is possible to discuss the operation of the balancing process among sovereign states, the relative value of different power positions, and, to some extent, the legal rights and duties of nations, without looking beneath the surface of the state.

In general, however, it is not possible to understand the course of international events without a careful study of the local factors and influences that enter into the formation of national policies.

9. All international relations can be described in terms of decision-making by identifiable individuals or groups of individuals.

This reveals the fact that the study of IR is basically the study of human behavior in a particular social setting.

. . . .

14. As a cultural subject, the aim should not be to turn out skilled decision-makers but to introduce the students to the general field and the methods available for analyzing its problems.

The subject-matter of IR has high cultural value both in teaching the ways of effective thinking and in enabling the student to come to terms with an important part of his environment. As a citizen in a democracy he is constantly faced with the necessity of arriving at sensible opinions on questions of foreign affairs.

15. As professional training for those who intend to follow careers in the field, IR contains an essential core of five subjects: international politics, international economics, international law and organization, diplomatic history, and political geography. In addition, it calls for some knowledge of the socio-psychological subjects—sociology, anthropology, psychology and social psychology, and ethics.

The IR analyst must acquire enough knowledge of the core subjects to enable him to move freely across the boundaries that separate them and to be able to think effectively about whole questions. In addition, he should have mastered at least one of the accepted disciplines so that he may become familiar with the basic intellectual virtues. Only after such training will he become sensitive to the need for maintaining the highest standards of rigorous scholarship if IR is to earn its place as a useful branch of higher learning.

4 • The Psychological Approach to War and Peace *

Quincy Wright

The author, Professor of Political Science at the University of Chicago, is one of the foremost American scholars of international relations. He is the author of such noted works as The Study of War *(1942),* The Study of International Relations *(1955), and numerous articles in journals of law, politics, and sociology.*

The psychological approach to war and peace must be distinguished from the economic, the ideological, the legal and the political approaches to those subjects. It searches for the cause of war and peace in the individual rather than in the group. The distinction between the individual and the group does not, however, indicate two wholly distinct entities but two different approaches to the problem of social man. The individual and the group are not distinct facts because the human individual exists only in groups, and groups exist only among individuals. This point of view, emphasized by the late C. H. Cooley, is now generally accepted by sociologists. It is not, indeed, a recent conception, but is at least as old as Aristotle's affirmation that man is a political animal. The individualism of post-Renaissance Europe, which tended to set the individual in opposition to society, as manifested in Herbert Spencer's *Man versus the State,* was an extreme position, as is Communism, which absorbs personality entirely in the group. A healthy view of man and society perceives that while neither can exist independently, neither should absorb the other. The points of view of both psychology and sociology are necessary to maintain a balanced conception of social man.

If we view the matter developmentally, we perceive that individuals in proximity with one another communicate, and from this emerges a *community.* Within the community, individuals interact with one another, developing common behaviour patterns from which emerges a *culture.* Once distinctive cultural patterns are established, the individuals bearing such patterns cooperate with one another to achieve common ends, and a *society* emerges. In order that cooperation may be more effective, the society develops an organization enabling it to act as a unit, and we have a *Government.*[1]

. . . .

...actually the members of a community through their associations develop a distinctive language and distinctive beliefs, values and ideologies, together constituting a culture and setting limits to

* *India Quarterly,* X (1954), 23–31. Reprinted by permission.

[1] Quincy Wright, editor, *The World Community* (Evanston, Ill.: University of Chicago Press, 1948).

easy communication. People of different cultures who speak different languages and have different beliefs and values are strangers to one another. Economic activity, trade and division of labour, tend to be confined to the culture. While there may be some trade with other cultures, strange groups are more likely to be regarded as rivals for the limited resources of nature. Cultural differentiation, therefore, added to the economic struggle against nature, leads to economic barriers, to rivalry, and to hostility among groups.

This tendency is augmented when the culture becomes organized into a society with a common law, and common institutions of family, religion and economy, and, finally, into a State with a common Government able to speak for the whole and to command the obedience of all members in defence or aggression.

The evolution of humanity from the economic grouping of people in communities, through the differentiation of cultures and societies, to the organization of people in States, each occupying a territory, and under a Government, marks the increasing probability of peace within the group and the increasing probability of war among groups. The 'in-group' becomes increasingly integrated and its members feel an increasing sense of solidarity not only because they understand one another and cooperate in many matters, but also because they are opposed to an 'out-group,' from which they expect opposition rather than cooperation and against which they must unite in defence. 'Hot' or 'cold' war with other nations, comes to be the price of peace within each nation, increasingly as the nations become larger and less homogeneous.

. . . .

The gravity of the situation is augmented in an age of atomic war and shrinking distances. Action to moderate the danger is not likely to succeed unless there develops some consciousness of universal solidarity and some sense of world citizenship among all peoples. A more general appreciation of the values of peace, of human rights, of national self-determination, and of economic and social cooperation set forth in the Preamble and the first article of the United Nations Charter, might contribute to these sentiments. Teachers of such appreciation, however, will not be listened to unless rivalries are moderated and the hope of peace is revived. An organization such as the United Nations can contribute to these ends, but to do so it must be strong enough to protect the nations by maintaining the basic law against aggression. It must also be equipped to facilitate universal co-operation for common ends, and continually to educate the peoples to an awareness of their common interests in maintaining its values. These are the momentous tasks before the United Nations. It is clear, however, that no artifices of structure can alone enable it to accomplish them. 'Wars,' as pointed out in the Constitution of the UNESCO, 'arise in the minds of men, and in the minds of men the defences of peace must be constructed.' The United Nations will lack power unless it lives in the minds of men everywhere, inspiring them with a determination to make it work. The sociological task of organizing the world politically must be accompanied by the psychological task of preparing the minds of men for such an organization. Only if the two tasks proceed together can either be successful.[2]

Let us, therefore, look at the problem of war and peace from the psychological

---

[2] Harold D. Lasswell, *World Politics and Personal Insecurity* (New York: McGraw-Hill, 1935), p. 237 ff, and "World Loyalty," in Q. Wright, ed., *op. cit.*, p. 200 ff; A. H. Feller, *United Nations and World Community* (Boston: Little Brown, 1952).

point of view. Can individuals, brought up in families and national cultures with parochial loyalties, be educated to an awareness of their citizenship in the world of which all nations are members? Is it possible for each individual to adjust his loyalties to family, occupation, religion, nation, region, and the world, so that the institutions of each group may function peacefully within a universal law and a universal organization?

Groups are composed of individuals, and their characteristics depend upon the existing motivations, attitudes, personalities and characters of individuals, however much the psychological characteristics of the individuals, whether leaders or followers, may have been formed by the group in which they have lived. The purposes which reason, looking to the future, attributes to a group can only be achieved by utilizing the interests and attitudes of individuals formed in the past.

The human individual, like his animal ancestors, is born with drives of self-preservation, sex, acquisitiveness and dominance. If his species is to survive he needs to avoid destruction, to propagate the race, to acquire food and shelter, and to lead or submit to leadership. Closely related to these primary drives are secondary drives. The tendency to defend a territory found among many animals, especially during the breeding season, aids in self-preservation and is at the root of the modern State. The tendency to associate into families and larger societies facilitates sexual functioning and is at the root of many civilized social institutions. The tendency to be active, curious, and inventive, assists in acquiring the necessities of life and is at the root of economic institutions. The sentiments of sympathy and compassion, aware of the urges for freedom, independence, and self-determination on the one hand and for dominance and power on the other,

contribute to institutions of religion and justice designed to maintain tranquillity of the spirit by sublimating the individual's desire for dominance through his identification with an all-powerful God, and by permitting him to realize his desire for freedom through subordination of all to law assuring justice.[3]

None of these motivations makes war inevitable. They are all attributes of universal human nature but they express themselves differently in different communities, cultures, societies and organizations. Any one of them can contribute to either war or peace, according to the mode and magnitude of its expression. Social philosophers are not wanting to show how mutual fears of attack, rival demands for territory, the urge for political power, and the desire for group self-determination have led to wars. It is also possible to find wars which have sprung from the drive of acquisitiveness and economic competition, emphasized by the Marxists; from crusades for defence of a way of life, an ideology, a religion or a society; and even from sexual jealousy, said to have motivated the Homeric siege of Troy, and undoubtedly a frequent cause of war among primitive peoples.

These same motivations, however, provide the psychological bases for peace. Thomas Hobbes insisted that mutual fears generated by the universal drives for gain, safety, and reputation, produced a war of all against all in a State of nature, and induced men to submit themselves to a Government able to give security to all. The same motivations have induced sovereign States at times to submit themselves, in a limited degree, to international organizations of collective security. The urge for dominance develops political men who organize States. The urge for freedom de-

[3] Quincy Wright, *A Study of War* (Evanston, Ill.: University of Chicago Press), p. 1456 f.

velops theories of justice and systems of law to maximize the liberty of all. The sentiment of compassion develops religious men who organize churches. The urge of sex develops the family and society, and also the sentiment of sympathy which provides the cement of organizations to preserve peace. The State, the law, the church and the social organizations have preserved peace in widening areas.[4]

As war becomes more destructive, the principle of reason increasingly demands that these basic urges be expressed in institutions of peace rather than of war. In the mature mind, the reality principle guides the wish principle, the *ego* controls the *id*, reason regulates emotions. It is the task of education to develop such knowledge and values in the culture, and in the personalities which compose it, that both will interpret the world as it is, and sublimate original drives to values that can be peacefully pursued in such a world.

· · · ·

In a world where security depends only on fear, peace is precarious. Prime Minister Winston Churchill, it is true, optimistically suggested that 'When the advance of destructive weapons enables everyone to kill everybody else, nobody will want to kill any one at all.'[5] Yet, with continuing anxiety, springing from the ever present possibility of sudden annihilation, apprehension that a rival is about to attack, may at some moment induce some Government to take the fatal step initiating atomic war.

Doubtless, the immediate remedy lies in the realm of international negotiation to increase confidence and relieve tensions, and of international organization to promote understanding and exert controls. These methods, however, cannot be successful unless the minds of men everywhere are educated to live in our changing and vulnerable world, to understand its dangers and its opportunities, and even more, to comprehend the motives, mechanisms and tensions of the individual mind and to acquire a maturity able to act in the light of the highest values and the most valid interpretations of reality. Such should be the goal of the psychological approach to war and peace.

---

[4] Q. Wright, A Study of War, op. cit., p. 273 ff.

[5] Winston S. Churchill, House of Commons Debate, 3 November 1953, Parliamentary Debates, Vol. DXX, col. 30.

PART I   THE STATE SYSTEM

I • Nationalism

National communities are the units of international relations. The state is the political organization of this community. It rests upon the sense of psychic and cultural identity which makes a people a nation. The nation is a culturally homogeneous social group which is conscious of its unity and distinctiveness. International politics would not exist, at least as we know it, if men were not organized into nations ready and willing to obey their governments' command. Though the territorial state as a physical shell has been shattered by the force of modern nuclear physics, nothing has thus far shattered the loyalty of people to their nation; and so long as this is true the motives, conduct, policy, and patterns of international relations will continue to be a function of the behavior of sovereign states. If we wish to understand the working of the nation-state system we must first understand the conditions that make the nation-state the fundamental unit and then examine the influence which these units exert on the system of international politics.

Man can only enjoy security and satisfy his needs within a community. The community, in turn, conditions his attitudes and evokes his loyalty. In modern times the nation-state is the community that most satisfies man's wants. Within it men have achieved the highest standards of life ever known, as well as order and security. As Reinhold Niebuhr described it:

> The modern nation is the human group of strongest social cohesion, of most undisputed central authority and of most clearly defined membership. The Church may have challenged its pre-eminence in the Middle Ages, and the economic class may compete with it for the loyalty of men in our own day; yet it remains, as it has been since the seventeenth century, the most absolute of all human associations.[1]

The nation-state as it is known in the West appears to have developed in two stages. The first, that of dynastic consolidation whereby feudalism in England, France, Spain, and Prussia was replaced by absolute monarchs who established their primacy over the supranational authority of the Church

---

[1] Reinhold Niebuhr, *Moral Man and Immoral Society* (New York: Charles Scribner's Sons, 1932), p. 83.

24

in the name of the state, had as its supreme function the establishment of law and order within the realm. The second stage—what Hannah Arendt terms "the conquest of the state by the nation"—witnessed a shift in the basis of legitimacy from divine right to popular representation and national sovereignty. Not all nations were so fortunate in achieving national unity and national self-consciousness at an early date. Over most of the world nation-building has been a slow and exceedingly painful process. Only the breakup of the German, Austrian, and Russian empires following the First World War permitted the submerged nations of Eastern Europe to achieve their national independence, and only the disintegration of the British, Dutch, and French empires has enabled the nationalist aspirations of Africans and Asians to find expression.

It is now possible to identify the three methods by which nation-states come into being in the perspective of history. (1) In terms of historical origin the state may precede the nation in which case national self-consciousness emerges as a function of the ruler's establishment of a new hierarchical and administrative system. (2) The nation may precede the state in which case the spirit of nationalism rebels against its submerged status until it achieves independent, sovereign statehood. These two processes are generally marked by a high level of violence and coercion. (3) A nation-state may also come into existence as a result of peaceful federation in which case the logic of perception, reason, and mutual advantage persuades a people of their common lot. Federation afforded the basis for Swiss and American national existence despite the geographical and/or cultural distances that separated the original components.

The social process leading to a sense of nationality, of belonging together, begins in the remote past of a people. We cannot say precisely when France and England became nation-states, i.e., when this political loyalty depended more on the feeling that their citizens had for one another than the feeling that they had for their king or prince. The growth of a sense of nationhood came about as a result of improved communications, of intensified social contact, of perceived economic advantage, and of the successful establishment of a common system of coercion. In his study of nationalism Karl Deutsch attributes the growth of a nation to "the transformation of a people, or of several ethnic elements, in the process of social mobilization." [2] Social mobilization refers to that stage in a people's economic and social evolution when they become conscious of the advantages that would flow from unity. The merit of Deutsch's formulation is that it focuses upon the conditions of economic and social change that are best suited to give a new idea such as nationalism its start. Nationalism does not spring up spontaneously; only men can sow ideas. When in the course of economic and social change the population becomes receptive to new appeals and new leaders bent on leading them to the promised land, nationalism emerges

---

[2] Karl W. Deutsch, "The Growth of Nations: Some Recurrent Patterns of Political and Social Integration," *World Politics,* V, No. 2 (1953), 169–170.

as a conscious focus of their attention only through the active efforts of a creative minority or a charismatic leader. Only when the appeal of nationalism captures their faith does the absorption of the uncreative majority into the movement become possible and lead to a new system of values and loyalties called nationalism.

Thus nationalism has at its roots an essentially irrational quality which may or may not become magnified by subsequent events. Once the process of national consciousness has started, cultural indoctrination and the legacy of common experience reinforce the growth of national integration. Renan described the process with poetic accuracy:

> A nation is a soul, a spiritual principle. Two things which are really only one, go to make up this soul or spiritual principle. One of these things lies in the past, the other in the present. The one is the possession in common of a rich heritage of memories; and the other is actual agreement, desire to live together, and the will to continue to make the most of the joint inheritance. The existence of a nation is a daily plebiscite, just as that of the individual is a continual affirmation of life.[3]

It is no exaggeration to say that, as a result of the security and well-being —psychological as well as material—that the nation affords to its members, nationalism has become the modern religion of a vast majority of people within every nation. In his study which follows, Morton Grodzins dissects the complex role that nationalism has come to play in the personalities and patterns of belief of millions of people. It is important to note that the sources, function, and objects of national loyalty are not the same for all people. Nor is loyalty to the nation-state necessarily an absolute, direct relationship. Loyalty to the state fulfills a psychological need for many people that might be served equally well by other entities. Similarly loyalty to the nation may be reinforced or strengthened by deriving from multiple sources—family, job, fraternal organization. Perhaps one of the best examples of this is the famous ending to the Yale anthem that goes— "for God, for Country, and for Yale." Studies of the psychological roots of nationalism indicate that loyalty to the nation-state need not be a barrier to loyalty to a regional or universal organization provided members of the national community can be encouraged to see that loyalty to such a group need not mean a decrease in loyalty to the nation-state.[4]

Historical experience indicates that there are several kinds of nationalism, each of which has a different impact upon international politics. For our purposes the typology defined by Carlton Hayes offers a suggestive basis of comparison. Hayes defines four types of nationalism: liberal, Jacobin, traditional, and integral. Liberal nationalism, which emerged in conjunction with the seventeenth and eighteenth century stress upon constitutionalism and individual rights, views the existence of the nation-state as indispensable

---

[3] Ernest Renan, *What is a Nation?*, 1862; quoted in G. Schwarzenberger, *Power Politics* (London: Stevens and Sons, 1951), p. 55.

[4] Harold Guetzkow, *Multiple Loyalties: Theoretical Approach to a Problem in International Organization* (Princeton: Center for Research on World Political Institutions, 1955), pp. 1–62.

to the fullest development of the individual. Jacobin nationalism is the expression of a community self-consciously dedicated to making the values of nationalism available to other people. In its determination to impart the values of freedom and national self-determination to others, it assumes an authoritarian and expansionist outlook.

Traditional nationalism urges the community to make itself invulnerable to alien doctrines that are threatening it from without. In this it seems to revert to an older tribal pattern in which group rights and values displace individual rights and values. However, traditional nationalism is an essentially defensive and isolationist reaction. By contrast integral nationalism, in which the individual loses significance and the right of the community to live and survive becomes the primary aim, is far more dynamic and expansionist. Integral nationalism usually calls for the totalitarian organization of society and seeks domination over others in the name of one's own national superiority. It is certainly possible on the basis of such a typology to make some predictions as to the behavior an international system can expect from its members.

Jacobin nationalism of the sort sponsored by the Convention of 1792 and taken over by Napoleon can be expected to call for the aggressive revision of traditional forms of government and of the international status quo. In a sense Colonel Nasser's pursuit of Arab unity represents a modern version of Jacobin nationalism insofar as he wishes to extend to the other Arab states the benefit of Egypt's new order. France has been the exponent of traditional nationalism for the past half-century, primarily because of a sense of declining national power in the face of Germany. While the United States has been the traditional exponent of Jacobin nationalism, in recent years it has become more cautious in its support of nationalist movements. The Soviet Union has become an outstanding advocate of nationalist movements, but as Stalin said, "It ought to be understood as the right of self-determination not of the *bourgeoisie* but of the toiling masses of a given nation. The principle of self-determination ought to be used as a means in the struggle for socialism and it ought to be subordinated to the principles of socialism." [5]

Not all people were as fortunate as the French, the English, or the Americans in establishing national homelands. In Eastern Europe where nations such as the Poles, Czechs, Slovaks, and Croatians remained submerged and oppressed until well into the twentieth century, nationalism acquired an intensely tribal and messianic quality. Yet it was precisely in Eastern Europe that the paradox of nationalism was most evident. The complicated ethnic distribution of peoples in Eastern Europe required that about 30 percent of the roughly one hundred million inhabitants of the Succession States (states created by the peace treaties following the First World War) dwell in states as specially protected minority groups, and in some

---

[5] Quoted in Isaac Deutscher, *Stalin: A Political Biography* (New York and London: Oxford University Press, 1949), p. 185.

of the Succession States the nationally frustrated minorities constituted 50 percent of the total population. As long as these people were convinced that true freedom, true self-expression, and true sovereignty were impossible without full national emancipation, they exposed the region to anarchy and to subversion by more powerful neighbors (such as Nazi Germany).

Similar patterns and problems beset the development of nation-states among the recently emancipated peoples of Africa, Asia, and the Middle East. While the imperial powers divided Africa and Asia into distinct territorial entities over which they established a common administrative superstructure, a legal system, and the rudiments of a new political community, they either did not or could not establish political boundaries which contained only one self-conscious cultural unit. As a result, while they broke the crust of tradition and set the processes of economic and social change in motion, they rarely succeeded in establishing the economic, cultural, or political conditions for the successful realization of nationalist aspirations. Nevertheless, the transformation brought about by Western imperialism was an indispensable precondition for the rise of nationalism. It transformed the economic, sociological, religious, political, and psychological character of African, Middle Eastern, and Asian societies in such ways as to foster nationalism. It intensified the degree of communications and economic interchange among the inhabitants. All of the conditions of social transformation that contributed to the growth of nationalism in Europe, plus factors connected with Western imperialism, are present among the peoples of Africa and Southeast Asia. This does not mean that a genuinely cohesive spirit of nationalism exists everywhere. Far from it. Many of these fledging states still are burdened by tribal and sub-national loyalties and other divisive forces.

While the conditions for the successful establishment of nation-states may not exist in many of these areas, the myth of national independence has created expectations which, if unrealized, threaten to produce highly explosive results. The deceptions and setbacks that have followed upon the disparity between promise, aspiration, and achievement have already produced in Egypt and elsewhere in the Middle East the most extreme manifestations of xenophobia and governmental instability. It is here that we touch upon one of the most dangerous consequences of modern nationalism for international relations. When these people discover that national independence is no guarantee of a better, happier life, many of them seek scapegoats among their leaders or among countries identified with Western colonialism. Others are attracted to new movements such as communism which promise to help them achieve their aspirations. The result is the creation of tension and instability in areas of the world such as the Middle East and Southeast Asia, which have become a focus of East-West rivalry.

1 • The Growth of Nations: Some Recurrent Patterns of Political and Social Integration *

Karl W. Deutsch

The author, Professor of Political Science at Yale University, received his Doctor of Law and Political Science from Charles University, Prague, and his Ph.D. from Harvard University. He was a Guggenheim Fellow, 1954–55; Fellow at the Center for Advanced Study in the Behavioral Sciences, 1956–57; Fellow, American Academy of Arts and Sciences; a former Chief of the Research Section, U.S. Department of State and Office of Strategic Services. His publications include Nationalism and Social Communication *(1953) and co-authorship of* Political Community and the North Atlantic Area *(1958).*

At many places and times, tribes have merged to form peoples; and peoples have grown into nations. Some nations founded empires; and empires have broken up again into fragments whose populations later attempted again to form larger units. In certain respects, this sequence appears to describe a general process found in much of history. This process shows a number of patterns which seem to recur, and which to a limited extent seem to be comparable among different regions, periods, and cultures....

Before discussing the recurrent problems of national integration, it may be well to note the use of a few terms. For the purposes of our discussion, a distinction is made between a *society,* which is defined as a group of persons who have learned to work together, and a *community,* which is defined as a group of persons who are able to communicate information to each other effectively over a wide range of topics. A similar distinction is adopted between a *country,* which denotes a geographic area of greater economic interdependence and thus a multiple market for goods and services, and a *people,* which is a group of persons with complementary communications habits. A *nation* is then a people which has gained control over some institutions of social coercion, leading eventually to a full-fledged *nation-state;* and *nationalism* is the preference for the competitive interest of this nation and its members over those of all outsiders in a world of social mobility and economic competition, dominated by the values of wealth, power, and prestige, so that the goals of personal security and group identification appear bound up with the group's attainment of these values.

While peoples are found at almost any period in history, nationalism and nations have occurred during only a few periods. A nation is the result of the

---

* *World Politics,* V (1953), 168–95. Reprinted by permission.

transformation of a people, or of several ethnic elements, in the process of social mobilization. Thus far, however, the processes of social mobilization and communication have at no time included all mankind. The "universal states" listed by A. J. Toynbee as stages in the disintegration of particular civilizations were superficial short-cuts, rather than solutions to the problem of the unity of mankind....

The process of partial social mobilization and of nation-building have been recurrent phenomena in history, at least in certain general characteristics. What uniformities can we find in this growth of nations in the past? And in what ways is our own age different in respect to the growth of nations from any age that has gone before?

SOME POSSIBLE SPECIFIC UNIFORMITIES

Uniformities which have been found in the growth of nations include the following:

1. The shift from subsistence agriculture to *exchange economies.*

2. The social mobilization of rural populations in *core areas* of denser settlement and more intensive exchange.

3. The growth of *towns,* and the growth of social mobility within them, and between town and country.

4. The growth of *basic communication grids,* linking important rivers, towns, and trade routes in a flow of transport, travel, and migration.

5. The differential accumulation and *concentration of capital* and skills, and sometimes of social institutions, and their *"lift-pump" effect* on other areas and populations, with the successive entry of different social strata into the nationalistic phase.

6. The rise of the concept of *"interest"* for both individuals and groups in unequal but fluid situations, and the growth of *individual self-awareness* and awareness of one's predispositions to join a particular group united by language and communications habits.

7. The awakening of *ethnic awareness* and the acceptance of *national symbols,* intentional or unintentional.

8. The merging of ethnic awareness with attempts at *political compulsion,* and in some cases the attempt to transform one's own people into a privileged class to which members of other peoples are subordinated.

Some of these similarities may be discussed briefly.

The Shift to Exchange Economies. The shift from subsistence agriculture to an exchange economy seems to have characterized all cases of wider national integration which I have been able to find. Where the exchange economy came to embrace the bulk of the population and to bring many of them into direct contact with each other in the interchange of a wider variety of goods and services, there we find a tendency to "national" or at least regional, linguistic, and cultural "awakening," provided only that sufficiently large numbers of individuals enter the exchange economy and its more intensive communication *faster* than they can be assimilated to another "alien" language or culture.

Where these shifts take place, the ethnic and in part the linguistic situation becomes, as it were, loosened or softened, and capable of settling again into new and different molds. The awakening of the Slavic population of the Balkans, and the rise of regions of greater intensity of trade and exchange around which the revived Serbian and Bulgarian languages and nationalities were constituted, may perhaps serve as illustrations.

Further Social Mobilization and Integration in Core Areas. The shift to an economy and culture based on wider interchange takes place at different times and different rates of speed in different regions. The result is often the existence of more "advanced" regions side by side with more "undeveloped" ones. The former are then often in a position to function as centers of cultural and economic attraction for some of the populations of the latter, and thus to become nuclei of further integration. The "when" is thus often as important and sometimes more important than the "where," and the processes of social mobilization and partial integration are truly historical in the sense that each step depends to a significant extent on the outcome of the step that went before.

Political geographers have sought to identify *core areas* around which larger states were organized successfully in the course of history. Characteristic features of such core areas are unusual fertility of soil, permitting a dense agricultural population and providing a food surplus to maintain additional numbers in non-agricultural pursuits; geographic features facilitating military defense of the area; and a nodal position at an intersection of major transportation routes. Classic examples of such core areas are the Ile de France and the Paris basin, or the location of London.

It should be noted that the density that makes a core area is one of traffic and communication rather than mere numbers of passive villagers densely settled on the soil. Thus the dense population of the Nile valley seems to have been less effective as a wider center of integration than the sparse population of the Arab territories beyond Mecca and Medina, who more than compensated for their smaller numbers by their proportionately far greater mobility, activity, and traffic.

The theory of core areas, however, cannot account for the persistence of some states and the failure of others. What counts for more may well be what happens within each core area, and perhaps particularly what happens in its towns.

The Growth of Towns, Mobility, and Ties Between Town and Country. There is no developed nation, it appears, without towns which have or have had a period of considerable growth, of mobility within the towns, and of increasing ties of social mobility, communication, and multiple economic exchange between town and country.

There have been towns, of course, where one or more of these conditions did not exist, and to that extent national development has been incomplete, absent, halted, or retarded. On the other hand, to the extent that there was such growing mobility and communication within towns and between town and country, national development was accelerated.

The Growth of Basic Communication Grids. Most nations do not seem to have grown from single centers. Many nations have had several capitals and have shifted their central regions several times in the course of their history. Even the classical example of growth around one center, France, has long had two capital cities, Paris and Orléans; and some significant phases of the unification of the French language took place at the Champagne fairs and along the trade routes leading through that region —not to mention the role of the North-South routes and connections in helping the North to consolidate its victory over separatist and Albigensian elements in the Midi during the religious wars of the thirteenth century.

A more extreme case, Germany, has no single core that could be easily identified, and it seems more helpful to think of Germany as essentially a grid of routes of traffic, communication, and migration....

The same notion of a basic grid seems to be applicable to the unification of China, Russia, Switzerland, Canada, and the United States. It would be interesting to investigate the relationship of such a grid to the incomplete unification and more recent separation of the areas that now comprise India and Pakistan.

It is not suggested that a grid in itself can make a nation. Also necessary, as a rule, are a minimum of cultural compatibility and, in many cases, sufficient similarity between spoken dialects to permit the emergence of a common language for large sections of the population. The cultural and linguistic data in themselves are given by history, of course, at each stage of the process. Yet we know how much of a difference in language or culture has been bridged successfully in the emergence of such nations as the Swiss, the British, or the Canadians, provided that enough tangible and intangible rewards and opportunities were present, ranging from greater wealth, security, freedom, and prestige to the subtler attractions of new common symbols, dreams, and ways of life.

The Differential Concentration of Capital, Skills, and Social Institutions. A major factor in national differences and national pride today are the differences in the general standard of living. To some extent such differences tend to cut across the differences between social classes; there is a social, moral, or traditional component in what is considered "bare subsistence" in a given community, or in what counts as "luxury" in another; and a significant part of what is considered the poor population in a relatively wealthy community may be appreciably better off in terms of physical goods and services than even many of the relatively well-off members of a poor or economically backward people. This difference between the generally prevailing standards of wealth, comfort, and opportunity among different regions or peoples has sometimes been called the

Kulturgefälle ("the drop in the level of culture") by German writers who have employed this concept to bolster claims to German supremacy or exclusiveness vis-à-vis the populations of Eastern Europe and the Balkans.

Behind the differences in the standards of living lie differences in levels of productivity and in the supply of factors of production, that is, in the material means to pursue any one of a wide range of conceivable ends regardless of the difference in importance assigned to some of these ends relative to others in some particular culture. These differences in productivity may involve geographic factors such as soils, water supplies, forests, mineral deposits, and the absence of obstacles to transportation. All such geographic factors, however, depend on specific technologies to give them significance. Every concentration of natural resources requires, therefore, a concentration of productive skills and knowledge if men are even to know how to use them; and resources as well as skills require a concentration of invested *capital* if they are to be used in fact.

It should be clear that, as technology progresses, the relative importance of the man-made factors of production, such as capital and skills, has tended to increase relative to the importance of the few natural facilities which once were the only ones that more primitive technologies could exploit. There is reason to believe that present-day differences in living standards are due far less to differences in natural factors of production, and far more to differences in the supply of skilled labor, schools, housing, and machinery.

Particular peoples and nations may then tend to crystallize, as it were, around particular concentrations of capital and technology, or of particular social institutions which offer individuals greater opportunities for the pursuit of the goods or factors which they have learned to desire. . . .

The effects of differential standards of living and of productivity operated long before the Industrial Revolution, but they were increased by its coming. Where large economic or industrial developments have taken place, they have had a "lift-pump" effect on the underlying populations. They have induced migrations of populations to the regions of settlement, employment, and opportunity, and put these newcomers into intensive economic and political contact with the locally predominant peoples, and with each other. This physical, political, and economic contact had one of two cultural and linguistic consequences: either it led to national assimilation, or, if national assimilation to the dominant group could not keep pace with the growing need for some wider group membership for the newcomer, then the "lift-pump" effect would tend to lead eventually to a new growth of nationalism among the newly mobilized populations. Eventually, it might result in the assimilation of some previously separate groups, not to the still-dominant minority, but to the "awakening" bulk of the population.

This rebellious nationalism of the newly mobilized population rejects the language or culture of the dominant nationality. Yet it shares many of its values and it desires to share or acquire its wealth and opportunities. The motives for this secessionist nationalism are thus to a significant extent the same motives that would lead, under different circumstances, to national assimilation. Nationalism and assimilation are, therefore, ambivalent in the economic as well as in the psychological sense. The same wealth and prestige are pursued by either method: in national assimilation they are to be attained through sharing, while in national resistance they are to be attained by power.

Both national assimilation and national resurgence thus respond in a "lift-pump" situation to the power of the "pump." The intensity and appeal of nationalism in a world of sharply differentiated income and living standards perhaps may tend to be *inversely proportional to the barriers to mobility between regions and classes,* and *directly proportional to the barriers against cultural assimilation, and to the extent of the economic and prestige differences between classes, cultures, and regions.*

Seen in this light, the rise of nationalism and the growth of nations have some semi-automatic features, even though they have other features which are by no means automatic. As the distribution of scarce rewards is made unequal by economic or historic processes; as men learn to desire the same kinds of rewards; as they fail to be assimilated to the language and culture of the dominant group; and as they succeed in becoming assimilated with other men who possess cultural and language habits more compatible with their own—as all these processes go on, situations conducive to nationalism are created without anyone's deliberate intention.

The Concept of Self-interest and the Experience of Self-awareness. The concept of a nation is bound up with that of a national interest. Already the non-national or proto-national institutions of the city-state and the princely state imply the notion of group interests and interests of state, and all these notions of national, state, or city interests imply in turn the interests of individuals. But this concept of individuals with interests has itself gained its present importance only gradually in the course of certain developments of history. Even today different regions and civilizations ascribe to it different degrees of significance, and it may lose again in the future much of its present importance. . . .

As men leave the relative security of villages and folk cultures for the mobility and uncertainty of travel, towns, and markets, and for the competition of wealth-getting, politics, and warfare, they may find greater opportunities and rewards for aggressiveness and self-assertion; and at the same time they may come to feel more poignantly the loneliness, the loss of security, and the loss of context and meaning in their lives which the transition to the new ways of life entails.

Nationalism is one peculiar response to this double challenge of opportunity and insecurity, of loneliness and power. Men discover sooner or later that they can advance their interests in the competitive game of politics and economics by forming coalitions, and that they stand to gain the firmer these coalitions can be made, provided only that they have been made with individuals and groups who have to offer in this game the largest amount of assets and the least amount of liabilities. To form the firmest possible connections with the most promising group of competitors would seem to be sound long-run strategy. With which group such firm connections can be formed is by no means arbitrary: in politics and economics such coalitions will depend to a significant degree on social communication and on the culture patterns, personality structures, and communications habits of the participants. Their chances of success will thus depend to some degree on the links that make a people, the ties of nationality. Machiavelli's advice to princes to rely on soldiers native to their kingdom was sound: a policy along these lines became the basis of the military power of the rulers of Brandenburg-Prussia in the century that followed, with results that were to lead eventually to the emergence of a German nation-state. The victory of the ethnic Turkish elements over the largely Slavic-speaking Janissaries in the struggle for the control of the Imperial Ottoman Court in the seventeenth century, and the emergence of the ethnic Turkish elements in the reform of the Ottoman Empire after 1908, and again in the salvaging of a much reduced Turkish state after 1918, may be other cases in point.

Organization along ethnic or national lines is by no means the only type of alignment which may be tried in the competitive game. Yet of all these probable patterns of organization, ethnic or national alignments often combine the greatest strength and resilience with the greatest adaptability to a competitive world. So long as competitive institutions continue to prevail, nationalism can mobilize more people and organize them more firmly than can many competing types of organization. The potential rewards of nationalism then grow in proportion to the potential resources of wealth and power to which members of a particular people have, or can gain, access on preferred terms.

To develop thus the economic, intellectual, and military resources of a territory and a population, *and to knit them together in an ever tighter network of communication and complementarity based on the ever broader and more thorough participation of the masses of the populace*—all this is sound power politics; and those who carry out such policies tend to be rewarded by the long-run outcome of this contest.

What may fit the necessities of the competitive game may also fit some inner needs of its participants. Ages of social mobilization, of rapid changes in the traditional social contexts, tend to be ages of increasing self-doubt and self-awareness for the individuals who live in them. The questions: Who am I? Whom do I resemble? In whom can I trust?—are asked with a new urgency, and need more than a traditional answer.

As a man seeks answers to these questions, he must try to take stock of himself, of his memories, his preferences, and his habits, of the specific images and indeed of the specific words in which they were conveyed and in which they are now stored in his mind. As old cultural or religious patterns, beliefs, and ceremonies become questionable, self-searching must lead back to the childhood memories and the mother tongue, in terms of which so many experiences have been acquired, and out of which, in a sense, the individual's character and personality have been built up. When men seek for themselves, they thus may come to find their nationality; and when they seek the community of their fellows, they may discover once again the connection between ethnic nationality and the capacity for fellowship. Instances of this process can be found even in antiquity: it is well known that Socrates enjoined upon his pupils the imperative, "Know thyself," and that Socrates' pupil, Plato, proposed that all Greeks should henceforth cease to plunder or enslave their fellow Greeks, but should rather do these things to the barbarians.

The phase of self-doubt and self-survey may end in conversion to a new religion or ideology, perhaps even one complete with a new language and traditions, such as was once the case in the matter of conversion to Islam, and sometimes to the Arab language; or in deliberate assimilation to a new nationality, as in many cases of emigration overseas, or in deliberate assimilation even in one's original country to the language and traditions one has now chosen to accept (e.g. Indians learning to speak Spanish and accepting Peruvian or Mexican national loyalties). In any case, the phase of self-doubt and self-appraisal tends to be followed by a phase of decision and of conscious or even deliberate identification with a group; and with the loosening of the ties of religion or status that group is likely to be a group delimited at least in part along national lines, in terms of habits of language and communication.

Our hypothesis finds some confirmation in a well-known pattern in the history of nationalism and the biographies of nationalist leaders. Many emotionally, culturally, and politically sensitive individuals react to a sojourn abroad, i.e. away from their native region or culture, with a far stronger assertion of nationalism and of allegiance to their own language, culture, and people. This precipitating crisis in the lives of many nationalists has been dubbed the *Fremdheitserlebnis* ("the experience of strangeness"), and it has been described repeatedly in the literature of nationalism.

From Group Awareness to the Nation-state. Individual awareness of one's language and people may appear to be a matter of personal psychology, even though there are social situations which make such awareness more probable. Group awareness, on the other hand, seems clearly a matter of social institutions. Some secondary symbols are attached to some aspects of group life and are repeated and disseminated over and over again by an organization or institution, often for a purpose that has nothing to do with nationality, or which might even be opposed to it. After a time, the institution may change or disappear, the organized repetition of the symbols may cease—but if there were enough of a primary reality capable of being symbolized, *and if there had been going on that basic process of social mobilization* which has been described earlier, then the results of the dissemination of those symbols may well prove irreversible. A stream of memories has been started that is partly self-regenerating, and so long as the foundations for the ethnic group exist, and social mobilization and communication continue to weld its members together, national group awareness may be there to stay. It can hardly be expected to give way to a wider supra-national allegiance until a basis for the appeal of wider symbols has again developed in the realm of objective fact, in experiences at least as real, as frequent in the daily life of individuals, and as relevant to their personal concerns, to their language, their communications, and their thoughts, as were those experiences which provided the basis for the awareness of nationality....

Reinforcing the impact of these symbols [of nationalism] there appear the institutions of modern economic life and of the modern state, all of which require more direct communication with large numbers of peasants, artisans, taxpayers, or conscripts than was the case before. In the eighteenth century, Austrian officers were taught Czech, so as to command better their Czech-speaking soldiers, and the revival of the teaching of the Czech language followed. Landowners in Wales and Scotland, interested in raising the productive skills of the population on their estates, founded societies to study the resources, languages, and cultures of their regions, and made the century of the "agricultural revolution" also the century of the "discovery" of the works of "Ossian."

No growth of nationalism was foreseen or desired in many of these cases, any more than in the more recent use of the Indonesian language by the Japanese in the administration of the Dutch Indies during World War II, or in the compilation of grammars and dictionaries of Hausa and other African languages by colonial administrators. Yet the growth of nationalism was facilitated by the consequences of these acts.

Once the process of group consciousness has started, however, there appear also the deliberate pioneers and leaders of national awakening. There appear grammarians who reduce the popular speech to writing; purifiers of language; collectors of folk epics, tales, and songs; the first poets and writers in the revised vernacular; and the antiquarians and historians who discover ancient documents and literary treasures—some genuine, some forged, but all of them tokens of national greatness.... Side by side with the awakeners of national pride and fashioners of symbols appear the first organizers....

Together with all this activity we find the gradual acceptance, or the deliberate proposal, of national symbols, of national colors, flags, animals, and flowers, of anthems, marches, and patriotic songs, from the "Rule Britannia" and the "Marseillaise" of the eighteenth century to the *"Nkosi sikelel i Africa"*—"God Save Africa"—of today's nationalist South African Negroes. How all these symbols, maps, anthems, flags, and flag-salutes are then taught and impressed upon the populations and their children by informal group pressure and the media of mass communication as well as by all the coercive powers of the state and its system of compulsory public education—this is a story that has been told often and well by students of these late stages of the nation-building process.

What does this process accomplish, and what does it aim at? When a nation has been built up, and when it has been reinforced finally by the full compulsive power of the state, then four things have been accomplished.

(1) A relatively large community of human beings has been brought into existence who can communicate effectively with each other, and who have command over sufficient economic resources to maintain themselves and to transmit this ability for mutual communication to their children as well. In

other words, there has been brought into being a large, comprehensive, and very stable human network of communication, capable of maintaining, reproducing, and further developing its channels.

(2) There has been both an effective accumulation of economic resources and a sufficient social mobilization of manpower to permit the social division of labor necessary for this process and to permit its continuation.

(3) There has been a social accumulation and integration of memories and symbols and of individual and social facilities for their preservation, transmission, and recombination, corresponding to the level of mobilization and integration of material and human resources, or even pointing beyond it.

(4) There has been at least some development of the capacity to redirect, re-allocate, or form a new combination of economic, social, and human resources as well as of symbols and items of knowledge, habit, or thought—that is to say, of the capacity to learn. Some of the social *learning capacity* is developed invisibly in the minds of individuals; some of it can be observed in the habits and patterns of culture prevailing among them; some of it finally is embodied in tangible facilities and specific institutions. Together, all these constitute the community's capacity to produce and accept new knowledge or new goals, and to take the corresponding action.

On all four counts, it should be evident, the nation represents a more effective organization than the supra-national but largely passive layer-cake society or the feudal or tribal localisms that preceded it.

On all these counts, there may be considerable contrasts between different nations. The social models accepted for imitation, the established institutions, the economic practices, and the methods of compulsion within each nation are all intimately connected with the cultural traditions and leading social classes currently prevailing there. Whether a leading class of businessmen or farmers or wage earners will prove more hospitable to accumulation of resources and to efficient dynamic innovation in their use may depend not merely on the general outlook to be found prevailing in each particular stratum, but also—and perhaps sometimes crucially—on the particular cultural goals and traditions which have become accepted by that particular class in that particular nation. Yet, the impression remains that even the worst-led nation represents, relative to its numbers of population, a greater amount of social communication facilities, of economic resources, and of social learning capacity than any pattern of ethnic or social organization preceding it.

Where does this process aim? The nation has been valued as a means of social advancement. In a world of extreme differences between living standards, men have tended to use the nation as an instrument to improve their own standards relative to those of their neighbors. The intrinsic bias of this process has been, where the opportunity offered itself, to produce in the temporarily most successful nation a sociological pattern reminiscent of a *mushroom cloud*. The stem of this social mushroom was formed by the "national solidarity" between the poorest and the lower-middle strata of the nation; the poorest strata, both rural and urban, however, tended to be somewhat less in relative numbers, and offered their members greater chances for "vertical mobility" than was the case in other less "successful" nations. The middle and upper strata, on the other hand, tended to form the crown of the mushroom; they tended to be somewhat larger in number than the corresponding group in other nations, with a greater propensity to spread out horizontally into new positions of privilege or control over new territories, populations, or capital resources, and correspondingly with at least somewhat greater opportunities to accept in their midst newcomers from the less favored strata of their own nation.

It is perhaps this sociological explosion into a mushroom cloud that has been at the heart of the transitory popularity of empire-building. Nationalism typically has led to attempts at empire or at least at establishing privileges over other peoples. The essence of this empire-building has been perhaps the attempt at ruling without sharing, just as the essence of nationalism has been the attempt at improving the position of one's "own" group without any sharing with "outsiders." To the extent that this process was successful it could only tend ultimately to transform the whole nation into a privileged class, a *Herrenvolk* lording it over servant peoples, as the Nazis dreamed of it, or a small, select population monopolizing vast natural resources or accumulations of technological equipment regardless of the fate of the rest of mankind. In reality, this state has probably never been achieved; and where it was even partially approximated, the results in the long-run were anything but lasting. Invariably, thus far, the same nation-building process which had permitted one nation to get temporarily on top of its neighbors subsequently raised up other nations to weaken or destroy it.

From this it might seem at first glance that the whole process of the rise and decline of nations has been cyclical, with only the names of the actors changing in an endlessly repeated drama. Closer scrutiny may show that this is not the case, and that some tentative inferences may be drawn from the events and processes surveyed.

THE UNIQUENESS OF THE PRESENT PERIOD

Our survey offers no support for the belief of many nationalists that nations are the natural and universal form of social organization for mankind. But neither does it confirm entirely the opposite view held by many thoughtful and distinguished observers—the view that nations are exclusively the product of the modern period and of Western civilization. Perhaps the impression that remains might be summed up by saying that the West has gone much farther on a road which all the world's great civilizations have traveled to some extent....

In a real sense, Western civilization is carrying on some—though certainly not all—of the traditions of all other civilizations, and its crisis in the world today is also their crisis, and not merely in externals.

It is this universal aspect that also characterizes the growth of nations in the present. During the last fifty years, there seems to have been growth in all the important regions of the world. Everywhere there has been growth in population, in gross economic wealth, and in national awareness. In no region has there been a decline to compensate for an advance elsewhere. Many of these advances in widely different areas have been the continuation of long-standing trends, which have been helped and speeded by the new resources and possibilities offered by the diffusion of science and technology during those last fifty years.

The result is that today all peoples are involved in the growth of national awareness, and that soon there will be no peoples left to play the role of submerged nationalities or underlying populations, or passive bystanders of history, or drawers of water and hewers of wood for their better organized neighbors.

The process has gone further. Within each people, all social strata have been mobilized, socially, economically, and politically, or are in the process of being so mobilized before our eyes. Wherever this social mobilization has progressed, it has undermined the patterns of authority and privilege inherited from an earlier day. The time can be envisioned now when the majority of all mankind will have shifted to non-agricultural occupations. There has never been a period like this in the history of the world.

. . . .

2 • The Basis of National Loyalty *

Morton Grodzins

The author is a member of the Political Science Department of the University of Chicago. He is the author of several outstanding books, including Americans Betrayed *(1949) and* The Loyal and the Disloyal; Social Boundaries of Patriotism and Treason *(1956).*

It is a contradiction in terms to speak of a man without loyalties. He does not exist. The human qualities that differentiate man from other mammals are the products of his social life. One with all the attributes of man, including his brain, is in isolation not a man. He is a beast.

This only says that when you scratch man you touch loyalty. For man means society. And society—social structures of every sort—rests upon loyalties: upon systems of mutual rights and duties, common beliefs, and reciprocal obligations. To accuse one of being devoid of loyalty can have only one meaning. His loyalties are antagonistic to your own.

The basic objective of this article is . . . : to show how factors of life situation tend to bind men's loyalty to their *nation;* . . .

FUNCTION OF LOYALTIES

Loyalties are a part of every individual's life because they serve his basic needs and functions. They are a part of his indispensable habit patterns. Loyalties provide him with a portion of that framework through which he organizes his existence. In the absence of such a framework, he could establish no easy, habitual responses. He would be faced with the endless and hopelessly complicated task of making fresh decisions at each moment of life. He would soon degenerate into wild and random inconsistencies or into a brooding state of confusion and indecisiveness, conditions that soon merge into the psychotic.

The propensity of man to organize the structure of his activities is apparent in every phase of his life. His very perceptions are so organized. Even what a man sees or smells or hears is determined in very large part by predisposing frameworks. This has been demonstrated in laboratory experiments, and the experiments are duplicated daily

* *Bulletin of the Atomic Scientists,* VII (1951), 356–59. Reprinted by permission.

in ordinary life situations. Drivers of cars which have collided have very different stories to tell. Two readers of the same book derive from it support for widely divergent points of view. Chinese music and Mohammedan paintings are displeasing or unintelligible to those who have not acquired the framework necessary to make them beautiful and meaningful.

This "structuring" of life's enormous range of potentialities begins from the very moment of birth. For the first years of life, when the plasticity of individuals is very great, the family is the dominant molding agency. Later, play groups, school, church, job, social class, government, all take important, sometimes parallel, sometimes conflicting, roles in shaping an individual's career, attitudes, and personality.

These groups that so crucially affect existence are the groups that demand and receive loyalty. They become the eye-pieces through which a person views his life and its relation to society. They actually and literally determine what he does and does not see, what he does and does not like, what he does and does not consider his life goals. Without the aid and comfort of these group ties, an individual would find existence impossible.

Loyalties are thus the source of great personal gratification. They contribute to making life satisfying. They protect the individual, reducing the area of his uncertainty and anxiety. They allow him to move in established patterns of interpersonal relations with confidence in the action expected of him and of responses that his action will evoke. By serving the group to which he is loyal, he serves himself; what threatens the group, threatens the self. There is no self outside group activity. "In so far as one identifies himself with a whole, loyalty to that whole is loyalty to himself; it is self-realization, something

which one cannot fail without losing self respect." [1]

Complete identification between individual and group does not often exist. Totalitarian governments attempt to accomplish this end by destroying all intermediary loyalties, or by fusing the activities of all other groups with those of the state.

In the Western democracies the case is different. Except in periods of extreme crisis, freedom to form and maintain group ties is cherished and encouraged, and individuals preserve strong loyalties to numerous non-national groups. These loyalties are given to family, friends, neighborhood, church, ethnic society, job, class, and to a host of other institutions, groups, and idea systems. They exist most frequently in situations that bring the individual face-to-face with others who share his views and situation; they may also exist where this immediate human contact does not exist. The relative strength and weakness of these numerous loyalties change with age, with shifts in life situation, with new experience, and especially under stress of crisis. They change as old relationships no longer serve biological needs or as they no longer supply satisfaction and security to the individual in the total network of his social existence.

Two Strands of National Loyalty

Individual satisfactions are related to *national* loyalty in an infinite number of ways. Almost the entire social structure is organized to promote and sustain this relationship. One of the prime reasons for the strength and universality of national loyalties is the virtuosity and deftness with which the connection between nation and happiness can be established. For convenience,

[1] C. H. Cooley, *Social Organization: A Study of the Larger Mind* (New York: Charles Scribner's Sons, 1909), p. 38.

one can distinguish between two broad strands which together tend to bind human satisfaction to national welfare.

DIRECT NATION-PERSON TIE

Patriotism as a Religion. On one plane the relationship between individual and nation is direct. Satisfaction springs from immediate identification with nation, from the acceptance of national symbols, the internalization of national ideals. There is delight in attaching oneself to a larger cause. Inner doubts are dissipated: the cause gives purpose and direction to life. The meanness and pettiness of everyday existence become unimportant; the nation is the dominant power unit in the modern world and it is involved in enterprises of grandeur. In this way, the nation acts to dissipate actual and imagined discontents and weaknesses; it simultaneously crystallizes the common faith which philosophers and politicians, sociologists and seers have argued is essential to any successful group life.

The world is organized territorially, and to some extent functionally, into national units. This very organization permits a complex flow of simple emotions to be woven into the sentiment of national loyalty. National states and the institutions within them conspire to promote and to sustain this loyalty.

Ethnocentrism: Death to the Porpoises. The tendency of man to prefer the familiar to the unfamiliar is a universal social phenomenon. The search for new experience and delight in the exotic must largely be understood in terms of the reassurance of the familiar and the habitual. As the world is presently organized, the familiar and the habitual are principally equated with the national. In this way affection for the scenes and experiences of childhood becomes identified with the nation. The familiar language, the familiar food, the

familiar humor, the familiar interpersonal responses—including, as Kipling wrote, the familiar lies—all are affectionately related to the nation.

Familiar misery is frequently more attractive than promised or actual, but unfamiliar, bliss. This is a function of what social anthropologists call ethnocentrism, the practice of judging foreign customs by familiar standards. Even the mean and savage regard their own way of life as the best and all others as sub-human or at least distinctly inferior. This mechanism has been described and documented in many ways. A classic example is in Anatole France, whose Penguin cottager affirms:

"He who says neighbours says enemies. ...Don't you know what patriotism is? For my part there are two cries that rise to my lips: Hurrah for the Penguins! Death to the Porpoises!"

The modern network of world-wide communications and other technological factors tend to weaken the force of ethnocentrism. But it remains potent because it lives on difference, real or imagined. It is strengthened by the structural qualities of the nation-state system. The great hostilities generated within nations are suppressed to every extent possible; they find outlets in bursts of patriotic fervor directed against other national units.[2] Man's love of community—his aim-inhibited libido, in Freud's term—is thus encouraged to stop at national boundaries. The ills of one's own person and one's own culture are projected outward: we are peaceful, they are aggressive; we are kind, they cruel; we aim for justice, they for conquest.

These mechanisms prompted the sardonic Sumner to comment that "the

---

[2] See Talcott Parsons, "Certain Primary Sources and Patterns of Aggression in the Social Structure of the Western World," *Psychiatry*, X (May, 1947), 167–81.

masses are always patriotic." They inspire the antagonisms and animosities that are basic to most patriotic endeavor. The process is self-generating and circular. National boundaries and patriotism to the nation establish convenient ethnocentric battle lines; the belligerencies so evoked add to patriotic fervor; the heightened patriotism produces new belligerencies. Thus patriotism can pour meaning into otherwise empty lives. The price may be individuality itself; but this seems cheap to those glorying in and suffering for great causes.

The Conspiracy of Institutions. The nation is not the only focal point for mass loyalties. Just as loyalty to a nation competes with loyalty to family, job, and friends, so it must compete with loyalty to race, religion, and class. The nation's advantage is based not only on the psychological processes just described: to some degree those energies are also available to other causes. The strength of national, rather than other, loyalties is also partly the result of objective facts: common language, common historical traditions, a definable territory. Finally, national loyalty is built strong as the result of the active role taken by social institutions in building a firm direct tie between individual and nation. The institution of government is of first importance in this effort.

Government is a powerful agency in setting up norms of behavior. By laws establishing limits of freedom and control, government defines general guidelines for life activities. Through control of the schools, government has a crucial lever for inculcating habits of thought, for encouraging some character traits and discouraging others, and for molding individuals to standards of thought and action. Through its multitude of substantive programs, the state purchases conformity and allegiance. By enforcing service in the armed forces, the state transforms citizens into soldiers and in the process brings about similarly striking changes in attitude and outlook. As the source of major news developments, government commands a large portion of the words and symbols transmitted to the public by press, radio, television, and film. By the encouragement of national holidays and festivals, government pounds home myths of national might and images of national glory. By fostering patriotic organizations and activities, government enlists citizens in active demonstrations of patriotism.

There are tremendous variations in the extent and manner that governments utilize the power they possess for building patriotism. There are even greater variations in the size and composition of the groups to which governments are responsible and thus in the final ends for which patriotism is utilized.

Democratic values and traditions do not countenance the ruthless exploitation of people by the state for the state. The power structure within democracies makes such exploitation impossible; it occurs only at the price of changing the character of the state itself. And in the United States, government power is further dispersed as the result of the federal system. Nevertheless, even in the United States, the patriotic theme is an essential ingredient of all public activity, even that at the state and local level.

Public education, for example, has been least affected in the United States by the insistent trend toward national financing and supervision. Yet, as the studies of Charles Merriam and Bessie Pierce have shown, the themes of patriotism and national service are consistently and insistently pursued.[3]

---

[3] Charles Edward Merriam, *The Making of Citizens* (Chicago: The University of Chicago Press, 1931); Bessie L. Pierce, *Civic Attitudes in American School Textbooks* (Chicago: The University of Chicago Press, 1930).

The total impact of the schools is designed certainly, if unwittingly, to conform to Rousseau's dictum: that education should direct the opinion and tastes of men so that they will be "patriots by inclination, by passion, by necessity."

This is true for all nations. Naturally enough, the truth has been demonstrated most graphically and most bleakly by the totalitarian governments. The Nazis showed that a state-operated educational system could be even more powerful than the family as a molder of attitudes and personality, supplanting or destroying the family's influence to a large measure.

The Nazis attempted to create a situation in which individuals received all their cues for action from a state or party agency. They did this by capturing or destroying all other institutions and groups—religious, professional, and social—that guide and control human action. The terrible efficiency of this fully mobilized state-controlled education cannot be doubted. It drastically altered the direction of the culture and the temper, the very personality of the people.

In the United States and other Western democracies, one does not find this total mobilization of state resources and state institutions for the purpose of constructing strong national allegiance. Yet state activities, with minor exceptions, move strongly toward cementing loyalty to the nation. Only a small portion of these activities aim at building direct emotional ties between individual and state. School programs illustrate this attempt, as do bond drives, ceremonies dramatizing the might of armed forces, the display and symbolic care of the flag. But in the democracies, unlike the totalitarian nations, the major impact of state activities is an indirect one: it strengthens national loyalties by strengthening the numerous voluntary groups through which so much of the life and politics of democratic people is organized and directed.

The effects of these programs do not, of course, stop with the voluntary groups. The groups have a vitality of their own. They, in turn, direct the emotions of group members toward the nation. In this circular fashion, virtually all groups contribute to national allegiance. Their members minimize or efface any antagonisms between their own group and the nation. They identify group and national welfare. "What is good for business is good for the nation," trumpets the National Association of Manufacturers. "High wages mean national health," responds the Congress of Industrial Organization.

The voices and forces all pushing in the same direction produce the religious quality of patriotism. It is a quality for which totalitarian nations strive continuously but which is known to democracies largely in periods of crisis—"an element of worship, of willing sacrifice, of joyful merging of the individual in the life of the nation." [4] Here the direct nation-individual linkage is most graphically expressed.

INDIRECT NATION-PERSON TIE

Non-National Loyalties as Filters of National Loyalty. The second strand relating individual to nation is an indirect one. Here satisfactions are experienced in the face-to-face relations of everyday living, in pleasurable interpersonal experiences, warm friends, sympathetic neighbors, the achievement of expectations in marriage and career. One's relationships to the nation are transmitted, or filtered, through these experiences. To the extent that they produce a satisfactory life situation, the individual's identification with his nation is positive. His loyalty may be presumed,

---

[4] Bertrand Russell, *Why Men Fight* (New York: The Century Company, 1917), p. 55.

though it is a loyalty different in kind from the loyalty fostered by direct ties with the state. Where a life situation does not produce a balance of gratifications, the individual's identification with the nation wavers. His loyalty may be more easily eroded.

Until the advent of modern totalitarianism, it is doubtful if the direct nation-person tie could have been built strong enough to sustain national loyalties over long periods of time. It involves, ultimately, the destruction of all privacy. Only with the techniques of modern political exploitation does this seem possible.

For the Western democracies, at least, patriotism cannot be maintained over long periods of time by the direct tie to the nation alone. No one has expressed this idea more clearly than George Washington, who wrote from Valley Forge in April, 1788:

Men may talk of patriotism; they may draw a few examples from ancient story, of great achievements performed by its influence; but whosoever builds upon it, as a sufficient Basis for conducting this Bloody war, will find themselves deceived in the end.... I do not mean to exclude altogether the Idea of Patriotism. I know it exists, and I know it has done much in the present Contest. But I venture to assert, that a great and lasting War can never be supported on this principle alone. It must be aided by a prospect of Interest or some reward.

Washington's concept of "interest" was largely a commercial one. The definition need not be so narrow. But Washington's point is basic.

Democratic nations cannot exist unless the "interests"—the life goals—of its citizens are at least approximately achieved. And these achievements are in areas where there is little or no direct nation-person relationship. National loyalty here becomes a by-product of satis-

factions achieved in non-public spheres of activity.

Indeed, from this view a generalized national loyalty is a misnomer. It does not exist. Loyalties are to specific groups, specific goals, specific programs of action. Populations are loyal to nation only because the nation is believed to symbolize and sustain these values.

Leon Trotsky once remarked that revolutions were not caused by the poor. If they were, he said, there would be revolutions going on all the time. This is one way of expressing the important fact that "life expectations" or "life goals" are not fixed or static concepts. Individuals define these terms in various and divergent fashions; their definitions are influenced in many ways, not least of all by parents, profession, sex, and social class.

To say that loyalty is dependent upon the achievement of life satisfactions is therefore not to say that the poor are the disloyal, the rich, loyal. The individual's own definition of satisfaction is of crucial importance. The fat men who do not make easy converts are those fat in satisfactions, not necessarily in body or other material possessions. A subtle tool to measure these satisfactions would be an index of the discrepancy, if any, between life expectancy and life achievements, as defined by the individual. Where the spread is a big one, deprivations are experienced and loyalty to the nation (not considering direct nation-person ties) is presumably less strong than where expectations are actually or approximately achieved.

This variety in definition of life satisfactions is crucial to understanding the interplay between those satisfactions and national loyalty.

A second general consideration is also of great importance. Life goals are achieved and life satisfactions are pursued within the framework of groups. The happy man in isolation does not exist. He may—and most frequently does—take his terms of reference, his cues for action, his definitions of the good and desirable from the small face-to-face groups with which he comes into most intimate contact: family, friends, business associates, professional colleagues, fellow-workers. Or these cues for life may be influenced by larger, less visible groups with which he identifies himself: social class, the universal church, the international workers. In these latter cases and even in those cases where frames of reference are derived from such apparent abstractions as "the good of mankind," there is usually a face-to-face group in existence, functioning to define and to clarify abstract goals in terms of day-to-day activity.

The principal loyalties of men in democratic states are directed toward these non-national groups and interests. Their very existence provides possibilities for sharp clashes between national and other loyalties. But these other loyalties are also the most important foundation of national loyalty.

Why this is so has already been sug-gested. The nation is the most important group with which all persons in a given geographic area are associated. It gives all citizens a common point of reference. It sustains their groups. A threat to a nation is interpreted as a threat to all groups within the nation and to the gratifications derived from those groups. The satisfactions springing from smaller groups are thus related to the nation and to national loyalty.

But in times of crisis, the national demands may easily conflict with the demands of non-national groups. Family welfare, professional status, career and job stability may be threatened or thwarted by governmental policy. In such circumstances, clean choices need not always be made. When they do, national loyalty may mean family or professional disloyalty. Where loyalty to family or to career or to profession is held foremost, then the result is national disloyalty.

The total configuration is a fine paradox: non-national loyalties are the bricks from which national loyalty is constructed; they are also the brickbats by which national loyalty is destroyed.

. . . .

II · The Nation-State and the State System

The organization of men's activities and loyalties into national communities, each possessed of sovereignty, has given international relations its distinctive form. A state is a body of people politically organized under one government with sovereign rights. Sovereignty refers to the exclusive jurisdiction that a state possesses within its territory and to its freedom to act in international affairs without subjection to the legal control of another state organization. The modern state system dates approximately from the Reformation when the temporal rulers of France, England, the German states, and the lesser powers of Europe took advantage of the anarchy accompanying the religious wars to assert their authority within their territorial domains. They had had to bow to the authority of the Pope in religious affairs, and to the Emperor of the defunct Holy Roman Empire in secular matters and to put up with the challenge of powerful feudal lords within their own kingdoms. Henceforth supreme authority or sovereignty was to be identified with the territorial state whose rights, independence, and power all derived from what Herz (see page 50) calls its "territoriality." Once established, sovereignty conferred upon each state the right to dispose of its people and its resources in whatever manner it deemed desirable, and to act without regard for any political superior either inside or outside the national territory. The result of this transformation was to create a world of sovereign, independent states, theoretically equal but varying widely in real power, each dependent for its survival upon its own ingenuity and resources. Henceforth individual security, diplomacy, international law, war, commerce, and the development of culture and civilization itself would take their form and content from the existence of the nation-state as the highest sovereign political entity.

Obviously not all states are equal in size or in the resources at their command. This inequality in the distribution of power has profoundly modified the operation of a system based upon the theoretical equality of each sovereign state. Samuel Grafton explained the distinction in his witty phrase: "Even after you give the squirrel a certificate which says he is quite as big as any elephant, he is still going to be smaller, and all the squirrels will know it and all the elephants will know it." [1] The book in which this quotation appeared, appropriately entitled *The Super-Powers*, sought to make Americans appreciate the fact that the Western state system has always been dominated by a few great states. The unequal distribution of power among states gave rise to classifications such as great powers and small powers. One author has defined a great power as "a Power with general interests, and with such strength that it can attempt to advance or protect those interests in every sphere." By contrast small powers are "Powers with the means of defending only limited interests...." [2] The same author introduces a category entitled Dominant Powers in order to denote those powers that have tried to dominate Europe and have only been prevented by a coalition of the majority of other powers, at the cost of an exhausting general war. "A Great Power is one that can afford to take on any other Power whatever in single combat; and a Dominant Power is one that can take on a combination of any other Powers." [3]

To this list can be added the category of "Superpower" which William T. R. Fox has defined as possessing "Great power plus great mobility of power." [4] In 1945 it looked as though there would be three superpowers, but postwar events soon revealed the weakness of Great Britain, leaving only Russia and the United States in this category. These classifications are important because trends in the distribution of power among nations largely determine the evolution of the pattern of international relations. If we know who the superpowers and great powers are, we know from whence we can expect the possibility of large-scale international violence.

Subject to no sovereign superior, the nation-states have traditionally been left to their own devices for regulating their relations and guaranteeing their security. This has given rise to the condition of "power politics" whereby each nation seeks to protect itself by employing its power to gain advantage over others. In order to protect themselves against the worst dangers of such a Hobbesian "state of nature," states have engaged in policies of alliance, whereby the strength of many is pooled to maintain a balance of power, and to assure collective security against the power of a more menacing member of the system. (See Chapter XI and XX.)

Until the United States and Japan entered the international arena towards the beginning of the twentieth century, the nation-state system was virtually limited to Europe. There a common culture and a common respect for the principle of dynastic legitimacy and (following the French Revolution) for the right of national self-determination, fostered a considerable measure of restraint in spite of power politics. However, as Herz points out, the foun-

---

[1] Quoted in William T. R. Fox, *The Super-Powers* (New York: Harcourt, Brace & Company, 1944), p. 3.

[2] Martin Wight, *Power Politics* (London: Royal Institute of International Affairs, 1946), pp. 18–27.

[3] *Ibid.*

[4] Fox, *op. cit.*, p. 21.

dation of European security rested upon the essential autonomy and defensibility of each national territory. Each of the great states was large enough to provide its citizens with living space and powerful enough to deter aggression. Since there was neither the necessity nor the opportunity for unlimited expansion, the European states were able to regulate their affairs by such devices as limited war and the balance of power. As a sense of security seeped across nineteenth century Europe, it became less necessary for states to organize the activities of their people for defense. The expectation of peace fostered peace just as today the expectation of war engenders those conditions which precipitate war. The European system also possessed a safety valve in the form of overseas expansion where nationalistic and economic pressures could find a less dangerous outlet and where even the most severe conflicts could be regarded as nonvital.

So long as the international system afforded the possibility for the major powers to develop in comparative peace and prosperity, the nation-state served a constructive function. But as Dr. Herz points out, beginning with the nineteenth century, certain trends became visible which threatened to undermine the principle of territorial impenetrability "which was the strongest guarantee of its independent coexistence with other states of like nature." In part these trends had to do with the difficulty of applying the principle of self-determination (i.e., one people, one territory) but also with the perfection of instruments of ideological-political penetration and of mass destruction.

World War I witnessed the breakdown of the European order of powers. The League of Nations' principle of collective security, which essentially sought to mobilize the collective interests of all in protecting the system against violation by one of its more aggressive members, proved unable to cope with the anarchy engendered by the extreme nationalism of the 1930's. Owing to the ethnic heterogeneity of Central and Eastern Europe which we mentioned earlier, it was impossible to erect viable national states. The conflicts between the new national states and their minorities soon became interwoven with the international ambitions of the revisionist powers—Italy and Germany. Germany in particular was seized by a virus of nationalism unlike anything that Europe had ever experienced. Among Germans the deprivations and insecurity incurred by industrialization, the dissatisfactions stemming from Versailles, the specter of Communism, and the unworkability of the Weimar Republic produced a traumatic condition in which millions of Germans threw themselves into the arms of Adolf Hitler. Hitler preached a doctrine of tribal (a mythical Aryan race) nationalism which promised to give Germans a more meaningful social existence. The fact that reactionary economic and social interest contributed to Hitler's rise and that liberals, workers, and Marxists had to be crushed does not change the fact that millions of Germans voluntarily rallied to the Hitlerian movement. Italy and Japan also stepped up the tempo of their expansion. By the mid 1930's it was easier to see the bankruptcy of a political system based upon nationalism than to do anything about it.

The post-World War I rivalry between the superpowers has demonstrated most dramatically the limits that exist to most nations' claims to equal political sovereignty and to any analysis based upon this assumption. Nation-states still exist as actors in the inter-state system, but the disparity of power among them has drastically modified the concept of a system composed of relatively equal sovereign entities. Even the strongest—the Soviet Union and the United States—are physically vulnerable to such devastating air-atomic attacks as to render the security function of the territorial state virtually meaningless for the millions of people who would be destined to die in an atomic war.

The transformation of the balance of power system into a bipolar system, which was inherent in the disparity of power between the superpowers and other nation-states, has greatly increased the instability of the present system. (See Chapter XI.) The monolithic organizational principles of the Communist bloc and the manifestations of Soviet expansionist intentions under Stalin quickly crystallized another bloc of powers around the United States. The inability or unwillingness of the superpowers to reach agreement on the terms for peaceful coexistence has brought about such a high degree of bloc integration that one student has been led to speak of "bloc actors" rather than nation-states to explain the operation of the bipolar system.[5] It is characteristic of the new system that many states—though by no means all, as Aron points out below—feel that their security can only be assured by integrating and concerting their behavior with that of the leading or directing member of the bloc. Although rarely ever complete, once such integration reaches a certain level it becomes extremely difficult for a bloc member to withdraw or to feel secure in doing so. Unlike the flexible balance of power system, the bipolar system is characterized by a deseparate struggle on the part of each bloc to secure a preponderant capability vis-à-vis its competitor. This has engendered a drive for spheres of influence and the enlistment of new members in each bloc. It goes without saying that in such a loosely integrated bloc as the Western, the divergent national values of its members are often a source of tension and disagreement, as the Suez crisis of 1956 demonstrated. Even within the Soviet bloc the vitality of the nation-state manifests itself in the varying experiences of Yugoslavia, Poland, and Hungary.

Two additional categories of states exist—the neutrals and the uncommitted. The neutrals like Switzerland and Sweden hope to preserve their independence by relying upon their natural strength (together with the interests which all antagonistic states have in preserving some "neutral" ground) to deter aggression. The uncommitted or neutralist powers like Egypt, India, and Indonesia regard the "cold war" as a selfish struggle between the superpowers in which they, themselves, do not need to be involved. The selection from Raymond Aron, (see page 60) conveys a

---

[5] Morton Kaplan, *System and Process in International Politics* (New York: John Wiley and Sons, 1957).

good impression of the variety of relationships that can exist even in a world characterized by an encompassing bipolar conflict.

The source of greatest potential revolutionary change in the nation-state system presently resides in the likelihood that additional powers will come into possession of nuclear weapons. In such an event, the concentration of most of the world's power (military and industrial) in two superpowers would give way to a system in which an indefinite number of lesser powers would exist on the basis of fundamental equality as possessors of the new weapons. Although such a development would tend to work a fundamental change in the present bipolarity, it would only deepen the anachronism of the nation-state and confront the world with the nightmare of uncontrolled atomic armaments.

1 • Rise and Demise of the Territorial State *

John H. Herz

The author, Professor of Government at the City College of New York, has also written Political Realism and Political Idealism *(1951). In his most recent study,* International Politics in the Atomic Age *(1959), Herz attempts to assess the profound impact of technological developments upon the concept and theory of sovereign nation-states.*

· · · ·

BASIC FEATURES OF THE MODERN STATE SYSTEM

Traditionally, the classical system of international relations, or the modern state system, has been considered "anarchic," because it was based on unequally distributed power and was deficient in higher—that is, supranational—authority. Its units, the independent, sovereign nation-states, were forever threatened by stronger power and survived precariously through the balance-of-power system. Customarily, then, the modern state system has been contrasted with the medieval system, on the one hand, where units of international relations were under higher law and higher authority, and with those more recent international trends, on the other, which seemed to point toward a greater, "collective" security of nations and a "rule of law" that would protect them from the indiscriminate use of force characteristic of the age of power politics.

From the vantage point of the atomic age, we can probe deeper into the basic characteristics of the classical system. What is it that ultimately accounted for the peculiar unity, compactness, coher-

---

* *World Politics,* IX (1957), 473–93. Reprinted by permission.

ence of the modern nation-state, setting it off from other nation-states as a separate, independent, and sovereign power? It would seem that this underlying factor is to be found neither in the sphere of law nor in that of politics, but rather in that substratum of statehood where the state unit confronts us, as it were, in its physical, corporeal capacity: as an expanse of territory encircled for its identification and its defense by a "hard shell" of fortifications. In this lies what will here be referred to as the "impermeability," or "impenetrability," or simply the "territoriality," of the modern state. The fact that it was surrounded by a hard shell rendered it to some extent secure from foreign penetration, and thus made it an ultimate unit of protection for those within its boundaries. Throughout history, that unit which affords protection and security to human beings has tended to become the basic political unit; people, in the long run, will recognize that authority, any authority, which possesses the power of protection.

Some similarity perhaps prevails between an international structure consisting of impenetrable units with an ensuing measurablility of power and comparability of power relations, and the system of classical physics with its measurable forces and the (then) impenetrable atom as its basic unit. And as that system has given way to relativity and to what nuclear science has uncovered, the impenetrability of the political atom, the nation-state, is giving way to a permeability which tends to obliterate the very meaning of unit and unity, power and power relations, sovereignty and independence. The possibility of "hydrogenization" merely represents the culmination of a development which has rendered the traditional defense structure of nations obsolete through the power to by-pass the shell protecting a two-dimensional territory and thus to destroy—vertically, as it were—even the most powerful ones. Paradoxically, utmost strength now coincides in the same unit with utmost vulnerability, absolute power with utter impotence.

This development must inevitably affect traditional power concepts. Considering power units as politically independent and legally sovereign made sense when power, measurable, graded, calculable, served as a standard of comparison between units which, in the sense indicated above, could be described as impermeable. Under those conditions, then, power indicated the strategic aspect, independence the political aspect, sovereignty the legal aspect of this self-same impermeability. With the passing of the age of territoriality, the usefulness of these concepts must now be questioned.

Thus the Great Divide does not separate "international anarchy," or "balance of power," or "power politics," from incipient international interdependence, or from "collective security"; all these remain within the realm of the territorial structure of states and can therefore be considered as trends or stages *within* the classical system of "hard shell" power units. Rather, the Divide occurs where the basis of territorial power and defensibility vanishes. It is here and now. But in order to understand the present, we must study more closely the origin and nature of the classical system itself.

THE RISE OF THE TERRITORIAL STATE

The rise of the modern territorial state meant that, within countries, "feudal anarchy" of jurisdictions yielded to the ordered centralism of the absolute monarchy, which ruled over a pacified area with the aid of a bureaucracy, a professional army, and the power to levy taxes, while in foreign relations, in place of the medieval hierarchy of power and authority, there prevailed insecurity, a disorder only slightly attenuated by a power balance that was forever being threatened, disturbed, and then restored. Such has been the customary interpretation.

It is possible to view developments in a somewhat different light. Instead of contrasting the security of groups and individuals within the sovereign territorial state with conditions of insecurity outside, the establishment of territorial independence can be interpreted as an at least partially successful attempt to render the territorial group secure in its outward relations as well. Especially when contrasted with the age of anarchy and insecurity which immediately preceded it, the age of territoriality appears as one of relative order and safety.

Indeed, the transition from medieval hierarchism to modern compartmentalized sovereignties was neither easy, nor straight, nor short. Modern sovereignty arose out of the triangular struggle among emperors and popes, popes and kings, and kings and emperors. When the lawyers of Philip the Fair propounded the dual maxim according to which the king was to be "emperor in his realm" (*rex est imperator in regno suo*) and was no longer to "recognize any superior" (*superiorem non recognoscens*), it was the beginning of a development in the course of which, in McIlwain's words, "Independence *de facto* was ultimately translated into a sovereignty *de jure*."[1] But centuries of disturbance and real anarchy ensued during which the problems of rulership and security remained unsettled. The relative protection which the sway of moral standards and the absence of highly destructive weapons had afforded groups and individuals in the earlier Middle Ages gave way to total insecurity when gunpowder was invented and com-

mon standards broke down. Out of the internal and external turmoil during the age of religious and civil wars, a "neutralist" central power eventually managed to establish itself in and for each of the different territories like so many *rochers de bronze*.

The idea that a territorial coexistence of states, based on the power of the territorial princes, might afford a better guarantee of peace than the Holy Roman Empire was already widespread at the height of the Middle Ages when the emperor proved incapable of enforcing the peace. But territoriality could hardly prevail so long as the knight in his castle (that medieval unit of impermeability) was relatively immune from attack, as was the medieval city within its walls. Only with a developing money economy were overlords able to free themselves from dependence on vassals and lay the foundations of their own power by establishing a professional army. Infantry and artillery now proved superior to old-style cavalry, firearms prevailed over the old weapons.

As in all cases of radically new developments in military technology, the "gunpowder revolution" caused a real revolution in the superstructure of economic, social, and political relationships because of its impact on the units of protection and security. A feeling of insecurity swept all Europe.[2] Though a

---

[1] Charles H. McIlwain, *The Growth of Political Thought in the West* (New York: The Macmillan Company, 1932), p. 268.

[2] Ariosto expressed the feeling of despair which invaded the "old powers" of chivalry when gunpowder destroyed the foundations of their system, in terms reminding one of present-day despair in the face of the destructive forces loosed upon our own world:
"Oh! curs'd device! base implement of
    death!
Framed in the black Tartarean realms be-
    neath!
By Beelzebub's malicious art design'd
To ruin all the race of human kind."
Quoted from *Orlando Furioso* by Felix Gilbert, in Edward M. Earle, ed., *Makers of Modern Strategy* (Princeton: Princeton University Press, 1943), p. 4.

Machiavelli might establish new rules as to how to gain and maintain power, there still followed more than a century of unregulated, ideological "total" wars inside and among countries until the new units of power were clearly established. Before old or new sovereigns could claim to be recognized as rulers of large areas, it had to be determined how far, on the basis of their new military power, they were able to extend their control geographically.

The large-area state came finally to occupy the place that the castle or fortified town had previously held as a unit of impenetrability. But the new unit could not be considered consolidated until all independent fortifications within it had disappeared and, in their place, fortresses lining the circumference of the country had been built by the new central power and manned by its armed forces. If we contrast our present system of bases and similar outposts surrounding entire world regions with what are today small-scale nation-states, perhaps we can visualize what the hard shell of frontier fortifications consolidating the then large-scale territorial states meant by way of extending power units in the age of absolutism. They became, in the words of Frederick the Great, "mighty nails which hold a ruler's provinces together." There now was peace and protection within. War became a regularized military procedure; only the breaking of the shell permitted interference with what had now become the internal affairs of another country.

In this way was established the basic structure of the territorial state which was to last throughout the classical period of the modern state system. Upon this foundation a new system and new concepts of international relations could arise. And as early as the second half of the seventeenth century a perspicacious observer succeeded in tying up the new concepts with the underlying structure of territorial statehood.

. . . .

The Territorial State in International Relations

From territoriality resulted the concepts and institutions which characterized the interrelations of sovereign units, the modern state system. Modern international law, for instance, could now develop. Like the international system that produced it, international law has often been considered inherently contradictory because of its claim to bind sovereign units. But whether or not we deny to it for this reason the name and character of genuine law, it is important to see it in its connection with the territorial nature of the state system that it served. Only then can it be understood as a system of rules not contrary to, but implementing, the sovereign independence of states. Only to the extent that it reflected their territoriality and took into account their sovereignty could international law develop in modern times. For its general rules and principles deal primarily with the delimitation of the jurisdiction of countries. It thus implements the *de facto* condition of territorial impenetrability by more closely defining unit, area, and conditions of impenetrability. Such a law must reflect, rather than regulate. As one author has rightly remarked, "International law really amounts to laying down the principle of national sovereignty and deducing the consequences."[3] It is not for this reason superfluous, for sovereign units must know in some detail where their jurisdictions end and those of other units begin; without such standards, nations would be involved in constant strife over

---

[3] François Laurent, as quoted by Walter Schiffer, *The Legal Community of Mankind* (New York: Columbia University Press, 1954), p. 157.

the implementation of their independence.

But it was not only this mutual legal accommodation which rendered possible a relatively peaceful coexistence of nations. War itself, the very phenomenon which reflected, not the strength, but the limitations of impermeability, was of such a nature as to maintain at least the principle of territoriality. War was limited not only in conduct but also in objectives. It was not a process of physical or political annihilation but a contest of power and will in which the interests, but not the existence, of the contestants were at stake. Now that we approach the era of absolute exposure, without walls or moats, where penetration will mean not mere damage or change but utter annihilation of life and way of life, it may dawn on us that what has vanished with the age of sovereignty and "power politics" was not entirely adverse in nature and effects.

Among other "conservative" features of the classical system, we notice one only in passing: the balance of power. It is only recently that emphasis has shifted from a somewhat one-sided concern with the negative aspects of the balance—its uncertainty, its giving rise to unending conflicts and frequent wars, etc.—to its protective effect of preventing the expansionist capacity of power from destroying other power altogether. But at the time of its perfection in statecraft and diplomacy, there were even theories (not lived up to in practice, of course) about the *legal* obligations of nations to form barriers against hegemony power in the common interest.

More fundamental to the conservative structure of the old system was its character as a community. Forming a comparatively pacified whole, Europe was set off sharply against the world outside, a world beyond those lines which, by common agreement, separated a community based on territoriality and common

heritage from anarchy, where the law of nature reigned and no standards of civilization applied. Only recently have the existence and role of so-called "amity lines" been rediscovered, lines which were drawn in the treaties of the early modern period and which separated European territories, where the rules of war and peace were to prevail, from overseas territories and areas.[4] There was to be "no peace beyond the line"; that is, European powers, although possibly at peace in Europe, continued to be *homo homini lupus* abroad. This practice made it easier for the European family of nations to observe self-denying standards at home by providing them with an outlet in the vast realm discovered outside Europe. While the practice of drawing amity lines subsequently disappeared, one chief function of overseas expansion remained: a European balance of power could be maintained or adjusted because it was relatively easy to divert European conflicts into overseas directions and adjust them there. Thus the openness of the world contributed to the consolidation of the territorial system. The end of the "world frontier" and the resulting closedness of an interdependent world inevitably affected this system's effectiveness.

Another characteristic of the old system's protective nature may be seen in the almost complete absence of instances in which countries were wiped out in the course of wars or as a consequence of other power-political events. This, of course, refers to the territorial units at home only, not to the peoples and state units beyond the pale abroad; and to the complete destruction of a state's inde-

---

[4] See Carl Schmitt, *Der Nomos der Erde* (Cologne, 1950), pp. 60ff.; also W. Schoenborn, "Über Entdeckung als Rechtstitel völkerrechtlichen Gebietserwerbs," in D. S. Constantinopoulos and H. Wehberg, eds., *Gegenwartsprobleme des internationalen Rechts und der Rechtsphilosophie* (Hamburg, 1953), pp. 239ff.

pendent existence, not to mere loss of territory or similar changes, which obviously abounded in the age of power politics.

Evidence of this is to be found not only in a legal and political ideology that denied the permissibility of conquest at home while recognizing it as a title for the acquisition of territorial jurisdiction abroad. For such a doctrine had its non-ideological foundation in the actual difference between European and non-European politics so far as their territoriality was concerned. European states were impermeable in the sense here outlined, while most of those overseas were easily penetrable by Europeans. In accordance with these circumstances, international politics in Europe knew only rare and exceptional instances of actual annihilation through conquest or similar forceful means.

Prior to the twentieth century, there were indeed the Napoleonic conquests, but I submit that this is a case where the exception confirms the rule. The Napoleonic system, as a hegemonial one, was devised to destroy the established system of territoriality and balanced power as such. Consequently, Napoleon and his policies appeared "demonic" to contemporaries, as well as to a nineteenth century which experienced the restoration of the earlier system. During that century occurred Bismarck's annexations of some German units into Prussia in pursuance of German unification. As in Napoleon's case, they appeared abnormal to many of his contemporaries, although the issue of national unification tended to mitigate this impression. Besides these, there was indeed the partition of Poland, and considering the lamentable and lasting impression and the universal bad conscience it produced even among the ruling nations in a century used to quite a bit of international skulduggery, again one may

well claim an exceptional character for that event.[5]

What, in particular, accounts for this remarkable stability? Territoriality—the establishment of defensible units, internally pacified and hard-shell rimmed —may be called its foundation. On this foundation, two phenomena permitted the system to become more stable than might otherwise have been the case: the prevalence of the legitimacy principle and, subsequently, nationalism. Legitimacy implied that the dynasties ruling the territorial states of old Europe mutually recognized each other as rightful sovereigns. Depriving one sovereign of his rights by force could not but appear to destroy the very principle on which the rights of all of them rested.

With the rise of nationalism, we witness the personalization of the units as self-determining, national groups. Nationalism now made it appear as abhorrent to deprive a sovereign nation of its independence as to despoil a legitimate ruler had appeared before. States, of course, had first to become "nation-states," considering themselves as representing specific nationality groups, which explains why in the two regions of Europe where larger numbers of old units stood in the way of national unification their demise encountered little objection. In most instances, however, the rise of nationalism led to the emergence of *new* states, which split away from multinational or colonial empires. This meant the extension of the European principle of "non-obliteration" all

---

[5] Except for these cases, we find only marginal instances of complete obliteration. The annexation of the Free City of Krakow by Russia eliminated a synthetic creation of the Vienna settlement. British conquest of the Boer Republics, if considered as an instance of annihilation of European polities in view of the European origin of the inhabitants, happened at the very rim of the world, as it were, remote from the continent where the practice of non-annihilation prevailed.

over the world. It is perhaps significant that even in our century, and even after the turmoil of attempted world conquest and resulting world wars, a point has been made of restoring the most minute and inconsiderable of sovereignties, down to Luxembourg and Albania.[6]

This hypertrophy of nation-states presented new problems—above all, that of an improved system of protection. For by now it had become clear that the protective function of the old system was only a relative blessing after all. Continued existence of states as such was perhaps more or less guaranteed. But power and influence, status, frontiers, economic interests—in short, everything that constituted the life and interests of nations beyond bare existence—were always at the mercy of what power politics wrought. Furthermore, much of the relative stability and political equilibrium of the territorial states had been due to the extension of Western control over the world. When what could be penetrated had been subjugated, assimilated, or established as fellow "sovereign" states, the old units were thrown back upon themselves. Hence the demand for a new system which would offer more security to old and new nations: collective security.

I propose to view collective security not as the extreme opposite of power politics, but as an attempt to maintain, and render more secure, the impermeability of what were still territorial states. To an age which took territoriality for granted, replacing power politics with collective security would indeed appear to be a radical departure. From the vantage point of the nuclear age, however, a plan to protect individual sovereignties

---

[6] Cf. also the remarkable stability of state units in the Western Hemisphere *qua* independent units; unstable as some of them are domestically, their sovereign identity as units appears almost sacrosanct.

by collective guarantees for continuing sovereignty appears questionable not because of its innovating, but because of its conservative, nature. Its conservatism lies in its basic objective: the protection of the hard-shell territorial structure of its members, or, as the core article of the Covenant of the League of Nations put it, its guarantee of their "territorial integrity and political independence" against external aggression. The beginning of air war and the increasing economic interdependence of nations had indicated by the end of World War I that the old-style military barriers might be by-passed. If territorial units were to be preserved in the future, it would be accomplished less by reliance on individual defense potentials than by marshaling collective power in order to preserve individual powers.

But since the idea of organizing a genuine supranational force—an international police force—was rejected, the League had to cling to classical arrangements insofar as the procedures of protection were concerned. The guarantee to the individual states was to be the formation of the "Grand Coalition" of all against the isolated aggressor, which presupposed the maintenance of a certain level of armed strength by the member states. A member without that minimum of military strength would be a liability rather than an asset to the organization—in Geneva parlance, a "consumer" and not a "producer" of security. Thus classical concepts (the sovereignty and independence of nation-states) as well as classical institutions (in particular, hard-shell defensibility) were to be maintained under the new system.

Whether there ever was a chance for the system to be effective in practice is beside the point here. It is sufficient to realize how closely it was tied to the underlying structure as well as to the prevailing concepts and policies of the territorial age.

THE DECLINE OF THE TERRITORIAL STATE

Beginning with the nineteenth century, certain trends became visible which tended to endanger the functioning of the classical system. Directly or indirectly, all of them had a bearing upon that feature of the territorial state which was the strongest guarantee of its independent coexistence with other states of like nature: its hard shell—that is, its defensibility in case of war.

Naturally, many of these trends concerned war itself and the way in which it was conducted. But they were not related to the shift from the limited, duel-type contests of the eighteenth century to the more or less unlimited wars that developed in the nineteenth century with conscription, "nations in arms," and increasing destructiveness of weapons. By themselves, these developments were not inconsistent with the classical function of war. Enhancing a nation's defensive capacity, instituting universal military service, putting the economy on a war footing, and similar measures tended to bolster the territorial state rather than to endanger it.

Total war in a quite different sense is tied up with developments in warfare which enable the belligerents to overleap or by-pass the traditional hard-shell defense of states. When this happens, the traditional relationship between war, on the one hand, and territorial power and sovereignty, on the other, is altered decisively. Arranged in order of increasing effectiveness, these new factors may be listed under the following headings: (a) possibility of economic blockade; (b) ideological-political penetration; (c) air warfare; and (d) atomic warfare.[7]

---

[7] Note: These new developments to which Professor Herz refers are treated in more detail in Chapters XII, XIII and XVII.

(a) *Economic warfare.* It should be said from the outset that so far economic blockade has never enabled one belligerent to force another into surrender through starvation alone. Although in World War I Germany and her allies were seriously endangered when the Western allies cut them off from overseas supplies, a very real effort was still required to defeat them on the military fronts. The same thing applies to World War II. Blockade was an important contributing factor, however. Its importance for the present analysis lies in its unconventional nature, permitting belligerents to by-pass the hard shell of the enemy. Its effect is due to the changed economic status of industrialized nations.

Prior to the industrial age, the territorial state was largely self-contained economically. Although one of the customary means of conducting limited war was starving fortresses into surrender, this applied merely to these individual portions of the hard shell, and not to entire nations. Attempts to starve a belligerent nation in order to avoid having to breach the shell proved rather ineffective, as witness the Continental Blockade and its counterpart in the Napoleonic era. The Industrial Revolution made countries like Britain and Germany increasingly dependent on imports. In war, this meant that they could survive only by controlling areas larger than their own territory. In peacetime, economic dependency became one of the causes of a phenomenon which itself contributed to the transformation of the old state system: imperialism. Anticipating war, with its new danger of blockade, countries strove to become more self-sufficient through enlargement of their areas of control. To the extent that the industrialized nations lost self-sufficiency, they were driven into expansion in a (futile) effort to regain it. Today, if at all, only control of entire continents enables major nations to survive economically in major wars. This implies that hard-shell military defense must be a matter of defending more than a single nation; it must extend around half the world.

(b) *Psychological warfare*, the attempt to undermine the morale of an enemy population, or to subvert its loyalty, shares with economic warfare a bypassing effect on old-style territorial defensibility. It was formerly practiced, and practicable, only under quite exceptional circumstances. Short periods of genuine world revolutionary propaganda, such as the early stages of the French Revolution, scarcely affected a general practice under which dynasties, and later governments, fought each other with little ideological involvement on the part of larger masses or classes. Only in rare cases—for instance, where national groups enclosed in and hostile to multinational empires could be appealed to—was there an opening wedge for "fifth column" strategies.

With the emergence of political belief-systems, however, nations became more susceptible to undermining from within. Although wars have not yet been won solely by subversion of loyalties, the threat involved has affected the inner coherence of the territorial state ever since the rise to power of a regime that claims to represent, not the cause of a particular nation, but that of mankind, or at least of its suppressed and exploited portions. Bolshevism from 1917 on has provided the second instance in modern history of world revolutionary propaganda. Communist penetration tactics subsequently were imitated by the Nazi and Fascist regimes and, eventually, by the democracies. In this way, new lines of division, cutting horizontally through state units instead of leaving them separated vertically from each other at their frontiers, have now become possible.

(c) *Air warfare* and (d) *nuclear warfare*. Of all the new developments, air warfare, up to the atomic age, has been the one that affected the territoriality of nations most radically. With its coming, the bottom dropped out—or, rather, the roof blew off—the relative security of the territorial state. True, even this new kind of warfare, up to and including the Second World War, did not by itself account for the defeat of a belligerent, as some of the more enthusiastic prophets of the air age had predicted it would. Undoubtedly, however, it had a massive contributory effect. And this effect was due to strategic action in the *hinterland* rather than to tactical use at the front. It came at least close to defeating one side by direct action against the "soft" interior of the country, bypassing outer defenses and thus foreshadowing the end of the frontier—that is, the demise of the traditional impermeability of even the militarily most powerful states. Warfare now changed "from a fight to a process of devastation." [8]

[8] B. H. Liddell Hart, *The Revolution in Warfare* (New Haven, Conn.: Yale University Press, 1947), p. 36. Suspicion of what would be in the offing, once man gained the capacity to fly, was abroad as early as the eighteenth century. Thus Samuel Johnson remarked: "If men were all virtuous, I should with great alacrity teach them all to fly. But what would be the security of the good, if the bad could at pleasure invade them from the sky? Against an army sailing through the clouds, neither walls, nor mountains, nor seas, could afford security" (quoted in J. U. Nef, *War and Human Progress* [Cambridge, Mass.: Harvard University Press, 1952], p. 198). And Benjamin Franklin, witnessing the first balloon ascension at Paris in 1783, foresaw invasion from the air and wrote: "Convincing Sovereigns of folly of wars may perhaps be one effect of it, since it will be impracticable for the most potent of them to guard his dominions.... Where is the Prince who can afford so to cover his country with troops for its defense, as that ten thousand men descending from the clouds, might not in many places do an infinite deal of mischief before a force could be brought together to repel them?" (from a letter to Jan Ingelhouss, reproduced in *Life Magazine,* January 9, 1956).

That air warfare was considered as something entirely unconventional is seen from the initial reaction to it. Revolutionary transition from an old to a new system has always affected moral standards. In the classical age of the modern state system, the "new morality" of shooting at human beings from a distance had finally come to be accepted, but the standards of the age clearly distinguished "lawful combatants" at the front or in fortifications from the civilian remainder of the population. When air war came, reactions thus differed significantly in the cases of air fighting at the front and of air war carried behind the front. City bombing was felt to constitute "illegitimate" warfare, and populations were inclined to treat airmen engaging in it as "war criminals." This feeling continued into World War II, with its large-scale area bombing. Such sentiments reflected the general feeling of helplessness in the face of a war which threatened to render obsolete the concept of territorial power, together with its ancient implication of protection.

The process has now been completed with the advent of nuclear weapons. For it is more than doubtful that the processes of scientific invention and technological discovery, which not only have created and perfected the fission and fusion weapons themselves but have brought in their wake guided missiles with nuclear warheads, jet aircraft with intercontinental range and supersonic speed, and the prospect of nuclear-powered planes or rockets with unlimited range and with automatic guidance to specific targets anywhere in the world, can in any meaningful way be likened to previous new inventions, however revolutionary. These processes add up to an uncanny absoluteness of effect which previous innovations could not achieve. The latter might render power units of a certain type (for instance, castles or cities) obsolete and enlarge the realm of defensible power units from city-state to territorial state or even large-area empire. They might involve destruction, in war, of entire populations. But there still remained the seemingly inexhaustible reservoir of the rest of mankind. Today, when not even two halves of the globe remain impermeable, it can no longer be a question of enlarging an area of protection and of substituting one unit of security for another. Since we are inhabitants of a planet of limited (and, as it now seems, insufficient) size, we have reached the limit within which the effect of the means of destruction has become absolute. Whatever remained of the impermeability of states seems to have gone for good.

What has been lost can be seen from two statements by thinkers separated by thousands of years and half the world; both reflect the condition of territorial security. Mencius, in ancient China, when asked for guidance in matters of defense and foreign policy by the ruler of a small state, is said to have counseled: "Dig deeper your moats; build higher your walls; guard them along with your people." This remained the classical posture up to our age, when a Western sage, Bertrand Russell, in the interwar period could still define power as something radiating from one center and growing less with distance from that center until it finds an equilibrium with that of similar geographically anchored units. Now that power can destroy power from center to center, everything is different.

. . . .

2 • Unity and Plurality of the Diplomatic Field *

Raymond Aron

The author, born in Paris in 1905, graduated from the Ecole Normale Supérieure, following which he undertook a period of study in German philosophy and historiography. After the French capitulation in 1940, he worked with General de Gaulle in London and became editor-in-chief of La France Libre. *Since 1947 he has been associated with* Le Figaro. *His views on social, political, and economic questions have won him recognition as Europe's ranking commentator on the contemporary scene, and his articles have appeared in many leading newspapers and journals throughout Europe and America. He is the author of a number of books, two of which—* The Century of Total War *(1954) and* The Opium of the Intellectuals *(1957) were published in America.*

The international situation at the end of the Second World War was characterized by four main features: the supremacy of Russia and the United States; the military presence of these two states at every point of the globe; their mutual ideological antagonism; and the development of weapons of mass destruction. None of these features, except the last, was unprecedented. But their conjunction was new, and the novelty can be shown in several different ways: the atomic weapon was introduced at a time when all the nations of the world constituted a single system dominated by two giants, each of which seemed pledged by its very nature to seek the destruction of the other.[1] When the collapse of European states and empires created a vacuum in Europe and Asia, two states faced each other, the one irresistible on land, the other, thanks to the atomic weapon, in the air, each convinced that it alone could show humanity the road to freedom.

Let us take as a point of departure the least original situation: the bipolar structure which historical memories—Athens and Sparta, Rome and Carthage, Caesar and Antony—charge with tragic overtones. When two states outclass all others, their relations are likely to take one of four different forms. They can rule together over the civilization to which they both belong; they can draw a dividing line between the zones which constitute their respective empires; they can engage in a struggle to the death; or they can coexist as enemies. These four possibilities might be boiled down to two: complete or partial agreement, total or limited conflict.

---

[1] The United States is pledged to seek the death of Communism only to the extent that the latter refuses to recognize and cannot recognize, according to its doctrine, the right of capitalism to exist.

* From *On War* (London:Secker & Warburg, 1958), pp. 38–63. Reprinted by permission.

There is another possible formula, less logical but historically more accurate: complete agreement or a struggle to the death being ruled out, the reality would consist of a combination between the partition of the world into zones of influence and competition for frontiers and the allegiance of neutrals. Cold war and peaceful coexistence are merely two variations of this same compound of tacit understanding and open rivalry. In one case, the leaders put the accent on rivalry, in the other on understanding. On the one hand, they encourage the fear that rivalry will lead to total war; on the other, they take pains to suggest that the tacit agreement will be transformed into an assured peace. The difference is real if one considers the psychology of peoples and the words of their leaders. It is insignificant if one sticks to the basic realities. One must passionately hope that the rivalry of the great powers will not lead to total war, but it is not certain that complete agreement would be preferable to rivalry. Men and states have always feared the hegemony of a single power. Would the hegemony of two be much better? Let us suppose that the Big Three directory which Roosevelt dreamed of, and which was merely a duumvirate in disguise, had lasted: would justice have been better preserved? In any case, a great-power directory would have reduced even further the freedom of maneuver and the autonomy of the small powers. The Cold War cut Germany in two, but the Grand Alliance had destroyed its very existence as a state. It is the Cold War which has restored to nations of the second rank a diplomatic role out of proportion to their resources. If and when the United States and the Soviet Union can or wish to come to an understanding, their representatives will confer alone without bothering about the fiction of equality between allies.

Is the division of the world into spheres of influence preferable to the rivalry of the Cold War or peaceful coexistence? The question is purely speculative, since the rivalry springs from the universality to which the official Soviet ideology lays claim and from the arbitrary lines of the frontiers between the two worlds. Whatever the meaning one ascribes to the Anglo-Russian agreements on the division of influence in Eastern Europe vaguely concluded in Moscow at the end of 1943 and repudiated by Roosevelt, world partition would have failed as the Russo-American directory has failed, and for the same reason. The rulers of Russia, in so far as they remain true to their faith, cannot *definitively* abandon any nation to capitalist exploitation. The West would deny its principles by recognizing as *definitive* the Sovietization of Eastern Europe. Would a world in which the Big Two had guaranteed the frontiers which separate their respective zones be greatly superior, politically and morally, to the world as it is? In this dream world, would Communist parties still be banned in the West? Would the West have to proclaim that the order which reigns in Warsaw represents the wishes of the Polish people?

Let us return to the real world. Incapable of reaching complete agreement, determined not to engage in a struggle to the death (atom bombs strengthen this determination if they do not actually create it: how much less likely is a Russo-American war than was the Peloponnesian War!), the Big Two neutralize each other and by this very fact restore some independence to other states. In balancing one another through disagreement, they themselves provoke the neutralities which they alternately welcome and denounce.

Nothing is more characteristic of this opportunity for neutrality than the Yugoslav adventure. Excommunicated by Stalin, who naïvely relied on the resolutions of the Cominform to demolish the walls of the dissident state, subjected to a Soviet blockade but determined (and condemned) to maintain a single-party regime, Tito's Yugoslavia would have been friendless and helpless had not the deserter from one camp automatically been welcome in the other. There is a sense in which Tito was more valuable from the West's viewpoint because he remained true to his faith. Did he not offer a living proof to the Communist elite of the other satellite countries that they could survive a break with Moscow? A state which declared itself Communist but not subject to the Soviet bloc represented in the long run the most dangerous heresy for Moscow, since it rejected the very principle of the Communist empire, namely the primacy of the Russian Bolshevik party. Its immediate effect was to seal the fate of the Greek guerillas and to restore the Western position in the eastern Mediterranean.

Ideological considerations apart, a bipolar structure guarantees, so to speak, the freedom of choice of any state providing it is favored by geography. The balance of power, the existence of another big power, tends to prohibit the use of military means against a dissident state. Would the invasion of Yugoslavia by the satellite armies have provoked a European war, a world war? No one knows, no one will ever know. The masters of the Kremlin would in any case have hesitated to bring a heretic state back to the fold by fire and sword. The essential fact remains: in certain areas at least, neither of the two great powers will dare to employ its armies against a small recalcitrant state, *because the other great power exists.*

The banal notion that the bipolar structure involves the formation of two blocs is first of all attributable to the situation of Europe after the war. This was characterized not so much by the concentration of power in two states as by a "power vacuum" in which the armies of the peripheral states came into direct contact with one another. Berlin, divided between the two camps, constituted a sort of island in the Soviet ocean. The countries west of the Iron Curtain, almost defenseless and torn by the memory of their struggles, felt the double need to perpetuate the American guarantee and to secure themselves against their own discords. Thus the hegemony exercised by Moscow over the countries of Eastern Europe determined first of all the establishment of the Atlantic Alliance and then, as a result of the Korean campaign, the constitution of NATO.

. . . .

...It is not altogether inconceivable that Europe may one day be in a position to declare itself neutral between the Big Two, that is, make use of the balance of power between them to reserve to itself as large an autonomy as possible. In 1949, at the time of the Berlin blockade, when neither Western Germany nor France nor Great Britain possessed an army worthy of the name, the *diplomatic* conception of European neutrality was simply absurd.

On the other hand, once the Atlantic Alliance was constituted, there was nothing to prevent certain solidly armed countries on the strategic side lines from remaining outside the military groupings. They gambled on the chance of being spared by the third holocaust as they had been by the first two.

What Sweden and Switzerland have been able to do in Europe, where any war that broke out would almost inevitably be a general one, the countries of the Near East, of Asia, of Africa, and perhaps of South America are in a position to do *a fortiori*. Each in its way can declare itself neutral and translate its neutrality into actions.

. . . .

... The ideological and power rivalry between East and West has altered the traditional Asian setup without making it entirely unrecognizable. Japan disarmed would be at the mercy of the Sino-Russians, were it not protected by the American alliance. Korea, the buffer between Japan and China, is today divided into two states, each of which is attached to one of the great power blocs: in the age of ideological warfare, partition is the substitute for neutrality.

But the situation is by no means stabilized. In accordance with its old habit of suddenly switching from one extreme to the other, Japan, the conquering hero of yesterday, has sworn never to fight again—to be the first on the royal road to peace since it could not be first on the road to war. Japan must accept the presence of American troops and live without means of defending itself or attempting to rearm. The country chooses to keep the American bases on her soil, but even those who make the choice rail against the consequences and expose themselves to the abuse both of the pacifists and the nationalists, the latter aspiring to a genuine rearmament, the former to the resolute application of the doctrine of "non-defense."

The substitution of more or less token American contingents for Japanese armed forces which would be scarcely less token is in itself of only minor importance. China (and the same applies to the Soviet Union) has no reason to invade Japan, where she would find no riches either above or below ground. But the American bases have an influence on the trend of Japanese internal politics. Left to herself, Japan might be attracted toward the Soviet bloc by the desire to find a source of raw materials and a market for manufactured products. Economic interdependence would eventually lead to political conversion.

In any case, the diplomatic situation in northeast Asia seems to conform to the logic of tradition and geography, a logic that has been altered but not destroyed by the conflict between the big powers and their ideologies. If the Russians and the Chinese had sacrificed North Korea, one might have said that the atomic weapon had paralyzed Communist action. In fact, the Chinese acted as if the Americans were incapable of destroying within a few hours the noble cities of the Middle Kingdom. They gambled on American reluctance, either from scruple or fear of a world war, to avenge Korean reverses on ancient stones and defenseless men: their gamble paid off.

The military power of the United States does not extend beyond the islands, or at most the neighboring peninsulas. In Southeast Asia the political and ideological rivalry between the United States and the Soviet Union is only one of several factors. The countries which are linked to the United States (the Philippines, Thailand, Pakistan, and South Vietnam) do not constitute a bloc comparable to the Atlanic Alliance. Korea and South Vietnam (which does not belong to SEATO) are linked to the United States because they are halves of countries: immediately confronting a fragment of the Soviet empire, they have the same impulse and the same need to seek support from the leader of the non-Communist universe. The Philippines are willing members of a Western-inspired alliance by reason of the links which bind them to their former American masters, perhaps also because of the exigencies of their island situation. Thailand, with a considerable Chinese minority, feels threatened by infiltration rather than invasion, and the Southeast Asian mutual assistance pact helps the country defend itself against the former rather than the latter. As for Pakistan, it expects from SEATO military aid which might reduce India's superiority rather than protection against a Communist attack, the possibility of which is fairly remote.

None of the considerations which explain and justify the Atlantic Pact—immediate confrontation of the Soviet and American armies, arbitrary demarcation lines, political solidarity of the Atlantic states—is to be found in the Southeast Asian situation.[2] One might, of course, assume a functional analogy: the Atlantic Pact restricts the belligerents in the Cold War to the use of political weapons alone, and the Southeast Asian pact might do the same. But the analogy is questionable. The threat of atomic bombardment in retaliation against an invasion of Western Europe is taken seriously, but it would be difficult to take it seriously in the case of Thailand, Laos, or Burma. This might just have been conceivable if one side enjoyed a monopoly of atomic weapons. Approximate equality once established, a threat from one of the Big Two would be considered genuine only in two cases: if the issue at stake were of decisive importance or if a counterthreat from the other great power were out of the question. In all other instances, the intervention of the Big Two in the regional systems will increasingly diminish or be restricted to traditional diplomatic methods. The two-bloc system would spring up in Southeast Asia if ever the small countries there came to feel the same way as, rightly or wrongly, the countries of Western Europe felt in 1946–47—in other words, if ever China seemed impatient to surround herself with satellite states.

At present, China is taking pains to give the opposite impression. Setting aside North Korea and Tonkin, traditional protectorates of the Chinese empire, China seems to have been more preoccupied since 1953 with industrial development than with external expansion. The leaders of Thailand, Burma, Laos, and Indonesia have to contend with their national Communist parties. They are perfectly well aware of these parties' links with Peking or Moscow, but they prefer to maintain good relations with the Communist powers and solemnly subscribe to Mr. Nehru's five principles, as if the Communist International was compatible with the principle of non-intervention in the internal affairs of states.

The mere fact that China shows no immediate inclination to expand is enough to make Asian diplomacy, the diplomacy which expresses itself in actions and not in world travel and fine speeches, entirely local and non-global. India's real diplomacy is concerned with Kashmir, which is claimed by Pakistan, and in this question Mr. Nehru behaves not as a disciple of Gandhi but as a traditional statesman. He can find plenty of high motives for refusing the plebiscite of which he fears the result. From Washington or Moscow, the conflicts between India and Pakistan, or between Vietnam and Cambodia, are local matters. From Saigon or New Delhi, the United States-Soviet Union rivalry, terribly real when it seems on the point of setting the world on fire, fades into the background as soon as it subsides. The fate of Tonkin affects the Cochin Chinese, just as the fate of the Pakistan Hindus affects the citizens of India and the fate of India's Moslems affects the citizens of Pakistan. As soon as the fear of general war recedes, the states recently promoted to independence—India, Indonesia, Burma—torn between resentment against colonialism and the fear of Communism, prefer neutrality to involvement, a preference which is as understandable and legitimate as the contrary preference of Pakistan or Thailand. The neutrals enjoy American protection gratis. Why should they pay

---

[2] Note: Compare this with G. Frederick Reinhardt's essay on SEATO in Chapter XXIII.

for something which they can have in any case? Since the Americans have a selfish interest in preventing the expansion of Communism, the non-Communist states are entitled to enjoy the benefits of good relations with both camps. On the traditional diplomatic plane, the whole question is to decide whether the advantages of non-involvement outweigh those of alliance. India decides in one direction, Pakistan in the other. If Mr. Nehru had wished, India might have decided in the same direction as Pakistan: the psychology of public opinion as well as that of the Prime Minister himself tended toward neutrality.

In fact, Mr. Nehru should thank heaven that the Cold War gives him the chance of playing the part he has assumed. If the Big Two reached an understanding, they would rule over the whole of mankind and lessons in morality would be relegated to the primary school. ...

III · Motivation in the Nation-State System: Power, Interests, and Ideology

One of the most difficult problems in the study of international relations is that of explaining why nations behave the way they do. The social scientist cannot be content with accepting the argument that the Germans went to war in 1914 because they are a militaristic people, or because France, England, and Russia were determined to keep Germany from enjoying a "place in the sun," or that World War II was inspired solely by the fanaticism of Adolf Hitler or that the cold war was brought on because of Communism or because of Stalin's lust for power. The variety of such explanations is so great that the social scientist seeks a common denominator or theory grounded in the uniformities of international life and human behavior that will enable him to order and explain a wide range of variables.

The so-called "realist" theory, the one most widely accepted by American theorists, holds that the struggle among nations for power is endemic in a system without a recognized authority, without common norms, and above all without security. We have included a passage from "The Pole of Power and the Pole of Indifference" by Arnold Wolfers because it is one of the clearest and most explicit summaries of the type of behavior which the system imposes upon the nation-states. According to this theory as expressed in a pioneer exposition of power politics, "It is the so-called sovereign independence of states, the absence of higher authority, and the freedom from external restraints that give to interstate relations their peculiar character of anarchy." [1] Under these circumstances, "There is no real security in being just as strong as a potential enemy; there is security only in being a little stronger." [2] Unquestionably a theory of motivation (power for the sake of survival and security) based upon the realities of the international system helps us to understand the intensity and persistence of conflict.

---

[1] Nicholas Spykman, *America's Strategy in World Politics* (New York: Harcourt, Brace & Company, 1940), p. 16.

[2] *Ibid.*, p. 21.

A more humanistic but equally valid formulation of this theory would be to start with the fact that the great majority of people in every nation-state believe that the security and integrity of their country is the condition of the good life, and they believe that a threat to its independence is a threat to their own way of life, their own private values. In a sense then, it is the function that the state performs in giving its members peace of mind and prosperity that makes them reluctant to trust their fate to other people.[3]

However, to believe that the conditions imposed by the system are the sole explanation for nation-state behavior is to leave unexplored several other sources of motivation. In view of the pathologic intensity of the hostility that exists between Russia and America there is a widespread disposition to believe that differences of economic and political organization and beliefs are the most important causes of international conflict. Nation-states appear to be influenced in their behavior by the antipathy that an alien ideology arouses in the minds and emotions of another people. Some observers have raised the question of whether ideology has not transformed the national conflicts of the past into international civil wars such as "those recently fought in Korea and Indo-China that partake of the character of international and civil war simultaneously." [4] From this perspective the "cold war" is a struggle between two competing moral philosophies. In contrast to this interpretation Hans Morgenthau argues that ideologies are but moral justifications for what is essentially the pursuit of power for its own sake. "In other words," he writes, "while all politics is necessarily pursuit of power, ideologies render involvement in that contest for power psychologically and morally acceptable to the actors and their audience." [5] However, Clyde Kluckhohn, the Harvard anthropologist, takes exception to this summary dismissal of conflicting moral values as a source of tension. "Values are something more than 'epiphenomena,' verbal rationalizations of existing conditions. Values influence and, on occasion, determine action." [6] In fact, no one is more emphatic than Professor Morgenthau in stressing that the intensity and totality of the power conflict in our day is due to the changed moral climate. "Nations no longer oppose each other as they did from the Treaty of Vienna to the First World War, within a framework of shared beliefs and common values, which imposes effective limits upon the ends and means of their struggle for power." [7] Historically or at least in the period following the Napoleonic Wars it is probably true that the policies of the European

---

[3] P. H. Partridge, "The Conflict of Ideologies," in *Paths to Peace,* ed. Victor H. Wallace (Melbourne: Melbourne University Press, 1957), pp. 98–99.

[4] Arnold Wolfers and Laurence W. Martin, *The Anglo-American Tradition in Foreign Affairs* (New Haven: Yale University Press, 1956), p. xviii.

[5] Hans J. Morgenthau, *Politics Among Nations* (2nd ed.) (New York: Alfred A. Knopf, Inc., 1954), p. 61.

[6] Clyde Kluckhohn, in *The American Style,* ed. Elting E. Morison (New York: Harper and Brothers, 1958), p. 146.

[7] Morgenthau, *Politics Among Nations: The Struggle for Power and Peace* (New York: Alfred A. Knopf, Inc., 1948), p. 230.

states were less influenced by ideological factors than other issues, but in our day the struggle has become unrestrained and total in part at least because conflicting systems of belief deny the existence of any basis for peaceful coexistence.

There should be nothing mysterious about this phenomenon. Ideologies or belief systems respond to one of the deepest intellectual and psychological needs of men—to know where they are going and to believe that what they are doing is right. To challenge belief systems is to challenge something that has the deepest meaning to human beings and thereby to thwart the desire for moral certainty and security. Foreign policy is no more immune than other social activity from the values which a people hold. It is even argued that people or states do not have interests apart from their moral or ideological convictions. "It is only from the point of view of moral ideas which they accept that they form a view of what their interests are." [8] This may be especially true when the foreign policy and international conduct of one of the superpowers is dominated by the doctrine that, because of the inescapable dynamics of capitalist society, conflict is inevitable and that it has the historical task of assisting every attempt by non-communist peoples to "free" themselves by revolutionary means from the existing status quo. Whether ideological values are the ultimate determinant of foreign policies or not, their influence poses an extremely difficult dilemma for statesmen and diplomats. In an article entitled "Strategy Versus Ideology," Louis Halle, a former high State Department official and policy planner, demonstrated how no statesman can afford to ignore the values held by a significant portion of his countrymen.[9] Similarly no theory of international relations would be realistic which failed to treat seriously the force of contending value-systems.

It seems unlikely that we can understand what motivates nations to compete with each other unless we pay some attention to the economic and political interests of influential groups or elites within each society. There are many people in every society whose loyalties and interests are more influenced by their identification with a business firm, or a labor union, or a patriotic or religious organization than by their responsibilities as citizens. While they claim to pursue objectives consistent with the national interest, the motives of such groups are sufficiently different to require examination in terms of a distinctive theoretical analysis. For example, are we to ignore the fact, well-established by studies of pressure group influence in domestic politics, that the objectives of large corporations, of religious and ethnic groups, and of superpatriotic organizations may call for the pursuit of policies which are not consistent with a rational or objective definition of the national interest? Then there are political leaders and chiefs of departments of government who, in quest of prestige or a larger share of the national budget, assert

---

[8] Partridge, *Paths to Peace*, p. 102.
[9] Louis Halle, "Strategy Versus Ideology," *Yale Review*, ILVI (1956).

their personal or bureaucratic preferences to be the expression of the national interest. "Teddy" Roosevelt is a good example of an American president who imposed his views upon American foreign policy in such a way as to antagonize Latin Americans for many years thereafter. Thus there are many groups or elites within a state whose values and interests can only be achieved by the extension of their state's power and authority. Indeed it is the paradox of the modern industrial society that while economic and technological organization now obliges people to pursue their interests at the world level, the political structure of the state cannot be extended indefinitely because it is based upon the loyalty of a unique national group and not upon the shared loyalties of a supra-national or universal community.

Lenin, in a book entitled *Imperialism: The Highest Stage of Capitalism*, attempted to construct a theory of nation-state behavior on the basis of the need of monopoly capitalism for safe investment outlets for surplus capital that can no longer find a profitable outlet within the developed home market. Although Lenin's theory does not constitute a completely scientific explanation of imperialism, it focuses upon the peculiar need of modern industrial and banking institutions to transcend the limits of national boundaries and secure access to the resources and markets of the world. While Lenin's explanation hardly accounts for the fact that Russia and the United States were active imperialists at a time (1900) when both were net capital importing countries, it forces us to be aware that within any nation there are indubitably individuals and groups who have a peculiar interest or belief in the virtue of extending their own nation's authority over the land, lives, and resources of another people.

The student who is genuinely interested in seeking the deeper causes that underlie the sequence of international events may rest assured that as yet we have no single theoretical explanation, a point which will become even more apparent in the discussion of the "Definition of Policy Aims" in Chapter IX. The field is so vast and complex that no one has yet seen it whole. Each of the following selections is but a partial explanation. Together they may suggest that the intensity of modern conflict stems from man's inability to give up his loyalty to the nation-state at a stage in history when his social and economic needs have begun to transcend the state itself.

1 • The Pole of Power and the Pole of Indifference *

Arnold Wolfers

The author, Sterling Professor Emeritus of International Relations, Yale University, is Director of the Washington Center for Foreign Policy Research. He is the author of Britain and France Between Two Wars *(1940), and co-author of* The Anglo-American Tradition in Foreign Affairs *(1956). He is a frequent contributor to leading journals in the field of international affairs.*

· · · ·

The realist image of the world has been presented in its essential features by a number of authors concerned with the theory of international politics. In its pure form it is based on the proposition that "states seek to enhance their power." In this brief statement are implicit the major assumptions of realist thought.

States are conceived as the sole actors in the international arena. Operating as a group of sovereign entities, they constitute a multistate system. The analogy of a set of billiard balls or chess figures comes to mind. All the units of the system behave essentially in the same manner; their goal is to enhance if not to maximize their power. This means that each of them must be acting with a single mind and single will; in this respect they resemble the Princes of the Renaissance about whom Machiavelli wrote. Like them, too, they are completely separate from each other, with no affinities or bonds of community interfering with their egotistical pursuit of power. They are competitors for power, engaged in a continuous and inescapable struggle for survival. This makes them all potential if not actual

enemies; there can be no amity between them, unless it be an alignment against a common foe.

Under these conditions the expectation of violence and even of annihilation is ever present. To forget it and thus to fail in the concern for enhanced power spells the doom of a state. This does not mean constant open warfare; expansion of power at the expense of others will not take place if there is enough counter-power to deter or to stop states from undertaking it. Though no state is interested in a mere balance of power, the efforts of all states to maximize power may lead to equilibrium. If and when that happens, there is "peace" or, more exactly, a condition of stalemate or truce. Under the conditions described here, this balancing of power process is the only available "peace" strategy.

While few would deny that the picture presented in these sweeping generalizations resembles the world we are living in at this time, it would not have passed for more than a caricature at other times. International relations within the Western world in the twenties or within the inter-American system today cannot

---

* *World Politics* IV (1951), 39–63. Reprinted by permission.

be fully understood in terms either of balanced power or an all-out struggle for survival. This does not preclude the possibility that the "pure power model" of the realists can render service at least as an initial working hypothesis. The actual world might never fully comply with the postulates of the model, yet to the extent to which it did, consequences deduced within its context would apply to the real world. Countries engaged in a race to enhance their power could, for example, be expected to align themselves in disrespect of earlier "friendships" or ideological affinities; expansion would be sure to take place wherever a power vacuum existed.

Of course, no such approximation of reality to "pure power conditions" can be taken for granted. It presupposes that the basic "realist" contention about state behavior is truly realistic. If an insatiable quest for power were not the rule, but represented instead an abnormality or marginal case, developments in the world might deviate drastically from those which the model leads one to expect. Peace strategies other than the balancing process might have a chance of success.

Realist scholars have sought to explain why it is that states do in fact behave as postulated or why they are compelled to do so. They have offered two different explanations. According to the first, human nature is such that men, as individuals and as nations, act like beasts of prey, driven by an insatiable lust for power or *animus dominandi*. Their will to power, moreover, when transferred from small and frustrated individuals to the collectivity of the state, takes on greater dimensions and generates an all-round struggle for survival.[1]

According to the second explanation, which is gaining adherents, the quest for power is due not to any desire for power as such, but to a general human craving for security.[2] The insecurity of an anarchical system of multiple sovereignty places the actors under compulsion to seek maximum power even though it run counter to their real desires. By a tragic irony, then, all actors find themselves compelled to do for the sake of security what, in bringing about an all-round struggle for survival, leads to greater insecurity. This "vicious circle theory" makes statesmen and people look less vicious than the *animus dominandi* theory; what it does is to substitute tragedy for evil and to replace the "mad Caesar," as Lasswell calls the *homo politicus* of the pure power model, by the "hysterical Caesar" who, haunted by fear, pursues the will-o'-the-wisp of absolute security.

The validity of these explanations of an alleged uniform behavior of states toward power need not be discussed here, because the realist scholars who started out with the assumption of such uniformity have not stuck to it after descending from the high level of abstraction of their initial propositions to the lower levels where the shape of actual things can be apprehended. All of them have found it necessary to "deviate" from their original assumption to the point of distinguishing between at least two categories of states with different attitudes toward power.

Few have stated more emphatically

---

[1] See Hans J. Morgenthau, *Scientific Man vs. Power Politics* (Chicago: University of Chicago Press, 1946), especially in the chapter on "selfishness and lust for power," pp. 191–201.

[2] John H. Herz, *Political Realism and Political Idealism*, (Chicago: University of Chicago Press, 1951), who expounds the theory of what he calls the "security dilemma" with much skill and vigor, says that "Basically it is the mere instinct of self-preservation which ... leads to competition for ever more power" (p. 4). This is the view held by Thomas Hobbes, which C. J. Friedrich discusses in *Inevitable Peace* (Cambridge: Harvard University Press, 1948), p. 126.

than Morgenthau that in international relations "power is pitted against power for survival and supremacy." [3] But more recently he has drawn a sharp distinction between two types of states, the "status quo powers" and the "imperialist powers." Of the former, he says that their policy tends "toward keeping power and not toward changing the distribution of power"; of the latter, that they aim "at acquiring more power." [4] Similarly, Frederick Schuman starts out with the assertion that in international politics "power is sought as an end in itself," but then goes on to differentiate between "satiated" and "unsatiated" states. His statements that "each state left to itself tends to extend its power over as wide a field as possible" and that "enhancement of state power is always the goal" are contradicted, it would seem, by his subsequent contention that states which benefit from the established status quo naturally seek "to preserve that from which they benefit," in contrast to those "which feel humiliated, hampered and oppressed by the status quo." [5] The authors of another recent text, Strausz-Hupé and Possony, follow a similar line. After stating at the outset that "foreign policy aims at the acquisition of optimum—and sometimes of maximum—power," the optimum remaining undefined, they go on to define, as a special type, the "natural aggressors" who in contrast to other states are "driven by a particularly pronounced dynamism, i.e., urge toward power accumulation." [6] Finally, Spykman, who did much to introduce the pure power hypothesis into the contemporary American discussion, deviates from his opening statement, according to which "the improvement of the relative power position becomes the primary objective of the...external policy of states," by speaking of the "dynamic state" which, as he puts it, "rarely sets modest limits to its power aims." [7] This implies that nondynamic states, on the contrary, do set such "modest limits." [8]

One consequence of distinctions such as these is worth mentioning. They rob theory of the determinate and predictive character that seemed to give the pure power hypothesis its peculiar value. It can now no longer be said of the actual world, e.g., that a power vacuum cannot exist for any length of time; a vacuum surrounded by "satiated" or "status quo" states would remain as it is unless its existence were to change the character of these states and put them in the category of "imperialist," "unsatiated," or "dynamic" states.

The idealist model, if such there be, cannot be as easily derived from writings

---

[3] Morgenthau, *op. cit.*, p. 71.

[4] *Ibid.*, p. 21. Actually, he adds a third type, described as a nation pursuing a policy of prestige. Prestige, however, in contrast to maintenance and acquisition of power, "is but rarely an end in itself," he says (p. 50); "it is rather an instrument through which the other two ends can be achieved."

[5] Frederick L. Schuman, *International Politics,* 3rd ed. (New York: McGraw-Hill Book Co., 1941), pp. 262–63, 274–75, 279.

[6] Robert Strausz-Hupé and Stefan T. Possony, *International Relations* (New York: McGraw-Hill Book Co., 1950), pp. 2, 9.

[7] Nicholas John Spykman, *America's Strategy in World Politics* (New York: Harcourt, Brace & Company, 1942), pp. 18, 20.

[8] Max Weber emphasizes the difference between more "isolationist" and more "expansive" powers, as well as their changing attitudes in his respect. (See *From Max Weber: Essays in Sociology,* trans. and ed. by H. H. Gerth and C. Wright Mills, New York: Oxford University Press, 1946, chapter VI on "Structures of Power," p. 159b.) "For general reasons of power dynamics *per se*," he writes, "the Great Powers are often very expansive powers." "But," he continues, they "are not necessarily and not always oriented toward expansion." See also William T. R. Fox, *The Super-Powers,* (New York: Harcourt, Brace & Company, 1944), who distinguishes between the "quest for security (power not to be coerced)" of some nations and the "quest for domination (power to coerce)" of others.

or statements of exponents of the idealist school itself. This school has been anything but theory-minded. Its attention has been focused on peace strategy and on blueprints for a better world. However, it would have made no sense for idealists to proffer advice on policy if they had held no general views about the existing world which permitted them to regard as practical the policies they sought to promote. As a matter of fact, Woodrow Wilson himself, with his predilection for broad generalizations, has expressed on one occasion or another all the main tenets of the "Wilsonian" school.

One feature of the idealist image strikes the eyes because of its contrast to the realist view. Here the basic propositions deal not with states, but with individuals, with peoples or with mankind. The idealist seems to be looking out not on a multistate system with its separate national entities, but on a nascent world community and the people who make it up. This precludes from the start that the emphasis be placed on national quests for power or on the struggle for power among nations. Instead, the accent is either on the "common purpose of enlightened mankind" [9] or on the common values which men hold as individuals. Because the vast majority of men are assumed to value the same things—such as individual freedom, the right to govern themselves, the safety of their homeland, and above all the absence of violence—it is concluded that there can exist no basic conflict between them even as nations. If it were not for extraneous interference—and a remediable measure of ignorance and misunderstanding—there would be harmony, peace, and a complete absence of concern for national power. "I sometimes think," said Wilson, "that...no

people ever went to war with another people." But he goes on to say that "governments have gone to war" with one another, thereby pointing to the darker side of the idealist picture.[10]

Only a dreamer could mistake for the existing order the vision of a world of independent nations in which there is no conflict, nor any drives for power. The idealist school does not do so. It not only fully recognizes the continued presence or threat of "power politics," but considers this discrepancy between "what is" and "what should and will be" as the crucial moral and political issue of international relations. The explanation for it is believed to lie in the operation of evil forces which violate the peace and law of the community.

There is no doubt about the character of these forces. They are conceived as anachronistic remnants of an age—now coming to an end—in which autocratic rulers rather than the peoples themselves controlled the destiny of nations. It was these rulers who were "playing the game of power," as Woodrow Wilson puts it; their ambitions, not the interests of their peoples, were in conflict and plunged the world into power politics and the struggle for survival. Whenever and wherever such autocracy asserts itself—or reasserts itself through a relapse into a bygone age—the community of peace-loving nations falls victim to the onslaught of aggressive power and violence.

One might suspect that when such aggression occurs, the world would return to conditions very much like those portrayed by the pure power model. The only difference would seem to be that now the power of aggressors would be pitted against the collective power of peace-loving nations. The idealist denounces such a comparison as superficial and dangerously misleading. It would be

---

[9] *The Public Papers of Woodrow Wilson: War and Peace,* ed. by Ray S. Baker and William E. Dodd (New York: Harper & Brothers, 1927), p. 259.

[10] *President Wilson's State Papers and Addresses,* introd. by Albert Shaw (New York: Review of Reviews, 1918), p. 177.

no less inappropriate, he maintains, to speak of a struggle for power or a balancing of power process when describing the defense of international peace and lawfulness than it would be to apply these same terms to the actions of a national police force engaged in fighting individual criminals.

According to idealist thought, then, the quest for collective international police power has taken the place of the obsolete quest for national power as far as the majority of the actors is concerned. One would be tempted, by way of contrast, to call this idealist image by some such name as the "pure solidarity model" were it not for the emphasis placed on the continued threat or presence of aggressive antisolidarity forces.

The idealist school has been taken to task by its critics for the illusory character of much of its interpretation of the existing world, especially for its *a priori* optimistic assumptions concerning human nature and the harmony of interest, as well as for its narrow explanation of the phenomenon which it terms aggression.[11] The validity of such criticism should become clearer, at least by implication, from what will be said later. It is more important, here, to point to some of the insights which the idealist approach suggests to the theoretical analyst.

By distinguishing from the outset between two types of behavior toward power, rather than introducing discrimination as an afterthought or deviation, the idealist has been more aware of the problems arising from this lack of uniformity.—If anything, he may be too much inclined to take the lack of uniformity for granted, for example, when

asserting categorically that democracies behave differently in foreign affairs than dictatorships.—Because of the important role he assigns to individuals and their values as well as to bonds of community transcending national boundaries, he has an eye for aspects of reality—such as the relative ease with which the English-speaking world has learned to collaborate—which are hard to reconcile with the image of a "billiard ball world." [12]

$\cdot \quad \cdot \quad \cdot \quad \cdot$

The two schools are obviously far apart, if not diametrically opposed on many issues. Yet, despite striking differences, their views are closely related to each other, at least in one significant respect. Both approach international politics on the same level—which might briefly be called the power level—though they approach it from opposite ends.[13]

---

11 For criticism of idealist thought in international relations, see E. H. Carr, *The Twenty Years' Crisis* (London: The Macmillan Company, 1939); Morgenthau. *Scientific Man;* Reinhold Niebuhr, *The Children of Light and the Children of Darkness* (New York: Charles Scribner's Sons, 1953).

12 Frederick S. Dunn, *War and Minds of Men,* (New York, Harcourt, Brace & Company, 1950) emphasizes the importance of supplementing the picture of international affairs that reveals itself when attention is focused on interstate relations by one that places social or human relations between individuals in the center of the scene (p. 12). He warns, however, against the illusion that a shift to the goals and values of individuals will help us to escape "from the sickening recurrence of international crises and war." "Political conflicts," he rightly insists, "arise from the existence of competing values among sovereign states."

13 The term "power" is used here and throughout this article in the restricted sense in which it occurs in the popular use of such word combinations as "power politics" or "struggle for power," meaning to cover the ability to coerce or, more precisely, to inflict depreviations on others. This leaves out other ways of exerting influence, e.g., by bestowing benefits which are not ordinarily connected with or condemned as "power politics." (See Harold and Margaret Sprout, in the new 2d rev. edition of *Foundations of National Power* (Princeton: Princeton University Press, 1951), p. 39, where they explain their reasons for choosing a much broader definition. The term "resort to power" will be used to mean reliance on the ability to inflict deprivations, "resort to violence" as actual coercion by the use of physical force.

By way of simplification, it can be said that while the realist is primarily interested in the quest for power—and its culmination in the resort to violence—as the essence of all politics among nations, the idealist is concerned above all with its elimination. On this level there can be no meeting of the minds....

Normally, power is a means to other ends and not an end in itself. Where it becomes an end, as it does in the case of the "mad Caesars," one is faced with what Toynbee would call an "enormity." Therefore, to treat the quest for power, positively or negatively, outside the context of ends and purposes which it is expected to serve, robs it of any intelligible meaning and, by the way, also makes it impossible to judge its appropriateness or excessiveness....

One gets a very different picture... if one considers first the values and purposes for the sake of which policy-makers seek to accumulate or use national power, as they may also seek alternative or supplementary means.

This suggests beginning with a "theory of ends" and proceeding from there to the analysis of the quest for power as it develops in conjunction with and under the impact of the ends it is meant to promote. It must be kept in mind, however, that one is not dealing with a simple cause-and-effect relationship. The degree to which power is available or attainable frequently affects the choice of ends. Prudent policy-makers will keep their ends and aspirations safely within the power which their country possesses or is ready and willing to muster.[14]

---

[14] Walter Lippmann has consistently advocated such prudence. "The thesis of this book," he says in reference to his *U.S. Foreign Policy: Shield of the Republic* (Boston: Little, Brown, and Company, 1943), "is that a foreign policy consists of bringing into balance, with a comfortable surplus of power in reserve, the nation's commitments and the nation's power. The constant preoccupation of the true statesman is to achieve and maintain this balance."

Statesmen with a respect for moral principles, or under pressure from people who have such respect, may hesitate to pursue goals which demand the sacrifice of these or of other values in the process of power accumulation or use....

The idealist school is correct in stressing the value which men in general place on peace and in insisting that such evaluations can affect the decisions of policy-makers. Whether of their own volition or under pressures from more peace-minded groups of the population, statesmen under certain circumstances will desist from pressing national demands through means of power or will limit their demands. Realists would not be so eager—as was Machiavelli himself—to impress their governments with the "necessity" of playing the game of power politics as consistently as their opponents, were it not for fear that these governments might act otherwise....

The extent to which there is a struggle for power is decided...by what might be called the "relationship of major tension," not by the attitude which nations not engaged in conflict take toward each other. In the same sense, it can be said that the degree of power competition and the expectation of violence rest not upon the behavior of countries concerned with self-preservation, but upon that of the "initiator." Idealist optimism in regard to the elimination of "power politics" is out of place, therefore, as long as the trend toward major tensions and toward the eruption of new and ambitious demands for self-extension is not reversed....

The realist school has merited its name for having appreciated the role which the quest for power plays in international politics though it has devoted little attention to the policy goals from which this quest for power springs. It has recognized that a multistate system —a term which still properly designates the outstanding feature of contemporary international politics—is heavily slanted toward struggles for power. Lying somewhere within a continuum which stretches from the pole of an "all-out struggle for power" to the pole of an "all-round indifference to power," the actual world tends to be pulled more strongly toward the former. This is true, whether the realist *a priori* assumptions concerning a universal human hunger for power or of a "security dilemma" arising from *la condition humaine* are correct or not. The main reason lies in the ever-recurring new incentives to demands for change and the equally strong incentives to throw power in the path of such change. By a curious irony, the same readiness to resist through power which is the prerequisite of any competition for power may, if strong, quick-moving, and determined enough, prevent the struggle from degenerating into violence. This is what the realists have in mind when placing their hopes for peace on the balance of power.

It is quite possible that most of the great drives toward national and revolutionary self-extension which at intervals have thrown the world into struggles of sheer survival could not have been presented by any means available to man. One can hardly escape a sense of fatalism if one asks oneself retrospectively whether the rise and aggressions of a Hitler could have been avoided. But this does not mean—as realist thought would seem to imply—that no influence can be brought to bear on policy-makers which would serve the interests of peace. Anything that bears on their value patterns and preferences, on their estimates of gains and deprevations, or on the scope of their identifications will, in principle, be able to affect the course of policy upon which they decide to embark.

It may be Utopian to expect that the causes accounting for resorts to power and power competition could ever be wholly eliminated—as it is Utopian to believe that defensive counter-force could be consistently held at sufficient strength to prevent the actual resort to violence; but there need be no resigned acceptance of the "enormity" of a continuous all-round struggle for survival. Through suitable policies, pressures, and appeals designed to attack the causes of intensive drives for enhanced power, the pulls toward the pole of all-round indifference to power can be strengthened. The main task of those engaged in developing a realistic theory of peace strategy is to discover policies and practices which offer most promise of turning nations away from goals that point toward power competition and violence.

2 • The Conflict of Ideologies *

P. H. Partridge

The author is Professor of Social Philosophy in the School of Social Sciences, The Australian National University, Canberra.

RUSSIA AND THE U.S.A.—POLITICAL AND ECONOMIC CONFLICT

...*In our own day, ideological cleavage does appear to be one of the major sources of international conflict.* It does seem to be true in some sense that two blocs of states have formed, and that the members of each bloc have aligned themselves according to the affinities of their political and economic constitutions and of the systems of values to which the respective communities adhere. It does appear that it is the spread of communist regimes throughout a large part of Europe and into Asia that is one of the chief causes of the present cleavage that divides the world. This is the problem to which I shall now turn.

I do not want to deny that ideology is one of the chief reasons for the conflict between Russia and its satellites and the United States and the Western powers.... It should be said that, in the cold war between the Soviet and the United States that has been proceeding since 1945, it is easy to exaggerate the role of the ideological conflict. Russia and America are two very great powers; and great powers have always been a threat to each other's security and vital interests, even where no ideological hatreds were involved. The rise of Ger-

many to the status of a first class highly industrialized power in the first decade of this century was immediately recognized as a threat by Britain and France, and would have been no less a threat if the three countries had possessed the same political and social constitutions.

There is no difference in principle between the present fear and hostility that prevail between Russia and America and the earlier fear of Germany by Britain and France. Given the system of independent sovereign states, we should expect a state of suspicion, fear and insecurity between the two superpowers, even if no ideological issues were in question. Because of the overwhelming power they have achieved, because of the vast areas they are able to dominate, and because their influence meets at so many parts of the globe, we might expect a degree of tension between them exceeding anything that has been seen in the past. Because they are vast industrial states, both have many interests, political, strategic and economic, beyond their own borders; both, therefore, can expect—as great powers have always done—a possible conflict of interests

---

* From *Paths to Peace*, edited by Victor H. Wallace (Melbourne: Melbourne University Press, 1957), pp. 104–117. Reprinted by permission.

in many parts of the world; both consequently have to fear for the security of their vital interests; and both will constantly manoeuvre for position. We are not in the least entitled to assume that if Russia were not a communist state, all other circumstances being the same, there would not be serious conflict of interests in Europe, in Asia and in other parts of the world.

COMMUNIST IDEOLOGY

However, there is obviously more to it than that. Since Russia appeared as one of the two dominating powers of the world in 1945, conflict between her and the United States has grown with extraordinary speed, has spread extraordinarily widely, and has been particularly acute; and there can be no question that ideological considerations have played an important part. It is perhaps the case that the ideological conflict that we are now concerned with, that between communism and capitalist-democracy, is different in kind from any that has before appeared in the history of sovereign states. In this case, we are not merely presented with an incompatibility of political and social constitutions and the bodies of belief which are associated with those constitutions. An example of that sort was the incompatibility between the government of imperial Germany and that of Britain in the years before World War I. Nor is it a conflict quite like that which prevailed in the period of the wars of the French Revolution where there existed in France and Britain not only different political ideologies but where the ideology that had sprung to life in France was a doctrine of social and political revolution which, because of its appeal to the peoples of autocratically governed European states, was a threat to the established order of government in those countries. Communism, of course, resembles the revolutionary doctrines of the France of 1790 in this respect, but it is something else besides.

The something else is that communism embodies a theory of world history, a theory of the future course of political and economic development throughout the world; and, in particular, it is a theory which postulates inevitable conflict between capitalist governments and their peoples, and between communist and capitalist states. If the leaders of a very great power are committed to the doctrine that, because of the inescapable dynamics of capitalist society, capitalist powers must sooner or later seek to destroy it, it is only to be expected that an ideology of this kind will play a very weighty part in world conflict. There has been no other ideology of international importance which has embodied such a theory of inevitable struggle and war. And when an ideology of this kind is officially enforced and professed by the government of a major world power, in such a case it is not possible, as Spykman and Morgenthau seem to recommend, that the definition of national interest should not be allowed to be influenced by ideological assumptions or sympathies. Obviously, the rulers of Russia cannot do other than define their national interest by reference to their theory of world politics; and Americans, in defining the vital interests of their state, cannot be unaffected by the thought that such a theory is professed officially by another great power.

The theory of Marx-Lenin-Stalin (and there is no good reason to believe that the theory has been discarded or substantially modified by the present generation of leaders, publicists and educationists in the Soviet Union) has always held to the inevitability of class war between bourgeoisie and proletariat, and hence to the inevitability of struggle between bourgeois and proletarian states. During the period of Russia's weakness and diplomatic isolation, the period of the theory of 'socialism in one country,' the revolution was prosecuted within the borders of Russia alone, and there was less disposition to insist on the international character of the communist revolution, or for the Russians to rely for their security and for the progress of their own revolution upon revolutionary upsurge in Germany and other countries.

During the thirties the Russian government sought, and succeeded sometimes in achieving, agreements with capitalist states. Yet, despite the fulminations of the Trotskyists, adherence to policies of short-term expediency implied no abandonment of fundamental theory. It was easy for Russian leaders to identify the interests of the Soviet Union itself with those of the world proletarian revolution, so that any policy aimed at the security of the Soviet could not conflict with the ultimate success of 'the revolution.' Russian leaders and theoreticians remained orthodox, at least to the extent of believing that advanced capitalist societies would be forced to seek solutions for the economic 'contradictions' in war; and no doubt Soviet foreign policy after the war has been influenced by the belief that the great capitalist states would be compelled to bolster their economies by preparation for war, and would sooner or later have to try to preserve themselves by attacking the Soviet Union and other communist states. 'To try to comprehend the Soviet outlook and to dismiss the inevitability of the world proletarian revolution is as idle as to try to comprehend the outlook of mediaeval man and to dismiss the reality of the Last Judgment.' [1]

---

[1] M. Beloff, *Soviet Foreign Policy*, quoted by Stone, Julius Stone, *Legal Controls of International Conflict* (Sydney, London, and New York: Reinhart and Company, 1954), p. 61.

RUSSIA AND WORLD REVOLUTION

The theory that communism is a continuing or, in Marxist language, 'permanent' revolution has produced in other ways a permanent hostility between Russia and the capitalist powers. The success of the Russian leaders in consolidating the revolution in their own country, and the failure during the twenties of similar revolutionary movements in Germany and other countries, allowed the Soviet through the Comintern to assert its leadership over communism throughout the whole world; and it induced in the Russian rulers a Messianic conceit which has not evaporated. It convinced them that they alone understood the nature of the revolution which is next on the agenda of history, that they alone are competent to organize and lead it. Here we get a mutual reinforcement of ideology and the ordinary expediencies of power politics. It is ordinary prudence that the Soviet, in order to strengthen its position against the U.S.A. and other potentially hostile powers, should try to gain the confidence of every anti-capitalist, anti-imperialist, anti-Western movement that might appear. It has been alleged that Britain in the nineteenth century followed a similar policy of encouraging popular and demagogic movements, and for a similar reason. In the case of the Soviet, such elementary tactical considerations are reinforced by a sense of revolutionary mission: the belief that there is *one* revolution which is to be accomplished throughout the world; that it is the revolution the mechanism of which has been explained for all time by Marx-Lenin-Stalin, and for which the leaders of the Soviet became after 1917 the organizing committee.

It has been pretty clear that the Russians have been determined that so far as possible the revolutions of the 'underprivileged' should be carried through under their patronage—the Russian intervention in the Spanish Civil War was a good example of how, and for what ends, the Soviet intervened in the revolutionary struggles of other nations—and should be guided to strengthen the interests of Russia itself. In this, there has been a mixture of great power politics and ideological proselytizing. But no state in earlier times has been able to compound quite the same mixture, since no state has before been placed in the same way at the centre of such a widespread revolutionary movement.

It is of course impossible to say how great is the attraction of communist ideology in itself in those countries of Europe and Asia which, since the end of the war, have been passing through a social revolution. In the countries of Eastern Europe which have been communized (the 'People's Democracies') it is very likely that communism would not have prevailed but for the presence or proximity of the Russian army or the ability of the Soviet to bring direct pressure to bear in other ways. Whether in China and other parts of Asia communism would have proved so great a force if the war had not turned Russia into a great world power is not easy to answer. However, there is no doubt that the existence of Russia as a power and as the protagonist of world revolution has been one of the main reasons for the post-war spread of the communist ideology. As Beloff says, 'it is communist power along with communist ideology that attracts adherents.'

In Asia and in other areas, communism as a movement gains support from the prestige of Russia, a prestige that comes, not only from its strength, but also from the fact that it is a great power which has proved its capacity and determination to carry through a tremendous revolution. The Soviet has established itself as a sort of school of revolution for the whole world, not only in that it has laid down the pattern of revolution for backward countries, but also in the sense that there were perfected in the Russian communist party techniques of revolutionary organization and leadership which the fascists and Nazis imitated, but which no rival revolutionary or popular movement has been able to surpass. The communists, with their ruthlessness, their immense self-righteousness, their conceit in believing that they are infallible technicians of social progress and that whatever they do is justified by the laws of social development, their great skill in building the machinery of political regimentation and social manipulation, are difficult to contend with.

NATIONALISM AND COMMUNISM IN ASIA

It is often argued that nationalism was one of the main forces behind the revolutionary movements of countries like China and Indo-China, the aspiration for national independence and the hatred of Western interference or domination, and that it is a mistake to regard these movements as being simply communist. No doubt, this is true; but in these countries communist intellectuals and political leaders have brought these movements into the communist stream partly because of the prestige they have derived from the fact that they have had the Soviet Union standing behind them, partly because Asian nationalism could not produce any other leaders with the same drive, skill and revolutionary thoroughness. It is also sometimes argued that there is a possibility of a clash between communism and nationalism both in Asia and in Eastern Europe, since the Russians as the self-appointed sponsors of international communism have always tended to assume that uniformity and subordination to the views and tactics of Russia are essential characteristics of the communist revolution.

It is argued that mere affinity of ideology is not sufficient to ensure that all communist countries will continue indefinitely to appear as a single bloc: that China will develop as a power in her own right, with policies that may not always run parallel with Russian interests. But this time is not yet; and because the struggle in China and in Indo-China has been in part a struggle against the West and against capitalist-imperialism, Russia and the Asian countries have been engaged in what is ideologically the same struggle. Russian expansion and Chinese revolution thus appear as parts of a single ideological movement, though if the common enemy were removed—the world of Western capitalist imperialism—ideology might not prove to be so strong a cement. It follows from this that if the Western democracies take communism as such to be their enemy, if they base their foreign policies on the postulate that wherever communism is, it is to be resisted or attacked, they will reinforce the binding properties of a common communist ideology.

Thus in backward, impoverished, semi-colonial countries fighting against Western domination and aiming at rapid and radical social reconstruction, the ideology of communism has great attraction, partly because of the revolutionary prestige of Russia, and especially because of the role she has in the struggle against the capitalist-democratic world. But the advantages of association with the Soviet in a common struggle, and the applicability of Russian patterns and techniques of revolution, are not the only explanations of the measure of success that communism has achieved in parts of Europe and Asia. Something of course must also be attributed to the content of the ideology. Communism, so doctrinaire and rigid in many ways, has shown great flexibility in adapting itself to the aspirations and problems of backward countries which had never succeeded in achieving an independent status among the nations of the world. It is evident that two of the main themes of Russian propaganda, the exaltation of the masses and the equality of races [2] are well aimed at countries carrying through simultaneously a social and national revolution.

ARE THE DEMOCRATIC STATES FIGHTING FOR DEMOCRACY?

This brings me to my final question. Is the main international conflict of our time not merely an ideological conflict but a conflict between communism and democracy? In organizing to protect themselves against the Soviet Union, in taking measures to 'contain' communism in Asia, are the democratic states fighting to preserve democracy? In an obvious sense of course they are. The Western states are organizing to protect their own security and vital interests, and one of those interests is their democratic way of life. But in Eastern Europe and in Asia is it an ideologically-motivated struggle they are waging, a struggle to preserve democracy, or the chances of a future democratic world against the triumph of communism? And is the extension of democracy into the threatened countries of Asia or into those parts of Europe which are at present within the Russian orbit a sensible objective of foreign policy?

It is impossible to believe either that American and Western policy is inspired by a desire to spread the benefits of democracy for their own sake, or that a policy of advocating democratic ideas (as they are understood in Britain or

---

[2] M. Beloff, 'No Peace, No War,' *Foreign Affairs*, vol. 27, 1948.

the United States) could be an effective way of contesting the advance of communism. On the first point, it is strange that the Western powers should be now concerned about the extirpation of democracy in the satellite countries of Eastern Europe or in China and Indo-China, when they showed no similar concern before the victory of the communist regime, and even supported in China a government which had little in common with democratic processes.

It may be that the democratic world has had a change of heart, and has been taught by the spread of communism in these countries or by its imposition upon them, that the introduction of democratic institutions in other countries is a necessary condition of a stable and peaceful world. That would be possible; but it looks rather like a case of 'the devil was sick'; and if America and the other democratic powers are now occupying themselves with the encouragement of democratic ideas and forces in these other countries, that is because they believe that democratic communities would be well-disposed towards themselves and unwilling to be drawn into the Soviet bloc. In other words, in Asia and in parts of Europe, the struggle is in no sense a struggle between communism and democracy. Or, rather, communists are struggling against democratic ideas and practices (in the British and American sense of democracy); and the Western powers are fighting against communism, partly because they are opposed to it as an ideology, partly because they see in it a threat to their own democratic systems. But it would be true to say on the whole that, in so far as America and the West try to support democratic movements or ideas in other countries, they do so in order to limit the power of the Soviet Union and in other ways to protect their own national security and their own interests. The struggle 'for democracy' is incidental to the protection of national interests as understood at the beginning of this chapter, as it was in the war 'to make the world safe for democracy' in 1914–18. In other words, the ideological struggle is instrumental, so far as the democracies are concerned, to the state's normal protection of its interests as a state. It is of course none the worse for that. We have seen that Russia's support for international revolution is equally an aspect of a struggle for power as a state. . . . In Asian countries and in other parts of the world the United States of America, because of her great economic resources, has great advantages in the struggle for influence, but not, probably, because of the American way of life, or of its democratic institutions and intellectual tradition. So far as the politically and economically backward areas are concerned, democracy as an ideology suffers from obvious disadvantages. It is especially identified with the civilization of the Western communities and with capitalism; and communism has been especially influential in countries which are fighting against Western interference. Secondly, in such countries, the cultural and economic conditions of democracy appear to be lacking; and it is doubtful whether such conditions will ever appear in the future in countries which have gone for so long without having developed these economic and cultural conditions.

In the West, liberal-democracy has been associated with a capitalist economy, at any rate with a wide distribution of wealth and property. And, in addition to that, the growth of democracy in the West was preceded or accompanied in its early stages by the religious and constitutional struggle of the sixteenth and seventeenth centuries. It is difficult to think of British or French or American democracy without that great upsurge of intellectual, cultural and social movements which marked the first two or three centuries of the modern period. And the growth of science in the modern period, too, contributed to the spirit of rationalism and social criticism, which has contributed so much to the development of the democratic ideology. It is difficult to conceive of the application of the ideas and methods of liberal-democracies in countries where the main social problem is the alleviation of the conditions of life of a vast, unorganized, impoverished peasantry.

It is difficult also to conceive how any regime which was and which remained democratic could carry out the tasks of economic and social reconstruction which the communists in China and elsewhere, with their characteristic lack of scruples and inhibitions, have undertaken. Much of Asia, we are told, is ripe for revolution. The masses want and are willing to support that drastic and very rapid remaking of economic life, and of political and social institutions which will raise their standards of life. It is certain that the methods and institutions of liberal-democracy are not adapted for this sort of revolutionary social surgery. In this century liberal-democracy is essentially cautious, experimental and conservative, and any regime which professed to be both democratic (in the Western sense) and to be carrying through the sort of wholesale revolutionary social reconstruction which was achieved in Russia and is said to be under way in China would clearly be hypocritical. For the forced transformation of backward and largely peasant societies the kind of revolutionary techniques that was pioneered in the Soviet Union is the obvious model. The prospects for the mere transplantation of liberal-democratic models to those countries where communism has already proved to have an appeal do not, therefore, appear to be good.

There is a great deal in what Butterfield says:

In the newly-awakened regions of the world, the issue of such a conflict can only be between alternative types of what we might call pseudo-democracy on the one hand, the 'guided' democracies of occupied countries (like Japan) or of British colonial areas; on the other hand, the 'guided' democracies of the type which communism establishes and to which Russia gives a similar protection. Once there is a question not merely of defence but of the spread of democracy by war, it is only this 'democracy under tutelage' which can be the issue of the conflict, whichever side may win; and the Russian form of this system possesses additional plausibilities and offers extra prizes if only because it can present all the show of freeing subject peoples from a foreign, imperial overlord.[3]

If there is any truth in this, it does not seem that the propagation of the classical ideology of liberal-democracy in Asia, or in those parts of Europe (e.g. Poland) where the communists have already gone a long way with agricultural reform and other phases of political and social reconstruction, is likely to have much effect. In those countries where it has established itself firmly, liberal-democracy preserves values which communism destroys; and it is plain that there are very few people in the majority of democratic countries who would prefer communism to democracy. But the values which democracy does offer are not now of great importance to the masses of countries which, for centuries, have been economically and culturally stagnant, impoverished and exploited by the more advanced countries. On the other hand, democracy if it remains true to its own methods and ideals can scarcely offer those masses what, in the present stage of history, they seem to want: a rapid and thorough-going achievement of elementary economic and social improvements.

[3] H. Butterfield, *Christianity, Diplomacy and War* (New York: Abingdon-Cokesbury Press, 1953), ch. 8, p. 117.

It remains true ... that the spread of communism is a threat to the stability and survival of the democratic world. What has been said in the last few paragraphs does not mean that the democracies should passively acquiesce in the dissemination of communism throughout Asia and Europe. It only means that an inflexible and doctrinaire repetition of democratic slogans or ideas is not likely to be a very effective form of opposition. If the democracies are to carry on a successful ideological struggle against communism in Asia and elsewhere, they will have to acquire a greater flexibility and originality in their social thinking than they have shown so far....

PART II CAPACITIES AND QUALITIES OF STATES

IV • The Influence of Geography Upon International Politics

Since force or the threat of force constitutes the ultimate recourse regulating international relations, no state can afford to neglect the elements of power. The statesman who plans to embark on a course of action must examine the means at his disposal as well as the means at the disposal of others if he is to evaluate accurately the chances for his nation's success. Unfortunately no one has ever devised an accurate means of measuring comparative national power. Although there is considerable agreement that geographical location, size, natural resources, population, industrial capacity, levels of technology, popular morale, and leadership, have something to do with national power, there is no common unit by which these components can be compared either with reference to each other or with reference to elements in the possession of other powers. In a vain effort to reduce this uncertainty various authors have attempted to distinguish between stable and unstable elements and between tangible and intangible elements. Among the stable or tangible elements are usually listed geography, population, natural resources, industrial capacity, and military strength, but even these are recognized to be subject to radical change and fluctuation owing to science, technology and changes in government. The unstable and intangible elements are too complex and ambiguous to bear measure in any but the most general terms.

In view of these limitations upon the measurement of national power it is best analyzed as a matrix in which the ingredients are always in flux both in relation to one another and in relation to the power matrix of other countries. Furthermore, the relative influence of different elements upon national power must be determined with regard to all countries that are engaged in relations with each other in international politics.

Perhaps as a reaction against uncertainty, analysts and statesmen have frequently indulged in errors or fallacies about power which have led to serious misjudgments. Hans Morgenthau lists the three most typical errors in assessing comparative national power: the first is to disregard the relativity of power by erecting the power of a particular nation into an absolute; the second takes for granted the permanency of a certain factor that has been historically important, thus overlooking the potentiality for change; and the third attributes decisive importance to one single factor to the neglect of all the others.[1]

Among deterministic theories of national power few have exercised a more seductive appeal than geography. Up until a half century ago the relationship of geographical position to national power appeared to be one of the most stable and predictable factors in international politics. Europe in particular was endowed with such a favorable combination of climate, population, and resources that its economic, technological, and social organization appeared destined to give it unlimited supremacy over the rest of the world. In fact with the exception of North America the rest of the world appeared to be hopelessly limited by geographic and climatic conditions.

The only significant transformation that anyone perceived was that envisaged by Halford MacKinder, who foresaw in the increasing efficiency of rail transportation a geographically predetermined struggle between the landpower of the Eurasian "heartland" (designated as the "Pivot Area" in 1904) and the seapower of the inner or Marginal Crescent [2] (termed the "rimland" by Spykman). MacKinder believed that the marked improvement in land transport would eventually enable one central authority to control the region running from roughly central Europe to the Siberian wastelands and that such control would offset the greater capacity and flexibility of movement by sea and thereby put the historically dominant Western European powers at the mercy of whoever controlled Russia and the North European Plain. MacKinder's view as well as the studies of Friedrich Ratzel inspired a whole host of geographic determinists, of whom the German geopoliticians were the most notorious with their claim that geographic factors entirely determine the growth and decline of nations. Most geographers are now highly conscious of the relativity of geography, and agree that geography is not the determining but merely one of many conditioning factors that shape the pattern of a state's behavior. Nor do contemporary geographers hold to any preconceived notions of what a nation is capable of achieving. The concept generally accepted today is "that the physical character of the earth has different meaning for different people: that the significance to man of the physical environment is a function of the attitudes, objectives, and technical abilities of man himself. With each change in any of the elements of the human culture the resource base provided by the earth must be re-evaluated." [3]

The selection "Environmental Possibilism" which we have included is

---

[1] Hans J. Morgenthau, *Politics Among Nations* (New York: Alfred A. Knopf, Inc., 1956),
[2] Halford J. MacKinder, "The Geographical Pivot of History," a paper read before the Royal Geographic Society in 1904.
[3] P. E. James, *American Geography, Inventory and Prospect* (Syracuse: Syracuse University Press, 1954), pp. 12–13.

designed to acquaint the student with the importance of recognizing that geography, far from being immutable, is capable of being molded to man's purposes. As the Sprouts point out, it is to be hoped that by achieving a more accurate conception of the man-milieu relationship the student of international relations will avoid the deterministic pitfalls that have beset geopolitics. Above all it should become clear that the mere analysis of data regarding geographic position, topography, resources, population, climate, industry, etc. has no intrinsic political meaning apart from the purposes for which men intend to exploit them. Geography becomes part of the analysis of international relations as a function of the "attitudes, objectives, and technical abilities of man himself." As men are able to view and control their environment in different ways so the relationship of geography to international relations changes.

In spite of the relativity with which its role must be viewed, geography is related to national power and strategy in many specific ways. The successive technological revolutions of the last half century may have changed, but they have not reduced the importance of location, topography, climate and size. For purposes of clarification Stephen B. Jones, in his article "Global Strategic Views," suggests that we look at the influence of geography upon international relations from two perspectives, "inventory" and "strategy." "Inventory" is Jones's shorthand term designating the power potential which a nation possesses by virtue of its size, population, resource endowment, and industrial base. What is important in "inventory" is the optimum combination of size and development, and aggregate wealth—widely diversified as to type of commodities produced, and distributed in such a manner as to permit a relatively high proportion of expenditure on capital and military goods. Thus Switzerland may have a higher standard of living but only the Soviet Union and the United States possess the massive economic base upon which power ultimately rests. "Strategy" refers to the implications that geographic position plus technology hold for international relations. The fact that the United States is separated from the Eurasian continent by several thousand miles of open sea and by the frozen Arctic Ocean still counts for something in the calculations of American and Soviet strategists. Similarly size has positive and negative strategic consequences for a country as large as the Soviet Union, depending upon the location of its resources and the efficiency of its transportation system.

The analytical value of the distinction between "inventory" and "strategy" becomes clear if we consider the historical record of the last century. The unification and rapid industrialization of Germany in the last third of the nineteenth century increased enormously its economic, demographic, and industrial "inventory." This enabled Germany to resort to war twice within a generation in the confident expectation of achieving a position of hegemony in Europe. From the standpoint of "strategy," unification and industrialization enabled Germany transform the disadvantages of a geographically vulnerable position into the advantage of centralized power. Belgium and Switzerland afford additional examples of the strategic consequences that location may have upon a country's existence. Belgium, because of its location at a point strategically vital to three great powers (Britain, France, Germany), found itself unable to remain neutral. Switzerland, located just off the main strategic axis of Western Europe, escaped involvement in two successive World Wars.

Canada and the Latin-America republics which until very recently had neither the population nor industrial base to be accounted great powers, were safeguarded from aggression by virtue of their isolation from the main centers of power. The United States and the Soviet Union are accounted superpowers because they enjoy the geographic advantages of both a favorable inventory of national assets and a strategic location. It was this combination of advantages that a century ago evoked from Tocqueville the prophetic observation that both Russia and America would one day hold within their hands "the destinies of half the globe" and that early drew MacKinder's attention to the potential of the Eurasian Heartland which the Soviet Union now possesses. And though MacKinder neither foresaw nor fully appreciated the strategic importance that the arctic region would assume with the development of air power, his concepts are so solidly rooted in geographic realities that the Rimland, that great belt or crescent of land that runs from the North Cape through Western Europe, the Middle East, and South East Asia to the Kamchatka Peninsula, is still the main arena of world conflict. The Arctic remains, for the time being at least, the great corridor through which the great strategic air blows would be struck in event of nuclear war.

The favorable conditions of climate, topography, resources, and communications by inland seas and overland routes that combined to make Europe and Southern Asia the oldest centers of civilization and power still give them a key position in international politics. Western Europe possesses the resources, social organization, industrial capacity, and trained manpower which in the hands of the Soviet Union would represent a dangerous accretion of power. Unfortunately climate has not dealt as favorably with the Middle East and Asia as it has with Europe; this fact, combined with an excess of population, has prevented Arabs and Asians from effectively developing their resources. As a result those regions remain more power vacuums than power centers. Thus geography establishes the foundations upon which capacity, interdependence and conflict are based, and its importance should not be underestimated. However, as the authors of the two selections below insist, it is the perceptivity, will, and creativity of men which ultimately determines the influence that geography will have upon international politics and strategy.

1 • Environmental Possibilism *

Harold and Margaret Sprout

Harold Sprout is Bryant Professor of Geography and International Relations at Princeton University and a Fellow of the Royal Geographic Society. Margaret Sprout has co-authored with her husband such outstanding works as Foundations of National Power *(1945),* Rise of American Naval Power *(1939), and* Toward a New Order of Sea Power *(1940).*

. . . .

The relationship hypothesis known as environmental possibilism, or simply possibilism, represents a reversal of attitude towards the man-milieu problem. In contrast to determinism and environmentalism, the initiative is held to lie with man, not with the milieu. The milieu is no longer conceived in terms of determinants, or controls, or influences impelling man along a road set by an active purposeful Nature. Environmental conditions, in the possibilist view, do not compel man to do anything. The milieu, is simply there, clay at the disposal of man, the builder. The milieu is thus conceived in terms of opportunities present but latent (i.e. inoperative) until man makes a decision and embarks on a course of action towards some chosen end.

The possibilist does not claim that man is omnipotent. His concept of opportunities always implies the complementary concept of limitations. The limitations, like the opportunities, are latent in the milieu, but inoperative until some decision is taken and implemented. These limits vary from place to place, and from one historical period to another. But limits there indubitably are, limits which will affect the outcome of any course of action undertaken, irrespective of whether or how perceived and reacted to by the actor in question.

This way of hypothesizing man-milieu relationships seems to have taken form in France early in the present century. It is usually identified with the French geographer, Vidal de la Blache. Possibilism is said to have arisen, at least in some degree, as a reaction against the strongly deterministic line of Ratzel and other German geographers who seemed to be laying the foundations for further "inevitable" expansion of the German Empire.

Possibilism also suited the mood of a generation which optimistically viewed the accelerating advance of science and technology as a "conquest of nature" and a "glorious liberation from environmental controls."

As an organizing principle for the study of man's relation to the milieu, possibilism represented both a step forward and a change of focus. Possibilism focussed on man's potentialities for

* From *Man-Milieu Relationship Hypotheses in the Context of International Politics* (Center of International Studies, Princeton, 1956), pp. 39–49. Reprinted by permission.

achievement rather than on the tasks which a teleological Nature set for him. The step forward was the increased emphasis on technology and other social factors in the milieu, which progressively enlarged man's ability to exploit and alter the physical environment to suit his purposes. In the possibilist view, the outcome of human effort usually depends on a whole complex of environmental factors, not merely on one set, for example, climate. It is of the essence of possibilism that the analyst must interpret the properties of the physical environment—the layout of lands and seas, the features of the landscape, distribution of earth materials, climate, etc.— in the light of human knowledge, equipment, and social organization.

Calculation of what is possible, or will become possible, at a given place and time always involves assumptions (frequently left implicit) or empirical findings with respect to the distribution and variation of these social factors of the milieu. Analysis of possibilities latent in the milieu requires special attention to the state of technology and to the prospects of technological change. If the analyst is sophisticated, he also pays close attention to the social structures which are requisites of technological change and advancement.

The factor of technology is strategic in virtually all calculations of environmental opportunities and limitations relevant to international politics. The vast North American deposits of coal, iron-bearing minerals, and other natural resources provided the basis for large-scale industrialization only after many interlocking advances in metallurgy, manufacturing, transportation, and the development of requisite social structures to sustain a modern industrial society. Insularity plus naval control of the water's surface in the Eastern Atlantic and Narrow Seas, enabled the British Isles to enjoy a high degree of security against military attack until a complex sequence of inventions—internal combustion engine, automotive torpedo, etc. —opened new opportunities to Continental enemies of Great Britain. Construction of the Suez Canal made it prudent for every European state to re-assess the strategic properties of its geographical position. Soviet mastery of nuclear science and its military applications rendered obsolete many of the assumptions and expectations upon which United States military strategy rested prior to 1949. In each instance, changes in one set of environmental factors have altered the properties of other environmental factors.

Of special interest to the student of international politics is the fact that calculations as to what is possible in technologically retarded areas always involve assumptions (again frequently left implicit) with respect to the mobility of equipment, skills, and theoretical knowledge from areas of higher technological advancement. What is possible, for example, in present-day United States, Western Europe, or the Soviet Union may lie well beyond the present indigenous capacities of Chinese scientists, engineers, administrators, and laborers. Sophisticated prediction of the rate of economic development in China or in any other under-developed country must take into account not only the indigenous capacity for technological advance but also the ability of the country in question to secure capital and technical assistance from more highly developed areas.

Statements regarding a given country's potentialities for future economic growth may leave the reader in doubt as to exactly what collateral assumptions underlie the conclusions presented. A recent example of this is G. B. Cressey's book on the present and potential strength of the Soviet Union. The "theme of this volume," stated in its preface, is "that permanent environmental restrictions of cold, drought, and continentality will never permit this part of the world to achieve strictly first-class rank." The author describes the Soviet geographical position in Eurasia, the Soviet landscape, the distribution of mineral and other resources, Soviet industrial plans and achievements to date, and prospects for future development. On every topic he comes out to about the same conclusion: physical environment sets permanent limits to Soviet economic growth and hence to Soviet power; these limits are more severe than is commonly believed; and if the Soviet Union should ever "overtake and surpass the capitalist world, including the United States," as Soviet spokesmen have predicted, "it would be because the Soviet people are more able, more loyal, and harder working than those of the Free World."[1]

It is not our intention to debate Cressey's image of the Soviet future. Whether one should accept, qualify, or reject his predictions is not the point at issue here. What is at issue is whether he has made sufficiently precise the basic assumptions and hypotheses from which his predictions of future possibilities are derived. For example, some assumption regarding future scientific discoveries and engineering applications thereof necessarily underlies any prediction of the limits of future economic development. It appears to us that Cressey's predictions rest upon some such assumption as: that technological advances are not likely to operate differentially to the advantage of the Soviet Union so as to offset the handicap which that country suffers because of differences between

the physical environments of the Soviet Union and the "Free World." If Cressey had been more specific on this point, one would run less risk of misinterpreting his estimate of future possibilities.

This example points up an important general conclusion with respect to environmental possibilism. Possibilist calculations consist of assessing the opportunities and limitations latent in one set of environmental factors viewed within a matrix of observations, assumptions, and hypotheses regarding other sets of environmental factors.

Conflicting interpretations or predictions of a simple event or a complex state-of-affairs can often be traced to variant assumptions regarding the matrix, or background, within which the phenomena are observed. Once during World War II, for example, two foreigners in the Soviet Union are said to have observed some idle freight cars on a railroad siding. One reported this as evidence of the weakness of the Soviet transportation system. The Russians, he reasoned, must be short of rolling stock, yet were so inefficient that they could not make full use of what they did have. The other observer reported the same state-of-affairs as evidence of Soviet strength. To him the idle cars implied that the Russians were utilizing their rolling stock so efficiently that they could keep some of it in reserve. A clear-cut case of contradictory assessments of possibilities derived from conflicting hypotheses regarding strategic factors in the milieu!

Always implicit, sometimes explicit in possibilist calculations is the concept of cost. In the words of George Tatham, Canadian geographer: "The opportunities offered by an environment are not all equal. Some demand little effort from man, others continual struggle; some yield large, others meager returns. The ratio between effort and return can be

[1] *How Strong is Russia?* (Syracuse: Syracuse University Press, 1954), pp. v, 26, 28, 42, 98, 119, 120, 140, and *passim.*

looked upon as the price..."[2] Isaiah Bowman put the same idea in the "punch line" that man "cannot move mountains without floating a bond issue," and he "conforms to many defective layouts because it would cost him too much to alter them."[3]

Bowman elaborated this theme as follows: "...the mind of man...remembers events, facts, and relationships, and actively experiments, observes, and generalizes to see how and why things work or can be made to work. This looks as if there were only the broadest bounds to man's spread and his power to use the earth. Time has taught him, however, that there is a higher law than that of making things work in spite of or against natural limitations. He can build a comfortable, well-lighted city and provide education, opera, and games at the South Pole.... But will it pay?"[4]

Lurking implicitly in Bowman's picturesque rhetoric is the very important proposition that calculation of what is possible is not to be confused with prediction of what will be attempted. That is to say, possibilism focuses attention on environmental opportunities and limitations, not on human motivations and criteria of choice. To such questions as: What will men pay for? How much will they pay? What constitutes a defective layout? Why do men differ as to which layouts are defective? Why do they try in some instances, but not in others, to improve layouts that they deem to be defective?—to none of these questions, we repeat, does possibilism provide any line of approach, any working hypothesis, or any criteria of judgment.

An analyst may make any assump-

tions, formulate any hypothesis, or carry out any investigations he desires with respect to the motivation, cognition, and decisional processes of the individual, group, or aggregate of individuals whose behavior is relevant to the problem being analyzed. He may assume, for example, that the human actors on the scene either have or have not substantially complete and accurate knowledge of environmental factors relevant to their decisions. He may assume that they are motivated by Christian charity, or by greed, or by lust for power, or by any other set of values. He may assume that they behave rationally or irrationally in their assessment of environmental opportunities (i.e., possibilities) relevant to whatever end they have in view.

The analyst, we repeat, can make these or any other assumptions he chooses with respect to the motivation, cognition, and decisional processes of the individual, group, or aggregate under study. But in doing so, he steps outside the possibilist frame of reference. For possibilism simply postulates that environmental limitations exist; and that these limitations will affect the course and outcome of any behavior that takes place, irrespective of whether or how these limitations are perceived and reacted to by the person or persons under consideration.

The outcome of action may take several forms. It may consist mainly of reactions on the part of other persons. In that case possibilism has limited utility for the reasons indicated above. Or the outcome of action may consist of alterations in the physical layout of the actor's milieu. Or it may take forms which bring the actor into other new relationships with non-human factors or with human beings who are not significant reactors in the particular situation. For explaining past results, or for predicting future possibilities, in these second and third categories, possibilism

---

[2] George Tatham, "Environmentalism and Possibilism" in *Geography in the Twentieth Century*, ed. Taylor Griffith (New York: Philosophical Library, 1951), p. 160.

[3] *Geography in Relation to the Social Sciences* (Scribner, 1934), pp. 3, 4.

[4] *Ibid.*, p. 164.

is a generally useful hypothesis—but subject to two provisos: One is that the analyst understands the requisites of the function being analyzed; the other is that he has adequate, though not necessarily complete, knowledge of the environmental factors relevant thereto.

To illustrate this conclusion, one might consider the problem involved in estimating the steel-making capacity of the Soviet Union. The analyst cannot proceed at all unless he knows the technological and other requisites of steel-making—raw materials requirements, equipment, skills, organization, etc. But this knowledge alone is useless unless he also has adequate knowledge of the quantities, location, and availability of coal, iron minerals, iron and steel scrap, limestone, and other essential raw materials; the capacity and other characteristics of Soviet mines, railroads, blast furnaces, coke ovens, steel mills, and other revelant equipment; the supply of skilled workers, the organization and management of Soviet industry; priorities and other values built into Soviet policy; etc.

The analyst's knowledge will usually be incomplete. His image of the milieu may fail in significant respects to correspond with what is "there," either because he lacks opportunity for observation, or because he perceives imperfectly or interprets inadequately what he has opportunity to observe. Hence his explanations of past events and his calculations regarding future events are generally no more than rough approximations. Despite these limitations, however, environmental possibilism is a useful tool for the analysis of state capabilities. It helps the analyst to keep constantly in view the proposition that opportunities and limitations implicit in the milieu of international politics may be operative irrespective of the cognition and anticipations of the participants in the action-interaction process.

A simple analogy will help perhaps to illustrate this position. A man enters an unlighted street in total darkness. Techniques of behavioral analysis may be helpful in explaining how he happens to be there (i.e., his motivation and purposes), how he conceives the layout of the street to be (i.e., his cognition of the milieu), and how he gropes his way forward in the darkness (i.e., his decisions and implementing actions). But there is an open manhole in his path. He does not know it is there. He cannot perceive it in the darkness. It forms no part of the apperceived milieu to which his decisions are oriented. Nevertheless, that manhole is a strategic factor in his milieu, for he will fall into it if he continues his present course. The unperceived factor sets limits on the results, or consequences, of the man's decisions and implementing actions. These limits operate irrespective of his cognition of them in advance. Indeed his ignorance of the unperceived factor makes it all the more strategic, since his ignorance excludes the possibility of his taking adaptive counter-action.

This hypothetical set of events has direct relevance to the applicability of possibilism to foreign policy analysis. The paths of politics are strewn with unperceived open manholes. That is to say, political decisions are constantly taken, and have to be taken, on the basis of incomplete or inaccurate knowledge of relevant phenomena in the milieu in which the decision-maker is operating. This is true of all politics. It is conspicuously true of diplomatic negotiations, military operations, and most other phenomena of international politics. This is so because of the efforts regularly taken to conceal relevant intelligence from adverse parties. The student of international politics has constantly to evaluate the consequences of discrepancy between actor-cognition and environmental "reality."

Any number of illustrations readily come to mind. A good one is the discrepancy between actor-cognition and environmental reality in the Japanese attack on Pearl Harbor. Admiral Kimmel and General Short made their decisions in ignorance of the approaching hostile fleet in the early days of December 1941. For them the Japanese fleet constituted no part of the milieu toward which their decisions were oriented. But the fleet was there all the same, and was approaching closer minute by minute. Though unperceived, and hence unrelated to their disposition of forces and other decisions, the hostile force was none the less a strategic "open manhole" in the milieu of the American high command. It indubitably affected the state-of-affairs that came into being on that fateful 7th of December.

Reasoning along possibilist lines underlies much of the discussion that goes on, regarding the "distribution of power" among states, the so-called "power position" of specific states, and the results to be expected from specific on-going or contemplated courses of action. So-called capability analysis, by which the military, diplomatic, industrial, or other capacities of states are described, evaluated, and compared, consists mainly of estimating the opportunities and limitations which the estimator judges to be significant with reference to various hypothetical contingencies.

All such estimates proceed from the possibilist thesis that action takes place within a matrix of environing conditions, circumstances, and events; and that these factors set limitations on the results of action irrespective of whether or how the limiting factors are known in advance, and irrespective also of whether the limiting factors are correctly evaluated by the decision-makers whose actions are under consideration.

But let us emphasize once again—possibilism is not a frame of reference and hypothesis for explanation or prediction

of decisions or the motivational and cognitive antecedents thereof. Possibilism does not provide any approach whatever to explanation or to prediction of motivation, choice, and decision, assertions to the contrary notwithstanding. *In the possibilist frame of reference, motives and decisions are taken as given,* not as phenomena to be analyzed and explained or predicted.

On both historical and logical grounds, this conclusion seems to us inescapable. Possibilism arose, as we have pointed out, in the reaction against environmental determinism, and its watered-down derivative, environmentalism. One of the attractions of possibilism seems to have been its explicit assumption of freedom of choice. As Febrve put it: "Necessities nowhere; possibilities everywhere: and man is the judge of their use." To take the opposite position— to argue that the milieu sets limits to what men can attempt as well as to what they can achieve—is to reintroduce the environmental determinism which possibilism was contrived expressly to supplant. In other words, there is no escape from the conclusion that possibilism *either has no relevance whatever to the analysis of motivation, choice, and decision, or else is conceptually indistinguishable from determinism.*[5]

To conclude, as we do on historical as well as logical grounds, that possiblism provides no basis for explanation or prediction of decisions, is not to contend that decision and achievement are unrelated. Calculation of the opportunities and limitations (i.e., the possibilities) latent in the milieu always proceeds

[5] The British geographer, A. F. Martin, arguing from premises which seem to us to be historically as well as logically untenable, reaches a conclusion somewhat at variance from ours. See his "The Necessity of Determinism: A Metaphysical Problem Confronting Geographers," in *Transactions and Papers*, Institute of British Geographers, 1951, No. 17, pp. 1, 6, 10.

from some assumption or some analysis of what the human actors upon the stage were trying, or are trying, or will try to accomplish. Given a decision—i.e., a definition of what was, is, or will be attempted—the possibilist hypothesis then becomes relevant. It is the essence of that hypothesis that the milieu sets limits to achievement of whatever is attempted; and that these limits are operative irrespective of whether or how they are perceived and reacted to by relevant persons on the scene.

This conclusion, that possibilist analysis starts from *actual or hypothetical given* ends (purposes, aims, goals, objectives), is highly relevant to the problem of estimating the military and non-military capabilities of states. Calculation of state capabilities is never calculation in the abstract. One cannot by-pass the question: capability for what?

Mere compilations of data regarding the layout of lands and seas, the configuration of landscapes, the distribution of material resources, the patterns of climate, the location and productivity of industries of all kinds, ways of living, forms of governing, etc. have no intrinsic political meaning or significance. Such data acquires political relevance only with reference to who wants what and how he proposes to try to get it within the system of action called politics. Similarly, elaborate and encyclopaedic data about specific states—their size, shape, location, terrain, climate, resources, stage of economic development, governmental system, military forces, civic attitudes, etc. acquires political significance only with reference to some set of policy assumptions regarding the demands which they are likely to make on other states and/or the demands which other states are likely to make on them.

Such policy assumptions may range from very general to very specific. Calculations may proceed with reference to alternative sets of policy assumptions, or with reference to one set only. But calculation of capabilities (i.e., opportunities and limitations in the milieu) inescapably proceeds *only from* some set of expectations regarding the behavior of specific states and/or the general course of international relations.

2 • Global Strategic Views *

Stephen Jones

The author, Professor of Geography at Yale University, is one of America's foremost students of political geography. He is the author of Geography and World Affairs *(1950).*

· · · ·

When Mackinder's "The Geographical Pivot of History" was printed in the *Geographical Journal*, the comments made by members of the audience were, according to the usual practice, printed also. Many readers have noted that one auditor, Amery, called attention to the airplane as possibly upsetting the as-

* *The Geographical Review*, XLV (1955), pp. 499–508. Reprinted by permission.

sumptions on which Mackinder's theory was based—this in 1904, only a few weeks after the Wright brothers had made their first flight.

Mackinder, we have seen, wrote of the seaman's and the landsman's points of view. The basic pattern of the physical world was of course the same for both, but the strategic forecast hinged on the belief that land transportation was overtaking sea transportation as a vehicle of power. We have also seen that putting, or seeming to put, seaman and landsman in strong contrast may have been a disservice to clear thinking. Now we have the airman. Must we add the airman's point of view? Or would that only increase the confusion?

For one thing, there is a wide range of thought about air power. Experience with air power is limited, and the pace of technological change has been extraordinary. We find variation from the "all-out" school, exemplified by such men as Douhet and Seversky, through moderate but firmly "air-first" men to the conservatives who hold that the main function of air power is to assist surface operations.

The conservative group holds that the surface battlefield remains the locus of decision. Sea power is vital to the supply of the battle front. Air power is vital to the security of sea routes, for observation and rapid transportation, and as long-range artillery to interdict enemy movements. Strategic bombardment, to this group, should be related to surface operations. Such a view of air power leads to no very new view of the globe. A third dimension has been added to the Mahan or Mackinder world, but its surface features have not been erased, and the travel-time scale has not been greatly altered, since surface movement dominates.

For an example of the air-first moderates, we may take Slessor, who holds that the strategic air force, with nuclear bombs, is "the Great Deterrent" which may prevent another general war.[1] But local wars are still possible, with ground forces bearing much of the load. Slessor sees a need for armies and navies and even for a special "semi-static" force or militia for local and civil defense. Slessor does not describe his global view, as we use that term here, but manifestly it must combine something like the Rimland—the locus of local wars—with a disbelief in heartlands. His views on heartlands seem like an echo of Amery's, amplified by half a century of aeronautical development:

Meanwhile do not let us be distracted by geopolitical talk about heartlands, which was all very well in Mackinder's day but ceased to be relevant with the advent of the long-range bomber. Russia's central position has some tactical advantages, vis-à-vis her neighbours, but in a world air war she would be at a decisive disadvantage. Air power has turned the vast spaces that were her prime defence against Napoleon and Hindenburg and Hitler into a source of weakness. In these days of near-sonic speeds, the depth of penetration necessary to reach some of her vital centres is offset by the size of the area to be defended and the fact that it can be attacked from almost all round the compass.[2]

In Slessor's view, the virtues of the Heartland—size, centrality, and inaccessibility—have become either of no advantage or disadvantageous. Have *Raum und Lage* gone into reverse, so to speak, in the air age?

In order that the Soviet power base be penetrable "from almost all round the compass," it is essential that the non-Communist powers maintain a strong position in the Rimland and in what Spykman called the "off-shore islands" of Great Britain, Japan, Africa, and

---

[1] John Slessor: Strategy for the West (New York: Morrow, 1954), especially Chapters 3 and 4.

[2] *Ibid.*, p. 34.

Australia. If these areas come under Communist domination, it will be the Americas that are penetrable "from almost all round the compass."

Whether centrality in Eurasia gives the Soviet Union a commanding position or only a strong one [has been discussed above].[3] The relative value of land power and sea power in the Rimland was held undecided. What of air power? It is incomparably fast, of increasing capacity, and less and less restricted by weather and surface features. But the very speed of the airplane may offset some of the advantages of position. At near-sonic speeds, to fly, say, from Tashkent to Delhi would take less than two hours. But from Singapore to Delhi would take only four. Would the difference be critical? Would not what Whittlesey calls "pace"[4]—the average tempo of operations—and timing be more important than the velocity of flight, at such speeds? Fuel remains a great problem until atomic energy is adapted to aircraft, but could not Singapore be supplied as readily as Tashkent? If one is ready and resolute, need one be despondent over geographical position? For that matter, may not the Battle of the Rimland be decided by politics rather than by war? Was Vietminh lost by war, or by French delay in freeing and arming Vietnam and American unwillingness to enter the fray?

How do nuclear weapons affect these matters? One may readily agree that in an all-out nuclear war, with cities blasted from the face of the earth and even the countryside polluted with radioactive fall-out, "Heartland," "Rimland," "land power," and "sea power" are words with little significance. But we hear much of the tactical use of nuclear weapons. Just what "tactical use" means is not clear. Should it be stretched to include use against docks, bridges, and freight yards, it comes perilously close to "strategic bombardment," involving or inviting the destruction of cities. If, however, it is possible to confine nuclear weapons to tactical uses, it is not certain that either land power or sea power is favored or that the Heartland-Rimland relationship is altered. Much depends on the relative improvement in methods of attack and defense and on the alertness of the belligerents and the astuteness of their commanders. [Note: these issues are discussed in Ch. XVII below.]

SEVERSKY'S VIEW

If there is a unique "airman's global view," it probably is essentially that of Seversky, and the azimuthal equidistant projection centered on the North Pole is its cartographic expression (Fig. 1).[5] The popularity of North Polar projections has been a valuable corrective to the overuse of the Mercator. The equidistant form, however, has the serious defect of stretching the latitudinal scale in the Southern Hemisphere, and this in turn has the visual effect of greatly exaggerating the width of the southern oceans.

Seversky definitely subordinates the army and navy to the air force. He believes that virtually complete air supremacy, not just local or temporary air superiority, is possible. The side that obtains air supremacy holds the other at its mercy. He does not expect this to come without enormous effort and losses, but he feels that a country such as the United States, with advanced technology but limited manpower, can better pay the price of air supremacy than that of

---

[3] In a section omitted from the present selection.

[4] Derwent Whittlesey: The Horizon of Geography, *Annals Assn. of Amer. Geogrs.*, Vol. 35, 1945, pp. 1–36; reference on p. 24.

[5] A. P. de Seversky: Air Power: Key to Survival (New York: Simon and Schuster, 1950).

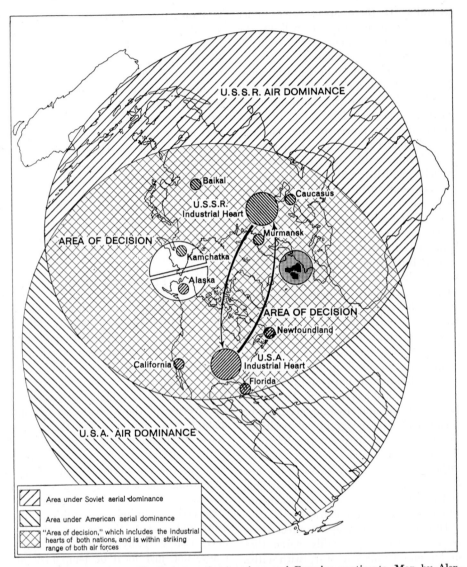

FIG. 1—The power equation between the American and Eurasian continents. Map by Alexander P. de Seversky, reproduced in black and white from colored insert map in his book *Air Power: Key to Survival,* (Simon and Schuster, New York, 1950), facing p. 312. An adaptation of this map also accompanied an article by Major de Seversky in *This Week* magazine, February 13, 1949. The dotted circle "denotes the British Isles, our only tenable overseas base. . . . The white circle embraces Alaska and Kamchatka, where land-sea-air teams will have valid application in an attempt at mutual neutralization as strategic bases."

superiority in three media.[6] Since he wishes the United States to avoid surface, and particularly ground, combat,

he regards overseas bases as undesirable, probably untenable, and, in an age of intercontinental flight, unnecessary. Besides the Soviet Union and the United States, Britain alone has the potentiali-

[6] *Ibid.,* p. 11.

ties of great air power. Only in the vicinity of Bering Strait does orthodox warfare seem justified. Latin America, within the circle of American air dominance, becomes the main reserve of American industry. Much of Africa and all of Southeast Asia are within the ellipse of Soviet air dominance. The overlap of the American circle and the Soviet ellipse is the "area of decision," where Seversky thinks the mastery of the air will be decided. Seversky's global view thus swings us back to the concept of Western Hemisphere defense, with a north-south rather than an east-west emphasis.

A number of American habits of mind favor acceptance of "the airman's view." A sort of "air isolationism" appears possible, the Western Hemisphere is revived, faith in machines and in American know-how is a string touched, the all-out air strategy seems economical in dollars and men. On the other hand, the conservatism of the Army and Navy and their civilian supporters is aroused. Dislike or disregard for "the frozen north" and habitual east-west thinking are strong. "The suggestive map" that speaks to most Americans is still likely to have the equator across the middle.

The choice among the conservative, moderate, and all-out air views is one of the most critical in the American future. The decision will determine the allocation of manpower and resources, the location of bases, policies toward Rimland countries and Latin America, and many other matters. It is beyond the reach of this paper to settle such weighty affairs. All we can do is to propound a few questions that bear on the evaluation of "the airman's view."

The first question concerns the reality of the Western Hemisphere and its self-sufficiency and defensibility. A report of a Senate subcommittee on strategic and critical materials says, as if it were axiomatic, "We belong in the Western Hemisphere." [7] The report demonstrates the present American dependence on sources of strategic and critical materials outside the Western Hemisphere but maintains that through stockpiling, exploration, subsidization, and scientific research the Americas could be made self-sufficient for a period of war. It is held that sea lanes to South America could hug the shore and be protected from enemy aircraft or submarines. "In the last analysis land transportation can be improved." [8] If we grant, if only for the sake of the argument, that the Americas could be made self-sufficient for a period of war, we must still question their complete defensibility by the strategy envisioned. Soviet planes in Central or even East Africa, beyond the circle of American air dominance, would be approximately as near the most vital parts of South America as planes based on Florida. South American cities, and particularly the influential metropolises of Brazil and Argentina, would be vulnerable unless their defenses were virtually perfect. American ability to retaliate, or to "neutralize" African airfields after a blow had fallen, would offer little solace. If substantial parts of Africa should come under Soviet control, it is not certain that Latin America would remain steadfast in support of the United States. We may thus have to defend large parts of the Rimland in order to protect Latin America, which the Senate subcommittee, possibly influenced by the polar projection, calls "our own backyard." [9]

Another question is that of defense against intercontinental bombardment. Perfect defense on both sides would

7 "Report of the Minerals, Materials, and Fuels Economic Subcommittee of the Committee on Interior and Insular Affairs," *83rd Congr., 2nd Sess., Senate Rept. No. 1627,* 1954, p. 12.

8 *Ibid.,* p. 28.

9 *Ibid.,* p. 23.

cancel out the offense. In that case, intercontinental bombardment would not even be "the Great Deterrent." True, perfect defense is improbable, but if defense is less than perfect, retaliation is to be expected, and thus to launch an intercontinental air attack entails great risks. Nevertheless, if a nation places all its defensive bets on this strategy, it must be prepared to use it.

The foregoing questions can be reduced to one: When, and under what circumstances, does a nation that adopts the all-out intercontinental strategy launch its aircraft? One choice would be preventive war, a choice that the United States is unlikely to make. Another would be to use the intercontinental air force in the event of any further aggression across the Iron Curtain. This would be containment by intercontinental means. It might succeed—even the threat might be enough—but it would require unlimited fortitude for an American commander in chief to stand ready to give the signal, risking retaliatory destruction of American cities, to halt, for example, Communist expansion in some country of southern Asia. Third, there is "air isolationism." A defensive perimeter, to use that unhappy term, might be drawn around the Americas, perhaps including some overseas areas considered particularly important. Intercontinental air war would be used or threatened only if this perimeter were crossed. Such a stand would require as much fortitude as the other. In fact, we have seen that large parts of the Rimland might have to be included within the defensive perimeter if Latin America were to be secure. Thus "air isolationism" approaches "containment."

The nub of the matter is that strategy and foreign policy are complementary and inseparable. This is particularly true of the key question of when to resort to armed defense.[10] Moreover, they are continuing processes and cannot be redirected overnight. If a state adopts a rigid strategy keyed to a single kind of war, its foreign policy is made rigid in major ways. This is not necessarily evil if the rigid view is sound, but history does not encourage the belief that man can foresee the precise course of future events. Some flexibility in strategic view seems wise. "Flexibility" should be forward-looking, however, not patterned on the past.

Recipe for a Composite View

We have examined ... a series of global views of politics and strategy. None of them, taken singly, is an adequate picture of the world. None can unhesitatingly be called "the best" or even "the best yet." There is no simple system of political geography, no single thought filter through which to strain all geographical information. We need a series of filters, a composite or an eclectic global view.

. . . .

... The "recipe for a composite view" that we give here makes no pretense to completeness or finality, nor does it contain anything that a geographer does not already know. It is merely an attempt to list the elements of a global view based on the concept of national power. No map of it is presented. This may be cowardice, engendered by our own warning ... that mapping an idea is likely to reveal its fuzziness. But much of the material in our list is already on maps, and for other items data are incomplete.

National power, as has been elabo-

---

10 Cf. W. W. Kaufmann: The Requirements of Deterrence, *Princeton Univ. Center of Internatl. Studies Memorandum No. 7, 1954.*

rated elsewhere,[11] has two components that may be called "inventory" and "strategy." The former is what one has, the latter what one does with it. The inventory component can largely be subsumed, we believe, under Mackinder's old term "man settling," the strategic component largely under his "man travelling." [12]

I. Man Settling
   A. Population
   B. Culture
   C. Material Base
II. Man Travelling
   A. The Atmosphere
   B. Oceans and Islands
   C. Continental Interiors and Peripheries
   D. The Northern Region

This list probably needs little explanation. What is left out may be more surprising than what is included. For example, climate, landforms, and mineral resources are not specifically mentioned. They are, however, implied under other headings and would appear in the higher orders of subdivision.

No one is likely to question the place of population or material base in a global view of national power. Population has been mapped many times, and its elements have been carefully outlined by Trewartha.[13] Among the more significant subdivisions are trends, in relation to total numbers and age groups, and urbanization. Urbanization is an indication of the kind of economy and of the tempting targets for nuclear bombs. The material base of course includes sources of food, energy, and essential raw materials. Athough maps of such items have been attempted, adequate and commensurable data for recent years are hard to find.[14]

The inclusion of culture as a major heading in a list based on the concept of national power may require some defense. But one element of culture is government, and the common political map is therefore a cultural map. The political interpretation of general culture is difficult and still in the experimental stage; thus it is perhaps faith that leads us to give culture so prominent a place. Culture has been placed between population and the material base because it is through culture that men make the material base economic, turn sources into resources, so to speak.

In subdividing "Man Travelling" our guiding principle has been that, for the immediate future at least, air, land, and sea movement are all of importance as means of projecting power. This is especially true because "projecting power" includes economic as well as military action. The relative importance of the three media varies for different kinds of action and in different parts of the world. The atmosphere, because of its global spread, its vertical extent, and

[11] S. B. Jones: The Power Inventory and National Strategy, *World Politics,* Vol. 6, 1953–1954, pp. 421–452.

[12] H. J. Mackinder: The Physical Basis of Political Geography, *Scottish Geogr. Mag.,* Vol. 6, 1890, pp. 78–84.

[13] G. T. Trewartha: A Case for Population Geography, *Annals Assn. of Amer. Geogrs.,* Vol. 43, 1953, pp. 71–97; reference on pp. 88–89.

[14] M. K. Bennett, in his book "The World's Food" (New York: Harper and Brothers, 1954), Chapters 12 and 13, subjects published data on national diets to considerable criticism. Excellent maps of energy production, consumption (1937, with estimates for 1948), and reserves accompany the study of "Energy Resources of the World" prepared under the direction of N. B. Guyol for the Department of State (*U. S. Dept. of State Publ. 3428, 1949*). The energy data in the *Statistical Yearbook* of the United Nations unfortunately do not include major Communist countries. The pending importance of atomic energy in industry further complicates the picture. Rapid strides in the beneficiation of lean iron ores make unreliable many published studies of the distribuiton of this basic metal.

the speed of the vehicles that use it, is of first and increasing importance. This is true whether or not "heartland operations" by strategic air forces are the pattern of future conflict. Every globe and relatively undistorted map gives an airman's view, but it takes imagination to see on them the useful and fearful canopy of air, so that emphasis is justified.

With the oceans we include the islands found in them. Every island is moated to a certain extent, and the defense of Britain in the Second World War and the delay the Formosa Strait imposed on the Chinese Communists show that the moating is still of some significance. But air power, and not just ships or water, is needed to make the moat effective. Not all islands or parts of the oceans are of equal importance. The islands and narrow seas off the Eurasian coast are of first importance today, those off the North American coast of second.

It is hardly news that the peripheries of continents differ from the interiors in ease of maritime access. In the age of nuclear weapons, peripheral location carries increased vulnerability from sabotage, ship- or submarine-launched missiles, and underwater explosion. It usually means a greater dependence on sea-borne supplies. But it also means wider economic contacts by the most capacious and economical of carriers. Only in Eurasia does the division into interior and periphery have great political significance, as Mackinder showed long ago. In the Americas the interior has been absorbed by the coastal states, with minor exceptions. Nearly all of Africa today is controlled from the shores, though its future political pattern is obscure.

The final item of our composite view is "the northern region," based on the nature of the Arctic Sea and the northern parts of North America and Eurasia and their relation to the great centers of power that are certain, for a long time at least, to lie in the Northern Hemisphere. In the northern region surface movement meets resistance for much or all of the year whereas air movement is relatively easy. The northern region may be, as we have said, an aerial "pivot area." There are other parts of the world where air movement is much easier than surface movement, such as the rain forests and the deserts, but these either are smaller than the northlands or offer less serious obstacles. The deserts, for instance, are traversed more easily than the northlands by conventional vehicles, and the Amazon and Congo basins have their immense, never-frozen rivers.

The global view just outlined is merely what the mythical German scientist is supposed to have written, *eine Einführung in das Leben des Elephanten,* though measurable in pages rather than in volumes. The whole elephant is too big for us to see in detail, but we are not blind, only myopic, and we can discern its outlines. And we can and do pursue it, though the path of our safari is beset by pitfalls. On one side is the flood of unfiltered information that rushes endlessly. On the other are the quicksands of oversimplification. To remain still is to be stung by the scholar's conscience. But hazards and discomforts are inevitable accompaniments of adventure, and the pursuit of the global view is the geographer's intellectual adventure.

V · Population Growth, Economic Change, and Education

There was a time not so long ago when the student of international relations studied population trends almost exclusively as an index of national power. The population profile, meaning the proportion of men and women in each age bracket, is still important not only because it tells us what proportion of the population is available for military service and for the labor force, but what these proportions are likely to be twenty or thirty years hence. It is often suggested that France's eclipse as a great power began in the nineteenth century when the birth rate of the German Empire began to exceed that of France. Yet population does not automatically determine a nation's power position: the swollen populations of India and China have been and may continue to be sources of weakness. The Soviet Union affords a good example of how a determined government may recoup population losses in one category by exploiting another category. Demographers were recently astounded by the revelation that Russia's wartime losses of men between eighteen and forty far exceeded original estimates. They can only surmise that the Soviet Union's remarkable recovery rests, in part at least, upon the working capacity of the Russian women.

Population is but one of the many variables that account for a nation's power and prosperity. If the size of the population exceeds the capacity of the existing productive resources to support it, or if it hinders the efficient exploitation of those resources, then it is a source of weakness rather than of strength. There must be some balance or equilibrium between population and resources which permits a society to generate an economic surplus over and above the subsistence level before a populous state can really become a great power. Before we can properly assess the relationship of population to power, we must know what proportion of the national wealth is available for capital investment and for education and science; what proportion of the population is educated; and what capacity it possesses for adapting to technological change.

However, population is important to the student of international relations from more than just the power point of view. One of the most intractable problems facing international relations today is the serious and growing imbalance between population and resources. There was a time when the swollen populations of India and China could be treated as little more than freaks of nature and dismissed as strategically unimportant. The United States and the European powers with the climate and resources conducive to industrial development were also those which had most successfully mastered the processes of population control. Beginning in the eighteenth and continuing through the nineteenth century, the European and North American resource base expanded more rapidly than the population, thereby providing a surplus for investment, education, and science. As a result the United States, Great Britain, and Germany emerged at the turn of the century as the leading industrial and military powers. By the end of the 1930's, the Soviet Union was industrially ready to join the select circle.

On the basis of favorable conditions of location, resources, climate, and size these countries have developed the social organization, capital, skills, science, and technology necessary to exploit their own resources and those of the rest of the world on a truly colossal scale. As a result of their superior technology much of the mineral wealth and raw materials of the rest of the world flows unceasingly towards these several centers. Meanwhile the incapacity of India, China, and the other underdeveloped countries to control their population growth relegates them to the status of second- and third-rate powers. So marked are the advantages accruing to the industrially developed countries that their economic lead relative to the underdeveloped countries is actually increasing. However, unlike the past, the plight of the underdeveloped countries can no longer be ignored. As Kingsley Davis points out in his article—and as we know from scenes of mob violence in Latin America, the Middle East, Africa, and Southeast Asia—the urban masses have become conscious of their power. Political independence has brought a rising demand for economic development and better standards of living. Although most of the underdeveloped countries are too weak to impose their will upon the richer countries, they are nevertheless a threat to world stability. As the inequalities of wealth, income, and education persist or continue to grow, we can expect their dissatisfaction to lead to political unrest and attacks upon Western interests. Events in Egypt and Iraq, the attacks upon United States interests in Latin America, and the struggle between blacks and whites in Africa are a preview of what we must expect in many parts of the world. Even if the West is prepared to deal with these problems with intelligence and moderation, we may expect a long period of revolutionary unrest and political instability.

International relations theory in the West has as yet failed to take sufficient account of what one Soviet theorist calls "the role of the masses in international relations." We are so accustomed to thinking of states and governments as the only legitimate international actors that the role of the street mobs in Cairo, Bagdad, Caracas, and Havana have taken us by surprise. The Soviet Union, unlike Western governments, frankly identifies itself with the explosive aspirations of the street mob in the hope of harnessing them to the chariot of world revolution. Time and again Soviet leaders have made it clear that they regard changes in the international status quo brought about by the masses as part of the price the West must accept for peaceful coexistence.

As a means of securing their authority we can expect the governments of the underdeveloped countries to exploit whatever advantages they possess to extort a larger share of the world's wealth for their people. In this regard Mossadegh's attempt to nationalize the holdings of the Anglo-Iranian Oil Company and Nasser's seizure of the Suez Canal are but examples of a pattern that is likely to become more familiar. In this way, the desperate plight of most of the nations of the world is being and will be forcibly projected into international relations, and the maldistribution of social values will become a prime focus of international politics.

Even for the industrially developed countries all is no longer clear sailing. As the report of the President's Materials Policy Commission, *Resources for Freedom*, points out, civilian and military consumption is so great that a country as rich as the United States already faces severe shortages of important resources. According to the report we have completed our transition from a raw materials *surplus* nation to a raw materials *deficit* nation, and our dependence upon overseas sources of supply threatens to increase. The countries of Western Europe are in an even more difficult position for obvious reasons. The Soviet Union, which is a relative newcomer to industrial maturity and about which we know comparatively little, has only begun to exploit its potential resources and is unlikely to face major resource problems for some time. Therefore, though the United States enjoys a large industrial lead over the Soviet Union, it faces the need to establish economic and trade relations with mineral-rich underdeveloped countries which will guarantee a continued supply of basic materials.

Since World War II, American companies have acquired large holdings in Latin America, Africa, the Middle East, and Southeast Asia, which are now threatened by the rising tide of nationalism. The United States government has pursued enormous stockpiling programs, particularly during the Korean War. These activities can only prosper if the underdeveloped peoples believe that they are getting a fair deal. Thus, far from being unrelated problems, the quest for economic development among the underdeveloped countries and the Western resource problem upon which its security and prosperity depend, are but two sides of the same coin. The following three selections should cast light not only upon the comparative power positions of the several national communities, but upon the difficult economic and diplomatic problems which underlie international relations between the industrial West and the underdeveloped countries.

1 • The Demographic Transition *

Kingsley Davis

The author is Professor of Sociology at the University of California, Berkeley, and a recent President of the American Sociological Society. He is one of America's foremost experts on population problems, and is author of The Population of India and Pakistan *(1951) and co-author of* Modern American Society *(1949).*

. . . .

A pattern of change through which, in a general way, every country achieving the industrial revolution has gone is the "demographic transition." It is a shift from one regime of negligible population growth to another, the first being characterized by *high* birth and death rates and the second by *low* birth and death rates. During the shift there is a rapid increase in numbers due to the lag of fertility decline behind mortality decline (the so-called "demographic gap"), but fertility eventually drops faster than mortality until it approaches the level of the latter. The shift represents an enormous gain in efficiency. When it is completed, each new generation of young adults is produced with a minimum number of pregnancies, child deaths, and woman-years, and with a maximum amount of educational attention. Furthermore, owing to the rapid decline of fertility in the later stages of the cycle, the age structure is temporarily characterized by an extremely high ratio of productive to dependent persons. For these reasons the demographic transition helped to foster the very industrial revolution with which it is so intimately linked.

This pattern, however, is more precise as an abstraction than as a reality. During the depression of the 1930's the cycle looked, in the industrial nations, as though it would soon end. Since then the birth rate has risen in nearly all these countries, giving rise in them to a second wave of population growth, especially persistent in the New-World industrial regions. Also, the magnitude and duration of the demographic gap have varied from one country to another.

Fortunately, an abstraction does not have to be borne out completely to be useful. The rise in birth rates in industrial nations has not been sufficient to bring back nineteenth-century levels, and in most of these countries it has fallen again. The recent phenomenal decline of fertility in Japan suggests that the pattern applies to an oriental as much as to a western industrializing country. In short, the model of the demographic transition has great utility, not as a complete description of reality, but as a device for allowing us to see

* "Identification of Fundamental Internal Social Changes which Condition Inter-Nation Relations," Paper presented at International Relations Conference, Northwestern University, April 1959. Reprinted by permission.

the interrelatedness of disparate facts and to raise basic empirical questions.

THE PRESENT TREND OF POPULATION GROWTH

A significant question is this: are today's underdeveloped areas repeating the demographic transition that the currently industrial countries went through? If so, we can compute the average time it took the latter to make the transition and the average number of times they increased their population in the process, and thus reach an estimate of when the present underdeveloped nations will finish and how many people they will have. But the answer to the question is, no. There are significant differences between then and now.

The most important of these differences are these: Today's underdeveloped areas are *not* showing a rate of natural increase similar to that shown earlier by the now industrial countries; they are showing a *much greater* natural increase —the fastest ever shown in human history. This speed-up derives from birth rates that remain extremely high in the face of sharper drops in the death rate than any industrial country ever experienced. The astonishing fall in mortality has come at a more primitive economic stage than did the fastest drop in the now industrial countries, where the main decline in death rates came early in the twentieth century. This speed and timing of the drop have been possible because, with international financial and technical help, the most advanced health procedures have proved effective on a mass basis even in the most backward areas. Whereas the peoples who first industrialized had gradually to invent and test the techniques now available for fighting death, the present peasant peoples are benefiting immediately from these techniques without any necessity of understanding or contributing to their scientific bases. At the same time, precisely because the imported health measures require little or no change in social organization, and because no effort of remotely equal magnitude is made to import fertility control measures, the birth rate has remained high—higher in most cases than it evidently ever was in Western Europe. As a consequence, the unprecedented population growth is not primarily a response to economic development within the agrarian countries themselves, as it was earlier in the now advanced countries, but is in spite of, and probably to the detriment of, such development. Further, it is occurring at a time when, in many of the underdeveloped regions at least, the density of population in relation to resources is far higher than was the case in northwestern Europe, and in a world that no longer has rich empty areas to fill by migration. Finally any poor country trying to industrialize now has numerous entrenched, competitively aggressive, and sometimes politically menacing industrial nations to deal with.

With the world experiencing an unprecedented and accelerating population growth, and with a disproportionate share of this increase occurring in the underdeveloped, or poor, nations, two international results can be briefly suggested. (1) The numerical increase, coupled with already excessive population density and with other formidable obstacles, is slowing down economic development in backward areas. Yet, for other reasons, the *aspirations* of the underdeveloped peoples are moving ahead rapidly. The resulting divergence between national goals and national means is causing a high degree of political instability in these countries. (2) The political instability, plus the slow and erratic character of their economic development, is weakening the underdeveloped countries vis-à-vis the developed ones. This is creating an international vacuum similar to, but in significant respects different from, the vacuum that once gave rise to the colonial system.

THE CHANGING AGE STRUCTURE

Affecting mainly the younger ages, the drastic decline of mortality has given the underdeveloped countries not only a fast-growing but also an exceptionally young population. This complicates the economic problem by increasing the burden of child-dependency, and contributes to political instability by swelling the cadres of energetic but disenchanted youth. When the waves of young people besieging the labor market each year cannot find jobs, the ebullient energy turns to agitation, revolution, and war. (Note: See article by Watnick, Ch. XVI.)

THE CONTINUING MALDISTRIBUTION OF PEOPLE

The population of agrarian countries has a territorial distribution exactly the opposite of what is required for industrial growth. During the process of economic development, therefore, a tremendous shift must take place in the location of persons—a shift in the direction of cities. Anything that impedes this shift also impedes economic advance. One such impediment is the fact that high fertility persists most tenaciously in the rural areas and thus obstructs the alleviation of excessive population density on farms and the modernization of agriculture. So great does the required magnitude of rural-urban migration become, and so politically troublesome does urban unemployment loom as compared to rural underemployment, that the government often pursues a policy of trying to discourage urbanization by decentralizing industry, subsidizing handicraft, investing in labor-intensive agricultural improvement, requiring official passes for internal movement, etc. In so far as such measures are successful, they dampen the rate of economic development and to this extent weaken the nation.

THE IRREPRESSIBLE URBANIZATION

Policies to the contrary notwithstanding, urbanization is rapid in virtually all underdeveloped countries, in response partly to economic advance and partly to rural overcrowding. Its political significance lies mainly in the multiplied potential it gives for rapid communication and collective interstimulation. In the swelling cities crowded with uprooted villagers and tribesmen, rumor spreads like a virus, popular aspiration soars with the visibility of the rich and the talk of demogogues, and close contact intensifies religious and ethnic hatreds. Under these circumstances the reaction to deprivation or insult or "injustice" is apt to be quick, massive, unenlightened, and violent.

NEW ROLES FOR EDUCATION

It is possible to detect in another crucial sphere—education—the enlarging inequality between industrial and nonindustrial nations. Consumption and national power both depend increasingly on advanced technology. Unless a people somehow acquire the innumerable skills needed to run an industrial economy, to make and apply scientific discoveries, to devise and manufacture nuclear weapons, to maintain public health, to accomplish engineering feats, it must depend on countries that do have these skills. The underdeveloped nations, as we have just seen, are unbalanced in their development. With too many untrained laborers and consumers already, they are adding to them at the expense of capital and skills. While replacement of the population is certainly required, a multiplication of people at the expense of their quality (their trained capacities) is shortsighted. Children are so numerous in some countries that, even with a large portion of the national budget devoted to education, only a fraction of them can receive even an elementary training; in others, mass education is spread so thin that, though it touches almost all, it affects very few.

Among the industrial nations, on the other hand, education is evolving rapidly in new directions. It is doing so in part as an incidental consequence of other social changes, but mainly as a result of awakening national policy. Not only are the industrial nations becoming aware that success in international competition is crucially dependent on the classroom, but they have the money to pay for the education they need.

Each nation, whether industrial or nonindustrial, is faced essentially with three different and somewhat antithetical tasks: to indoctrinate the young with the sentiments of national loyalty and ideology of the state's structure; to give the young the knowledge and lore for living in the particular society with its unique institutions and culture; and to teach the different skills required by variegated groups making up the extraordinarily complex occupational structure. Of the three tasks, the last is technically the most difficult and the most expensive, because it requires not one kind of education but hundreds of kinds. Further, it requires not only a knowledge of present needs but also an estimate of future needs, and a mechanism for altering the supply of trainees in each speciality according to the future need for it from the national standpoint....

Obviously, ... a nation ... has to have productive skills and performance. In modern times the realization has grown that a nation's strength depends overwhelmingly on science and engineering. As a result, national efforts are being made to ensure that the schools turn out the necessarily enormously increased supply of people trained in scientific and technical fields. This movement continues, in a way, the already established vocational trend in education, but with some major differences. Whereas the older trend was individualistic and indiscriminate, emphasizing the individual's own choice of an occupation and treating one vocational subject as being just about as important as another, the new trend is for the occupational needs of the nation to be emphasized, the important ones being given high priority. The fact that the high-priority education is expensive, and that it demands great effort and self-discipline by the student over many years, is no bar to the policy, because the necessity is beyond dispute.

We find, then, that the industrial nations on the whole are exercising more control over the schools to guarantee loyalty and to supply their need for highly trained manpower. This is but another facet of their increased mobilization of resources for national purposes. The movement has of course gone farther in communist countries than in the democracies, but the latter must perforce follow suit if they are to meet the competition. It is worth noting, too, that the underdeveloped countries in the communist camp are taking firmer ideological and vocational control of education than their counterparts in the free world....

2 • The Role of the Popular Masses in International Relations *

Y. Arbatov

The author, a Soviet citizen, is a contributor to the Soviet English-language journal International Affairs.

...the greater role played by public opinion in foreign policy is one of the major manifestations of the growing role of the masses in history. The popular masses—the genuine creators of material and spiritual values—always have been the decisive factor in history. But never has their role been so great as it is now in our epoch, the epoch of proletarian revolutions, the epoch of building socialism over a considerable part of the earth's surface, when they, headed by the proletariat and its party, act as a particularly vigorous force, accelerating the social movement.

The proletariat is the chief motive force of social development in our time —it is the most numerous of all classes who have ever headed society and the only class in history capable of leading all the oppressed masses of the people —the overwhelming majority of society —to victory. The millions of peasants and oppressed peoples of the colonies— the natural and lawful allies of the proletariat, not transient fellow-travellers but allies for all time—are being won for active and consistent political struggle under the leadership of the proletariat, for the proletariat alone can emancipate them and show the way to happiness.

Lenin, drawing attention to the enormously accelerated world development, showed that the chief reason for this was that additional hundreds and hundreds of millions of people, comprising the majority of the population of the world, had been brought into its orbit. "This majority," he wrote, "has now awakened and is in motion, which cannot be halted by the strongest and 'mightiest' of Powers."

The invaluable source of the strength of the proletariat and of the working masses led by it is that, alone of the oppressed classes, the proletariat, thanks to Marxist-Leninist theory, has a scientific understanding of its historical aims, of its class interests, and has scientifically developed ways and means of realizing its aims.

The awakening of the peoples to active political struggle and the involvement in it of increasingly wider masses of the working people, equipped for the first time with a scientific understanding of their aims and of how to achieve them, are accompanied by deep-going changes in all spheres of life including international relations.

---

* *International Affairs* (Moscow), September 1955, 54–67.

The general reasons for the development in international relations of what the bourgeois theorists describe as the "emotionalization" of foreign policy are, as we have seen, the increased role of the popular masses in history, a growth which has become particularly impetuous in the specific conditions of our time, during the extreme sharpening of all the imperialist contradictions, the collapse of the system of exploitation and the triumph of the new, socialist society.

. . . .

Historical development, in addition to heightening popular interest in the issues of war and peace, in matters of foreign policy, has resulted also in a considerable growth of the influence of the masses on foreign policy.

Among the factors, which in their totality determine the lengths to which it is possible to go in foreign policy—in addition to economic potential, the system of alliances, the state of other countries, and *so on—the sentiment of the masses of the people and their attitude to a particular measure or course in foreign policy are acquiring an increasing significance....*

The exploited working masses, in addition to participation in elections, have other means of influencing the foreign policy of their rulers. They are working tirelessly for peace. The modern peace movement, which has assumed unprecedented dimensions and embraces large sections of the population in all countries, is a striking testimony to the active intervention of the people in international relations. The working people also possess such a tried weapon of class struggle as strikes, widely varied forms of political action, and so on. History is rich in examples of successful action of this kind.

Modern wars are waged not by a handful of mercenaries or by professional armies. "Wars," in Lenin's words, "are fought nowadays by nations." Huge ar-

mies, without which it is impossible to wage war in modern times, are recruited from widest strata of the population and, in the first instance, at the expense of the working people. The role of the masses has grown immeasurably on the home front too, where they face privation and danger and where the fate of any military campaign depends largely on their labour and their morale. Because of this the attitude of the masses to war and to the foreign policy preceding it has become a vital factor, determining to a considerable extent the military potential of the country, particularly the morale of its army, the quality of the divisions, stability of the home front, etc.

These circumstances add up to an important political factor and have a sobering effect even on the more bellicose military circles in the capitalist countries and give rise, naturally, to very serious disquiet among them.

It is not mere chance that ever since the First World War numerous concepts, such as "wars of machines" and "wars without armies," have gained wide circulation and to this day determined one of the main trends in the military-political thinking of the imperialists. Its essence was expressed most clearly by the British General Fuller who, in a book published in the twenties, stated that the ideal army, for which it was necessary to strive, was not the armed people, but the single soldier capable of pressing a button and setting the machines in motion. However, all these and similar projects, ranging from the aircraft war of the Italian Douhet and the American General Mitchell and the tank war of the British General Fuller and the German General Guderian, right up to modern plans of a "push button" war with weapons of mass annihilation, proved empty fantasy. Not even the best military technique can replace mass armies, the armed people, as demonstrated on the battlefields of the Second World War and later during the war in Korea.[1] The weight of the facts has forced many of the advocates of these concepts to recognize this (for example, Fuller in one of his latest works has completely revised his views). Experience has shown that the development of military technique (which, like any other technique, is dead without people who create it and set it in motion) by no means leads to the abolition of the dependence of the imperialist Powers on the broad masses of the people. Indeed, it adds to this dependence, because with the increase in the means of destruction and annihilation the masses are becoming increasingly alert to the intrigues of the war-makers.

As the experience of the two world wars has shown, the attitude of public opinion to foreign policy and to wars is restricted not to the moral factor, which is of vital significance for the outcome of any military operation; it can also accelerate abolition of the rule of the classes hurling the peoples into the shambles of war.

In this respect the success of the national-liberation movement in the colonial and dependent countries and the liberation of the peoples of a number of countries from the colonial yoke are of tremendous significance. Thanks to this a new and important force has appeared in international relations,

facilitating the struggle for peace and for a democratic foreign policy.

As things are today the rise of the world peace movement, a new form of popular struggle against the danger of war, uniting in its ranks all to whom peace is dear, irrespective of nationality, social status, political views or religious convictions, cannot but be regarded as a perfectly natural phenomenon. It is the material embodiment of the role of public opinion in foreign policy and in recent years has developed into a powerful factor in international relations.[2]

It is an incontestable fact that in our times conditions are highly favourable for the struggle of the masses in all countries for preserving and strengthening peace, for a genuinely democratic and peaceful foreign policy....

This concept of strength is the source of the close and intimate bonds with millions of people which make the socialist state invincible and ensure popular support for its policy.

It is plain for all to see that the increased role of the popular masses, of public opinion in international relations is not a chance matter, nor is it the outcome of some subjective miscalculation on the part of bourgeois politicians and diplomats. The natural result of objective historical development, it is a vital factor of our time, the fruit of the selfless struggle waged by millions of working people. It is a social phenomenon favouring the progressive, peace-loving forces of mankind and their foreign policy. The increased influence of the masses on foreign policy simultaneously acts as a hindrance to the realization of

---

[1] Note: There is a great deal of evidence from the Soviet side that controverts this dictum. Following the death of Stalin, Soviet military doctrine underwent a revolution. Today Soviet strategic doctrine is focused upon "pre-emptive" war designed to frustrate a preventive war coming from the "imperialist" camp. Such a doctrine necessarily places supreme emphasis upon strategic nuclear power. See H. S. Dinerstein, *War and the Soviet Union: Nuclear Weapons and the Revolution in Soviet Military and Political Thinking* (New York: Praeger, 1959).

[2] Note: In the light of Khrushchev's visit to the United States no one would deny that public opinion can be moved to exert an influence upon foreign policy. Whether the consequences are a "natural phenomenon" or the result of skillful manipulation is a debatable point.

the reactionary, aggressive designs. Never will the peoples of the world relinquish this splendid gain. And most certainly they will not be forced into doing so by the senile mouthings of ideologues of reaction....

3 • Processes of Economic Change in America *

The President's Materials Policy Commission

William S. Paley, Chairman of the Commission, is a prominent radio executive. The Commission was assisted in the survey and preparation of their report by a number of outstanding economists. Their report, often referred to as the "Paley Report," fills two large volumes and constitutes one of the most comprehensive surveys ever prepared of the United States resource position.

...Each American consumes, on an average, 18 tons a year. He uses about 14,000 pounds of fuel for heat and energy—warming houses and offices, running automobiles and locomotives, firing factory boilers, smelting metals, and hundreds of other tasks. He uses 10,000 pounds of building materials—lumber, stone, cement, sand and gravel, and so on—800 pounds of metals (winnowed from 5,000 pounds of ores). He eats nearly 1,600 pounds of food; this, together with cotton and other fibers for clothing, and with pulpwood for paper, and other miscellanous products mounts up to 5,700 pounds of agricultural materials. In addition he uses 800 pounds of nonmetallics, such as lime, fertilizer and chemical raw materials.

Such levels of consumption, climaxing 50 years of phenomenal economic progress, levy a severe drain on every kind of resource we have: minerals, forests, soil and water. In the first 50 years of the 20th century, as population doubled and our total national output reached five times the 1900 level, the stream of raw materials increased in volume and value until, in 1950, it was worth two and one-half times as much (in constant dollars) as it was in 1900. In the mixture that made up this stream there were some significant differences, of which the most startling was that whereas our use of forest products actually declined one percent in 1950 compared to 1900, our consumption of minerals, including fuels, was six times 1900 totals. In 1950 we were taking from the earth

two and one-half times more bituminous coal;
three times more copper;
three and one-half times more iron ore;
four times more zinc;
twenty-six times more natural gas;
thirty times more crude oil;

than in the year 1900. *The quantity of most metals and mineral fuel used in the*

* Resources for Freedom, Summary of Vol. I of a Report to the President's Materials Policy Commission (Washington, D.C.: U.S. Government Printing Office, 1952), pp. 6 ff.

United States since the first World War exceeds the total used throughout the entire world in all of history preceding 1914.

This vast drain, greater today than yesterday, and inescapably greater tomorrow than today, upon resources that cannot be renewed has become the most challenging aspect of our present-day economy. A ton of ore removed from the earth is a ton gone forever; each barrel of oil discovered means one less remaining. Neither the next 50 years nor even the next 25 can see a growth in minerals consumption at the same increasing swift rate unless profound changes in trade and technology occur; in their absence, such increases could not be stood.

Even though they have been less urgently demanded, "renewable" resources have also felt the strain. Ninety percent of our virgin timber stand in the commercial forest area has been cut, and thus far we have done a poor job in growing replacement crops. At present we are using up our inventory of saw-timber at a rate 40 percent faster than its annual growth. Millions of acres are no longer in forest; other millions have gone to brush and inferior trees. Upon our agricultural land we have imposed a heavy burden of depletion; we have opened it, exploited it heavily, abandoned much of it after its fertility had been drained, and moved on to repeat the process elsewhere. Partly because of soil erosion, even water, once regarded as a "free commodity" of virtually unlimited supply, has become a problem.

The time has clearly passed when we can afford the luxury of viewing our resources as unlimited and hence taking them for granted. In the United States the supplies of the evident, the cheap, the accessible, are running out. The plain fact is that we have skimmed the cream of our resources *as we now understand them;* the pause must not be too long before our understanding catches up with our needs.

With less than 10 percent of the free world's population and 8 percent of its land area, the United States has come to consume almost half the free world volume of materials. It is such growth of demand that is at the core of our materials problem; it is mainly our unwillingness to accept the status of a "mature economy," that challenges the adequacy of our resources to meet our needs. All the copper ever discovered in the United States up to now would last only 25 years at the rate of consumption projected for 1975; all the lead would similarly last only 18 years, all the zinc only 30 years. In short, handing over the United States mineral deposits, intact and pristine as they were in Columbus' day, to our children in 1975 would scarcely help them solve their materials problem at all.

As a Nation we have yet to face squarely such growing inconsistencies between our ambitions and the domestic bases upon which they rest. How did we get this way? And what are we going to do about it?

OUT OF THE PAST; INTO THE FUTURE

The United States has never been completely self-sufficient in raw materials: had we insisted on being so, our economic output and living standards today would be considerably lower than they are. We began as an "underdeveloped" Nation, with rich resources but a shortage of manpower and capital, and little industry. It made good sense for us then, as it does for many underdeveloped countries today, to concentrate on the export of raw materials and agricultural products as the best means of acquiring purchasing power abroad with which to buy foreign manufactured goods to support better living standards and economic growth. Our own manufacturing grew; our foreign trade burgeoned and its composition underwent drastic change. United States exports of crude materials slowly fell in proportion as exports of manufactured products slowly rose. Opposite changes occurred in our pattern of imports. Finally, the decade of the 1940's marked a turning point in the long-range material position of the United States; historical trends long in the making came to a climax when the national economy moved just prior to the war from a long period of depression into a period, still continuing, of high employment and production. By the mid-point of the 20th century we had fully entered an era of new relationships between our needs and resources; our national economy had at last not merely grown up to our resource base but in many respects had outgrown it. We had completed our slow transition from a raw materials *surplus* nation to a raw materials *deficit* nation.

The symptoms of this changed materials position are today numerous; we have become the world's largest importer of copper, lead, and zinc, whereas once we were huge exporters. We have begun to meet from foreign sources a sizable and growing portion of our needs for petroleum and iron ore, long the hallmarks of United States self-sufficiency. We have shifted from net exporter to net importer of lumber. There are today only two metals (magnesium and molybdenum) used by United States industry for which we are not partially or wholly dependent on foreign supplies. At the start of the century we produced some 15 percent more raw materials than we consumed (excluding food); by midcentury we were consuming 10 percent more materials than we produced.

WHAT SHALL WE ASSUME?

The size of future materials demands, and the adequacy of supplies, will depend upon the rate at which the United States economy and that of the whole free world expands. If we assume for the moment a favorable set of materials supply conditions, the size of our national output by 1975 will depend mainly upon the size of total population and working force, the number of hours worked per week, the accumulation of capital that has occurred by then, and the rise of man-hour productivity.

Estimates of United States population for the future range between 180 million and 220 million; the Commission has assumed, after consultation with the Bureau of the Census, a population of 193 million by 1975 and a working force of 82 million, in contrast with the 1950 figures of 151 million and 62 million. It has assumed a work week perhaps 15 percent shorter than in 1950. It has further assumed an annual rise of about 2.5 percent in production *per man-hour* against a somewhat smaller past rate of 2.1 percent, because the Commission thinks it reasonable to expect steadier levels of employment and economic activity in the future, in line with the avowed national objective of making major depressions a relic of the past. This does not preclude, however, the possibility of milder fluctuations.

The fundamental assumption, drawn from this, may be wrong, but seems unquestionably conservative: it is that the rate of growth of the economy in the next 25 years will be neither more nor less than what it has averaged over the last century, or about 3 percent per year. Three percent compounded results in a doubling every 25 years; thus, by 1975 our total output of goods and services (the Gross National Product or GNP) is assumed to be twice what it actually was in 1950.

Based upon the foregoing, the Commission has projected the general magnitude of demand in the decade 1970–80 for various major materials. These projections do *not* predict how much of each material will actually be available and consumed. Instead, they are estimates of what might be demanded *if relative prices of various materials remained the same as in early 1950,* which they are most unlikely to do. Moreover, the projections can make no allowance for unforeseeable new uses, sharp substitutions or dramatic technological improvements. Their value is solely as a starting point; they give only the roughest measure of the general magnitudes involved.

These projections may look high by today's standards; they may well look too low by tomorrow's. Far from assuming faster growth rates, they reflect in some cases a somewhat *smaller* annual rate of increase for the future than has characterized the past. Although it is assumed that our Gross National Product will double in the next 25 years, past experience indicates that less than a doubling of total materials input can achieve this owing to the fact that GNP will reflect more value added to materials by higher fabrication and a greater proportion of services. It thus seems that an increase in the total materials stream of between 50 and 60 percent will suffice to achieve a doubling of the GNP by the 1970's. But demands for various materials may be expected to rise most unevenly, in some cases going up as little as one-quarter, in others rising fourfold or more. Demands are assumed to vary according to the main uses which the materials fill today, but to reflect the effect of large substitution trends already clearly in motion. On these assumptions, the year 1975 would show something like this:

Demand for minerals as a whole would be 90 percent higher than in 1950.

Within this figure, demand for iron, copper, lead and zinc might rise only 40 to 50 percent, but other increases might be: fluorspar, threefold; bauxite

for aluminum, fourfold; magnesium, eighteen to twentyfold (the largest projected increase for any material).

Demand for timber products would be 10 percent higher than in 1950.

Without changes in the rate of improvement in forestry there would be a serious situation in saw timber, with an annual growth of 40 to 42 billion board feet falling far short of a projected annual drain of 66 billion. Demand for saw logs might rise 10 percent over 1950; a pulpwood increase of 50 percent would be the heaviest demand increase projected for a timber product category by 1975. For such things as poles, piling and hewn railroad ties, changing conditions might make 1975 demand actually less than today's.

For agricultural products of all kinds, demand would be about 40 percent higher than in 1950.

Industrial water needs might rise from 80 billion to 215 billion gallons a day —an increase of 170 percent.

Demands for total energy would double over 1950.

Within this figure, demand for electricity would more than triple—from 389 billion kilowatt-hours in 1950 to a possible 1,400 billion in 1975. The demand for liquid fuels would more than double; for natural gas would possibly triple; the demand for coal, for all uses including synthetic liquid fuels, would rise 60 percent.

These figures apply in the United States alone. What of the rest of the free world? Such estimates as the Commission has been able to make for "other free world" are necessarily much rougher than those made for the United States. But they suggest that demand in other free nations, building as it will on a smaller base, will be even larger in percentage increases than United States demand during the next generation, and that the United States, although its total of materials consumption will increase greatly, will probably consume a somewhat smaller share of the free world's total supply.

In the difficult matter of projecting future demands one point of overriding importance stands out: despite wide differences of judgment as to whether demand for some material will rise 50 percent, or 100 percent, or 200 percent, the central point is that demand for everything *can be expected to rise substantially.* This may not be a popular dictum, particularly among some businessmen who may be more fearful of creating too much future capacity than of having too little. But the economic history of our times records more estimates of the future that were too small than those that erred on the other side. Many unexpected turns of fate will occur in the next quarter-century; one or more of them may have some deplorable effect upon business. But this Commission sees no reason to assume that a world that has been growing economically by leaps and bounds for many generations will suddenly become static in this one. If we are to believe in growth, it is essential that we show our faith.

III

The threat of the Materials Problem is not that we will suddenly wake up to find the last barrel of oil exhausted or the last ton of lead gone, and that economic activity has suddenly collapsed. The real and deeply serious threat is that we shall have to devote constantly increasing efforts to acquire each pound of materials from natural resources which are dwindling both in quality and quantity; thus finding ourselves running faster and faster in order to stay standing still.

In short, the essence of the Materials Problem is *costs.*

The real costs of materials are not measured primarily in money; they lie *in the hours of human work and the amounts of capital required to bring a pound of industrial material or a unit of energy into useful form.* These real costs have for some years been declining, and this decline has helped our living standard to rise. In this Commission's view, there is a serious possibility that this downward trend in real costs may be stopped or reversed tomorrow—if, indeed, this has not already occurred.

. . . .

RELIEF THROUGH FLEXIBILITY

If costs are the problems, what is the solution? The answer of this Commission is that there is no *one* solution. There are, however, many flexibilities in our materials position—in what resources we use, in where we get our supplies, in how we use them—and we can succeed in averting the threat in the Materials Problem if we undertake a series of simultaneous actions which utilize these flexibilities to the full.

Consider for a moment what would happen if the United States were forced to live rigidly within its present materials position. We would have to meet all future needs from the resources we now have and know how to utilize. Our technique of producing and using materials would be frozen in its present mold. Each successive year would further deplete reserves, materials costs would rise geometrically, production would shrink, and the clock of economic progress would run down.

Fortunately, the outlook, although serious, is not that bleak. If we are sufficiently adroit, we can exploit the flexibilities in our materials situation more fully than ever in the past to the end of providing an expanding flow of materials in a "mix" to suit our needs, at costs we can afford to pay. In so doing, we can proceed along three main lines:

We can get more materials and more energy from domestic resources by pushing back the technological, physical and economic boundaries that presently limit the *supply*.

We can alter our patterns of materials *use* by more efficient designs and processes—and by shifting the burden of use away from scarcer materials, toward more abundant ones.

We can get more materials from abroad, on terms beneficial to ourselves and other free nations.

These opportunities are real and promising, but their full benefits will never be realized except by earnest and unremitting effort. To consider them, it is also necessary to consider the problems that go with them.

More Materials From Domestic Resources

The United States even today makes practical use of only a small fraction of its total resource base. Past depletions notwithstanding, we still possess a broader and stronger usable fraction of our resource base than ever before—mainly because, over the years, we have discovered resources and uses unsuspected by our ancestors. The bayberries of Cape Cod and the sperm whales off Nantucket were vital resources to the early inhabitants of Massachusetts; so was the buffalo to the plainsmen. It was irrelevant to them that nature had created huge pools of petroleum under the soil of Texas, great bodies of iron ore in Minnesota, waterfalls in Washington, and phosphates in Florida. It is equally irrelevant to us today that the candles, the whale, and the buffalo have all but vanished; it is of high importance that the resources of the West have been opened up, that the invention of the internal combustion engine has made petroleum a valuable resource, that technology has taught us how to make aluminum from bauxite, and plastic from such abundant resources as coal, water, and air. By discovery, development, and technology, the materials stream which flows from our resources has been enlarged and its composition vastly altered, while the cost of materials measured in human effort has, until recently, steadily declined....

IV

...Our strongest weapons for accomplishing improvements in supply and use, and in fighting the threat of rising real costs wherever encountered, are in the application of larger quantities of energy to *work*, and larger quantities of technology to *working methods*. How well supplied are we with energy and technology, *as resources*, to give us the flexibility we must have to support the burdens of the future? As of today the simple answer is: not well enough.

Energy and Technology as Resources

If we are to double our Gross National Product by 1975, we must be able to double the supply of energy, at real costs we can afford to pay. Our petroleum and natural gas industries have grown with remarkable vigor and are still growing, but they are working against a resource which is exhaustible, and there will be a strong upward pressure on their cost. Our coal reserves are much more abundant, but economically coal is far from being an all-purpose source of energy as things stand today, and for many purposes and in many places it is not sufficiently cheap to buck the rising tide of energy costs. Favorable hydroelectric sites are limited in number, and although we have not yet used them to the full, the opportunities they provide for enlarging our supply of low-cost energy fall far short of matching our expanding electric needs....

Technology similarly presents a problem of far-reaching importance. The rate of technological progress depends heavily upon the supply of scientifically trained personnel and upon the expansion of basic scientific knowledge on which applied technology is founded. The available evidence shows, however, that the prospective flow of new scientific and engineering personnel from the universities is alarmingly below apparent needs. Men far wiser than this Commission in the affairs of science warn us that particularly since 1940, the Nation has been far more industrious in putting scientific facts to work than in increasing basic knowledge.

The previous contributions of technology to materials supply have been great, but the future contributions must be greater still. Most Americans have been nurtured on the romantic notion that technology will always come to the rescue with a new miracle whenever the need arises; after all, it gave us synthetic rubber and the atomic bomb in a hurry when the need was urgent. But isolated solutions of problems relating to individual materials are no substitute for the broad frontal attack which technology needs to make on the materials problem as a whole. The criticism here is not of our technologists but of our lack of national concern for the materials problem.

SECURITY AND MATERIALS

In time of war the overriding problem of materials is to have enough safely available, and the question of costs becomes subordinate. In the period of preparation against the threat of war, however, the question of costs remains a major concern.

Every war consumes more and more massive amounts of materials. The United States is becoming increasingly vulnerable through the growing military importance of metals and mineral fuels and our shrinking resources for supplying them. Of more than 100 mineral materials we use, about one-third—for example, sulfur, coal, phosphates, magnesium, molybdenum—are at present fully supplied from our domestic resources. Another third of the list we get almost entirely from other lands; this fraction has assumed greater importance as advances in the technology of high-temperature alloys and electronics have brought into greater prominence such minerals as columbium, cobalt, high-grade quartz-crystals, and others we do not possess. The final third of the list we obtain partly from abroad and partly from domestic output—materials like iron ore, petroleum, copper, and lead.

To meet or anticipate our needs from the supply side, we stockpile, and we seek reserve materials capacity in safe areas, domestic and foreign. On the supply side, civilian authority remains more or less in control. But on the demand side, the military, particularly in wartime, is in a commanding position. With each successive war, and now with preparation against the contingency of another, the military has become a greater and greater claimant against the materials of the whole economy. It would be impossible to fix a maximum percentage of military claims to the total economy and say "beyond this point you may not go." But even though the point cannot be fixed, it is known to exist. The military thus carries a heavy responsibility to hold its drain against the Nation's materials supply to the lowest levels consistent with adequate military strength; although progress has been made here, there is room and pressing need, for much more.

The demands of security are imperative—but they do not by any means provide us with the only reason for achieving greater flexibility in our materials position. Even if no threat of war overhung today's world, the United States would still have to face the fact that our high-consumption economy no longer makes our domestic resource base adequate even to our civilian needs. The United States will find it increasingly worth while to turn abroad for more supplies of basic materials.

Some alterations in political thought may be necessary before such a policy becomes accepted as an everyday matter. Actually, however, there is little to be lost and enormous advantages to be gained by importing a much greater volume of raw materials in the future than we have in the past. We are in a good position to make bargains advantageous to buyer and seller alike. Where import conditions are unattractive, we can always raise domestic output (at higher costs), develop substitutes or, if need be, use less. But where conditions for international economic cooperation are favorable, we can not only benefit ourselves but, by shifting to more imports, also benefit the supplying countries whose receipts from sales would provide them with exchange to expand their own economies and thus help raise their peoples' standard of living.

There is today extreme variation among the free nations in their current living standards and in the prospective relationship of needs to resources. The industrial nations of Western Europe and Japan have strong industrial capacity and labor skills but severe resource limitations. At the other extreme are numerous nations of South America, Africa, South Asia, and the Middle East whose average living standards are low but who possess rich and relatively undeveloped natural resources. In between these two groups are such nations as the United States, Canada, Australia, and New Zealand whose resources are relatively strong, whose industry is advanced, and whose living standards are high.

These three groups of nations could cooperate economically over the next 25 years to the tremendous advantage of each. The more advanced nations could export the tools of growth to the less developed areas. The less developed nations, by expanding their exports and by attracting foreign capital and management skills, could put themselves on the road to accelerated economic growth.

The fact that nature distributed resources very unevenly over the face of the earth in relation to human population and consumption alone argues in favor of increasing integration of the various national economies of the free world. But the hard political facts of mid-twentieth century add further great weight to the proposition that it will be to the mutual advantage of all freedom-loving peoples of the earth to achieve a greater measure of economic and political cooperation than ever before, founded on the principles of mutual help and respect. Such cooperation can succeed only if it is based on a clear understanding of the varying needs and resources of all the nations concerned, and the opportunities which lie in mobilizing the strength of all to meet the particular weaknesses of each.

On paper, the economic opportunities in free world cooperation are tremendous; they suggest a possible new era of world advancement dazzling in its promise. Unfortunately many obstacles, mostly man-made, lie in the path. Underdeveloped nations today are highly conscious of the disparity between their own standards of living and those of more highly developed countries. They resent the stigma of "colonialism" which often attaches to economies heavily dependent on raw material exports. They remember the great depression of the

1930's when falling prices for their big raw material exports wiped out their ability to buy the goods they needed from their more industrialized neighbors.

Potential investors, on the other hand, wonder whether foreign countries will keep their bargains. The individuals and corporations with capital to invest in foreign raw materials production hold back for fear of legal uncertainties, fear of expropriation and the possible impermanence of governments with whom they might make contracts. They fear arbitrary administration of import and export controls and limitations on the convertibility of their earnings into American dollars. At home, tariffs and certain aspects of our tax laws add to the obstacles.

It would be folly for policymakers in this or any other nation to assume that the present turmoil of the world will work itself out in ideal fashion. The violent political upheavals of this century clearly have not yet spent their force. What happens internally in the less developed nations, and to their economic and political relations with the industrially advanced nations of the free world, will largely determine whether materials development can be used to help world progress.

VI · Economic Potential, Technology, and Science

As the last article in the preceding chapter indicated, no matter how rich a country may be, its power ultimately depends upon the effectiveness with which it utilizes its natural resources, and this in turn depends on its level of economic development and social organization. In 1914 the German armies, though heavily outnumbered by the Russians, were able to defeat them in part at least because of the superior productivity of German industry. A generation later German armies of equally superb equipment and morale were incapable of subduing a Russia which had by then acquired modern weapons and supporting industry. In the intervening two decades, the new Soviet government had carried out the forced industrialization of backward Russia to bring it abreast of its most dangerous Western foes. To achieve this goal Stalin had concentrated upon the development of Soviet heavy industry at the expense of light industry and consumer goods. From a level of steel production less than one quarter that of Germany's in 1914, the Soviet leaders raised Russian production until it exceeded Germany's in 1940. That, plus American lend-lease, was enough to give Russia the industrial means necessary to establish mastery over Germany.

Today only a few nations possess the industrial productivity indispensable to a great power, and of these only the Soviet Union and the United States possess an industrial base sufficient to support large-scale armaments, nuclear and missile development, and large-scale economic assistance to the underdeveloped countries, while maintaining substantial levels of capital investment. As Allen Dulles, director of the Central Intelligence Agency points out (see page 125), the great question facing the United States is whether it will continue to develop at a pace rapid enough to meet Soviet competition. "Whereas Soviet gross national product was about 33 percent of that of the U. S. in 1950, by 1956 it had increased to about 40 percent, and by 1962 it may be about 50 percent of our own. This means that the Soviet economy has been growing, and is expected to continue to grow through 1962, at a rate roughly twice that of the economy of the United States."

Neither Great Britain nor Germany appears capable of developing the industrial base upon which these phenomenal economic achievements rest. Britain and Germany are so vulnerable to air atomic and missile attacks that their ability to survive an all-out nuclear war is debatable, and Communist China, which possesses limitless manpower and considerable natural resources, is likely to be restricted to land operations until it develops an industrial base, unless, of course, it is to be equipped with Soviet air material. Although there are many obstacles to China's developing an economic strength comparable to that of the United States or the Soviet Union, a considerable accretion of industrial power can be expected within the next two or three decades. The potential rate of Communist China's industrial growth should not be underestimated.

The resources, population, skills, and industrial base of a country together constitute what is traditionally known as economic potential for war, which Knorr defines as "the capacity to produce military forces and supplies in time of war and thus to add substantially to, and often to multiply, the amount of combat power maintained in peacetime" (Knorr, "Economic Potential for War," page 137). However, in view of the fact that the line between war and peace has become increasingly blurred, we must begin to treat economic potential as the wherewithal to support a whole spectrum of security programs ranging from the narrowly military through defense support and economic assistance to education and scientific research. Differences in economic potential then would refer to the relative capacities of two or more powers to provide the necessary productive resources to support foreign economic aid and development programs and a high level of investment in appropriate industries as well as a military establishment.

The range of wars that may confront a nation renders the traditional concept of war potential somewhat ambiguous. In the old days a nation had only one type of war to reckon with, and the security equation could be calculated in terms of fairly predictable military factors. In preparing for the maximum possible security challege, one also prepared for lesser wars. This is no longer possible, for the new military technology has not only created arms of unprecedented destructive power but also reduced the protective function of time and space to a matter of hours. If the modern nation is to stand ready to wage an all-out nuclear war it must maintain forces of an enormous magnitude and weapons such as intercontinental bomber fleets which are subject to constant technological obsolescence. At the same time a nation must be prepared to wage "brush fire" wars and, in the case of NATO, all-out conventional war with tactical nuclear weapons. The magnitude of this dual function necessitates not only a high level of taxation and commands a big slice of the gross national product, it requires the existence of a structure of output and flexibility of production that will provide a high level of speed and ease in the modification of output patterns. War potential as it was understood between wars is no longer a fully comparable concept. The present armed stalemate has the revolutionary character of giving a possibly decisive advantage to the rival which devotes the biggest share of its technology and industrial base to war production *in advance of actual hostilities.*

As wars have become more and more total and peace itself nothing but "cold" war, elements of national life that at an earlier time were taken for granted must now be assigned an important weight. Nowhere is this more evident than in the tempo of change which science has imparted to the arts both of peace and war. As Warner R. Schilling points out in "Science, Technology and Foreign Policy," the connection between science, technology, and war is not a new one. War has always inspired new social and scientific innovations, and the achievements of science have always been a double-edged sword. But it is only recently that science has been consciously employed to solve problems selected with a view to their military importance. Until World War II the scientific method had been applied but haphazardly to the advancement of military weapons. Britain secured certain military advantages against Germany by the application of scientific techniques to the development of radar in the late 1930's. However, the most significant application was the development of the atomic bomb by American and British scientists in time to end the war against Japan. Since then the United States and the Soviet Union have become locked in a gigantic arms competition based upon the development and conscious direction of scientific research.

But war is not the only focus of scientific competition. The Soviet Union is presently leading in the struggle to mass produce scientists upon whom depends the whole process of technological development. Eventually it hopes to supplant the United States as the main source and symbol of technological achievement. The outcome of this competition will be either the profound modification of the pursuit and attainment of economic and social goals throughout the world or the destruction of modern civilization. It is currently in a society's capacity to respond to the new challenge of science that its institutions and social system are most forcefully tested. Even if the incentive of peaceful competition with the Soviet Union did not exist there is another respect in which the development of our economic and scientific skills would relate to international relations. International politics will be increasingly effected by the revolutionary upsurge of the newly emergent states of Asia and Africa. Whatever capacity we possess to ease their economic and social transition may well depend upon our ability to provide them with indispensable scientific support and skills. A viable international society in which the United States can continue to enjoy its present favored status may depend upon our willingness to produce a high proportion of skilled physical and social scientists.

1 • Khrushchev's Challenge *

Allen W. Dulles

The author, a wartime member of the Office of Strategic Services, is Director of the Central Intelligence Agency.

...To understand the seriousness of the Soviet economic threat, it is essential to understand the Soviet economic and industrial base on which they are developing their economic penetration program.

Since 1928 the Soviet Union has developed rapidly from a predominantly agricultural and industrially underdeveloped country to the second largest economy in the world. Forced draft industrialization, emphasizing heavy industry, was carried out by Stalin to prevent, to quote his words, another beating of backward Russia by the more economically advanced capitalist countries. Forced draft industrialization continues in Russia today, and now the emphasis is more positive: namely, to meet Khrushchev's goal of, "catching up and surpassing the United States in per capita production within the shortest possible historical period of time." This theme is being used not only as internal propaganda but also to propagate the Soviet faith abroad.

Comparison of the economies of the US and the USSR in terms of total production of goods and services indicates the USSR's rapid progress.

Whereas Soviet gross national product was about 33 percent of that of the US in 1950, by 1956 it had increased to about 40 percent, and by 1962 it may be about 50 percent of our own. This means that the Soviet economy has been growing, and is expected to continue to grow through 1962, at a rate roughly twice that of the economy of the United States. Annual growth over-all has been running between six and seven percent, annual growth of industry between 10 and 12 percent.

These rates of growth are exceedingly high. They have rarely been matched in other states except during limited periods of postwar rebuilding.

A dollar comparison of USSR and US gross national product in 1956 reveals that consumption—or what the Soviet consumer received—was less than half of total production. It was over two-thirds of the total in the US. Investment, on the other hand, as a proportion of GNP in the USSR, was significantly higher than in the US. Furthermore, investment funds in the USSR were plowed back primarily into expansion of electric power, the metallurgical base, and into the producer goods industries. In these fields, it was over 80 percent of actual US investment in 1956, and in 1958, will probably exceed our own. Defense ex-

* Excerpts from an address delivered by Mr. Dulles on April 28, 1958, at Washington, D.C. to the 46th Annual Meeting of the Chamber of Commerce of the United States. Reprinted by permission.

penditures, as a proportion of GNP in the USSR, were significantly higher than in the US; in fact about double.

Soviet industrial production in 1956 was about 40 percent as large as that of the US. However, Soviet heavy industry was proportionately larger than this over-all average, and in some instances the output of specific industries already approached that of the US. Output of coal in the USSR was about 70 percent of that of the US, output of machine tools about double our own and steel output about half.

Since 1956, Soviet output has continued its rapid expansion. In the first quarter of 1958, Soviet industrial production was 11 percent higher than a year ago. In comparison, the Federal Reserve Board index shows a decline of 11 percent in the United States.

According to available statistics, in the first quarter of 1958, the Sino-Soviet Bloc has for the first time surpassed the United States in steel production. The three months figures show that the USSR alone turned out over 75 percent of the steel tonnage of the US.

A recession is an expensive luxury. Its effects are not confined to our own shores. Soviet propagandist have had a field day in recent months, pounding away at American free enterprise.

Every Soviet speech, magazine article, or radio broadcast beamed to the underdeveloped nations plays up and exaggerates our economic difficulties. The uncommitted millions are being told by the Communists—"see, we told you so. Crises and unemployment are inevitable under capitalism. Communism is the only true road to social progress." Our economy is giving the Communists a propaganda target as damaging, and I trust, as transitory as their own Sputniks.

Continued Soviet industrial growth has had a counterpart in increased trade with the free world. Over the past two years, their trade with the West has been moving ahead far more rapidly than it has within the Bloc itself. About 70 percent of the USSR's increase in non-Bloc trade in 1957 was with the industrial nations of Western Europe and, under agreements such as that just concluded with Germany, will expand still more.

Recent speeches by Soviet leaders— Khrushchev, Mikoyan, and Deputy Foreign Minister Zahkarov—stress the USSR's desire to expand trade with the Free World. Mikoyan, for example, said that the USSR is "confident that with the establishment of normal trade relations a significant forward step will be taken along the road leading to the establishment of cooperative relations between the Soviet Union and the United States." This month, Zahkarov told the United Nations' Economic Commission for Europe that Western trade ministers should devote their energies to bringing about a long-run increase in East-West trade.

Soviet capabilities to export petroleum and metals—aluminum, tin, zinc, and ferro-alloys—is increasing. The USSR is already a supplier in a few traditional Western metal markets. Over the years, the USSR may well become a major source of many such industrial necessities to Western Europe.

This seems particularly likely if Khrushchev's 1972 commodity goals prove to be realistic.

Take, for example, petroleum. By 1972, the Soviets plan to produce as much crude oil as we in the United States do today. Even allowing for substantial increases in domestic consumption, they could export about 2 million barrels a day. Today, all of Western Europe consumes about 3 million barrels a day.

A start has already been made on the pipeline needed to bring the crude oil from the Ural-Volga basin to the Baltic. Soviet ability to use trade as a weapon to advance its political aims will increase in a direct ratio to their success in realizing their economic goals.

For example, once they have penetrated Western European markets to the extent that these markets become substantially dependent on Soviet industrial raw materials, they will have available a new and formidable weapon of economic warfare. By withholding supplies, by capriciously raising prices, or by dumping commodities, the Soviets in effect will have a seat at the council table of the great industrial nations of Europe.

During the Suez Canal crisis, we saw a brief glimpse of Soviet capabilities to grant or withhold economic favors through the forms of its own petroleum exports. The increase in sales of metals and petroleum to Free World countries, which moved sharply upward in 1958, is not an economic flash in the pan. It is a reflection of growing Soviet industrial capacity.

Further, their governmental setup is well adapted to waging economic as well as political warfare. They have no budgetary controls when it comes to diverting funds to particularly urgent national policies. There need be no prior consultations with parliaments or the people.

This, briefly described, is the Soviet economic base and foreign trade program, as we analyze it today. It is to this base that Moscow is adding its foreign economic penetration deals designed to wean to its camp the uncommitted and newly developing areas of the world....

2 • Science, Technology, and Foreign Policy *

Warner R. Schilling

An assistant professor in the Department of Public Law and Government at Columbia University, Mr. Schilling is also Research Associate in the Institute of War and Peace Studies and is an Associate Director of the Council for Atomic Age Studies of Columbia.

This paper is meant to stimulate some general ideas about how the development of scientific knowledge and its technical application will influence the future direction of American foreign policy. The first part of the paper will survey the impact that science and technology have had on world politics in the recent past. This is perhaps the best way to alert one's self to the full range over which future change may be expected to occur. The second part will list some of the constant as well as the changing characteristics of this historical relationship. Finally, in the third part, an effort will be made to indicate a few of the foreign policy problems and opportunities posed by present and prospective scientific and technological developments.[1]

---

[1] Recent conversations with William T. R. Fox stimulated much of the content of this paper and the arresting phrase "the endless frontier of politics" should in particular be acknowledged.

* *Journal of International Affairs*, XIII (1959), pp. 7–18. Reprinted by permission.

I

The dominant technological development of the past 300 years has been the large-scale and increasing substitution of inanimate for animate energy as the motive force for man's machines. This substitution had its early beginnings in the use of wind and water, but it was only with the discovery of how to convert the heat from the burning of fossil fuels into mechanical energy and how to convert mechanical into electrical energy and back again that inanimate energy became both plentiful and transportable. It is this energy base that has made possible that whole complex of technological, economic and social developments that we associate with modern industrial civilization.[2]

Clearly, none of the key elements in the international political process has been untouched by the industrial revolution. The structure of the state system and of states themselves, the purposes and expectations moving state policy, and the means available to states for securing their purposes have all been significantly altered.

Consider the changes in the structure of the state system, that is, in the number and relative power of its members. As the industrial revolution transformed the bases for military power, the hegemony of the industrial states over the non-industrial areas of the world became virtually complete. Indeed, the Europeans had already been able to impress their rule over the better part of the globe with such rudimentary energy advantages as the sail and gunpowder, and, until the industrialization of Japan and the United States, world politics was essentially European politics.

The structure of the European state system was no less affected by the new technology. The enhanced opportunities for union, voluntary or involuntary, saw the number of states in Europe reduced from 400 at the time of the peace of Westphalia to less than 100 by 1815 and a mere 30 in 1878.[3] The disparity in power between large and small states was greatly increased (contrast the vulnerability of the Lowlands in 1914 and 1940 with their military exploits against Spain in the late 16th century), and drastic changes occurred in the distribution of power among the Great Powers themselves, most notably by the early industrialization of England and the later displacement of France by Germany as the dominant power on the Continent.

These changes in the number, relative power, and location of the states making up the system have had great consequence for both the stability of the system itself and the character of the strategies pursued by individual states within it. Two world wars testify to the instabilities introduced by the rise of German power. Similarly, the whole character of American foreign policy has been altered as the United States moved, from a position where its sheer survival was dependent upon the commitment of European power and interest elsewhere than the North American continent, to a position where its military potential exceeded that of all the European powers combined.

Equally striking have been the changes in the political structures of states themselves. The development of the urban industrial nation has made possible the rise of a variety of new elites and new political relationships be-

---

[2] For an effort to put history in an energy perspective, see Max Born, "Europe and Science," *Bulletin of the Atomic Scientists,* February 1958. Hereafter cited as BAS.

[3] See Quincy Wright, "Modern Technology and the World Order," in W. F. Ogburn (ed.), *Technology and International Relations* (Chicago: The University of Chicago Press, 1949), p. 181, for this point and a rewarding general treatment of the subject.

tween elites and masses. The impact of these new modes of government on foreign policy is to be understood by virtue of the fact that the manner in which foreign policy decisions are made can affect the content of policy itself. Thus, for those states in which technical advances in transportation and communications have been followed by a wider diffusion of political power, the possibilities for unstable or inconsistent policies (or indeed no policy at all) have been significantly increased.

The impact of changing technology on the purposes of state policy has perhaps been most marked on what might be considered the "intermediate" level of the ends-means chain. Thus, while states may have been continuous in their pursuit of such general goals as "power" and "welfare," there has been considerable variation in the operational definition of these goals. Consider, for example, the changing evaluation that states have assigned to particular areas of real estate on the globe. The success of the American Revolution owes much to France's decision that her power relative to England's would be better increased by depriving England of her North American colonies than by taking the opportunity that was also present to accomplish her traditional aim of conquering the Lowlands. Similarly, the present focus of interest on the Middle East is not unrelated to the increased dependence of Western Europe on that area's oil reserves. Among many of the so-called underdeveloped states in the world today, the effort to secure an industrial technology has itself become one of the major preoccupations of foreign policy. As for the contribution of technology to changes in the more "ultimate" purposes of state policy, it must be noted that just as technological change makes possible all sorts of new arrangements of things and people, it also gives people an opportunity to differ

as to how these new arrangements are to be made. Thus, the present conflict between the Soviet Union and the United States owes much to the fact that they have evolved differing conceptions of the proper arrangement of things and people in an industrial society and that they seem persuaded that their conception of the good life must and should prevail elsewhere.

The relation of science to foreign policy is for the most part indirect, since society usually experiences new additions to scientific knowledge in the form of the technical applications of that knowledge. This is not the case, however, with respect to man's general expectations about the course of human events. Here, new knowledge about man and the universe in which he lives can lead directly to a reorientation of such expectations. The belief of 17th and 18th century statesmen in the balance of power as the natural order of state relations was in part a reflection of their appreciation for the picture of measured order and equilibrium that science then presented of the physical world. Similarly, international politics by the turn of the 19th century was conditioned by a whole host of expectations concerning the "natural" struggle of states and the "inevitability" of selection against the weaker that had been stimulated by Darwin's concepts concerning the evolutionary process.[4]

The major alternatives available to states for securing their purposes (persuasion, bargaining and coercion) remain the same, but the techniques through which states may employ these means have been greatly altered by recent technology. The history of Anglo-American relations turned on two occasions upon the slowness of trans-Atlantic communication in the day of sail, in

---

[4] Point and illustrations from Llewellyn Woodward, "Science and the Relations Between States," BAS, April, 1956.

1778 when British concessions "raced" against the French offer of an alliance, and again in 1812 when news of the impending British repeal of the orders-in-council arrived only after the Congressional vote for war.[5] Today the words of governments can be spread almost instantaneously around the world, and their agents are only hours away from the most distant foreign capitals. There have been accompanying changes in both the content of international communications and the personnel of the communicators and the audience, and there are those who maintain that negotiation has become all but impossible when undertaken by quickly assembled major figures before the attentive publics of the world.

What technology has given with one hand, by increasing the speed of communication, it has taken with the other by decreasing the time available for decision. Not even the telegraph was able to offset the pressures placed upon diplomats in 1914 by the mobilization tables of the general staffs, whose own time bind was the result of the contribution that the railroad had made to the speed with which large armies could be assembled on enemy frontiers.

Since, in Nicholas Spykman's classic phrase, "international relations are conducted to the constant accompaniment of the drums of battle," the relationship between technology and foreign policy is nowhere more evident than in the innovations made in the instruments for coercion.[6] In fact, the changes here have been broadly reflected in all of the elements previously discussed. Note has

already been taken of the changes in the structure of the state system that resulted from the near synonymity of great military power and great industrial power. The development of governmental structures capable of controlling every sphere of human activity and the conduct of diplomacy for its impact on domestic, as well as foreign, audiences likewise reflect the increased military importance of the civilian labor force. And nowhere has the reciprocal relation between ends and means been better demonstrated than by the advent of 20th century total war. As technology increased the number and destructive scope of the weapons of war, thereby increasing the costs in blood and treasure entailed in their production and use, compensation was sought through enlarging the purposes of war, which, in turn, served to stimulate the belligerents to still greater destructive efforts. Understandably enough, the last two wars have also left their mark on some of the general expectations of mankind, most notably that prevalent in the late 19th century concerning the inevitable progress of Western civilization.

II

The preceding discussion has endeavored to show that no element in the international political process (actors, ends, expectations, means, or field) has been untouched by the technological developments of the past two centuries.[7] Attention may now be directed to some of the general characteristics of this relationship. Seven in all will be considered, the first three of which have been constant over time and seem likely to remain so, whereas the last four appear to be trend developments.

(1) The technical developments in-

---

[5] Samuel Flagg Bemis, *A Diplomatic History of the United States* (New York: Appleton-Century-Crofts, Inc., 1949, rev. ed.), pp. 31, 157–158.

[6] Nicholas J. Spykman, *America's Strategy in World Politics* (New York: Harcourt, Brace and Co., 1942), p. 25.

[7] These ordering concepts are a modified version of those advanced by Gabriel Almond some years ago.

volved in political change are usually multi- rather than mono-factor. Thus, in seeking an explanation for the British decision in 1912 to cancel plans for a close blockade of Germany, attention must be directed to a multiplicity of developments (torpedoes, mines, submarines, steam engines) rather than to any single technical innovation.[7]

(2) Major changes in the character of international relations have been the result of a multiplicity of non-technical factors as well as technical. The end of the limited warfare of the 18th century can only be partially explained by such important technical changes as better roads, increased metal production, or the increased efficiency of firearms and artillery. Reference must also be made to critical changes in political goals (the displacement of territorial and commercial objectives by the ideological issues of the American and French Revolutions); changes in military doctrine (organizational innovations making more easy the direction of large armies, and the development of more aggressive and sustained campaign tactics, which were in turn made possible by changes in the number and social character of troops as a result of the changes in political goals); and even changes in the general cultural ethos (lessened belief in the sinful character of man with a consequent loosening of the inhibitions against weapons development, and a shift from an interest in making products of artistic beauty to a concern for low-cost and quantity production).[8]

(3) The political advantages of technological change have been unequally distributed among states, both temporarily and permanently. Economic de-velopment in Asia and elsewhere is greatly complicated by the fact that its industrialization (unlike Europe's) must follow the spectacular decline in death rates made possible by medical science. Another example is afforded by the American experience with nuclear weapons. The advantages of short-lived monopoly have been followed by a revolutionary decline in the American security position. Unlike Germany, the Soviet Union has no need to conquer the Old World before it can command the resources necessary to strike a mortal blow at the United States. The destructiveness, range and cheapness of nuclear weapons systems have stripped America of her cushions of allies, time and space and have canceled out the industrial superiority that meant defeat for her enemies in the last two world wars.

(4) In the early years of the industrial revolution technology developed independently of advances in basic scientific knowledge. Steam engines were built long before the basic scientific laws governing their behavior were formulated. However, since the turn of the last century, the development of technology has been increasingly dependent upon advances in basic knowledge about the physical world. The atomic bomb was not only contingent upon basic research in nuclear physics; many of the technical applications of this new knowledge were actually carried through by the theoretical physicists themselves.

(5) Both technological innovation and the growth of new scientific knowledge appear to be increasing at an exponential rate. Scientific knowledge (as crudely measured by the volume of scientific publication) is apparently doubling every ten to fifteen years. In the first 300 years after the invention of firearms, the improvement of the original crude product was so slow that Benjamin Franklin apparently seriously considered arming the Continental Army

---

[8] See Bernard Brodie, *Sea Power in the Machine Age* (Princeton: Princeton University Press, 1941), pp. 18–19, 76–77.
[9] See John U. Nef, *War and Human Progress* (Cambridge: Harvard University Press, 1952, chs 9–11, 14, 16.

with bows and arrows.[9] In contrast, only 90 years passed between the first successful steamship and the disappearance of sails from warships, and a bare 55 years will separate the flight of Orville Wright from the first rocket to the moon.

(6) Both the costs of acquiring new scientific knowledge and the costs of product innovation appear to be increasing, at least in a number of key areas. One reason why university research budgets have become so dependent on federal funds is that no other source is rich enough to meet the costs of new research. The situation in some fields of nuclear physics was well expressed by the scientist who observed that "it costs a million dollars even to ask the question." Similarly, a fighter plane could be produced for 17,000 engineering hours in 1940, but 1,400,000 hours were required by 1955.[10] The point to these trends would seem to be that not only Great Powers alone can have great technology but that in the future only Great Powers will have great science.[11]

(7) In World War II science was for the first time directly mobilized in support of foreign policy. Science in its purest form (the discovery of the facts of nature for knowledge's sake alone) had developed since the 17th century into an essentially autonomous social institution. The scientific community had certain canons with regard to the conditions of their work. Science was international (the facts of nature were open to all who chose to discover them through the methods of science) and the advancement of knowledge was dependent on freedom of research, i.e., freedom of choice with respect to the research problem and freedom to communicate the results of research. But except for the general assumption that new knowledge would ultimately benefit mankind, the scientific community largely disassociated itself from whatever practical applications that might come from their discoveries.[12]

During the great ideological wars of the early 19th century, scientists and their ideas were allowed to pass freely across political frontiers, both in time of peace and war. This practice is more understandable when it is realized that as late as 1900 states also permitted the free circulation of detailed plans of their major weapons and most recent weapon innovations.[13] During World War I states made some primitive efforts to apply scientists to the problems of war, but it was only with the advent of World War II that the resources of the scientific community were brought to bear on such problems in any extensive fashion. The results of this effort (radar, the proximity fuse, the A-bomb) were such as to guarantee that its value would not be forgotten with the war's end.

III

Turning now to a brief list of foreign policy problems and opportunities, the

---

[10] Publication point from Ellis A. Johnson, "The Crisis in Science and Technology and its Effect on Military Development," *Operations Research*, January–February, 1958, pp. 14–15. Franklin reference from Brodie, "Implications of Nuclear Weapons in Total War," RAND Memorandum 1842, p. 2.

[11] Victor Weisskopf, as quoted in Theodore H. White, "U.S. Science: The Troubled Quest," *The Reporter*, September 23, 1954, p. 14. Engineering figures from Johnson, *op. cit.*, p. 16.

[12] Note, however, that by a pooling of their scientific effort the states, for example, of Western Europe could achieve "great science" without necessarily achieving any of the other attributes of "Great Powerhood."

[13] See Margaret Smith Stahl, "Splits and Schisms: Nuclear and Social," Unpublished Doctorial Dissertation, University of Wisconsin, 1946, ch. 4.

[14] On the early political experience of scientists, see Sir Henry Dale, "Freedom of Science," BAS, May, 1949; on 19th century military disclosures, Brodie, "Military Demonstrations and Disclosures of New Weapons," *World Politics*, April, 1953, pp. 283–288.

last four developments discussed above clearly give first priority to the relationship between government and science. Had the victorious coalition against Germany not so emphatically followed the historical pattern, perhaps science could have regained some semblance of its prewar autonomy. As it was, by 1955 about 50 per cent of the nation's engineers and 25 per cent of its scientists were in the employment of the government, either directly or on contract; in universities some 70 per cent of the research budget was government financed; and scientists were invited into the highest councils of government.[14] This activity simply reflects the fact that as the two Super Powers throw one weapons system after another into the effort to maintain at least a balance of terror, neither deems it prudent to fall behind in either the discovery of new scientific principles or the application of scientific knowledge to military hardware and political-military strategy.

In the present and the future world, "the science potential of nations" must take its place alongside such traditional items as the production of steel or electric energy as a meaningful index of military potential. In 1945 and 1946 the wartime experience of scientists stimulated considerable discussion of the question of whether the government could or should influence the direction of scientific development. This is now a dead issue; the government does and must. To be sure, neither the generation of brand new ideas nor the derivation of gadgets from extant ideas follows directly in proportion to the number of scientists at work or the amount of equipment at their disposal. But the supply of scientific talent is rather limited (the debate

in 1949 over whether and how to undertake a "crash program" to make an H-bomb was operationally concerned with the allocation of no more than thirty and perhaps as few as five individuals), and allocation of this talent's time (and therefore to a considerable extent the character of its product) is obviously influenced by the extent and direction of the government's appeals and support.

The question of whether our science potential is being developed in the most desirable or efficacious manner will be a continuing issue. Here the concepts developed for the analysis of war potential may prove quite useful.[15] Applying Klaus Knorr's major categories—resources, motivation and administrative skill—to the current scene, it is clear that the United States is quite favorably situated vis-à-vis the Soviet Union with respect to the basic resource, students. Thus, in 1954, despite the fact that only one out of five high school graduates ended up as a college graduate, the United States still had more than twice as many college graduates as the Soviet Union. While there is some cause to believe that the "state of the arts" was better in the Soviet Union, i.e., that their students received the better education, the main point is that about 50 per cent of the Soviet students majored in science and engineering, in contrast to about 15 per cent in the United States. Accordingly, our output of scientists and engineers was only 70 per cent of that of the Soviet Union.[16]

If one could be sure that we "want" more scientists and engineers than we graduate, some examination of our ad-

15 Lee A. DuBridge, "The American Scientist: 1955," *Yale Review*, Spring, 1955, p. 13, and American Association for the Advancement of Science, "Interim Committee Report," BAS, March, 1957, p. 82.

16 See Klaus Knorr, *The War Potential of Nations* (Princeton: Princeton University Press, 1956).

17 Joint Committee on Atomic Energy, 84th Congress, 2nd Session, Committee Print, *Engineering and Scientific Manpower in the United States, Western Europe and Soviet Russia* (Washington, D.C.: U.S. Government Printing Office, 1956), pp. 66, 78, 81.

ministrative skills would be in order. However, the major explanation for the continued greater Soviet output would seem in any case to be a matter of motivation. The complex that makes up the American "we" in this instance has simply placed a much lower value on the production of such graduates. One way in which foreign policy can serve to compensate for America's lesser motivation is by expanding the resource base to include the NATO countries. The addition of the scientists and engineers graduated in these states would produce a total nearly equal to the Soviet output. Truly effective scientific coordination with the NATO states would require at least a partial restoration of the "international community" of science that existed before World War II, and this would entail some loss in our ability to impose and maintain secrecy. But in return we would gain in knowledge, and the progress of Soviet science is such that most of our "secrets" are really not secret anyway.[17]

The variable of administrative skills is most evident in the distribution of the Russian and American effort between applied research and basic research, the discovery of new knowledge. The Soviet Union has between 20 to 30 per cent more scientists engaged in basic research than the United States. The percentage allocated to basic research in the budgets of Russian scientific academies has been estimated at 20 to 30, which is, interestingly enough, approximately the same percentage that the Russians allocate of their gross national product to gross investment. The American emphasis on applied research would pay military dividends if a war comes soon (or if this is the only way we can maintain the balance of terror), but otherwise we shall be left to face the costs of a narrower knowledge base in the future. Superior administrative skills would also seem evident in the estimate that the Russians develop new weapons systems in about half the time it takes the United States.[18]

The end result of greater motivation and superior administrative skill can be read in Edward Teller's predication that in ten years scientific leadership will pass into the hands of the Soviet Union. Reconsidered "wants" and administrative changes can not now prevent this from happening, although they can affect an American endeavor to regain that leadership.[19] The Soviets appear to have duplicated in science what Germany did before World War II in military power (mobilizing a superior force from an inferior resource base) while at the same time avoiding Germany's failure to expand their productive capacity. The political consequences of Soviet leadership will not be restricted to the

---

[17] For some specific proposals in this connection, see the account given of a report prepared in October 1957 for Senator Henry M. Jackson in *The New York Times*, October 23, 1957. For the issue of secrecy, see Edward Teller, "Alternatives for Security," *Foreign Affairs*, January, 1958, pp. 207–208.

[19] Figure on scientists from the report of the National Science Foundation, October 16, 1957, as summarized in BAS, December, 1957. Figure on budgets provided by Professor M. D. Hassialis, Columbia University, and based on discussions with Russian scientists. Figure on development time from Johnson, *op. cit.*, p. 16.

At his press conference on October 30, 1957, President Eisenhower said he had been "astonished" to learn that the major concern of his Scientific Advisory Council was where American science would be in ten years and whether the government would take the initiative in securing more funds and effort for basic research. See text, *The New York Times*, October 31, 1957.

[20] Testimony of Edward Teller, Preparedness Subcommittee of Senate Committee on Armed Services, 85th Congress, 1st and 2nd Sessions, Hearings, *Inquiry Into Satellites and Missile Programs* (Washington, D.C.: U.S. Government Printing Office, 1958), Part I, pp. 42–43.

fact that the Russians will have a larger knowledge base from which to develop new weapons. Just as a reputation for military power yields political results above and beyond the actual forces on hand, so too may the Soviet Union be expected to reap political benefit from its "scientific prestige," especially among the undeveloped states where scientific and technological achievements stand as symbols of the good life they hope to achieve.

The discussion of the "production" of scientific knowledge should not conclude without observing that it would be unrealistic to expect scientists to be as responsive to the demands of national policy as is the output of Hoover Dam, and it would be extremely short-sighted to wish that they were. The character of modern weapons is such that additions to or innovations in our military capabilities mainly serve to keep our security from deterioriating. Unless we should decide to remedy our long-standing deficiencies for limited war, they promise little in the way of enhanced security. If we are to produce real improvements in security, it must be in the realm of the political perspectives of our enemies, their goals and expectations. In the furtherance of such an intent-oriented (as compared to capability-oriented) security policy, the image we present of ourselves to the outside world is most critical. The scientific tradition (its freedoms and its dedication to liberating the "human mind from ignorance and consequent fear"),[20] is both an attractive and long cherished part of our "self." It, too, can bring "security," and we should not forget it.

Should the greater number of Soviet scientists result in their having a significant edge in the qualitative and quantitative production of knowledge, it by no means follows that hideous ruin

and combustion will overtake our foreign policy. What is certain is that the science of all nations will continue to stimulate new technological and political developments. The structure of the state system is still in a state of flux from the advent of nuclear power; its impact has yet to be made in Western Europe, much less in the great continental areas of India and China. Nor have secrecy, security risks and the increased influence of scientific and military elites (and hence the influence of their policy perspectives) exhausted the changes that the prospect of thermonuclear ruin will bring to internal state structures. And we may confidently expect the intermediate goals of American foreign policy to be quite different now that we have moved from an era where the enemy's conquest of Europe was the *sine qua non* for even a fifty-fifty chance to invade us, to an era where such conquest will only make somewhat more cheap the cost of his "America-bomb."

Nuclear technology has compelled the Russians to revise their expectations about inevitable war, but man's expectations have yet to react fully to relativity theory or anti-matter, not to mention machines that are capable of creative thought. Nuclear weapons systems promise a whole host of new political issues, of which test fall-out and the probability of satellite "downings" may be only a harbinger. The character of these systems can also be expected to lead to considerable proliferation among the non-violent techniques for pursuing and resolving interest conflicts, including more than a few more words about surrender.

Certainly the contribution that we can make to the economic development of India and less important states can capitalize on the potentiality of medical science to develop more effective techniques for birth control. Similarly, the fact that automation can now be sub-

21 Quotation from DuBridge, *op. cit.*, p. 4.

stituted for the deficiencies in the human nervous system, just as inanimate power was substituted for the deficiencies of the human muscle, requires us to re-examine our theories regarding the economic prospects and problems of these countries.[21] In short, there is clearly room in our foreign policy for "scientific aid" programs, although we may here find the Soviet scientists as worrisome as we have found their "surplus" engineers and conventional weapons.

The list of possibilities and problems could be multiplied were we to venture further into the scientific future and consider such prospects as weather control, psycho-chemistry, controlled thermonuclear power, or the variety of communications which can be made from satellites. But it must be remembered that man has never been the passive tool of his technology. When the idea of the A-bomb came to Washington in 1939, it found the concept of strategic bombing waiting for it, and, as such classic instances as the divergent development of French and German military doctrine before 1940 amply demonstrate, it can make considerable difference which ideas man brings to his technology.[22]

Important as the scientific discoveries and technical innovations of the past century have been, so too have been man's social and political discoveries and innovations. The history of these years must also be written with reference, for example, to the Protestant ethic, nationalism, bureaucracy, the balance of power, collective security and Marxist-Leninist doctrine, not to mention the content of the social sciences. In brief, there is an "endless frontier" to politics, as well as science, and man's fate will be determined as much by his "adventures" along the one as the other.

---

[22] For this conception of automation, see Gerald Piel, "Science and the Next Fifty Years," BAS, January, 1954. Some economic possibilities are outlined in Richard L. Meier, "Automation Technology and Economic Development," BAS, April, 1954.

[23] For a very stimulating discussion of the contribution that political science can make in this connection, see Harold Lasswell, "The Political Science of Science," *American Political Science Review,* December, 1956.

3 • The Concept of Economic Potential for War *

Klaus Knorr

The author is Professor in the Woodrow Wilson School of Public and International Affairs, Princeton University, and a frequent government consultant. He is an outstanding authority on the economics of international resources, and indeed on the economic aspects of international relations in general. He has written several books and numerous articles in this field.

...Military potential...is the ability of a nation to divert resources to defense in both formal peace and war. Economic (including technological) capacity is, of course, one constituent of military potential in this sense. But before concentrating on this particular factor, its relation to other major constituents must be clarified. The production of military power demands an input of manpower and other productive resources which would otherwise be directed to non-military output, or marginally, remain idle. But at no time, not even when engaged in total war, can a nation allocate all resources to the production of combat power. The proportion which can and will be diverted to this purpose depends (a) on the structure and productivity of these resources and (b) on the nation's will to provide for military power, i.e., to pay the price for military strength. This price is to be paid not only financially but in terms of foregoing the satisfaction of a wide range of interests— consumption, leisure, comfort, safety, etc.—that conflict with the commitment of resources to the production of military power. The will to provide for military power is therefore another constituent of a nation's defense potential.

Furthermore, given any degree of willingness to pay this price (including the discipline with which the population supports government measures), the output of military power depends upon the efficiency with which the diverted resources are employed. Hence, organizational ability and especially administrative competence represent a third major constituent of military potential. To illustrate, the amount of military power maintained by the United States at any one time is not only a function of the country's productive capacity. It also depends on the size of the defense budget (which permits a proportion of this capacity to be allotted to the output of combat power, and which is contingent upon a political decision reflecting the price the American people are willing to pay for defense), and on the efficiency with which every defense dollar—and, indeed, every non-defense dollar—is spent. As will appear in the following, any realistic analysis

---

* "The Concept of Economic Potential for War," *World Politics,* X (1957), 48–62. Reprinted by permission.

of economic and technological potential for defense must pay heed to these inter-relationships.

II

While it is useful to theorize on the general meaning of military potential and on the general ways in which this concept can be put to predictive and manipulative use, practical application calls for an immediate descent from the general to the particular. In real life, a nation has no such thing as a military potential or an economic defense potential which is the same for all possible situations calling for the use of military power in formal peace or war. At present, for example, there are countries which have a relatively high potential for fighting with non-atomic weapons on their own territory or in nearby theaters of war; but they have a very low potential for conducting war with non-atomic arms in distant theaters of operations and a still lower, or zero, potential for waging thermonuclear war. It cannot be stressed too strongly that the analysis of the war potential of any particular country or alliance must begin with specific assumptions about the kind of situation demanding the use of military power. If we are interested in military potential, we must relate our analysis to the likely situations that require, or will require, a military effort. At the present time, and using the United States as an example in the following analysis, it is reasonable to concentrate on three such situations: (1) the long-run maintenance of an adequate defense establishment (which, in fact, it is hoped will deter aggression without jeopardy to vital American interests abroad); (2) involvement in limited wars; and (3) the outbreak of unlimited war. For illustrative purposes, we may furthermore assume that the first two situations demand a diversion of resources from the civilian to the military sector of the economy amounting to from 8 to 12 per cent and from 14 to 18 per cent of the Gross National Product (GNP), respectively.

Obviously, the basic factors governing economic defense potential are the same for the two first situations, in the sense that a nation endowed with a high economic defense potential for fighting limited war usually also enjoys a high potential for maintaining a strong military posture in the absence of formal war. The main conditions that make up economic defense potential for limited war are:

(1) The volume of the GNP. The absolute volume is patently significant, since the economic effort for defense will be measured as a proportion of total capacity for producing goods and services. The volume of GNP per capita, or per head of the labor force, is a rough index of the productivity of labor and helps in estimating how much civilian consumption can be compressed in an emergency in order to release productive factors for the defense section. Clearly, it makes a difference whether the GNP per capita is the equivalent of $2,000, $800, or $100 per year.

(2) The rate of growth of the GNP. This datum will help in estimating changes in economic defense potential over time. Growth will result chiefly from increases in the labor force, from the rate of savings and investment, and from technological innovation. These three factors each have their own bearing on economic defense potential—e.g., a country with a high rate of savings and investment may be able to sustain the conduct of limited war by temporarily switching resources to the military sector entirely or largely from investment, rather than from consumption.

(3) The structure of output. The most relevant condition is the degree

to which the normal product mix approaches the output mix required for waging limited war. This includes the value of industrial as against agricultural, mining, and service production; of heavy as against light industrial production; within these categories, of production of the many goods of special importance to defense such as arms, aircraft, electronics, and fuels; and the growth rate for all of these key products.

(4) The flexibility of output. It is important to know the relative ease and speed with which output patterns can be modified and, especially, the output of key military supplies be expanded. To the extent that this depends on the flexibility of an economy rather than on government policy, the main factors are the organizational ability of management, the mobility of labor, and the state of such industries as construction, transportation, and machine tools which facilitate the conversion of plant from one output mix to another or the shift of labor from one plant or locality to another.

(5) Science and technology. The current pace of technological innovation in weapons production is unprecedented in history and is indeed so swift that a nation's endowment in scientists and technicians, the rates and quality of their training, the distribution of this precious personnel over various research fields, and its division between pure and applied research have become major constituents of economic defense potential.

(6) Size and structure of the defense budget. This factor will in large measure determine a country's ready capacity for producing military supplies and skills required in limited war.

(7) The size and structure of the tax burden. Both the magnitude of tax revenues in relation to the national income and the tax pattern affect the ease with which the financial instrument can be used in an emergency for allocating additional resources to defense production.

It should be noted that the degree of national self-sufficiency, as against dependence on foreign supplies, is considered as part of the "structure of output." For industrial nations, this problem is chiefly one of foodstuffs and primary commodities. Normally, there should be no problem so far as the long-range maintenance of defense forces in time of formal peace is concerned. But as the Suez Canal crisis and the sharp rises of raw materials prices during the Korean War showed, dependence on foreign supplies may be a very serious handicap in time of limited war. Yet, since most primary materials are storable, and since participation in international trade tends to raise labor productivity and the GNP—another determinant of economic defense potential—self-sufficiency achieved by a deliberate cut-back of foreign trade is distinctly less of an asset than when it is the natural outcome of comparative production advantages.

In view of the number of main conditions affecting the economic war potential of nations, it is immediately apparent that there is no magic key to the estimation of war potential. An estimate of any one condition cannot be expected to yield more than partial results. For instance, a mere comparison of the GNP of two countries—although it offers valuable information—is not only difficult technically but also of narrowly limited value by itself.

When the conditions of economic defense potential are discussed, reference is often made to conditions that are not actually economic, but constituents of administrative capacity or of the nation's will to provide for military power. Thus, how large an input of productive resources is needed to generate a given amount of military strength depends in large measure on the administrative efficiency with which defense dollars are spent. The flexibility of the output mix depends on administrative competence, which is a considerable element in lead-times, whenever new admixtures of military end-items are urgently required.

The maintenance of a large-scale defense effort in time of formal peace must, in the long run, rest on a commensurate degree of taxation, so that there are no consumption and investment dollars in excess of what can be spent on consumption and investment goods at current prices. If the defense effort is not put on a pay-as-you-go basis whenever full employment prevails, inflationary pressures will result and, if strong and prolonged, they will have various debilitating consequences. Whether the defense effort will or will not be mounted on a pay-as-you-go basis is not, of course, an economic but a political and psychological problem (and, since public attitudes are subject to government leadership, it is an administrative problem as well). This crucial factor of the will to provide for defense is frequently slighted in American discussions of how large a defense budget the "economy" can stand. What the "economy" can stand is something quite different from, though not unrelated to, what the electorate will stand. Provided the electorate agrees to be taxed for a defense effort requiring year after year, say, 12 per cent of the GNP, the question is whether or not this tax load (in addition to taxes for the civilian purposes of government) will undermine the "soundness" of the economy. The economy might suffer if high taxes engendered a fall in the rate of savings and investment (public as well as private) and, in a private enterprise economy, weakened the incentive to work, innovate, and employ productive resources efficiently. Such ill consequences would slow down the rate of economic growth in, and reduce the flexibility of, the economy and thereby diminish economic defense potential over time.

Contrary to the assurance with which such deleterious effects are frequently predicted, we know unfortunately little about the circumstances under which they would represent a serious risk. We do know that the high tax rates levied in the United States since the outbreak of the Korean War have not prevented a very high rate of economic growth; that the effects on the incentives and the savings of high-income groups as a whole have been minor; that harmful effects of severe taxation depend on the structure of taxation as well as on its level; and that, in democratic communities, the slackening of the electorate's will to provide for defense in peacetime is likely to keep taxes from reaching the level at which these subversive risks to the economy would become serious....

VII • Military Power

Anyone living in today's world must wonder if Clausewitz's famous aphorism that "war is nothing but the continuation of political relations by other means" retains its original meaning. After all Clausewitz wrote in an age when the concept of limited war was rooted in the temper and technology of the times. During the past half century the political interests of victor and vanquished alike have been swept away by the passions of total war. And now to the arsenal of total war man has added nuclear weapons and inter-continental ballistic missiles, the destructiveness of which reduce to a mockery the idea that there would be any political relations worth continuing after the next war. As one wit has pointed out, the verdict of any future war will not be who's right but who's left.

Knowing this we must still examine international relations in the light of war because neither human nature nor the nation-state system have changed much since Clausewitz's day—"no single weapon—however revolutionary—suffices to change human nature; political trends depend on men and societies as much as on weapons...." [1] The fact that nuclear weapons developed at a moment when two states were overwhelmingly more powerful than all the others has only reduced the anarchy of the nation-state system to a precarious bipolar balance of nuclear terror. It is one of the mockeries of the modern age that peace itself seems to rest upon the mutual fear inspired by the magnitude of nuclear destructiveness. Nations have arrived at such a deadlock in their search for security that peace seems to depend upon the degree to which the rival camps can maintain the so-called balance of terror. The diabolic fatalism of the situation may be exaggerated, and it may well be within human hands, even American hands, to break the vicious circle.

However, so long as war lurks in the background of international politics, the relevant issue seems to be one of how much and what kinds of military power are most appropriate to one's objectives. In examining these questions we are not forgetting the vital political issues underlying international rela-

---

[1] Raymond Aron, *On War* (New York: Doubleday Anchor Books, 1959), p. 2.

tions. We must realize that the answers to these questions involve more than calculations of relative technological capacity. The psychology engendered by an arms race has an intense and, as yet, unexplored impact upon the total environment in which international relations are carried on. An arms race, like war itself, seems to possess its own inner dynamic: military superiority soon becomes an end in itself. However, unless we are to succumb to a doctrine of inevitability even in the grip of an arms race with all its diabolic potential there may exist opportunities to intersect the vicious spiral with some strategic choices that lead away from war. These considerations are all the more vital when one is told that "the most serious wars are fought in order to make one's own country militarily stronger, or more often, to prevent another country from becoming militarily stronger, so that there is much justification for the epigram that 'the principal cause of war is war itself.' " [2]

Louis Halle offers the following criteria by which nations might sanely and safely measure their military power: (1) to have adequate force available and known to be available for deterring or successfully meeting any threats to its vital interests; (2) to leave no doubt in the minds of others that it has the will and competence to use its force effectively ... ; and (3) to leave no doubt in the minds of others that force is under responsible control....[3] Valuable though such guidelines may be, they only hint at the real problems of military power; problems which are far more complex and far less amenable to such rational but ambiguous postulates. The policy-maker confronted by an enormous range of weapons in the hands of a potential enemy and restricted by the scarcity of resources for his own purposes must choose among a baffling host of weapons systems which do not lend themselves to any ready determination of adequacy. Military power costs money, and few nations, unless their national survival is clearly at stake, are willing to forego the indefinite sacrifice of other values in order to be militarily secure. (See Wolfers' article in Chapter IX.) Furthermore no nation can afford to neglect a wide range of ancillary conditions upon which modern military power ultimately rests: education, health, basic scientific research, capital investment, strategic intelligence, foreign aid as a means of supporting alliances and overseas bases, etc. However compelling the concept of an adequate level of military power may be it is ultimately weighed against corresponding values in other directions.

Then there is the question of mobilized versus potential military strength. Historically, no nation, and least of all the United States, has ever been fully mobilized in peacetime. Normally nations set the peacetime level of their combat strength according to the prevailing goals for which military power is a means and according to prevailing assumptions about the amount of military power necessary to achieve these goals. The higher a nation rates goals which are only attainable by military power or the greater its sense of insecurity "the larger will be the amounts of military strength that are

---

[2] E. H. Carr, *The Twenty Years Crisis: 1919–1939* (London: Macmillan and Company, 1939, 1946), p. 111.

[3] Louis Halle, "The Role of Force in Foreign Policy," *Social Science*, XXX (1955), 203–08.

preferred." [4] Large-scale mobilization of military power invariably means the sacrifice of economic, moral, and cultural values. The classic case is Sparta, but history has known many other such examples. Some societies such as the German may place a high value on military virtues and military life in which case the costs of mobilization are more readily sustained. Soviet society has been in a quasi-mobilized state since the October 1917 Revolution as an accompaniment of the transformation to Communism. Hence Soviet citizens have been obliged to make far greater sacrifices in peacetime as well as in war for the attainment of national goals. Only in recent years have Soviet leaders been forced to acknowledge that the burden of all out military preparedness cannot be sustained indefinitely in the face of a restless and impoverished population.

In a sense the importance of the distinction between mobilized and potential military strength has been whittled away by the need for the "great powers" to devote such an enormous share of their productive resources, even in peacetime, to military purposes. Events of the last two wars demonstrated that superiority in armed manpower and matériel is hard to beat in a prolonged war. What Klaus Knorr calls the "industrialization of warfare" has been one of the most revolutionary developments of the twentieth century. The advent of nuclear striking power now requires that the industrial might of the nation be devoted to military ends long before war becomes a reality if they are to serve their purpose of protection and deterrence. Hence only nations possessing large, advanced industrial systems can hope to compete in the struggle for power and security. Finally the decision as to levels of military expenditure and output which have a very high priority in time of war assumes a far more ambiguous and contingent aspect in time of peace.

Nor does the problem of the policy-maker end with the simple determination of the military slice of the pie in relation to other areas of expenditure. Since few countries can normally afford to possess all possible ranges of weapons, the policy-maker must make some fairly drastic choices which may or may not be appropriate when the showdown occurs.

The magnitude of the threat and the rapidity and destructiveness of nuclear weapons necessitates that we estimate beforehand what weapons systems may be most appropriate. Uncertainty as to what constitutes the most effective distribution of the components of military power obliges the major powers to prepare for more than one type of war. The superpowers must arm for conventional wars in the hope that atomic wars can be avoided. Finally the price of modern weapons and the rapidity of obsolescence add up to astronomical sums.

A second and closely related problem in appraising military power is that of defining one's objectives. The decision to rely upon massive retaliation as our principal deterrent involved a choice between alternatives which had

[4] Klaus Knorr, *The War Potential of Nations* (Princeton: Princeton University Press, 1956), p. 21.

far-reaching consequences that were not fully understood at the time the decision was made. Preparation for small wars or guerrilla warfare requires quite a different focus from that which envisages nuclear war as the sole strategy. Partly because the United States did not understand this relationship between objectives and means, it persisted in regarding a large strategic air force as an efficient and sufficient answer to the danger of Soviet aggression. Instead of developing our military potential along diversified lines designed to contain the Soviets at a minimum cost to ourselves, we based our military strategy upon the fleeting superiority of atomic air power which, in the end, we were unwilling to employ and which, as Korea showed, did not make us invulnerable to aggression. Military power is only meaningful in relation to strategy, and strategy is only meaningful in relation to national objectives. It is a course of ruination for a country to develop costly strategies which have little or no relation to the permissible or attainable goals of national policy. In his article "Military Forces and National Objectives," Charles M. Fergusson, Jr., demonstrates that if a nation is uncertain about its objectives it will squander its economic substance and engage in untenable and irresponsible strategies which sow confusion at home and alienate its allies.

Halle describes a third way in which the appraisal of military power is related to international relations: the assurance that military power is under responsible control. As the magnitude of the security problem grows and the claims of the military upon the lives, resources, and direction of society increase, there is the latent danger of the transformation of national life in the direction of the "garrison state." But there is an even more subtle aspect to the problem and that is the risk that military considerations will take precedence over the political in the conduct of foreign policy. The misplaced emphasis in American strategy over the last decade is nothing new. Other societies have suffered the disastrous consequences of letting a narrow, military perspective dominate national strategy. Such perspectives are usually tuned to the circumstances of the last war, provided it wasn't a defeat, and to interservice rivalries. "When we recall," writes Bernard Brodie, "that both sides prior to the First World War failed utterly, with incalculable resulting costs, to adjust adequately their thinking to something as evolutionary as the machine gun, and that such failures have been characteristic rather than exceptional in the history of war, we can hardly be sanguine about the adjustments likely to be made to such a change as represented by developments in nuclear weapons."[5] Time and again societies turn the most crucial decisions affecting their destiny over to incredibly busy men, limited by training and experience, with little or no motivation to examine the basic issues of strategy or of international politics. In 1914 European diplomats handcuffed themselves to the mobilization schedules of the general staffs; in 1939 it was the folly of the Maginot Line; in 1949

---

[5] Bernard Brodie, "Nuclear Weapons: Strategic or Tactical?," *Foreign Affairs*, XXXII, No. 2 (January 1954), 219.

it was our surprise at the rapidity with which the Soviet Union achieved a nuclear explosion; one wonders what other blunders of political strategy have been or will be made in the name of military planning. Soldiers are often the first to recognize their limitations, but they usually operate in a political and intellectual vacuum. As a result they gradually lose all awareness of the limits to their thinking that result not only from the curbs on their own knowledge and curiosity but also from the protection accorded their views. Those views are screened off from criticism arising outside the tight corporate structure of a military hierarchy governed by habit, tradition, interest, and formal authority.[6]

In summary, the assessment of military power must be carried out within the context of political purposes and human values, not outside it. The costs and risks involved are too great to be left to the generals and admirals. The honest realist who accepts the proposition that military preparedness is a rational concomitant of the nation-state system assumes the obligation to appraise military power according to the strictest canons of political necessity and human values.

1 • Military Forces and National Objectives *

Charles M. Fergusson, Jr.

The author, a West Point graduate of 1942, saw military service during the Second World War with the 6th Cavalry Squadron and 1st Cavalry Division. He was Assistant Professor of Social Sciences at West Point until 1954, when he was assigned to the Command and General Staff College, Fort Leavenworth, Kansas. In addition to his other academic work, he is a 1950 graduate of the Princeton University post-graduate course in Public and International Relations.

. . . .

This article is concerned with military force and its relationship to the attainment of . . . national objectives.

. . . .

The purpose of this article is not to suggest the specific military force that should be committed under any given set of circumstances. The purpose is a

more modest one of examining briefly some of the various capabilities of military force, some of its limitations, and of suggesting some implications for mili-

* *Military Review,* XXXV (1955), 114–32. Reprinted by permission. The original article carried the note that the views expressed are the author's and not necessarily those of any official branch of the American government.

---

[6] *Ibid.,* p. 219.

tary policy based upon these capabilities and limitations.

. . . .

I. MILITARY CAPABILITIES

The capabilities of military force in supporting national policy will be discussed under the following major headings: offensive war capability, defense capability, deterrent capability, and other capabilities.

Offensive war capability. Since time immemorial states have frequently waged offensive war against their unfortunate neighbors. States have resorted to the overt use of military force for political, economic, and other advantages that are often obscure. Particularly during the nineteenth century, the United States herself was not unwilling to employ military force in this manner as evidenced by the War of 1812, the Mexican War, the Indian wars, and, most particularly, the Spanish-American War. Incidentally, all of these were quite limited operations.

It cannot be denied that many aggressive wars have paid handsome dividends to the aggressors. Most nations, including the United States, owe their independence to the overt use of military force. Many have expanded their territory and increased their wealth through force of arms. The United States expanded to the West—and elsewhere—at the expense of the Indians, the Spanish, and the Mexicans. Thus it seems accurate to conclude that—at least under certain circumstances in the past—military force used overtly has provided an effective means of seeking state objectives. Recent history marked by World Wars I and II and the Korean conflict indicates conclusively that the day of overt use of military force is not over. It also indicates a rather consistently dismal series of failures for the aggressors. There are probably many reasons for these failures. Any overt application has tended to unify the defenders and stimulate their greatest efforts. Acts of aggression have tended also to alienate neutrals and former allies from the aggressor.

The failures of some recent aggressions do not of course prove that future acts of aggression would be equally disastrous. The aggressor has always enjoyed a great advantage in his ability to determine the time, the place, and the type of attack. Some observers feel that special purpose—chemical, biological, and radiological, as well as atomic and thermonuclear—weapons so strengthen this advantage as to make it decisive.

Any aggressor must make a number of important decisions about his attack: what objectives to seek; what weapons or forces to apply; what geographic areas to include or exclude; and whether to employ tactical warfare, strategic warfare, or both. The terms "tactical" and "strategic" are subject to considerable confusion. As used herein, tactical warfare describes an attack directed on the enemy armed forces while strategic warfare is directed on the enemy economy and home-front. The choice of weapons makes little, if any, difference. Special purpose weapons, for example, could be used tactically or strategically depending on the nature of the target.

The aggressor may choose to wage unlimited warfare: unconditional surrender of the enemy, special purpose weapons, no geographic limitations, and both tactical and strategic warfare. Or he may choose to limit his operations in one or more ways. He may choose to seek limited objectives, he may limit his choice of weapons, he may avoid certain geographic areas, or he may concentrate his attack on enemy armed forces rather than on strategic targets or vice versa.

The many possible variations of aggressor attacks seem to fall logically into four major categories: mass destruction attacks, conventional attacks of the World War II and Korean vintage, cold war penetrations as exemplified by Czechoslovakia, Indochina, Malaya, and Greece, and bonafide civil wars. In practice it is becoming almost impossible to differentiate between the latter two because any civil war almost immediately attracts the attention of one or both of the two great powers.

. . . .

Defense capability. Defense against enemy attack is the military capability most consistent with the more recent American military tradition and one many Americans would consider *the* capability of military force. Since about the turn of the century until World War II and even after, the United States placed almost exclusive reliance on latent defense in time of peace. There was some logic in this strategy because of the existence of relatively strong friendly forces—particularly the British Fleet on the Atlantic—and the absence of strong nations anywhere near our borders. However, the continued reliance on latent defense got us into the difficulties of World Wars I and II—wars which might well have been averted had the United States and the other Allies wisely used even a small fraction of their great power in what we shall later discuss as the "deterrent capability."

Today an effective defense requires a larger, more diverse, better prepared force than ever before, inasmuch as an attack can come at any time, at any place, in a variety of forms, and our allies are far weaker relative to the potential enemies than ever before.

To the extent that defense forces are ready, they obviously contribute to the "deterrent capability" as well as to the defense capability. As in the case of the aggressor, the defender must arrive at certain decisions relative to weapons, objectives, strategy, and geography.

Some of these decisions are literally forced upon the defender by the actions of the aggressor, some of these choices are narrowed by the actions of the aggressor, and some are relatively unaffected.

Initially the defender does have the choice of whether to defend or not, as did the United States at the outset of the Korean conflict. Once he has chosen to defend, however, he has lost the initiative to the extent that he must fight, and fight at the time and probably—although not necessarily—at the place and with the weapons chosen by the aggressor.

The defender may choose to wage unlimited warfare or he may choose to limit his operations in one or more ways. He may choose as his objective the unconditional surrender of the enemy— as the Allies did in World War II—or he may choose to limit his objective in any one of a number of respects. He may choose merely to throw the aggressor behind the line from which the aggression was launched, or he may attempt to punish the aggressor sufficiently to force an armistice, thus settling for less than unconditional surrender.

The defender has a similar choice between limited and unlimited courses of action in the geographical areas and in the choice of tactical or strategic targets. He may choose to set no geographical limits as to the theater of operations or he may for various political or military reasons exclude certain areas. He may choose to wage both tactical and strategical warfare or he may select one and not the other. If the aggressor is waging strategical warfare, however, public opinion might refuse to accept any decision not to employ strategical warfare against the enemy, however wise the decision might otherwise be.

The weapons the aggressor chooses

to employ strongly influence—although they do not determine—the choice of weapons by the defender. An appropriate defense against a mass destruction attack would by no means necessarily be effective in defending against a civil war in some allied or neutral country. In the weapons area the defender has lost the initiative to the extent that his weapons must be effective in defeating the attack.

An effective defense against a mass destruction attack would seem to require all the weapons that a society could muster.

• • • •

A conventional attack might or might not be countered by special purpose defensive weapons. It would certainly require a combination of air-ground-sea forces as committed in World War II and Korea. A defense against a cold war penetration or a civil war requires conventional forces coordinated with political, economic, and psychological tools and techniques. Here the special purpose weapons may be worse than useless.

It is important to point out here that the use of special purpose weapons does not necessarily imply the choice of unlimited warfare in the other areas. The United States could, for example, have chosen to employ special purpose weapons in North Korea with no objective other than that of forcing the Communists to the north of the 38th Parallel. Whether or not this course of action would have worked is another question, but it does illustrate the fact that an unlimited choice of weapons can be employed to seek limited objectives.

Although limited warfare may constitute the most logical course of action for a defender, even in a mass destruction war, it may in practice be difficult to adopt. In order to enlist the complete support of the society to the war effort, it may be necessary—or at least the leaders may feel that it is necessary—to arouse public antipathy toward the enemy to such a point that total victory alone will satisfy. Any limitation of the objective or any negotiation may be subjected to the charge of "appeasement."

• • • •

There are several possible solutions to this dilemma. The leadership of a nation must be aware of the possibilities of limited application of military force. They must be careful not to overstate the results which the military operations will bring. The military commanders themselves must be ready, willing, and able to employ their forces as ordered by responsible political authority. Also, it may be helpful to point out that limiting the objectives against an enemy or conducting negotiations with him does not indicate approval of that enemy. It merely indicates that a compromise is preferable to the costs of more ambitious objectives.

• • • •

Passive nature of defense. Defense against an external attack is essentially a passive application of military force. Planning for defense involves an estimate of the capabilities, intentions, or the overt acts of other nations. Military forces are established and maintained on the actions of potential aggressors rather than upon the objectives of the defender.

Some military observers argue that defense planning must be based upon the *capabilities* of other nations. This view seemingly stems from an inexact analogy between tactics and grand strategy. It may be possible for a division commander to plan against the various capabilities of the enemy force confronting him. It is entirely a different matter for a nation to plan against the various capabilities of potential enemy nations. Other observers, agreeing that defense planning cannot provide against every enemy capability, argue that the *intentions* of the potential enemies must determine the level of defense—and most particularly the defense spending—required. As a matter of fact, United States defense planning seems to have been based neither upon capabilities nor intentions but primarily upon the overt acts of other nations.

For example, in 1945 the United States had no intention of matching the capabilities of the Soviet Union. Even after diplomatic relations worsened and the expectations of postwar harmony faded into oblivion, there was still no response in United States defense spending in 1946, 1947, and into 1948. The overt *coup d'état* in Czechoslovakia in February 1948 did cause a minor ripple in military policy, but it was not until the invasion of South Korea in June 1950 that military planning and spending was materially accelerated.

Planning for defense is complicated in another way; defense can be accomplished by a combination of offensive and defensive means which are at the same time complementary and conflicting. Consider, for example, the air defense of the continental United States. In defending against an air attack, it would be useful to possess offensive strategical airpower to strike the enemy airfields and launching areas; defensive air capability in the form of warning nets, fighter planes, and antiaircraft guns to fight the enemy planes that did get through; and passive defensive measures such as dispersion, bomb shelters, and civil defense to lessen the damage caused by enemy attacks. The conflict stems in large part from budgetary considerations. How much should be spent on each of the three defense measures listed above? This widely debated question illustrates the fact that planning for defense alone has many facets and is subject to wide controversy.

Deterrent capability. To summarize, defense against external attack constitutes the major traditional use of military force by most democratic nations in recent years. Its importance remains undiminished but its realization is infinitely more difficult. It remains to be seen whether there can be anything like an effective defense in the traditional sense when each nation possesses the capability of raining unprecedented devastation on any other nation at any time. Whatever the importance of defense, it is by no means the only contribution or even the most important contribution that military force can make to the attainment of national objectives. Few would deny that deterring an attack is far preferable to the most successful defense.

It would be inaccurate to say that the deterrent capability of military force is a new concept, unique to this era. The Swiss, among others, have long recognized that a ready military force would tend to increase the costs of an aggressor attack to such an extent that it was not worth the effort. In fact, the deterrent capability is inherent to some extent in any sizable military force, past or present. It can be said, however, that the deterrent is more important than ever before in this era of special purpose weapons; that until very recently the United States had not made effective use of it, either in theory or practice; and that as a consequence much more needs to be known of the techniques of using military force as a deterrent.

A successful deterrent would seem to require:

1. That the defender possess appropriate forces designed to meet the specific type of attack the potential aggressor is capable of launching.

2. That the defender be willing actually to use that force if sufficiently

provoked. (Cold war penetrations, apparently, do not provide sufficient provocation for the commitment of special purpose weapons.)

3. That the potential aggressor have a reasonably accurate estimate of the capabilities and intentions of the defender. (This presents an interesting conflict with the conventional military attempt to keep all information out of the hands of the enemy.)

4. That the defender take into account the values of the potential aggressor if they differ materially from those of the defender. (A force that would deter State A might not be equally effective in deterring State B.)

5. That the potential aggressor be rational.

Two factors merit additional attention: the kind of attacks that are to be deterred and the military forces appropriate for deterring these attacks. The attacks may be classified once again as mass destruction, conventional, cold war penetration, and civil war. A force effective for deterring one kind of attack may or may not be effective in deterring others.

Much of the attention currently devoted to the deterrent capability concerns the possibilities of special purpose weapons in deterring attack. It is a fact that there has been no overt use of military force either of a mass destruction or conventional nature in Europe since 1945. Considering the disproportionate conventional military strength existing on each side of the Iron Curtain, this is a remarkable accomplishment for which we should be thankful. Much of the credit must be accorded to the United States Air Force with its special purpose weapons and its capabilities of delivering these weapons. The development and maintenance of mass destruction forces is an essential military requirement into the foreseeable future.

Special purpose weapons alone, however, will not suffice. They may effectively deter a potential aggressor from launching a mass destruction attack and in some instances a conventional attack. Recent history, nevertheless, provides abundant evidence that special purpose weapons have not and probably cannot deter all conventional attacks, and they provide practically no deterrent against cold war penetration and civil wars. An effective deterrent against these types of attacks requires conventional military forces coupled with other tools and techniques.

Few would deny the vital importance of deterring a mass destruction war. However, it is almost equally important to deter the other threats. These threats are well worth deterring for the costs that they would inflict alone. Even more important, mass destruction war would be more likely to develop from a conventional war or cold war situation than from a period of relative peace.

One of the difficulties inherent in the deterrent capability is the impossibility of proving the success of the mission. The greatest success of a deterrent force may be rewarded by a clamor for the reduction of the very force that has been responsible. It can hardly be overemphasized that military force may be quite productive even when it is not actively employed against an enemy. It may be at that time producing its greatest success....

...the deterrent capability in itself provides no real solution to the basic problems besetting the world. A combination of mass destruction and conventional forces may provide the time necessary for other forces and the surge of history to provide the solutions. This provision of time would in itself constitute no small accomplishment, the possibilities of which indicate that we should devote much greater attention to perfecting the deterrent capability....

Guerrilla capability. Guerilla warfare can be used in conjunction with any degree of military force from mass destruction operations to civil wars. In World War II the Allies gained relatively little experience in antiguerrilla operations—most guerrilla action favoring the West. The Soviet guerrillas behind the German lines, the French *maquis*, the Italian partisans, the Chinese Communists—all supported the Allied cause to a greater or lesser extent. In Korea the United Nations forces did gain some valuable, if unpublicized, experience in combating guerrillas.

The fact that the West did not have to fight guerrillas during World War II and did have to fight them in Korea is explained in large part by the fact that the Communists supported the West in World War II and opposed it in Korea. The Communists have long recognized the importance of guerrilla warfare and have by all accounts employed it successfully. Mao Tse-tung himself is probably the world's foremost authority on guerrilla warfare. His pamphlet, *Guerrilla Warfare*, published in 1937 in China, advanced the doctrine that has been widely followed not only by the Chinese Communists but also by the Soviets and by Communists everywhere.

Any future war between the East and the West would almost certainly be characterized by extensive guerrilla and antiguerrilla operations. To be effective these operations must be coordinated with conventional military operations and must to a considerable extent be commanded by military officers.

Guerrilla operations might prove more effective in a mass destruction war than in the past. Guerrilla forces operate widely dispersed and offer a poor target for special purpose weapons; they are capable of providing invaluable information about atomic targets; and the dispersal of enemy ground forces due to the atomic threat should facilitate the success of the guerrillas. In fact, in a mass destruction war, guerrilla type operations might prove the most practicable method of employing ground forces.

· · · ·

II. LIMITATIONS

Like the other tools and techniques of statecraft, military force suffers important limitations, costs, dangers, and disadvantages. Some of these have been implicit in our discussion of military capabilities, but they merit additional, systematic consideration. First of all the overemployment of military force in the form of wars has in the past resulted in the destruction of the very values which the military force was supposedly utilized to protect. Arnold Toynbee, the British historian, offers this as one of his major conclusions in his 10-volume *Study of History:*

In studying the breakdown of civilizations, the writer has indeed subscribed to the conclusion—no new discovery—that war has proved to have been the proximate cause of the breakdown of every civilization which is known for certain to have broken down, insofar as it has been possible to analyze the nature of these breakdowns and to account for their occurrence. There have been other sinister institutions besides war with which mankind has afflicted itself during its age of civilization ... yet ... war stands out among the rest as man's principal engine of social and spiritual self-defeat during a period of his history which he is now beginning to be able to see in perspective.

This is a sobering statement for soldiers and civilians alike to ponder. If older civilizations have broken down through the intemperate application of military force, there would appear to be no logical reason why ours might not follow. Furthermore, these previous breakdowns have resulted from the employment of a rather medieval military technology. The modern military technology could prove much more efficient in destroying civilization, unless of course it is used in such a manner as to prevent the disasters of the past.

. . . .

Next it is extremely important to remind ourselves that increasing the military strength of a nation does not necessarily increase its security. This seeming anomaly may result in several ways: first, the increase in military power of State A relative to State B may motivate State B (and its allies) to an even greater military effort, with a consequent decrease in security to State A. Or, State A, having increased its military force, may be tempted to employ it to overcome supposedly weaker nations, only to find that these nations were not as weak as expected. The recent history of Germany, Japan, and Italy provides excellent examples. In each case there is no question that the nations increased their military forces, at least initially. However, these forces through overt commitment precipitated an unexpected increase in strength by the defenders which led to ultimate disaster for the aggressors.

It is of great significance that the German military forces possessed a high level of technical military competence. The German Army has been widely admired and imitated. Yet the employment of this technically competent German Army brought disaster on the society it was designed to protect. Much the same can be said of Napoleon, Alexander, and perhaps most of the great captains of history. Thus the development and maintenance of technically competent military forces does not alone provide security for the society concerned. These forces must be used wisely in the pursuit of feasible objectives. In other words we are suggesting the existence of two related but nevertheless

quite distinct fields of endeavor: one, the development and maintenance of technically competent military force; and the other, grand strategy or the rational employment of military forces along with the other tools and techniques in pursuit of feasible objectives. Either may be present without the other. The fact that an individual possesses great competence in one does not mean that he is equally competent, or at all competent, in the other.

Another limitation of military force lies in the many surprises which war brings in its wake. Seldom if ever have wars ended the way the participants—particularly the aggressor—anticipated. If the results could have been foreseen, the losers presumably would not have chosen to participate, assuming them to be rational. Moreover, in order to win a war, nations must—or at least feel that they must—make numerous agreements and concessions, many of which they have not foreseen and many of which they later regret. Thus during World War II the United States contributed to the building up of Soviet power and prestige, a fact that was regretted later.

. . . .

Another limitation of military force involves the danger of overmobilization of nations who are weak economically. As we shall see later, this danger is far less likely in the United States than in many allied nations. This conflict between economic health and mobilization provides the basic assumption underlying the extensive American military aid programs to allied nations since the end of World War II. If many nations devote too much of their production for military purposes, they may thereby further depress an already low standard of living so as to precipitate apathy, distress, or even revolt. Assuming full employment, mobilization adversely affects the economic situation in a number of ways: it lowers the standard of living, shifts manpower from productive to unproductive pursuits, diverts production from civilian to military goods with a consequent unfortunate effect on exports and on the balance of payments, creates inflationary pressures, and necessitates an increase in costly imports, further worsening an already unfavorable balance of trade.

Finally, military force alone cannot suffice in the absence of some minimum degree of political and economic viability. Or perhaps it would be more accurate to say that the costs of employing military force are not commensurate with the probable results when the requisite political and economic institutions do not exist. For example, military force could conceivably have succeeded in saving North Vietnam from the Communists. However, the lack of effective indigenous political and economic institutions would have so increased the size, costs, and duration of the military effort required and also rendered so uncertain the ultimate results, that these results were not deemed commensurate with the costs.

III. STRATEGIC IMPLICATIONS

What can we conclude from examining the capabilities and limitations of military force? What guidelines for strategy and policy follow from our analysis?

1. It cannot be repeated too often that military force is a means, an instrument, and a tool for obtaining objectives—it is not an objective in and of itself. There is nothing inherently good in military force or in military operations. These are good only to the extent that they contribute to the objectives of the society which they serve. Moreover, military force is not the only means available for achieving objectives.

2. An examination of the various capabilities of military force suggests that there is no one set way in which military force must be utilized, any more than there is any one set way that the political, economic, and psychological tools must be utilized. Like the other tools and techniques, military force can be used to help your friends or potential friends and hurt your enemies or potential enemies. Like the other tools and techniques, military capabilities cover a wide spectrum of possibilities, from the mere hint of a threat on one pole to mass destruction war on the other.

... our organization, training, research, personnel policies, and weapons must envisage the various types of missions which are likely to develop. It would be the height of folly to base our military plans on the assumption of a mass destruction war, only to encounter a threat of a different nature. In fact, the more successful our deterrent of mass destruction war, the more likely the threat will take the form of conventional war, cold war, or civil war.

The other tools and techniques of statecraft—in the form of diplomacy, economic warfare, and psychological warfare—have played important roles in full-scale war in the past and would certainly play an important part in any future all-out war. Whatever the importance of these tools in all-out war, it seems that they are of progressively greater importance as the threat changes from mass destruction war to conventional or cold war. If our efforts to deter mass destruction war are successful—which is quite possible—we will be confronted by situations requiring an even greater coordination of military force with the other tools and techniques of statecraft.

3. Our analysis of capabilities and limitations conflicts squarely with the so-called concept of "pure war." "Pure

war" has never—to the author's knowledge—been clearly spelled out by United States writers, but apparently its proponents hold that military operations should in no way be limited by political and economic factors but should be pursued to victory—victory being defined presumably as the unconditional surrender of the enemy. While a number, although by no means a majority, of American military officers have professed adherence to this concept from time to time, a frequent and eloquent spokesman has been General Douglas MacArthur.

. . . .

General MacArthur's concept seems questionable on a number of counts. The statement that limited war is a new concept in military operations simply is not true. States have fought limited wars down through the ages of history. For relatively long periods of time, wars fought for limited objectives were the rule rather than the exception. As a matter of fact, most wars have been limited in one respect or another and as indicated earlier the United States itself has often fought for quite limited objectives.

"Pure war" is also vulnerable in its failure to recognize the political and economic content of military objectives. A strong implication extends throughout the concept that somehow military victory is separate and distinct from the other aspirations of society and is a goal worth seeking for its own value rather than for any other advantages which might be brought about as its result.

We may also question the description of war as "when politics fail, and the military takes over." This seemingly overlooks or subordinates the many important short-of-war capabilities of military force, some of which were discussed earlier. It also overlooks or subordinates the contributions that diplomacy and the other tools and techniques can make during the actual conduct of military operations.

Moreover, there seems to be an interesting inconsistency between "pure war" and the traditional military philosophy frequently expressed in the United States services that military commanders will carry out any orders in a cheerful, willing manner regardless of their personal views. If one is obsessed with the idea that there is one way and only one way to employ military force, then can he really be relied upon to exercise strategical judgments when ordered to carry out missions not in accordance with his personal views? ...

In short, "pure war" is no longer, if indeed it ever were, an adequate philosophy for the employment of military force. It has produced many unfortunate results in the past, not the least of which is the muddying of our thought processes. It is likely to prove even more disastrous in the unlikely event that it governs future strategy.

4. Our military capabilities suggest that there is no bargain basement economy possible for United States military forces. No one service alone, no one weapon alone, can possibly succeed in accomplishing the various tasks which may have to be accomplished. Into the foreseeable future the United States must continue to develop and maintain both conventional military forces and forces trained to employ special purpose weapons. The question, "Can we afford it?" naturally follows.

We are often told that military spending is likely to "wreck the American economy." Precisely how this "wrecking" is going to come about has never been explained, and it is remarkable that so many people continue to believe and repeat this allegation so frequently without subjecting it to the critical analysis to which it is so vulnerable.

If anything can be said about military spending and the American economy, it is almost exactly opposite to the above: that military spending has been instrumental in maintaining the high levels of production and employment that the United States has enjoyed since about 1941. In 1940 we should not forget the United States still had over 8 million men—14.6 percent of the civilian labor force—unemployed. Certainly without war this level of unemployment would not have decreased anywhere near as rapidly as it did under the stimulus of military spending.

Let us make it abundantly clear that this does not mean that only huge military expenditures can ensure prosperity. ...It does mean that the United States can afford to develop and maintain the necessary military force, both conventional and otherwise, to carry out our objectives.

Certainly there is a level of military spending which would result in a lower standard of living, a decrease in capital investment, and a consequent danger to our national economy. Since the end of World War II military spending has not come anywhere near the point where it would "wreck" the economy. This conclusion has been reached by several inquiries into the matter. One objective study has concluded that the United States can sustain an annual defense program costing up to 70 to 75 billion dollars without undue strain.

. . . .

What the United States cannot afford is a mass destruction war which would almost certainly be accompanied by considerable, if not catastrophic, devastation, and which would certainly decrease the standard of living here and everywhere else. It is a strange anomaly that some who emphasize the danger to the American economy from the post-Korean level of military spending, suggest a preventive war as a solution to the problem. Such a war would certainly stimulate strong inflationary pressures, decrease civilian investment, and result in devastation, all of which *would* tend to weaken the economy. Thus to solve a problem that does not in fact exist, some would choose a course of action which would be most likely to make the assumed danger a reality.

To summarize, the United States can afford to develop and maintain the military forces, both conventional and otherwise, that will reasonably contribute to the attainment of national objectives. In fact it can hardly afford not to maintain such forces as will provide reasonable security against war, because war is the one thing which the United States can least afford.

5. Finally, the capabilities of military force on the one hand and Toynbee's thesis on the other pose a great dilemma for the United States and for all other nations—not excluding the Soviet Union. The dilemma is how can we take advantage of the capabilities of military force in the pursuit of feasible objectives without precipitating that overuse of force which has proved disastrous in the past and which promises even greater disaster in the future? To be sure, this problem far transcends the responsibility of military leaders. It is instead a problem for the entire society and particularly the political leaders—both elected and politically appointed—who represent the people....

2 • Military Power and War Potential *

Klaus Knorr

MOBILIZED VERSUS POTENTIAL MILITARY STRENGTH

The ratio between the mobilized force and the war potential of nations will differ greatly from nation to nation and, for the same nation, will vary over time. When peace seems dependable, a nation's mobilized force may be extremely small compared with its war potential. In the early 1930's, Great Britain and the United States were in this position. When intent on aggressive war or fearing involvement in a major conflict, nations will transform an increasing proportion of their potential into ready strength. This happened in Germany in 1938 and in the United States in 1940. But even on the eve of recent wars, this conversion has been far from complete. At the beginning of the last two world wars, all major belligerents had mobilized only a small part of their potential. In 1939, for example, when Germany set out on her aggressive enterprise, she produced only 20 per cent of the volume of combat munitions which she was to turn out in 1944. In 1940, this percentage was only 35. In that year Great Britain manufactured a supply of matériel equivalent to 34 per cent of what she was to manufacture in 1944. As late as 1942, the United States and Japan each produced a quantity of combat equipment somewhat less than half of what they produced in 1944.[1]

How much military strength a nation can mobilize in wartime, or shortly before war breaks out, is the main subject of this study. How much mobilized strength a nation chooses to set up in peacetime depends on the politically effective expectations of its members about how their various interests will be best served in the aggregate. These expectations result from a cost-gain calculation or, in other words, from a balance of advantages and disadvantages foreseen from the maintenance of military power at different levels. The desirability of ready combat strength depends, first, on the importance of the prevailing goals for the achievement of which military power is a means and, secondly, on the prevailing assumptions about the amount of military resources necessary to achieve these goals. Thus, security against aggression or benefits anticipated from aggression are typical goals which military power can serve. The higher such goals are ranked in the structure of goals that are politically effective in the nation, the larger will be the amounts of mobilized strength that are preferred.

Instrumental considerations are concerned with the functions which mobilized combat strength is expected to perform in specific international situations. For nations not intent on aggression, mobilized forces chiefly serve to deter the aggression of others by ready strength

---

[1] All these figures are taken from R. W. Goldsmith, "The Power of Victory: Munitions Output in World War II," *Military Affairs,* x (1946), p. 72.

* From *The War Potential of Nations* (Princeton: Princeton University Press, 1956), pp. 20–32. Reprinted by permission.

or by facilitating the conversion of war potential into fighting power, and affording time for this conversion. The speed of conversion in the face of need depends, first, on the ease with which manpower and productive resources can be released from previous employment and, secondly, on the ease with which the existing armed forces can absorb this influx of men and matériel and weld them into an efficient fighting organization. This latter facility varies with the size and structure of the existing military establishment. Expansion of a very small force is a formidable task, requiring many years for building up cadres of officers and other personnel, creating efficient organization, planning and acquiring equipment, providing facilities for housing and training, etc. On the other hand, to increase a very large army, air force, or navy by a mere fraction of its strength is a far easier undertaking. Clearly, the larger the existing force, the greater is its capacity for quick expansion. Much, however, also depends on the nature of the initial establishment, i.e., on whether it is a replica in miniature of a large force or whether it is specifically designed as a framework for an army to be swiftly expanded.

By protecting a country against attack when war is imminent or when it has broken out, mobilized power affords time for converting potential into ready strength. The mobilized power of the enemy, the speed with which he can launch dangerous attacks, and the ease with which a threatened country can mobilize its war potential will determine what constitutes an adequate military establishment for this purpose. Thus, if a nation feels menaced by the military build-up and the behavior of other powers, it may want to add to its own ready strength in order to prepare for defense against sudden attack against itself or other countries, as well

as to demonstrate its intention not to yield to military threats and thus to counter the use of such threats by aggressive nations and perhaps reduce the chances that war will break out.

For nations planning to precipitate or threaten war, mobilized force has an aggressive function which replaces or is superimposed on the protective function. This aggressive function is met when the ready strength of the aggressor can force a decision before the enemy has had time to mobilize his war potential, or when it can at least cripple his war potential at the outset of war. Given this capacity, the aggressive country may be able to gain foreign policy objectives by the overt or implied threat to resort to violence.

However, any preference for a large military establishment in peacetime which is motivated by attachment to important foreign policy objectives and by considerations of instrumental efficiency is more or less checked by unwillingness to bear the costs. This largely explains why mobilized military power in peacetime has usually been kept at a small proportion of potential strength.

These costs consist of the frustration of other effective goals and preferences which must be de-emphasized or suspended for the sake of providing military strength. Important moral, cultural, and political values may be involved on the debit side. For example, a society which attaches a high value to personal freedom will be reluctant to conscript its youth in the event that voluntary enlistment proves insufficient. Or, there may be a deep-seated fear that a large peacetime army is dangerous to the political system. In other societies, to be sure, such costs may be small or entirely absent. Thus, some societies may place a high value on military virtues and military life.

There are also economic costs, and—

with a strong attachment to high material standards of living prevailing nearly everywhere—these costs are registered sharply. Increases in military expenditures reflect real material sacrifices. The additional manpower and other economic resources that are allocated to furnish more men and supplies to the military establishment obviously are no longer available to produce goods and services for civilian consumption or economic development. Depending on the magnitude of this resource diversion and on whether the nation's manpower and other resources are currently fixed, declining, or growing, consumption and investment levels either must fall or will not rise as much as they might have otherwise.

. . . .

Unless war is imminent, nations are often unable to prepare for precisely the war which they may have to fight in the future. In order to prepare for a specific war, they would have to make correct assumptions about the identity and strength of enemies and allies, about theaters of war, weapons, and the duration of the possible conflict. Such assumptions would have to be based on predictions which are necessarily hazardous and hence require frequent checking and revision. In 1939 the United States did not foresee—and hardly could have foreseen—the proportion of its forces which would be committed to fighting in the tropics or in desert country or in western Europe or in Italy; or the most effective balance of army, air force, and navy in the war to come; or the weapons and types of equipment that would be of greatest importance.

However, the resources which go into fashioning military strength-in-being are the more effectively employed—that is, a nation is militarily the more powerful—the more closely that force is adapted for the specific conditions of the war

actually to be fought, if war breaks out at all. Preparation for just any war is far from perfect preparation for any particular war. As a safety device, nations find it expedient to build up "balanced forces" which are likely to be neither particularly well-adapted nor particularly ill-adapted to waging a specific war. However, since a realistic rebalancing of these forces cannot be undertaken, in many instances, before war is imminent or has actually broken out, it is less wasteful to keep the balanced force relatively small until the need for expansion is urgent and what is needed can be more clearly foreseen. ...No doubt it is often far easier for some nations than for others to arrive at fairly reliable predictions about a future war. It is obviously easier for aggressor countries than for those on the defensive. In general, it has also been easier for land-locked countries than for those whose military power has been seaborne. But some element of uncertainty there will always be.

Finally, modern technological change is so speedy and continuous, and now so readily applied to munitions, that old weapons are almost constantly being improved and new ones invented. The tanks and planes built in one year may be markedly inferior to those produced two or three years later. Indeed, when new weapons are delivered to the armed services, they may be already more or less obsolete when compared with those on the drawing board or those being tested in laboratories and on proving grounds. On the other hand, the equipment of modern armed forces represents a huge investment of resources for any nation, even for the largest industrial countries. They will find it exceedingly onerous, if not prohibitive, to undertake a continuous substitution of new for old matériel. This dilemma, too, argues against the maintenance of large ready strength before its use is imminent, provided sufficient allowance is made for the difficulty of recognizing "imminence" and excepting supplies whose output can be quickly expanded only with great delay. The problem of obsolescence is, of course, of lesser importance to a country which intends to engage in war in the foreseeable future and win it speedily by a knock-out blow made possible by a preponderance of mobilized power. The Nazi leaders nursed such expectations in 1939.

These three problems indicate the limited usefulness, from the viewpoint even of instrumental efficiency, of mobilized strength as it is increased, in time of peace, beyond a certain point. At this optimum point, it would be a disadvantage to a nation's power position to convert either more or less of its potential into mobilized strength. The optimum point sets that ratio between mobilized and potential strength which maximizes military power, comprised of both mobilized and potential strength, at that time. To locate this point—even approximately, to be sure —is not easy, especially in view of the difficulty of appraising, at any one time, the precariousness of peace. To cover this risk, governments often feel induced to expand their military resources when other countries increase theirs. The magnitude of the risk also depends on the relative capacity of nations for quickly converting potential into ready force. The greater this capacity, the greater will be the mobilized fighting strength that can be readily obtained from a given war potential, and the smaller will be the risk of keeping mobilized power relatively small in time of peace.

It is clear that the atomic age has brought a marked increase in the risks of deficient preparedness in time of peace. As military equipment has become more complicated—airplanes, for instance—the expansion of output tends to require more time than before. The training of additional personnel has likewise become more time-consuming. More important, the offensive, and perhaps also the defensive, means for fighting all-out atomic war (but not for fighting any war in the atomic age) must be in full readiness at all times if they are to serve their purpose of deterrence and protection. By the middle 1950's, this increased emphasis on mobilized strength was further reinforced by the dangerous tensions between the Soviet bloc and the NATO nations and, from the viewpoint of either camp, by the high degree of military readiness which the other maintained in time of formal peace. However, this pronounced shift toward maintaining peacetime military establishments at a level that is unusually high in relation to war potential has made these nations sharply aware of the costs involved. Moreover, the rapid technological pace maintained in the development of weapons has also increased the burden of obsolescence. These developments have by no means mitigated the problem of ascertaining the proper size of ready military power in time of peace.

It is with reference to these technical considerations and the costs of military preparations, on the one hand, and to foreign policy goals, on the other, that government leaders—and through them, the influential members of the community, be they few or many—must choose the size of their military establishments in time of peace. The cost-gain calculations on which the choice rests must obviously deal with a very complex situation. Since the object of foreign policy is to influence the behavior of other governments, foreign policies, to be successful, must be related to the means of influence on hand. To the extent that military power is vital to the exercise of influence, the more ambitious the foreign policy objectives are—whether of an essentially aggressive or of a defensive nature—the more mobilized strength will be required. How much will be needed in absolute terms depends mainly upon the ready strength and presumed intentions of prospective allies and opponents, and on the expected speed with which all protagonists can convert further potential into ready combat power. Potential strength counts only if hostilities last long enough for war potential to be converted into armed force. How much mobilized strength can be afforded depends on the sensitivity of nations to the costs of providing for it. If there is a gap between what is needed and what will and can be provided, foreign policy objectives must be retrenched in order to bring them into a proper relation with the means available for their implementation, or the conduct of foreign policy may suffer from the lack of effective power.

. . . .

THE CONSTITUENTS OF MILITARY POWER

Short of battle, there is no precise test or measurement of mobilized military power. To be sure, quantitative comparisons of divisions, naval vessels, air units, and supporting personnel are readily made—both as to men and as to major items of equipment—if information is complete. However, the introduction of qualitative factors robs such comparisons of conclusiveness. Allowance must be made for differences in the balance of the quantitative components. How much, for instance, will superiority in the air compensate for inferiority on land and on the sea? How, especially, do atomic bombs and long-range bombers compare in military worth with surface forces? How much will superiority in men be offset by a

larger number of tanks and cannon? Then there are likely to be differences in the performance of generals, men, and weapons. How much weight in the total equation should be attributed to good or bad generalship, good or bad organization of supply; how much to the physical endurance, training, and morale of troops; how much to differences in the performance of planes and guns? Finally, these qualitative differences cannot be evaluated simply in the abstract if even the roughest comparison of armed forces is to be meaningful, for their bearing will obviously depend on where and against whom a war may have to be fought. If realistic assumptions can be made in these respects, then it becomes somewhat less hazardous to compare mobilized forces. The problem of weighing superiority on land against superiority on the sea or in the air, and of allowing for differences in the firepower, armor, and mobility of tanks, and in the physical stamina, training, and morale of troops becomes less intractable. But if dependable assumptions of this kind cannot be made, and often they cannot, ignorance of many of the factors that render battles and wars unique—location of the theater of war, duration of hostilities, identity of allies and enemies, etc.—seems to permit comparison of the quantifiable factors—numbers of divisions, air wings, submarines, nuclear missiles, etc.—to yield little information on relative combat strength.

However, the problem of comparison is somewhat less forbidding than it appears to be at first sight. Past experience suggests certain hypotheses which are plausible under many circumstances and which, if contrary circumstances do not prevail, permit a narrowing of the margin of error inevitably involved in net comparisons of military forces. First, unless there is knowledge or presumptive evidence to the contrary, it can be assumed not only that some errors in evaluating particular qualitative factors may cancel each other, but also that not all differences in the qualitative determinants of ready strength will favor one nation or group of nations over another. Regarding major military powers, it is unlikely that with respect to weapons, generals, military morale, troop training and stamina, and military organization, one power will be superior in every category to another. Secondly, as the industrial revolution has progressed and war itself has become more and more industrialized, sheer quantity of equipment, irrespective of all but major differences in quality, has become more important than before in determining military strength compared with such qualitative elements as generalship, physical stamina, and valor, or even compared with mere numbers of men in the armed forces.[2] More than ever before, war has become a matter of machines rather than of men. Thirdly, unless there is specific knowledge or presumptive evidence to the contrary, certain qualitative factors can be expected to vary directly with a nation's capacity for making large quantities of heavy and complicated equipment. A nation capable of producing huge amounts of matériel is also likely to produce munitions of good quality and to supply manpower for the officer corps and ranks which is skilled in the use, maintenance, and transport of intricate equipment and has received formal education facilitating the acquisition of new skills. These three considerations tend to reduce the weight to be accorded to the total of qualitative factors in estimating the mobilized strength of nations. They suggest a lesser margin of error if comparisons of armed forces deal largely with quantities of military manpower and supplies.

This is not to say that qualitative factors are unimportant in modern warfare. History abounds with examples of forces inferior in numbers, and sometimes in equipment, snatching victory from what appeared to be prospects of certain defeat.

. . . .

...striking superiority in the qualitative constituents of military power can produce victory when two contending forces are roughly similar in numbers of men and equipment. At a time such as the present, when immense advances are being made in the technology of weapons, a decisive superiority in weapons and in their tactical employment may well offset, and perhaps more than offset, any inferiority in the size of the armed forces or in the other qualitative ingredients of combat power such as troop morale or military leadership. In the atomic era, it may happen that, for a time at least, one nation develops missiles, planes, or ships greatly superior to those at the disposal of other nations.

The margin of combat superiority which accounts for victory may be provided by any, or any combination, of the constituents of military strength, qualitative or quantitive. Yet, these possibilities do not necessarily contradict the experience of the big and prolonged wars since the beginning of the nineteenth century which suggests that no net superiority in qualitative attributes can in the longer run make up for a substantial inferiority in the quantity of military manpower and equipment, provided the theater of war permits these to be put to efficient use. It seems plausible that the industrial progress made during the last century and a half has given the quantitative factors a larger weight in the balance of the constituents of which combat power is the joint result. ...

---

[2] This argument is affirmed by B. H. Liddell Hart, *The Revolution in Warfare* (New Haven: Yale University Press, 1947).

VIII · Society, Public Opinion, and Leadership

In Chapter VI we noted that it was not until the Soviet government assumed control that Russia was able to develop its power or capability in such a fashion as to win victory over Germany. The geography, population, and resources of Russia were much the same in 1941 as in 1914. What had happened to account for the transformation in Soviet fighting capacity? Essentially a new government had taken power which was determined to mobilize the primitive energies of backward populations and transform them into cadres of trained workers, engineers, bureaucrats, and party members who in turn knew how to organize and develop Russia's vast natural resources. With Communist ideology as a guideline and supported by the fanaticism of Communists dedicated to carrying out the projected transformation of society, Soviet leaders were able to impose a new type of society upon Russia, and to imbue, albeit brutally, the Russian people with a will to work and to fight for the Socialist Motherland.

Their success points up the importance—vital at any time and crucial in an age of conflict—of human will, organization, and leadership to the successful achievement of national power and diplomacy.

> And in one way at least these mental factors are far more weighty than in Napoleon's day. For behind the army lies the nation; and the whole unwieldly mass, army and nation, is more a mental unit than in any previous war, each dependent on the courage and good-will of the other. In no war has human quality counted for so much: the endurance, the initiative, the power of sacrifice, the loyalty, the ability to subordinate personal interest and pride, the power of taking the measure of the event, of discounting the unfavorable turn, of responding to frightfulness with redoubled resolution rather than with fear, of appreciating the real emergency and rising instantly to meet it. It is these qualities of mind and character which in the ensemble go by the name of "morale"; and it is these qualities that hold the balance of power in war.[1]

If one were to attempt to analyze the conditions upon which these qualities rest, one would have to know a great deal about the social system by

---

[1] W. E. Hocking, *Morale and Its Enemies* (New Haven: Yale University Press, 1918).

which a society maintains its cohesion and governs the vast range of relations that go untouched by the government. The social system is comprised of a complex of customs, values, reciprocal relations, institutions, and laws by which a society lives and maintains its cohesion. It exerts so profound an influence that we often are unconscious of its existence. Yet no nation can bind its whole population into a functioning society without the unseen web of social roles and social motivation that society provides. It is only when society breaks down as it did in Russia in 1917, or when race or class violence, strikes, or group rivalry becomes intense, or where social cohesion has never existed, as in some of the newly independent states, that we immediately become conscious of its importance. As Klaus Knorr points out in the following selection, "Government and War Effort," where basic consensus is strong in peacetime, and where government leaders have a reputation for pursuing the interests of their people with courage and intelligence, national morale will reflect itself—as in the Battle of Britain and in the battles of Moscow, Leningrad, and Stalingrad—by courage and tenacity.

However, state capability also depends upon the effectiveness with which a nation analyzes its national interests and devotes its resources to their attainment. If a people or their leaders are unable to define feasible objectives or to implement their policies so as to achieve the most favorable state of affairs, the country will be as badly off as if it possessed neither the means nor the will to assert itself. Time and again great nations have misjudged their power or pursued dangerous and fatal chimeras because they lacked the wisdom or statecraft to make the most efficient use of their power by peaceful means or they failed to take a sufficiently realistic view of their opponent's power. Both the Germans and Japanese underestimated the social cohesion and the moral fiber of the Americans (Hitler thought of Americans as a "rootless" people) and thereby contributed to their own defeat. This aspect of the problem relates to the much-neglected relationship between the domestic and foreign policies of the nation-state. How does the internal constitution of the state, the distribution of power and wealth within the community, and the values and skills of the elite affect the policies of the state? What are the channels of information leading to the government and the amount of independence of the policymakers from the rest of society? What are the origin, patterns of education, and ideas of the decision-makers, and what are their views about the ends of policy and about the means to be employed?

American statecraft has been under criticism for two decades because of its supposed inability to participate in international politics or define its war aims in anything but idealistic, moralistic, and legalistic terms. As a result the United States is alleged to have fought two wars for goals which, victory won, were impossible to implement. By contrast the Marshall Plan and Point Four afford examples of policies that were highly successful precisely because many post-war problems responded to the sort of economic enterprise and power which are the hallmarks of American civilization. And so it goes: each country is better or worse equipped to develop and implement its foreign policy strategy according to the traditions, values, and habits created by its history.

One of the most controversial aspects of this whole question is the comparative ability of democracies and dictatorships to mobilize their national power, define their national interests, pursue effective policies, plan military strategy, maintain their armed forces, and wage war. There can be no general answer to this question because each system is geared to a different set of principles and goals which may or may not have a bearing upon its overall capacity to pursue its national interests. A well-established and effective democracy such as the British, American, Swiss, or Scandinavian may be as fully capable as a dictatorship provided the government leaders are able and willing to make politically courageous decisions. Certainly what evidence we have of the German and Italian dictatorships suggests that the façade was often more impressive than the reality. In the case of the Italians the situation was hopeless to begin with because the Italians were neither materially nor psychologically endowed to fight a modern war—Mussolini or no Mussolini. The case of the Germans is more complex. The verdict of J. K. Galbraith based upon the findings of the U. S. Strategic Bombing Survey is that the "Germans were no better organizers than their democratic opposition...." [2] They began to prepare for war sooner and they took advantage of the initial unpreparedness and moral disarray of the western democracies, but once alerted Britain did a considerably better job of facing up to the sacrifices and austerities of total war than Germany. The root of the German failure which, in view of its initial success, was spectacular, resides in the particular inefficiencies to which a dictatorship is prone: overconfidence, incompetence, irrationality. The Soviet leadership has been zealously on guard against those attitudes which in the end defeated Hitler. Victory, though their creed may take it for granted, must be earned, and the role of the Communist Party as the watchdog of the system is indicative of the impressive institutional arrangements by which the Soviets maintain the dynamism and reliability of their society. Klaus Knorr, in the selection that follows, sums up the merits of the democracy-versus-dictatorship controversy very well: "The motivation of the individuals in the mass and in government, and the influence and skill of leaders, weigh far more heavily in the balance than differences in the form of authority."

Nevertheless there are certain problems and disadvantages that a democracy faces in an all-out power competition which cannot be ignored. The article from *The Economist* of London which we have included speaks bluntly of the weakness of American democracy in the field of foreign affairs. This was written at a low ebb in American leadership, before the Marshall Plan had been proposed and at a time when the government had to manufacture a crisis atmosphere and employ shock tactics to arouse

---

[2] J. K. Galbraith, "Germany Was Badly Run," *Fortune*, December 1945, pp. 173–179, 196, 198, 200.

public opinion. Nevertheless it sums up rather well the difficulties that democracies face, at least in time of peace, of maintaining among its people a steady unwavering commitment to a line of action. Either democracy must afford a high level of informed public interest, intelligent and courageous leadership, and newspapers and other media of communication dedicated to their responsibilities, or government will more and more resort to secrecy and the manipulation of opinion. The United States government has employed both techniques in recent years to achieve important policy decisions which it felt could not be safely left to the determination of sober thought.

It is encouraging to note that so far as the direction of American foreign policy is concerned the Presidency has emerged as the focus of effective leadership provided the incumbent is intelligent and willing to use his powers of leadership to the utmost. This does not mean that the United States must accede to presidential dictatorship or that bureaucratic decisions must be obscured behind a cloak of secrecy, but rather that the President is in a position to use the elements of intelligence and judgment at his disposal to present the public with honestly reasoned and well-conceived policies. His ability to accomplish this task is very much dependent upon the intellectual resources at his disposal and the ability of the administrative system to employ them effectively.

In this regard, it is perfectly clear that the ability to avoid war or defeat is intimately dependent upon strategic intelligence. One of the most dangerous traps into which a nation can fall is the choice between war or appeasement. The risks of this dilemma can be minimized only by maintaining adequate levels and types of power consonant with the potential trend of the enemy's policy. This requires a type of strategic intelligence which is based upon an intimate knowledge of the enemy's philosophy or "operational code," his culture, the psychology of his leadership, and the long-range relationship between the development of his power and his capacity to use it. It also requires that the product of intelligence research be employed by its consumers—the decision-makers—if it is to be worth anything. In a study of "Intelligence and Policy-Making in Foreign Affairs," Roger Hilsman found American decision-makers to be obsessed with activism (action for action's sake), simplism, organizational tinkering designed to secure more wisdom by introducing more bureaus, a fetish for facts (a mechanistic faith that enough facts will produce a correct solution), anti-intellectualism, and a naive faith in "know-how"—a striking illustration of how a nation's cultural values may permeate the most rational processes of government.

In the end the ability of a nation to employ its resources effectively, to formulate and conduct foreign policy, and to make a lasting impression upon international relations depends upon the will of people. In a dictatorship it will depend upon the small group at the top who command society; in a free society it will depend upon the intelligence and responsibility of the individual.

1 • Government and War Effort *

Klaus Knorr

Once the decision to fight has been made, government leaders must organize the war effort needed for attaining the tentative military objective. Toward this end, they must define the instruments and intermediate objectives and thereby translate the prevailing motivation for war into the detailed and specific activities by which individuals will honor their commitments. The main task is that of reconciling the need for military power with the resources which the nation is willing to provide, and of effecting this reconciliation continuously, since both these factors may change over time. If the amount of military power which government leaders deem necessary for achieving the military objective exceeds the resources which the nation is willing to spare, then they must either lift the prevailing motivation for war to a higher level or retrench the military objective. They must also choose policies, in these circumstances, which will extract a maximum military effort from the resources which the nation is prepared to make available for waging war.

In bolstering the prevailing motivation for war, government leaders can attempt to influence the goal striving of individuals and groups in three ways: by information, by persuasion, and by bargaining.[1]

Government leaders need not be passive agents, merely accepting the goals of individuals and groups. They are usually in a position to influence choices. By means of an adroit policy of information, the government can assist citizens in gaining a picture of reality which is conducive to a high personal commitment to wage war. Although the members of the nation may pay heed to other sources of information, modern government is usually able to affect, if not largely determine, the manner in which the war situation is perceived. The way government leaders represent the war effort will, in effect, limit the individual's choice and guide his response. In accordance with their assessment of the war situation, the leaders of government must propose what level, manner, and speed of mobilization are needed. To exact the necessary effort, they must explain and justify, and perhaps even "oversee," the instrumental requirements of victory. Through skillful information, government may be able to prevent a relaxation of effort in the face of military reverses or, for that matter, military success. Especially at the outset of war, great efforts may be required in order to make the nation face unpleasant facts, if it is addicted to a wishful underestimate of the war effort ahead.

In addition to merely imparting information about the facts of war, gov-

[1] Motivation for war cannot be improved by force even where its use is tolerated. By force, or the threat of force, leaders can hope to extract an increment in war-supporting behavior from whatever relevant motivation prevails.

* From *The War Potential of Nations* (Princeton: Princeton University Press, 1956), pp. 81–96. Reprinted by permission.

ernments can boost the individual's identification with the nation and its leaders. Before the First World War, for example, Kaiser Wilhelm II of Germany had publicly referred to the Social Democrats as "those fellows without a fatherland who are not worthy of being called Germans." On the first day of war in 1914, he declared: "I no longer know any parties, I know only Germans." Thus, government can stress unifying, and play down divisive, symbols and issues. During the Second World War, Propaganda Minister Goebbels noted in his diary that "the German people must remain convinced—as indeed the facts warrant—that this war strikes at their very lives and their national possibilities of development...." [2] Governments, in other words, may persuade the nation that the interests of all are in basic agreement with each other and with a resolute war effort. Government is also in a position to clarify the community obligations of the individual in a wartime emergency, for these obligations may be only vaguely defined by prevalent values and dispositions.

These functions of leadership are of obvious importance, for failure in this area may be fatal. To take Germany again as an example, after the first flush of martial enthusiasm, it became increasingly clear that the masses of the population did not think the war aims of Imperial Germany worthy of the sacrifices which the First World War exacted. During the Second World War, Hitler became increasingly preoccupied with the military problem and failed to give persistent leadership on the home front. Though deeply devoted to Hitler, Goebbels refers repeatedly to this curious lack of leadership in the Führerstaat. "Our problem today is not the people but the leadership." "We are

living in a leadership crisis." "We are without a governing hand at home." [3] During the Second World War, the Italian war effort no doubt suffered because a great many Italian people refused to embrace the values cherished by the Fascist elite.

The government can also affect the selected goal of individuals by bargaining with interest groups. It may secure their consent to certain deprivations placed on their members in exchange for agreed limits to such sacrifices, or for an assurance to tolerate, or even to promote, other interests of the groups concerned....

On the other hand, the bargaining situation may be such that the war effort can be boosted by giving substantial concessions to a particular class or group which feels keenly that its particular interests have been slighted in the past and which will agree to full cooperation in exchange for long-run improvements in its position. Thus, during both world wars, the British working class received important concessions to its interests.

In general, the sacrifices inherent in modern war are on such a scale that an equitable distribution of the burden is incumbent on any government bent on maximizing the war effort. If any special group refuses to shoulder its share, the deprivations inflicted on all others obviously increase, no matter whether the level of mobilization is high or low. In the United States and Britain, public sensitivity to profiteering and pressure for sharp excess profit taxes (in Britain raised to 100 per cent in 1940) were indicative of this concern. It manifests itself acutely in the matter of the rationing of consumers' goods, harshness being far more bearable than unfairness. Solidarity is in part predicated on a fair distribution of hardships, and morale begins to soften when people realize

---

[2] Louis P. Lochner (ed.), *The Goebbels Diaries* (New York: Doubleday, 1948), p. 147.

[3] *Ibid.*, pp. 269, 326, 396.

that others are carrying a lighter burden than they are themselves.

How much a government will want to strengthen the war effort by means of information, persuasion, and bargaining will depend on the goals of its leaders and, of course, on their conception of the prevailing attitudes in the nation, which may be more or less favorable to the desired level, manner, and speed of mobilization. How well a government uses these devices depends on the skill and power of its leaders.

Sometimes, a leader is able to create intensive dedication to a united effort by the mere fact of charismatic authority, springing from unquestioned emotional response rather than hard-headed consensus. Some element of charismatic leadership is often present, especially in wartime, even where government is ordinarily based on the democratic consent of the governed. The personal genius of Lloyd George and Winston Churchill during the last two world wars functioned in part through this ability to command devotion. In general, however, the power of leadership is founded on the degree to which the nation—among its parts and with the government—is agreed on its most cherished interests. Where such basic consensus is strong in peacetime, and where government leaders have a reputation for pursuing these interests with efficiency, they are able to exercise a substantial power of appeal.

Because the need to cope with a crisis demands vigorous leadership, it is usual for the power of government to be increased in time of war. The reins of government can then be tightened precisely because war activates value patterns which reinforce individual and group identification with the nation, and because individuals and groups realize that a rarely occurring exigency like war creates situations and requires actions which ordinary citizens are not as well prepared to define and organize as they are the ever-recurring and familiar problems and tasks of peace.

No matter how powerful the leaders of a government, their control over society is always in some measure reciprocal and hence restricted. No matter how skillful and respected they are, their ability to manipulate the level, speed, and manner of mobilization is limited. The basic goal striving of individuals and groups is the raw material, as it were, which the power, skill, and prestige of leaders can transform into more military power than would be forthcoming spontaneously. If government leaders ask for too much, if they assign to personal security, comfort, and safety too low a value, identification with the nation's leaders and war issues is weakened, and the demands of government may be rejected by active or, where this is not feasible, by passive resistance. At best, obedience will then be no more than formal and grudging; at worst, there will be apathy.

In adapting military means to military ends, government leaders must continuously face the problem that, whatever the motivation for war which individuals and groups display at the outset—when the basic decision to fight or not to fight is made—those individuals and groups must still come to terms with the many specific deprivations to which they will be subjected at a later date.

Initially, individuals may favor an exacting level of mobilization. The enthusiasm with which an initial general commitment may be undertaken is shown by the readiness with which legislators appropriate huge funds for the prosecution of a war. In one instance, the United States House of Representatives passed in 1943 a naval appropriation bill for $32 billion, without debate and without a single question from the floor, in twenty minutes. It is clear, however, that people may make rash choices based on untested preferences. The bill is presented to them later, in the form of personal deprivation, piecemeal and over a long period of time. The individual will find his desire for self-direction impaired in numerous and sometimes unexpected ways. He may be drafted into the armed services, his peacetime job may disappear, his right to strike be suspended, his consumption seriously curtailed, and his leisure time reduced. Although he supports a high scale of commitment for the nation as a whole, he may balk at the specific ways in which he himself is asked to honor the commitment....

Indeed, the government's and the public's knowledge of the present, and their ability to forecast, are so limited that the rational adaptation of means to ends is far from a simple matter. Even if all citizens were agreed to do everything to ensure victory, there would still remain the problem of stating the requirements of victory in terms of so and so many divisions, airplanes, and ships, such and such a percentage of the gross national product, or just so many casualties. Few particular figures and policies are demonstrably right or necessary. The government's plans are not "facts" but contingent predictions of the future course of events. They contain a great deal of guesswork, thus making it easy for the individual to disagree and to resent specific deprivations which he is asked to undergo, but which he does not think essential to win the war.[4]

To make matters more difficult, a lengthy time lag usually intervenes before a decision to mobilize resources comes to fruition in the form of ready combat power. Throughout the war, therefore, planning decisions must be

[4] Samuel A. Stouffer, et al., *The American Soldier: Adjustment During Army Life* (Princeton, N.J.: Princeton University Press), 1949, I, pp. 430, 452.

made ahead, often far ahead, of the actual allocations of resources; they call for forecast of what is militarily necessary and politically feasible in the more or less remote future....

Equally important is the skill with which government leaders settle on mobilization policies that will obtain the utmost war effort from individuals whose motivation for war is limited and who go on pursuing private goals that are at odds with a high level of mobilization. Evidence of such limited commitments to the war effort can be found in the history of all wars. During the Second World War, for instance, the large majority of American workers, businessmen, farmers, politicians, civil servants, and soldiers were obviously eager for their country to win the war. Yet none of these groups was ready to make more than a limited personal commitment to the war effort. With a sellers' market for labor, workers were reluctant to stay in unpleasant jobs, such as foundry work and lumbering, and acute labor shortages developed in these industries. Any thought of industrial conscription was deeply repugnant to labor and industry. At the beginning of mobilization, businessmen were reluctant to shift to defense production, for they did not want to leave normal markets to their competitors. The government faced widespread resistance when it came to the problem of containing inflation. Congress was reluctant to raise taxes as much as the administration demanded. Various people and pressure groups favored higher taxes, but only for others, not for themselves. Farmers opposed ceilings on farm prices, and workers ceilings on wages. But the farm bloc approved of wage controls, and labor unions of price ceilings on farm products. Many Congressmen exerted influence to divert a satisfactory share of war contracts to their constituencies. While "big business" wanted to win the war, some of its representatives also continued to fight "big government" and "big labor." The War Production Board was subject to numerous clashes between the viewpoints of industry and labor representatives. In Washington, the "in-fighting" for personal and group power continued among the big bureaucrats. In most cases, such pursuit of special interests was rationalized as necessary to winning the war.

American soldiers, too, exhibited a limited personal commitment. Before long, a great many of them began to talk of "having done their share," a phrase connoting not only that there should be limits to personal sacrifice but also that these limits had been reached. It implied that "the desire to be safe, or to be home, or to be free to pursue civilian concerns, was stronger than any motivation to make a further personal contribution to winning the war." [5] The very weighing and measuring of their contribution by individuals testify to the grudging of further sacrifice.

High as the desire to win the war ranked as a motivation for social action, the war revealed a large and irregular gap between that desire and what Americans were willing to accept as necessities justifying personal sacrifices. There was a sharp conflict in dominant motivations "between (1) the general desire to win the war, to hasten its conclusion, and to minimize the attendant toll in human suffering...and (2) the persistent effort of each section of the population to maximize its own wartime prosperity, comfort, and independence and to safeguard itself against post-war threats to its continued well-being." [6] ...

Thus, although most government activity in directing the nation's war effort is of a technical and administrative type, and although these activities receive primary, and often exclusive, attention when the war effort of nations comes under study, the vital essence of governmental performance is in political leadership. Helping the nation to orient itself to the war, clarifying the involvement and obligations of citizens, bargaining with individuals and interest groups, calculating the course of action most likely to maximize the war effort—these are essentially political tasks.

To be sure, mobilization in all its myriad details must be planned and administered by experts, technicians, and administrators, and the administrative capacity of the nation is a major determinant of its military prowess. Yet the plans which the technicians draw up and the complex of policies which they administer are apt to frustrate the goal striving of individuals and groups insistently and at numerous points. Direct responsibility for the actions of administrators and technicians must devolve, therefore, on the politician who ultimately makes the top administrative decisions. He makes them not by formulating plans but by backing the plans formulated by technicians.

This was, for example, one of the points at issue in the controversy between Bernard Baruch, who was always concerned with the administrative issues of mobilization, and President Roosevelt, who was preoccupied with its political problems. [7] When the President

---

[5] *Ibid.*, pp. 449–51. Of soldiers interviewed in 1945, when they were fairly well agreed that there was a long, hard struggle ahead, 46 per cent felt that they had done their share and should be discharged; another 36 per cent felt that they had done their share but were ready to do more. *Ibid.*, p. 158.

[6] Bela Gold, *Wartime Economic Planning in Agriculture* (New York, Columbia University Press, 1949), pp. 488–89, 493.

[7] Eliot Janeway, *The Struggle for Survival* (New Haven: Yale University Press, 1951), pp. 185–87.

made James Byrnes Director of War Mobilization and established him in his own office, he finally entrusted an experienced politician with the top job of coordinating the war effort of the United States. At this high level, "... policy decisions and coordination are the very essence of politics." [8] Only the political leader can commit the nation to the policies which the administrators and technicians need in order to do their part of the job.

WAR POTENTIAL AND FORM OF GOVERNMENT

The foregoing analysis is applicable to all modern political communities, no matter whether their form of government is of the democratic, authoritarian, or totalitarian type. Since the chapter has so far focused on the problem as it presents itself in democratic states, we shall next discuss special applications to the authoritarian and totalitarian types.

In an authoritarian country—unlike the totalitarian—tradition, customs, and possibly law limit the hierarchical authority wielded by monarch, dictator, ruling clique, or aristocracy. Compared with democratic societies, the masses of the population have less influence over government policy and are expected to obey the decisions made by their autocratic ruler or rulers. Whether this difference tends to increase or lower motivation for war will depend, aside from the degree of unity among the elite, on the goals and preferences of the people. If obedience is firmly rooted in their personal goal estimates or if individuals are persuaded that the purpose of any particular war is as important to their own goal achievement as to that of their

[8] Herman M. Somers, *Presidential Agency: The Office of War Mobilization and Reconversion* (Cambridge, Mass.: Harvard University Press, 1950), p. 231.

governmental leaders, then there is clearly no reason why such a society should be incapable of a high level of mobilization. On the other hand, should large sections of the population be discontented with their status and find competent leaders behind whom to rally, loyalty and obedience will become shaky and very slowly or quickly fade under the strains and stresses of war, especially when the disaffected groups or masses recognize no stake in the war aims of their overlords. During the First World War, such conditions prevailed in the Austro-Hungarian monarchy and the Russian empire. But where, as in Japan, during the Second World War, the masses remain loyal and obedient to their rulers, wartime morale and obedience may be of the highest.

In totalitarian countries also, level, manner, and speed of mobilization and the stamina of the people to outface the deprivations and hazards of war are determined ultimately by the motivation of individuals—at the top, in the middle ranks, and at the bottom of the hierarchical structure. As in authoritarian states, influence on the making of decisions is less evenly shared than in democratic communities. But there are notable differences in the circumstances under which the goal striving of individuals and groups affects the war effort.

To begin with, in modern totalitarian countries, mobilization does not conflict, or conflicts less, with the pursuit of various specific private interests than in democratic societies, for the pursuit of such private interests is in totalitarian countries prohibited or sharply restricted even in time of peace. The area of permissiveness granted to many kinds of private goal achievements is normally smaller than in democratic communities. Instead of granting considerable freedom for self-direction, rulers in the totalitarian state reach searchingly into the life of individuals and subject it to severe discipline. In the USSR, freedom in personal goal-seeking is considered "petty bourgeois."[9] Even to the extent that war brings further encroachment on personal freedoms, citizens in totalitarian countries are accustomed to see the areas of private permissiveness expand or contract with capricious suddenness.[10] Furthermore, in the Soviet Union and Nazi Germany, the proportion of the national income devoted to defense and investment together was far higher in the late 1930's than in the democratic countries, and was in fact so high that consumption could not be lowered a great deal when war came.

War nevertheless exacted new sacrifices of personal values. It did so in the form of threats and destruction to life and property, and increased military service and family separation. In many other respects, the life of the German and Russian civilians in 1943 and 1944 was a far cry from what it had been in 1938. Although consumption levels in the USSR had been low before the war, they were cut further during the war; the work week, long before, was lengthened; and the freedom to choose employment, normally very limited, became even more restricted.

There are differences also in the conditions governing the individual's identification with the nation's leaders and with their war policy. If totalitarian propaganda were highly successful in terms of its objectives, it would engender an intense spontaneous identification of the individual with his official leaders and their war effort, for it is the purpose of this propaganda to make this identity absolute, and to inculcate

the unquestioned conviction that the interests of the individual coincide fully and at all times with those of his leaders. Monopolizing all channels of mass communication, totalitarian propaganda does not so much help the individual to relate himself to government and war effort as implant in his mind the one and only picture of the war situation which the rulers think suitable. Its purpose is not so much to persuade people to exercise choice in a suggested manner as to foreclose all choice; to organize the motivation of individuals in a rigid and mechanical pattern; or—as one writer has put it—to destroy individuality itself.[11]

In Nazi Germany and Soviet Russia, official indoctrination has no doubt been an effective instrument of power in the hands of the leaders and, to that extent, an intense motivation for war rested on the conviction of most individuals that they were fighting ultimately for their own interests. Both systems rested in large part—and the Soviet system still does—on the loyalty of their subjects; for no regime could display as much wartime strength as these did on the basis of terror and repression alone. There were elements in their official ideologies attractive to large sections of the population. To some extent, however, wartime loyalty was rooted in traditional values of patriotism and in hatred and fear inspired by the enemy. Even if disaffected citizens despised the regime, they often took pride in its military achievements, and patriotic attachment to the homeland caused them to support the government.[12]

It is clear, however, that totalitarian propaganda has so far failed everywhere

[9] Cf. Barrington Moore, *Terror and Progress: USSR* (Cambridge, Mass.: Harvard University Press, 1954), p. 206.

[10] *Ibid.*, p. 157.

[11] Hannah Arendt, *The Origins of Totalitarianism* (New York, Harcourt, Brace & Co., 1951), p. 426.

[12] Cf. Merle Fainsod, *How Russia Is Ruled* (Cambridge, Mass., Harvard University Press, 1953), pp. 452, 497.

to achieve complete success. It has not succeeded in crushing the unique identity of the individual, nor has it instilled in the masses a sense of identification with the leaders so solid that it can withstand all tests. Its method is the widespread use of terror, to which democratic societies do not resort. Totalitarian rulers thus rely to a far greater extent than democratic leaders on enforced solidarity. Moreover, compulsory conformity rests less on the informal controls operating in democratic communities than on legal and police power. Repressive control is inherent even in official information, for it tolerates no sources but its own.

Yet terror and repression need not be ineffective in compelling wartime sacrifices from disaffected individuals. Totalitarian rule may have considerable tensions and weaknesses of its own,[13] but the desire to escape punishment may provide a powerful motive to accept deprivation in time of war or of peace. So long as terror cannot be escaped, the performance of the masses may remain substantially unaffected despite smouldering resentments, cynicism, and personal insecurity. The totalitarian system is designed, after all, to function with a measure of efficiency in the face of widespread discontent.[14]

Finally, it remains to be acknowledged that the political machinery of the totalitarian state is formally an effective instrument through which the decisions of a small ruling group may be translated into the coordinated activities of the masses.[15] It is a system of government which, as regards the complex and integrated interference of

government in the life of citizens, and the relative centralization of decision-making, democratic communities emulate to some extent in time of large-scale war. Here is again a problem of conversion, and its costs, which looms larger in liberal and democratic than in totalitarian countries.

Yet totalitarian countries tend to have weaknesses of their own which may be a liability in time of war. In the Soviet Union, for example, totalitarian rule instills a fear of taking the initiative in many tasks and an escape from assuming personal responsibility on the part of many bureaucrats as well as soldiers, workers, and farmers. The suppression of open political rivalry, and hence of public criticism, may be costly in terms of official errors, and the more prone a government is to policy errors, the more must military, political, and economic strength suffer. The mere existence of a highly centralized administration does not guarantee efficient government. German wartime government, for instance, showed greater deficiencies than administration in Britain or the United States. To the extent that terror is exercised for enforcing desirable behavior, mere obedience may shade off into apathy, and apathy may diminish the productivity of workers and officials. Popular dissatisfaction may suddenly reveal itself in the wake of military reverses, as was evident in the Ukraine when the German armies occupied the region in 1941 and 1942.

There is no valid reason for supposing that democratic communities are unable to muster the intense devotion to military enterprise which national survival in total war may require, or that totalitarian countries will always be able to do so. During the Second World War, a high motivation for war prevailed in Nazi Germany, Japan, and, after 1942, in Soviet Russia, but not in Fascist Italy or in the Soviet Union at

---

[13] Cf. *ibid.*, chs. 15–17; Moore, *op. cit.*, pp. 175–77.

[14] W. W. Rostow, *The Dynamics of Soviet Society* (New York, W. W. Norton, 1953), p. 174.

[15] Cf. Moore, *op. cit.*, p. 185.

the beginning of the war. Similarly, a high motivation for war was generated in the United Kingdom and the United States, but not in France. The mere form of government and the type of the social structure upon which these forms rest are far from decisive in determining war potential. The motivation of individuals in the mass and in government, and the influence and skill of leaders, weigh far more heavily in the balance than differences in the form of authority. Wartime virtues—such as courage and skill in battle, high economic productivity, endurance in putting up with the severe and petty hardships of war, consensus and solidarity—are not peculiar to any particular kind of political regime. This is not to say that the type of government is a matter of indifference when it comes to estimating a nation's war potential. But the motivation of individuals is a much more important factor, and a high or low motivation for war is, as history reminds us and the above analysis suggests, possible under any form of political regime. Nor can a case be made for expecting that a relatively low or high motivation for war is more likely to prevail under one kind of government than under another.

2 • Democracy and Dictatorship *

Excerpts from two editorials, written in May 1947, in The Economist *highlight some of the major distinctions between the participation of democratic and authoritarian states in international relations.*

I

"Imperialism or Indifference"

The nation-wide debate that followed President Truman's request for the Greek and Turkish appropriations was the most impressive testimony to the emotional and institutional obstacles that lie in the way of canalising America's overwhelming economic strength into a sustained and effective foreign policy.... Even an America that was fully conscious of its strength would be held back from using it by some of its most deeply rooted patterns of thought. The brake would be applied impartially to any active policy, whether of aggression or of cooperation. The old combination of liberalism at home and isolationism abroad, of a forward policy in domestic matters and of no policy at all in foreign affairs, still holds good....

...opposition to direct American intervention abroad on moral grounds fuses at the political level with the amoral but even more effective force of mere selfish isolationism. When Mr. Joseph Kennedy remarked that the best way to defeat Communism was to make the American system work at home, he did not speak only for himself. And when the House of Representatives, in a single day, gave Mr. J. Edgar Hoover all the funds he wanted for tracking down Communists in America and threw out the entire appropriation for

---

* Editorial, "Imperialism or Indifference," *The Economist,* May 24, 1947, 786–787; and Editorial, "Russia's Strength," *The Economist,* May 17, 1947, 746–747. Reprinted by permission.

the "Voice of America,"...they demonstrated their relative concern for the internal and external aspects of America's anti-Communist crusade.

The more difficult and distasteful the problems of the outside world become, the greater is the temptation to Americans to concentrate on the world they really control and understand—which is their own United States. It is easier and possibly more rewarding to build a TVA for the Missouri than for the Danube.

This is the emotional context in which the American political and economic system works. The structure of the system adds further impediments of its own to the development of a consistent, sustained and aggressive foreign policy. It is difficult to believe that the next few years will abolish the old economic instability of the United States, the cyclical recurrence on its economy of recessions and depressions. The importance of these dislocations is not, as is sometimes supposed, the possibility that they will allow other nations, in particular the Soviet Union, to outstrip America in industrial strength. The loss of wealth represented by even the most severe depression is not more, in real terms, than, say twenty per cent, and with a national income running at some $160 billions a year [Ed.: it is close to 3 times that at this point], the United States' margin of superiority over its competitor is far larger than that. The importance of a depression to America's external relations is that it would enormously reinforce the instinct to concentrate on American problems to the exclusion of the outside world....

But perhaps the greatest single obstacle to the emergence in America of a sustained and positive foreign policy is the nature of its political system. The division of power between President and Congress, the possibility of different parties controlling the one and the other, the lack of a Cabinet responsible to the legislature, the working of the party system, are all weighted against the present pursuit of long-term national or international objectives. So long as the essence of the political struggle in the country is the conciliation of minorities and the avoidance of controversial topics, the great issues of foreign policy cannot be fairly placed before the electorate and later confidently worked out....

II

"RUSSIA'S STRENGTH"

. . . .

The pure doctrine [of Soviet Communism] says that a crisis in western capitalism, a failure by the Americans to maintain their power by production and full employment, must lead to Fascism —or a new version of it. And Fascism, as the simplest Soviet citizen can understand, means war against the Soviet Union. For that he must be prepared. The goal is therefore industrial and technical equality with the Americans and their satellites. That equality, added to the disruptive power of Communist parties abroad, to the political strength of the Soviet way of government, and to the compact vastness of Soviet territory, would ensure military superiority....

Over-simplified though it may be, it is in some such deliberate view of the future that the main strength of the Soviet Union lies. Its planning aims at power for the state, power to reach the final stage where every external and internal human agency is under control; whereas western planning is so far content to aim at social justice, the good life, more money and less work—happiness for the individual, not power for the state. It is this ruthless concentration on power that lures efficient and intelligent men into the Communist party; it is the spell which holds eastern Europe, which fascinates the Germans and which spreads in most parts of the world that vague and irritable fear which is at once the enemy and the ally of Russia.... [In spite of the death and destruction wrought by the war against Germany and the utter weariness and exhaustion of the Russian people, no sooner had the war ended than the Soviet leadership demanded an effort comparable to that which the Politburo had extracted during the 1930's]: That the Soviet Government should be able, against such a background, to appeal for the same shock-worker spirit and for the same effort to rebuild for power rather than for circuses that it did fifteen years ago shows the strength of its emotional and administrative hold over the people. There is clearly nothing comparable in this country or in the United States—a fact which is important in any weighing of relative strengths. That hold gets part of its strength from the confidence of the ruling group that they can achieve all their aims, provided they are left alone....

Those who make their assessments of comparative power by statistical calculations of national production and wealth will not have much difficulty in convincing themselves that it will be a very long time before the Soviet Union is likely to "catch up" to the West in any real sense.... But when the analysis passes from economic comparisons to the political field, Russian diplomacy has enormous advantages. First and foremost, the Soviet leaders can be absolutely certain that no government which is in the western sense democratic can suddenly declare aggressive war. It cannot even secretly prepare defensive war. It cannot even face the possibility of hostilities without discussion of the issue and the possible enemy. This means that the Soviet rulers (unless they are the slaves of their own propaganda) need only concern themselves with their own policy; they can move silently and fast towards any military or diplomatic action which they think security demands: it is sufficient to recall the invasion of Finland, the pact of 1939 with Germany or any of the major political moves...in eastern Europe.

Secondly, they need fear within the USSR itself no organised criticism through recognised constitutional or public channels—no strikes, demonstrations, passive resistance or sabotage. In their use of police methods they are as far ahead of the British and Americans now as they were behind them in industrial methods twenty-five years ago. They have the power to direct movements of industry and population where strategy demands—for instance east of the Urals—whatever the cost in money, efficiency or human life.

Thirdly, they can be certain of denying to the major industrial countries of Europe precisely those advantages; they can count on Communist parties everywhere, or effective sections of them, to play the fifth-column role if ordered to.

Lastly, the directors of Soviet foreign policy have an advantage of inestimable value: they can control most of the information on the outside world which reaches the Russian public. They can therefore prepare the ground for any move that might be unpopular, or inconsistent, or unfamiliar. Whereas it is inconceivable—for example—that any French statesman should publicly work for or sympathise with a German nationalist point of view, [Russian statesmen] can and do so. What is more, Soviet statesmen can choose their own pace in policy; they need promise no quick results or neat compromises. The millions they rule will probably be content with an endless vista of hard and patient work....

There is, therefore a real sense in

which time is on Russia's side.... time may well bring out some of the inherent weaknesses of the western position, the weaknesses from which any democracy and still more a collection of democracies, suffers when it comes to the game of power politics. For that game demands patience, resolution, clear sight, a lack of illusions, a refusal to be frightened by tactical moves, a determination not to be taken in by appearances or yield to emotions.... What made Hitler strong was not any great accumulation of economic resources but the flabbiness of the democracies, their lack, as Paul Reynaud told them, of *la lucidité et l'audace*—of clear thinking and courage. The answer to the riddle of Russia's strength is to be found in Washington.

PART III   OBJECTIVES AND METHODS OF STATES

IX · The Definition of Policy Aims

In Chapter III we spoke in general terms of the problem of motivation in the state system, inquiring into the meanings of such concepts as "power," "interests," and "ideology," which are said to shape the behavior of states in international relations. Chapters IV through VIII were addressed to the task of identifying selected capacities and qualities of states which influence both the formulation of goals and the possibilities of attaining them. It now becomes necessary to turn more specifically to the problem of definition and implementation of the policy objectives of states. The task of analyzing the *implementation* of such objectives, which forms the subject matter of Chapters XI through XIV, is in a sense easier than that of analyzing the considerations entering into the initial definitions of policy aims. This difficult task is the subject matter of the present chapter.

Let it be said at the outset that in this area of the study of international relations we operate on the basis of many assumptions but little tested knowledge. It is temptingly easy to base an entire theoretical construct of international relations on assumptions about the motivations of individuals, groups, governments, and states. But it is very difficult to prove that those assumptions correspond to objective reality in an invariable and therefore predictable fashion.

To begin, we make the assumptions: 1) that the activity of individuals and groups is, consciously or not, goal-oriented; 2) that varying factors, internal and external to the actor, influence the definition of the goal for which he strives, as well as his chances for attaining it; and 3) that all groups involved in international relations have multiple objectives, the ingredients of which may at times be contradictory or mutually exclusive. For example, if a statesman were to say that "our objectives are peace, security, and the fulfillment of our legitimate aspirations" (and stranger statements are on record!), he would have made a meaningless utterance unless we—and he—knew what definition and what priority was to be given to each item on this list.

One of the most important points to bear in mind in an analysis of objectives is that the terms which are in common usage are not without seriously disqualifying ambiguities. For instance, "survival" or "self-preservation" of a given state is often cited as the *sine qua non* of its policy. But, one might well ask, what is the "self" that is to be preserved? For that matter, what do terms such as "preservation" or "survival" mean? Do they refer to the maintenance of a momentary *status quo,* or do they also take into account changes in the internal composition or external position of states? Another term frequently used is "independence." It has, to be sure, referents in real life, as Sayre's article, reprinted in this chapter, makes clear. We find that especially for the newer countries, the stress on independence is extremely strong, which in part explains the emphasis on "neutralism" discussed in Chapter XVI. But if one wishes to be wholly realistic about it, one is forced to the conclusion that no country, not even the most powerful one, is ever fully independent of decisions made in other countries, over which only very imperfect control can be exercised. (Sayre's article, incidentally, tends to look at this question very much from the Western point of view, rather than from the point of view of the new countries and the territories presently claiming separate statehood. This is even more true of the selection by Jessup, who addresses himself quite specifically to the task of defining ends of American foreign policy. A similar essay could be written about the ends of any other nation's policy.)

"Territorial integrity," another term often used to define state objectives, is no more free of ambiguity than the terms already mentioned, since it fails to specify precisely which territory is to be protected, and against what. Taking the case of the United States as an instructive example, does the term "territorial integrity" imply that this country would defend only its own territorial boundaries? If so, what does one make of the foreign bases which were established for the specific reason of protecting the national realm? Would these not also have to be defended? The underlying difficulties with many of these terms, especially "national security," are treated brilliantly in the selection by Arnold Wolfers.

There are other problems in this field. As indicated in Chapter III, many students of politics maintain that all human behavior—especially in the field of international relations—is characterized by a "power-drive." Thus, Professor Morgenthau speaks of the drive for power as "bio-psychological." [1] Bertrand Russell says that "of the infinite desires of man, the chief are the desires for power and glory," and adds that some human desires, unlike those of animals, "are essentially boundless and incapable of complete satisfaction." [2] Other competent analysts take much the same view, and although some might not classify the power-drive as either unlimited or omnipresent, they feel that the concept of power provides the best organizing focus for the study of relations among individuals and groups, including the

---

[1] Hans J. Morgenthau, *Politics Among Nations* (New York: Alfred A. Knopf, 1949), p. 17.
[2] Bertrand Russell, *Power: A New Social Analysis* (New York: W. W. Norton & Co., 1938), pp. 9–11.

massive and complex groups whose interaction is the subject matter of the study of international relations.

Yet one should be cautious before accepting any single-motive explanation of behavior. Certainly considerations of power are important; probably they are never completely absent from the minds of statesmen engaged in international relationships. But this is not quite the same as claiming for them a priority in each and every type of situation. Much, of course, depends upon one's definition of "power." If it is equated with physical force alone, one finds that many contemporary international relationships cannot be explained at all by sole reference to relative possession of physical strength. If "power" takes in, as it must, not only physical, but also psychological, economic, and even moral ingredients, then one may wonder whether the concept has not become so broad as to become useless for purposes of analysis.

Among other objectives frequently mentioned, we find those of aggrandizement and expansion—either physical, economic, cultural, or ideological. Again, no doubt, this is frequently an important goal of states in international relations, and it might be an interesting exercise to establish categories of states according to the frequency with which they engage in actions designed to achieve one or more of these aims. Yet, again, one should hesitate before drawing conclusions from such categorizations. It is not easy to divide the states of the world into neat categories on any basis.[3] A presently non-expansionary state may simply be one that is content with the fruits of past expansionary policies.

"Well-being" is another goal often cited in the literature of international relations. For many countries, particularly those which depend on international trade for a substantial segment of their income, economic considerations may indeed be the most significant objectives of foreign policy. Since all countries are becoming, in greater or lesser degree, "welfare" states (that is, actively concerned with the personal security and well-being of their citizens), the economic factor is certainly important and cannot be neglected.

The problems inherent in the task of defining goals of state behavior are clear; the solution to these problems is less obvious. Given the complexity of the subject, Professor Morgenthau suggests a way out by employing the concept of "National Interest" as a guide to the analysis of a country's behavior in international relations. In alerting us to distinctions from subnational or supra-national interests, the concept undoubtedly has its usefulness. The difficulty with it is that it is vague and that it differs from country to country, and within countries from period to period. Thus, even after one has said "national interest," one has really only pushed back the definition of the motivation of state behavior. The next task must inevitably be

---

[3] Attempts to divide the states of the world into such categories as peace-loving vs. aggressive, satiated vs. unsatiated, "haves" vs. "have-nots," etc. almost invariably suffer from serious shortcomings.

the precise definition of that "national interest" in time and space. Indeed, some students of the subject reject the concept altogether. Professor Wolfers obviously belongs to the latter group.

The more adequate conceptualization and categorization of objectives thus seems to be an outstanding need for the student of international relations. This is especially the case since it is difficult to distinguish between "objectives" and "policies"—ends and means. Much semantic confusion ensues as a result of this difficulty. The various categories have a way of shading off into one another. Some policies may be so long-range in nature as to be tantamount to objectives of state policy.

One possible way out of this problem is to distinguish between objectives and policies in terms of *time*. This would involve the distinction between immediate objectives, corresponding to short-term policies; intermediate objectives, corresponding to longer-but-still-limited-term policies; and long-range objectives, corresponding to permanent policies. Another tool of analysis which may be useful in the interpretation of state objectives would be to distinguish a given society's aspirations from the point of view of their objects. Thus, a country's objectives for itself would presumably differ from those it has for its close allies, which might in turn differ from those for potential allies, neutral states, and potential or actual adversaries. (Note, however, the ambiguity of the terms "potential," "allies," and "adversaries." One's allies at one time may become one's adversaries at other times, one's potential adversaries are, conversely, also one's potential allies.)

Relatively few professional students of international relations have grappled with this complex topic. The selections reprinted in this chapter constitute some of the best thinking on the subject to date. But more work must be done before the student of international relations can have cause to be satisfied with his knowledge concerning this key question.

1 • Another "Great Debate": The National Interest of the United States *

Hans J. Morgenthau

II

. . . .

. . . what is the national interest? How can we define it and give it the content which will make it a guide for action?

. . . .

It has been frequently argued against the realist conception of foreign policy that its key concept, the national interest, does not provide an acceptable

* *American Political Science Review*, XLVI (1952), 971–78. Reprinted by permission.

standard for political action. This argument is in the main based upon two grounds: the elusiveness of the concept and its susceptibility to interpretations, such as limitless imperialism and narrow nationalism, which are not in keeping with the American tradition in foreign policy. The argument has substance as far as it goes, but it does not invalidate the usefulness of the concept.

The concept of the national interest is similar in two respects to the "great generalities" of the Constitution, such as the general welfare and due process. It contains a residual meaning which is inherent in the concept itself, but beyond these minimum requirements its content can run the whole gamut of meanings which are logically compatible with it. That content is determined by the political traditions and the total cultural context within which a nation formulates its foreign policy. The concept of the national interest, then, contains two elements, one that is logically required and in that sense necessary, and one that is variable and determined by circumstances.

Any foreign policy which operates under the standard of the national interest must obviously have some reference to the physical, political, and cultural entity which we call a nation. In a world where a number of sovereign nations compete with and oppose each other for power, the foreign policies of all nations must necessarily refer to their survival as their minimum requirements. Thus all nations do what they cannot help but do: protect their physical, political, and cultural identity against encroachments by other nations.

It has been suggested that this reasoning erects the national state into the last word in politics and the national interest into an absolute standard for political action. This, however, is not quite the case. The idea of interest is indeed of the essence of politics and,

as such, unaffected by the circumstances of time and place. Thucydides' statement, born of the experiences of ancient Greece, that "identity of interest is the surest of bonds whether between states or individuals" was taken up in the nineteenth century by Lord Salisbury's remark that "the only bond of union that endures" among nations is "the absence of all clashing interests." The perennial issue between the realist and utopian schools of thought over the nature of politics, to which we have referred before, might well be formulated in terms of concrete interests vs. abstract principles. Yet while the concern of politics with interest is perennial, the connection between interest and the national state is a product of history.

The national state itself is obviously a product of history and as such destined to yield in time to different modes of political organization. As long as the world is politically organized into nations, the national interest is indeed the last word in world politics. When the national state will have been replaced by another mode of organization, foreign policy must then protect the interest in survival of that new organization. For the benefit of those who insist upon discarding the national state and constructing supranational organizations by constitutional fiat, it must be pointed out that these new organizational forms will either come into being through conquest or else through consent based upon the mutual recognition of the national interests of the nations concerned; for no nation will forego its freedom of action if it has no reason to expect proportionate benefits in compensation for that loss. This is true of treaties concerning commerce or fisheries as it is true of the great compacts, such as the European Coal and Steel Community, through which nations try to create supranational forms of organization. Thus, by an apparent paradox, what is historically relative in the idea of the national interest can be overcome only through the promotion in concert of the national interest of a number of nations.

The survival of a political unit, such as a nation, in its identity is the irreducible minimum, the necessary element of its interests vis-à-vis other units. Taken in isolation, the determination of its content in a concrete situation is relatively simple; for it encompasses the integrity of the nation's territory, of its political institutions, and of its culture. Thus bipartisanship in foreign policy, especially in times of war, has been most easily achieved in the promotion of these minimum requirements of the national interest. The situation is different with respect to the variable elements of the national interest. All the cross currents of personalities, public opinion, sectional interests, partisan politics, and political and moral folkways are brought to bear upon their determination. In consequence, the contribution which science can make to this field, as to all fields of policy formation, is limited. It can identify the different agencies of the government which contribute to the determination of the variable elements of the national interest and assess their relative weight. It can separate the long-range objectives of foreign policy from the short-term ones which are the means for the achievement of the former and can tentatively establish their rational relations. Finally, it can analyze the variable elements of the national interest in terms of their legitimacy and their compatibility with other national values and with the national interest of other nations. We shall address ourselves briefly to the typical problems with which this analysis must deal.

The legitimacy of the national interest must be determined in the face of possible usurpation by subnational, other-national, and supranational interests. On the subnational level we find group interests, represented particularly by ethnic and economic groups, who tend to identify themselves with the national interest. Charles A. Beard has emphasized, however one-sidedly, the extent to which the economic interests of certain groups have been presented as those of the United States.[1] Group interests exert, of course, constant pressure upon the conduct of our foreign policy, claiming their identity with the national interest. It is, however, doubtful that, with the exception of a few spectacular cases, they have been successful in determining the course of American foreign policy. It is much more likely, given the nature of American domestic politics, that American foreign policy, insofar as it is the object of pressures by sectional interests, will normally be a compromise between divergent sectional interests. The concept of the national interest, as it emerges from this contest as the actual guide for foreign policy, may well fall short of what would be rationally required by the overall interests of the United States. Yet the concept of the national interest which emerges from this contest of conflicting sectional interests is also more than any particular sectional interest or their sum total. It is, as it were, the lowest common denominator where sectional interests and the national interest meet in an uneasy compromise which may leave much to be desired in view of all the interests concerned.

The national interest can be usurped by other-national interests in two typical ways. The case of treason by individuals, either out of conviction or for pay, needs only to be mentioned here; for insofar as treason is committed on behalf of a foreign government rather

---

[1] *The Idea of National Interest: An Analytical Study in American Foreign Policy* (New York: The Macmillan Company, 1934).

than a supranational principle, it is significant for psychology, sociology, and criminology, but not for the theory of politics. The other case, however, is important not only for the theory of politics but also for its practice, especially in the United States.

National minorities in European countries, ethnic groups in the United States, ideological minorities anywhere may identify themselves, either spontaneously or under the direction of the agents of a foreign government, with the interests of that foreign government and may promote these interests under the guise of the national interest of the country whose citizens they happen to be.

. . . .

The usurpation of the national interest by supranational interests can derive in our time from two sources: religious bodies and international organizations. The competition between church and state for determination of certain interests and policies, domestic and international, has been an intermittent issue throughout the history of the national state. Here, too, the legitimate defense of the national interest against usurpation has frequently, especially in the United States, degenerated into the demagogic stigmatization of dissenting views as being inspired by Rome and, hence, being incompatible with the national interest. Yet here, too, the misuse of the issue for demagogic purposes must be considered apart from the legitimacy of the issue itself.

The more acute problem arises at the present time from the importance which the public and government officials, at least in their public utterances, attribute to the values represented and the policies pursued by international organizations either as alternatives or supplements to the values and policies for which the national government stands. It is frequently asserted that the foreign policy of the United States pursues no objectives apart from those of the United Nations, that, in other words, the foreign policy of the United States is actually identical with the policy of the United Nations. This assertion cannot refer to anything real in actual politics to support it. For the constitutional structure of international organizations, such as the United Nations, and their procedural practices make it impossible for them to pursue interests apart from those of the member-states which dominate their policy-forming bodies. The identity between the interests of the United Nations and the United States can only refer to the successful policies of the United States within the United Nations through which the support of the United Nations is being secured for the policies of the United States.[2] The assertion, then, is mere polemic, different from the one discussed previously in that the identification of a certain policy with a supranational interest does not seek to reflect discredit upon the former, but to bestow upon it a dignity which the national interest pure and simple is supposed to lack.

The real issue in view of the problem that concerns us here is not whether the so-called interests of the United Nations, which do not exist apart from the interests of its most influential members, have superseded the national interest of the United States, but for what kind of interests the United States has secured United Nations support. While these interests cannot be United Nations interests, they do not need to be national interests either. Here we are in

---

[2] See, on this point, Hans J. Morgenthau, "International Organizations and Foreign Policy," in *Foundations of World Organization: A Political and Cultural Appraisal,* Eleventh Symposium of the Conference on Science, Philosophy and Religion, edited by Lyman Bryson, Louis Finkelstein, Harold D. Lasswell, R. M. MacIver (New York, 1952), pp. 377–383.

the presence of that modern phenomenon which has been variously described as "utopianism," "sentimentalism," "moralism," the "legalistic-moralistic approach." The common denominator of all these tendencies in modern political thought is the substitution for the national interests of a supranational standard of action which is generally identified with an international organization, such as the United Nations. The national interest is here not being usurped by sub- or supranational interests which, however inferior in worth to the national interest, are nevertheless real and worthy of consideration within their proper sphere. What challenges the national interest here is a mere figment of the imagination, a product of wishful thinking, which is postulated as a valid norm for international conduct, without being valid either there or anywhere else. At this point we touch the core of the present controversy between utopianism and realism in international affairs; we shall return to it later in this paper.

The national interest as such must be defended against usurpation by non-national interests. Yet once that task is accomplished, a rational order must be established among the values which make up the national interest and among the resources to be committed to them. While the interests which a nation may pursue in its relation with other nations are of infinite variety and magnitude, the resources which are available for the pursuit of such interests are necessarily limited in quantity and kind. No nation has the resources to promote all desirable objectives with equal vigor; all nations must therefore allocate their scarce resources as rationally as possible. The indispensable precondition of such rational allocation is a clear understanding of the distinction between the necessary and variable elements of the national interest. Given the contentious manner in which in democracies the variable elements of the national interest are generally determined, the advocates of an extensive conception of the national interest will inevitably present certain variable elements of the national interest as though their attainment were necessary for the nation's survival. In other words, the necessary elements of the national interest have a tendency to swallow up the variable elements so that in the end all kinds of objectives, actual or potential, are justified in terms of national survival. Such arguments have been advanced, for instance, in support of the rearmament of Western Germany and of the defense of Formosa. They must be subjected to rational scrutiny which will determine, however tentatively, their approximate place in the scale of national values.

The same problem presents itself in its extreme form when a nation pursues, or is asked to pursue, objectives which are not only unnecessary for its survival but tend to jeopardize it. Second-rate nations which dream of playing the role of great powers, such as Italy and Poland in the interwar period, illustrate this point. So do great powers which dream of remaking the world in their own image and embark upon world-wide crusades, thus straining their resources to exhaustion. Here scientific analysis has the urgent task of pruning down national objectives to the measure of available resources in order to make their pursuit compatible with national survival.

Finally, the national interest of a nation which is conscious not only of its own interests but also of that of other nations must be defined in terms compatible with the latter. In a multinational world this is a requirement of political morality; in an age of total war it is also one of the conditions for survival.

In connection with this problem two mutually exclusive arguments have been advanced. On the one hand, it has been argued against the theory of international politics here presented that the concept of the national interest revives the eighteenth-century concept of enlightened self-interest, presuming that the uniformly enlightened pursuit of their self-interest by all individuals, as by all nations, will of itself be conducive to a peaceful and harmonious society. On the other hand, the point has been made that the pursuit of their national interest by all nations makes war the permanent arbiter of conflicts among them. Neither argument is well taken.

The concept of the national interest presupposes neither a naturally harmonious, peaceful world nor the inevitability of war as a consequence of the pursuit by all nations of their national interest. Quite to the contrary, it assumes continuous conflict and threat of war, to be minimized through the continuous adjustment of conflicting interests by diplomatic action. No such assumption would be warranted if all nations at all times conceived of their national interest only in terms of their survival and, in turn, defined their interest in survival in restrictive and rational terms. As it is, their conception of the national interest is subject to all the hazards of misinterpretation, usurpation, and misjudgment to which reference has been made above. To minimize these hazards is the first task of a foreign policy which seeks the defense of the national interest by peaceful means. Its second task is the defense of the national interest, restrictively and rationally defined, against the national interests of other nations which may or may not be thus defined. If they are not, it becomes the task of armed diplomacy to convince the nations concerned that their legitimate interests have nothing to fear from a restrictive and rational foreign policy and that their illegitimate interests have nothing to gain in the face of armed might rationally employed....

2 • National Security as an Ambiguous Symbol *

Arnold Wolfers

Statesmen, publicists and scholars who wish to be considered realists, as many do today, are inclined to insist that the foreign policy they advocate is dictated by the national interest, more specifically by the national security interest. It is not surprising that this should be so. Today any reference to the pursuit of security is likely to ring a sympathetic chord.

However, when political formulas such as "national interest" or "national security" gain popularity they need to be scrutinized with particular care. They may not mean the same thing to different people. They may not have any precise meaning at all. Thus, while appearing to offer guidance and a basis for broad consensus they may be permitting everyone to label whatever policy he favors with an attractive and possibly deceptive name.

* *Political Science Quarterly*, LXVII (1952), 481–502. Reprinted by permission.

In a very vague and general way "national interest" does suggest a direction of policy which can be distinguished from several others which may present themselves as alternatives. It indicates that the policy is designed to promote demands which are ascribed to the nation rather than to individuals, sub-national groups or mankind as a whole. It emphasizes that the policy subordinates other interests to those of the nation. But beyond this, it has very little meaning.

When Charles Beard's study of *The Idea of National Interest* was published in the early years of the New Deal and under the impact of the Great Depression, the lines were drawn differently than they are today. The question at that time was whether American foreign policy, then largely economic in scope and motivation, was aimed not at promoting the welfare interests of the nation as a whole but instead at satisfying the material interests of powerful sub-national interest or pressure groups. While it was found hard to define what was in the interest of national welfare or to discover standards by which to measure it, there could be no doubt as to what people had in mind: they desired to see national policy makers rise above the narrow and special economic interests of parts of the nation to focus their attention on the more inclusive interests of the whole.

Today, the alternative to a policy of the national interest to which people refer is of a different character. They fear policy makers may be unduly concerned with the "interests of all of mankind." They see them sacrificing the less inclusive national community to the wider but in their opinion chimeric world community. The issue, then, is not one of transcending narrow group selfishness, as it was at the time of Beard's discussion, but rather one of according more exclusive devotion to the narrower cause of the national self.

There is another difference between the current and the earlier debate. While it would be wrong to say that the economic interest has ceased to attract attention, it is overshadowed today by the national security interest. Even in the recent debates on the St. Lawrence Seaway, clearly in the first instance an economic enterprise, the defenders of the project, when seeking to impress their listeners with the "national interest" involved, spoke mainly of the value of the Seaway for military defense in wartime while some opponents stressed its vulnerability to attack.

The change from a welfare to a security interpretation of the symbol "national interest" is understandable. Today we are living under the impact of cold war and threats of external aggression rather than of depression and social reform. As a result, the formula of the national interest has come to be practically synonymous with the formula of national security. Unless explicitly denied, spokesmen for a policy which would take the national interest as its guide can be assumed to mean that priority shall be given to measures of security, a term to be analyzed.[1] The

[1] Hans Morgenthau's *In Defense of the National Interest* (New York: Alfred Knopf, 1951), is the most explicit and impassioned recent plea for an American foreign policy which shall follow "but one guiding star—the National Interest." While Morgenthau is not equally explicit in regard to the meaning he attaches to the symbol "national interest," it becomes clear in the few pages devoted to an exposition of this "perennial" interest that the author is thinking in terms of the national security interest, and specifically of security based on power. The United States, he says, is interested in three things: a unique position as a predominant Power without rival in the Western Hemisphere and the maintenance of the balance of power in Europe as well as in Asia, demands which make sense only in the context of a quest for security through power.

question is raised, therefore, whether this seemingly more precise formula of national security offers statesmen a meaningful guide for action. Can they be expected to know what it means? Can policies be distinguished and judged on the ground that they do or do not serve this interest?

The term national security, like national interest, is well enough established in the political discourse of international relations to designate an objective of policy distinguishable from others. We know roughly what people have in mind if they complain that their government is neglecting national security or demanding excessive sacrifices for the sake of enhancing it. Usually those who raise the cry for a policy oriented exclusively toward this interest are afraid their country underestimates the external dangers facing it or is being diverted into idealistic channels unmindful of these dangers. Moreover, the symbol suggests protection through power and therefore figures more frequently in the speech of those who believe in reliance on national power than of those who place their confidence in model behavior, international coöperation, or the United Nations to carry their country safely through the tempests of international conflict. For these reasons it would be an exaggeration to claim that the symbol of national security is nothing but a stimulus to semantic confusion, though closer analysis will show that if used without specifications it leaves room for more confusion than sound political counsel or scientific usage can afford.

. . . .

...attention should be drawn to an assertion of fact which is implicit if not explicit in most appeals for a policy guided by national security. Such appeals usually assume that nations in fact have made security their goal except when idealism or utopianism of their leaders has led them to stray from the traditional path. If such conformity of behavior actually existed, it would be proper to infer that a country deviating from the established pattern of conduct would risk being penalized. This would greatly strengthen the normative arguments. The trouble with the contention of fact, however, is that the term "security" covers a range of goals so wide that highly divergent policies can be interpreted as policies of security.

Security points to some degree of protection of values previously acquired. In Walter Lippmann's words, a nation is secure to the extent to which it is not in danger of having to sacrifice core values, if it wishes to avoid war, and is able, if challenged, to maintain them by victory in such a war.[2] What this definition implies is that security rises and falls with the ability of a nation to deter an attack, or to defeat it. This is in accord with common usage of the term.

Security is a value, then, of which a nation can have more or less and which it can aspire to have in greater or lesser measure.[3] It has much in common, in this respect, with power or wealth, two other values of great importance in international affairs. But while wealth measures the amount of a nation's material possessions, and power

[2] Walter Lippmann, *U. S. Foreign Policy* (Boston, 1943), p. 51.

[3] This explains why some nations which would seem to fall into the category of *status quo* Powers *par excellence* may nevertheless be dissatisfied and act very much like "imperialist" Powers, as Morgenthau calls nations with acquisitive goals. They are dissatisfied with the degree of security which they enjoy under the *status quo* and are out to enhance it. France's occupation of the Ruhr in 1923 illustrates this type of behavior. Because the demand for more security may induce a *status quo* Power even to resort to the use of violence as a means of attaining more security, there is reason to beware of the easy and often self-righteous assumption that nations which desire to preserve the *status quo* are necessarily "peace-loving."

its ability to control the actions of others, security, in an objective sense, measures the absence of threats to acquired values, in a subjective sense, the absence of fear that such values will be attacked. In both respects a nation's security can run a wide gamut from almost complete insecurity or sense of insecurity at one pole, to almost complete security or absence of fear at the other.[4]

The possible discrepancy between the objective and subjective connotation of the term is significant in international relations despite the fact that the chance of future attack never can be measured "objectively"; it must always remain a matter of subjective evaluation and speculation. However, when the French after World War I insisted that they were entitled to additional guarantees of security because of the exceptionally dangerous situation which France was said to be facing, other Powers in the League expressed the view that rather than to submit to what might be French hysterical apprehension the relative security of France should be objectively evaluated. It is a well-known fact that nations, and groups within nations, differ widely in their reaction to one and the same external situation. Some tend to exaggerate the danger while others underestimate it. With hindsight it is sometimes possible to tell exactly how far they deviated from a rational reaction to the actual or objective state of danger existing at the time. Even if for no other reasons, this difference in the reaction to similar threats suffices to make it probable that nations will differ in their efforts to obtain more security. Some may find the danger to which they are exposed entirely normal and in line with their modest security expectations while others consider it unbearable to live with these same dangers. Although this is not the place to set up hypotheses on the factors which account for one or the other attitude, investigation might confirm the hunch that those nations tend to be most sensitive to threats which have either experienced attacks in the recent past or, having passed through a prolonged period of an exceptionally high degree of security, suddenly find themselves thrust into a situation of danger. Probably national efforts to achieve greater security would also prove, in part at least, to be a function of the power and opportunity which nations possess of reducing danger by their own efforts.

Another and even stronger reason why nations must be expected not to act uniformly is that they are not all or constantly faced with the same degree of danger. For purposes of a working hypothesis, theorists may find it useful at times to postulate conditions wherein all states are enemies—provided they are not allied against others—and wherein all, therefore, are equally in danger of attack.[5] But, while it may be

---

[4] Security and power would be synonymous terms if security could be attained only through the accumulation of power, which will be shown not to be the case. The fear of attack—security in the subjective sense—is also not proportionate to the relative power position of a nation. Why, otherwise, would some weak and exposed nations consider themselves more secure today than does the United States?

Harold D. Lasswell and Abraham Kaplan, *Power and Society* (New Haven: Yale University Press, 1950), defining security as "high value expectancy" stress the subjective and speculative character of security by using the term "expectancy"; the use of the term "high," while indicating no definite level, would seem to imply that the security-seeker aims at a position in which the events he expects—here the continued unmolested enjoyment of his possessions—have considerably more than an even chance of materializing.

[5] For a discussion of this working hypothesis—as part of the "pure power" hypothesis—see my article on "The Pole of Power and the Pole of Indifference" in *World Politics,* vol. IV, No. 1, October 1951. [Reprinted, in part, in Chapter III, above.]

true in the living world, too, that no sovereign nation can be absolutely safe from future attack, nobody can reasonably contend that Canada, for example, is threatened today to the same extent as countries like Iran or Yugoslavia, or that the British had as much reason to be concerned about the French air force in the twenties as about Hitler's *Luftwaffe* in the thirties.

This point, however, should not be overstressed. There can be no quarrel with the generalization that most nations, most of the time—the great Powers particularly—have shown, and had reason to show, an active concern about some lack of security and have been prepared to make sacrifices for its enhancement. Danger and the awareness of it have been, and continue to be, sufficiently widespread to guarantee some uniformity in this respect. But a generalization which leaves room both for the frantic kind of struggle for more security which characterized French policy at times and for the neglect of security apparent in American foreign policy after the close of both World Wars throws little light on the behavior of nations. The demand for conformity would have meaning only if it could be said—as it could under the conditions postulated in the working hypothesis of pure power politics—that nations normally subordinate all other values to the maximization of their security, which, however, is obviously not the case.

There have been many instances of struggles for more security taking the form of an unrestrained race for armaments, alliances, strategic boundaries and the like; but one need only recall the many heated parliamentary debates on arms appropriations to realize how uncertain has been the extent to which people will consent to sacrifice for additional increments of security. Even when there has been no question that

armaments would mean more security, the cost in taxes, the reduction in social benefits or the sheer discomfort involved has militated effectively against further effort. It may be worth noting in this connection that there seems to be no case in history in which a country started a preventive war on the grounds of security—unless Hitler's wanton attack on his neighbors be allowed to qualify as such—although there must have been circumstances where additional security could have been obtained by war and although so many wars have been launched for the enhancement of other values. Of course, where security serves only as a cloak for other more enticing demands, nations or ambitious leaders may consider no price for it too high. This is one of the reasons why very high security aspirations tend to make a nation suspect of hiding more aggressive aims.

Instead of expecting a uniform drive for enhanced or maximum security, a different hypothesis may offer a more promising lead. Efforts for security are bound to be experienced as a burden; security after all is nothing but the absence of the evil of insecurity, a negative value so to speak. As a consequence, nations will be inclined to minimize these efforts, keeping them at the lowest level which will provide them with what they consider adequate protection. This level will often be lower than what statesmen, military leaders or other particularly security-minded participants in the decision-making process believe it should be. In any case, together with the extent of the external threats, numerous domestic factors such as national character, tradition, preferences and prejudices will influence the level of security which a nation chooses to make its target.

It might be objected that in the long run nations are not so free to choose the amount of effort they will put into security. Are they not under a kind of compulsion to spare no effort provided they wish to survive? This objection again would make sense only if the hypothesis of pure power politics were a realistic image of actual world affairs. In fact, however, a glance at history will suffice to show that survival has only exceptionally been at stake, particularly for the major Powers. If nations were not concerned with the protection of values other than their survival as independent states, most of them, most of the time, would not have had to be seriously worried about their security, despite what manipulators of public opinion engaged in mustering greater security efforts may have said to the contrary. What "compulsion" there is, then, is a function not merely of the will of others, real or imagined, to destroy the nation's independence but of national desires and ambitions to retain a wealth of other values such as rank, respect, material possessions and special privileges. It would seem to be a fair guess that the efforts for security by a particular nation will tend to vary, other things being equal, with the range of values for which protection is being sought.

In respect to this range there may seem to exist a considerable degree of uniformity. All over the world today peoples are making sacrifices to protect and preserve what to them appear as the minimum national core values, national independence and territorial integrity. But there is deviation in two directions. Some nations seek protection for more marginal values as well. There was a time when United States policy could afford to be concerned mainly with the protection of the foreign investments or markets of its nationals, its "core values" being out of danger, or when Britain was extending its national self to include large and only vaguely circumscribed "regions of spe-cial interest." It is a well-known and portentous phenomenon that bases, security zones and the like may be demanded and acquired for the purpose of protecting values acquired earlier; and they then become new national values requiring protection themselves. Pushed to its logical conclusion, such spatial extension of the range of values does not stop short of world domination.

A deviation in the opposite direction of a compression of the range of core values is hardly exceptional in our days either. There is little indication that Britain is bolstering the security of Hong Kong although colonies were once considered part of the national territory. The Czechs lifted no finger to protect their independence against the Soviet Union and many West Europeans are arguing today that rearmament has become too destructive of values they cherish to be justified even when national independence is obviously at stake.

The lack of uniformity does not end here. A policy is not characterized by its goal, in this case security, alone. In order to become imitable, the means by which the goal is pursued must be taken into account as well. Thus, if two nations were both endeavoring to maximize their security but one were placing all its reliance on armaments and alliances, the other on meticulous neutrality, a policy maker seeking to emulate their behavior would be at a loss where to turn. Those who call for a policy guided by national security are not likely to be unaware of this fact, but they take for granted that they will be understood to mean a security policy based on power, and on military power at that. Were it not so, they would be hard put to prove that their government was not already doing its best for security, though it was seeking to enhance it by such means as international coöperation or by the negotiation of compromise agreements—means which in one instance may be totally ineffective or utopian but which in others may have considerable protective value.

It is understandable why it should so readily be assumed that a quest for security must necessarily translate itself into a quest for coercive power. In view of the fact that security is being sought against external violence—coupled perhaps with internal subversive violence— it seems plausible at first sight that the response should consist in an accumulation of the same kind of force for the purpose of resisting an attack or of deterring a would-be attacker. The most casual reading of history and of contemporary experience, moreover, suffices to confirm the view that such resort to "power of resistance" has been the rule with nations grappling with serious threats to their security, however much the specific form of this power and its extent may differ. Why otherwise would so many nations which have no acquisitive designs maintain costly armaments? Why did Denmark with her state of complete disarmament remain an exception even among the small Powers?

But again, the generalization that nations seeking security usually place great reliance on coercive power does not carry one far. The issue is not whether there is regularly some such reliance but whether there are no significant differences between nations concerning their over-all choice of the means upon which they place their trust. The controversies concerning the best road to future security that are so typical of coalition partners at the close of victorious wars throw light on this question. France in 1919 and all the Allies in 1945 believed that protection against another German attack could be gained only by means of continued military superiority based on German military impotence. President Wilson in 1919 and many observers in 1945 were equally convinced, however, that more hope for security lay in a conciliatory and fair treatment of the defeated enemy, which would rob him of future incentives to renew his attack. While this is not the place to decide which side was right, one cannot help drawing the conclusion that, in the matter of means, the roads which are open may lead in diametrically opposed directions. The choice in every instance will depend on a multitude of variables, including ideological and moral convictions, expectations concerning the psychological and political developments in the camp of the opponent, and inclinations of individual policy makers.

After all that has been said little is left of the sweeping generalization that in actual practice nations, guided by their national security interest, tend to pursue a uniform and therefore imitable policy of security. Instead, there are numerous reasons why they should differ widely in this respect, with some standing close to the pole of complete indifference to security or complete reliance on nonmilitary means, others close to the pole of insistence on absolute security or of complete reliance on coercive power. It should be added that there exists still another category of nations which cannot be placed within the continuum connecting these poles because they regard security of any degree as an insufficient goal; instead they seek to acquire new values even at the price of greater insecurity. In this category must be placed not only the "mad Caesars," who are out for conquest and glory at any price, but also idealistic statesmen who would plunge their country into war for the sake of spreading the benefits of their ideology, for example, of liberating enslaved peoples.

. . . .

3 • The Quest of Independence *

Francis B. Sayre

The author began his career as Professor of Law in the Harvard Law School and went on to a distinguished career in the diplomatic service. He held such posts as High Commissioner to the Philippines (1939–1942), and U.S. Representative to the Trusteeship Council of the UN (1947–1952). During the war, he was responsible for much economic planning in the State Department. He was a frequent contributor to journals of international relations and foreign affairs.

NOTE: *The following constitutes an abridgment and not the complete text of the article.*

Americans seem not to realize what an important place dependent peoples and underdeveloped areas hold in the world today or what urgent problems are raised by their desire for independence and a larger share in the prosperity of our modern age. There is a tendency to consider these as secondary questions, not comparable in importance to the acute political problems of the day. But anyone who has served, as I have, as United States Representative in the Trusteeship Council of the United Nations, wrestling with the problem during more than five crowded years, will know the contrary. The policies which we adopt toward the backward areas of Asia and Africa will have consequences quite as far-reaching and profound as will the more spectacular decisions which we make in the stupendous struggle now raging between Soviet Russia and the free world. On their outcome hangs the future of civilization.

The situation is perilous today in large parts of Asia and in most of Africa because of the conjunction of three poison-breeding factors:

First, a condition of appalling human need. Living standards in most of Asia and Africa are the lowest in the world. In many sections, life expectancy at birth is only 32 years. One out of every three babies dies before reaching its first birthday. Those suffering from malaria in Asia today equal the total population of the Western hemisphere— and every year 3,000,000 of these sufferers die. Tuberculosis, malaria and yaws are rampant: all are controllable diseases. Monstrous illiteracy bars the door to spiritual or technological advance. More people in Asia and Africa are unable to read a word from a printed book or direction than inhabit the whole of Europe and of the United States.

Second, embittering memories of the cruel racial discrimination and exploitation which often accompanied nineteenth century colonialism. These have left livid scars. The feelings of racial inferiority which have been generated

* Excerpted by special permission from *Foreign Affairs*, XXX (July 1952), 564–69. Copyright by Council on Foreign Relations.

offer serious hindrances to Western attempts to build bulwarks for freedom. Racial hatreds have bred among many people in Asia and Africa profound distrust of all white peoples, and in some cases fear of them.

Third, surging forces of nationalism. The earlier conditions which isolated underdeveloped peoples have been largely swept away by modern commerce, the radio and military activities on a world scale. Asia and Africa today, emerging from the primitive conditions which locked them in for centuries, are being confronted with twentieth century problems which they scarcely understand and for which they are quite unprepared. Out of a welter of new conceptions and new aspirations the high explosive of nationalism is emerging. Peoples which have recently achieved independent statehood often remain rabidly nationalistic. Many of them, freed from the fetters of colonialism and awakening to the world around them, are beginning to feel the striking disparity between the peoples of the Western World, in their eyes luxuriating in plenty, and themselves, lacking even the bare essentials of existence. Millions of men and women in the underdeveloped areas of Asia and Africa are asking more and more insistently why they should live as the disinherited of the earth.

It is the conjunction of these three inter-related factors—desperate human need, the feeling of resentment bred by long years of racial discrimination and a new-found and explosive nationalism—that constitutes the problem of underdeveloped areas in Asia and Africa. Even if the Soviet régime collapsed tomorrow this problem would remain, and there could be no assurance of world peace until it had been mastered. For peace depends upon human freedom; and where there are desperate hunger and need, where racial hatreds are deep-rooted, and where peoples quite unprepared for the responsibilities of power acquire it suddenly, genuine freedom is impossible.

. . . .

The issues that come to the surface in the debates in the Fourth Committee are basic. Certain peoples, isolated from the busy pathways of mankind, lack the modern resources, training and experience to govern themselves competently or to defend themselves against attack by a possible aggressor. Leading Western nations, with or without right, have entered the territories of many of these peoples in the past and successfully established control and government over them. Under the system of national sovereignty as developed in international law they consider today that their right to control and rule these people is legally and constitutionally unassailable.

But during the last 100 years a new social consciousness has arisen throughout the world, a deepening sense of the sanctity of the human rights which must lie at the foundation of any lasting world order. As a result, men and women everywhere are questioning the right of one people to govern and control another people without its consent; and the challenge is being pressed not only by dependent peoples but also by many sovereign nations which themselves possess no colonial territories. However strongly entrenched in law and in constitutional theory may be the right of colonial Powers to rule alien peoples, there is a growing tendency in the public mind to shift the issue from constitutional to moral considerations.

Within recent years, then, the march toward political independence has been assuming dramatic proportions. Moved by a complex of motives and forces, hastened by the pressures of world opinion, the great colonial Powers today are in numerous instances giving up former possessions or putting a time limit on the continuance of their rule. Since the Second World War some 500,000,000 people—a fifth of the entire population of the world—have won political independence.

But with independence come new problems; and genuine freedom is not to be had until a way can be found to solve them. Examples of this abound. As a result of the vote of the General Assembly in 1949, Libya has now become a "united independent and sovereign state," and the former occupying Powers, Great Britain and France, have transferred all their governmental powers to the new Libyan Government as from December 24, 1951. Free and democratic national elections have already been held there and a new constitution has been inaugurated.

But independence carries with it responsibilities. Defense calls for large outlays of money. Necessary buildings and public works cost large sums of money. So do adequate educational programs and public health measures. So do schools and hospitals and training institutions for indigenous schoolteachers and doctors and nurses. In Libya, thus far, the necessary revenues have for the most part come out of the treasuries of the administering Powers, Great Britain and France. Libya itself lacks sufficient revenues. The United Nations budget is not large enough to support the necessary expenditures. For the time being, Great Britain and France have promised to make good the deficits in the Libyan budget. During the current year the United Nations is advancing to Libya more than $1,000,-000 in technical assistance, the United States is advancing about $1,500,000. But the question remains how the Libyan people will in the long run meet the necessary costs of economic and social and educational advancement. Whence will come the money?

. . . .

Problems such as these face us today in many similar areas. Men and women are questioning the right of any nation to govern an alien people against their will, but they forget that the maintenance of independence and the development of economic and industrial resources cost money and require trained personnel. Where are these to come from? Surely the answer is not simple abandonment of the countries in question. Underdeveloped peoples cannot be left to live on in ignorance and want even if they would. In many of the underdeveloped areas in Asia and Africa we today have perhaps our last opportunity to meet these problems with humane and Christian solutions. If we fail, can we be surprised if Communism moves in?

. . . .

World peace can be built only upon human freedom. Yet at present some 200,000,000 people do not govern themselves. What is the solution of this paradox?

The easy but superficial answer is prompt independence for all. This, the answer which the Soviets beguilingly espoused at San Francisco when the United Nations Charter was being framed in 1945, carries an instant emotional appeal to almost everyone. It wins support in every General Assembly— particularly among the Latin American groups and those Middle Eastern states which have achieved their independence after long years of struggle. And we Americans, perhaps more than any other people, believe that freedom is the rock upon which all human progress must be built. Without it, we know, democracy cannot exist and stable world peace cannot be attained.

Under its Charter, the United Nations is consecrated to the task of assisting all non-self-governing peoples in their progressive development toward independence or self-government. This is the avowed purpose of every people outside the Soviet ring. Since the setting up of the United Nations, as has already been pointed out, some 500,000,000 people have acquired political independence. Seven new nations of Asia—India, Pakistan, Ceylon, Burma, the Philippines, the Republic of Korea and Indonesia—have come into existence.[1] To these must be added Syria, Lebanon, Jordan and Israel in the Middle East; and in Africa, Libya, which was given independence.[2] Somaliland, Nepal, the new states of Indo-China and others stand in the offing.

But what many fail to understand is that political independence is not synonymous with human freedom. In 1783 the wresting of American independence from the British Crown was only the first step toward freedom. There had to be many more steps. There had to be a constitutional bill of rights to guarantee freedom of speech and of the press, freedom of religion, freedom of assembly, freedom from illegal process. Thereafter it took the people of the independent nation many years of sustained effort to build the social and cultural foundations necessary to establish American freedom and make it reasonably secure. And still we are in the process of building. As we move forward we continually gain new vision and adopt new goals.

Genuine freedom cannot be achieved by a mere political grant or by a military victory. It comes only as adequate political, economic, social and educational foundations can be made ready. ...Political independence is a notable step along the way. But surely it is only a step, and in no sense the goal itself. Men can be as effectively manacled by economic and social forms of servitude as by political oppression. Among the peoples living in many primitive parts of Asia and Africa the real problems therefore go far deeper than political status. In such areas genuine solutions can come only through steady processes of education and training in the fundamentals upon which successful self-government must be built.

When we undertook the administration of the Philippine Islands in 1898, we did not, in spite of insistent Filipino demands, give them independence for almost half a century. Instead we sent among them armies of schoolteachers and doctors and road-builders. We helped them to learn the meaning of democracy in action. We gave them practical experience in the exasperating art of self-government. Even today we must continue to assist them as they learn to stand alone.

The premature grant of political independence, before a people have had adequate economic and social preparation, can do them untold harm. Indigenous leaders who are not subject to the restraint of the civic standards that come with popular education can exploit their compatriots as ruthlessly as aliens, or even more so. Nor is the cause of international peace served by giving full independence to a people who are not able to defend themselves. Large parts of Asia and Africa which today possess immense natural resources and exceedingly valuable strategic bases are inhabited by people quite unable to hold their own against lawless aggressors armed with twentieth-century weapons.

If we are to build for human welfare and for the peace of the world, our course is, therefore, clearly marked. We must stimulate and help the peoples in all underdeveloped areas, self-governing as well as non-self-governing, to construct the kind of economic and social and educational foundations necessary to prepare them for maintaining their

---

[1] More have been added since this article was written: Viet-Nam, Laos, Cambodia, Malaya.

[2] Since joined by Ghana, Guinea.

political freedom and to qualify them for increasing self-government. Only thus can we rid ourselves of the inherent dangers now existing in every under-developed country—dangers due to Communist infiltration, to the possible rise and spread among such peoples in the future of ideologies even more devastating than Communism, to deepening cleavages among those who must stand together if peace is to be stabilized in the world. Only thus do we make our own freedom.

Many will ask why we should force a twentieth-century culture upon peoples who through the centuries have developed their own cultures and found happiness in them. Would it not make for the happiness of all to leave them unmolested in their own ways of life? The answer is that we in fact have no

choice. No one can stay the hand of advancing cultures—least of all in an age when insistent commercial and military demands knit all peoples into an inescapable unity. Western Samoa during the whole of the second half of the nineteenth century struggled to preserve its indigenous culture and to remain in isolation from Western civilization. The effort was of no avail. Other attempts tell the same story. In the shrunken world of the twentieth century no people can successfully isolate their native culture behind a Chinese wall. Each people has contributions of incalculable value to make to the human race. The conditions of our twentieth century demand that every people make its own contributions and share the differing cultures of others.

. . . .

4 • Ends and Means of American Foreign Policy *

Philip C. Jessup

The author has been on the faculty of Columbia University since 1925. Since 1946 he has occupied the position of Hamilton Fish Professor of International Law and Diplomacy. From 1948–1952 he served as U.S. representative to the General Assembly, and in 1949 he was appointed Ambassador-at-large. He is the author of A Modern Law of Nations *(1948),* Transnational Law *(1956), and frequent articles in scholarly journals.*

. . . .

CATALOGUE OF FOREIGN POLICY OBJECTIVES

Security. There is no doubt that foreign policy must have as an objective— a prime objective—the defense of the

United States from devastation by an enemy or defeat in war. There have been times in our history when the danger

* The American Assembly, *International Stability and Progress: United States Interests and Instruments* (New York, Columbia University, 1957), 18–21. Reprinted by permission.

was not so acute as to lead us to put this objective in the first place. Other countries—let us say Uruguay or Venezuela for example—may be in that same happy situation today. For the United States, however, the danger is very real. The problem is to prevent this danger from driving out of our minds other long-range objectives. During World War II, concentration upon the objective of winning the war in some instances prevented our paying due heed to the problems of the postwar era. The United States must not permit concentration upon the necessity of winning the Cold War to obliterate other objectives or to cause it to subordinate them so that they are merely considered means to this one end. Perhaps the problem is most easily envisaged if one assumes that the communist menace is removed and if one then asks what are the other objectives of our foreign policy.

Economic prosperity. Despite some echoes from our isolationist past and despite occasional plaints inspired by self-interest, it is hardly necessary any longer to argue that the American economy is affected by foreign trade and by economic conditions in other parts of the world. It is clear that international economic problems fall within the scope of our foreign policy even though as a matter of our governmental organization the decisions are not all made in the Department of State but are shared with, for example, the Treasury, Commerce, and Agriculture Departments, and the Export-Import Bank; and such international agencies as the International Bank of Reconstruction and Development, and the International Monetary Fund. Our foreign aid programs are, or should be, definitely linked to the general problem of maintaining international economic and financial stability and to promoting world-wide economic development in the benefit of which we will share. The fact that the aid programs may serve other ends as well cannot obscure this consideration.

Opportunity for self-improvement. This objective is closely related to security and to economic prosperity but it contains other elements. We would like to be able to devote ourselves to various domestic reforms such as slum clearance, better education, care for the aged and disabled, better hospitals, more recreation facilities. We are aware—sometimes rather vaguely—that a successful foreign policy, which diminishes the danger of war, can contribute to these ends. If we succeed in evolving a workable plan for the limitation of armaments, this contributes not only to security but also to the reduction of the national defense budget so that more of our resources can be devoted to these domestic goals. It is less often appreciated that progress toward these goals is also a contribution to the foreign policy of a great power. As George Kennan said in his Stafford Little Lectures:

Blighted areas, fiithy streets, community demoralization, juvenile delinquency, chaotic traffic conditions, utter disregard for esthetic and recreational values in urban development, and an obviously unsatisfactory geographic distribution of various facilities for homelife and work and recreation and shopping and worship; these things may not mark all our urban communities in conspicuous degree; but they mark enough of them to put a definite imprint that leads others to feel that we are not really the masters of our own fate, that our society is not really under control, that we are being helplessly carried along by forces we do not have the courage or the vitality to master.... Peoples of the world are not going to be inclined to accept leadership from a country which they feel is drifting in its own internal development and drifting into bad and dangerous waters.

An environment conducive to freedom. This objective is also closely related to the three already described, but it suggests a positive American interest in the fruitful development of free institutions elsewhere in the world. It is sought not only to avoid the constrictions on our own lives of a "garrison state," but also because it permits our society to benefit from the healthy interchange of ideas, peoples, and values with other societies. It is in a sense the international counterpart of our faith in the domestic ideal of an "open society."

Prestige and influence. It may well be argued that prestige and influence are sought merely because they are means to other ends. Unquestionably they are such means, but they are something more. In one degree or another almost every state seeks these ends just as individuals do, nor is this reprehensible. One sees constantly in the United Nations the intense rivalry for positions of prestige which have only a remote connection with the advancement of other national interests. A small state, member of the United Nations, is eager to have one of its nationals chosen as a judge of the International Court of Justice for example, not because it expects to be a litigant before the Court and hopes to have a sympathetic member on the bench, but because of the general prestige factor. As a state grows in power and influence it may well disregard some of the minor insignia of prestige, but the prestige factor itself is not cast aside. This is not to say that United States foreign policy should be directed toward the absurd goal of winning a popularity contest as if Uncle Sam were competing for selection as "The Man of the Year." It is one of the popular fallacies, for example, that our foreign aid programs are designed to "buy friends," bound to us by ties of grati-

tude and affection. Millikan and Rostow have dealt effectively with this misconception. It is doubtful whether any responsible United States official has ever labored under the delusion that such a policy could ever achieve such a result. The prestige of a nation is not based on popularity; it rests far more upon respect. To be respected and to have the prestige and influence which flow from such respect is a natural and legitimate objective of foreign policy.

Satisfying a sense of justice. Many will challenge the inclusion of "satisfying a sense of justice" as an objective of foreign policy, but it represents something substantial from the point of view of the American people. The American people are not likely to consider a foreign policy successful if it secures some material gain at the expense of principles which they consider part of their heritage. Here looms the whole debate over the proper role of morality in the making of foreign policy.... Without rearguing here the dilemma of the policy-maker, it is asserted that there is such a thing as an American national conscience, which does not rest easy if it feels that the United States has failed to show a "decent respect to the opinions of mankind." There is a persistent uneasiness about the justification for the use of the atom bomb on Hiroshima and Nagasaki. The anti-imperialists were able to build on a like uneasiness in opposing McKinley's Philippine policy. Congress has reflected this call of conscience in resolutions adopted on such occasions as the Jewish pogroms in Russia and the massacre of Armenians in Turkey. The reception of Kossuth in Washington a century ago, like the reception of the Hungarian refugees today, is further illustration. In framing its policy on the issues of colonialism today, it is clear that the Department of State feels the necessity of taking into account the sympathies of the American people for groups which are seeking independence. Whether or not the policy-maker be influenced by expediency or necessity in deciding upon a certain course of action, the results of the policy will be judged by the American people at least partly in terms of whether they feel they can look the world in the eye and say, "This was the right thing for the United States to do."

.   .   .   .

X • Diplomacy

In recent years there has been renewed interest in using the diplomatic method for the purpose of resolving international conflict. This interest may be the counsel of despair on the part of persons who feel that since nothing else seems to be working very well to reduce tensions, established methods of adjusting international conflicts might as well be given another chance. It may, on the other hand, be a recognition of the possibility that diplomacy really *is* a promising method, that the old practitioners of this ancient art were right all along.

The most basic definition of diplomacy is that it is a form of contact between nations based on permanent representation of each state in the capital city of each other state. Other definitions may serve to delineate the nature of diplomacy. Thus we find a dictionary definition of diplomacy as "the management of international relations by negotiation; the method by which these relations are adjusted and managed by ambassadors and envoys." A British diplomat, Sir Ernest Satow, defined the concept in terms of its *method* as "the application of intelligence and tact to the conduct of official relations between governments"; and a recent American text points to the *substance* of diplomacy by describing it as "the accumulative political, economic, and military pressures upon each side, formalized in the exchange of demands and concessions between negotiators." [1]

The professional diplomat has a two-fold function. He presents the views and advances the interests of his government toward the government of the state to which he is accredited; and he interprets the latter's policies, capabilities, and ambitions to his own government. These tasks are extraordinarily difficult, requiring the utmost in skill and craftsmanship. A 19th century Austrian diplomat put the needed qualifications in the following terms:

> What a hard trade is the diplomatist's! I know of none which demands so much abnegation, so much readiness to sacrifice one's interests for the sake of duty, so much courage. The ambassador who properly discharges his obligations, never betrays fatigue, boredom, disgust. He disguises the emotions which he feels, the temptations

[1] Ernst B. Haas and Allen S. Whiting, *Dynamics of International Relations* (New York: McGraw-Hill Book Co., Inc., 1956), p. 135.

to succumb which assail him. He knows how to pass over in silence the bitter deceptions which are dealt to him, as well as the unexpected satisfactions with which his
fortune, though rarely, rewards him. Jealous of his dignity, he never ceases to be
cautious, takes care to quarrel with nobody, never loses his serenity, and in all the
great crises, when the question of war arises, shows himself calm, impassive, and sure
of success.[2]

As the selections reprinted in this chapter make clear, there have been
a number of changes in the practice of diplomacy during the present century.
These changes include 1) greater publicity for diplomatic negotiations; 2)
less freedom of action for the professional diplomat; 3) more direct negotiations between foreign ministers and heads of state. Not all observers are
convinced that these changes have been for the better. Consequently, some
of them argue forcefully that we should revert to some extent to previous
diplomatic methods. The great evil of such methods was, of course, the
secrecy which attended negotiations and resulting agreements. This secrecy
contributed to the general tension and uneasiness, because no state could
ever be sure that it was not the victim of some arrangement of which it knew
nothing—or, in any event, of which it did not know enough to set up counteracting secret arrangements of its own. Most students of the subject would
agree that except in wartime not much can be said for secret agreements
which poison the international atmosphere and contribute to general tension.
But an increasing number argue that there is a great deal to be said for
negotiations which are kept confidential until a final agreement is reached
and made public.

Another innovation which has not found universal acclaim is the habit
of foreign ministers and heads of states to participate personally and frequently in negotiations ("summit-meetings," to use a current phrase). Certainly there are advantages to this procedure: top decision-makers may
benefit by knowing one another personally—not because acquaintance necessarily leads to friendship, but because it provides a chance to size up one's
counterpart in another government. Also, when differences in position have
been narrowed down to manageable proportions by lower-level negotiators,
ultimate decisions will have to be made, and these can be made only by top
personnel. Under such circumstances, a personal meeting may play a positive
function in settling specific international problems.

There are, however, certain disadvantages. If negotiations take place at a
very high level, it is impossible to conduct them in complete confidence,
except during wartime. There are bound to be information-leaks, or indeed,
official briefings of the press. The negotiators, having to state their positions
publicly, will do so in maximum terms, backed by appeals to morality,
legality, or ideology—and then they are unable to back down. Public opinion will be aroused. Expectations will be raised. Since the essence of negotiation is compromise, the effects of this publicity are thus obviously de-

---

[2] Quoted in R. B. Mowat, *Diplomacy and Peace* (New York: Robert M. McBride & Co.,
1936), pp. 56–57.

structive. One might go so far as to say that public negotiations are no negotiations at all. Then, too, a summit-negotiation is a race against time. Top decision-makers are seldom able to take several weeks or even months from their demanding tasks. Pressure for time leads to pressure for results and imprecision in the agreements which are made.

A number of these problems are discussed in the ensuing selections. Charles Burton Marshall cautions against the unrealistic assumption that negotiation in itself gives assurance of a desired outcome. Sir Harold Nicolson puts much of the blame for current misuses of diplomatic methods on Americans. He refers, in passing, to Soviet methods (which he does not deem worthy of the term "diplomacy" at all). One may question how useful it is to place blame. Western and Soviet diplomats work under different conditions, with different objectives and assumptions. This leads to misunderstandings and misinterpretations of intention and method. Even if it does promote "understanding" of one another—as Marshall aptly points out —the chances for resolving conflict are not automatically enhanced. One might even go so far as a recent editorial which states:

> The old diplomacy of persuasion, compromise, and patient conciliation has come to a dead end, even if diplomats must pretend to the contrary. When the differences between two parties are as profound as they are between the West and the Soviet world—when the political assumptions, economic beliefs, and the very modes of individual existence are so far removed as to be incomparable—then the very basis of this old diplomacy is abolished. It can only operate now within the alliances; between the two blocs, it falls freely in a vacuum.[3]

This point of view is basically similar to that ably expounded by Charles Burton Marshall in this chapter.

And yet, one easily under-estimates the real potentialities of diplomacy in performing a number of important tasks in international relations. Diplomats are useful tools for collecting information concerning the views and policies of other countries and for communicating their own countries' views and policies to other governments—with politeness and restraint, but with accuracy and precision. The diplomatic method can, if the policy-makers so desire, provide a convenient and easily accessible way to solve specific international problems. Finally, diplomacy and diplomats can teach us how to live patiently and in good humor with unresolved problems.

In a sense, the selection from Nicolson, in spite of its sharply critical tone, provides certain criteria for a revival of effective diplomacy. He obviously, if by indirection, advocates attention to building a competent and respected diplomatic service. He argues for honesty and probity on the part of diplomats in their relations with one another. He stresses the need for continuous and confidential negotiations and for precision in thought, terms, and actions. If these suggestions could be implemented, one might look forward to the emergence, or re-emergence, of a method of conduct-

---

[3] *The Reporter*, August 20, 1959, p. 2.

ing international relations which would be more effective than diplomacy has been permitted to be in recent decades.

In his provocative text, *Politics Among Nations,* Professor Morgenthau advances as fundamental rules for a successful diplomacy the propositions that diplomacy must be divested of the crusading spirit, that it must look at the political scene from the point of view of other nations, and that nations must learn to compromise on all non-vital issues.[4] He concludes with a most appropriate quotation from Winston Churchill, speaking in 1948:

> I will only venture now to say that there seems to me to be very real danger in going on drifting too long. I believe that the best chance of preventing a war is to bring matters to a head and come to a settlement with the Soviet Government before it is too late. This would imply that the Western democracies, who should, of course, seek unity among themselves at the earliest moment, would take the initiative in asking the Soviet for a settlement.
>
> It is idle to reason or argue with the Communists. It is, however, possible to deal with them on a fair, realistic basis, and, in my experience, they will keep their bargain as long as it is in their interest to do so, which might, in this grave matter, be a long time, once things are settled. . . .
>
> There are very grave dangers . . . in letting everything run on and pile up until something happens, and it passes, all of a sudden, out of your control.
>
> With all consideration of the facts, I believe it right to say today that the best chance of avoiding war is, in accord with the other Western democracies, to bring matters to a head with the Soviet Government, and, by formal diplomatic processes, with all their privacy and gravity, to arrive at a lasting settlement. There is certainly enough for the interests of all if such a settlement could be reached. Even this method, I must say, however, would not guarantee that war would not come. But I believe it would give the best chance of coming out of it alive.[5]

---

[4] Pp. 439–441.

[5] *Parliamentary Debates (Hansard), House of Commons,* Vol. 446, No. 48, 562–3.

1 • The Problem of Incompatible Purposes *

Charles Burton Marshall

The author, who holds degrees from the University of Texas and Harvard University, has a varied background. He has worked as a newspaperman, a teacher (at Harvard University and Radcliffe College), an officer in the U.S. Army during World War II, a consultant to the Committee on Foreign Affairs of the House of Representatives (1947–1950), and a member of the Policy Planning Staff of the Department of State from 1950 to 1953. Since that time he has published The Limits of Foreign Policy *(1954) and has held positions with The Washington Center of Foreign Policy Research and The Carnegie Endowment for International Peace.*

In international affairs, as in other fields, simple terms are used to communicate about hugely complex, shifting, multifarious situations and relationships. There never would be time enough to think, to remember, or to discuss if one had always to describe fully the phenomena concerned. So to keep tabs on ideas, we put tabs on them. The tabs then tend themselves to become legal tender in the exchange places of ideas as if they had independent meaning and validity. This leads to a great deal of fallacy, and it becomes necessary from time to time to refresh comprehension of the processes for which the tabs are only symbols—in a shift of metaphor, to restore the edges of words dulled by ill usage.

A number of words and phrases in the common lexicon of international affairs come to mind as illustrations—*the cold war, balance of power, the rule of law, the battle for men's minds, containment, liberation, the free world, aggression, peace with justice, alliance,* and so on and on. Anyone can make his own list of the poster words which publicists, professors and practitioners use often with careless regard for the complex actualities.

Just now an overworked tab is *negotiation,* closely attended by *disengagement* and *relaxation of tensions.* It is to negotiation that I wish to give academic attention.

A catalogue of the vapid, inapposite things said with high solemnity... [about] negotiations on both sides of the Atlantic would be as long as your arm. I can deal here with only a few of them.

"What harm would there be in our talking to the Russians?" is a question put by a Midwestern newspaper. The same issue contained two long news items demonstrating that in fact our Government was doing just that already, and being talked to voluminously in turn. The idea that negotiation is necessary to cure Washington or Moscow

* *East-West Negotiation* (The Washington Center of Foreign Policy Research, 1958), 68–73. Reprinted by permission.

of being tongue-tied is obviously specious. Has there ever been a time of fuller communication between adversaries than the present?

"Negotiation at least might lead to better understanding even if it did not produce agreements," a professor said at a dinner meeting. One hears this idea repeatedly. It is as if a reservoir of reconciliation were secreted in the rock waiting only to be smitten by negotiation, whereupon it would gush forth in abundant streams. The nub, I suspect, is that in fact our Government and the one in Moscow actually understand each other quite well.

One current notion about negotiation attributes to it qualities of an intercollegiate debate—an exercise in histrionics and logic, with the decision going to the side scoring best in presentation. It is as if at a certain point in the argument across the table Khrushchev might say to Mr. Dulles, "All right, you've got me! I can't answer that one. So what are your terms?"

Another notion attributes to negotiation the characteristics of a one-shot business deal. Let us call this the haggling theory of negotiation—or the Yankee trader theory. One can imagine the American and the Russian arguing about prices and the quality of the goods—Mr. Dulles making for the door in feigned scorn with Mr. Khrushchev turning around with a shrug to put the fabrics on the shelf and then each turning back to renew the bargaining until at last the price is right.

A third notion conceives of negotiation in terms of a Quaker meeting—as if the spirit of togetherness descends upon a gathering, bringing new insights, new efficacy, and a new spirit of reconciliation through the interaction of souls in propinquity. This view of negotiation let us label as the inspirational theory.

In searching for illustrations of these views of negotiation, I happened to come across all three in one context. It is an item in a recent issue of *Saturday Review*. It refers to a speech by Alf Landon to a teachers' meeting in Kansas and characterizes him as sounding "more like a yeasty young liberal than a former Republican candidate for President." The article then quotes him as urging "that we should use our Yankee ingenuity in a summit meeting," continuing, "Instead of saying no-no-no to the Soviet's proposal for a summit conference, why don't we sit down and start arguing?" The quotation then goes on: "The Secretary of State says we can't trust them. Who wants to? Americans were famous once as Yankee traders who always got their money's worth. They didn't bother about the religion, the political philosophy, or sincerity of the other party, just so the deal suited them." The *Saturday Review's* writer endorses all that and adds on his own: "The time seems ripe for a fresh, imaginative, and inspired approach to international relations."

There we have the three—sit down and start arguing, get your money's worth and don't worry about sincerity, and finally get inspired.

According to my dictionary *negotiate* means "1. To treat for, obtain, or arrange by bargain, conference, or agreement. 2. To transfer for a value received, as a note, bond, or other written obligation. 3. To accomplish or cope with successfully, as to *negotiate* an obstacle. 4. To treat or bargain with others." Negotiation embraces then the process of talking about terms, the achievement of terms, and the terms.

Clearly we are already in the midst of negotiations, and long have been, if we mean only the process of talking about terms—at least about the terms for talking about terms. The Russians have been busily propounding the conditions for a spider's feast. Mr. Eisenhower and Mr. Dulles have been assiduously—and properly—rejecting these. In this Mr. Dulles has been accused of inflexibility—which is the pejorative word for firmness.

The reason why negotiations have not progressed to the achievement of terms (in this case even the achievement of terms for trying to achieve terms) is not a lack of inspiration or yeastiness. It is not even a lack of understanding.

We do understand the Russians.

Basically, and quite clearly, the Russians do seek world domination. A great many experts on Russia may deny this. They will point to the remoteness and theoretical character—and hence the supposed irrelevancy—of the ultimate aspirations of the Marxist ideology and contend that there is no active desire whatsoever in the Kremlin rulers really to subjugate Western Europe, etc. This is really not the point. The point is that the Russian rulers do set as their goal and actively pursue the condition that all problems exterior to Russia deemed important to them are to be settled their way. This does not mean that the Russian rulers aspire to see the Red flag over the Quai d'Orsay or Whitehall. It merely means paramountcy for Russian purposes when the issues are drawn.

On the other hand the Russians understand us quite well. I can state this only as a supposition. I cannot give personal assurance about it. Our own purposes and interests make unacceptable to us the condition of world relations coveted by the Russians.

This mutuality of understanding is what impinges upon negotiation in the sense of achievement of terms.

In a negotiation which advances to terms, each side seeks ends and brings means. Each side conceives its ends in terms of means to be tendered by the other. In a one-shot deal—the Yankee trading sort of negotiation—means and ends settle out in an exchange if the price is right, and the seller awaits other customers while the buyer takes home the goods or goes to other markets. This has no bearing on the sort of negotiation which the U.S. is being exhorted to undertake. The point at issue is the conditions for a continuing relationship. Whether at the summit or elsewhere the basic bargaining must be on how in broadest terms the entities concerned are to relate themselves to each other. If we wish to draw a metaphoric parallel, the most apt would be the sort of negotiation which took place between the U.A.W. and General Motors in 1937. Here the issue was whether the company and the union would thenceforth relate themselves to each other in a continuing bargaining relationship. That issue setled, the other elements in contention fell into place more or less readily.

The conditions of successful collective bargaining shed some light on the problem of negotiating with the Russians. In collective bargaining that works, the adversariness of the parties is limited by their recognized need of each other. Their ends are not the same. They may even be opposite, but they are compatible. Each side seeks satisfaction of its own ends at a minimum practicable expenditure of means to satisfy the ends sought by the other, but neither hates or fears *per se* the ends which the other seeks, and so neither feels compelled to suspect or distrust the use which the other might make of a success.

Between the Russians and us such conditions do not exist. Debate is not likely to convince either party to the contrary. A basis for Yankee trading is lacking. The inspiration of tête-a-tête is not likely to cause either side to forget the facts.

In this perspective the argument about locus—whether to negotiate at a mysterious summit or along even more mysterious corridors of professional diplomacy—becomes as derivative and arid as a question whether Neville Chamberlain or Nevile Henderson was the best man for doing business with Hitler. If a universe of discourse making for compatible ends were shared, negotiations at whatever level might be productive of the longed-for solutions. If this were so, moreover, the problems and dangers which men of good will wish to abate would not exist.

This brings us to the vaunted relaxation of tensions. One hears that the Russians harbor thoughts of bringing this about and need to be met only halfway. If by the phrase one means a sag along our side of the confrontation—a disengagement, an abatement of the challenge which we carry to Russian purposes—then the answer is that, of course, the Russians are ready for it and want it the worst way. If it means that the Russians are in a mood for modifying the intensity and constancy of their own desires, one can only answer that the mood is deeply concealed, and its existence a matter of guesswork.

This does not mean an endlessly static situation. The material relevancy of certain means may alter from one stage to another, and problems may move up or down in the scale of negotiability; particular impasses may become unblocked, as occurred, for instance, in the case of the Austrian Peace Treaty. The time when it will become possible to transform the situation by putting means of high importance into the bargain and to reconcile ends seems remote, however.

If there is to be relaxation of tensions otherwise than on terms of capitulation, it will be only in the inward sense: a reassertion of captaincy over our own spirits and resolving to live calmly in danger for a long time to come. I am not hopeful that this will be done easily. I can almost hear the yeasty throngs chanting:

> One-two-three-four
> Terminate the cold war!
> Five-six-seven-eight
> Hurry and negotiate!

The problem is how to restore balance to our side, how to dispel the beguiling notion that negotiation of itself is a means of redressing dangers and achieving harmony of interest, rather than merely an avenue along which one may proceed to success, impasse, or catastrophe, depending on the ratios of will and resources between the adversary parties. To counter the surge of demand for negotiation under conditions of high disadvantage to our side it will be necessary to abandon the secondary and unattractive propositions that clutter up the American case and to concentrate on a few basic and sound propositions: a proper insistence on the baleful character of the adversary, the necessity of American interposition, in fact and not merely in promise, on the continent; and the indispensability of NATO. Above all, it will be necessary to correct our imprudent strategic reliance on a thermonuclear weapon that frightens our friends more than it cows our putative enemies.

2 • The Faults of American Diplomacy *

Sir Harold Nicolson

Educated at Oxford University, the author served in the British Foreign Service from 1909 to 1929, both at the Foreign Office in London and at various posts abroad (Constantinople, Madrid, Teheran, Berlin). He was a member of the British delegation to the Peace Conference of 1919, and a member of the League of Nations Secretariat 1919–1920. Among his numerous works are Peacemaking 1919 *(1933);* Curzon; The Last Phase *(1934);* Diplomacy *(1939); and* The Evolution of Diplomatic Method *(1954).*

Since the close of the first world war, international diplomacy has been dominated—or at least heavily influenced—by what might be called "the American method." It has almost completely replaced the Old Diplomacy—the French method, which was originated by Richelieu and adopted by all European countries during the three centuries that preceded 1919. Yet it would hardly be accurate to speak of a New Diplomacy. I prefer—since the Americans have not yet discovered their own formula—to call it "The Transition between the Old Diplomacy and the New."

The French method, in my opinion, was best adapted to the conduct of relations between civilized states. It was courteous and dignified; it was continuous and gradual; it attached importance to knowledge and experience; it took account of the realities of existing power; and it defined good faith, lucidity, and precision as the qualities essential to any sound negotiation. The mistakes, the follies, and the crimes that during those three hundred years accumulated to the discredit of the old

diplomacy can, when examined at their sources, be traced to evil foreign policy rather than to faulty methods of negotiation. It is regrettable that the bad things they did should have dishonored the excellent manner in which they did them.

I am not of course proposing to scrap all existing machinery and to return to the system of the eighteenth and nineteenth centuries. The conditions on which the old diplomacy was based no longer exist. I am suggesting only that as a method of negotiation it was infinitely more efficient than that which we employ today.

Let me therefore consider five of the chief characteristics of the old diplomacy.

In the first place Europe was regarded as the most important of all the continents. Asia and Africa were viewed as areas for imperial, commercial, or mis-

---

* *Harper's,* CCX–CCXI (1955), 52–58. Reprinted by permission of The Macmillan Co., publishers of *The Evolution of Diplomatic Method,* from which the present essay was taken.

sionary expansion. Japan, when she arose, appeared an exceptional phenomenon. America, until 1897, remained isolated behind her oceans and her Doctrine. No war, it was felt, could become a major war unless one of the five Great European Powers became involved. It was thus in the chancelleries of Europe alone that the final issue of general peace or war would be decided.

In the second place it was assumed that the Great Powers were greater than the Small Powers, since they possessed a more extended range of interests, wider responsibilities, and, above all, more money and more guns.

The Small Powers were graded in importance according to their military resources, their strategic position, their value as markets or sources of raw material, and their relation to the Balance of Power. There was nothing stable about such categories. At one moment Egypt, at another Afghanistan, at another Albania, would acquire prominence as points of Anglo-French, Anglo-Russian, or Slav-Teuton rivalry; at one moment the Baltic, at another the Balkans, would become the focus of diplomatic concern. The Small Powers were assessed according to their effect upon the relations between the Great Powers; there was seldom any idea that their interests, their opinions, still less their votes, could affect a policy agreed upon by the Concert of Europe.

This axiom implied a third principle —that the Great Powers possessed a common responsibility for the conduct of the Small Powers and the preservation of peace among them. The principle of intervention was generally accepted. The classic example of joint intervention by the Concert of Europe in a dispute between the Small Powers was the Ambassadors Conference held in London in 1913, at the time of the Balkan Wars. That Conference—which provides the last, as well as the best, example of the old diplomacy in action— prevented a Small-Power crisis from developing into a Great-Power crisis.

DIPLOMACY BY PROFESSIONALS

The fourth characteristic bequeathed by the French system was the establishment in every European country of a professional diplomatic service on a more or less identical model. These officials representing their governments in foreign capitals possessed similar standards of education, similar experience, and a similar aim. They desired the same sort of world. They tended to develop a corporate identity. They had often known each other for years, having served in some post together in their early youth; and they all believed— whatever their governments might believe—that the purpose of diplomacy was the preservation of peace. This professional Freemasonry proved of great value in negotiation.

The Ambassadors, for instance, of France, Russia, Germany, Austria, and Italy, who managed to settle the Balkan crisis of 1913, each represented national rivalries that were dangerous and acute. Yet they possessed complete confidence in each other's probity and discretion, had a common standard of professional conduct, and desired above all else to prevent a general conflagration.

It was not the fault of the professional diplomatists that the supremacy of Europe was shattered by the first world war. The misfortune was that the advice of these wise men was disregarded at Vienna and Berlin, that their services were not employed, and that other, nondiplomatic influences and interests assumed control of affairs.

The fifth main characteristic of the old diplomacy was the rule that sound negotiation must be continuous and confidential. It was a principle essentially different from that governing the itinerant public conferences with which we have become familiar since 1919. The Ambassador in a foreign capital who was instructed to negotiate a treaty with the government to which he was accredited was already in possession of certain assets. He was acquainted with the people with whom he had to negotiate; he could in advance assess their strength or weakness, their reliability or the reverse. He was fully informed of local interests, prejudices, or ambitions, of the local reefs and sandbanks, among which he would have to navigate. His repeated interviews with the Foreign Minister attracted no special public attention, since they were taken for granted as visits of routine. Since his conversations were private, they could remain both rational and courteous; since they were confidential, there was no danger of public expectation being aroused while they were still in progress.

Every negotiation consists of stages and a result: if the stages become matters of public controversy before the result has been achieved, the negotiation will almost certainly founder. A negotiation is the subject of concession and counter-concession: if the concession offered is divulged before the public are aware of the corresponding concession to be received, extreme agitation may follow and the negotiation may have to be abandoned. The necessity of negotiation remaining confidential has never been more forcibly expressed than by Jules Cambon—perhaps the best professional diplomatist of this century.

"The day secrecy is abolished," writes M. Cambon, "negotiation of any kind will become impossible."

An ambassador negotiating a treaty according to the methods of the old diplomacy was not pressed for time. Both his own government and the government with whom he was negotiating had ample opportunity for reflection. A negotiation that had reached a deadlock could be dropped for a few months without hopes being dashed or speculation aroused. The agreements that in the end resulted were no hasty improvisations or empty formulas, but documents considered and drafted with exact care. We might cite as an example the Anglo-Russian Convention of 1907. The negotiation between the Russian Foreign Minister and our Ambassador in St. Petersburg occupied a period of one year and three months; and at no stage was an indiscretion committed or a confidence betrayed.

VICES OF THE OLD AMBASSADORS

I trust that my preference for professional to amateur methods of negotiation will not be ascribed solely to the chance that I was myself born and nurtured in the old diplomacy. I am fully conscious of the many faults that the system encouraged. The axiom that all negotiation must be confidential did certainly create the habit of secretiveness, and did induce men of the highest respectability to enter into commitments which they did not divulge. We must not forget that as late as 1914 the French Assembly was unaware of the secret clauses of the Franco-Russian Alliance or that Sir Edward Grey (a man of scrupulous integrity) did not regard it as wrong to conceal from the Cabinet the exact nature of the military arrangements reached between the French and British General Staffs. Confidential negotiations that lead to secret pledges are worse even than the televised diplomacy that we enjoy today.

Nor am I unaware of the functional defects which the professional diplomatist tends to develop. He has seen human folly or egoism operating in so many different circumstances that he may identify serious passions with transitory feelings and thus underestimate the profound emotion by which whole nations can be swayed. He is so inured to the contrast between those who know the facts and those who do not know the facts, that he forgets that the latter constitute the vast majority and that it is with them that the last decision rests. He may have deduced from experience that time alone is the conciliator, that unimportant things do not matter and that important things settle themselves, that mistakes are the only things that are really effective. He may thus incline to the fallacy that on the whole it is wiser, in all circumstances, to do nothing at all.

He may be a stupid man or complacent; there are few human types more depressing than the self-satisfied diplomatist. He may be of weak character, inclined to report what is agreeable rather than what is true. He may be vain, a defect resulting in disaster to all concerned. And he often becomes denationalized, internationalized, and therefore, an elegant empty husk. A profession should not, however, be judged by its failures.

The speeding up of communications has done much to alter the old methods of negotiation. In former days it took many months before a dispatch could be received and answered, and ambassadors abroad were expected to use their own initiative and judgment in carrying out the policy outlined in the instructions they had received on leaving home. Some ambassadors profited by this latitude to pursue a personal policy.

"I never," wrote Lord Malmesbury, "received an instruction that was worth reading." Other highly gifted ambassadors, such as Sir Hugh Elliott and Sir Henry Bulwer, relished their independence as enabling them to indulge in personal eccentricities and romantic affairs.

Yet these were exceptions. Most ambassadors during the period of slow communications were so terrified of exceeding their instructions or of assuming an initiative that might embarrass their home government, that they adopted a purely passive attitude, missed opportunity after opportunity, and spent their time writing brilliant reports on situations that had entirely altered by the time their dispatches arrived.

Today a Foreign Secretary from his desk in Downing Street can telephone to six ambassadors in the course of one morning or can even descend upon them quite suddenly from the sky. Does this mean that a diplomatist today is no more than a clerk at the end of a line? Such an assumption would be much exaggerated. An ambassador in a foreign capital must always be the main source of information, above all the interpreter regarding political conditions, trends, and opinions in the country in which he resides.

In every democracy, in every cabinet or trade union, power at any given moment rests with three or four individuals only. Nobody but a resident ambassador can get to know these individuals intimately or be able to assess the increase or decrease of their influence. It must always be on his reports that the government base their decision about what policy is at the moment practicable and what is not. That in itself is a most important function and responsibility.

But the ambassador also remains the chief channel of communication between his own government and that to which he is accredited. He alone can decide at what moment and in what terms his instructions can best be executed. Moreover he remains the intermediary who alone can explain the purposes and motives of one government to another. If he be foolish, ignorant, vain, or intemperate, great misunderstandings may arise and damaging indiscretions be perpetrated. Important results may depend upon the relations that he has been able to cultivate and maintain, upon the degree of confidence with which he is regarded, upon his skill and tact even in the most incidental negotiation.

Nor is this all. An ambassador should possess sufficient authority with his home government to be able to dissuade it from a course of action which, given the local circumstances, he knows will prove disastrous. Governments who allow themselves to be represented in foreign capitals by ambassadors to whose judgment and advice they pay no attention are wasting their own time and public money. No newspaper, no banking firm, would consider for one instant being represented abroad by a man in whose opinion they placed no confidence.

I do not agree, therefore, that improvements in means of communication have essentially diminished the responsibility of an ambassador, or to any important extent altered the nature of his functions.

WILSON'S DANGEROUS IDEALS

No, it was not the telephone that, from 1919 onward, brought about the transition from the old diplomacy to the new. It was the belief that it was possible to apply to the conduct of *external* affairs, the ideas and practices which, in the conduct of *internal* affairs, had for generations been regarded as the essentials of liberal democracy.

It was inevitable, after the first world war, that some such experiment should be made. On the one hand, the ordinary citizen—convinced that the masses in every country shared his own detestation of war—attributed the breach of the peace to the vice or folly of a small minority, which must in the future be placed under democratic control. On the other hand, when the Americans arrived as the dominant partners in the coalition, they brought with them their dislike of European institutions, their distrust of diplomacy, and their missionary faith in the equality of man.

President Wilson was an idealist and —what was perhaps more dangerous— a consummate master of English prose. He shared with Robespierre the hallucination that there existed some mystic bond between himself and "The People" —by which he meant not only the American people but the British, French, Italian, Roumanian, Yugoslav, Armenian, and even German peoples. If only he could penetrate the fog-barrier of governments, politicians, and officials and convey the sweetness and light of his revelation to the ordinary peasant in the Banat, to the shepherds of Albania, or the dock-hands of Fiume, then reason, concord, and amity would spread in ever widening circles across the earth. He possessed, moreover, the gift of giving to commonplace ideas the resonance and authority of Biblical sentences, and, like all phraseologists, he became mesmerized by the strength and neatness of the phrases that he devised.

During the long months of the Paris Peace Conference, I observed him with interest, admiration, and anxiety, and became convinced that he regarded himself, not as a world statesman, but as a prophet designated to bring light to a dark world. It may have been for this reason that he forgot all about the American Constitution and Senator Lodge.

I have no desire at all to denigrate President Wilson, who was in many ways inspiring and inspired. He assumed a weight of responsibility greater than any single human being is constituted to support, and he was tragically crushed. Yet if we read again the tremendous sermons that he delivered during 1918 we shall find in them the seeds of the jungle of chaos that today impedes and almost obliterates the processes of rational negotiation.

The first of his Fourteen Points of

January 8, 1918, providing that in the future there should be nothing but "open covenants of peace openly arrived at" and that "diplomacy should proceed always frankly and in the public view." On reaching Paris, President Wilson quickly decided that by "diplomacy" he had not meant "negotiation," but only the results of that negotiation, namely treaties. He also decided that the phrases "openly arrived at" and "in the public view" were relative only and contained nothing that need deter him from conducting prolonged secret negotiations with Lloyd George and Clemenceau—while one American marine stood with fixed bayonet at the study door, and another patrolled the short strip of garden outside. I can well recall how startled I was, on first being admitted to the secret chamber, to discover how original was the President's interpretation of his own first rule. Today, being much older, I realize that the method he adopted was the only possible method which, in the circumstances, could have led to any result.

The general public, however, were not similarly constrained to test the validity of the President's pronouncements against the hard facts of international intercourse. They continued to assume that by "diplomacy" was meant both policy and negotiation, and to conclude that, since secret treaties were demonstrably evil things, negotiation also must never be secret but conducted always "in the public view." This is perhaps the most confusing of all the fallacies that we owe to President Wilson.

In the second of his Four Principles of a month later, the President announced that the system of the Balance of Power was now for ever discredited and that subject populations must be granted their independence, irrespective of the wishes of other states. In the Four Ends of the following July he fore-shadowed the creation of a League of Nations which would establish, to quote his words, "the reign of law, based upon the consent of the governed and sustained by the organized opinion of mankind."

He failed to realize that the public is bored by foreign affairs until a crisis arises; and that then it is guided by feelings rather than by thoughts. Nor did he foresee that it would be impossible to organize the same opinion in every country simultaneously—or that the conscience of mankind, as a means of sustenance, might prove inadequate when faced by a dictator controlling all means of information.

In the Five Particulars on September 27 he pronounced that the rule of justice which America must achieve would be one that "plays no favorites and knows no standards but the equal rights of the several peoples concerned." This commandment was subsequently misinterpreted to signify that not the rights merely but also the opinions and the votes of even the tiniest country were of a validity equal to that of a Great Power. Egalitarianism was thus for the first time extended to imply equality among nations—an idea which does not correspond to reality and which creates mixed ideas.

If read as a whole, the successive pronouncements made by President Wilson during those months of 1918, constitute a magnificent gospel. They embody conceptions which no man should either ignore or disdain. The misfortune was that the public imagined that what was intended as a doctrine of perfectability was in fact a statement of American intentions. Thus when America repudiated her own prophet, a regrettable dichotomy was created between the realists and the idealists in every country. The former concluded that the whole of the Wilson doctrine was sentimental nonsense, and the latter floated off into vague imaginings that what they wanted to happen was likely to occur. As the latter were in the majority, the practical politician found himself in an invidious position. It was the endeavor to reconcile the hopes of the many with the doubts of the few that brought such seeming falsity to foreign policy in the twenty years between 1919 and 1939.

· · · ·

Two important changes were introduced into diplomatic method in the period that followed the war of 1914–18. The first was the refusal of the American legislature to ratify a treaty negotiated and signed by their own chief executive in person. That assuredly was an innovation of the utmost significance and one that dealt a heavy blow to the sanctity of contract and the reliability of negotiation.

The Curse of Conferences

The second was the increasing practice of indulging in the method of diplomacy by conference. By that I do not mean merely the several *ad hoc* conferences, such as Spa, Cannes, Genoa, Lausanne, Stresa, and so on: some of these were necessary and some were not. I am referring rather to the permanent state of conference introduced by the League system and later by the United Nations.

These conferences do little to satisfy the vague desire for what is called "open diplomacy." But they do much to diminish the utility of professional diplomatists and, since they entail much publicity, many rumors, and wide speculation—since they tempt politicians to achieve quick, spectacular, and often fictitious results—they tend to promote rather than allay suspicion, and to create those very states of uncertainty which it is the purpose of good diplomatic method to prevent.

The defects (or perhaps I should say the misfortunes) of the new diplomacy are today magnified for us as if on some gigantic screen. The theory that all states are equal, even as all men are equal, has led to lobbies being formed among the smaller countries (as for instance between the Asians and the Latin Americans) the sole unifying principle of which is to offer opposition even to the resonable suggestions of the Great Powers. The theory that "diplomacy should proceed always frankly and in the public view" has led to negotiation being broadcast and televised, and to all rational discussion being abandoned in favor of interminable propaganda speeches—addressed, not to those with whom the delegate is supposed to be negotiating, but to his own public at home.

I have made but slight reference to the diplomacy of the Soviet Union. Mr. W. P. Potjomkin, in his history of diplomacy, assures us that the Russians possess one powerful weapon denied to their opponents—namely "the scientific dialectic of the Marx-Lenin formula." I have not observed as yet that this dialectic has improved international relationships, or that the Soviet diplomatists and commissars have evolved any system of negotiation that might be called a diplomatic system. Their activity in foreign countries or at the international conferences is formidable, disturbing, compulsive. I do not for one moment underestimate either its potency or its danger. But it is not diplomacy; it is something else. This may be a sad conclusion. But it is not my final conclusion.

It would, in my view, be an error to take as an example of modern diplomatic method the discussions that are conducted in the Security Council and the Assembly of United Nations. We may resent the wastage of time, energy, and money; we may regret that, in transferring to external affairs the system of parliamentary argument, a more efficient type of parliament should not have been chosen as a model. We may deplore that the invectives there exchanged should add to the sum of human tension and bewilderment. Yet it would be incorrect to suppose that these meetings are intended to serve the purpose of negotiation: they are exercises in forensic propaganda and do not even purport to be experiments in diplomatic method. Such negotiation as may occur in New York is not conducted within the walls of the tall building by the East River: it is carried out elsewhere, in accordance with those principles of courtesy, confidence, and discretion which must forever remain the only principles conducive to the peaceful settlement of disputes.

It is not therefore either diplomacy by loud-speaker or diplomacy by insult that we need consider, since these contain a contradiction in terms. It is whether the changes inspired by President Wilson in 1919 do not repeat and emphasize the defects of previous systems and render more difficult what must always remain the chief aim of diplomacy—namely international stability.

Woodrow Wilson, with his academic intelligence and missionary spirit, did not realize that foreign affairs are *foreign* affairs, or that a civilization is not a linotype machine but an organic growth. He believed that the misfortunes of mankind are due to the faults of statesmen and experts and that "the people" were always right: he did not realize that, although it may be difficult to fool all the people all the time, it is easy to fool them for a sufficient period of time to compass their destruction. Thus the "Wilsonian," or the "American," method omits many of the merits of the earlier diplomatic systems and exaggerates many of their faults.

WHO HAS THE LAST WORD?

For example, the chief fault of democratic diplomacy as practiced by the Greek City States was its uncertainty. Not only were their diplomatic missions composed of delegates who betrayed each other, but the final decisions rested with an Assembly whose members were ignorant, volatile, impulsive, and swayed by emotions of fear, vanity, and suspicion. No negotiator can succeed unless reasonable certainty exists that his signature will be honored by his own sovereign. If either the conduct or results of negotiation are subject to irresponsible intervention or repudiation on the part of an assembly or even a Congressional Committee—then uncertainty is spread. My first criticism therefore of the American method is that it weakens certainty.

Again, the fault of the method perfected by the Italians of the Renaissance was that it lacked all continuity of purpose and represented a kaleidoscope of shifting combinations. It may be, for all I know, that the President, the State Department, the Pentagon, and Foreign Affairs Committee of the Senate, are unanimous regarding the aim to be achieved; but they are not unanimous as to the means to be adopted. The variability of the diplomatic method employed suggests opportunism rather than continuity; this is an unfortunate impression, a Machiavellian impression, for a great good giant to convey.

The French system possessed the great merit of creating a centralized authority for the formation of foreign policy and a professional service of experts through whom that policy could be carried out. The misfortune of the American system is that no foreigner (and few Americans) can be quite positive at any given moment who it is who possesses the first word and who the last. Although the Americans in recent years have been in the process of creating an admirable service of professional diplomatists, these experts do not yet possess the necessary influence with their own government or public. The egalitarian illusions of the Americans— or if you prefer it, their "pioneer spirit" —tempts them to distrust the expert and to credit the amateur. I am not just being old-fashioned when I affirm that the amateur in diplomacy is apt to be suspicious.

"Gullibility," as Sir Edward Grey once said to me, "is in diplomacy a defect infinitely preferable to distrust."

Now that the old disciplines of Pope and Emperor, the old correctives of the Concert of Europe and the Balance of Power, have been dispensed with, it is regrettable that the authority exercised by the United States is not more consistent, convincing, and reliable. Yet I am not pessimistic about the evolution of their diplomatic method. I know that the Americans possess more virtue than any giant Power has yet possessed. I know that, although they pretend to deride the lessons of history, they are astonishingly quick at digesting the experience of others. And I believe that the principles of sound diplomacy— which are immutable—will in the end prevail, and thus calm the chaos with which the transition between the old diplomacy and the new has for the moment bewildered the world.

3 • The Art of Diplomatic Negotiation *

Hans J. Morgenthau

. . . .

...we are entering into the positive task of ascertaining what the functions of traditional diplomacy are and in what its permanent value consists. A nation, existing as it does as an equal among other nations, can deal with the outside world in one of three different ways. It can deny the importance of the other nations for itself and its own importance for them and retreat into the impotence of isolation. Or it can deny the equality of the other nations and try to impose its own will upon them by force of arms. In either case, at least in its pure, extreme realization, a nation can afford to dispense with diplomacy. Or a nation can want to pursue its interests in active contact and on the basis of equality with other nations, assuming the universality of that desire. In that case it cannot do without the constant redefinition and adjustment of its interests for the purpose of accommodating the interests of other nations.

Conflict of interests—actual, seeming, or potential—is the overriding fact of international society, as it is one of the overriding facts of all societies, even those most highly integrated and centralized. Diplomacy in all its diverse historic and social manifestations is the technique of accommodating such conflicting interests. That technique proceeds in two stages: the ascertainment of the facts of conflict and the formulation of the terms of settlement.

Nation *A* pursues certain interests,

* From Leonard D. White, ed., *The State of the Social Sciences* (Chicago, The University of Chicago Press, 1956), 408–11. Reprinted by permission of the publisher.

and so does nation B, and the interests of A and B are on the face of them in conflict. Both nations want to settle this conflict peacefully. How can they go about it? They have to define their respective interests and ascertain the point of conflict. That investigation may lead them to one of three possible conclusions.

If what A wants, being vital to itself, B cannot cede without endangering its vital interests, if not its very existence, because of the intrinsic importance of the territory, frontier, port, or air base at issue, diplomatic accommodation is impossible. When Francis I of France was asked why he always made war against Charles V of Austria, he is reported to have answered: "Because we both want the same thing: Italy." As long as both kings wanted Italy badly enough, they could either go to war over it or else leave the issue unsettled, hoping for future developments to deflect the energies of both sides toward less contentious objectives. Often in history nations have indeed avoided war over their vital interests by allowing time to take the sting out of their conflicts. Yet in such cases it is to the restraint of warlike passions and the renunciation of quick and radical solutions rather than to the practices of diplomacy that the credit for the preservation of peace must go.

Nation A may again pursue an objective vital to itself, which nation B could cede only at the price of a vital interest of its own. Yet in contrast to the type of conflict just discussed, the importance of the objective to both sides is here not intrinsic to the objective itself but rather the result of a peculiar configuration of interests which are subject to manipulation. For instance, the Soviet Union has a vital interest in preventing a united Germany from joining the Western alliance, and the United States has a similarly vital interest in preventing such a Germany from being absorbed by the Soviet bloc. Taken by themselves, these positions are obviously incompatible and, as the history of East-West negotiations has thus far shown, not subject to diplomatic accommodation. Yet one can well imagine, without committing one's self to its practical feasibility in the immediate future, an over-all European or world-wide settlement of which a German settlement would form an organic part, satisfactory to the interests of both sides which could not be reconciled to the unification of Germany considered in isolation. In situations such as this, it is the vital task of diplomacy to redefine the seemingly incompatible vital interests of the nations concerned in order to make them compatible.

This task of diplomacy is, as it were, strategic in nature and truly creative, not often attempted and rarely successful. It yields in practical importance to that function with which diplomacy is typically associated in the popular mind: the function of bargaining issuing in a compromise. In conflicts to which this function applies, nation A seeks an objective which nation B either is willing to grant only in part or refuses to grant at all without compensation. Conflicts of this kind concern non-vital interests of which nations are willing to dispose by way of negotiations. The technique of diplomacy consists here in ascertaining the interests of both sides and in allocating the objective at issue in view of these interests and of the power available for their support.

The same diplomatic technique serves not only the peaceful settlement of conflicts among nations but also the delineation and codification of common interests. In this respect it performs its classic function for the negotiation of treaties serving a common purpose of the contracting parties. Called upon to settle a conflict between two nations, diplomacy must create out of the conflicting interests a community of interests, a compromise which cannot satisfy all parties completely, but with which no party will be completely dissatisfied. When the representatives of two nations meet to negotiate a treaty, say, of commerce or alliance, they must discover and make precise an already existing community of interests. This community of interests, before it is crystallized in legal stipulations, is amorphous and inchoate, obscured and distorted by seeming and real conflicts. It is the task of diplomacy to define the area of that pre-existing community of interests and to express it in terms sufficiently precise to serve as a reliable foundation for future action. It need only be mentioned in passing that this function of diplomacy is identical with that of contractual negotiations on all levels of social interaction.

It must be obvious from what has been said thus far that the traditional methods of diplomacy are of vital importance to a nation which seeks to pursue its interests successfully and peaceably. A nation which is unwilling or unable to use diplomacy for that end is of necessity compelled either to forsake its interests or to pursue them by war. As pointed out before, nations have always had a choice among three alternatives: diplomacy, war, and renunciation. Which one of these alternatives a nation would choose in a concrete situation was a matter of rational calculation; none of them was *a priori* excluded on rational grounds.

Modern technology, especially in the form of all-out atomic war, has destroyed this rational equality among diplomacy, war, and renunciation and has greatly enhanced the importance of diplomacy. In view of that technology, there is no longer safety in renunciation or victory in war. From the beginning of history to World War II the risks inherent in these three choices were commensurate with the advantages to be expected. Nations would miscalculate and suffer unexpected losses; but it was never rationally foreordained that they could not win. War, in particular, was a rational means to a rational end; victory would justify the risks and losses incurred, and the consequences of defeat were not from the outset out of all proportion to the gains to be expected from victory.

The possibility of all-out atomic war has destroyed these rational relationships. When universal destruction is the result of victory and defeat alike, war itself is no longer a matter of rational choice but becomes an instrument of suicidal despair. The pursuit of a nation's interests short of all-out atomic war, then, becomes a matter of self-preservation. Even on the assumption—at present a moot one—that limited wars can and will still be safely waged, the risk of such a limited war developing into an all-out atomic one will always be present. Hence, the imperative of the avoidance of all-out atomic war at the very least gives unprecedented urgency to the pursuit of a nation's interests by peaceful means. Such peaceful pursuit, as we know, spells diplomacy. Neither diplomacy nor all-out atomic war is today one among several rational choices available to a nation. As all-out atomic war is tantamount to suicide, so successful diplomacy provides the only certain chance for survival. A nation which under present conditions is either unwilling or unable to take full advantage of the traditional methods of diplomacy condemns itself either to the slow death of attrition or the sudden death of atomic destruction.

. . . .

XI • The Balance of Power

We have noted that the international scene is characterized by the presence of a large number of autonomous units (states), each of which pursues certain self-defined goals. These goals are formulated separately, although, of course, in their formulation the power and position of one's own and various other states, as well as the entire nature of the international environment, must be taken into consideration. Nevertheless, the important point is that there is no assurance that the goals of the various units—especially those units which are in close contact with one another—will always harmonize. Indeed, the precise opposite is frequently the case, and this fact leads to potential or actual international conflict.

Confronted with the ever-present possibility of conflict with other states or with a combination of states, each state must constantly be aware of and concerned with its power position vis-à-vis actual or potential opponents. This awareness, and the attempt to adjust power positions is referred to as awareness, and the attempt to adjust power positions is referred to as the pursuit of "balance of power" policies.

In the following selection, Ernst Haas brilliantly clarifies the various meanings and usages of the term "balance of power." Fundamentally there are two alternatives: "balance" may mean equilibrium, as when two sides of a scale are "in balance"; or it may mean preponderance, as when one speaks of a "balance in the bank," in the sense of a surplus of assets over liabilities.

The use of this term depends on the state under discussion and on the specific relationships with other states in which it is engaged. For many states in their relations with many others, equilibrium may be all they can aspire to. For some, indeed, even this is beyond their capacities, and they can only hope that the more powerful opposing unit may be engaged elsewhere or be otherwise unable to bring its whole power to bear. This is, in fact, a quite common situation, which explains why smaller and weaker states can "get away" with much in their relations with larger and more powerful units. The United States benefited from precisely this kind of situation—a European preoccupation with balance of power throughout the 19th century; weak states benefit by it today in their relations with the Soviet Union, the United States, and other powerful countries.

In other situations, there may be real opportunities and contests for superiority—for "equilibrium *plus*." Such contests take place for two reasons: first, a given power position is difficult, even impossible, to measure with precision. (This problem was discussed in Part II of this book.) Hence, since there is always a chance for error, each state wishes to make *its* error on the side of safety. Second, a surplus of power, if attainable, is—like a surplus of funds—desirable even if one has no immediate plans for its use. It provides psychological satisfaction, and, more significantly, it constitutes a reserve on which one can draw should there be necessity or opportunity to do so.

The basic purposes which underlie the pursuit of balance of power policies are, first of all, to prevent another state or group of states from becoming so powerful as to threaten one's own security (however defined), or even one's values; in short, one's existence. Secondly, one wishes to see one's own state powerful enough to withstand demands which others may make upon it. Thirdly, one may indeed hope to enable one's own state to make certain demands on others and have those demands honored.

Historically the most common form of balance of power is that of the multiple balance, in which a number of states, fairly evenly matched, participate in the struggle by shifting their alignments to correspond with their interests. This system, as Elder points out in his selection in this chapter, is quite successful in preventing conflicts which would destroy one or more of the participating states. Each state is interested not only in maintaining or improving its own power position in absolute terms, but also in preventing other states from becoming so strong that they might at some future time become dangerous. Hence participants in such a multiple balance of power structure tend to coalesce against stronger members and come to the aid of weaker states which are threatened. Since coalitions are flexible, all participants proceed with caution and circumspection, lest the impression of unreasonable ambitions on their part antagonize other members of the system and bring about a coalition between them.

In our day, as in some previous historical periods, we have a different situation, referred to as a simple balance of power, or a bipolar distribution. This type is, according to Elder and others, inherently brittle, unstable, and dangerous. To be sure, the stark bipolarity of the immediate postwar era is apparently giving way to a different situation in which a growing number of states refuse to commit themselves to either side.

States employ a variety of methods to establish or maintain either a fairly equal power distribution with other states or a situation of preponderance. Among these methods we find the following: 1) Compensation, which consists in giving a state the equivalent of something of which it has been deprived. A good example is the manner in which the Soviet Union undertook to compensate Poland for the loss of territorial claims on its Eastern frontier by extending its Western Frontier into territory historically claimed by Germany. 2) Division of states among other states in such a way that power relations among the dividing countries are maintained. The various divisions of Poland in the 18th and 20th centuries are again instructive examples, as was the division of Africa among contending European colonial powers during the past century. This is a fine method for keeping power relations constant—for everyone, that is, except the unfortunate victim! 3) Agreements to establish buffer zones or states between actual or potential antagonists—areas over which both parties exercise agreed-upon degrees of influence. Persia (Iran) has been an example of this, and present proposals for "disengagement" contemplate this type of solution to the conflict between the Soviet Union and the anti-Soviet coalition. (See Chapter XIX.) 4) Attempts within a society to strengthen one's own state against others by increasing or improving social cohesion, industrial and economic productivity, economic self-sufficiency, and armaments. 5) Attempts to weaken the other side through the use of economic, psychological, political, and even military means. Such attempts often take the form of trying to split up existing coalitions; they may even take the form of war. 6) Finally and most frequently, balance of power policies are pursued through the conclusion of alliances with other states whose interests and intentions are similar to one's own. Such alliances may be purely defensive, to protect and preserve a given power position; or they may be offensive, designed to bring pressure to alter a given power situation and construct a new one, more in line with one's own preferences.

It is possible to criticize the concept of balance power, for its unreality, its imprecision, and its inherent danger. In spite of all such criticisms, the term denotes processes which actually *do* exist in international relations. Indeed, regardless of one's value preferences (and recognizing the inappropriateness, suggested by Haas, of picturing balance of power policies as the sum total of all international politics), it may be argued that policy-makers of all countries really have no choice but to pursue some type of balance of power policies in order to protect and advance the interests of their state in a context in which these interests are constantly subject to challenge.

1 • The Balance of Power: Concept, Prescription or Propaganda *

Ernst Haas

The author, Associate Professor of Political Science at the University of California (Berkeley), is the co-author of an outstanding text, The Dynamics of International Relations *(1956). More recently he has published* The Uniting of Europe: Political, Social, and Economic Forces, 1950–1957 *(1958), an original study of the underlying problems and forces working for and against European unity. He is a frequent contributor to journals in the field of international relations and organization.*

NOTE: *In preceding sections of this article, not reprinted because of lack of space, Professor Haas discusses the following possible meanings of the term "balance of power": 1) distribution of power; 2) equilibrium; 3) hegemony; 4) stability and peace; 5) instability and war; 6) power politics; 7) a universal law of history; 8) a system and guide to policy-making. He now addresses himself to the task of analyzing the meanings and intentions of those who use the term:*

. . . .

BALANCE OF POWER AS DESCRIPTION

Forswearing any theoretical or analytical purpose, writers commonly have recourse to the term "balance of power" in discussing international affairs. Current references to the balance of power by journalists and radio commentators most frequently fall into this category. And in most instances the meaning to be conveyed to the audience merely implies "distribution" of power, rather than "balance" in anything like the literal sense. . . .

On other occasions, however, the descriptive use of the term implies more than a mere distribution of power. It may then come to mean "equilibrium" or even "hegemony" or "preponderance" of power, still without implying more than a descriptive intent. It is quite possible that the political motivations of the particular user may make their entrance at this point. Thus Lisola, writing in the seventeenth century, saw in the balance of power the equilibrium between Hapsburg and Bourbon interests. But he used his description to counsel war on France in order to maintain that very equilibrium. Austrian writers again invoked the balance of power principle during the wars of the Polish and Austrian Succession in order to secure allies against France and Prussia, represented as seeking hegemony. During the preceding century, French

* *World Politics,* V (1953), 459–74. Reprinted by permission.

writers had used the equilibrium connotation of the term to demand war on Austria. And it might be pointed out parenthetically that during the Seven Years' War British officials frowned on the use of balance of power terms to justify British aid to Prussia, since it was Frederick II who had "disturbed the balance" with his attack on Austria. In all these writings and statements the term "balance of power" is used and abused as a descriptive phrase, connoting the existence or non-existence of equilibrium and the actual or threatened hegemony of some state or alliance. The same easy transition in meaning from "distribution" to "equilibrium" and finally to "hegemony" can sometimes be detected in contemporary references to the balance of power. These usages are rarely kept in their separate compartments. And, when the users' intentions go beyond that of mere description, clarity of thought and purpose may be seriously jeopardized.

BALANCE OF POWER AS PROPAGANDA AND "IDEOLOGY"

A precise understanding of the verbal meaning of the term "balance of power" becomes especially important when it is used as a propagandistic slogan or as an ideological phrase.... The meanings of "balance" as being identical with either "peace" or "war" fall into this category. Obviously, while it might be correct to speak of a state of balance or imbalance *implying* or *engendering* either war or peace, the balance as such cannot logically be equated with conditions which might arise as a consequence of the balance, i.e., war or peace. In the cases in which the authors employed it to mean "peace" or "war," "balance of power" then became no more than a convenient catchword to focus individual aspirations into a generally acceptable mold; and there can be no doubt

that at certain times the concept of balance was an extremely popular one, whether it was used for policymaking or not. If used in a patently forced manner, the term becomes indistinguishable from plain propaganda....

(Professor Haas cites some examples of the usage of the term for progaganda purposes. Ed.)

It is apparent that ... the balance of power was invoked in such a way as to serve as the justification for policies not *ipso facto* related to balancing anything. In some instances it was used to cloak ideological conflicts, in others to sanctify the search for hegemony over Europe, and in still others to "justify" the continued strength and size of a defeated state. The significance of this invocation, then, lies not in any theoretical belief, but in the fact that the users of the term felt so convinced of its popularity as to make its conversion into a symbol of proper policy propagandistically profitable.

Propaganda assumes the dishonest use of facts and the distortion of concepts devised on intellectually sincere grounds. It implies conscious and deliberate falsification.[1] Ideology, as defined by Mannheim, however, postulates belief in a set of symbols which, even though they may be "false" objectively, still characterize the total myth system of social groups and are essential

---

[1] My conception of propaganda may be expressed in Leonard W. Doob's definition: "Intentional propaganda is a systematic attempt by an interested individual (or individuals) to control the attitudes of groups of individuals through the use of suggestion and, consequently, to control their actions." *Propaganda* (New York: Holt, 1935, p. 89). It is clear that this postulation does not assume that the propagandist himself accepts the material or shares the attitudes he attempts to disseminate. I cannot accept the definition of propaganda offered by Doob in *Public Opinion and Propaganda* (New York: Holt, 1948, p. 240), since it seems almost indistinguishable from the more general concept of ideology.

to the spiritual cohesion of a ruling group which would lose its sense of control if it were conscious of the "real" state of affairs. It is therefore possible to raise the hypothesis that the balance of power may have served such "ideological" purposes. It may have been used to explain policies in terms of natural laws, in terms of moral rightness, or in terms of historical necessity if the symbol chosen to "put it over" was a sufficiently widely accepted one; indeed, if it was a symbol—even a metaphorical one—which the ruling groups themselves tended to accept. In this sense, the term "balance of power" would not serve a strictly propagandistic purpose, since the element of falsification yields to the element of self-deception.[2]

In a remarkable eighteenth-century essay the whole concept of the balance of power was criticized in these very terms. In his *Die Chimäre des Gleichgewichts von Europa*, Justi concluded that the balance of power theory is nothing but the ideological justification adopted by statesmen eager to hide their real motives, motives usually described by the term "aggression."...

. . . .

...he urges what he considers the real *raison d'être* of the usage, thus, incidentally, coming perilously close to characterizing the balance of power as a purely propagandistic device:

When a state which has grown more powerful internally is attacked...in order to weaken it, such action is motivated least of all by the balance of power. This would be

a war which is waged by the several states against the strong state for specific interests, and the rules of the balance of power will only be camouflage under which these interests are hidden.... States, like private persons, are guided by nothing but their private interests, real or imaginary, and they are far from being guided by a chimerical balance of power. Name one state which has paritcipated in a war contrary to its interests or without a specific interest, only to maintain the balance of power.[3]

The distinction between the propagandistic and ideological uses is thus a tenuous one. The "camouflage" is ideological only if the actors on the international stage are themselves convinced, to some extent, of the identity of "private interest" with a general need for balancing power *qua* power.

BALANCE OF POWER AS ANALYTICAL CONCEPT

At the opposite pole of the propaganda-oriented application of the term "balance of power" lies the user's intention to employ the term as a tool of analysis. It is in this area of intentions that the term rose to the status of a theory of international relations during the eighteenth and nineteenth centuries, no less than it has in our own era. It is also true, however, that in this area as well as in the other fields of intentions analyzed so far, not one but several of the verbal meanings of the term find application. Even as a tool of scholarly

[2] For a masterful analysis of this aspect of the balance of power, see Alfred Vagts, The Balance of Power: Growth of an Idea, *World Politics*, I (October, 1948), pp. 88–89, 100 ff. I have explored the ideological significance of the concept with respect to European diplomacy in the 1830's in my doctoral dissertation, *Belgium and the Balance of Power*, Columbia University Library.

[3] J. H. G. von Justi, *Die Chimäre des Gleichgewichts von Europa*, Altona, 1758, p. 65. Albert Sorel's estimate of the invocation of balancing terminology by statesmen is a similar one. Since he denies that balancing policies are deliberately chosen by diplomats and since he urges that only the search of unilateral hegemony motivates policy, he argues in fact that the use of the term by statesmen implies a disguised hankering for superiority and no more. Albert Sorel, *L'Europe et la Revolution française* (Paris: 1908), p. 34.

analysis the term has been used to mean "power politics," "equilibrium," "hegemony" and, finally a "universal law" of state conduct.

"The basic principle of the balance of power," wrote Réal de Curban, "is incontestable: the power of one ruler, in the last analysis, is nothing but the ruin and diminution of that of his neighbors, and his power is nothing but the weakness of the others."[4] And in a Hobbesian state of nature which was presupposed to exist among sovereign states no other conclusion seemed possible. This reasoning has led numerous writers to equate the balance of power with power politics or *Realpolitik* generally. The struggle for self-preservation in the state of nature implies the formation of alliances and mutually antagonistic blocs which in turn make negotiations in "good faith" a contradiction in terms. Power politics are the only discernible pattern in which balancing is an inherent process. As such, it is not separate from but identical with competitive power struggles. Consequently, in dispassionate analyses of international affairs the "balance" of power carries no significance other than that usually associated with "power politics," unrefined by any conception of equilibrium or deliberate balancing measures.[5]

Furthermore, the concept of evenly balanced power, or "equilibrium," finds frequent application as a tool of analysis. In the preceding discussion the equilibrium concept found application merely as a descriptive phrase implying no generalized behavior patterns in international relations. In the present context the reverse is true. Lasswell, in speaking of the "balancing process," for instance, assumes that under conditions of expected future violence—domestic as well as international—any increase in the coercion potential of one power unit will lead to a compensatory increase in the competing unit or units. Further increases on the part of one side will always bring corresponding increases on the part of its competitors, so that in effect a rough equality of power potential will always prevail, a factor which may make for either open conflict or induce fear of refraining from hostilities, depending on circumstances, the nature of the elites in question, and the accuracy of intelligence reports concerning the degree of "balancing." The analytical application of the equilibrium-meaning of the balance of power, in short, generalizes the basic assumption of the absence of international consensus and the consequent inherent presence of conflict into a pattern of balancing.

Carrying the equilibrium-meaning one step further results in the application of the balance of power concept as implying the search for hegemony. This application again finds its counterpart in the intentions of detached analysts striving for a generalized understanding of phenomena rather than for description. Spykman, ... clearly sets forth the assumptions of this approach. His argument is that the search for power by sovereign states is an end in itself, since conflict—actual or potential—is the only consistent pattern in relations between state units. While the search for power originally implied the desire for self-preservation, a generalized desire for power-seeking over a long period of time converts this process into an end in itself. On this level, the discussion of the balance of power is identical with power politics generally. As in the case of Lasswell's balancing

---

[4] Gaspard de Réal de Curban, *La science du gouvernement* (Paris: 1764, VI), p. 442.

[5] See, e.g., H. N. Brailsford and G. Lowes Dickinson, as quoted in Georg Schwarzenberger, *Power Politics*, London, 1940, p. 123, and also the author's own comments, which also tend to equate power politics with power balance.

process, however, the generalized process of competitive power-seeking must result in equilibrium if war is avoided—temporarily. But statesmen, as indicated above, seek a margin of safety in superiority of power and not in equality of power. Hence the search for equilibrium in effect is the search for hegemony, and the balance of power as an analytical concept becomes another term for the simultaneous search for preponderance of power by all the sovereign participants. No wonder Spykman exclaims that

He who plays the balance of power can have no permanent friends. His devotion can be to no specific state but only to balanced power. The ally of today is the enemy of tomorrow. One of the charms of power politics is that it offers no opportunity to grow weary of one's friends. England's reputation as *perfide Albion* is the inevitable result of her preoccupation with the balance of power.[6]

In this refined analysis, the balance of power comes to be considered as a special case—either in its equilibrium or its hegemony connotation—in the general pattern of power politics, though Spykman in the passage just cited again tends to use the two terms interchangeably.

The supreme attempt to use the balance of power as an analytical concept arises in the case of those writers who make the balance the essence of a theory of international relations. It is here that the balance attains the quality of a "law of history," ... Professors Morgenthau and Schuman, for instance, in giving the balance of power this extended meaning, go beyond the characterization of equilibrium and hegemony. They develop the thesis that it is inherent in the nature of a multi-state system based on sovereignty to engage in

mutually hostile policies, for whatever motives. In this process the search for balanced power, the need to form blocs and counterblocs to prevent the feared attainment of hegemony by one or the other of the participants in the conflict is a natural, if not instinctive, choice of policy. A group of revisionist states always lines up against a group of states devoted to the maintenance of the status quo in such a way that approximate balance results. So general is this pattern that it attains the quality of a historical law. And the characteristic feature of this law is that it does not necessarily assume a conscious intention on the part of statesmen to "balance power with power" in a sense which would imply the official acceptance of a balance of power theory by governments. Statesmen, to be sure, may be consciously motivated by balancing notions. But, if they are not, the policies which they would most logically adopt would be those consistent with the balance of power. As Professor Morgenthau indicates, if they fail to do so, they do not make "logical" policy and thereby violate historically proven and generalized modes of conduct. The distinctive feature about the balance of power applied as a tool of analysis, then, is its possible separation from the motivations of governments.

BALANCE OF POWER AS PRESCRIPTION

While the analytical application of the term does not imply conscious acceptance of balancing rules by governments, there is a large body of thought —historical and contemporary—which does insist that the balance of power is —or should be—a guiding principle for decision-making on the part of governments. It is this application of the term which makes use of the meaning defined above as "guide-and-system." Once more international relations are pic-

---

[6] Nicholas J. Spykman, *America's Strategy in World Politics* (New York: Harcourt, Brace and Co., 1942), pp. 1–21, 103–4.

tured, in one version, as being in the Hobbesian state of nature, so that survival dictates the formation of alliances among those states committed to "preserving the balance" against the onslaught of the state(s) allegedly seeking world or regional domination or, as the eighteenth-century writers put it, "universal monarchy." In this sense, the balance is a conscious guide dictating the rules of survival. In another sense, however, the world (or Europe, in the earlier writing) is represented as a "system" of states tied together by mutual interdependence, common institutions, and a common system of law (the law of nations), and the search for hegemony of a single member of this "system" was then represented as an attack upon the whole organic unit. The system was based on the continued independence of all members and their common will to resist the search for hegemony by any one of their number. The balance of power was inherent in the very system itself and also acted as a body of rules dictating the proper policies for preventing the attainment of hegemony, i.e., it acted as a "guide."

That Metternich subscribed in principle and in considerable detail to the theory of the balance of power as a guide to foreign policy-making is beyond any doubt. Consistent with his overall political philosophy of the value of historically sanctioned social and political traditions, of the need for preserving what the historical process had created and for protecting it against the fanaticism and stupidity of misguided men, i.e., the liberals, Metternich considered the balance of power as another of these time-hallowed doctrines, and as an international institution vital to the preservation of the total institutional status quo which he so cherished. As he wrote:

Politics is the science of the life of the state, on its highest level. Since isolated states no longer exist ... it is the society of states, this important condition of the contemporary world, which has to be watched carefully. Thus each state, in addition to its particular interests, has certain common interests, either with the totality of the other states or with certain groups among them. The great axioms of political science derive from the understanding of real political interests, of all states; the guarantee for their existence rests in these general interests, whereas particular interests ... only possess a relative and secondary value. History teaches that whenever the particular interests of one state are in contradiction with the general interest and whenever the latter is neglected or misunderstood, this condition ... is to be regarded as exceptional and pathological.... The modern world is characterized, in distinction to the old world, by a tendency of states to approach one another and to enter into the bonds of society in some manner; so that the resulting bond rests on the same foundations as the great society which developed in the shadow of Christianity. This foundation consists of the command of the Book of Books: "Do not do unto others what you would not have others do unto you." Applying this basic rule of all human associations to the state, the result is reciprocity, politically speaking, and its effect is ... : mutual respect and honest conduct. In the ancient world, politics sought pure isolation and practiced absolute egoism, without any control save common sense.... Modern history, however, shows us the application of the principle of solidarity and the balance of power offers us the drama of the unified efforts of several states in restraining the hegemony of a single state and limiting the expansion of its influence, and thus forcing it to return to public law.[7]

This formulation of international relations in general as necessary and close rapport between the states of Europe, which he regarded in the then custom-

---

[7] Metternich, *Aus Metternichs Nachgelassenen Papieren* (Vienna, 1882), I, pp. 32 ff., a section entitled, "Maxims on Which the Actions of My Political Career Have Been Based."

ary manner as so many atoms in a universe held together by Christian moral rules and the dictates of international law, and of the balance of power as the *ad hoc* regulating mechanism of this system, is in almost all respects identical with the formulation of Ancillon, of Castlereagh, of Brougham, and of Gentz. Thus Ancillon, Prussian court chaplain in the 1820's, tutor to Frederick William IV, and State Secretary for Foreign Affairs from 1832 until 1835, argued:

All forces are similar to the nature of expanding bodies; thus, in the society of large states in which law does not enjoy an external guarantee, we take as our point of departure the possible or even probable misuse of force. What will be the result? Mutual distrust, fear and restlessness, always recurring and always effective. Each state can have no other maxims in its external relations than these: whoever can do us damage through an excessive balance of power in his favor, or through his geographical position, is our natural enemy, but whoever in view of his position and forces is able to harm our enemy, is our natural friend. These simple maxims which the need for self-preservation has given to man, are and have been at all times the anchors on which all of politics rests.[8]

Nor was Castlereagh's understanding of the balance of power much different, even though he indicated that "my real and only object was to create a permanent counterpoise to the power of France in peace as well as in war." The Concert of Europe through its regular conferences was merely to be the consultative mechanism whereby the *ad hoc* balance could be maintained through timely negotiations.[9] However, the likelihood of the guide-and-system version of the balance implying different "rules for different states is here betrayed.

Gentz's theory of the balance of power was stated in his *Fragmente aus der neusten Geschichte des politischen Gleichgewichts in Europa* (1806), the purpose of which was to give the Austrian and British governments an excuse for unleashing a new war on Napoleon without having been attacked first. Gentz, it might be added, was in the pay of the British cabinet to produce writings of this type. He rejected the arguments that an exact equilibrium is impossible and that power cannot be measured as irrelevant to the system, since all the system requires is eternal vigilance that no state acquires enough power to overawe all of Europe.[10] Also, he thought that the certainty of a strong counterforce being mustered against the hegemony-seeker was a sufficient deterrent and that actual war would usually be unnecessary. And

Only when one or the other state, with open violence, invented pretexts, or artificially concocted legal titles undertakes enterprises which, directly or in their inevitable consequences, lead to the enslavement of its weaker neighbors, or to the constant endangering, gradual weakening and eventual demise of its stronger neighbors, only then there will come about a breach of the balance, according to the sound conceptions of the collective interest of a system of states; only then will the several states combine in order to prevent the hegemony of a single state, through a timely contrived counterweight.[11]

---

[8] Paul Haake, *J. P. F. Ancillon and Kronprinz Friedrich Wilhelm IV, von Preussen* (Munich, 1920), p. 40. Of Ancillon's own works, see his *Ueber den Geist der Staatsverfassungen und dessen Einfluss auf die Gesetzgebung* (Berlin, 1825), pp. 16–19, 313–14, 317–31, and *Tableau des révolutions du système de l'Europe* (Paris, 1806), IV, pp. 5–19.

[9] Sir Charles Webster, *British Diplomacy, 1813–1815*, London, 1921, pp. 62, 218; and Castlereagh's memorandum of October 30, 1814, for Alexander I, cited in Angeberg, *Les traités de Vienne*, Paris, 1864, pp. 399–401.
[10] Gentz, *Fragmente aus der neusten Geschichte des politischen Gleichgewichts in Europe* (St. Petersburg, 1806), pp. 1–8.
[11] *Ibid.*, pp. 10–14.

Yet Gentz opposed policies of partition and compensation as violating the true conservative character of the theory. Moreover, there could be no such thing as indifference to a given issue, since under the power rules all issues had to be of equal interest to all states in the system.[12] His comments on the right to intervene in the domestic affairs of other states are of the highest interest. Gentz urged that ideological distastes for internal changes elsewhere did not in themselves constitute a ground for balance of power intervention and war. But as soon as such changes had the necessary consequence of upsetting the balance of power, i.e., as soon as the new ideology seemed to suggest the search for hegemony, then the right to intervene existed, as in 1793.[13]

The case of Lord Brougham is a fascinating one for the study of the theory of the balance of power. In his essay on "The Balance of Power," written in 1903, he urged that the balance was the only tenable theory of international relations. He defined it in the same terms as Gentz and Ancillon and added:

Had it not been for that wholesome jealousy of rival neighbors, which modern politicians have learned to cherish, how many conquests and changes of dominion would have taken place, instead of wars, in which some lives were lost, not perhaps the most valuable in the community and some superfluous millions were squandered! How many fair portions of the globe might have been deluged in blood, instead of some hundreds of sailors fighting harmlessly on the barren plains of the ocean, and some thousands of soldiers carrying on a scientific and regular and quiet system of warfare in countries set apart for the purpose, and resorted to as the arena where the disputes of nations might be determined.

The old argument of the tacit federation of Europe, the common system of law and morals, and the need for the regulating mechanism of the balance to keep one of the "federated" states from absorbing the others is restated in full.[14] The principle, as well as the detailed application of the theory in its guide-and-system form, were stated by the young Brougham in the classical manner, and with unsurpassed and brief lucidity:

It is not then in the mere plan for forming offensive or defensive alliances; or in the principles of attacking a neighbor in order to weaken his power, before he has betrayed hostile views; or in the policy of defending a rival, in order to stay, in proper time, the progress of a common enemy; it is not in these simple maxims that the modern system consists. These are indeed the elements, the great and leading parts of the theory; they are the maxims dictated by the plainest and coarsest views of political expediency: but they do not form the whole system; nor does the knowledge of them ... comprehend an acquaintance with the profounder and more subtle parts of modern policy. The grand and distinguishing feature of the balancing theory, is the systematic form to which it reduces those plain and obvious principles of national conduct; the perpetual attention to foreign affairs which it inculcates; the constant watchfulness which it prescribes over every movement in all parts of the system; the subjection in which it tends to place all national passions and antipathies to the views of remote expediency; the unceasing care which it dictates of national concerns most remotely situated, and apparently unconnected with ourselves; the general union, which it has effected, of all the European powers in one connecting system —obeying certain laws and actuated, for the most part, by a common principle; in fine, as a consequence of the whole, the right of mutual inspection, now universally recognized among civilized states, in the appointment of public envoys and residents [sic]. This is the balancing theory.[15]

---

[12] *Ibid.*, ch. II.
[13] *Ibid.*, ch. IV.

[14] Brougham, *Works* (London, 1872), VIII, pp. 4–12.
[15] *Ibid.*, pp. 12–13, 33–38.

Intervention in domestic developments of other states, of course, is legal if the balance of power is really and truly threatened by these changes. The superiority of the balance to all ideological considerations, so plainly stated here, is especially striking. This principle he repeated in his "General Principles of Foreign Policy" (1843) in most emphatic terms:

But the mere circumstance of our preferring a democratic to an aristocratic or a monarchical to a republican scheme of government, can never afford any good ground for uniting with others who have the same preference, against a community or a league of states, whose views of national polity are of a contrary description.[16]

Hence the Holy Alliance—or the Western bloc against it after 1832—was not consistent with the rules of the balance. Not only is ideological intervention condemned, but Brougham urged that

It is the bounden duty of all rulers to discourage sentiments in their subjects leading to national enmities; and when a popular cry arises against any foreign people, a general clamor of war, there is no more sacred duty on the part of the government than to resist such a clamor and keep the peace in spite of it.[17]

In short, any manifestations of public opinion had to be rigorously excluded from policy-making under balancing rules, a sentiment heard more and more frequently in our present epoch.

Whether the balance of power is regarded merely as a set of rules to be applied to the preservation of the state or whether it is expanded into the defensive mechanism of some "system"— and by analogy the United Nations system might today be considered the successor to the European system postulated by the earlier writers—the rules laid down by Gentz and Brougham remain the same. The statesman who is anxious to preserve his state must have recourse to balancing principles in averting the hegemony of his rival. The perusal of the contemporary literature on this subject confirms this conclusion. George F. Kennan's *American Diplomacy* is merely the latest and best-known example of the continuing importance ascribed to balancing in rules international relations. And the fact that the examples cited concerned statesmen conscious of the balance as a motivating force underlines the possible importance of the concept as prescription.

. . . .

---

[16] *Ibid.*, pp. 70–71, 77, 79–80, 80–83.
[17] *Ibid.*, pp. 91–93, 100–2.

2 ● Factors Affecting Stability of the Balance of Power *

Robert E. Elder

The author received his Ph.D. from the University of Chicago in 1947. He has taught at Colgate University since 1946. He has contributed to the Western Political Quarterly, American Political Science Review, and the American Journal of International Law.

I

As the territorial boundary between the East and West begins to harden, there is some evidence that a balance of power, whether in fact or only in effect, soon will be established, with the Soviet Union and its satellites on one side and the United States and those nations which have accepted American economic aid or other forms of cooperation on the other.

With the freezing or stabilizing of the frontiers, the limits of peaceful expansion will have been reached, and it is quite likely that the efforts of the super powers then will be turned, momentarily at least, to consolidation of their positions within their respective spheres of influence.

This occurrence would follow the classic pattern of power politics, for it has been observed that in one stage of the struggle between great powers in a state of international anarchy—"that of alignment in preparation for the actual duel for supremacy" [1]—nations effect ententes and alliances which often have resulted in the formation of the opposing groups into what was recognized as an equilibrium or as a balance of power.

If one grants the probability of establishing an equilibrium or balance of power between the East and West, it would seem that the duration of any period of peace which such a balance might bring would depend upon the type of balance of power formed and other related factors which contribute to or detract from the stability of any given equilibrium.

Once a balance of power is established, it may be accepted as almost axiomatic that war is preferable to peace whenever a great power is threatened by an unfavorable breakdown of the balance. This is because any departure from equilibrium tends to lead to further conquest. It seems likely that only an abrupt and complete destruction of a balance could occur without war. The degree of stability of the Soviet-American balance of power, therefore, will help determine the immediacy of possible armed conflict and will affect the chances for peace.

II

When a balance of power is multipolar in nature, involving a large num-

[1] Arthur W. Spencer, "The Organization of International Force," *American Journal of International Law,* IX (1915), p. 64.

* *The Western Political Quarterly,* III (1950), 155–60. Reprinted by permission.

ber of states, each possessing a moderate degree of strength, each interested in preserving its own security, each willing under certain conditions to shift its position in the balance for the sake of maintaining the equilibrium, a stable balance of power exists. If one state or complex power unit becomes aggressive and seeks to gain increasing power, other states or complex power units combine against this threat to their security.

When the number of states or power units in balance is small, when there is considerable disparity in the strength of the states within the power units, and when states are bound by permanent alliances or rigid neutrality obligations, the degree of stability is low. As a rule, there are few states available to shift position, and these are unlikely to do so because of lack of strength, because of alliances or because of rigid neutrality.

When there is disparity in power between the weights on either side of the scales no equilibrium can exist in fact. Any factor which contributes to this disparity decreases the stability of a balance of power. For example, if other factors cannot compensate, the sudden development of a new military technique, an ideological or economic movement which tends to regroup nations, or the entrance of a powerful new state into the balance affects the stability of an equilibrium. If the new element is introduced slowly, there is opportunity for the adjustment of other factors and the balance may be maintained.

The power disparity factor has become more important in recent years with the increased mobility of military forces and the resultant decrease in the defensive value of geographic separation. At one time a mountainous frontier or an ocean channel was a real military asset. Modern weapons of war can now overreach most geographic defenses. It is true that modern means of communication and transportation make possible more rapid movement to the defense of an attacked state, but the speed with which an aggressor can overrun a weak state tends to be greater than the speed with which other states can rally to the defense.

The stability of any balance of power is affected by the adjustability of the factors which contribute to the equilibrium, because the character of even a relatively stable balance of power is continuously changing. If all factors in a given balance were constant except one, the variation of a single factor would tend to upset the equilibrium, but possibly at a slow rate. Where a number of factors are variable, it is possible that adjustments will take place which will counterbalance change, but it is just as likely that the balance will be lost more rapidly.

When a great disparity in power exists among states participating in an equilibrium, the stability of the equilibrium is decreased, since there is a tendency for weaker states to be drawn into the orbit of one or another of the stronger states. This leads to polarization into rival alliances and to the formation of complex power units. Such a development necessarily reduces independence of action by the smaller individual states. It is upon this independence of action by several simple or complex power units that much of the stability of an equilibrium must be predicated. Carl Friedrich, among others, has placed great emphasis upon the necessity of at least a third power unit in a balance to serve as a makeweight between the two major units in equilibrium. A bi-polar balance is considerably less stable, other factors being equal, than a tri-polar or a multi-polar equilibrium.

The geographic area encompassed by a balance of power should not be overlooked in computing the stability of the equilibrium. A local balance of power which shows elements of instability may be redressed by the entrance of neighboring states into the equilibrium. Similarly, a continental balance which is failing may be reinvigorated by the entrance into the balance of a state or a power unit from another continent. However, where an equilibrium is global in nature, already involving most of the important states in the world, there is no longer an outside territorial force which can intervene to maintain the balance of power.

Also valuable in calculating the stability of any balance of power are an accurate knowledge of the degree of rationality used by responsible government leaders of the states or power units in balance to compute their own strength and that of their possible adversaries, and an accurate knowledge of the degree of pragmatism with which they are prepared to act in maintaining the equilibrium. Inaccurate computations of strength lead to armament races, war, and breakdown of balance of power. Lack of pragmatism in shifting the position or the policy of a state to support the balance, likewise, will endanger the stability of an equilibrium.

III

In the Soviet-American balance of power there is at the present time relative equality rather than great disparity between the weights on either side of the balance. Temporarily, perhaps, the balance lies with the United States and its allies on the basis of American industrial production, leadership in research on the atom and hydrogen bombs, and the American surface navy. This situation is counterbalanced by the size of the Soviet army, the Soviet submarine power, the greater dispersal of Soviet industry, the entrance of the People's Republic of China into the equilibrium

and the fact that the Soviet Union now has the atom bomb and may soon have the hydrogen bomb. [*Editor's Note: This article was written before the advent of IRBM's, ICBM's, and Sputniks.*]

. . . .

Many states are involved in the Soviet-American equilibrium, the effective scope of which is global, with the United States, Japan, Western Europe, Latin America, and most of the British Commonwealth of Nations pitted against the Soviet Union, Eastern Europe, and the People's Republic of China. There is a great disparity of power among the states in this balance. The result has been the formation of two complex power units, each dominated by a super power. This has curtailed independence of action by lesser states. Worse yet, there remains for the time being no state or complex power unit capable of entering into the present bi-polar balance to play the role of balancer between the East and West in order to create a more stable tripolar equilibrium. The most serious threats to the stability of the Soviet-American balance of power are its bipolarity and global nature.

How accurate the leaders of the Soviet Union and of the United States are in calculating each other's strength —both offensive and defensive—is problematical. However, the Soviet Union, with its small ruling elite, is likely to be more pragmatic in its attempts to maintain the equilibrium or to attain a favorable balance of power than the United States, which must be responsive to public opinion. The men who make American policy are not less pragmatic than those who form Soviet policy, but the policies which American planners recommend must be modified to stay within the limits of change possible in American public opinion. Since American public opinion is based, in some measure, on emotional rather than on rational grounds, American foreign policy incorporates moral or other highly subjective considerations. This may decrease the stability of the balance of power. However, if one grants that the United States has a slightly favorable balance of power and, for reasons of public opinion, will not engage immediately in war—even though feeling a present superiority and sensing that time is on the side of the Soviet Union —the stability of the Soviet-American equilibrium will be temporarily increased by the decreasing disparity in power between the weights on either side of the balance. Although the global bi-polar nature of the Soviet-American balance of power is a threat to the stability of the equilibrium, this is partially counteracted by a slight American margin of power and a lack of complete pragmatism in American foreign policy.

The balance of power which now exists between the East and the West, either in fact or in effect, is neither so lacking in stability that its sudden collapse will avert war nor so stable that war will be permanently postponed. At best, it would seem that this balance can preserve peace only temporarily and thus—unless implemented by strenuous efforts to sublimate the Soviet-American balance into a stronger international organization—it is in no manner different from preceding balances which have been of only passing value as instruments of world order.

XII • Psychological Methods

Psychological methods in international relations are designed to serve two purposes. Domestically, they rally the people of a country in support of the policies of their government, thus adding strength to the pursuit of those policies. Internationally, such policies are designed to have certain consequences within other states. These desired consequences may be of two types: negative, to create internal dissensions and weaken the support which policies of other governments enjoy on the part of their people; and positive, to promote and foster policies which are advantageous to the state employing the psychological methods.

The use of psychological means is not a new development in international relations (see the article by Padover in this chapter) although its scope depends on the availability of communications channels. The only real innovation is "the frank recognition of propaganda as a regular branch of government alongside economic and military departments." [1] Bismarck used the press in order to bring about a certain state of affairs between Prussia (Germany) and France. During the First World War, stories of atrocities, reports of starvation due to blockade, and even President Wilson's Fourteen Points were designed, in whole or in part, to bring about changes in the policies of important countries. The Second World War saw an extension and refinement of such methods, and in the contemporary Cold War period, its use has proliferated. As Bolsover's article makes clear, whether psychology can be as effective as other methods will depend largely on the skill with which it is applied and the responsiveness of the audience to which these psychological efforts are addressed. (On the latter point, White's article is very significant.) It must also be stressed that psychology is unlikely to replace policy in terms of effectiveness: what is *said* is not as important as what is *done*. It is perhaps best to speak of psychological methods as supplementary to other policies rather than as substitutes for them. They can help attain certain ends if their employment is skillfully combined with the use of other methods of policy.

---

[1] John B. Whitton, "Propaganda in Cold Wars," *Public Opinion Quarterly*, XV (1951), 142–44.

The term "psychological methods" refers to a variety of activities. The first of these, obviously, is propaganda—the manipulation of facts and symbols to attain desired results in the minds of the audience. The dividing line between "propaganda" and "psychological warfare" is shadowy, if indeed it exists at all. The element of hostility is perhaps more marked in the latter than the former. Still another term used in this context is "subversion." While subversion may take overt physical forms, its relevance to the present discussion is that it represents an attempt to enlist individuals and groups within countries to work for the advantage and interests of another country.

For a number of reasons, democratic societies find themselves at a disadvantage in psychological contests with non-democratic adversaries. The pursuit of effective psychological warfare, as a special committee reported to President Eisenhower during his first term, is based on certain preconditions. These include fanaticism, utmost flexibility and maneuverability, and money, with no holds barred and no questions asked. An inspection of this list will reveal that autocratic regimes are more likely to satisfy these requirements, with the possible exception of money, than are democracies. Furthermore, there are no democratic equivalents to the well-disciplined Communist parties which are found in most countries of the world. Finally, an autocratic government can always conceal its failures, while a democratic country finds it impossible to do so.[2]

Since the use of psychological methods is essentially an exercise in communications, one may suggest that the crucial questions to be answered about it are contained in the formula "*Who* communicates *what* to *whom*, through what *media*, and with what *results?*" The following selections do not provide exhaustive answers to these questions, but they will serve to outline some of the potentialities and problems of the use of psychological methods in international relations.

---

[2] Arthur Krock, "Why we are losing the Psychological War," *New York Times Magazine*, August 8, 1957, p. 12 ff.

1 • Psychological Warfare and Foreign Policy *

Saul K. Padover

The author, Professor of Politics and History and Dean of the School of Politics of the New School for Social Research, has had a broad background of service in the United States Government, as editorial writer for the newspaper PM, *and visiting professor at the University of Paris. His publications include* The Washington Papers *(1955) and* French Institutions: Values and Policies *(1954).*

"What is so furiouse or mad a thinge as a vaine sounde of wordes of the best sort and most ornate, contayning neither connynge nor sentence?"
SIR THOMAS ELYOT, The Boke of the Governour, 1534

. . . .

...Of psychological warfare one can say that it is neither psychology nor war. The term covers a field of activity in the realm of politics, foreign affairs, communications, publicity and propaganda. In essence, it means the use of all available media of communications for the purpose of destroying the enemy's will to fight.

Modern psychological warfare is more inclusive than old-fashioned propaganda in its sphere of operations, and less naive in its faith in the efficacy of one-sidedness and calculated falsehood. It tends to place some confidence in the teachings of the sciences of man, notably social psychology and cultural anthropology. It tries to understand the audience and acts on the assumption that words alone do not win wars or campaigns. To be effective, words must be coupled with action. Hence psychologi-

cal warfare is closely tied to political or military policy.

In the United States, as elsewhere, psychological warfare is a part of foreign policy....

. . . .

Psychological warfare, about which we are going to hear more and more as the Cold War intensifies (and still more if and when general shooting begins), is not merely an exercise of the vocal chords or the printing press. Physical devices can also be used to achieve propaganda effects, as is illustrated by the recent case of the right arm of the Jesuit missionary, St. Francis Xavier. When St. Francis died on his way to China in 1552, his fellow-Jesuits sliced off his right arm and sent it to Rome. In 1949, the sacred relic, well-preserved in a gold and glass case, was sent by the Catholic Church to Japan to help General MacArthur fight communism there. *Life* magazine, awestruck by the propagandistic possibilities of the holy bone, reported:

---

* *The American Scholar*, XX–XXI (1950–52), 151–61. Reprinted by permission.

An ancient, awe-inspiring relic last month took its place in the mounting struggle between paganism and Christianity in Japan. ... There was good reason for the arm's return. St. Francis himself had had plenty of opposition from the Buddhists during his campaign to Christianize Japan. Now, in a different form, opposition was still strong. ... Communism was gaining more converts than Christianity.... General MacArthur asked for more Bibles to aid in the fight and the Catholics were exhibiting Xavier's arm to vast crowds in many cities... to dramatize their campaign for converts.

World War II, when the phrase "psychological warfare" became current, saw two new developments. One was the use of loudspeakers and other devices, such as leaflet bombs, on the field of battle, in order to induce the enemy to surrender. The other was the large-scale and systematic application of radio to political warfare. In terms of the history of war, this young medium of communication which can encircle the earth and cross all man-made borders was as much of a new weapon as the atomic bomb. Today this "whispering gallery," as Woodrow Wilson described radio, is the main instrument of ideological warfare and propaganda. It is aimed essentially at civilian audiences over the face of the earth.

Both the Americans and the Russians are fully engaged at present in the battle of the vocal chords. Sound is reinforced by print and picture. It is a war to which the average, even reasonably well-informed American has paid too little attention. Yet in its implications and repercussions, the psychological warfare now being waged may be at least as important as the fighting in Korea.

No one is more keenly aware of the value of political progaganda than are the Communist Russians. They know that underlying the diplomatic-political-economic-military aspects of the global cold war, is the ideological struggle, the conflict for human loyalties and beliefs. They are alert to the possibilities of using human emotions, hopes and fears and aspirations, as prime political ammunition. They give the impression of being convinced that, in the end, the struggle between East and West will not be won so much on the field of battle as in the hearts and minds of men.

The Soviet Union's propaganda machine, for use both at home and abroad, is one of the most formidable instruments for the shaping of beliefs in the world today. It employs hundreds of thousands of professionals at home. Abroad it has fervent and devoted allies who repeat the Soviet arguments and carry out its policies. When one keeps in mind that there are more than twenty million Communist party members outside the Soviet Union, not to mention the tens of millions of their fellow-travelers, one begins to realize what an immense pro-Russian propaganda force exists. Everywhere and at all times these people propagate the line laid down by the Kremlin. They may, indeed, be regarded as the Soviet Union's powerful foreign legion in psychological warfare.

What do they say in their propaganda? As is well known, the United States has become Moscow's chief devil. Against America, Soviet propaganda follows three main themes:

1. U. S. is corrupt, run by Big Business.
2. U. S. is imperialist, determined to dominate the world economically.
3. U. S. is a warmonger, out to destroy "the people's democracies."

The Communists' anti-American propaganda is not mere hate or willfulness or words spoken out of ignorance. On the contrary, it is a long-range strategic offensive against the free world; it is part of the far-reaching policy of undermining the United States even before a single bullet is fired, and thereby substantially weakening the one power capable of resisting or blocking Communist imperialism. In other words, the Kremlin propaganda line is not a conventional name-calling affair, but an integral instrument of total aggression on a global scale.

Consider, for example, the theme that the United States is a warmonger. Propaganda-wise, nothing could be more clever. As a smoke screen, it enables communism to cloak its planned aggressions as a supposed defense against so-called American warmongering machinations. Thus in the case of Korea, the Soviet and Chinese line has been that imperialist Americans with the aid of South Koreans invaded the innocent "people's democracy" of North Korea. This is the well-known technique of the Big Lie. As George Orwell put it, in the Communist language night is day, black is white, war is peace, brutality is love. This particular Big Lie about United States aggression is of particular importance with regard to the future, for it is a strategic maneuver intended to destroy either America's will to action or its moral ground before action. Should, for example, Communist aggressions and provocations become so intolerable as to move the United States to take armed steps, the Russian will be in a position to announce to the world a triumphant, "I told you so."

. . . .

We can now attempt to evaluate the whole psychological warfare program from the point of view of its effectiveness as a foreign policy instrument. In other words, does it achieve what it attempts to do?

One must emphasize that psychological warfare in itself is not a policy, but an instrument. These are things it cannot do. It cannot, in the long run, get away with systematic falsehoods. It cannot impose an alien system of values on one that already exists. It cannot alter basic institutions or satisfy physical needs or permanently substitute words for deeds.

But properly used—which means always in coordination with action—it can encourage friends and discourage enemies. It can undermine and disrupt. It can neutralize the potentially hostile or wavering. Tied to military action, it can help to confuse the enemy, damage his morale, put him on the defensive. In wartime, for example, it can make systematic appeals to the latent nationalisms in the Soviet orbit and stimulate discontent that would lead to disruptive action.

Looked at from the foreign policy point of view, the American psychological warfare program has not been effective. Indeed, quite the contrary. Two chief misconceptions are largely responsible for the failure. One is the idea that psychological warfare or propaganda is just like advertising. The other is that foreigners think, or wish to think, like Americans.

. . . .

. . . There is in the United States a tendency to disregard the basic interests and outlooks of the foreign audiences to which America addresses itself. The American inclination is to assume that what is good for the United States is good for everybody. Effective propaganda, however, must take into account the hopes, demands and expectations, not of the propagandist, but of the audience. Instead of telling a Malayan, for example, about the daily life of a worker in the Ford factory, or a Turk about the Christmas spirit in America, it would be more fruitful to inform him of his own plight and what American democracy is ready to do for him.

Even in Western Europe, American propaganda fails in its effects when it describes—truthfully, to be sure—the gleaming kitchens, labor-saving devices, and assorted gadgets which the middle-class housewife of the United States has at her disposal. Since the overwhelming majority of European housewives could not possibly afford or ever hope to possess such equipment, the result is either disbelief or resentment. This is particularly true in our propaganda to the Russians, whose standard of living is so low compared to that of the United States that they simply cannot conceive the vastness of the difference. Consequently, statements of American superiority in material things sound to the Russians like sheer lies. The Russians plainly cannot imagine that such things as carpets in every home and cars in workingmen's garages could possibly be true. This is clearly brought out by the comment of Moscow's *New Times:*

What the Voice of America has to say about workers' housing conditions is no less phony and unconvincing.... He [the commentator] wants to assure us that Americans—all Americans!—live like princes. Here is the rosy picture he paints: "The American worker," he says, "lives either in a separate house or in a separate apartment with kitchen and bathroom. Very many married people prefer to live in the suburbs in a detached cottage with a garden." And he further asserts that the 25 per cent of earnings paid in rent includes gas and telephone and even carpet-cleaning. Carpets, of course, are mentioned here not by chance. The Voice of America wants to insinuate that carpets are as common a thing in America as gas rings.[1]

Even the most truthful statement can boomerang, if it is not geared to the range of the audience's beliefs and expectations.

All reports from Europe and Asia indicate that the United States has failed to win over the masses of the people in those parts of the world. This is notably true in Asia, where our policy-makers

have failed to take into proper account the revolutions that are now convulsing that continent. Leadership of the revolutionary movements there has been virtually abandoned to the Communists. Despite all that, as Reinhold Niebuhr pointed out, "The American nation is grossly overestimating its moral standing in Asia." The truth is, the United States has little prestige left there. Washington's psychological warfare program has hardly made a dent among the masses of the colored and undernourished peoples.

It is clear that the best radio transmitters in the world and the most far-flung organization of information specialists are no substitute for policy and leadership. United States policy has been singularly deficient in this moment of world crisis. It has been largely negative: *against* communism, *against* Sovietism, *against* dictatorship. But *for* what? To a world in fear and in need, a humanity in the agony of upheaval, the rich and powerful United States has offered no inspirational ideal or positive social program. As Maury Maverick once said: "You cannot fill the baby's bottle with liberty." Faced with a Communist-led ideological challenge, we have offered no Wilsonian Fourteen-Points program, no Rooseveltian Four-Freedoms appeal. And it is an axiom that you cannot beat something with nothing.

In consequence, our psychological warfare, even as our foreign policy, which it reflects, suffers from intellectual and spiritual emptiness. Perforce it must continue to do so until such a time as the United States shall have formulated a positive program for action, an ideal around which to rally men. Short of that, we are in danger of talking only to those of our friends who already share our expectations, and of losing the great majority of mankind that is still searching for a hope and a vision.

[1] Note: Compare this to Soviet comments concerning the American Exhibit in Moscow, 1959.

2 • Soviet Ideology and Propaganda *

George H. Bolsover

The author is head of the School of Slavonic Studies at the University of London and one of Britain's leading Soviet experts.

In keeping with their belief that although intellectual and cultural activity arises out of the social system it can and must be used to influence social development, the Soviet leaders have created a vast propaganda machine to spread their ideas and theories both at home and abroad. There is no Soviet Ministry of Propaganda. But the Communist Party has a widely ramified network of propaganda bodies ranging from the administration of propaganda and agitation of its Central Committee through provincial and district departments of propaganda and agitation to individual propagandists and agitators in primary party organizations. Their function is to explain and interpret Soviet and party policy to the general public and particularly to ordinary party members who are called on to serve as a leaven among the non-party masses. Mainly through them and the party groups which are expected to act as the leading force in all State and public institutions, organizations and bodies, the Soviet leaders are able to ensure that the press and wireless and all other visual and oral means of spreading the written and spoken word will be preaching the same views about the same things from Brest Litovsk to Vladivostok and from Murmansk to Alma-Ata. The Chief Administration for Literary and Publishing Affairs and the use of a single Soviet news agency to collect and distribute news, particularly foreign news, provide further powerful aids to uniformity.

The Communist Party also has an elaborate system of party schools and courses giving instruction in Marxism-Leninism. Marxism-Leninism is even made a compulsory subject for study and examination in all Soviet universities and higher education institutions. The output of party and political literature is on an unbelievable scale. For example, in spite of the war and although not published until 1938, *The Short History of the Communist Party of the Soviet Union* has already been issued in thirty-one million copies in every conceivable language. Writers, scholars and all other members of the Soviet intelligentsia are expected to use their talents and energies not only to pursue their own particular specialities but to pursue them in a way which will conform to and promote Marxist-Leninist ideas and help the Soviet leaders to make the Soviet people more ideologically aware of and therefore more

---

* *International Affairs,* the Journal of The Royal Institute of International Affairs, London, XXIV (1948), 176–80. Reprinted by permission.

intent on fulfilling the tasks set before them. "In Soviet society," we are told in *Bolshevik*, No. 21, November 1946, "science and the arts collaborate with the policy of the Party and State and under the guidance of this policy... serve... the cause of building communism... only if guided by this policy can literature, the arts, science and philosophy fully achieve their real purpose,... and play an active role in the creation of new forms of life." As the Central Committee of the Communist Party made brutally clear in August and September 1946 in its decrees on literature, drama and the cinema, etc., all forms of intellectual activity in the Soviet Union must serve political ends and there can be no art or science for its own sake or for the sake of beauty and truth.

Soviet propaganda to the outside world is naturally on a somewhat less massive scale than propaganda at home. But it pours out in a broad and steady stream through the press, the wireless, the Soviet news agency and various less obvious channels, giving maximum currency to Soviet views and theories and inspiring maximum criticism of everything and everybody thought to stand in their way. Some of it is crude and unskilfully angled, particularly for more sophisticated audiences. But those responsible for it probably feel that the masses to whom it is mainly directed will prefer bluntness to subtlety.

During the early years of the war Soviet propaganda was carefully coordinated with and subordinated to the needs of the fronts and seemed to acquire a much less ideological flavour. This encouraged some foreign observers who confused tactics with strategy to believe that the Soviet revolution had already passed its climax and that the post-war period would see the capitalist and Soviet systems co-operating more and more closely and influencing each other more and more profoundly until the worst features of both had disappeared and each had grown very like the other. But since the end of the war Soviet leaders have been making it increasingly clear that they still base their policy on a strictly Marxist-Leninist analysis of world development and have been giving their propaganda a more and more stridently ideological tone. Their view of the general world situation is simple and follows logically from dialectical and historical materialist principles. They continue to think in terms of a struggle for mastery between what they regard as the rising forces of socialism and the declining and decaying forces of capitalism. They hold that the war has strengthened the forces of socialism partly by demonstrating the strength and stability of Soviet socialism, partly by increasing the influence of Communist Parties, particularly in the States of Eastern Europe, and partly by encouraging the struggle of colonial peoples for freedom and independence. Similarly, it has weakened the forces of capitalism by leading to the defeat and overthrow of Nazi Germany, fascist Italy and imperialist Japan. But capitalism continues on a wide scale and remains powerful, and the Soviet leaders believe that the laws of its development will lead it to resist the rising forces of socialism, and try to overcome its inherent contradictions by circumscribing the working classes politically, intensifying imperialism, and opposing the Soviet Union as the home and bulwark of socialism. In their view this calls for action by the anti-capitalist and anti-imperialist forces both on an international and national scale and for unremitting efforts to uncover and sharpen the struggle for mastery and to make people aware of it. The result is that they bitterly oppose nonrevolutionary socialists and trade unionists who refuse to act on the theory of the class war and continue to believe in the policy of slow and gradual transition from capitalism to socialism.

One of the major themes of present Soviet propaganda has been the immense political, economic and cultural superiority of Soviet Socialism over Western bourgeois Capitalism and the need for carrying the October Revolution to completion by pressing on with the transformation of Soviet Socialism into Soviet Communism. This has led, on the one hand, to increasing stress on Soviet patriotism and to mounting attacks on imitation or praise of the West and, on the other hand, to efforts to root out what are described as "capitalist survivals in people's minds" and nationalist ideas of the traditional kind, both of which are said to be retarding the movement of the Soviet Union towards communism. These "capitalist survivals" include trying to take from the community more than is given to it, laziness, lack of discipline at work, lack of concern for socialist property, selfishness, self-indulgence, and nationalist ideas which might serve to disunite the Soviet peoples. The stress on Soviet patriotism has also been accompanied by frequent assertions that the Soviet Union is the leader of the progressive forces of humanity and enjoys tremendous prestige and support among ordinary folk everywhere and, conversely, that any opponent or critic of Soviet policy is a reactionary opposed to progress.

A second major theme of present Soviet propaganda has been praise and support for the new régimes which are developing in the countries of Eastern Europe. Their "people's front" Governments, based largely on a communist-socialist bloc, are regarded as Governments of a new type and, as such, more truly democratic than Western bourgeois Governments. In Soviet eyes they give the clearest proof of their democratic and progressive character by na-tionalizing industry, breaking up big estates and sharing them among the peasantry, weakening and wherever possible destroying opposition parties, pursuing a pro-Soviet policy, and resisting what are considered to be imperialist penetration and control by capitalist countries like the United States. This campaign of support for the new régimes in Eastern Europe is closely linked with the All-Slav movement, which has no real basis in Marxist-Leninist ideology, though it has now come to be an important aspect of Soviet propaganda.

A third major theme of present Soviet propaganda has been the intensification of capitalist imperialism with its internal strains and its fierce hostility to the Soviet Union and the consequent need for "peace-loving" folk everywhere to support the "peace-policy" of the Soviet Union. The Soviet leaders regard events in Indonesia and Indo-China as proof that the imperial and colonial Powers have no intention of relaxing their grip on their subject peoples. They even interpret British policy in India and Burma, not as an abandonment of empire, but as clever and sinister manoeuvring designed to bolster up the imperial connection. They also believe that within the capitalist world the United States is the rising Power and Britain and her empire a declining Power, and that the United States will find herself becoming increasingly imperialist and driven to look for overseas markets and sources of raw materials partly at Britain's expense. They feel that she is already facing a serious crisis of overproduction and is striving to meet it in advance by expedients like the Marshall Plan, which they regard as a scheme not so much for trying to make Europe economically healthy again as for turning her into a field for American exports and economic exploitation. At the same time they retain their old fear that in spite of its internal rivalries and crises the capitalist world may try to find a temporary solution of its internal contradictions by joining forces for an attack on the Soviet Union and the new régimes in Eastern Europe. They see the United States in possession of the atom bomb and American policy falling more and more under what they consider to be the dictation of the military and the monopolists and establishing its influence at sensitive strategic points like Greece and Turkey, where it supports régimes which the Soviet Government castigates as reactionary and hostile to itself. They also believe that the British Government is always ready to support American policy in blocking the Soviet Union and trying to undermine the new and pro-Soviet régimes in Eastern Europe, and they even suspect the existence of an Anglo-American military alliance partly based on an agreement over spheres of influence in various parts of the world. They similarly interpret the Marshall Plan as an attempt to build up a Western anti-Soviet bloc of nations with a resurrected Germany as the spearhead of an anti-Soviet policy. All this feeds their fear of a joint capitalist crusade against the Soviet Union, inspired and led by an increasingly imperialist United States. It was not for nothing that in May 1947 Generalissimo Stalin emphasized in his interview with Mr. Harold Stassen that the American and German economic systems were identical.

A fourth major theme of present Soviet propaganda has been criticism of the leaders of the Western European Socialist Parties and the British Labour Party, whom the Soviet authorities accuse of acting as capitalist hirelings and traitors to the working classes. Soviet policy has aimed at co-operation and joint action between communists and socialists on both a national and international plane against reactionaries and all the forces of the Right. But socialist leaders like Blum, Attlee, Bevin, Morrison and Saragat have refused to agree to the reproduction of the East European pattern of development in Western Europe and have preferred instead to hold the communists at arm's length and to adhere to the traditional social-democratic policy of a slow gradual transition from capitalism to socialism. The inevitable result has been that Soviet propaganda has revived the old Bolshevist charge that the right-wing socialist leaders of the West are betraying socialism and helping the capitalists to maintain their position by mitigating the class struggle and splitting the forces of the Left.

An examination of the main principles of the guiding ideology of Stalin and his colleagues cannot bring much comfort to those who may still hope for a swift and easy solution of present-day world problems. But it should at least contribute to a clearer realization of the ideas and motives which inspire the Soviet Government, help to dispel the view that Soviet policy is enigmatic and incomprehensible, and enable Soviet pronouncements about the possibility of co-operation between different economic and social systems to be fitted into their general ideological setting. It has sometimes been argued that Stalin and his colleagues no longer believe in the ideology which they preach and merely use it as an instrument for maintaining their power at home and extending their influence abroad. This is a tempting theory if only because it seems to reduce the fundamental problems which confront us to problems of power politics and suggests the possibility of solving them by various international "deals" among the Big Three or at least the Bigger Two. But Stalin at any rate has been speaking and writing in terms of dialectical and historical materialism for the past half century, and it would be incredible if his thinking had been cast in entirely different terms. This suggests that it would be mistaken and dangerous to assume that he no longer believes in dialectical and historical materialism, especially as Soviet policy, which makes nonsense if interpreted in terms of a merely cynical desire to retain power, becomes much more coherent and intelligible if interpreted in terms of Marxism-Leninism in its present form.

3 • The New Resistance to International Propaganda *

Ralph K. White

The author, a former member of the Department of Psychology at Cornell and Stanford Universities, has more recently been professionally concerned with the propaganda aspects of the "cold war." His special field of competence is the analysis of Soviet propaganda.

The world is more and more tired of "propaganda." This is the fundamental, all-embracing fact which every propagandist must face, and the implications of which he must recognize, if he is even to have an entree into the minds of those who are not already emotionally on his side. The psychological resistances of a skeptical, propaganda-weary world must be respected and intelligently taken into account; they cannot be simply battered down.

American propagandists have been from the beginning more aware of these resistances than their Communist opponents have been. Recent evidence, however, suggests that they should be given even more weight than they have been given in the past. There is accumulating evidence that the special antagonism felt by neutralists toward "propaganda" coming from either side in the present East-West conflict is the greatest single obstacle to our effectiveness, and that the greatest single factor in our being able to beat the Communists at their own propaganda game will be our ability to understand this neutralist skepticism and to see its practical implications.

Recent evidence, in other words, suggests that the following propositions are, if anything, more true today than ever before:

First, our Soviet opponents have lost more than most Americans realize by their almost continual use of the battering-ram technique. The idea prevailing in some quarters that we lose by being less crude, less repetitious, less "emotional" than the Russians is in the main a dangerous misconception. Second, the chief weakness of our own propaganda is not, as some Americans assume, that we are too gentlemanly to descend to Soviet tactics and "fight fire with fire." It is that—at least in what we say to the non-Communist world—we too often give the impression of being "propagandistic." Third, the psychological resistances which the Communists fail to batter down by sheer crude repetition are equally incapable of being circum-

* *Public Opinion Quarterly*, XVI (1952), 539–51. Reprinted by permission.

vented by subtlety or deviousness. The way into the heart of the skeptical neutralist lies not through artifice but through candor.

This does not mean that on the most essential points, such as the danger of Soviet aggression or the necessity of collective strength to deter Soviet aggression, we need to soft-pedal our own convictions. It does not mean that we need to have any sense of guilt or apology in our role as propagandists—in the better sense of that word, involving only a large-scale effort to persuade or convince. (Probably there are few listeners to the Voice of America who do not take it for granted that it is a propaganda arm of the American Government in this non-condemnatory sense of the word propaganda. Of course we are propagandists.)

It does mean two things. First, our *actions* must be in line with our words. The propaganda of the deed is more potent than the propaganda of the word, and the propaganda of the word is effective in direct proportion to the deeds which it is able to publicize. As Secre-

tary Acheson has put it, "what is even more important than what we say to the world is how we conduct ourselves, at home and abroad. The force of example and action is the factor which finally determines what our influence is to be."

Second, it means that our words will be most effective—at least in what we say to the non-Communist world—when the *manner* of our effort to persuade and convince is modest, reasonable, discriminating, sensitive to the kinds of skepticism existing in the minds of any particular audience, and prepared to meet that skepticism candidly and factually, as neighbor might talk to neighbor. It means that we are most effective when we depart freely, wherever the facts warrant it, from a simple black-and-white picture of the world, when we avoid all of the stock ballyhoo techniques of the radio or television advertiser as well as the manners of the table-pounding orator and the finger-wagging schoolmarm, when, instead, we cultivate the highest standards of journalism.

. . . .

XIII · Economic Policies

At a time when weapons of physical destruction have become so enormous that violent resolutions of conflict become less and less rational, statesmen naturally turn their attention to other means of conducting international relations. Diplomacy, various policies suggested by balance of power considerations, and psychological warfare have been discussed in preceding chapters. Economic policies provide another alternative. As in the case of psychological means, economic policies may be (and are) employed in various ways and for varying reasons. They are apt to be most effective when they are combined with the use of other methods of policy.

Because of Dr. Abbott's thorough and specific discussion of certain types of economic policies which are used in international relations, a lengthy introduction seems unnecessary. Since his topic is that of "economic penetration," he concentrates on such activities as cartels, industrial penetration, the interchange of patents, the uses of government corporations, and foreign loans. Other methods of economic policies in international relations include preemptive buying and stockpiling, tariffs, subsidies and dumping, embargoes and boycotts, quotas and licenses, the use of exchange controls, and even forgery and sabotage!

Professor Abbott makes a very important point when he says that every type of international commercial transaction can have both political and economic implications. But it would be a mistake to explain all commercial actions in purely political terms, just as it would be erroneous to disregard the political element altogether. It should also be noted that certain economic policies may not be directed against another country at all, but may simply have the purpose of bolstering some sector of the internal economy of the country which institutes them. The damage to others may be a regrettable by-product.

Certainly the use of economic policies to achieve domestic or international goals is not new, although their scope, and certain aspects of the manner in which they are employed, have no precedent. Thus, for example, the use of foreign aid in the form of grants from the government of one country to that of another for development purposes is, in its present scope, a new development in international relations. Similarly, the concept of technical assistance is new in the sense that governments have not previously been involved in this type of activity. Obviously, as economic policies become increasingly important, a country's success will depend upon the level of economic production and overall capacity which it has attained.

One of the numerous difficulties in the use of economic policies in international relations is that interests within a given country are always affected by them—favorably or otherwise. Thus a tariff which "punishes" another country may benefit some but will injure other segments of the imposing country's economy. The same is true of such weapons of economic policy as embargoes, boycotts, etc. Since economic interests are easily combined into powerful pressure groups, especially within democratic countries in which the economic function is privately performed, governments seldom enjoy a free hand in the application of economic policies vis-à-vis other countries. To the extent that in societies such as the Soviet Union private economic interest groups do not exist (and probably would not be very effective in influencing government action if they *did* exist), America's "cold war" adversary enjoys certain advantages in the application of economic methods to international relations. This aspect of the problem is closely tied to questions which were discussed in Chapter VIII: national morale, a positive attitude toward innovation, and a willingness to make sacrifices.

The foregoing considerations are particularly significant within the present context of world affairs, which finds a majority of the world's population living in countries characterized by underdeveloped economies and consequent low rates of production and low standards of living. These countries are placing economic development high on the list of their national objectives. (For a more detailed discussion, see Chapter XVI.) For this reason it is quite understandable that impressive American economic programs—such as the Marshall Plan, the Point Four program, and various foreign aid programs of the 1950's—have probably forced the Soviet Union to emulate us, so that today underdeveloped countries may have an opportunity to receive aid from both blocs. The Soviet effort in the field of economic assistance is, overall, far smaller than American programs. Yet, since it is pin-pointed toward a small number of countries, it has at times exceeded local American efforts, and in a number of instances seems to have been more effective. It may be useful to bear in mind that since the end of World War II, American foreign aid programs have averaged around $5 billion per year. Approximately 20% of this has been in the form of repayable loans. Of the remainder, slightly over one-third has been for military aid, the balance going for economic assistance. While these figures look (and are) impressive, it is worth noting that the average share of the American gross national product devoted to foreign aid has been less than 2% and has diminished rather than increased in recent years.[1]

---

[1] 85th Congress, 1st Session, Senate Report #300, *Report of the Special Committee to Study the Foreign Aid Program* (Washington, D.C.: U.S. Government Printing Office).

Finally it should be mentioned that not all economic aid programs are sponsored by individual states. There are international groups, such as the Colombo Plan, which operate in this area; and numerous general international agencies, affiliated with the United Nations system, are active in this field.

Inasmuch as economic policies can be and are used to strengthen one's own country and one's friends and to weaken one's adversaries, it seems realistic to predict that they will continue to be widely used in the international relations of the second half of the 20th century.

1 • Economic Penetration and Power Politics *

Charles C. Abbott

The author is Dean of the Graduate School of Business Administration of the University of Virginia. He was Professor at Harvard University and also served as lecturer to the Naval War College and as consultant to the Office of the Secretary of Defense.

. . . .

In its extreme form economic penetration may be defined as the manipulation, by one sovereign power, of the business and economic ties that connect its economy with those of other powers, for the purpose of achieving political or military advantage. In instances where commercial links have been scanty or ill-suited to political objectives the tactics of economic penetration have included the negotiation of treaties, the establishment of trade connections, and the construction of business arrangements that were primarily designed to further political policy and were only secondarily intended to result in financial gain. In such cases the national interest, as interpreted by the Foreign Office or the equivalent agency, has often had a voice stronger than that of the bankers. In other instances, par-

ticularly where commercial relations were well developed, power politics and the profit motive have been able to make common cause in a way that benefited both.

Looked at from the point of view of power politics, every type of international commercial connection possesses political as well as economic significance. Foreign loans, the control of raw materials, patent-interchange agreements, and other well-publicized forms of economic penetration are only the more obvious means by which one nation influences the course of business and the economic process of another sovereignty. The establishment of branch plants across the border, the use of foreign subsidiaries, even the ordinary business

---

* *Harvard Business Review*, XXVI (1948), 410–24. Reprinted by permission.

connections necessary for the conduct of foreign trade contain political implications. Furthermore, the existence of such trade relationships is ordinarily a prerequisite for economic warfare; in their absence preclusive buying, dissemination of propaganda, or the redirection of established, peacetime channels of trade become commensurately more difficult.

In short, the student of this subject views the business world, and particularly the world of international business, from a vantage-point radically different from that occupied by the financial analyst or the economist. The economist studies his universe for the purpose, let us say, of forming generalizations regarding the results of the economic motive; the financial analyst is concerned with determining the prospect of gain. The student of economic penetration is intent upon discovering how particular forms of commercial organization and how specific types of business operations serve to embarrass or undermine the political position and military potential of sovereign powers.

A word of caution is perhaps appropriate here. It is a mistake to try to *explain* all or even the great bulk of commercial conditions and business actions in terms of political purpose. Economic interest and the search for gain are sufficient bases for most business practices, even those of German cartels. Too persistent a search for sinister motives and for explanations that lie outside ordinary business procedure only confuses the issue. Yet we must not forget that even normal business arrangements and spontaneous trade connections do provide the mechanisms of economic penetration, of international power politics.

Objectives. The specific objectives which at one time or another have been sought through tactics characteristic of economic penetration are numerous.

Four general categories of purposes, however, may be distinguished:

(1) The weakening of the political position and military strength of rival states. To go back into history, the British Navigation Acts of the seventeenth and eighteenth centuries were aimed in part at this objective. What is even more to the point, so were some of the practices of German cartels in the interwar period.

(2) The creation of an economy that is self-sufficient, particularly in a military sense. Self-sufficiency, of course, may be achieved either by acquiring control of the necessary raw materials or by technological advances that permit the creation of substitute materials through the magic of modern science. Imperial Germany strove both for colonial expansion and for dominance in synthetic chemistry. In Hitler's Reich the Balkans were exploited systematically at the same time that synthetic rubber was produced.

(3) The close integration of the economies of satellite countries to that of the dominant nation through such means as commercial ties, the use of branch plants, cartel operations, and international loans. The ultimate goal of such coordination, of course, is to achieve an integration so binding that satellite countries cannot pursue independent political policies. Present Russian activities in the Baltic and in the Balkans clearly come in this classification.

(4) The increase and extension of foreign trade, with emphasis upon the expansion of either imports or exports, depending on the dictates of time and circumstance....

Some of these objectives are complementary. The expansion of foreign trade and the integration of the economies of satellite countries with that of a dominant power are closely allied policies. It was no accident, for example, that both colonial expansion and foreign lending marked the foreign policy of the great nations of western Europe at the end of the nineteenth and the beginning of the twentieth century. The two operations complemented each other, and loans to colonial areas served both to expand trade and subordinate one territory to the needs of another. Indeed, many of the particular methods of economic penetration, such as foreign loans, export bounties, and international patent pools, typically serve more than one purpose.

On the other hand, some of the objectives are mutually exclusive. Policies aimed at creating a militarily self-sufficing state generally result in diminished opportunities for profit in foreign trade, as may many actions aimed at weakening the military potential of another power. For example, a policy of reducing United States shipments of scrap iron to Japan in the years before the Second World War seemingly would have been inconsistent with the policy of building up United States trade with that country, which was pointed toward another objective of economic penetration, equally logical in its own right. Whether the decision made between these two policies was sound is another question.

. . . .

UNDERMINING FOREIGN POSITIONS

Virtually all the mechanisms of economic warfare have the immediate purpose of weakening the economic power and military strength of foreign nations. Blockades, preclusive buying, the seizure or purchase of sources of strategic materials, export licensing, the blocking of currencies and transfer payments —all are intended to undermine the economic and perhaps the political position of other states.

The potentialities of economic war-

fare were perhaps seen clearly for the first time during the First World War. Notwithstanding the great commercial connections built up in earlier periods by England and France through the expansion of their trade and the extension of foreign credits, and despite the supplies of raw materials provided by their colonial empires, in 1914 these countries found themselves in some embarrassment. German commercial interests were discovered to be more extensive than most people had realized. Plants and factories located in France, Italy, Spain—in fact all over the world—were, it was found, not only controlled by Germany but of military consequence. In particular, many products of great importance in modern war were soon seen to be, whether by accident or design, virtual monopolies of the Germans. Acute shortages suddenly appeared in significant fields: dyestuffs, nitrates, potash, medicines, military optical goods, surgical instruments, heavy ordnance, magnetos, and certain electrical specialties. In each instance a German company or cartel occupied a dominant position. The Germans' control of salvarsan was commonly cited as an example of their Machiavellian planning.

Immediately much talk was heard about German industrial penetration in time of peace for the purpose of military advantage, and the "key industry" method of economic conquest. The truth was, of course, that quite irrespective of whether the German General Staff had planned it that way, technological advance had been so rapid and far-reaching that control of raw materials and a creditor position in international finance—upon which for decades England and France had relied—were no longer, by themselves, sufficient to provide a nation with an impregnable economic position.

Henri Hauser, the French economist,

had a clearer perception of the meaning of German commercial policy than did many of his contemporaries. In 1915 he wrote:

Economic warfare, conquest of markets, are phrases which, applied to Germany, are far from being m taphors. More than ever do we feel that Germany during unclouded peace was waging war with the elements of peace.

Dumping, export bounties, import bonuses, combined sea-and-land transport rates, emigration measures—these are the various methods which were employed by Germany, not as the normal procedure of economic activity, but as means of strangling, crushing and terrorizing her adversaries.[1]

It is too bad that in the interim between the two great wars the world did not bear in mind Hauser's dictum, that the nature of German industry was such that German economic penetration of other countries would inevitably continue after hostilities ended, whether Germany won the war or not.

Cartels. An essential element in the "key industry" method of penetration—assuming it was a conscious policy—were the German cartels. And no aspect of German economic policy has been more discussed, particularly since 1933 and the advent of the Third Reich.

Some of the more lurid statements regarding I. G. Farbenindustrie, the so-called "master plan" of the Third Reich, and the hidden power of the German industrialists appear extravagant. Yet even so measured a commentator as Dr. Corwin Edwards has recently stated:

A cartel may readily be used for political ends if one nation's participating enterprises are politically minded....

In cartel policy, as in that of national states, trade relationships often have diplo-

matic and military as well as economic significance....

After the Nazi government came into power, cartels were extensively used for trade penetration, political propaganda, collection of strategic information about foreign industries, and efforts to suppress the development of strategic industries in areas which might be hostile to Germany.[2]

. . . .

...We may properly note...that the more extreme forms of penetration are possible only under an authoritarian government and, by the nature of things, are hardly feasible in democracies. In Hitler's Germany the whole economy was brought under the most careful and detailed control by the government, and distinctions between government and business to which we are accustomed were in large measure obliterated. The fact that many business operations became in substance activities of the state greatly aided the Third Reich's pursuit of economic and political ends.

In general it is clear that there have been many instances in which cartels, whether for purposes of commercial conquest or not, have taken actions which inevitably have had a military significance. To cite a case: Bunge & Born, an Argentine company, during the 1930's gave evidence of its intention to commence the manufacture of sulphuric acid (an industrial chemical of great importance in war), which had hitherto been supplied to the Argentine by Duperial, the jointly owned subsidiary of DuPont and Imperial Chemical Industries. At the crucial time the Duperial Company, in its own words:

[1] Henri Hauser, *Germany's Commercial Grip on the World* (New York, Charles Scribner's Sons, 1918), p. ix.

[2] A study made for the Subcommittee on War Mobilization of the Committee on Military Affairs of the U. S. Senate, Pursuant to S. Res. 107, *Economic and Political Aspects of International Cartels*, Senate Committee Print, Monograph No. 1, 78th Congress, 2nd Session (Washington, D. C., Government Printing Office, 1944).

...proceeded to tell Bunge & Born that ...our shareholders had decided that our existing share in the sulphuric acid market would be protected quite irrespective of the level to which prices might decline during the ensuing period of competition. We explained that this information was being proffered in order that Bunge & Born might visualize the effect on their own prospective returns from sulphuric acid manufacture, but that, quite apart from the effect of their entry into the sulphuric acid field, it is now our definite policy to bring about a reduction in acid prices by progressive stages to the point where that business would no longer provide a constant invitation to others to enter the same field.[3]

The record does not show whether the military importance of sulphuric acid was a critical consideration in the situation. Yet it is obvious that an action of this type, taken by companies owned outside the country affected, particularly when that country is relatively undeveloped industrially, may readily be looked upon as imbued with political connotations and will be interpreted as an act of economic imperialism.

Other instances cited by Edwards seem to be of definite military consequence, such as the prewar control of the price of tungsten carbide shared by General Electric and Krupp Aktiengesellschaft and the prewar difficulties experienced by the Hercules Powder Company in its attempts to construct a synthetic ammonia plant. The difficulties in the latter instance were apparently attributable to the indirect control of the necessary patents by I. G. Farbenindustrie.

It would seem wise, therefore, for the United States to judge its cartel policy not only on economic and ideological grounds but also in the light of military considerations. In view of this country's traditional stand against monopoly of trade our objective ought to be the negative one of blocking the effects of other countries' use of this medium, rather than one aimed at securing positive advantages through encouraging active participation of American businesses in cartels.

Interchange of Patents. Agreements for the interchange of patents and the results of scientific research are the types of arrangement that have perhaps been most commonly criticized during and since the war. The criticism has in substance alleged that representatives of foreign companies have wormed out of domestic corporations technical information that was of military value, and that the unsuspecting domestic concerns have in return secured information that was of little if any use. Cross-licensing agreements and their attendant arrangements in this view are looked on as a vehicle for high-class espionage.

Commonly cited in this connection are the prewar relations between Bausch & Lomb and the German firm of Carl Zeiss and between the American Bosch Corporation and the German Robert Bosch Company, as well as the exchange of information regarding synthetic rubber that took place between the Standard Oil Company of New Jersey and I. G. Farbenindustrie. The position of the American companies referred to has in general been that on balance they gained, and many of their arguments are persuasive. Establishment of the facts in these and similar cases is very difficult, even for the trained technician. It seems evident, however, in view of the increasing part played in modern warfare by scientific and industrial technology, that such arrangements must be scrutinized with great care in the future.

MILITARY SELF-SUFFICIENCY

A line of demarcation cannot be drawn that clearly separates practices

---

[3] *Ibid.*

designed to weaken the military potential of foreign powers from policies designed to create military self-sufficiency at home; nor can measures intended to produce military autarchy be wholly distinguished from those whose object is to subjugate the economies of satellite countries. The overlapping of these two types of action can easily be indicated by one or two examples.

The traditional interest of the German Government in the progress of technology, particularly in the field of synthetic chemistry, certainly increased the German military potential at the same time that it was greatly reducing Germany's dependence on imported raw materials. Some of the practices of I. G. Farbenindustrie and of other cartels tended to check industrial development in other countries, and thereby the growth of military and economic strength; hence support of the chemical industry served two purposes. On the other hand, although the American tariff system has made some contribution to industrial development in this country during the last 150 years, and has thus strengthened the United States militarily at home, it does not appear that progress fostered in this way was at the expense of other countries, or that American tariffs were an instrument which impeded technological development abroad.

. . . .

Government Corporations. A[nother] striking characteristic both of the present time and of the seventeenth and eighteenth centuries is the narrow margin separating political and economic activities. One of the points where these two types of action most clearly merge is in the government-owned or government-sponsored corporation.

In a period when the governmentally sponsored chartered trading company, such as the East India Company, the Royal African Company, or the Hudson Bay Company, was the great instrument for extending both commercial and political relations, it was general to find economic and political motives closely intertwined. The British ambassadors to Turkey or to Russia were commonly also members of the Levant or Muscovy companies and presumably acted in dual capacities. Sir Thomas Roe, when undertaking his diplomatic missions to India in the seventeenth century, was a member of the East India Company and was chiefly interested in obtaining additional privileges for its merchants. Dupleix, when defeated by Clive in India, was not only Governor-General of the French possessions but also a member of the French East India Company. Interesting similarities may be traced between the positions of such men and the positions of heads of modern government trade missions, such as the British Runciman mission to Czechoslovakia just before the war or Ribbentrop's numerous trips to the Balkans. Indeed, the administrators of the Marshall Plan are reminiscent, in a number of respects, of seventeenth and eighteenth century forerunners.

EXTENSION OF FOREIGN TRADE

The governmentally owned or sponsored corporation is, of course, a traditional means of extending foreign trade, of exerting political pressure under the guise of commerce, and of accomplishing some of the purposes of economic penetration. The great seventeenth and eighteenth century trading companies of Great Britain, France, and the Netherlands, equipped with their own diplomatic representatives and fortified with their own armed forces, were admittedly engines of political as well as economic maneuver. Throughout the nineteenth century, in the colonial areas of the world, developmental companies played important roles that cannot always be appraised in terms of dollars and cents or of returns on investment.

Such British concerns as the Delagoa Bay Development Corporation, the Mozambique Chartered Company, and the British South Africa Company clashed repeatedly with German interests in East Africa prior to the First World War. In the Far East various concerns such as the Chinese Engineering and Mining Company in the Kaiping Basin were able on more than one occasion to enlist official aid. Politically the two most striking instances of the confluence of British financial and political interests were: (1) the series of events that followed the bankruptcy of the Khedive of Egypt in 1876 and which led to the British control of Egyptian finances and of the Suez Canal, and (2) the conflict of ambitions that precipitated the Boer War. Of equal dramatic quality, and perhaps of even greater present-day significance in view of the areas concerned, was the long series of French, British, and Turkish intrigues that ultimately thwarted the Teutonic dream of a German-controlled "Berlin to Bagdad" railway.

Nor has the governmentally sponsored company disappeared from the present international scene. During the last three years the Soviet Government has turned to that characteristic instrument of capitalistic imperialism, the holding company. Eastern Europe and the Balkans have been studded with a dozen such companies as the Soviet-Rumanian Petroleum Company, the Soviet-Rumanian Civil Aviation Company, the Hungarian-Soviet Bauxite-Aluminum Company, and the Hungarian-Soviet River Transportation Company; and more of these organizations are apparently contemplated.[4]

Ordinarily these companies are jointly owned by the Soviet Government and the government of the country in question, and they control all or a major portion of a particular industry. Typically the Russians have at least a 50% representation on the board of directors. In most cases the Russian contribution to these undertakings has been property seized by the Soviet Government from German nationals or from others. In any event, these corporations constitute a most effective mechanism for control by the Russian Government of key industries in the satellite countries, particularly industries with military significance.

Americans also are making use of trading or developmental corporations as a means of expanding commercial or financial interests; while in most cases these are private rather than governmental in form, they often have semiofficial government backing. Since the war a number of companies jointly owned in the United States and Latin America have been created.... One former Secretary of State has announced the formation of two corporations intended to operate in the international field: the World Commerce Corporation and the Liberia Development Corporation. Another former Secretary of State has become a director of an American investment trust that has very large foreign holdings, particularly in the mining field. Finally, it seems possible that Federal Government corporations may play a considerable part in the implementation of the Marshall Plan and in American efforts to reconstruct the European economy. Time alone can reveal the outcome of these developments, but it is worth while recognizing that these so-called experiments are not so new as is sometimes alleged, and it may even be worth while studying the history of their predecessors, as one means of understanding existing conditions.

---

[4] See *Preliminary Report Twenty* of the House Select Committee on Foreign Aid, pursuant to H. Res. 296, *The East European Economy in Relation to the European Recovery Program* (Washington, D. C., Government Printing Office, March 7, 1948).

Foreign Loans. Historically, as a method of promoting foreign trade, the foreign loan has been of fully as much consequence as has the government corporation. Indeed, the two devices have commonly gone hand in hand, particularly in the period of colonial expansion beginning after the Franco-Prussian war and ending in 1914. During that interval enormous amounts of capital were exported from London, Paris, Berlin, Amsterdam, and the other money markets of Europe as diplomacy sought the aid of finance and the profit motive made common cause with power politics.

. . . .

The great bulk of the funds exported by Britain went to finance private enterprise. It is generally thought that as of 1914 no more than one-fourth of the British foreign investment was represented by loans to governmental bodies. Such undertakings as Argentine railways, South African mines, Ceylon tea and Malayan rubber plantations were typical investments. Developmental and extractive corporations of all types, located both within and without the Empire, were common.

By their nature such undertakings had, and have, social and political connotations not possessed by, say, an assembly plant of General Motors or a sales office of International Harvester. For example, the former type of operation tends to remove real wealth from the country in question, whereas the latter brings wealth to it. Furthermore, such an undertaking as a mine in the last analysis is at the mercy of the government of the area in which it is located. The operations of a General Motors assembly plant in Africa or South America, however, are primarily dependent upon the continuous flow of parts from this country, and only secondarily dependent upon the goodwill of the sovereignty within which the asset is located.

The character of foreign loans made by France and Germany prior to 1914 was quite different from that of the British. Here there was no pretense that the extension of credit did not constitute a branch of foreign policy, or that the privilege of utilizing the capital market in Paris or Berlin need not be compensated by economic or political advantages.

In France virtually every international loan was preceded by diplomatic negotiation, by a long-continued process of haggling over minute provisions in the loan agreement, and by bargaining over the procedural as well as the substantive aspects of the financing. The French loans to Turkey, to the Balkan countries, to the North African states, and elsewhere were allowed only after numerous and meticulously considered economic and political concessions had been granted by the borrower. One of the important bases of the Franco-Russian Alliance, of course, was that French capital should be available to the Czar's government, a privilege of which the Czar took full advantage. How revealing was the statement of Minister of Finance Caillaux, in 1913, as he looked back over his long career:

I have conducted the public finances for six years; I have admitted to quotation only those foreign loans which assured France political and economic advantages. . . .

In Germany governmental control over foreign lending was perhaps less direct than in France, but no less sure since foreign loans formed a recognized part of the expansionist policies that characterized Imperial Germany. The intimate relations of the Foreign Office and the banks furnished a conduit by which the government made its desires known. In general, governmental influence strove to direct capital into, and wrest concessions from, those areas where Germany hoped to acquire colonies or gain control of raw materials, particularly Africa, the Balkans, Turkey, and China.

The part played by foreign investment in economic penetration may be summed up by two quotations from Herbert Feis:

The traditional theory of capital movements given in the economic texts, wherein capital is portrayed as a fluid agent of production put at the service of those who paid or promised the most, is inadequate to account for the direction capital took before the war. In the lending countries international financial transactions were supervised in accord with calculations of national advantage, which were often unrelated to the direct financial inducement offered the owners of capital. Peoples and governments exerted themselves to direct the capital to those purposes which were judged likely to strengthen the national state, especially in time of war, or increase the chances of extended dominion. Capital was called upon to abstain from investment in the lands of potential enemies. It was urged or commanded into the service of allies... it came to be commonly regarded as a servant of national purposes rather than an ordinary private possession... it became an important instrument in the struggle between national states.[5]

... official circles of lending countries gradually came to envisage the foreign investments of their citizens, not as private financial transactions, but as one of the instruments through which national destiny was achieved. Financial force was often lent or withheld in accordance with political calculations.[6]

The applicability of many of these observations to the foreign financial policy of the United States since 1945 is clear.

As America increasingly comes to play the role of capitalist for the rest of the world, it is evident that our foreign loans will, inevitably, be used more and more as an instrument of national policy and will lose—if they ever had—the characteristics of "pure" capital described in the economic textbooks. If lending can be used to maintain peace, our foreign loans can be a source of great good. The fervent hope is that we may learn from the mistakes of the past and avoid, on the one hand, the Scylla of economic exploitation and, on the other hand, the Charybdis of unrealistic and ill-conceived sentimentality.

---

[6] *Ibid.*, p. xvi.

. . . .

---

[5] Herbert Feis, *Europe: The World's Banker* (New Haven, Yale University Press, 1930), pp. 465–66.

2 • Widening Boundaries of National Interest *

Nelson A. Rockefeller

The author has had a long and distinguished public service career. He served as coordinator of Inter-American affairs, 1940–44, as Assistant Secretary of State, 1944–45, Chairman of the International Development Advisory Board, 1950–51, and as Special Assistant to President Eisenhower on economic affairs. In 1958 he was elected Governor of New York.

NOTE: *The following constitutes an abridgment and not the complete text of the original article.*

In a few paragraphs, the fourth point of President Truman's inaugural address in January 1949 phrased a concept that sparked an electric response along the great circuit that links the minds and imaginations of human beings throughout the world. The concept was basically simple. It declared that:

1. Mankind for the first time in history possesses the knowledge and skills to make his environment yield an adequate and progressively improving return to all peoples.

2. Despite this knowledge, more than half of the world's people still live under economic systems which provide less than minimum needs for food, clothing and shelter, and lack the promise of betterment.

3. Since the security and continued prosperity of the United States and other relatively industrialized nations can be maintained only if there is complementary progress in the economically backward areas, we should assume the leadership in a concerted productive effort which will promote both their interests and ours.

4. Basic to the accomplishment of this purpose is a flow of investment capital, carrying with it technical and managerial skills, to create and harness mechanical power and production tools and equipment so that they supplement the work of human muscles. Our policy should focus on creating conditions that permit and encourage such transfers, under procedures that avoid imperialism or any form of exploitation on either side, and are founded upon mutual respect and recognition of a mutual interest.

5. "Democracy alone can supply the vitalizing force to stir the peoples of the world into triumphant action, not only against their human oppressors, but also against their ancient enemies— hunger, misery and despair."

The wide and extraordinarily warm response invoked everywhere outside of the Communist world by this formulation of a new phase of American foreign policy merits examination. Seemingly, it stemmed in part from a recognition that we were thereby taking a further step

---

* Excerpted by special permission from *Foreign Affairs,* XXIX (July 1951), 523–38. Copyright by Council on Foreign Relations, Inc., New York.

away from our traditional isolationism. Our acceptance of a common interest between United States and Western Europe had been attested by our participation in two world wars and by direct military and economic aid, amounting to some 55 billion dollars, given to Europe during and after the second of these struggles. Point Four was a declaration that our interest included a concern for the well-being and progress of the entire world.

Furthermore, this interest was defined not in military or even in political terms. The pronouncement placed it squarely upon economic considerations that linked the continuing progress of our system to a correlative development in the economies of all democratic peoples. As a nation, we have 6 percent of the world's peoples and 7 percent of the world's land area, but more than half of the world's industrial output. Yet we possess only one-third of the raw materials, so that we depend upon others for a large part of our strength. These economic ties have a way of persisting through periods of peace, war or the uneasy half-war, half-peace, in which the world now lives.

Thus, the principles stated in Point Four were accepted as an assurance that we have moved from self-contained sufficiency to a recognition of our responsible partnership in a free-world effort. This emphasis has tremendous import. Its implications should be thoroughly understood here as well as abroad.

There already was no lack of evidence that the United States stood ready to coöperate with other nations in time of need. Over the past ten years the total of its military and economic assistance to other nations has amounted to the staggering sum of approximately 80 billion dollars. But the money was spent for emergency measures to meet successive crises. One after another, lend-lease, UNRRA, the United Kingdom loan, Philippine rehabilitation, Greek and Turkish, Japanese and Korean aid, the Economic Recovery Program, and even to a major degree our subscriptions to the International Bank and Monetary Fund arrangements agreed upon at Bretton Woods—each was submitted to and accepted by the people of the United States as something that must be done to avoid catastrophe, with a strong implication that once it was done the situation would be well in hand and our responsibilities discharged.

It is unfortunate that the presentation of the Point Four concept to the American public and the specific steps implementing it have taken a form that carries the dual connotation of a "give-away program" and one that is principally concerned with sending technicians abroad to offer advice. Humanitarian motives are deeply ingrained in the United States tradition and have been nourished by the religious and democratic heritage of its people. But the tendency to accept the giving of grants and advice as an all-embracing definition of what is implied in the Point Four program does a major disservice to its basic principles.

Such an interpretation narrows the broad pronouncement of community of interests put fourth in the President's original statement, and it even now clearly whittles down the statement of purpose given to the program by Congress in Title IV of its Act for International Development (Public Law 535). In Section 403(a) of this law, Congress states: "It is declared to be the policy of the United States to aid the efforts of the peoples of economically underdeveloped areas to develop their resources and living conditions by encouraging the exchange of technical knowledge and skills and the flow of investment capital to countries which provide conditions under which such technical assistance and capital can effectively and constructively contribute to raising standards of living, creating new sources of wealth, increasing productivity and expanding purchasing power." In a preceding paragraph [Section 402 (a)] it is stated: "The peoples of the United States and other nations have a common interest in freedom and in the economic progress of all peoples. Such progress can further the secure growth of democratic ways of life, the expansion of mutually beneficial commerce, the development of international understanding and good will, and the maintenance of world peace."

It is this emphasis upon community of interests that gives significance to Point Four as an important forward step in the evolution of our foreign policy. Once accepted, it is clear that any program for carrying out our intent must be broad enough to embrace *all* of the aspects in which our economy exerts important impacts upon the economies of others in the free world, not merely the giving of gifts and technical advice. It is equally clear that the program must be a continuing one—geared to the deliberate pace of economic development rather than to the bell-clanging rush of apparatus designed to put out fires.

The pressure of compelling political or security considerations will necessarily change the focus and the emphasis of our economic policies at home and abroad. The policy of Soviet Russia and her dominated satellites is to organize a tightly-contained economic area having the least possible trade with free-world areas. This necessarily restricts our community of economic interest to those countries outside the Soviet orbit. The militarily aggressive Soviet policy forces us at the present time to give precedence at home and abroad to those aspects of economic activity which will assure successful resistance to that aggression either through direct production of armaments or through correcting deficiencies that make certain areas peculiarly vulnerable to pressure from without or subversion from within.

But the *aim* of our foreign economic policy should remain constant—in peace, in emergency, or in war, if war cannot be avoided. If we live up to our pronouncements, we shall conduct our economic affairs as a whole in a way to further the healthy, balanced development and the progressively larger yield of the economies of all peoples who elect to belong to the free-world trading system.

II

Is the concept of an economic policy based upon community of interest valid? To answer this, we must know the importance of our economic ties to the so-called underdeveloped areas and whether it entitles them to high priority among the competing demands being made upon scarce resources in the present emergency period. First, let us demarcate the areas we are talking about.

The term underdeveloped may be applied to areas of the non-Communist world inhabited by the 1.75 billion people living in Latin America, Africa, Greece, Turkey, the Middle East, South Asia, Southeast Asia and the Pacific Islands of Oceania. The term has never been given precise definition; and obviously any descriptive term applied to the above areas will mask the widest disparities in ethnic groups, cultures, religious values, population densities and social and economic institutions, as well as in climates, topographies and resources. A few of the countries situated in these general regions have attained per capita income levels that remove them from the "underdeveloped category," except in the sense that all countries might make better use of their material and human resources. Perhaps they account for about 40,000,000 people. It may be said of the remainder that per capita incomes are appallingly low—generally under $200 per year and averaging perhaps $80 a year. Further, their annual outputs in few cases are increasing faster than their populations, and hence they offer little current promise for bettering levels of living; they are largely agricultural, with low yields per person employed and per acre, so that they seldom produce sufficient foodstuffs to provide a satisfactory domestic diet; and their manufacturing and industrial activity is generally rudimentary.

Despite the meagerness of their individual and collective economic output, the economies of the underdeveloped areas are of crucial importance to the United States and to Western Europe. The very imbalance which limits their production and makes them so vulnerable to world commodity market fluctuations gives them a weight in world trade quite disproportionate to their over-all economic performance. They supply 57 percent of the United States' imports and 65 percent of Western Europe's. Of the critical and strategic materials upon which armaments depend, they supply three-quarters of all United States imports and an even higher percentage of those of our European allies. Clearly, the success of the industrial mobilization plans of the North Atlantic Treaty countries is contingent upon the continued and increasing supply from underdeveloped areas of such strategic minerals as bauxite, chrome, copper, lead, manganese, tin, uranium and zinc. The same is true for natural rubber and a variety of important fibers. Our civilian economies are equally dependent upon the same sources for such items as coffee, tea, cocoa and bananas and other fruits and

foodstuffs. Seventy-five percent of Western Europe's supply of petroleum comes from the Middle East, and the cutting off of even the 25 percent supplied by Iran would have a most serious impact upon the petroleum economy of the entire Western World.

The interdependence is equally impressive when viewed from the perspective of the underdeveloped areas themselves. Their highly specialized economies depend for more than 70 percent of their total imports on the United States and Western Europe. Any important curtailment of this supply would create chaos for most of them. Their imports represent a decisive proportion of their ever-deficient supplies of manufactures and foodstuffs for consumers, and a preponderant proportion of all of the basic equipment needed both for maintenance and for development.

Here we have a striking example of the principle set forth above, that the Point Four policy must have regard for the total impact of industrialized economies upon the less developed. As our NATO programs for munitions production bite deeper into our available supplies of materials, manufacturing capacities and manpower skills, there will be—there already is—increasing pressure to tighten up on our export licensing. The underdeveloped areas are dependent upon the United States and Western Europe for imports valued last year at more than 12 billion dollars; and for most of these they have no presently feasible alternate sources of supply. Cutbacks of these exports, even to the degree that we curtail our own output of civilian goods, will have a far more disruptive effect upon their economies, habitually starvation-thin, than we can imagine. Any reckless handling of this problem can create such chaos in the underdeveloped areas that our present imports of raw materials from them may be completely upset, and future imports perhaps lost as a result of their being thrown into the closed economic orbit of the enemy.

One of the strongest arguments for setting up an administration for the whole foreign economic program, including development, is that through export controls alone the United States can do the underdeveloped countries 5 billion dollars' worth of damage. This could never be compensated for by an aid program totalling a few hundred millions, however well intentioned it might be in concept. If we choke off the equipment upon which their industrial progress depends, any program of economic coöperation designed to stimulate economic development in underdeveloped areas will be an act of hypocrisy.

If we look beyond the present emergency to our long-term economic prospects we see that the stake of the United States and Western Europe in an expanding economy throughout the free world is even more impressive. The United States accounts for more than one-half of the heavy industry production of the world, but it mines only about a third of the 15 basic minerals upon which such production depends. Even so, it is depleting its mineral reserves at an exorbitant rate. On balance, the mineral reserves now within Soviet Russia's effective control are larger than those available to the United States within her own borders and from other parts of the Western Hemisphere. Our industry will become increasingly dependent upon imports. If access to the raw materials of the underdeveloped areas were to be denied to us and to Western Europe, our current industrial outputs would be devastatingly affected. Unless development in those areas keeps pace, it simply will not be possible for the United States and Western Europe to continue to expand their economies in the future in the manner which has given them their strength in the past.

Thus both the security of our free world and our own continuing economic growth are dependent upon the development of the underdeveloped countries. But we should be under no illusions that we could, even if we wanted, expand them as raw material suppliers exclusively, retaining ourselves the more lucrative operations of transferring such materials into manufactures. The history of the United States shows conclusively how stubbornly the people of a nation and of its several segments insist upon the prerogative of diversification, and how wise they are to do so.

Thus while we must seek to expand the free world's raw material production, our policy must be sufficiently broad and sufficiently wise to encourage an industrial expansion as well. The chief incentive of the underdeveloped areas to produce additional raw materials for export will be the desire to acquire the exchange to purchase the equipment for building healthily-balanced economies. Initially they must purchase such heavy equipment from industrialized areas, since machine tools and machinery generally are the product of relatively mature economies. Eventually, they will produce such machines themselves. Those who fear the impact of such competition would do well to consider the volume of market demand if the billion people of the underdeveloped free-world areas could raise their per capita incomes from the present average of $80 per year to the $473 level of Western Europe or to the $1,453 level of the United States.

III

When once the fact of interdependence and community of interest among the United States, Western Europe and the underdeveloped areas of the free world is accepted, two questions thrust themselves forward. The first: Is it within the practical range of our power and resources to aid effectively more than a billion people to move their economies off dead center and imbue them with a dynamism to match our own? If this question can be answered affirmatively, the second is: How?

The 150,000,000 people of the United States have devised an economy which currently produces a national income of well over 250 billion dollars per year.[1] The 270,000,000 people of Western Europe are producing an income totaling 150 billion dollars. The billion people with whom we are concerned live on an income estimated at, perhaps, 80 billion dollars. The several economies are all interrelated. Looking at their magnitude instead of at the numbers of population, we see that the 400 billion dollar economy of the industrialized West can obviously exert a decisive impact on the 80 billion dollar economies to which it is so closely linked. Thus the question of "whether" can be quickly resolved. The answer is affirmative. The question of "how" is far more difficult. Here any answer must take cognizance of the fact that our past relationships with these areas have not, except in a few cases and upon a limited scale, sufficed to plant the seeds of organic growth. But the barrenness of the past record need not be regarded as an index of future possibilities, since until now there has been but little recognition of the need to concentrate on such a goal and no focussed effort to achieve it. The essential job is one of organizing all of our economic relationships with the underdeveloped areas in a fashion to lead consistently toward economic progress. For maximum effectiveness there must be close coordination of policy and practice between the United States and Western Europe.

[1] Note: Present figures are in excess of 400 billion dollars per year. The population, too, has increased by approximately 30 million.

. . . .

The major immediate objectives of our foreign economic policy must include:

1. A drive to increase food production in the underdeveloped areas by 25 percent, which would bring them barely above the minimum needed for health.

2. An increase of 50 percent in the production of raw materials for export by the underdeveloped areas as a means of meeting the needs of the industrialized world and of giving the underdeveloped areas the exchange they need to maintain their economies and to further their own agricultural and industrial progress.

3. The maintenance of essential exports from the United States and Western Europe at levels which avoid disruptions that might threaten national security; and the accordance of due weight to development needs which would improve the internal economies of the receiving states, giving them positive incentives for adhering to free institutions.

4. A foundation for broad economic development which will increase production and make possible a rising standard of living in the underdeveloped areas.

Under the pressure of current emergency mobilization requirements, our foreign economic policies and procedures are inevitably governed by considerations of national security. Nevertheless, in order to be successful our strategy must take account of the need of preserving the cohesion of the countries of the free world against either external aggression or subversion. To accomplish this, it must embrace far more than the production of arms, although that is essential. For both the emergency and the long-term the instruments for promoting economic progress are the same. They are: the furnishing of capital goods upon which productive efficiency depends; the exchange of consumption goods produced under the advantages derived from the specialized employment of resources and skills; and the coöperation to achieve more efficient methods of production and management. At all times the problem is to see that these instruments are used in a way that promotes the combined strength of all the coöperating nations and the individual strength of each within the group....

. . . .

It is obvious that the major impetus for economic progress in the underdeveloped areas must come from local initiative and local resources. Foreign capital, economic and social coöperation, and technical aid can be extraordinarily useful—they may even be essential in the initial development stage—but they can never have a decisive effect unless the people concerned show a will for improvement and offer genuine hospitality. Within each region, development plans must be worked out on a country-to-country basis; within each country, they must be worked out coöperatively with the citizens and their government representatives. The regional representatives in the central United States establishment should help develop over-all plans with respect to each country through a joint commission containing strong local representation in addition to those who are assigned from the United States. They would have the continuing responsibility of seeing that the sum of American economic relationships serves a constructive end.[2]

---

[2] *Author's Note:* For a more complete exposition of the above ideas see "Partners in Progress," a Report to President Truman," by the International Development Advisory Board (Simon and Schuster, New York, 1951). The author of this article gratefully acknowledges his debt to the other Board members and to its staff in the formulation of most of the concepts here set forth.

IV

In the above sections an attempt has been made to answer in the space available, the questions of "whether" and "how." There remains the overridingly important question of "what." The following paragraphs will attempt to outline the steps which might be taken to answer that question.

Economic progress in the underdeveloped areas as elsewhere depends upon three main factors.

The first is the production and distribution of goods. This is primarily a function of private enterprise, from the smallest farmer to the largest industrial corporation. It is logical, therefore, that we should help others in these fields by encouraging private direct investments abroad or joint investments with private domestic capital.

The second factor is that of the basic services of health and sanitation, education, agriculture, public administration and training people in basic skills. A variety of philanthropic and religious groups pioneered in carrying American procedures in these activities abroad. Now these are becoming more and more subject to government initiative. Our Government is best equipped to coöperate in these fields with government agencies abroad, either through its own technicians, those of the United Nations or experienced voluntary agencies.

The third factor is public works such as roads, railways, harbors and irrigation projects. These are primarily the responsibility of governments, but in many areas are developed by private capital.

Efficient agricultural and industrial production depends upon capital investment. The underdeveloped areas, with an average per capita income of $80 a year, simply do not generate sufficient savings to provide the needed capital equipment. Few of them have the will or the mechanisms to channel even their limited savings into productive uses.

Pioneer economies everywhere have depended for their initial forward impetus upon the foreign private investments provided by relatively mature economies. Investment in frontier areas has always entailed great risks. Historically, however, the large returns from successful ventures have more than offset the losses from those that failed. At the height of Britain's economic power, private foreign investment amounted to a fabulous 10 percent of her total national income, and it averaged almost 2.5 percent for a period of more than 30 years. Private foreign investment from the United States has lately been averaging less than .5 percent; and the United Kingdom and other countries of Europe no longer have any considerable margin of funds to commit abroad.

One major reason for the decline in foreign private investment is to be found in the new tax structures of industrialized countries. Corporation and individual income taxes absorb so much that what is left from bonanza enterprises no longer compensates for the capital lost in ventures that fail. Hence, a premium has been placed upon security in investments; investment in high-return, high-risk ventures has been discouraged. This has militated particularly against foreign investments in frontier areas, where the business risks remain as high as formerly and the nonbusiness risks— political disturbances, expropriation, discriminatory treatment, exchange losses, transfer difficulties and the like—are even greater than formerly. Underdeveloped areas obviously could do much to reduce such hazards, and should be encouraged to do so. But it is well within the power of the United States, the leading creditor nation, to take steps that, at relatively modest cost, would greatly increase the incentives for private investors to renew their interest in foreign investments.

The simplest, most effective and cheapest way would be for the United States to adopt the general principle that corporate taxes will be imposed on earnings only in the country in which they are realized, without requiring that the difference between the foreign corporate tax and the United States corporate tax be paid when they are repatriated. Tax rates are generally low in underdeveloped areas, and this is one of the few genuine incentives they can hold forth. But the incentive is completely discounted by the United States tax law. Although the loss in tax revenues to our Treasury through the immediate adoption of this measure would be small ($200,000,000 on the basis of 1947 figures, the latest available), it would probably be expedient during the current budgetary stringency to restrict the concession to *new* foreign corporate investments only, with the provision that it should automatically apply to all foreign corporate investments when the emergency is officially declared ended. A partial exemption should be offered to individual investments abroad that would offer incentives comparable to those granted corporations.

In addition to such tax incentives, there is genuine need for a banking facility not now in existence. Its job would be to furnish senior or equity capital to cover the domestic currency costs of establishing an enterprise. Many potential investors are willing to hazard the exchange risks of the dollar (usually the equipment) cost of a foreign project but hesitate to transfer additional dollars to cover land, building and labor costs and working capital. There is a similar difficulty, though for other reasons, in finding local investors to carry the domestic costs.

The International Bank for Reconstruction and Development has long been interested in the above problem. There is reason to believe that it would be glad to operate, as an affiliate, an International Finance Corporation, which would make loans in local or foreign currencies without requiring government guarantees and likewise make non-voting equity investments in local currencies in participation with private investors. Obviously, the Finance Corporation would select its investments upon criteria of soundness; and there is expectation that it would realize sufficient profit from the sale of its equity holdings in successful ventures to compensate it for all risks taken. Such sales should be to domestic investors, who would acquire full voting rights with all equity stock purchased. This would be an effective step—long urgently needed —toward bringing about the local marketing of securities.

A still further step that might help to renew interest on the part of United States investors in gilt-edge foreign portfolio securities would be for the Export-Import Bank to exercise the authority it already possesses to underwrite, for a proper fee, the transfer risks of the interest and amortization on dollar debt securities of highest credit rating. The issuing corporation, which would be responsible for the risks of exchange depreciation, would thus have the advantage of obtaining long-term credit that is seldom to be had in its local market; and United States investors would again have reason to look favorably on at least some foreign offerings. If a recently-petitioned modification of the rigid New York State restrictions upon the type of investments eligible to insurance reserves is allowed, United States insurance companies will be enabled to invest 5 percent of their funds in high-grade securities abroad.

No one can state with certainty what influence the above-recommended measures would have on our private invest-ment in underdeveloped areas. At the current rate it averages about $700,-000,000 per year. Perhaps this would be tripled. Private foreign investment then would still represent less than 1 percent of our national income. We invested about twice that abroad during the 1920's, and more would be desirable now.

In making recommendations concerning the second factor—basic services, such as health, sanitation, education, training—the International Development Advisory Board studied various types of coöperation. Technical assistance alone is not sufficiently broad in concept or operation to achieve the necessary results. Nor would a United States program operated by United States personnel and paid for by the United States do the job; even if it succeeds momentarily, such a project creates jealousies among local officials; and when the United States stops, the whole project stops. Joint planning and operations in which United States and local government personnel work together, using joint resources, are needed. A specific target must be selected, and the people and resources of the country used fully. At a rate set in advance, the United States share of financing would be reduced and the local share would rise, so that at the end of the fixed period service would be entirely in local hands.

The third field—that of heavy public works—presents the most problems, and yet it is of basic importance. Huge sums can be wasted on such projects through bad planning, bad construction, bad operation. The inherent weakness here lies in the fact that the money of American taxpayers is spent for projects to be run by governments other than their own. Yet the more we try to assure high standards, the more resentment we are apt to generate on the ground that we are intervening in the internal affairs of another government.

Yet there are many cases where basic public works must precede or accompany any progress in agricultural or industrial development. Even in an emergency period, when long-term projects are subordinated to immediate needs, it becomes necessary to build highways, railways or port facilities to get out raw materials or to support new domestic production in vulnerable areas which are difficult to supply through normal exports. Since the governments of underdeveloped areas have limited ability to raise capital, outside aid is needed. The problem is to organize public works aid in a manner to avoid corrupting our political relationships— easy money, slush-fund politics on an international scale—and outraging the tolerance of our Congress and our people.

Perhaps the best way to organize assistance in this field is through an International Development Authority, which in turn could organize local authorities to carry out approved projects. The administration of its activities might well be entrusted to the International Bank for Reconstruction and Development, which has had much experience and knows how to exercise sound business judgment in assuring the feasibility of projects and in analyzing national development needs and credit potentials. There is no need to duplicate its staff work. In the course of its investigations it has turned up many useful development projects which it cannot accommodate because local credit cannot support the entire cost. Its officials believe that a number of sound loans could be made, for example, to support large-scale mining projects, if the access roads or port facilities could be given grant assistance.

If such an International Development Authority were set up—supported by major contributors to the International Bank for Reconstruction and Development in the same proportion that they subscribe to the Bank's capital, *i.e.* 40 percent by the United States and 60 percent by the other participants—the apparently insoluble problem of organizing efficient support for public works in underdeveloped areas might be overcome. There would be no need for a big "giveaway program" by the United States, with all the accompanying pressures and strains upon good will and all of the difficulties of imposing proper controls. The funds would be administered by the World Bank, which is in a position to turn down unsound projects and accommodate useful ones with far less strain than arises when the negotiators are separate national sovereignties.

Under the auspices of such an international agency, it would be possible to establish a Jordan Valley Authority, for example, which could help settle the 750,000 Arab refugees from Palestine, one of the grave sources of unrest in the Middle East. At present, these people are being barely kept alive by some 30 or 40 million dollars of relief expenses a year. This is a palliative, not a solution. The reclamation of several million potentially fertile acres is possible, both in the Arab countries and Israel, but it is expensive. It could be accomplished through the combination of a loan from the International Bank, meeting the costs that could be repaid over a period of years, plus a grant from the International Development Authority, meeting the costs which would not be a sound banking risk. Furthermore, this would be an international loan and grant, representing a genuinely coöperative effort of the whole free world.

V

What would be the cost of a program like that here set forth? It would not be inconsiderable. But neither are the costs that we shall have to bear if major areas of the world which form part of the fabric of our national economic life and our political security are alienated....

.   .   .   .

What might the expectations be from such a program in the flow of funds to underdeveloped areas? All the measures combined, including the release of savings in the underdeveloped areas themselves, might mean a flow of capital into productive channels of 3 or 4 billion dollars a year.

An annual flow of funds of this dimension would not accomplish miracles overnight. It would not result in European levels of living for most of the billion people in the underdeveloped areas for many weary years. But its potential force should not be under-

valued. Not much is known about domestic capital accumulation in the underdeveloped areas, but the total is probably not more than 6 to 7 billion dollars annually. Only a small fraction of that total is channeled into new *productive* enterprise. If 3 billion dollars annually were directed wisely into crucially productive channels, if it were supplemented by additional grants or investments from other relatively advanced economies, if our procurement and export policies are handled with due regard to the interests of the whole free world—the tempo of economic advance in the areas in question would be, in truth, revolutionized. The hope of discernible progress would replace the despair of stagnation. And we should have gone far toward giving meaning to the institutions of democracy, and a sense of a living and deepening community of interest to free nations.

PART IV   TENSION, CONFLICT AND VIOLENCE

XIV • Theories of International Conflict

The problem of conflict and violence between states is as old as recorded history. Therefore it is hardly surprising that it has engaged the attention of students of human affairs since earliest times. The aspects of this problem are so many and so varied that this chapter represents only an attempt to present a few contemporary ideas on the subject, and these introductory comments can do no more than call attention to some additional theories on the nature of international conflict, not covered in the subsequent readings. War is not the only, or even the most frequent, conflict relationship in international relations, although it is the most dramatic expression of tensions which exist on all levels and at all times. For the moment, we are primarily interested in identifying certain assumptions about the nature of conflict as such. In subsequent chapters, we shall deal with two specific conflict situations: that between the Soviet Union and the anti-Communist group of nations, and that between the more and less developed countries.

Certainly conflict is a ubiquitous social phenomenon. Stuart Chase has identified no less than fifteen types or levels of conflict: personal quarrels, family against family, quarrels between family groups or clans, community quarrels, sectional quarrels, workers *vs.* management, political contests, race conflict, religious conflict, ideological quarrels, occupational conflicts, competition within a given industry, competition between industries, national rivalries, and conflicts between cultures.[1] The two last types are, of course, of special interest to the student of international relations.

Although the present nature of weapons technology is such that the negative consequences of international conflict overshadow its positive functions, not all expressions of social conflict are necessarily destructive. Social conflict may increase the adaptation or adjustment of relationships within and —occasionally—between groups. Few states exist today which do not owe either their original formation or their continued existence to acts of overt

---

[1] Stuart Chase, *Roads to Agreement* (New York: Harper and Brothers, Publishers, 1951). Psychiatrists might add that the most formidable conflicts take place within the individual himself.

or covert conflict and violence. External conflicts tie the members of a group more closely together and may even preserve that group. (An example of this notion can be found in Secretary of State Seward's suggestion to President Lincoln just before the outbreak of the Civil War: to preserve the Union by starting a war with Western European nations!) This cementing function is true within national societies, but at times may also be true of groups of states. Surely, for example, the relationship between Great Britain and the United States is closer today than it would have been were it not for the experiences of World War II. The same may be said for the relationship between the Soviet Union and some of the Eastern European satellite states! Within states, conflict may serve as a safety-valve for accumulated pressures and tensions, while between states, conflict may serve to establish or maintain desired power distributions.[2]

In spite of the fact that conflicts may have positive and beneficial functions, the bulk of contemporary attention naturally focuses on their destructive consequences, and upon ways of avoiding them. UNESCO has sponsored a great deal of current research on conflict and its possible resolution. The orientation of the organization is in the direction of a psychological or social-psychological explanation of the phenomenon, as evidenced by the controversial theme expressed in UNESCO's Constitution that "wars begin in the minds of men." (See Dunn's discussion in Chapter XVIII.) This approach conceives group conflict to be the function of a combination of individual behavior patterns. It is closely related to the "frustration-aggression" hypothesis, which holds that frustration always engenders aggressive behavior (not necessarily either immediate or directed against the frustrating agent), and conversely, that any given act of aggression can be traced back to some preceding frustrating experience.[3] Stated in such absolute terms, the hypothesis has been found wanting,[4] but social psychologists are in broad agreement that aggression is indeed likely to be one of a number of possible consequences of a frustrating experience. This is a provocative theory, even though one must be careful in applying such findings from individual or small-group research to the explanation of behavior of large and complex units, such as nations, states, and governments.

For what it may be worth (and bearing in mind the same need for caution), evidence from the behavior of apes and children suggests three types of causes for exhibitions of aggression and outbreak of fighting: 1) competition over possession of some external object or objects; 2) the intrusion of a stranger of the same species into the group; and 3) failure or frustration in a given activity. On the basis of such findings, psychoanalysts usually draw attention to the existence of *unconscious* aggressive impulses in indi-

---

[2] Lewis A. Coser, *The Functions of Social Conflict* (Glencoe: The Free Press, 1956).

[3] Dollard, Miller *et al.*, *Frustration and Aggression* (New Haven: Yale University Press, 1939).

[4] S. Stanfield Sargent, "Reaction to Frustration—A Critique and Hypothesis," *Psychological Review*, LV (1948), 108–13.

viduals, to the possibility of ambivalence in personal relations, and to the impact of feelings of shame and guilt which may lead to a projection of hostile intent to others.[5] Such theories, by the way, are not completely in contrast to those advanced by Professor Ichheiser in this chapter.

Another conceptualization of conflict is based on the findings of "learning theory" as interpreted by Social Psychologists. Professor Mark A. May is perhaps the outstanding exponent of this school of thought. In his book *A Social Psychology of War and Peace*[6] he proposes that war and peace "are basically and fundamentally the products of the types of social conditioning that have occurred in the large masses of people of the leading nations of the world." He investigates such sequences as "Learning to Hate and Fight"; "Learning to Fear and to Escape"; and "Learning to Love and Defend." This theory is remarkably close to that of Malinowski, reprinted in this chapter.

In an excellent study, written under UNESCO auspices,[7] Professor Jessie Bernard discusses yet another conceptualization of conflict, namely the semanticist view which holds that conflict is the result of misunderstanding between individuals or groups. The conclusion which follows from this view is that the resolution of conflict lies exclusively in the establishment of accurate and adequate channels of communications, and that true understanding of views or policies of others would automatically make those views and policies acceptable.

This concept is in sharp contrast to the view that in international relations one is confronted with *real*, not imaginary, conflicts of interest and policy among units which decide on their goals and methods independently of one another. This view, which was expounded in Chapters III and IX, may be referred to as the "sociological" conceptualization of conflict (according to Professor Bernard). But if politics is conceived, in whole or in part, as conflict between groups and systems, it might be termed a "political" conceptualization as well.

There are two things wrong with the semanticist concept that all countries really want the same thing because they express their goals in the same terms, and therefore conflicts between them are artificial and can be prevented once the coincidence of objectives is understood. In the first place, all countries do *not* desire the same things, even if they do use identical or similar terms to describe their policy-objectives. The problems of ambiguity concerning common terms in this area were fully covered in Chapter IX. At the very least, the objectives of various countries are bound to differ in terms of priority and emphasis. And secondly, even if all countries *did* desire the same thing in a given situation, no statement could

---

[5] E. F. M. Durbin and John Bowlby, *Personal Aggressiveness and War* (New York: Columbia University Press, 1939).

[6] (New Haven: Yale University Press, 1943.)

[7] *The Nature of Conflict: Studies on the sociological aspects of international tensions,* UNESCO, Paris, 1957.

as yet be made concerning the likelihood of agreement or conflict between them. If "the same thing" were a scarce commodity—such as relative influence over a given area, a base, access to raw materials, etc.,—then the very identity of desires would promote conflict.[8] Ichheiser's article, although taking its point of departure from the issue of "misunderstandings," is a refreshing contrast from those who see in such misunderstandings the only, or even the major, source of conflict and tension. In linking this problem to the processes of perception (how, for example, can the United States ever convince the Soviet Union that American bases ringing Soviet territory are *not* aggressive? Would *we* be convinced if the situation were reversed?), he suggests that there is no natural harmony between various countries, and that a necessary first step is the acknowledgment of one's own limits of perception and understanding. Similar positions are held by Kecskemeti and Dunn in Chapter XVIII, which in a sense forms the counterpart of the present discussion.

All of the views represented in these comments and in the readings below have adherents and critics. The student of international relations must, above all, understand the varying points of view, evaluate them, study them, and attempt to arrive at ever more complete and comprehensive formulations.

---

[8] See, for example, Morgenthau, "The Art of Diplomatic Negotiation," p. 217 *supra:* "When Francis I of France was asked why he always made war against Charles V of Austria, he is reported to have answered: 'Because we both want the same thing: Italy.'"

1 • Common Statement *

Gordon W. Allport, *Professor of Social Relations, Harvard University.*

Gilberto Freyre, *Professor of Sociology, University of Bahia, Brazil; Professor at the Institute of Sociology, University of Buenos Aires, Argentina.*

Georges Gurvitch, *Professeur de Sociologie, Université de Sorbonne; Administrateur du Centre d'Etudes Sociologues, Paris.*

Max Horkheimer, *Director of the Institute of Social Research, New York.*

Arne Naess, *Professor of Philosophy, University of Oslo.*

John Rickman, M.D., *Editor,* British Journal of Medical Psychology.

Harry Stack Sullivan, M.D., *Chairman, Council of Fellows, Washington School of Psychiatry; Editor,* Psychiatry, Journal for the Operational Statement of Interpersonal Relations.

Alexander Szalai, *Professor of Sociology, University of Budapest; President, Hungarian Institute of Foreign Affairs.*

Man has now reached a stage in his history where he can study scientifically the causes of tensions that make for war. The meeting of this little group is itself symptomatic, representing as it does the first time the people of many lands, through an international organization of their own creation, have asked social scientists to apply their knowledge to some of the major problems of our time. Although we differ in the emphases we would give to various parts of our statement and in our views as to its comprehensiveness and implementation, no one of us would deny the importance of any part of it. We agree to the following twelve paragraphs:

(A) To the best of our knowledge, there is no evidence to indicate that wars are necessary and inevitable consequences of "human nature" as such. While men vary greatly in their capacities and temperaments, we believe there are vital needs common to all men which must be fulfilled in order to establish and maintain peace: men everywhere want to be free from hunger and disease, from insecurity and fear; men everywhere want fellowship and the respect of their fellowmen; the chance for personal growth and development.

(B) The problem of peace is the problem of keeping group and national tensions and aggressions within manageable proportions and of directing them to ends that are at the same time personally and socially constructive, so that man will no longer seek to exploit man. This goal cannot be achieved by surface reforms or isolated efforts. Fun-

* Hadley Cantril, ed., *Tensions that Cause Wars* (Urbana: University of Illinois Press, 1950), pp. 17–21. Reprinted by permission. The editor, Professor of Psychology at Princeton University, served as director of the UNESCO project on International Tensions. He was co-author of the pioneering study in national stereotypes, *How Nations See Each Other* (1953).

damental changes in social organization and in our ways of thinking are essential.

(C) If we are to avoid the kind of aggression that leads to armed conflict, we must among other things, so plan and arrange the use of modern productive power and resources that there will be maximum social justice. Economic inequalities, insecurities, and frustrations create group and national conflicts. All this is an important source of tensions which have often wrongly led one group to see another group as a menace through the acceptance of false images and oversimplified solutions and by making people susceptible to the scapegoating appeals of demagogues.

(D) Modern wars between nations and groups of nations are fostered by many of the myths, traditions, and symbols of national pride handed down from one generation to another. A great many current social symbols are still nationalistic, hindering the free movement of thought across political boundaries of what is, in fact, an interdependent world.

(E) Parents and teachers find it difficult to recognize the extent to which their own attitudes and loyalties—often acquired when they were young and when conditions were different—are no longer adequate to serve as effective guides to action in a changing world. Education in all its forms must oppose national self-righteousness and strive to bring about a critical and self-disciplined assessment of our own and other forms of social life.

(F) The development of modern means of swift and wide range communication is potentially a great aid to world solidarity. Yet this development also increases the danger that distortions of truth will reach a great many people who are not in a position to discriminate true from false, or to perceive that they are being beguiled and misled. It must

be a special responsibility of U.N. organizations to utilize these means of mass communication to encourage an adequate understanding of the people in other countries. This must always be a two-way traffic. It will aid the cause of peace if nations are enabled to see themselves as others see them.

(G) The prospect of a continuing inferior status is essentially unacceptable to any group of people. For this and other reasons, neither colonial exploitation nor oppression of minorities within a nation is in the long run compatible with world peace. As social scientists we know of no evidence that any ethnic group is inherently inferior.

(H) Many social scientists are studying these problems. But social scientists are still separated by national, ideological, and class differences. These differences have made it difficult for social scientists to resist effectively the emergence of pseudo-scientific theories which have been exploited by political leaders for their own ends.

(I) Objectivity in the social sciences is impossible to achieve whenever economic or political forces induce the investigator to accept narrow, partisan views. There is urgent need for a concentrated, adequately financed international research and educational programme.

(J) We recommend, for example, the cooperation of social scientists on broad regional and international levels, the creation of an international university and a series of world institutes of the social sciences under international auspices. We believe that international scientific fact-finding studies could contribute useful information concerning the cultures of all nations and bring to light dangerous insecurities and sources of tension, as well as legitimate aspirations of people all over the world. Equally certain to be rewarding are studies of educational methods in the home, the school, and in youth organizations and other groups by which the minds of the young are oriented toward war or toward peace. From the dissemination of the information resulting from these studies, we may anticipate the emergence of concrete proposals for the guidance of national programmes of education.

(K) The physical and biological sciences in recent years have provided impressive demonstrations of the effect of research. Some of the practical results have been rather to dismay and disquiet the civilized world than to reduce its tensions. The scientists whose research has been used in the development of atomic and biological warfare are not themselves responsible for launching a curse upon the world. The situation reflects the forces now determining the uses to which science can be put. While other factors are concerned, we hold that the chances for a constructive use of the potentialities of scientific and technological developments will improve if and when man takes the responsibility for understanding the forces which work upon him and society both from within and from without.

(L) In this task of acquiring self-knowledge and social insight, the social sciences—the sciences of Man—have a vital part to play. One hopeful sign today is the degree to which the boundaries between these sciences are breaking down in the face of the common challenge confronting them. The social scientist can help make clear to people of all nations that the freedom and welfare of one are ultimately bound up with the freedom and welfare of all, that the world need not continue to be a place where men must either kill or be killed. Effort in behalf of one's own group can become compatible with effort in behalf of humanity.

2 • Misunderstandings in International Relations *

Gustav Ichheiser

The author, an Austrian by birth, has taught and done research in Austria, Poland, and at the Institute of Sociology in London. He came to the United States in 1940, and after serving as a Psychologist at a State Hospital, became Professor of Psychology and Sociology at Talladega College. He has written perceptive articles on the problem of misunderstandings in various types of human relationships.

Since I agree with those who insist that social science is not only a science but also an art, I shall start my paper not with facts and concepts but with two metaphorical stories. These stories will point, symbolically, in the direction of those facts and issues which I shall later discuss conceptually.

The first story: A friend is visiting

---

* *American Sociological Review,* XVI (1951), 311–16. Reprinted by permission.

your city for the first time and he wants to gain a general view of the city. You take him first to the north end where there is a tall tower with a view commanding the whole area. Then you take him to a similar spot at the south end. At that point your friend exclaims with great amazement, "How very strange! The city looks quite differently from here!" Now, what is your reaction? Something of shock, for you rightly assume that every normal adult understands that things in physical space look differently from differing points of view. You probably conclude that your friend is, to say the least, a bit unbalanced and in need of psychiatric attention.

Now, the really strange thing is that what every normal person understands by himself as far as things in *physical* space are concerned, most people do not understand, and even do not want to understand, so far as phenomena in *social* space are concerned. And any attempt to explain the relativity of social perspectives, and its full implications, usually meets with strong psychological resistance.

The second story: Here we approach the core of our problem. Assume that, pointing to a desk, I should say, "This is a chair," and in spite of all attempts on your part to correct me, I still insist it is a chair. You determine that I do know the English meaning for desk and chair. You prove my eyesight is not faulty. Still I insist. Now further assume that it is of utmost importance to you, both in terms of your own personal welfare and your moral values, to maintain for yourself and others that this is a desk, not a chair. Thus, my insistence to the contrary would threaten your whole external and inner security system. How then will you react to my insistence? You will probably contend that I am insane and suffer from hallucinations or that I am a dangerous and subversive person—in either case need-

ing to be locked up; or being yourself a "tolerant" person you decide that, at the very least, I am a "queer" person and am to be avoided.

Does this story seem to you pointless? People, by and large, do agree as to what is a desk and what a chair; what a blackboard or a window, a pipe or a cigarette. So long as *physical* objects are concerned, we agree, but if we turn from physical objects to *social* facts then our story becomes pertinent and very realistic—in symbolic terms. For what to members of the one ethnic groups looks like "aggression," to members of another group looks like "defense" or "revolt"; what to the one group looks like "liberation," to the other group looks like "enslavement"; what to the one group looks like "re-education," to the other group looks like "persecution"; what to the one group looks like "dictatorship," to the other group looks like "true democracy"; what to the one group looks like a "hero," to another group looks like a "criminal"—the list could be continued *ad infinitum*. The real problem is, why do people of different cultural and, particularly, national background see the social world in entirely different ways?

Before I answer this question by translating the metaphorical stories into the language of facts and concepts, two prefacing points are pertinent.

First, most of what will be said in discussing the social psychology of misunderstandings in international relations would apply also, with some slight modifications, to other intercultural relations; and some would apply as well to all human relations.

Second, I shall refrain from discussing at this time those misunderstandings which have their roots in differences of ideologies which are not primarily culturally conditioned....

I shall proceed now to discuss first what might be called the two basic "dynamic systems" which are at the bottom of intercultural and international misunderstandings. These two "dynamic systems" are not the only ones which produce misunderstandings, but I am inclined to believe that they are two of the most important. And second, I shall discuss two types of nationalism, the *conscious* and the *unconscious,* which distinction is, in my opinion, also of crucial importance for an understanding of the whole problem.

The first of the two "dynamic systems" which are causing misunderstandings in international relations is related to a certain definite interdependence between culture, emotions, perceptions and again emotions; the second "dynamic system" is related to what I called recently the limits of insight.

1. CULTURE—EMOTIONS—PERCEPTIONS —EMOTIONS

Cultural background is among the major factors which influence how we feel about things, i.e., about the various aspects and contents of our immediate experience.

The way we feel about things, i.e., our likes and dislikes, our hopes and our fears, and so on, influence not only our motives, ideas, and actions, but our perceptions as well. This means that the way we perceive the world, what we see and to what we are blinded, what we emphasize and what we neglect, and a host of valences and characteristics of the perceptual world, are the expressions, projections, manifestations of our emotions. The scientific realization that our emotions significantly determine and thus distort our perceptions, seems to be comparatively new, and is not yet fully understood in its far-reaching theoretical and practical implications.

Not only do our emotions influence our perceptions but, in turn, our perceptions evoke our emotions. We are confronted here with one of those numerous vicious circles operating frequently in human affairs. In consequence of this interdependence, not only do our emotions, culturally conditioned as they are, influence the organization of our perceptions but in turn our thus emotionally conditioned perceptions influence certain of our emotional reactions.

Of particular importance in this context is the fact that the law of the emotional, and thus indirectly cultural, conditioning of our perceptions and conceptions applies, of course, also to our perceptions and conceptions about other people and about ourselves. Hence, to limit our discussion here to the collective level only, and using an example, being a Frenchman means, among other things, having certain definite, collectively distorted perceptions and conceptions about, let us say, Englishmen on the one hand, and Frenchmen themselves, on the other, which distorted images, in turn, evoke certain specific emotional reactions.

As a rule, we are completely unaware of the silent organization of our perceptions (and conceptions) by our culturally conditioned emotions, and of the far-reaching implications of this state of affairs. Instead, we believe that we simply see things "as they really are." It is even fair to say that the culturally conditioned organization of our emotions and thus also of our perceptions is among those mechanisms which are the most hidden from our explicit awareness. (Particularly naive in this respect are the Marxians: they see that our "consciousness" is determined by the socio-economic system, but are altogether blinded to the more deep-seated fact that it is determined by our culture.)

If, therefore, members of two groups influenced by two different cultures meet, both, by and large, take it for granted that they themselves see the things, including themselves and each other, "as they really are." When they find, as they are bound to find, that others see things differently, both reach the conclusion that it is the other fellow who is unable to see the things "as they really are" and who has distorted conceptions about himself as well as about others.

The final step which, in a way, closes the cycle of the inter-cultural misunderstandings (and irritations), consists in developing various defense-mechanisms which serve the purpose of maintaining the belief in the validity of our own perception of reality by insisting and "proving" that something, intellectually or morally or both, is wrong with the others. In order to prove that we are right and true and even sane, we have to prove that others are wrong and false, if not outright insane.

The intensity and amount of misunderstandings (and irritations) which will actually develop in this situation will depend, among other things, on the degree of the incompatibility of the respective cultural patterns; on the underlying ecological configuration; and on the distribution of power among the groups which are irritating each other.

Let us now turn to the second "dynamic system."

2. LIMITS OF INSIGHT

We can, of course, communicate adequately only with those people whose symbols, i.e., whose "language" in the broadest meaning of this term, we understand.

We have to distinguish with reference to our problem in this context four types of symbols: first, those symbols which we are able to identify as symbols and whose meaning we understand—for instance, a foreign language which we speak; second, those which we are able to identify as symbols the meaning of which we do not understand, yet are fully aware of our lack of understanding—for instance, a foreign language which we do not speak; third, those which we fail to identify as symbols, thus not understanding that we do not understand—for instance, not understanding that certain districts have a certain symbolical prestige for the members of another group; and fourth, those which we are able to identify as symbols but misinterpret as to their real meaning—for instance, misunderstanding of the meaning of certain religious symbols for those who share another creed.

It is the last two forms which are the sources of the most important misunderstandings in intercultural and international relations. Not to understand is a frustrating experience, especially if we cannot help being in contact with those whom we do not understand and with whom we possibly have to cooperate; it leads to disappointments when the false expectations are disproved by the experience.

This being the case, it is inevitable that between members of different cultural groups who have different symbols expressing different meanings, certain peculiar forms of non-understanding and misunderstanding are likely to develop in addition to those which are operating even among the members of the same cultural (national) group. This state of affairs is aggravated by the fact that, in order to overcome their perplexity, people who are confronted by disagreements arising from misunderstandings tend to develop certain forms of pseudo-understanding in order to maintain the belief that it is the others and not they themselves (or both) who are responsible for all those disagreements, irritations, and disappointments.

Hence, again, the vicious circle is closed: differences in the systems of symbols lead to non-understanding and misunderstanding; non-understanding and misunderstanding lead to irritations; these, in turn, evoke defense-mechanisms which serve the purpose of maintaining the belief that "we are right" and "they are wrong."

In approaching the same problem of misunderstandings in international relations from a somewhat different angle, I shall discuss now two types of nationalism, namely, the conscious and the unconscious, a distinction which, as already mentioned, is of great importance for an understanding of certain misunderstandings in international relations.

We are dealing with a *conscious* type of nationalism if members of a national group profess and emphasize in an open way certain particular national ideals, if they strive consciously and overtly towards certain particular national goals, at the same time rejecting in a more or less aggressive way the values, ideals, symbols and goals of other national groups.

If, on the other hand, members of a national group are so deeply involved in a set of nationally determined assumptions, interpretations, conceptions that, even though not expressing in an articulate way any particular beliefs and ideals, they see in fact and judge everything from their own national point of view, then we are dealing with an *unconscious* type of nationalism.

The conscious nationalist, if he fights, fights in concrete terms and with full awareness—for America, or for France, or for Japan, or for whatever country. The unconscious nationalist, if he fights, fights always in the abstract for "humanity," or "justice," or "freedom," and remains completely blinded to the fact that the way he defines these ideas and ideals is determined by his unconscious nationalistic frame of reference.

To put it another way, the conscious nationalist *is* a nationalist and *knows* that he is a nationalist. The unconscious nationalist is also a nationalist, but he either does not know it, or denies it, or even professes to be "against nationalism." He is, in a way, the "partner in crime" of the notorious "unprejudiced man" in the domestic scene, and is among the most dangerous types of our age.[1]

In trying to understand the misunderstandings in international relations in the light of social psychology, we have, therefore, to analyze national attitudes, motives, conceptions, and actions on two levels. Ethnic and similar groups which, on the conscious level, believe themselves, or even appear, not to be nationalistic at all, nevertheless are often profoundly nationalistic as far as their unconscious presuppositions and motivations are concerned. This unconscious nationalism may manifest itself on the conscious level in the disguise of most perplexing and confusing transformations and rationalizations. So, for instance, "pacifism" may be sometimes only a rationalization of a nationalistic or even chauvinistic attitude of privileged ethnic groups which, being satisfied with the status quo, wish to enjoy it in peace. Or again, "internationalism" may be only a distorted manifestation of deep-seated, unconsciously nationalistic attitudes of certain ethnic or similar groups or sub-groups which may hope, by participating in a pseudo-internationalistic movement, to improve the status of their ethnic group.

---

[1] *Morris Ginsberg* in his book *Reason and Unreason in Society* (Harvard University Press, 1948), p. 165, mentions that the famous German writer, G. E. Lessing, wrote in 1767 that the Germans seem not to have any national characteristics. Oddly enough, notes Ginsberg, David Hume, Lessing's contemporary, made almost an identical statement about the English, which clearly shows how blinded we are to our own cultural characteristics.

In spite of Marxian theories, unconscious nationalism is more deeply rooted in the personality structure than is class-consciousness. The Frenchman, for instance, might have some doubts as to whether he is a bourgeois or a proletarian; he might have his doubts as to whether he ought to be a democrat, a communist, or a fascist; but he cannot have any doubts as to whether he "is" (or whether he "ought to be") a Frenchman. His nationality is so basically a part of his personality that it can never become a "problem" to him. He takes it for granted. A problem and dilemma can be only something which might be in doubt. Orthodox Marxism is mainly responsible for the confusion in the mind of many intellectuals concerning these obvious facts.

To repeat and summarize, the unconscious nationalist, not being aware of his own nationalistic frame of reference and its hidden presuppositions and motivations, believes that he is simply a "human being," that he sees the facts "as they really are," and as they are seen by all other "reasonable people." He feels irritated that there are other ethnic groups who do not have the same "objective" and "correct" conceptions which he is happy to possess; he does not realize that he, in turn, irritates those others who are as sure as he is himself that not he but they themselves have "objective" and "correct" conceptions. Our unconscious nationalist then wonders how it happens that other people fail to realize their "false" ideas about things "as they really are." Are these other people bad? Or are they stupid? Or are they misguided?

Now, some people might say that what I call "unconscious nationalism" is only another term for "ethnocentrism." However, it seems to me, that my concept emphasizes different aspects of the respective attitudes. First, the main point I am stressing is not that the unconscious nationalist sees things from his own point of view but that he is not aware of it. Second, I am calling attention to the fact that it is one thing to know about ethnocentrism "in principle," and it is quite another story to know of what, concretely, our own ethnocentric attitudes, motives, assumptions, interpretations, and conceptions consist. And third, I insist upon the importance of an analysis of the relationship between the conscious and the unconscious aspects of nationalism.

The question arises as to whether this present diagnosis refers to all inter-ethnic relations or merely and specifically to the situation with which we are confronted in our age. My answer is that the described features of inter-ethnic relations, and particularly of international relations, appear in our age in an aggravated form. There are several causes which are responsible for this aggravation. I wish, however, to mention briefly only two of them.

First (and this has been often said) the revolution of the technology of communication and transportation brought in its wake *physical* contacts among ethnic and similar groups which, psychologically, not only do not understand each other but, what is still more confusing, do not even understand that they do not understand each other. I hope and pray that we all shall begin as soon as possible to understand at least that we do not understand each other.

Second (and this point is often overlooked), social reality has become more and more complex, ambiguous, elusive, "invisible." In consequence, the social world we are confronted with looks more and more like an ink-blot, like a Rorschach test which everybody can shape according to his own hopes, fears, hatreds, suspicions, and the like. And nobody knows in fact who is who, and what is what. This, it seems to me, is one of the most fundamental, if not actually the most fundamental, dilemma of our age.

Now, what should we do about this situation, especially in terms of a sociology of education? My first, and very personal, answer is that I do not adhere to a radically pragmatic philosophy of life. This means that I would insist upon discussing this issue and upon maintaining, at least "esoterically," our intellectual integrity in a confused world even if I knew we could do little about this matter in terms of effective action. In contradiction to many colleagues, I am both for research and reflection without action and for action without research. However, I submit the following five practical suggestions:

1. It is a basic fact and fate of mankind that it is subdivided into ethnic and similar groups. This fact and fate must be recognized and acknowledged. Men are not simply "human beings"— they are Americans, Frenchmen, Germans, Chinese, Japanese, Gentiles, Jews, Protestants, Catholics, and so on. This variety of cultural backgrounds is an essential and integral part of human personality. Hence, if we consider ourselves and each other simply as "human beings," then we either deceive or misunderstand ourselves and each other.

2. Since people *are* in fact nationalists, i.e., since their perception of social reality is profoundly influenced by their cultural-national background, it would be much better if they would be at least aware of this state of affairs. What I actually suggest is that the best thing to do is to transform unconscious nationalists into conscious nationalists who are aware that they actually see things in the particular perspective of their national group. I repeat, not the conscious but the unconscious nationalist who strives for a "one world" defined

in terms of his own nationalistic frame of reference to which he himself is blinded, is the most dangerous fellow of our age.

3. We should discard our naively optimistic presupposition that there is some kind of a "pre-established harmony" among various cultural patterns and among various ethnic groups. This presupposition—upon which, incidentally, the current trends in intercultural education are largely based—is obviously a counterpart of the presupposition of the classical (liberal) economists who assumed that there is kind of a pre-established harmony among various classes and between self-interests of the individuals and the interests of the society as a whole. Both presuppositions are entirely unrealistic. We should rather recognize the fact that tensions, antagonisms, conflicts, misunderstandings among various cultural groups are a *normal* state of affairs. This fact should not be camouflaged but should be taken into account in framing our ideas and actions.

4. I also suggest that we cease lamenting and denouncing the "irrational factors" in personality and society. These so-called "irrational factors" are in the very core of our personality and many sacred meanings and values of life are rooted in them. A society without irrational beliefs is an unknown entity and in practical terms a complete impossibility.

5. Finally—and this is the most practical suggestion—I urgently suggest that we should establish a committee, or a research group, in which social scientists (including psychologists, of course) of different cultural background would reach a solemn "gentleman's agreement" that, in a "permissive atmosphere," they will tell each other frankly what they consider in each other to be a bias, false silent assumption, blind spot, culturally distorted interpre-

tation, prejudice, and the like. For, obviously, not only the common man but also the social scientist is profoundly affected by his cultural background and his conditioned emotions in his perceptions and conceptions, in his research and theory. The illusion of a culturally independent objectivity is probably the most serious occupational disease of social scientists. I have not the slightest doubt that, if this suggestion would be accepted and translated into practice, what would come out of such an experiment would be of such a nature that, as compared with it, the Kinsey Report would pale into insignificance.

Should I have the privilege of being invited to take part in such a discussion, in a permissive atmosphere and after a gentleman's agreement has been reached for being frank with one another, then, being of cautious nature, I would still ask for the special permission of being allowed to reveal only approximately fifty per cent of what I consider to be the truth.

3 • An Anthropological Analysis of War *

Bronislaw Malinowski

The author rose to great eminence as Professor of Anthropology at the University of London. Founder of the functional school of anthropology, his studies include Myth in Primitive Society *(1926)*, The Dynamics of Culture Change *(1945)*, Freedom and Civilization *(1944) and more than a dozen other books and monographs.*

· · · ·

There is ... a legitimate role for the anthropologist. Studying human societies on the widest basis in time perspective and spatial distribution, he should be able to tell us what war really is. Whether war is a cultural phenomenon to be found at the beginnings of evolution; what are its determining causes and its effects; what does it create and what does it destroy—these are questions which belong to the science of man. The forms, the factors, and the forces which define and determine human warfare should, therefore, be analyzed in a correct anthropological theory of war.

...the main problem of today is simple and vital: shall we abolish war or must we submit to it by choice or necessity? Is it desirable to have permanent peace and is this peace possible? If it is possible, how can we implement it successfully? There is obviously a price and a great price to be paid for any fundamental change in the constitution of mankind. Here, clearly, the price to be paid is the surrender of state sovereignty and subordination of all political units to worldwide control. Whether this is a smaller or greater sacrifice in terms of progress, culture, and personality than the disasters created by war is another prob-

* *The American Journal of Sociology*, XLVI (Chicago: University of Chicago Press, 1941), 522–43. Reprinted by permission.

lem, the solution of which may be foreshadowed in anthropological arguments.

I think that the task of evaluating war in terms of cultural analysis is today the main duty of the theory of civilization. In democratic countries public opinion must be freed from prejudice and enlightened as regards sound knowledge. The totalitarian states are spending as much energy, foresight, and constructive engineering on the task of indoctrinating the minds of their subjects as in the task of building armaments. Unless we scientifically and ethically rally to the counterpart task, we shall not be able to oppose them. At the same time the full cultural understanding of war in its relation to nationality and state, in its drives and effects, in the price paid and advantages gained, is necessary also for the problem of implementing any fundamental change.

The problem of what war is as a cultural phenomenon naturally falls into the constituent issues of the biological determinants of war, its political effects, and its cultural constructiveness. In the following discussion of pugnacity and aggression we shall see that even preorganized fighting is not a simple reaction of violence determined by the impulse of anger. The first distinction to emerge from this analysis will be between organized and collective fighting as against individual, sporadic, and spontaneous acts of violence—which are the antecedents of homicide, murder, and civic disorder, but not of war. We shall then show that organized fighting has to be fully discussed with reference to its political background. Fights within a community fulfil an entirely different function from intertribal feuds or battles. Even in these latter, however, we will have to distinguish between culturally effective warfare and military operations which do not leave any permanent mark either in terms of diffusion, of evolution, or of any lasting historical aftereffect. From all this will emerge the concept of "war as an armed contest between two independent political units, by means of organized military force, in the pursuit of a tribal or national policy." [1] With this as a minimum definition of war, we shall be able to see how futile and confusing it is to regard primitive brawls, scrimmages, and feuds as genuine antecedents of our present world-catastrophe.

WAR AND HUMAN NATURE

We have, then, first to face the issue of "aggressiveness as instinctual behavior"; in other words, of the determination of war by intrinsically biological motives. Such expressions as "war is older than man," "war is inherent in human nature," "war is biologically determined" have either no meaning or they signify that humanity has to conduct wars, even as all men have to breathe, sleep, breed, eat, walk, and evacuate, wherever they live and whatever their civilization. Every schoolboy knows this and most anthropologists have ignored the facts just mentioned. The study of man has certainly evaded the issue concerning the relation between culture and the biological foundations of human nature.

Put plainly and simply, biological determinism means that in no civilization can the individual organism survive and the community continue without the integral incorporation into culture of such bodily functions as breathing, sleep, rest, excretion, and reproduction.

. . . .

Can we regard pugnacity and aggressiveness and all the other reactions of hostility, hate, and violence as comparable to any vital sequence so far discussed? The answer must be an em-

[1] Cf. my article, "The Deadly Issue," *Atlantic Monthly*, CLIX (December, 1936), 659–69.

phatic negative. Not that the impulse of aggression, violence, or destruction be ever absent from any human group or from the life of any human being. If the activity of breathing be interrupted by accident or a deliberate act of another individual, the immediate reaction to it is a violent struggle to remove the obstacle or to overcome the human act of aggression. Kicking, biting, pushing, immediately start; a fight ensues, which has to end with the destruction of the suffocated organism or the removal of the obstacle. Take away the food from the hungry child or dog or monkey and you will provoke immediately strong hostile reactions. Any interference with the progressive course of sexual preliminaries—still more, any interruption of the physiological act—leads in man and animal to a violent fit of anger.

This last point, however, brings us directly to the recognition that the impulse of anger, the hostilities of jealousy, the violence of wounded honor and sexual and emotional possessiveness are as productive of hostility and of fighting, direct or delayed, as is the thwarting in the immediate satisfaction of a biological impulse.

We could sum up these results by saying that the *impulse* which controls aggression is not primary but derived. It is contingent upon circumstances in which a primary biologically defined impulse is being thwarted. It is also produced in a great variety of nonorganic ways, determined by such purely cultural factors as economic ownership, ambition, religious values, privileges of rank, and personal sentiments of attachment, dependence, and authority. Thus, to speak even of the *impulse* of pugnacity as biologically determined is incorrect. This becomes even clearer when we recognize ... that the essence of an impulse is to produce a clear and definite bodily reaction, which again pro-

duces the satisfaction of the impulse. In human societies, on the contrary, we find that the impulse of anger is in almost every case transformed into chronic states of the human mind or organism—into hate, vindictiveness, permanent attitudes of hostility. That such culturally defined sentiments can lead, and do lead, to acts of violence, simply means that acts of violence are culturally, not biologically, determined. Indeed, when we look at the actual cases of violent action, individual, or collective and organized, we find that most of them are the result of purely conventional, traditional, and ideological imperatives, which have nothing whatsoever to do with any organically determined state of mind.

. . . .

When we are faced with the question where, how, and under what circumstances, acts of purely physiological aggression occur among human adults, we come again to an interesting result. Cases of sound, normal people attacking, hurting, or killing one another under the stress of genuine anger do occur, but they are extremely, indeed, negligibly, rare. Think of our own society. You can adduce an indefinite number of cases from a mental hospital. You can also show that within very specialized situations, such as in prisons or concentration camps, in groups cooped up by shipwreck or some other accident, aggression is fairly frequent. Such a catastrophe as a theater on fire or a sinking boat has sometimes, but not always, the effect of producing a fight for life, in which people are trampled to death and bones broken through acts of violence, determined by panic and fear. There are also cases in every criminal record, primitive or civilized, of homicidal injuries or bruises which occur under outbursts of anger and hatred, or a fit of jealousy. We see that "aggressiveness" within the framework of an adult cultural group is found under the headings of "panic," "insanity," "artificial propinquity," or else that it becomes the type of antisocial and anticultural behavior called "crime." It is always part and product of a breakdown of personality or of culture. It is not a case of a vital sequence which has to be incorporated into every culture. Even more, since it is a type of impulsive sequence which constantly threatens the normal course of cultural behavior, it has to be and is eliminated.

THE HARNESSING OF AGGRESSION BY CULTURE

Another interesting point in the study of aggression is that, like charity, it begins at home. Think of the examples given above. They all imply direct contact and then the flaring-up of anger over immediate issues, where divergent interests occur, or, among the insane, are imagined to occur. Indeed, the smaller the group engaged in co-operation, united by some common interests, and living day by day with one another, the easier it is for them to be mutually irritated and to flare up in anger. Freud and his followers have demonstrated beyond doubt and cavil that within the smallest group of human co-operation, the family, there frequently arise anger, hatred, and destructive, murderous impulses. Sexual jealousies within the home, grievances over food, service, or other economic interests occur in every primitive or civilized household. I have seen myself Australian aborigines, Papuans, Melanesians, African Bantus, and Mexican Indians turning angry or even flaring into a passion on occasions when they were working together, or celebrating feasts, or discussing some plans or some issues of their daily life. The actual occurrence, however, of bodily violence is so rare that it becomes statistically negligible. We shall see shortly why this is so.

Those who maintain that "natural aggressiveness" is a permanent cause of warfare would have to prove that this aggressiveness operates more as between strangers than between members of the same group. The facts taken from ethnographic evidence give an entirely different answer. Tribal strangers are above all eliminated from any contact with one another.

. . . .

...We have to conclude that, contrary to the prevailing theoretical bias, aggression as the raw material of behavior occurs not in the contact between tribal strangers but within the tribe and within its component co-operative groups.

We have seen already that aggression is a by-product of co-operation. This latter organizes human beings into systems of concerted activities. Such a system, or institution, as we can call it, is the family. A small group of people are united under the contract of marriage. They are concerned with the production, education, and socialization of children. They obey a system of customary law, and they operate conjointly a household—i.e., a portion of environment with an apparatus of implements and consumers goods. The clan and the local group, the food-producing team and the industrial workshop, the age grade and the secret society are one and all systems of concerted activities, each organized into an institution.[2]

Let us try to understand the place of aggressiveness within an institution.

[2] I have suggested, in the...article "Culture," that this concept of institution is, in anthropological analysis, preferable to that of culture complex. This point will be more fully elaborated in a forthcoming article entitled "The Scientific Approach to the Study of Man," to appear in a volume entitled *Man and Science,* of the "Science and Culture Series," edited by Dr. R. N. Anshen.

There is no doubt at all that, within these short-range co-operative and spatially condensed forms of human organization, genuine aggressiveness will occur more readily and universally than anywhere else. Impulses to beat a wife or husband, or to thrash children, are personally known to everybody and ethnographically universal. Nor are partners in work or in business ever free of the temptation to take each other by the throat, whether primitive or civilized. The very essence of an institution, however, is that it is built upon the charter of fundamental rules which, on the one hand, clearly define the rights, prerogatives, and duties of all the partners. A whole set of minor and more detailed norms of custom, technique, ethics, and law also clearly and minutely lay down the respective functions as regards type, quantity, and performance in each differential activity. This does not mean that people do not quarrel, argue, or dispute as to whether the performance or prerogatives have not been infringed. It means, first and foremost, that all such disputes are within the universe of legal or quasilegal discourse. It also means that the dispute can always be referred, not to the arbitrament of force, but to the decision of authority.

And here we come upon the fact that the charter—the fundamental customary law—always defines the division of authority in each institution. It also defines the use of force and violence, the regulation of which is, indeed, the very essence of what we call the social organization of an institutionalized group....

It is characteristic once more that most fighting on the primitive level occurs between smaller units of the same cultural group. The members of two families or two clans or two local groups may come to blows. We have instances of such fighting among the Veddas, the

Australian aborigines, and other lowest primitives. Such intratribal fighting is always the result of the infraction of tribal law. A member of a clan or a family is killed. A woman is abducted or an act of adultery committed. Only in the rarest of cases, a spontaneous brawl or fight ensues immediately. For there exist rules of tribal law which define the way in which the dispute has to be fought out. The whole type of fighting between families, clans, or local groups is conventional, determined in every detail by beliefs and elements of material culture, or by values and agreements. The collective behavior in such fighting, which is characteristic of the primitive level of lowest savages, is guided at every step and is controlled by factors which can be only studied with reference to the social organization, to customary law, to mythological ideas, as well as to the material apparatus of a primitive culture.[3]

When there is a strong rivalry between two groups, and when this leads to a general state of mind—generating frequent outbursts of anger and sentiments of hatred over real divergencies of interest—we find an arrangement in which occasional fights are not only allowed, but specially organized, so as to give vent to hostile feelings and reestablish order after the feelings have been overtly expressed. Such occasional tournament fights take sometimes pronouncedly peaceful form. The public songs of insult, by which the Eskimo even up their differences and express hatred, grievances, or hostility, are a well-known example of this. In Central

---

[3] If space would allow, we could show that witchcraft, which is also an important tool of expressing anger or hatred, is a characteristic substitute mechanism. The use of direct violence is eliminated by translating the reaction of anger into a sentiment of hatred, and expressing this, not by any fighting or use of force, but by mystical acts of hostility.

Europe the institution of Sunday after-noon drinking and fighting fulfils the function of an organized and regulated exchange of insults, blows, at times injuries and casualties, in which accu-mulated resentments of the week are evened up. We have a good description of such regulated fights within the group among the Kiwai Papuans, among the Polynesians, and among the South American Indians.

Anthropological evidence, correctly interpreted, shows, therefore, that there is a complete disjunction between the psychological fact of pugnacity and the cultural determination of feuds and fights. Pugnacity can be transformed through such cultural factors as propa-ganda, scare-mongering, and indoctrina-tion into any possible or even improb-able channels. We have seen the change in France: the pugnacity of yesterday has overnight become a lukewarm alli-ance, and the friendship of the most recent past may, at any moment, flare up into the pugnacity of tomorrow. The raw material of pugnacity does ad-mittedly exist. It is not in any way the biological core of any type of organized violence, in the sense in which we found that sex is the core of organized family life, hunger of commissariat, evacuation of sanitary arrangements, or the main-tenance of bodily temperature a biologi-cal factor around which center cultural adjustments of clothing and housing. Anger and aggressiveness may flare up almost at any moment in the course of organized co-operation. Their incidence decreases with the size of the group. As an impulse, pugnacity is indefinitely plastic. As a type of behavior, fighting can be linked with an indefinitely wide range of cultural motives.

Everywhere, at all levels of develop-ment, and in all types of culture, we find that the direct effects of aggressiveness are eliminated by the transformation of pugnacity into collective hatreds, tribal or national policies, which lead to organ-ized, ordered fighting, but prevent any physiological reactions of anger. Human beings never fight on an extensive scale under the direct influence of an aggres-sive impulse. They fight and organize for fighting because, through tribal tra-dition, through teachings of a religious system, or of an aggressive patriotism, they have been indoctrinated with cer-tain cultural values which they are pre-pared to defend, and with certain col-lective hatreds on which they are ready to assault and kill. Since pugnacity is so widespread, yet indefinitely plastic, the real problem is not whether we can completely eliminate it from human nature, but how we can canalize it so as to make it constructive....

THE CONTRIBUTION OF ANTHROPOLOGY TO THE PROBLEM OF WAR

Glancing back over our previous arguments, we can see that we have arrived at certain theoretical conclu-sions, new to anthropological theory. It will still be necessary to show where our gains in clarity and definition are related to modern problems.

As regards the theoretical gains, we have shown that war cannot be regarded as a fiat of human destiny, in that it could be related to biological needs or immutable psychological drives. All types of fighting are complex cultural responses due not to any direct dic-tates of an impulse but to collective forms of sentiment and value. As a mechanism of organized force for the pursuit of national policies war is slow in evolving. Its incidence depends on the gradual development of military equipment and organization, of the scope for lucrative exploits, of the for-mation of independent political units.

Taking into account all such factors, we had to establish, within the genus of aggression and use of violence, the following distinctions: (1) Fighting, private and angry, within a group belongs to the type of breach of custom and law and is the prototype of criminal behavior. It is countered and curbed by the customary law within institutions and between institutions. (2) Fighting, collective and organized, is a juridical mechanism for the adjustment of differences between constituent groups of the same larger cultural unit. Among the lowest savages these two types are the only forms of armed contest to be found. (3) Armed raids, as a type of man-hunting sport, for purposes of head-hunting, cannibalism, human sacrifices, and the collection of other trophies. (4) Warfare as the political expression of early nationalism, that is, the tendency to make the tribe-nation and tribe-state coincide, and thus to form a primitive nation-state. (5) Military expeditions of organized pillage, slave-raiding, and collective robbery. (6) Wars between two culturally differentiated groups as an instrument of national policy. This type of fighting, with which war in the fullest sense of the word began, leads to conquest, and, through this, to the creation of full-fledged military and political states, armed for internal control, for defense and aggression. This type of state presents, as a rule, and for the first time in evolution, clear forms of administrative, political, and legal organization. Conquest is also of first-rate importance in the processes of diffusion and evolution.

The types of armed contest, listed as (4) and (6) and these two only, are, in form, sociological foundations, and in the occurrence of constructive policy are comparable with historically defined wars. Every one of the six types here summed up presents an entirely different cultural phase in the development of organized fighting. The neglect to establish the differentiation here introduced has led to grave errors in the ap-

plication of anthropological principles to general problems concerning the nature of war. The crude short-circuiting—by which our modern imperialisms, national hatreds, and world-wide lust of power have been connected with aggression and pugnacity—is largely the result of not establishing the above distinctions, of disregarding the cultural function of conflict, and of confusing war, as a highly specialized and mechanized phenomenon with any form of aggression.

We can determine even more precisely the manner in which anthropological evidence, as the background of correct understanding and informed knowledge, can be made to bear on some of our current problems. In general, of course, it is clear that since our main concern is whether war will destroy our Western civilization or not, the anthropological approach, which insists on considering the cultural context of war, might be helpful.

Especially important in a theoretical discussion of whether war can be controlled and ultimately abolished, is the recognition that war is not biologically founded. The fact that its occurrence cannot be traced to the earliest beginnings of human culture is significant. Obviously, if war were necessary to human evolution; if it were something without which human groups have to decay and by which they advance; then war could not be absent from the earliest stages, in which the actual birth of cultural realities took place under the greatest strains and against the heaviest odds. A really vital ingredient could not, therefore, be lacking in the composition of primitive humanity, struggling to lay down the foundations of further progress.

War, looked at in evolutionary perspective, is always a highly destructive event. Its purpose and *raison d'être* depend on whether it creates greater values than it destroys. Violence is constructive, or at least profitable, only when it can lead to large-scale transfers of wealth and privilege, of ideological outfit, and of moral experience. Thus, humanity had to accumulate a considerable stock of transferable goods, ideals, and principles before the diffusion of those through conquest, and even more, the pooling and the reorganization of economic, political, and spiritual resources could lead to things greater than those which had been destroyed through the agency of fighting.

Our analysis has shown that the work of cultural exercise is associated with one of the two widest groups, the tribe-nation. The work of destroying and also of reconstructing in matters cultural is associated with the tribe-state. Here, once more, it will be clear to every social student that, in giving this ethnographic background to the concepts of state and nation, of nationalism and imperialism, we may have contributed to the theoretical clarification of the corresponding modern facts.

What matters to us today, as ever, is human culture as a whole, in all its varieties, racial and religious, national or affected by regional differentiation of interests and of values. Nationhood in its manifold manifestations, today as always, is the carrier of each culture. The state should be the guardian and the defender of the nation, not its master, still less its destroyer. The Wilsonian principle of self-determination was scientifically, hence morally, justified. It was justified to the extent only that each culture ought to have full scope for its development—that is, every nation ought to be left in peace and freedom. Self-determination was a mistake, in that it led to the arming of new nations and more nations, while it ought to have meant only the disarming of dangerous, predatory neighbors. Self-determination can be perfectly well brought about by the abolition of all states, rather than by the arming of all nations.

Thus, the general formula which anthropological analysis imposes on sound and enlightened statesmanship is the complete autonomy of each cultural group, and the use of force only as a sanction of law within, and in foreign relations, a policing of the world as a whole.

XV • The Cold War

From a theoretical discussion of the problem of international tension, we now turn to some practical examples. We began with the "cold war." In almost every one of the preceding as well as the succeeding chapters, reference has been or will be made to the present state of tension between the Soviet Union and her associated states and the non-Communist coalition of states. This tension, which has been labelled "cold war" is a cardinal fact of international life in the mid-20th century and thus must affect any analysis of contemporary international processes.

It is important to see the present tensions in proper perspective. Conflicts between great powers or great systems of powers are not new in world history. The many precedents to the current crisis appear in some ways remarkably similar [1] in that they involved not only power considerations but also ideological compulsions. As is the case at present, so in previous instances the existence of a great power conflict colored and affected all the lesser conflicts of the period. The one authentic new element in the current situation is that of a weapons technology which makes possible the complete—and mutual—destruction of the participants as well as of "by-standers."

One generally speaks of the "cold war" as originating after the close of World War II. As a result of that conflict, all but two major states were either vanquished or, even if nominally victorious, greatly weakened. The Soviet Union found herself in a position of relative superiority vis-à-vis all countries except the United States—which, for a variety of reasons was never able or willing to translate its military superiority vis-à-vis the Soviet Union (provided by a temporary atomic monopoly) into strategic or political advantage. The attempts of the Soviet Union to ratify and extend the position of strength in which she found herself in 1945, by infiltrating and dominating adjacent areas and other countries, encountered the opposition of the United States and its allies; and overt friction soon replaced

---

[1] See, for example, H. R. Trevor-Roper, "A Case of Coexistence: Christendom and the Turks," *Horizon*, I (1958), 46–47; and Alfred Cobban, "An Age of Revolutionary Wars: An Historical Parallel," *Review of Politics*, XIII (1951), 131–41.

the wartime partnership which had, at best, been an uneasy marriage of convenience. Soviet ideology views wars as creators of fluid, revolutionary situations which are to be fully exploited. Surely, the situation following both the First and the Second World War must seem to the Soviets to bear out that theory.

From a broader perspective, the conflict between the Soviet Union and other states antedates the Second World War by more than twenty years. It dates back to the assumption of power by a Communist regime in Russia in 1917. At no time since that date—not even during the 1930's, when a common front against Hitler was widely advocated—were relations between Russia and the important countries of the West (or, for that matter the East), close or cordial. Objectives as well as methods of policy have been in conflict ever since. One might inquire as to the reasons for this inability of Soviet leaders to cooperate with their counterparts in other countries. In part it is undoubtedly a result of their personal and Russian historical experiences both before, during, and immediately after the Revolution. In part it is due to Marxist theory which pre-supposes an inevitable struggle between states which are dominated by different class interests. As a result of both history and ideology, therefore,

> It is clear that the United States cannot expect in the foreseeable future to enjoy political intimacy with the Soviet regime. It must continue to regard the Soviet Union as a rival, not a partner, in the political arena. It must continue to expect that Soviet policies will reflect no abstract love of peace and stability, no real faith in the possibility of a permanent happy co-existence of the Socialist and capitalist worlds, but rather a cautious, persistent pressure toward the disruption and weakening of all rival influence and rival power.[2]

Numerous explanations for the emergence of the "cold war" are advanced. The Soviets, of course, blame it upon Western distrust, as expressed in attempts to deprive Russia of what she considered to be legitimate fruits of victory. In this connection it is interesting to note that American policy-makers during World War II generally assumed that the Soviet leaders desired only "security"—especially since the security of Russia had so often been jeopardized in the past; that they were entitled to that security in compensation for their magnificent contributions to the war effort; and that the West could indeed afford to establish a postwar situation in which Russia would feel—and be—secure.[3] Only much later did the American government and other Western governments come to the conclusion that Soviet aims were not thus limited. In this connection it is important to note that no "socialist-capitalist" dichotomy can be established, since Great Britain's Labor government found it just as impossible to get along harmoniously with the Soviets as did more conservative regimes elsewhere.

---

[2] George F. Kennan, "The Sources of Soviet Conduct," *Foreign Affairs*, XXV (1947), 566–82.

[3] Herbert Feis, *Churchill-Roosevelt-Stalin: The War They Waged and the Peace They Sought* (Princeton: Princeton University Press, 1957).

The blame for the eruption of the "cold war," according to the West, lies with Soviet violations of her pledges, especially those relating to the independence of the newly re-established states of Eastern Europe; Soviet suspicion; and Communist subversion in many parts of the world. The non-Soviet world conceives the eventual aim of the Soviet Union as that of bringing about the downfall of capitalist economies and democratic societies. According to Marxist ideology, the Soviets consider this downfall to be an inevitable historical process, which need only be helped along. They oppose political systems which they consider to be dominated by capitalist ruling groups, deemed to be inherently hostile to the Soviet Union and her policies. Although the precise meanings are far from clear, terms such as "world domination," "world revolution," and "world conquest" are commonly used to describe Soviet aims against which other states must protect themselves.

In conducting the contest between the two systems, two facts emerge: first, that it is conducted on many levels and with economic, psychological, cultural, and political methods as well as military force; and, second, that both the West and the Soviet Union have established "blocs" of states tied to each other by contractual arrangements. The United States is a member of NATO, SEATO, and other alliances which tie it to more than forty other states. The purpose of such alliances is to pool strength and deter the Soviet world from attempting to take over one country at a time.

However, as the contest between the Soviet and non-Soviet blocs has ever more closely approached a stalemate (for reasons elaborated by Professor Mason below), other tensions have risen to the surface, including those characterizing relations between countries within the various non-Soviet alliance systems as well as those within the Soviet bloc proper. We may well be witnessing the process of "multilateralization" of the stark bi-polar contest which dominated the first postwar decade.

The policy of the anti-Soviet bloc is essentially defensive—although the Russians, looking at the bases encircling their continental realm, find this hard to believe. The future course of the "cold war" seems to depend less on decisions made by the anti-Soviet coalition than on those made by the Soviets themselves. This is inherent in any contest between status quo and revisionist states. The key questions are these: What are Soviet objectives? How far will their leaders go to achieve these objectives? Are the objectives limited, or are they all-embracing? Is "hot war" being contemplated to replace the present cold or lukewarm varieties? Can there be a lasting shift from traditional Soviet methods of subversion, sabotage and coups, to methods of peaceful competition in the economic and cultural fields? Are there possibilities for a *detente*, for mutual recognition of the status quo, or are the Soviets bound to violate all arrangements in their quest for ever more power and influence? What are the most promising alternatives for the West in coping with the problems of the "cold war"?

Some of these questions may be partially answered from materials in other chapters of this book—as, indeed, the existence of the "cold war," being one of the outstanding characteristics of present-day international relations, affects all analyses of those relations. (See, for example, the selection from Partridge in Chapter III.) The following essay by Aron also clarifies the world-wide scope of the contest. (Cf. his article in Chapter II.) All the questions which are raised invite the most careful thought of students of world affairs. The selections in this chapter, written respectively from a European, a Soviet, and an American point of view, may serve as a useful introduction to further reflection.

1 • The Cold War—Preparation or Substitute for Total War? *

Raymond Aron

Is the "cold war" a preparation or a substitute for total war? If the former, the two camps are simply maneuvering for position until the day of final settlement. If the latter, the propaganda battles, the struggles among national parties, the fighting localized in Greece or Korea, constitute the war itself—inevitable because of the incompatibility of the two worlds, but limited so as to reduce the ravages of violence.

These distinctions have never been drawn by statesmen. The current alternative is: war or peace. But what magic wand would produce peace throughout Asia and Europe, the former in revolution, the latter divided, impoverished, disarmed? Why should Stalinism stop exploiting subversive movements in the four corners of the earth? How could the two great powers agree to partition the world as long as the Stalinist gospel claims to be universal? How would they agree to "control" atomic weapons as long as each is convinced of the other's bad faith and as long as the Soviet empire prevents the free exchange of ideas and persons?

Surely, no peace was or is conceivable unless the Kremlin abandons the fight against heretics. Pending such a conversion, which is improbable for years to come, cold war is the normal state of the world, and this limited war must continue till Stalinism acquires a new soul, either of its own accord or under external pressure.

Is it an illusion, this hope that the cold war may be a substitute for total war? History may indeed render such a verdict, but the verdict is not to be foreseen. The Stalinists, in accordance with their doctrine, anticipate terrible struggles between capitalists and socialists before the final victory of the latter; but there is still reason to believe that for some time they will not deliberately provoke the upheaval. Accordingly, a new map of the world can take shape, and a new order emerge from the chaos in Asia and Europe. Political aggression should prove less and less profitable, military aggression will be seen to be

---

* *The Century of Total War* (Boston: The Beacon Press, 1955), 226–38. Reprinted by permission.

more and more dangerous. The peace that resulted from the third world war would be all the more solid because that war had not been waged, or at least had been limited.

I. In Asia the Soviet Union has scored sensational successes, but certain of the means employed amount to a violation of the unwritten conventions of the cold war. With Communist expansion the recourse to regular armies tends to wear down the brakes that still keep the violence from increasing.

Western victories would have increased the chances of warlike peace. The Soviet victories have reduced those chances. The West is not animated by any crusade or desire to conquer. If it had succeeded in checking the advance of Stalinism, it would not have taken advantage of its success to press on and attack the vital interests of the Soviet Union. On the contrary, having become more self-confident and less apprehensive about the future, it would have agreed more readily to discussion.

On the other hand, the ambitions of Stalinism are excited, not appeased, by partial satisfactions. The more the Soviet empire extends, the more the men of the Kremlin become convinced of their superiority and inclined to use their power as a means of extortion. Under the bi-polar structure of world politics, the danger is not that the Soviet Union might be driven by weakness to desperate acts. The danger is that every chance of equilibrium will disappear when regimes faithful to Moscow fill the European or the Asian void. Thanks to the Sovietization of China, Stalinism is able to push toward Southeastern Asia and India under conditions such that the chances of halting it without a general war have diminished.

The crossing of the 38th parallel by the North Koreans was an event whose symbolic import even surpassed its real import: for the first time a line of demarcation traced by agreement between the Soviet Union and the United States of America had been crossed, for the first time the camp claiming to be that of peace had embarked on military aggression pure and simple.

II. The hope of prolonging the cold war and of arriving little by little at some sort of stabilization depends on reinforcing the West, on restoring a balance between the two worlds, on consolidating the political and social structure of the free countries, and on establishing armed forces. We are still far from that goal.

...the partition of Europe has not been effaced but reinforced. Eastern Germany has become a People's Republic, consolidated to such a degree that it would be very difficult to undo its Sovietization. Western Germany has regained economic prosperity, but its political regime is weak. The Communist parties act freely west of the Iron Curtain, and maintain secret armies whose function would be to act as a fifth column when the time comes.

The cold war has not been lost in Europe, for Soviet expansion has not exceeded the limits fixed by the agreements between the victors. But neither has it been won, for the Red Army has not been pushed back, Germany is not unified, and the nations west of the Iron Curtain remain politically and, even more, militarily weak.

III. It is true that the West has at last awakened to a sense of danger. The United States has undertaken rearmament on a large scale, and the countries of Europe themselves are beginning to shake off their lethargy. Two or three years hence the disproportion between ground forces will be less, and Western Europe and the Middle East will be sheltered, if not from invasion, at least from a surprise attack, with a chance of repelling local aggression. In the past Russia did not consider that the presence of Japan in the Far East and of Germany in Europe was an infringement of her security, but the temporary effacement of these two powers is sufficiently in her interest for her to try to make it permanent.

General and total war would be an unforeseeable venture for the Soviet Union: the atomic and industrial superiority of the United States is hardly in doubt. War would become inevitable on the day when one of the two great powers had come actually to want it, or to look upon it as inevitable. That is not the case today. Rulers and peoples alike see the abyss toward which mankind is slipping. The United States is preparing for an eventuality which it judges probable. This foresight, in its turn, forms an element in its deliberations, but does not suggest resignation to the worst.

Rearmament, if pushed beyond a certain point, spreads or risks spreading a war psychosis; but primarily it comforts and encourages those who were previously inferior and without defense. An armament race has often preceded an explosion, but without being its principal cause: the race itself was the effect of conflicts which ultimately led to war. It did, however, create a supplementary cause of a psychological order. This time, rearmament is to be considered neither as the anticipation of an approaching apocalypse, nor as the promise of certain peace, but as the price of security, payable not in one installment but annually for a generation or more. The effort embarked on by the United States can be continued indefinitely without the collapse or dislocation of its economic life. The maintenance of armed forces, even on a considerable scale, in time of peace, would not absorb more than about twenty per cent of the gross national income. More-

over, at the end of a few years this proportion would decrease. Economic considerations will no more make total war necessary for the Soviet Union or for the United States than they did for Hitler.

It must not be imagined that there exist tactics, infallible but unknown, that will change the world situation at a stroke. All that can be done is to improve a line of action which can hardly be changed in essentials, because it results from the very structure of the two opposing camps.

Today as yesterday it remains true that, in every sector of the periphery, the Soviet empire has forces that are locally superior. Today as yesterday the West can prevent the *military* expansion of Communism only by threatening, in certain events, to reply with general war.

What can be done to improve this strategy? The first task, as everyone agrees, is to reduce the inequality of the present forces in the two camps. Pushed beyond a certain point, this inequality eventually inclines the aggressor to doubt the resolution of his adversaries. Already he knows that the capitalists, the bourgeoisie, and the democrats have a mortal dread of total war. (And why should they not dread it, after two experiences of it?) He tends to minimize a threat which the Westerners use simply in order not to have to carry it out. This skepticism is in danger of provoking the explosion through misunderstanding.

The West must not only possess actual forces sufficient to impress the men of the Kremlin; but instead of being concentrated beyond the seas, their forces must be spread over the theaters of operations which, in case of unlimited war, would suffer the first attack. The Stalinists know that the United States will find difficulty in committing itself unconditionally as long as Europe is defenseless. One does not abandon to the enemy one of the essential stakes of the struggle, a stake that is lost whatever the final result if it serves as a hostage for some years to Stalinist imperialism.

At the same time, the West ought to review rigorously the decisions that it would take in certain eventualities. It is not necessary to proclaim publicly that the crossing of the Yugoslav frontier by Bulgarian and Rumanian armies would constitute a *casus belli;* but if, as seems probable, such an aggression would unleash general war, it would be best to intimate this probability, discreetly but firmly, to the masters of the Kremlin.

Once this general principle is laid down, there remain some uncertainties. The most serious of these concerns the attitude to be adopted toward Communist China: must she be considered henceforward as an enemy, bound body and soul to the Soviet enterprise, or as a great power, allied to the U.S.S.R. but perhaps capable of an autonomous diplomacy?

India and Great Britain have assumed the second alternative, and acted accordingly. By recogizing the Peiping regime they aimed at encouraging a development which they held to be possible. The Soviet Union, while claiming the admission of Communist China into the United Nations, seems nonetheless to have exerted itself to prevent contact being made between the new regime and the West. These maneuvers gave some weight to the British argument in spite of the invectives hurled against the West by Peiping propaganda. Some American diplomats themselves were inclined to the same opinion. The Chinese intervention in Korea brought that position to an abrupt end. Regardless of mistakes, history is irreversible. It is unlikely that Communist China would retrace her steps to the point where Washington would consent to renew the effort at reconciliation.

Supposing that Mao Tse-tung ended by accepting the original compromise— the re-establishment of the two Koreas —the State Department would hesitate for a long time before sacrificing Formosa. Not only a strategic position is at stake, but also the fate of Chiang Kai-shek and the remains of the Nationalist Army and administration. Was it really a mistake to have supported the former generalissimo? Probably—even though experience of Communism may have lessened the unpopularity which the Kuomintang ultimately suffered because of its inefficiency.

Does the Washington administration contemplate waging total war against Communist China? It is certainly not wished, but it is considered possible. Above all, Washington will give up nothing that will be militarily useful in the hope of appeasing Mao Tse-tung. Impressed by the outbreak of Chinese nationalism, and by the hate campaign against America, the leaders of the United States see no chance of coming to terms with the present Chinese leaders; Washington does not believe that a regime tied to Moscow will be satisfied with partial concessions.

The United States is in a position to impose an economic blockade on China, to interrupt sea traffic, to supply the partisans, to arm the troops in Formosa. China is in a position to invade Indo-China, Burma, Siam, and perhaps Malaya. None of these steps would imply world war; the Soviet Union would not be responsible for Chinese aggression in Indo-China, and would not be obliged to intervene in the event of American bombing of Manchuria. But should such steps be taken, no one can foresee exactly their ultimate consequences.

In the Far East, the Soviet Union has succeeded in conferring on the conflict the character that suits its preferences. Europeans are fighting directly against

Asians, and thus contribute to the strengthening of the anti-white feelings which Moscow promotes for its own purposes. The Chinese can keep the troops of Ho Chi Minh supplied indefinitely with arms and ammunition. Although there is no *casus belli*, certain local conflicts, as in Indo-China, hardly portend a happy outcome for the West.

To determine clearly the cases in which the threat of general war is applicable, to implement that threat by rearmament, to fill gradually the European gap, to abandon the Asiatic outposts whose local defense is too expensive, to maintain a line of resistance while leaving open the possibility of negotiations with Peiping—these are the lines of action in the immediate future which are indicated by good sense.

After basing excessive hopes on economic aid, it is now unduly depreciated. Although in Europe it has greatly speeded recovery, clearly it has neither eliminated Communism nor given the political systems an artificial robustness. Nevertheless, it has created conditions such that a military effort appears possible without serious troubles, even for the parliamentary democracies. Has economic assistance been ineffective in Asia? It has been in places where feeble rulers have failed to prevent either inflation, or the squandering of dollars, or distress among the masses. Distributed without guarantee and without precaution, money or supplies could no more weaken Communist strength than lessen American unpopularity in the Far East.

The distribution of American aid between Asia and Europe has been in inverse proportion to the poverty of the recipients. Europe has received the most by far, while Asia had stronger claims, if claims are equated to needs. When one thinks of how the millions of Indian, Chinese, or Persian peasants live, one is tempted to say that Europeans have been given luxuries while elsewhere necessities are lacking. That statement is materially correct, but is open to criticism on many counts. Needs are measured with reference to habits and not to physiological data. Complex economic systems resist certain privations with more difficulty than more primitive systems. The European populations do not resign themselves to disaster; they blame the evil works of men and not the cruelty of fate. The immensity of the needs in China and India tends to discourage good will. It can be maintained that, in return for aid, the economic, political, even human, yield from some 20 billion dollars has been higher in Europe than it would have been in Asia.

And yet, if certain guarantees about its administrative management had been demanded and obtained, substantial aid to China would perhaps have stopped the decay of the Nationalist regime. Substantial assistance to India and Pakistan would help to revive the energy of the rulers, and to overcome the alternative of apathy and revolt among the masses. The haughty nationalism of the rulers in countries recently given over to self-government will resist everything that looks like a *quid pro quo* or a political condition for aid. Money will be refused rather than privileges granted to foreigners. If these latter are sufficiently clear-sighted not to desire discrimination in their favor, they will perhaps obtain indirectly the reforms without which the dollars would be spent in vain.

I shall be careful not to present the "Marshall Plan for Asia" or Point Four as a miraculous cure. Perhaps Chinese expansion will assume such a military character that resistance by force of arms will supersede resistance by economic aid. Yet the dominant idea remains no less valid. The intellectuals of the West are at liberty to vituperate technology and its monstrous development; but for four fifths of mankind, technology means the application of scientific knowledge to the struggle for existence, the promise not of abundance but of a decent life or of less fearful poverty. The West, far more than the Soviet Union, has the means of translating this promise into reality.

The Soviet Union employs even during the pretended peace all the devices of propaganda, sabotage, and infiltration, often described by sociologists but rarely recognized by the victims. We must wage this war, imposed on us by Stalinist aggression; and military means are only one of the arms of this Protean combat. The Western military experts are not sufficiently freed from traditional conceptions, and keep wondering whether war will come, when it is raging all the time. The battle against propaganda and infiltration must be waged indefatigably; the elimination by trade unions of Stalinist ringleaders often signalizes a victory comparable with the formation of an additional army division.

James Burnham's central idea in *The Coming Defeat of Communism* seems therefore correct. But one question must be asked: What results could the West secure from a psychological offensive in countries already subject to the Communist regime and in threatened countries? Burnham is certainly right when he refuses to accept the current view that tyranny and terror make the "popular democracies" invulnerable. That the West retains allies on the other side of the Iron Curtain is shown by the flood of refugees. In 1941, in the Ukraine, there were elements of the civil population who put hatred of their masters above hatred of the invader. It would be playing the enemy's game to accept the myth of unanimous populations. Modern technique permits the production of Communist militants, of resigned crowds, of fanaticized youths, but it is

not infallible. It is possible to shake the conviction of the militants, restore hope to the crowds, and penetrate the armor of juvenile fanaticism. What remains doubtful is the degree of possible success.

Consider Eastern Europe, apart from Albania—the feeblest of the satellites, and the only one (except North Korea) with which the Soviet Union has not concluded a treaty of mutual assistance. Is it conceivable that psychological warfare, even aided by clandestine infiltration, could imperil the Communist state in Poland or Czechoslovakia? We may recall the partisans who continued the war in the Ukraine. But the mass of the Czechs and Poles have no thought of liberation, except conceivably through a general war. The militants, the party officials, the leaders of the people's democracies, or at least some of them, probably have doubts about the merits of the regime. The longing for national independence is found in the elites as well as in the masses. Personal quarrels and rivalries, even more than differences of ideas, rage within the new ruling classes. But as long as the Russian forces are actually present, and the remote Western forces only potentially so, no imitation of Stalinist methods will suffice to batter down the walls of the Communist fortress.

The Stalinists know well that political warfare is efficacious, that it levels obstacles and wears down resistance, but that it is no substitute for civil war or invasion by the Red Army. Surely the inadequacy of these means is still more evident when they are employed by the West, which in this respect is obviously in a position of inferiority.

The strength of the psycho-political activity carried on by the Stalinists does not lie in their exceptional skill, but in another sort of advantage. Once in power, they monopolize the dissemination of news and propaganda. It is easier to persuade or stupefy men when they are submitted exclusively to one propaganda line. An obsession cannot be fully created unless all those who would hinder unanimity are reduced to silence. A system of interpretation, however stupid and absurd, ends by leaving its mark on men's minds when it is applied every day, every hour, every minute, to the innumerable events that occur in the four corners of the earth; so that the public learns of those events only after they have been refracted through the official doctrine. The democracies renounce on principle the creation of such a monopoly which would be fatal to the very values for which they are fighting.

In the long run, it may be that the beliefs slowly acquired and founded on traditions are more solid than the attitudes imposed by techniques of violence and dehumanization. But in the ordeal of limited war the democracies clearly reveal all their weaknesses, while the totalitarian regimes hide and partly suppress theirs up to the end when disaster strikes for all the world to see.

In clandestine action, as was seen in the course of the second war, the Communist Party is an incomparable instrument. Organized for secrecy and disciplined more and more tightly through the years, it obtains from the militants unreserved devotion, nourished by faith and obedience comparable to that of a soldier. Even when the insurgents against Stalinism are animated by an equal devotion, they have to learn the rules necessary to underground activity, and to find leaders. But as they are never in agreement about long-term objectives, their united efforts are deprived by conflicting views of the monolithic unity characteristic of the Stalinist movement.

Nowhere is the United States supported by an American party. In liberated countries Fascists and collaborators were removed, and then the democrats were told: "And now go and argue." What wonder that the Stalinists exploit the disputes of political parties and labor difficulties when the politicians and the public alike seem more concerned about rivalries and ambitions than about the unity needed to combat the Stalinist menace.

In Asia the American influence is, at bottom, more revolutionary than any other. Consider the policy followed during the first years of occupation in Japan. The worship of the Emperor was shaken, women's suffrage and trade union organization were encouraged, entire freedom of party propaganda and activity was recognized, and private persons were invited to take part in public affairs. The process of secularization and rationalization that required centuries to evolve in Europe was carried through in a few years. But the essential fact was forgotten: the democratic institutions thus transferred—parties, trade unions, freedom of persons and ideas—tend to develop social divisions rather than social unity. Formal liberties sometimes destroy nations, they never create them.

Group demands and social conflicts are softened by expression. The working classes adhere to a government that gives them the right to make themselves heard and allows them a better chance to improve their condition. Trade unions and political parties, as long as their disputes are kept within certain limits, contribute to the protection of the governed. There is no incompatibility between liberal institutions and industrial civilization.

But neither is there a pre-established harmony. Liberal institutions have accompanied the development of industrial civilization only in countries where political democracy was a continuation of national traditions. Respect for others and their rights, when felt by every citizen as an obvious duty, contributes more to the survival of parliaments than the words of a constitution or even economic progress. Liberal institutions are no exceptions to the rule: they are founded on unprovable convictions, "transrational" if not irrational, and transmissible only with difficulty.

Rebels against the colonial domination of the Europeans, rebels also against any secular hierarchy, the Americans create an emptiness which Communism tries to fill. They upset ideas which for ages have governed people's attitude toward parents or rulers. Freed from the old conditions, everyone tends to push egalitarian claims to the limit. Communism adopts and exaggerates these claims in theory, while preparing to deny them in practice. At least it offers a kind of society to those whom the factory, the dissolution of the family, or the beginning of religious disbelief has left in a soulless solitude. Stalinism completes the revolution created by that Western influence, and brings it temporarily to an end through a new regimentation of the masses adapted to the exigencies of the industrial age.

What is required to avoid such a development and strengthen conservative governments? Obviously, it is necessary to satisfy the peasants by giving them the land, or by exacting a smaller part of their crops, finding efficient administrators, augmenting the common resources by economic progress, checking the rise in population, and slowing down the revolution in ideas and beliefs. But such a program is difficult to carry out and would not give immediate or sensational results.

The American influence, in itself revolutionary, does not immediately replace the abolished regime with a new order, whereas the Communist action revolting against the past is exercised through a sect capable of administering the new regime and organizing the masses.

This difference explains why, even where the transfer of authority from the former colonial power to an independent state took place without disturbance, military impotence results from the liberation. British India was able to contribute 2 or 3 million men to the defense of the Middle East and of its own frontiers. In the Kashmir dispute India and Pakistan now employ their few divisions (whose officer corps is still partly British). But in a general war it is to be feared that India, too, would be helpless. No such result seems to have been produced by the Communist victory in China.

It is often said that the weakness of the West in the political war is due to the absence of a leading doctrine. It is easier to rally the crowd to a false idea, so long as it seems attractive, than to a whole number of ideas that are true but prosaic. Freedom and a higher standard of living are genuine aspirations of the European peoples, and perhaps of the Asiatics. But Communism itself makes capital out of the hope of better conditions of existence, and transfigures that hope through a sort of religion of the machine and the proletariat. In Europe the reality of Stalinism is sufficiently understood or suspected for more people to see through its fictions. But in countries where poverty and overpopulation are rampant, where inequality is spectacular and offensive, and where independence was acquired quite recently, while poverty was left undiminished, the traditional disciplined resignation is upset, so that any sect, even a small one, has a chance of instigating popular revolts and, under cover of the disorder, establishing itself in power.

Are the ideas themselves at fault? Yes, when we think of the Western intellectuals, or even of the simple folk who, lacking a transcendental faith, have a vague longing for some revelation. But the West is not as destitute of ideas as that. When the battle is waged in Europe with equal weapons, the West wins consistently. The things it lacks are the weapons of violence, the monopoly of propaganda, and the support of parties on either side of the Iron Curtain.

There is no doubt that Communist Russia, allied with Communist China and protected by the European satellites, is in a position to maintain for years the pressure of the cold war, without starting a total war or accepting a general settlement. Europe west of the Iron Curtain will never completely re-

cover as long as the Soviet Army occupies Eastern Germany. The limited wars in Indo-China and in Malaya will never be won as long as Russia and Red China agree to support them. The economic system of the free world will always be threatened by the disproportion of resources between the United States and its European allies, by the contraction of the zone open to normal trade and the expansion of the Soviet zone.

Only unpredictable events such as the retreat of Russian troops into the frontiers of Russia or a peaceful solution to the Asiatic conflicts could bring a decisive improvement.

2 • Soviet Views on the Cold War

I

*The following excerpts are taken from an article by Professor P. Fedoseyev entitled "Sociological Theories and The Foreign Policy of Imperialism." ***

. . . .

The imperialist "positions of strength" policy is covered by a variety of screens. In recent years it has been widely advertised as "containment" and "liberation."

What is the essence of this policy?

"Containment" is the name given by the monopolists to the policy which aims at halting the growth of socialism and the national-liberation movement, at holding back and preventing the growth of the progressive forces. This policy, the substance of which, according to its architects, is the "use of counter-force," is formulated particularly in the writings of George Kennan and other ideologues of imperialism.

The victory of the people's democratic

system in a number of countries of Europe and Asia, and the mighty growth of the national-liberation movement have demonstrated the futility of the policy of "containment," its inability to stem the rising flood of socialism and the national-liberation movement. Consequently, international reaction has replaced it by the still more reactionary policy of "liberation." "Liberation" has become the slogan of the reckless policy designed to bring about the downfall of the socialist countries and the restoration of colonial regimes in the East. Its features are intensified espionage and

---

* *International Affairs* (Moscow), 1957, #3, pp. 14–15.

subversive activity and ideological sabotage against the countries of socialism, and interference in the internal affairs of independent and sovereign states. The United States rulers have arrogated to themselves the right to decide which social system a people should choose.

The aims of the "liberation" policy are proclaimed with perfect candour in James Burnham's *Containment or Liberation?* Describing his plan for offensive action against communism, Burnham says that the offensive should be all-embracing, with the final aim of weakening and crushing the adversary. The main blow, according to Burnham, should be delivered in Eastern Europe. This policy, he writes, reflects the viewpoint that "the key to the situation is what happens and what can be made to happen in Eastern Europe, Europe from the Iron Curtain to the Urals. So far as possible, therefore, actions in every sphere (military, psychological, diplomatic, economic) and every geographical area will be selected and judged in terms of their direct or indirect effect on Eastern Europe." Burnham wants the Communist parties in the non-socialist countries to be made illegal and the organized democratic movement banned and suppressed.

The "liberation" doctrine enjoys official blessing; it was proclaimed as the cornerstone of the foreign policy of the United States and elevated to the level of national policy. Congress allocates hundreds of millions of dollars for propaganda and subversion against the socialist countries. The U.S. imperialist circles and their Western allies dream of restoring the capitalist system in the countries which have taken the road to socialism and of crushing the national-liberation movement in the colonial and dependent countries.

In a vain endeavour to strangle the Chinese revolution the American aggressive circles encouraged and supported the reactionary Kuomintang clique in its war against the Chinese people. They supplied it with vast quantities of armaments. But neither terror nor military effort saved the Kuomintang clique from destruction. The military attack launched by the imperialists against the Korean People's Democratic Republic likewise ended ingloriously. The imperialist aggressors suffered heavy defeat in Viet-Nam. The colonialists' attempts to intimidate the peoples of the East and to break their will in the struggle for freedom and independence failed miserably. The peoples of India, Indonesia, Burma and a number of other countries are now stepping out along the highway of independent development.

More recently the aggressive nature of the policy of imperialism was most clearly manifested in the Anglo-French-Israeli attack upon Egypt, and in the organization of the counter-revolutionary uprising in Hungary. The collapse of the military gamble in Egypt and the failure of the attempts to destroy the achievements won in the building of socialism in Hungary once more demonstrate the futility and hopelessness of the ideology and policy of strength.

The American monopolists, however, have not learnt their lesson. They have now advanced the Eisenhower Doctrine, the aim of which is to provide a basis for colonialism and to subordinate the countries, which have won liberation or are in the process of being liberated from Anglo-French domination, to American imperialism. The most revolting expression of the aggressive policy of the American rulers is their intention to quarter American atomic forces in the countries under their control in Europe and in Asia for the purpose of preparing atomic war against the Soviet Union and the People's Democracies.

The rich international experience of the post-war years shows that the ideology and policy of force have suffered defeat after defeat, and that they can but accelerate the final collapse of imperialism. The events of recent years have demonstrated more and more that there are now powerful social and political forces possessing means capable of preventing the imperialists from unleashing war and of delivering a crushing rebuff to the aggressors should they attempt to do so.

. . . .

II

The following excerpts are taken from answers which Soviet Premier Nikita Khrushchev gave to questions submitted by P. Dampson, correspondent of the Toronto Telegram.*

Question: Does the Soviet Union consider that the winding-up of foreign military bases in all European countries would be an effective contribution to the relaxation of international tension?

Reply: Yes, undoubtedly. The winding-up of military bases abroad is one of the most important issues in solving the problem of disarmament and the relaxation of international tension. It would be most reasonable to begin precisely with this. Judge for yourself—can the peace-loving peoples believe in the sincerity of declarations about disarmament made by statesmen of countries which maintain military bases in foreign countries?

If the Western powers had really wanted to solve the disarmament problem and to achieve a relaxation of international tension, they should have wound up their military bases abroad and withdrawn their armed forces. It would also be logical to reduce armed forces by an amount at least equivalent to the number of troops at present manning these bases. The whole world is aware that the overwhelming majority of the military bases are to be found close to the frontiers of the Soviet Union, the People's Democracies, and the peace-loving countries of Europe, Asia and Africa. If the United States of America and the other Western countries were to wind up their bases, then the Soviet Union and the other peace-loving countries would immediately carry out measures for further disarmament. All this would facilitate the strengthening of peace and the abolition of international tension.

Furthermore, it should be said frankly that the time is not far distant when all will be obliged to acknowledge that military bases abroad no longer have the importance ascribed to them by some immoderately boastful generals and other aggressively-inclined Western statesmen. It is necessary to take sober and realistic account of the development of present-day technology, as a result of which the situation has changed radically. The production of intercontinental ballistic missiles has solved the problem of delivering a thermonuclear warhead to any point on the globe. Distance is now no obstacle. As for the military bases in Europe, Africa and Asia, missiles which can reach any part of

---

* *International Affairs* (Moscow), 1957, #11, pp. 14–18.

these continents have already been in existence for a long time. I think that it is no secret that there now exists a range of missiles with the aid of which it is possible to fulfil any assignment of operational and strategic importance. Nor, of course, is it any secret that such missiles now have both atomic and hydrogen warheads. Let us not play hide-and-seek with the facts: let us look them in the face. Can it be supposed that military bases are known only to those who established them? But if their location is known, then, given the present level of missile and other technology, they can speedily be rendered ineffective.

We are convinced that very soon the peoples of those countries in which American military bases have been set up many thousands of kilometres from America herself, will come to realize more fully what a terrible danger these bases constitute for their countries and will resolutely demand the immediate abolition of foreign bases on their territory.

. . . .

Question: Do you personally consider that the danger of war is less than, for example, a year or two ago?

Answer: At first sight a concrete question, this is at the same time an enigma. It is very difficult to give a short answer. From the point of view of common sense, there now exist conditions which are not fraught with the danger of war in the near future. We can say that the peoples are anxious for peace, that we do not have an eve-of-war situation like that, for example, prior to the Second World War. Then the aggressive actions of Hitler Germany went unpunished and the aggressors were encouraged in their attacks upon peace-loving countries. There are today imperialist, militarist groups who would like to unleash war, but the peoples do not support their aggressive aspirations and are fighting back. And furthermore, great changes have taken place in the countries against which the imperialists would like to launch war, and therefore an attack upon them would be fraught with serious dangers for the assailant.

The imperialist monopolies have a vested interest in profits and for them war is a most profitable undertaking. But the people, of course, have no interest in war.

The socialist countries, which express the will of the people, the working class, the working peasants and intellectuals, have no interest in war. The governments of these countries are doing everything to ensure not only that there shall be no war but also that the state of tension shall be abolished and normal conditions for competition between the two systems on the basis of peaceful coexistence created.

We deny that war is inevitable. But it is also impossible categorically to declare that there will be no war. In some capitalist countries there are those occupying high governmental posts who are calling for war. Can anyone say what madmen will do?

. . . .

3 • Reflections on the Changing Nature of Current International Relations *

John Brown Mason

Dr. Mason has held offices in the State Department and with the U.S. High Commission in Germany. Formerly in the Department of Government at Georgetown University, he is now affiliated with the Orange County State College in California. His many contributions to the literature of international relations include Hitler's First Foes *(1936),* The Danzig Dilemma *(1946), and numerous articles in international journals.*

Until recent times a government finding itself at war against its wishes was always able to fall back on its armed forces in a final attempt to succeed by might where it had failed by diplomacy, and to try to salvage national security on the battlefield. By invasion of the enemy's territory and by cumulative attrition of his power it could hope to achieve military victory and thus assure itself of a position of superiority and at least temporary safety. The attack on Pearl Harbor was a deadly blow to Secretary Hull's hopes and efforts, but as a military disaster its proportions were limited. Recovery was a matter of time and effort. In fact, because of the insidious character of the aggression, it served to rally the country to unity and to greater exertion. Physical efforts and national fortitude increased greatly in scope and impact and, in the end, decided the outcome.

Man's great advance in science and technology has resulted in a basic change in international relations. Aside from regional conflicts, the next war threatens to be one of annihilation rather than attrition. It does not promise victory for one side but suicide for both. It "can secure only the dubious comfort of having one's enemy reduced to the same level of prostration as one's self ...when both sides have the same weapon yielding substantially the same order of power, then neither side has any real advantage, and its use only serves to make the war more terrible and costly. Mere destruction is not decision, no matter how it may be calculated." [1]

If military victory is out of the question, we must not base national security on a mirage. National superiority in armaments loses in importance when mere sufficiency in atomic and thermonuclear weapons is enough to bring collapse. The true test of national defense at the fatal moment of supreme international crisis, therefore, will be its power to deter the enemy, to keep a hostile government from engaging in total war, rather than mere ability to

---

* *Confluence,* VI (1957), 255–63. Reprinted by permission.

[1] Ralph E. Williams, Jr., "America's Moment of Truth," *United States Naval Institute Proceedings,* Vol. 81, No. 3, March 1955, pp. 248, 253.

inflict greater destruction. The purpose of American armaments will be served best when they are so awe-inspiring that they need not be used; when total war does not begin because a potential enemy realizes that, even with the advantage of surprise, he could not survive.

The rational conclusion that war is completely destructive, that it constitutes the classical, deadly boomerang among nations, does not, by itself, constitute a guarantee that war cannot happen. Man does not act upon the basis of reason alone, but is often moved by fears, suspicions and hatreds. The task of diplomacy, therefore, is to exert all possible power and skill to the end that cold reason keeps the cold war under control. Statesmen must avoid supreme crises and strive for alternatives to total war based on a new type of relations between the two super power blocs.

Basic changes have occurred in history before. A hundred years of devastating war—as total as possible at the time—taught both Catholics and Protestants in Europe that neither could conquer the other. Somehow, they learned to get along with each other, though after three hundred years difficulties still remain. Christianity and Islam have coexisted now for several centuries, though they had been deadly enemies for ages, fanatically convinced that one of them had to disappear from this earth. As Commander Ralph E. Williams, Jr., put it: "...two missionary faiths, each of them claiming to be universal, had finally to recognize the inconvenient fact that, neither being able to extirpate the other, they had to find some basis for living together in the same world." And as Commander Williams continues: "Today the same compulsion for a *modus vivendi* between the Free World and the Soviet Bloc exists, but for exactly the opposite reason. The two earlier belligerents lacked the capacity and the power to destroy one another;

the two protagonists of the Twentieth Century do have the power to destroy one another, and to do it mutually and completely. In these circumstances neither side has the power to achieve victory; it has only the power to deny it to the enemy." [2]

The question, therefore, is whether the two power blocs can live in what may be called "simultaneous existence" long enough to allow the impact of historical forces on human institutions to affect their relationship deeply and make peaceful co-existence possible. The changes called for do not demand the absence of rivalry. Rather they require, if self-defeating mutual destruction is to be avoided, that competitive struggles take place primarily on the diplomatic, political, economic and cultural fronts, though conceivably peace might be interrupted by limited conflicts which neither side would allow to get out of bounds. The big task is to keep the atomic hounds confined to the role of safeguards, ready for action if needed for defense, but not needed because they are ready.

The next question naturally would be whether both sides would be able to keep their mutual relations fluid rather than allow them to become rigid to the point where an irresistible force meets an immovable object. Specifically, are both the Soviet Union and the United States capable of enough diplomatic flexibility to adjust to the new nature of international relations, instead of moving toward a head-on collision?

At first sight, Soviet communism and its governmental institutions would seem to be of the inflexible type. Its doctrine is all-inclusive in scope and its modern technological means of mass communication and control over its subjects are powerful. Actually, while Moscow has been consistent in pursuing

---

[2] *Ibid.*, pp. 253–54.

its goal of world rule—whether the motive was ideology, old time imperialism, fear for its security or a combination of these—it has shown great adjustability in its tactics. Its methods are whatever promises the best results at the moment and, therefore, they differ greatly according to time, place and circumstances. They have ranged from collaboration with Hitler to co-belligerence with the Allies, from suppression of small nationalities in Soviet Russia to fanning nationalist fires in Asia, and from underground subversion to smiles at the summit. Some of the methods have been used simultaneously, without regard to apparent contradictions. The Kremlin specializes in exploring all possibilities for advancing its aim and pushing toward its goals wherever success seems likely; it also retracts and withdraws wherever opposition is too strong, where it does not feel safe or where the ground seems insufficiently prepared. It yields to realities and adjusts its measures and policies accordingly. It realizes that its program is determined not only by its own strength but also by the weakness or strength of others.

Soviet communism is not the irresistible force which it claims and which it often appears to be. The Kremlin will use brutal force where they think it will serve a purpose, as in East Berlin and in Hungary. It will avoid it where the price threatens to be out of proportion in a potentially dangerous situation, as in Poland. It will do so even when such policies conflict with its totalitarian claims.

American foreign policy is by no means a lethargic force but is mobile and, at times, agile. We were the world's leading isolationist power and became the pillar of NATO. The outstanding architect of high tariff walls, we lowered them through reciprocity treaties; and preoccupation with prosperity at home changed to sponsorship of the Marshall Plan and large-scale economic and technical assistance overseas. We helped to smash Hitler's Germany and made the Bonn Republic one of our major allies. We fought side by side with the Soviet Union and assisted her in the process of liberation from the invader. We also opposed her expansionism and encroachments upon the free world. While her policy is hostile we seek a base for greater Western security in political and military alliances. But we are not satisfied with policies of containment or cold war objectives. On the lookout for new diplomatic approaches, we support President Eisenhower's readiness to collaborate with the Soviet Union in regard to the restriction of armaments in the hope that eventual success will lead to calm consideration of other common problems and to a general improvement in our relations.

II

The year 1955 will be remembered as a time which gave the appearance of a thaw in the cold war. The sunshine at the Geneva summit had encouraged hopeful attitudes in a Western world which was weary of turmoil and tensions and eager for relief from an atmosphere of strife. A New Optimism ranged from cheerful talk about "peaceful coexistence," carefully undefined, to rash conclusions regarding changes in the goals of Soviet communism. To be sure, there was some puzzlement when the Geneva meeting was followed by another unfriendly Soviet initiative in the international scene. Promises to the West to cut down oversize armies were accompanied by bitterly hostile speeches in India and elsewhere against the Geneva conference partners and by continuous broadcasts directed toward Africa and inciting the populace to revolution. And there were sales of arms to Egypt, in an area thick with explosive possibilities. But while Western perplexity deepened into a frown, much basic optimism remained. Hope does not die easily, and so much was at stake.

The Hungarian revolt served to dispel the mirage of Soviet smiles. A world rudely awakened from daydreaming witnessed brutal reality as the Red Army shot down Hungarian national freedom fighters. It was clear once more that Soviet communism had not changed with the death of Stalin; that its goal continued to be worldwide domination; and that the Soviets intended to hold onto power wherever possible, by any means that promised results. Kremlin affability had looked pleasant while it lasted but, like a Moscow summer, it was seasonal and short.

The smoldering ashes of the Poznan uprising and the Hungarian revolt called for a fresh look at Soviet communism, our own system of values and our relations with other nations, both within and outside the Soviet orbit. While Americans were more cautious after the dismal experience with the New Optimism, some did seem to discern new perspectives, new prospects and some possible changes.

Many in the West had appeared resigned to Kremlin success in exploiting for its own ends the nationalism of Asian peoples, as in North Vietnam, Indonesia, Egypt and elsewhere (while overlooking Moscow's lack of success in India, Burma, South Vietnam, the Philippines, etc.). Some in the Free World had even approached despair. Surprise was widespread, therefore, when nationalism proved again that it is as live a force on one side of the Iron Curtain as on the other. Events in Poland and Hungary showed that nationalism could defy the imperialism of Moscow, as it had done earlier in Yugoslavia. Too many in the West, it appeared, had accepted the notion that anti-communism depended primarily upon the property-

sense of the peasants, the aspirations of the middle classes and the religious needs of the older generation. To the astonishment of Communists and anti-Communists alike, the national patriots of Poznan and Budapest, as earlier of East Berlin, were members of communism's privileged class. They were workers. They were the men and women whom communism had considered its avant-garde.

Also, the fighting and dying were done by youths who had been exposed to Communist indoctrination for a decade, who had never lived in a democratic society and whose parents, too, had precious little knowledge of one. Among the rebels there were students from working-class families who had been admitted to university training only after careful screening and ideological testing and with a solid background of active, eager participation in party-controlled youth organizations; who had been herded into strictly supervised studies of Marxist-Leninist-Stalinist doctrine, in a social environment which did not include free speech, a free press or other opportunities for the untrammeled exchange of ideas. The world witnessed with amazement the anti-Soviet fervor of workers and youth—two groups considered basic to the future of communism.

Budapest thus taught two valuable lessons.

One: Soviet communism possesses less inherent, basic strength than had been widely assumed after its vast expansion of recent years. At least outside the Soviet Union, in the "satellite" countries, it cannot count indefinitely on containing forces hostile to its totalitarian nature—such as the desire for national independence and personal freedom. Individuals can be brainwashed but nations cannot. Fetters of indoctrination can snap. Physical force does not suffice to keep the lid down indefinitely because spiritual and intellectual forces are dynamic: pressing against soft spots they explode with elementary violence. Political loyalties do not remain shatter-proof as even Communists join the national opposition and freedom fighters. The reliability of the police and armed forces becomes questionable. Defeated workers can be driven to factory gates by threats and hunger, but they cannot be made to produce efficiently and sufficiently. Production suffers in the ruins of an oppressed cause. Heavy losses from both destruction and under-production increase the difficulties of "building socialism" and drastically reduce the contributions of the satellite nations to the economy of the Soviet Union. Instead, its resources are drained as it must advance economic aid to those who formerly gave it. The myth of almighty communism is dispelled among captive peoples who now bide their time. Brutal revenge against workers and youths builds up new underground pressures. The strength of patriotism is added to dissatisfaction with economic conditions in the workers' paradise. Among defeat and traces of despair, hope and consolation are sought more than ever in the belief in and practices of religion which, by communism's own admission, is its strongest single enemy.

Two: Western ideals have more vitality and attractiveness than critics had believed. Ideas of both national and personal freedom are stronger and more robust than many thought in moments of weariness, or remembered from history. They are harder to extinguish when oppressed and quicker to recover. Despite disagreements over policy, the West possesses basic unity and great vigor. It has tensile strength which enables it to meet and welcome the pressures of free inquiry, criticism, non-conformity, search for alternatives and all the other freedoms of the mind. It values the individual and his worth. In our own struggle for a better world we do not need to suppress writers, poets, novelists, painters, philosophers or students. Our intellectual and political freedoms are an expression of innate strength. They have a strong appeal to the captive nations, and they offer a basis to the "uncommitted" nations of Asia and Africa for free national development according to their native genius that totalitarian and dictatorial communism cannot match.

In the meantime, the cold war goes on. Its ups and downs, hot spells and relaxations and its apparent endlessness have caused many Americans to reflect upon its nature and its value. Certainly it cannot be ended by unilateral action or lack of action; but also, it does not seem to be the last word in international relations any more than is total war.

.   .   .   .

XVI • Relations Between Developed and Underdeveloped Countries

If one compares a map of the world in 1939 and 1959, one finds many changes. The most significant of these changes reflect the fact that since World War II a large number of territories have changed their status from colonial possessions to independent statehood. Even as this book goes to press, other territories are on the threshold of a similar transition.

The vast majority of the new states lie in Asia and Africa. While no two states are ever completely alike, the newly independent countries show enough similarities to permit the student of international relations to make some general statements about them. All of these areas have a history of Western domination of varying length and varying degrees of severity and/or benefit. All of them also fall into the category commonly referred to as "underdeveloped." [1] This means that these countries are characterized by low standards of living, widespread illiteracy, much disease. Their economies have traditionally been almost completely dependent on the production of agricultural commodities and raw materials; there has been little industrial development. The inhabitants of these countries, in short, lack most of the necessities and amenities of life which citizens of the more highly developed older states have long since come to take for granted. In a pithy, if tragic, phrase, two thirds of the world's population are ill-fed, ill-clothed, ill-housed, illiterate and ill. [2]

Many efforts are afoot to improve conditions in the underdeveloped areas of the world. The United States and other Western countries have aid and development programs which provide needed assistance to these states, albeit on too small a scale to bring about a rapid transformation of the economy. The Soviet Union has more recently developed a highly concentrated and selective foreign aid program, which has been quite effective in

---

[1] The term "underdeveloped", although preferable to the term "backward" which has fortunately been abandoned in the 1950's, is not without ambiguities. In a sense, every country is "underdeveloped" if present conditions are viewed in relation to future potentials.

[2] This phrase was used by Leonard Kenworthy at a Quaker Meeting in Philadelphia.

achieving some of its aims. Numerous programs, too, are under the auspices of the United Nations and its specialized agencies, such as the World Health Organization, the Food and Agriculture Organization, the United Nations Educational Scientific and Cultural Organization, and many others.

Nevertheless, none of these programs by themselves—nor all of them together—suffice to bring about needed improvements as rapidly as the peoples living in these areas desire. The world is confronted with what has been termed a "revolution of rising expectations"—a set of demands by the peoples of these underdeveloped countries, composing a majority of the world's population, and growing at a rapid pace (see Kingsley Davis' article in Chapter V) who want improvement in their condition. They want it quickly, and they are not dogmatic or choosy on the question of where the aid is to come from. Yet, for a variety of reasons, long-range rapid improvement in living standards is extraordinarily hard to bring about. The medical revolution which characterizes our century has made it easy to fight disease and thereby decrease death rates dramatically, which decrease is reflected in sharply rising population curves. (See Chapter V.) This fact means that the rate of increase in economic productivity must outpace the population explosions which are characteristic of underdeveloped countries in their present stage of development. To bring about greatly increased productivity requires vast capital investments—many of them in activities which will not be immediately profitable. By definition, the societies themselves do not contain surplus capital in amounts sufficient for such investment. Private investors are reluctant to invest money where there is political and social unrest (particularly when investment opportunities at home are good). Governor Rockefeller outlines the specific reasons for this reluctance, with some suggestions for change, in his article in Chapter XIII. Thus the only feasible alternative is aid from other governments, but on a scale vastly larger than any contemplated thus far.

The relations between the underdeveloped and the more highly developed areas of the world constitute one of the most serious contemporary and future problem areas in international relations. The tensions thus generated would exist irrespective of the Soviet-anti-Soviet conflict; but the fact that the more highly developed states of the world *are* antagonists further contributes to the tension. For the most part, the underveloped states have refused to commit themselves to one or the other side in the power struggle, for reasons explained by Prime Minister Nehru (whose arguments, incidentally, are reminiscent of those used by President Washington in his *Farewell Address*), and analyzed by Professor Scalapino in the selections reprinted in this chapter. Both sides assiduously attempt to win the approval and support of these areas. It has been suggested that the outcome of the "cold war" between the two contending blocs will be decided in the presently underdeveloped countries.

If this is so, then it must be said that for a number of reasons the outlook for a democratic triumph seems problematical as Professor Partridge has already indicated in Chapter III. As Professors Watnick and Scalapino make clear, most of the countries here under discussion react strongly against close ties with the West, because they still identify the West—even the traditionally anti-colonialist United States—with their former colonial masters. To be "pro-Western" in some of these countries is tantamount to being "pro-Communist" in the United States or "bourgeois" in the Soviet Union! These new states are intensely nationalistic, and their nationalism expresses itself primarily in terms of opposition to former colonial powers and distrust of any states allied with those colonial powers. While Communism pretends to be a universal doctrine, and would therefore seem to be in opposition to nationalism, the Soviets and their Allies (including the Chinese Communists) have been skillful in identifying their interests with those of the emergent and victorious nationalist movements in underdeveloped countries, especially their educated leadership groups.

Furthermore, most of these countries feel, perhaps not unjustfiedly, that their hopes for short-term economic improvement depend upon close government control of the economy—in brief, a socialist rather than a capitalist system. Americans who are persuaded of the values and advantages of capitalism may find it difficult to adjust to regimes which do not share these preferences. On the other hand, the Soviet system provides an example of rapid economic development, and—in spite of conflicting reports by different observers—the Chinese experience seems to be similar. Hence it is not altogether surprising that an increasing number of people in the underdeveloped countries find the thought of imitating the economic programs of the Soviet Union and China less and less uncongenial. The advantages which the Communists thus seem to enjoy in the contest for the underdeveloped areas could be erased only by far-reaching programs on the part of Western powers; and by such proofs of naked aggression on the part of Communist states as to convince presently uncommitted nations that the danger from that source far outweighs the problems of closer cooperation with the West.

Whatever the outcome of the crucial contest between the Soviets and the anti-Soviet world may be (and surely there are steps that the West can take, above and beyond what it has already done, to enhance the chances of success for *its* type of program), the relationship between underdeveloped and more highly developed areas promises to be one of the tension-areas of the international scene for decades to come.

1 • The Appeal of Communism to the Peoples of Underdeveloped Areas *

Morris Watnick

The author, a member of the staff of the Russian Research Center at Harvard University, was formerly associated with the Office of Intelligence Research in the Department of State.

If time is a power dimension in any political strategy, the odds facing the West in the underdeveloped areas of the world today are heavily weighted against it. The effort to capture the imagination and loyalties of the populations of these areas did not begin with the West in President Truman's plea for a "bold new program" of technical aid to backward areas. It began more than a generation earlier when the Communist International at its second world congress in 1920, flung out the challenge of revolution to the people of colonial and dependent countries, and proceeded to chart a course of action calculated to hasten the end of Western overlordship. We thus start with an initial time handicap, and it is a moot question whether we can overcome the disadvantage by acquiring the radically new appreciation of the human stakes involved necessary to meet the challenge of the Communist appeal to the peoples of these areas.

Fortunately, there is no need to trace out the tortuous course of the careers of the various Communist parties in the backward areas of the world in order to gain some appreciation of the extent and intensity of their indigenous appeal. For purposes of this discussion we can con-fine ourselves to China, India and the area of southeast Asia where they have had their greatest successes to date. Despite the blunders and ineptitudes which marked their initial grand play in China in 1924–27, ending in almost complete disaster for their most promising single party organization in these areas, they have emerged today as a political magnitude of the first order, boasting a seasoned leadership, a core of trained cadres and a mass following recruited mainly from the peasant masses of the region. It is the purpose of this paper to indicate the nature of the Communist appeal to the peoples of these areas and to suggest some of the sociological factors which have made that appeal so effective.

It was once the wont of certain continental writers, preoccupied with the problem of imperialism, to refer to the peoples who form the subject of our deliberations as the *history-less* peoples. Better than the Europa-centric term, "underdeveloped peoples," it delineates in bold relief all the distinctive features which went to make up the scheme of

* Reprinted (in part) from *Economic Development and Cultural Change,* Volume I, Number 1 (March 1952), pp. 22–36. Reprinted by permission.

their social existence: their parochial isolation, the fixity of their social structure, their tradition-bound resistance to change, their static, subsistence economies and the essential repetitiveness and uneventfulness of their self-contained cycle of collective activities. With a prescience which has not always received its due, these theorists of imperialism also called the right tune in predicting that the isolated careers of these archaic societies would rapidly draw to a close under the impact of economic and social forces set in motion by industrial capitalism, and that these *history-less* peoples would before long be thrust onto the arena of world politics, impelled by a nascent nationalism born of contact with the West and nurtured by a swelling resentment against the exactions of its imperialism.

The final result of this process is unfolding today with a disconcerting force and speed in almost all the backward regions of the world. We can see its culmination most clearly among the classic exemplaries of *history-less* peoples in China, India and the regions of south Asia where the political and economic predominance of western Europe is being successfully challenged by forces unmistakably traceable to the forced absorption of these societies into the stream of world history. Their internal cohesiveness, largely centered on self-sufficient village economies, has been disrupted by enforced contact with the West, giving way to a network of commercialized money transactions in which the strategic incidence of economic activity has shifted from subsistence agriculture to plantation production of raw materials and foodstuffs for the world market. Their economies thus took on a distorted character which rendered the material well-being of the native populations peculiarly subject to the cyclical fluctuations of the world market. All this, coupled with rapid population increases which the existing state of primitive technique, available area of cultivation and customary allocation of soil could not adjust to the requirements of maximum output, have conspired to create wide-spread rural indebtedness, abuses of plantation and tenant labor and other excrescences traditionally associated with the prevalence of a raw commercial and financial capitalism super-imposed on a predominantly agricultural economy.

Given the fact that the new economic dispensation in these regions was fashioned under the aegis, if not active encouragement, of the Western imperialisms, it should occasion no surprise that these regions, particularly southeast Asia, have seen the efflorescence of a distinctive type of nationalism, especially after the debacle of western rule during the second World War, differing in many crucial respects from the historical evolution of nationalism as experienced by western Europe. Indeed, the employment of a term like "nationalism" with all its peculiarly western connotations to describe what is going on in south Asia today is in a sense deceptive precisely because it diverts our attention from some of the distinctive attributes of native sentiment which set it apart from the nineteenth century manifestations of nationalism in Europe. It is moreover a particularly inappropriate characterization because it inhibits a full appreciation of the potency of the Communist appeal among the populations of these regions. Historically, nationalism in western Europe has flourished with the burgeoning of an industrial technology, the urbanization of the population, the growth of a self-conscious middle class and an industrial proletariat, the spread of literacy and the multiplication of media of mass communication. Now it is one of the distinctive features of the movements of revolt in southeast Asia today that they lack any of these marks of Western nationalism. The indigenous "nationalism" of southeast Asia today lacking any of these props, nevertheless derives its peculiar potency from a universal reaction of personalized resentment against the economic exploitation of foreign powers. Whether all the economic and social dislocations of this region are directly attributable, in refined analytic terms, to Western rule is quite beside the point. The simple and crucial datum which we must take as the point of orientation in our thinking is that to the mind of masses of indigenous peoples they do stem from this common source. The Indochinese intellectual debarred from a higher post in the government service, the Burmese stevedore underpaid by the *maistry* system of contract labor all tend to attribute the source of their grievances to the systems of government and economy imposed on them from without. The distinctive and novel aspect of the native movements of southeast Asia, then, is that they represent a mass collective gesture of rejection of a system of imposed economic and social controls which is compelled by historic circumstances to take the form of a nationalist movement of liberation from foreign rule.

It is this distinctive coalescence of two sources of resentment which offers Communist parties the opportunities they lack elsewhere to any comparable degree. The two-dimensional direction of native resentment lends itself ideally to Communist appeal and manipulation for the simple reason that Communists can successfully portray Soviet Russia both as a symbol of resistance to political imperialism imposed from without as well as a model of self-directed and rapid industrialization undertaken from within. This twin appeal gains added strength from the multi-national composition of the USSR which enables indigenous Communists of south Asia to confront their audience with the glaring disparity between the possibilities of ethnic equality and the actualities of western arrogance and discrimination. Communist propaganda has accordingly exploited this theme in almost all important policy pronouncements directed to the people of Asia.

With the victory of the Chinese Communists, the incidence of these appeals has perceptibly shifted the symbolism of successful resistance and internal reconstruction from Russia to China which is now being held up as a model for emulation by the other areas of southeast Asia. The shift is not without its tactical and propaganda value since the adjacent region of southeast Asia is now regarded as the "main battle-front of the world democratic camp against the forces of reaction and imperialism." Success in this case carries its own rewards beyond the frontiers of China itself for it is altogether probable that Mao-Tsetung will take his place alongside Lenin and Stalin as a fount of revolutionary sagacity for these movements in India and southeast Asia.

Unfortunately, recent discussions of the Communist movement in Asia have done more to obscure than to clarify the nature and direction of its appeal to the indigenous populations. All too frequently, the tendency has been to fall back on the blanket formula that Communists have sought to identify themselves with local nationalism and demands for agrarian reform. We have already seen that their identification with nascent nationalism, if such it must be called, derives its peculiar strength from certain of its unique qualities. It is no less important to an appreciation of the problem to recognize that the Communist appeal does not by mere virtue of this process of identification, acquire the same uniform access to all sectors of the population. Indeed, the most striking and disconcerting feature of much of the propaganda appeal emanating both from Moscow, Peking, and other centers is that it is not, and in the nature of the case, cannot be designed for peasant or worker consumption. The appeal of Communism as such in these areas is first and foremost an appeal which finds lodgment with indigenous professional and intellectual groups. Its identification with native nationalism and demands for land reform turns out to be, when carefully scrutinized, not so much a direct appeal to specific peasant grievances, powerful though its actual results may be, as it is an identification with the more generalized, highly conscious and sharply oriented outlook of the native intelligentsia.

Given the entire range of sociological and economic forces at work in these areas, the very logic and terms of the Communist appeal must of necessity filter through to the peasant masses by first becoming the stock-in-trade of the intellectual and professional groups. To revert to the terminology suggested at the outset of this paper, we may say that by and large, it is the old *history-less* style of social existence which still claims the loyalty and outlook of the bulk of the indigenous populations. It is still the old village community which serves as the center of peasant and worker aspirations, and if they have taken to arms it is because European rule has destroyed the old securities and values without replacing them by new ones. Without leadership and organization their unrest would be without direction and certainly without much chance for success, quickly dissipating itself in spontaneous outbursts against individual landowners and achieving no lasting goals. Whatever else it may be that we are facing in southeast Asia today, it certainly does not resemble the classic uprisings of peasant *jacquerie*, but a highly organized and well-integrated movement, with a leadership that

has transcended the immediate urgencies of its mass following and can plan ahead in terms of long range perspectives.

That leadership is supplied by the new indigenous intelligentsia. It is from this group that native Communist and non-Communist movements alike recruit their top leadership as well as the intermediate layers of cadres for, of all the groups which make up the populations of these areas, it is the intelligentsia alone (taking the term in its broadest sense) that boasts an ideological horizon which transcends the *history-less* values of the bulk of the population and makes it the logical recruiting ground for the leadership of political movements. For this, it can thank the formal schooling and intellectual stimulus provided by the West, which not only brought such a group into existence but also—and this is crucial—condemned large sections of that intelligentsia to a form of *déclassé* existence from the very beginnings of its career. The new intelligentsia was in large measure consigned by the imperial system to hover uneasily between a native social base which could not find accommodation for its skills and ambitions, and the superimposed imperial structure which reserved the best places for aliens. There were, of course, considerable variations and differences in the various areas of south Asia—India, for example, did succeed in absorbing a good many of its professionally trained native sons—but by and large, the picture is one of a rootless intellectual proletariat possessing no real economic base in an independent native middle class. The tendency in all these areas, moreover, has been to train technicians, lawyers, and other groups of professional workers in numbers far out of proportion to the absorptive capacity of the social structures of the home areas, even if more of the higher posts in industry and administration were thrown open to native talent. In any case, those who did find such employment were frozen in minor posts, the most coveted positions going to Europeans.

But if these groups could not be integrated into the social structure of these dependent areas, the same does not hold true of their acclimatization to the cross currents of political doctrine. Western education exposed many of them to the various schools of social thought contending for influence in Europe, and from these they distilled the lessons which seemed to offer the best hope for their native communities. Western capitalism was necessarily excluded from their range of choices if for no other reason than that its linkage with imperialist rule over their own societies debarred it from their hierarchy of values. The anti-capitalist animus is common to the intellectual spokesmen of these areas, whatever their specific political allegiance or orientation may be. Nor does it appear that any populist variety of Gandhism, with its strong attachment to the values of a static subsistence economy, has won any considerable following among these intellectual groups. Soeten Sjahrir voiced a common sentiment when he wrote:

We intellectuals here are much closer to Europe or America than we are to the Boroboedoer or Mahabrata or to the primitive Islamic culture of Java or Sumatra. ...For me, the West signifies forceful, dynamic and active life. I admire, and am convinced that only by a utilization of this dynamism of the West can the East be released from its slavery and subjugation.

The sole possibility, then, which appeared acceptable to them was one or another of the forms of state-sponsored reconstruction and industrialization, for which liberation from the rule of European states was naturally considered to be a prerequisite. Liberation and internal reconstruction thus came to be two inseparable operations, intimately tied together as they seldom have been before.

We can now appreciate the enormous initial advantage which was thus offered the Communist movements in these backward areas. The Russian Revolution of 1917 and the subsequent course of planned industrialization could not but fail to impress native intellectuals as offering a model pattern of action by which they could retrieve their communities from precapitalist isolation and backwardness without repaying the price of continued foreign exploitation. There is doubtless a large measure of self-revelation in Mao's reaction to the Russian experience in his statement that:

There is much in common or similar between the situation in China and pre-revolutionary Russia. Feudal oppression was the same. Economic and cultural backwardness was common to both countries, Both were backward. China more so than Russia. The progressive waged a bitter struggle in search of revolutionary truth so as to attain national rehabilitation; this was common to both countries....The October Revolution helped the progressive elements of the world, and of China as well, to apply the proletarian world outlook in determining the fate of the country.... The conclusion was reached that we must advance along the path taken by the Russians.

It should also be noted, in passing, that the Comintern lost no time in launching a large number of international front organizations such as the Red International of Trade Unions, International League Against Imperialism, International of Seamen and Dockers, International Red Aid, etc., all of which provided the necessary organizational scaffolding and support for facilitating the dissemination of propaganda. Finally, ...the Comintern provided a rallying point for their aspirations by outlining a program of revolutionary action in the colonies and dependent areas which was ideally calculated to provide them with a mass peasant following.

The result, though viewed with some misgivings by the leadership of the Comintern, was merely what might have been expected under the circumstances. The Communist parties of these under-developed areas of Asia were from their very beginnings, initiated, led by, and predominantly recruited from (prior to their conversion into mass organizations as has been the case in China after 1949) native intellectual groups. Though this vital sociological clue to the nature of the Communist appeal in the colonial areas has not received the recognition it deserves, amidst the general preoccupation with the theme of Communist appeals to the peasantry, its implication was perfectly plain to the leaders of the Comintern. One of the most revealing (and to date largely un-noticed) admissions on this score is contained in the Sixth Comintern Congress in 1928 in its resolution on strategic policy in the colonies and semi-colonies in which the point is very clearly made that:

Experience has shown that, in the majority of colonial and semi-colonial countries, an important if not a predominant part of the Party ranks in the first stage of the move-ment is recruited from the petty bour-geoisie, and in particular, from the revolu-tionary inclined intelligentsia, very fre-quently students. It not uncommonly hap-pens that these elements enter the Party because they see in it the most decisive enemy of imperialism, at the same time not sufficiently understanding that the Com-munist Party is not only the Party of strug-gle against imperialist exploitation ... but struggle against all kinds of exploitation and expropriation. Many of these adherents of the Party, in the course of the revolution-ary struggle will reach a proletarian class point of view; another part will find it more difficult to free themselves to the end, from

the moods, waverings and half-hearted ide-ology of the petty bourgeoisie....

The fact that this did not accord with the idée fixe of this and all other Comin-tern pronouncements that leadership of colonial revolutionary movements is properly a function of the industrial urban workers should in no way blind us to the fact which Comintern leader-ship was realistic enough to acknowl-edge, namely that membership of these Communist Parties is heavily weighted in favor of the intelligentsia. One may, in fact, go one step further and say that in accepting the predominance of the "colonial" intelligentsia, the Comintern was closer to the *genus* of Leninist doc-trine than were any of its endorsements of the leadership role of the urban prole-tariat. No other group in these areas but the intelligentsia could be expected to undertake the transformation of the so-cial structure under forced drafts and in a pre-determined direction and thus ful-fill the main self-assigned historical mis-sion of Leninism.

If we bear this key factor in mind, it throws a new light on the nature of the grip which Communists exercise on the political movements of these areas. The usual formulation of the character of these movements is that they stem from mass discontent with the prevailing sys-tem of land distribution, with the labor practices in force, with the overt or indi-rect political control of these areas by foreign governments, etc. These are per-fectly valid empirical descriptions of the necessary conditions for the rise of lib-eration movements in these areas. But they obviously fail to take notice of the specific social groups that give these movements their *elan,* direction and whatever measure of success they have had thus far. As matters stand today, the intellectuals are the sole group in these areas which can infuse these raw social materials of agrarian discontent, etc., with the necessary organization and leadership necessary for their success. And it is largely this group which has acted as the marriage broker between the international Communist movement and the manifestations of indigenous revolt.

. . . .

As matters stand, then, the organization and leadership of Communist parties in colonial areas do not accord with their accepted doctrinal precepts. For over a generation now it has been a standard item of doctrine, reiterated again and again, that the leadership of these parties must rest with the industrial working class. The realities of the situation in these areas have not been very obliging to this formula though it still occupies its customary niche in all their pronouncements. From the standpoint of their own strategic imperatives and long-term objective however, the Communist parties of these areas have not hesitated to draw the necessary practical conclusions. They have acquiesced in the primacy of the intellectuals in the movement because the acceptance of any alternative leadership coming from the ranks of the peasantry or of the industrial workers (assuming the possibility of such leadership), would entail the sacrifice of the prime objectives of the party—viz., the seizure of power and the launching of a long-range plan for internal planning and reconstruction. Gradual and piecemeal reforms and certainly basic reforms designed to bring immediate relief to the masses (for instance in the credit structure of an area) undertaken by non-Communist regimes would be welcomed by the mass of the peasantry because they are in accord with their immediate and most pressing interests. A program of seizing political power followed by prolonged industrialization, economic planning, recasting of the social structure, re-alignment of a country's international position in favor of the USSR—these are considerations

of the type which can attract intellectuals only.

Accordingly, if the main appeal of Communism *per se*, in underdeveloped areas, has been to the native intelligentsia, a transgression has apparently been committed against an expendable item of party dogma, but the fundamental spirit of the Leninist position with regard to the relation between leadership and the masses, has actually been preserved in its pristine form. There is no need to labor this point since there is enough evidence to indicate that the leadership of Communist parties in underdeveloped areas is acutely aware of the conflict between its own long-range objectives and the "interests" of its mass following, as well as of the conclusions to be drawn for the practical guidance of their parties' activities. Thus a recent party document issued by the Malaya Communist Party to cope with internal criticism of its leadership and policies contains this cogent passage:

Regarding these masses, our responsibility is not to lower the Party's policy and to accede to the selfish demands of small sections of the backward elements, but to bring out a proper plan to unite and direct them courageously to carry out the various forms of struggle against the British. If this course is not followed we will retard the progress of the national revolutionary war, and will lose the support of the masses. The proper masses route is not only to mix up with them [mingle with them?] but to resolutely and systematically lead them to march forward to execute the Party's policy and programme. By overlooking the latter point, we will not be able to discharge the historical duty of a revolutionary Party.

If we discern the central driving force of Communism in the underdeveloped areas to be its appeal to a considerable number of the indigenous intelligentsia, we are also in a position to reassess the meaning and changes of its mass appeal, most notably its program of land redistribution. To no inconsiderable extent, much of the confusion which attends thinking and discourse on the subject in this country can be traced to a widespread impression, still current, that the Communist movement in underdeveloped areas owes its success to the fact that it is finely attuned to the most urgent and insistent "land hunger" of millions of the poorest peasants living on a submarginal level of existence. There is just enough historical truth in this impression to make it a plausible explanation of Communist strength. It is unquestionably true that the mass base of the Communist parties in south Asia can be accounted for by the almost universal prevalence of local agrarian unrest which thus constitutes the necessary precondition for the activities of the Communists. But if—as is not infrequently done—this is offered as the crucially strategic element in the complex of circumstances which have served the cause of the Communist parties, we are once again confronted with the old confusion of necessary with sufficient causes. For there is no intrinsic reason which compels the groundswell of agrarian discontent to favor the fortunes of the Communist parties—unless that discontent can be channelled and directed in predetermined fashion by the intervention of a native social group capable of giving organized shape to its various amorphous and diffused manifestations. If the foregoing analysis has any merit, the balance of the sociological picture in these areas will have to be redressed in our thinking to give greater weight to the Communist-oriented intelligentsia, and to its role as the prime mover of the native Communist movements.

. . . .

To say, ... that the Communist program in the underdeveloped areas of Asia is designed purely and simply as an appeal to the poorest and landless sections of the peasant population is to indulge in an oversimplification of the facts. The Communist appeal is rather a complicated function of the total interplay of political forces in these areas, and has therefore tended to shift both in direction and content with the degree of influence and political power exercised by the Communist parties. The only constant element among all these changes has been the abiding appeal of the Communist system to certain sections of the intelligentsia. Whether the new dispensation of the appeal can be expected to evoke the same degree of sympathetic response from the "national bourgeoisie" and the more prosperous peasantry as the discarded slogan of outright land confiscation had for the impoverished peasants is open to considerable doubt. The avowed transitional character of the program of the "People's Democracy" is alone sufficient to rob these appeals of any sustained response. It does not require any high degree of political sophistication on the part of the "national bourgeoisie," for example, to realize that a full measure of cooperation with a Communist-controlled regime would only serve to hasten its own extinction. How seriously such a withdrawal of support would affect the fortunes of a Communist regime would depend to a crucial extent on the speed with which it could find a substitute support in newly evolved social groups with a vested stake in its continued existence. Some indication of how the problem is visualized by the leaders of the Communist regime in China may be gleaned from the following remarks made by Li Shao-chi in a speech to Chinese businessmen (in 1951. Ed.).

As Communists we consider that you are exploiting your workers; but we realize that, at the present stage of China's economic development, such exploitation is unavoidable and even socially useful. What we want is for you to go ahead and develop production as fast as possible and we will do what we can to help you. You may be afraid of what will happen to you and your family when we develop from New Democracy to Socialism. But you need not really be afraid. If you do a really good job in developing your business, and train your children to be first-class technical experts, you will be the obvious people to put in charge of the nationalized enterprise and you may find that you earn more as managers of a socialized enterprise than as owners.

For the time being the challenge which confronts the West in its efforts to deny the underdeveloped areas of south Asia to the Communist appeal is therefore of two distinct elements. The more obvious of these is, of course, the problem of depriving the Communists of their actual and potential "mass base" by an adequate program of technical aid and economic reform designed to remove the blight of poverty and exploitation from the scheme of things heretofore in force in these areas. The other and more imponderable aspect of this twofold challenge requires the development of an ethos and system of values which can compete successfully with the attraction exercised by Communism for those sections of the native intelligentsia which have been the source and mainstay of its leadership. To date, there is little evidence that the West is prepared to meet either of these challenges on terms commensurate with its gravity.

2 • Prime Minister Nehru on "Neutralism" *

Following are excerpts from speeches made by Prime Minister Nehru, chief spokesman for the neutralist position, at the Asian-African Conference in Bandung, Indonesia, 1955. The excerpts are joined together, without indications of omissions.

The distinguished leader of the Turkish Delegation gave us an able statement of what I might call one side representing the views of one of the major blocs existing at the present time in the world. I have no doubt that an equally able disposition could be made on the part of the other bloc. I belong to neither and I propose to belong to neither whatever happens in the world. If we have to stand alone, we will stand by ourselves, whatever happens (and India has stood alone without any aid against a mighty Empire, the British Empire) and we propose to face all consequences. I am afraid of nobody. I suffer from no fear complex; my country suffers from no fear complex. We rely on nobody except on the friendship of others; we rely on ourselves and none others.

We have to face the position as it is today, namely, that whatever armaments one side or the other might possess, war will lead to consequences which will result in, not gaining an objective, but ruin. Therefore, the first thing we have to settle is that war must be avoided. Naturally, war cannot be

* As quoted in George McTurnan Kahin, *The Asian-African Conference*, Bandung, Indonesia, April 1955 (Ithaca: Cornell University Press, 1956), p. 64 ff. Reprinted by permission.

avoided if any country takes to a career of conquest and aggression. But that is a different matter. Secondly, we countries of Asia have to consider whether we can, all of us put together, prevent the great powers or big countries going to war. We certainly cannot prevent the big countries going to war if they want to, but we can make a difference. Even a single country can make a difference when the scales are evenly balanced. What action are we going to take?

The first step is to make our view clear that these things should not happen. So far as I am concerned, it does not matter what war takes place; we will not take part in it unless we have to defend ourselves. If I join any of these big groups I lose my identity; I have no identity left. If all the world were to be divided up between these two big blocs, what would be the result? The inevitable result would be war. Therefore every step that takes place in reducing that area in the world which may be called the unaligned area is a dangerous step and leads to war. It reduces that objective, that balance, that outlook which other countries without military might can perhaps exercise.

Every pact has brought insecurity and not security to the countries which have entered into them. They have brought the danger of atomic bombs and the rest of it nearer to them than would have been the case otherwise. They have not added to the strength of any country, I submit, which it had singly. It may have produced some idea of security, but it is false security. It is a bad thing for any country thus to be lulled into security.

Two big colossuses stand face to face with each other, afraid of each other. Today in the world, I do submit, not only because of the presence of these two colossuses but also because of the coming of the atomic and hydrogen-bomb age, the whole concept of war, of peace, of politics, has changed. We are thinking and acting in terms of a past age. No matter what generals and soldiers learned in the past, it is useless in this atomic age.

Now, therefore, are we, the Asian and African countries, going to work on it passively or are we going to take a step which will upset the balance on one side or the other? This is not a question of security. Will not security be damned if war comes? Who is going to protect us if war comes and if atomic bombs come? Are we going to continue to be dragged and tie ourselves to Europe's troubles, Europe's hatred and Europe's conflicts? I hope not. Of course, Europe and Asia and America are all dependent on one another. It is perhaps not quite right to think in terms of isolation because we are not isolated, we have to live together and to cooperate with each other. Nevertheless, Europe has got into the habit of thinking—also other great countries in America or Europe, whatever their political persuasions may be —that their quarrels are the world's quarrels, and therefore the world must submit to them this way or that way. Well, I do not quite follow that reasoning. I do not want anybody to quarrel in Europe, Asia, or America, but if at least others quarrel, why should I quarrel and why should I be dragged into their quarrels and wars? I just do not understand it. Therefore, I hope we shall keep away from these quarrels and exercise our will not to quarrel. I realize that we cannot exercise tremendous influence over the world. Our influence will grow no doubt; it is growing, and we can exercise some influence even today. But whether our influence is great or small, it must be exercised in the right direction, in an intelligent direction, in a direction which has integrity of purpose and ideals and objectives. It represents the ideals of Asia, it represents the new dynamism of Asia, because if it does not represent that, what are we then? Are we copies of Europeans or Americans or Russians? What are we? We are Asians or Africans. We are none else. If we are camp followers of Russia or America or any other country of Europe, it is, if I may say so, not very creditable to our dignity, our new independence, our new freedom, our new spirit and our new self-reliance.

3 • "Neutralism" in Asia *

Robert A. Scalapino

The author, a member of the University of California (Berkeley) Department of Political Science, is a specialist in Far Eastern Government and Politics and the author of several notable articles.

Many Americans view "neutralism" as a new type of social disease. Its probable causes: intimacy in some form with communism; its symptoms: mental confusion and moral dereliction; its cure: unknown. This is a somber diagnosis, filled with implications of doom for the "victims." But our warnings and protests have been to little avail. Most "neutralists" have deliberately rejected them, and the "disease"—if that be its proper designation—has approached epidemic proportions in many areas. Among the centers of infection, Asia is certainly the region where "neutralism" has shown its most consistent strength and taken its most diverse forms. And however much they may lament it, Americans must recognize the fact that Asian "neutralism" can be neither ignored nor talked out of existence. In our own interests, therefore, we should seek a more complete understanding of this highly complex force—its causes and effects, and possibly its implications for future American policy. Understanding does not necessarily mean accept-ance; it does permit a more accurate calculation of alternative risks, and this is the vital element in decision making.

At the outset, the problems of definition and terminology must be raised. It is not easy to define or describe "neutralism" in such manner as to obtain the largest measure of agreement from all parties concerned. Frequently, the word is intended as an epithet, with connotations similar to those suggested in our opening sentences. In other cases, the expression is used as if it were a symbol of virtue, a literary badge of honor. To attempt a dispassionate definition, it can perhaps be said that Asian "neutralism" in its current usage is a term applicable to those policies and attitudes representing a rejection of extensive commitment to either side now engaged in the cold war. It must be recognized, however, that while most of the Asian "neutralists" would accept this description of their position, many re-

* *American Political Science Review*, XLVIII (1954), 49–62. Reprinted by permission.

sent the label attached to it. Opposition to the term "neutralism" by those for whom it is intended stems from several considerations. There is the insistence that even when given its most generous interpretation, such an appellation is too negative and too passive. There is also the feeling that it suggests unfairly a lack of responsibility concerning world affairs. Some of the "neutralist" arguments on these points might be set forth briefly as follows: Ours is a position based upon positive actions and equally positive beliefs. Sometimes these coincide with Western desires and interests, sometimes with those of the Soviet Union, on many occasions with those of neither country. Our main objective, of course, is to maintain a position toward international affairs consistent with our own interests and values as we see them. We are confident, however, that it is not only a positive position, but one which contains constructive proposals for reducing world tension and developing a firmer basis of cooperation among nations. We have participated in international affairs to the limit of our capacities as long as it was consistent with our clearly-stated views. Indeed, we have achieved some measure of leadership in pressing for a solution to certain current world problems. We have followed the practice of abstention only when any other course would jeopardize our basic beliefs, not because we are afraid to stand up and be counted. The record will bear out the fact that we have not been neutral in terms of issues and principles, rather, we have been independent.

It is the word "independent" which climaxes this defense, for those whom we call "neutralists" generally think of their policies and attitudes not as "neutralism" but as "independence." The above arguments are probably a fair representation of the views held by most of the leaders in India, Burma, and In-donesia—the so-called "neutral bloc" in East Asia. Modified somewhat, they could also be used by most of the individuals and groups espousing "neutralism" throughout Asia, although one of the complexities with which we must deal is the fact that "neutralism" stems from diverse interests and philosophies. It differs greatly in orientation and degree, and knows no single line of defense. The position outlined so briefly above comes closest to expressing some of the views of the moderates—those "neutralists" whose general opinions have the most in common with the values of the Western democracies.

Even so, this defense would not satisfy most Americans, including many who consider themselves sympathetic to the problems of modern Asia. Instead of seeking to present their rebuttal, however, let us turn directly to the basic issues. I shall continue to use the word "neutralism" in quotation marks, for while I do not accept its implications fully, neither do I find an adequate substitute in such a phrase as "independent policy."

. . . .

What, then, are the foundations upon which "neutralist" policy in South Asia rests? The Asian "neutralist" would answer this question by invoking that much debated concept, the national interest. It is not necessary here to explore the controversy which has raged over "the national interest" theme. It is sufficient to emphasize as forcefully as possible that the first line of defense for "neutralism" in India, Burma, and Indonesia has been built around this concept. To rely successfully upon such a broad thesis as "the national interest" is on obvious advantage as compared with such alternatives as reliance upon a thesis of class or group interest, or any given ideological adherence. It is also extremely difficult, and yet to a remarkable extent it has been accomplished, thus far at least, in the above countries. Any central explanation must focus upon what might be described as the two massive facts of these societies: first, the recency and nature of the nationalist revolution; second, the serious domestic problems of this transitional period.

The implications of nationalism will be discussed more fully later on, but here it must be noted that the so-called "neutral bloc" of South Asia share both a common timing and relatively common circumstances in their emergence from colonialism. And as a result of these factors, the nationalist argument can reach a level of intensity as an appeal comparable to that of arguments resting upon a thesis of religion or class, with the further advantage of being much more comprehensive in its coverage. While this is a significant aspect of all Far Eastern politics, conditions have given it particular force in the countries under discussion.

With regard to the second factor, it is certainly no exaggeration to describe the general domestic situation in the South Asian countries as critical. Political and economic stability remain to be achieved, and even national unification is incomplete. Economic problems are particularly pressing in India and Indonesia, and no basic solutions have been discovered. In all three of these countries, the political situation is precariously balanced, with the present governments in power representing a middle-of-the-road position and being subject to assaults of varying intensity from both right and left. The moral fervor and political unity achieved in the heat of the independence movement have shown an inevitable decline. Leadership faces the serious problem of combatting moral and political disintegration. And naturally the military strength of the present governments is scarcely equal to the task of preserving order even on the home

front; in most cases it is a weak and uncertain element in the political picture. Even so, it is a serious drain upon the limited resources of the society.

Thus the immediate situation in these countries tends to reduce possibilities in the field of foreign policy to two broad alternatives. One is active partisanship in world affairs combined with extensive military and economic support from foreign sources. The other is a policy of international participation strongly conditioned by its possible influence upon the domestic scene and its impact upon the major powers. Both policies involve substantial risks. Any success with the first alternative depends upon such factors as the consistency of action by the major powers; the military feasibility of foreign protection; and, perhaps most important of all, the internal repercussions of dependency and a certain amount of foreign supervision and control. All of these risks, and especially the last, militate strongly against its being adopted at present by such countries as India, Burma, and Indonesia. There is grave uncertainty in Asia as to which general course American foreign policy will follow with regard both to the Far East and to the world; there are equally serious doubts as to the strength of the other Western democratic powers, and about some of their actions. In any case, grave doubts have been entertained as to how adequately and at what cost nations on the continent of Asia could be defended by means of Western power, even if events caused or forced them to consider it desirable. The lesson of Korea may not be a valid one for the future, but at this point it has been an impressive one to many continentals, and it is extremely doubtful whether it would have been less impressive had we scored a greater military victory, in view of the enormous sacrifices of the Korean people. On the other hand, the power of nearby Communist China is now treated as a fact by many Asian leaders besides Nehru.

But the greatest problem to be surmounted, should the first alternative be chosen, would undoubtedly be that of losing control of the nationalist movement. Practically all the statesmen of these three countries are both leaders and prisoners of that movement. At present, it is not merely advantageous to cast political appeals in nationalist terms; it is a necessity. The political struggle in these areas still focuses around the battle to capture the nationalist symbols. Each competing group must claim to have inherited that revolutionary movement which had as its central emblem the struggle against Western imperialism. In South Asia, such epithets as "imperialist" and "supporter of Western exploitation" are as dangerous as terms like "fellow-traveler" and "Communist" in America. Thus a foreign policy which can be easily defended as "independent" is the most potent weapon available to men like Nehru and U Nu against some of their opponents, particularly the domestic Communists. Moreover, any other policy would represent a break with a tradition composed of concrete pronouncements and actions as well as generalities. An examination of the numerous foreign policy statements of the Indian Congress party during the period of British rule reveals clearly the strong element of continuity involved in present Indian foreign policy. In this connection, one must not forget that leadership for the most part is in the hands of first generation "revolutionaries," including men whose prestige in South Asia is connected with a lengthy public record on most of the current issues. In this as in other respects, the colonial era still casts a long shadow over the policies of people who have just gained political independence.

Hence the second alternative, despite its obvious risks, becomes the most natural choice, and in the eyes of present leaders the most reasonable. Its dictates are simple but compelling. It must take account of internal weakness and the urgent nature of domestic problems. Thus, foreign partisanship, at either the individual or the national level, is regarded as a development likely to produce further cleavages in an already confused situation. And under the circumstances foreign policy must be the pillar of strength, capable of being sustained on the basis of its own emotional and political appeal, so that the governments in power can fight with some advantages the inevitable crucial battles over domestic policy. Involved in this second alternative also is the necessity for appraising in realistic fashion power abroad, both actual and potential, and then seeking to reduce any threats by relying largely upon a policy of conciliation and compromise, at least until that time when military strength and internal stability may permit the consideration of other approaches. But it need not be a policy resting upon moral suasion and compromise alone. There is also the possibility of creating a position of power not through military strength but rather through a strategic political position attuned to the nature of power politics in the modern world.

. . . .

"Neutralist" exponents do not push the claim that their policy will prevent involvement should another world war occur, although popular hopes in this direction generally accrue to their advantage. Much of the nineteenth-century optimism that participation in war could be avoided has gone with the tide of recent events, and the classical defense of isolation on this score represents a relatively minor part of "neutralist" arguments. The present defense of "neutralism" is that it can help prevent war. A substantial part of this theory is based upon the old balance of power theme, though that phrase is rarely used. It is the "neutralist" contention that we now have a bi-polar world and that this represents the most dangerous political form in terms of reducing tensions and avoiding conflict. Most "neutralists" like to consider themselves a "third force" holding a position that can save the world from self-destruction.

The "third force" concept deserves close examination, so important is it to the general attitudes and actions of all "neutralists." Once again, our initial discussion will revolve largely around its strategic implications, with the vital ideological-attitude factors reserved for a later point. Again, the problem of power is centrally involved. The idea of a "third force" can be attractive as a method of developing influence and power in the international scene despite internal conditions of great weakness. The political advantages of non-commitment—the power of the floating vote— are not inconsiderable under contemporary conditions. In addition, there is the prospect of becoming an important channel of communication between major power blocs and the initiator of both the ideas and institutions of international compromise. If these possibilities could be translated into realities, it would be the supreme vindication for leaders who have only recently emerged from the status of subversives. And like most leaders, these are not men without ego and ambition. Moreover, the prospect of importance is a great stimulant to the society as a whole, coming as it does so soon after the colonial era and the complexes produced thereby.

The "third force" idea is also an ally of regionalism, an objective of both historic and current importance to many people in the Far East. In its indigenous forms, the drive for Asian regionalism has been closely connected with the struggle against Western control. Under

Japanese aegis, such slogans as "Asia for the Asians" and even "The Greater Co-Prosperity Sphere" had potency because of this fact. But now the concept of regionalism has new and dynamic implications. Many Asians would like to think of the "third force" as a group of nations recently freed from colonial status which together with people still under foreign control would act in concert on the international level. Such a union, they believe, can serve as a formidable pressure group to secure justice and recognition for its members. Actually this is an idea that goes beyond regionalism in many cases, to conceive of incorporating societies from diverse areas facing common problems of timing and development. Its basis for political unity supposedly lies in common nationalist aspirations and opposition to dictation by major powers, and in its common economic interests in such problems as technological development and safeguards against foreign exploitation. In some respects, the so-called "Arab-Asian bloc" has symbolized the bond between a "third force" and a "regionalism" of under-developed societies. The record of this group, together with the growing Asian interest in the African nationalist movements, has been hailed as evidence of the practicality of such a plan.

. . . .

Already we have moved toward a discussion of attitudes, and the preceding comments may serve as the transition. In this connection "neutralism" must be viewed at its broadest and most complex level, one encompassing philosophy, ideology, prejudice, and emotionalism. The setting can no longer be restricted to a few countries, but must extend to the whole of the Far East and, by inference, to many other areas as well. At the beginning, one must admit that there is no easy method whereby every pertinent factor can be included and assigned its appropriate weight. It may be wise to start with an attempt to relate to the problem three comprehensive forces which have been so important in contemporary Asian thought and life: the forces of eclecticism, nationalism, and Marxism.

The first of these, eclecticism, might be called the "tolerant component" of the modern Far East. It is deeply imbedded in the entire traditional background, and finds its current expressions in both the philosophies and the institutions of Asian societies. The quest for the greater harmony, for the complete synthesis of conflicting ideas, is still a primary objective. Challenges, to be sure, have not been absent in the modern period. Whatever its ultimate possibilities, Western science in its philosophic reaches has thus far been mainly the science of differentiation, with an emphasis upon empirical research aimed at identifying and categorizing the vast body of fact and ideas. Tendencies toward exclusivism have gained considerable strength from this trend. Out of the process of rigid logical and value distinctions, theories essentially exclusivist in nature emerged. If Western society has been generally characterized by exclusivism at the level of individual theories, it has, by the same token, emphasized vigorous competition among such theories, rather than placing any great premium upon harmonization. And certainly, in their impact upon Asia, Western ideology and religion have presented the case for such competition and the necessity for rigorous selectivity in very powerful terms. This has had a significant influence, and in fact the area is not without some subordinate traditions which lend support.

At the same time, however, the nature of modern Asian problems and certain recent trends in the West itself have served to sustain the eclectic tradition in general, and actually increase its appeal in some important respects. The Asian problem of adjustment to modern Westernism is the largest and most complex problem of synthesis that has ever faced these societies. The difficulties of adopting Western patterns intact and the impossibility of duplicating earlier Western evolution have strengthened the conviction among many Asians that they cannot use the old roads to reach their objectives, but only the old implements used to build those many roads, now to be borrowed from the diverse Western sources and refashioned into a uniform set of equipment for future tasks. If there is a fundamental logic in this position, there is also the risk of very great confusion at both the academic and the operating political levels on such issues as basic values and the degree to which seeming incompatibles can be rendered compatible. To many of us, this type of confusion is an impressive aspect of the Asian scene, ranging in form from simple naïveté to the tormented ambivalence of some of the most powerful minds in the Far East. But perhaps the supreme irony lies in the fact that most Asians do not recognize the degree to which the West now shares in this problem. The reaction here against exclusivism has been compounded out of many forces, but essentially it comes from the pressing necessity of developing new approaches to current problems, approaches involving synthesis and running similar risks of confusion. Still, Asia sees us—and particularly America—largely in the old image, the image of a rigid, inflexible society governed by a set of exclusive principles, and basically intolerant whether of people or ideas. Communist interpretations of us have certainly contributed to this belief; their attempt to posit our rigidity as the only alternative to theirs often produces a firmer desire on the part of Asia to avoid both if possible. But our interpretations of ourselves are often a great disservice to truth and to our own interests; if we were to take our stand with the concept of selective synthesis more positively, there would still be differences, some of them basic, but the real issues could be more easily posed.

The preceding discussion is closely connected with the psychology of "neutralism." The tendency of the "neutralist" is to regard each contemporary Western ideology as in and of itself inapplicable, and to see all as having a common denominator in their absolutist base. The commitment, therefore, to any specific ideological position as reflected either through a single Western nation or through a group of allied countries, is limited. There is a natural urge to maintain independence toward political and ideological lines that are considered in some measure artificial, and certainly incomplete. But complementing this critical attitude is a kind of broad tolerance toward rival ideologies which many Western liberals feel is indiscriminate. In this connection, I would venture the somewhat heretical view that in an important sense the bent of contemporary Asia is more practical than ideological, to the extent that such a distinction has validity. The primary test of an idea is its success in the practical field of governing, not its inner consistency or its adherence to the body of thought from which it sprang. There is, to be sure, a strong element of conflict in some cases between the desire for ideological consistency and policy defenses couched in terms of "ideological purity" on the one hand, and the urgent necessity for pragmatic action at the policy level on the other. But it is the latter course which largely governs actual policy in Asia, including its Communist as well as its non-Communist spheres.

If eclecticism can be called in some respects the "tolerant component" of the modern Far East, then nationalism is the "intolerant component." This is not to deny the Asian nationalist movement its justification and its quota of laudable goals. Nor is it to ignore the fact that Asian nationalism in many of its forms is striving for some type of synthesis with internationalism. It is simply to make the point that Asian nationalism like nationalism everywhere rests centrally upon an emotional appeal with hate, prejudice, and general irrationality playing an important part. And in connection with Asian nationalism, two facts are significant in analyzing "neutralist" attitudes. First, it has been a movement directed quite naturally against the West. Secondly, in its "progressive" forms, it has had considerable stimulus from Marxism in general and communism in particular. To mention this latter fact is to introduce the third and final comprehensive factor relating to Asian "neutralism."

It is obvious to anyone that nationalism is the only political movement that has approached mass proportions throughout modern Asia. It is also a movement dominated by the concept of a counterattack against Western power and attitudes of superiority; in recent decades, this attack has been fierce, unrelenting, and operating at all levels of sophistication. It still contains some of the most appealing symbols for the Asian mind. This is partially because they are symbols with continuing validity. But in any case the recency and the intensity of the attack make difficult any re-evaluation of the current Western position which would give full credit to the West when credit is due, and would raise before the public the more recent evidences of Communist imperialism. Consequently, the Western threat in both its political and its economic forms still looms up before many Asians, including almost all "neutralists," as the most immediate threat to be faced; as compared with it, the dangers of communism, and particularly external Communist aggression, are frequently considered remote. The term "imperialism" is still reserved almost exclusively for the West; even when the native Communists show sufficient power to make themselves respected or feared, the movement is viewed largely as an internal problem and a part of the indigenous revolution.

Actually, it is possible to make two broad divisions in the Asian nationalist movement, with reference to groups stemming from it. The first group might be called the traditionalists. In seeking to defend their society against the onslaughts of Westernism, they have relied largely upon traditional values and presented a defense that is distinctly anti-modernist. Their attack has ranged broadly over the fields of urbanism, commercialism, liberalism, and secularism. Their portrait of the West has placed its emphasis upon the surfeit of materialism and the paucity of cultural or spiritual values, and it has achieved particular depth of feeling when dealing with American society. It must never be forgotten that "neutralism" has its "right-wing" as well as its "left-wing" derivations; in Asia, this can be found wherever "neutralism" exists as an important force.

The traditionalist approach has complemented in a sense the attack of the modernists upon the West. If the latter group have accepted as desirable many of the end-products of Western civilization, such as industralization and centralized power, they have been equally vigorous in opposing what they consider to be the use of these by the West against their own societies. And in many respects they have been strongly influenced by Marxism. The concepts of economic exploitation and of the state as an instrument of oppression fitted well into the pattern of nationalist attack upon the Western powers. Capitalism

has borne odious connotations in the Far East partly because it was under simultaneous attack by both the traditionalists and the modernists; in Asia, certain forces of the Western seventeenth and twentieth centuries seem almost to be joined together under anti-imperialist banners.

In a broader sense, however, the influence of Marxism in Asia, especially among the intelligentsia, must be ascribed to the fact that Marxism has had greater applicability to the Asian scene than any other Western philosophy. The refinements of modern Western economic and political thought have generally been tailored to the problems of societies reaching increasingly complex levels within the industrial process. Thus the issues have been more and more removed from those societies whose basic economic and political forms are still relatively simple as related to this particular stage. The West has had the greatest opportunity to reveal the inadequacies of Marxism, with regard both to its initial premises and to its subsequent evolution. But in Asia Marxism has not only achieved a measure of integration with the nationalist revolutionary movement; it has also benefited from the degree to which some of its central theses fit this stage of Asian development. As a result, while only a small portion of the Asian intellectuals are Communists, a very substantial number are deeply influenced by Marxism. And the intellectuals are important in the Asian "neutralist" movement not only because they are well represented in its ranks, but also because they are the leading publicists in many Asian countries, interpreting to the people their own and foreign societies.

Thus far we have been considering the broad forces of eclecticism, nationalism, and Marxism, in an attempt to discern the various sources of "neutralist" thought. Though these are what might be called the massive factors in the picture, there are other elements of importance. Certainly one is the great weariness of conflict and the omnipresent fear of involvement in another war. This is a widespread sentiment in the Far East, and while it does not represent automatic support for "neutralism," there can be no doubt that many consider the risks increased under conditions of open dependence upon or alliance with the United States or any bloc of Western powers. Another aspect of "neutralist" thought is related to economics: there is an inevitable desire on the part of most Asian business groups, and particularly those in Japan and overseas Chinese communities, to have trade and financial relations with all possible sources. While this does not always lead to a "neutralist" attitude, it frequently contributes to a position of political aloofness on the major issue here posed. And it must not be forgotten that such a position has had a certain historic rationality for the Asian business class. A basically apolitical attitude or opportunism has often been the staff of life for the Far Eastern entrepreneur. Another factor lies in the political realm, and is perhaps connected more with policy than with attitude, though in reality it is an excellent representative of that element of fusion between the two. "Neutralism" in Japan, for instance, is promoted by some socialist groups because it appears to be a promising issue by which to attack those in power. This is not to belie the obvious sincerity of many Japanese "neutralists," but merely to underline the fact that policy-attitudes are affected by the degree of responsibility held and by the dictates of opposition strategy. And a final factor—to which various names might be applied—is, basically, indifference or ignorance. The greater number of "common men" in Asia are, for all real purposes, "neutralists" by default; their only deep commitments are to the immediate problems of livelihood and personal tension which contact with modernism has introduced. Mass indoctrination on an intensive scale has just begun in parts of the Far East, and in any case is likely to follow government policy in most areas.

Implicit in this analysis of "neutralism" both as a policy and as an attitude has been the fact that the causal factors presented have application in regions other than Asia. The emphasis, to be sure, would vary with different areas, and some points would have to be modified or omitted, but in spite of diversity and complexity "neutralism" in all parts of the world has its connecting links.

. . . .

XVII • The Changing Nature of War

Of all the types of relationship which may exist between states, war is at one and the same time the least attractive and the most significant. In recent times, the nature of war has changed drastically, primarily because of the changing technology of war, but also due to changing concepts about the purposes of war. In former times (e.g. the 16th through 19th centuries) wars were, on the whole, fought with limited means—partly because no other means were available—and for limited objectives. The participants in an armed conflict took it for granted that, with minor rectifications and changes, the postwar environment would resemble the pre-war scene. War, in other words, was important but not crucial; its outcome made a difference, but it did not make the difference between survival and extinction. With the coming of total war of, by, and against whole populations and for total stakes, previous concepts of war have become inapplicable, and there has developed a pressing need for re-evaluating war as an instrument of policy in international relations.

There are many theories on the causes and occasions of war. Most of them leave much to be desired. Thus we can identify a "who-done-it" theory of war, which assumes that there is a villain or group of villains who can be identified and properly and conveniently punished. These villains may be governmental leaders, the press, an inflamed public, big businessmen, warlords, or munitions-makers. Unfortunately the problem of war is too complex to lend itself to such easy explanation.

Another misconception is the idea that countries are either at war or at peace with one another. In this view, the presence of war is identified by a formal declaration of hostilities. But many wars are, and always have been, fought without formal declarations. The United States alone has been engaged in more than twenty such undeclared wars, of which the Korean War was only the latest example. Also, the distinction between war and peace runs into difficulty in terms of "warfare" by means other than armed forces—such as psychological, political, subversive, economic. The very term "cold war" indicates that the simple war-peace dichotomy is insufficient. It is probably more useful to think of relations among states as lying along a continuum where one finds complete amity and absence of violence on one end, and total violence without restraint on the other. Both extremes are seldom reached, but somewhere along such a continuum it may be possible to place specific inter-state relationships.

Among other faulty ideas about war, we find the Marxist-Leninist view which holds that wars are caused by economic motivations; more specifically, by capitalism in a certain phase of its development. Others believe that wars are caused by racial, religious, or cultural differentiations which give rise to frictions.

The Marxist-Leninist thesis has been discredited by evidence that in many instances capitalists have opposed war as an undersirable disturbance of normal economic processes. There is no evidence to substantiate the view that *inter* racial, religious, or cultural (broadly defined) wars are more frequent than *intra* racial, religious, or cultural conflicts.

Moving to somewhat more plausible explanations, we find the idea that wars are caused by individuals and groups who desire it for some reason. The reason may be their genuine attachment to certain symbols or ideals. It may be the fact that an incident has occurred, or a situation exists for which war appears to be the only suitable remedy. Thus, "revolutionary" wars of "proletarian liberation" seem to be accepted as useful by the Soviet Union. One also hesitates to discard altogether the idea that individuals may desire war as a means of escape from unsatisfactory conditions,[1] although it should be said that popular enthusiasm for war has steadily waned in recent decades. Yet, it has not been possible to make "peace" as meaningful a symbol as war, in the sense that men are willing to work and sacrifice as much for one as for the other.

Emery Reves has advanced the thesis that the real cause of all wars has always been the fact that groups of men form social units, and that these social units, exercising unrestricted sovereign power, come into contact with one another. He proposes that wars will cease the moment sovereign power is transferred from states to larger units. "War takes place whenever and wherever nonintegrated social units of equal sovereignty come into contact." [2] This may be the formulation of a necessary cause, but it is hardly in itself a sufficient one. It fails to explain the incidence of civil wars, or the existence of long-range amicable relationships between many "nonintegrated social units of equal sovereignty."

In a real sense it may be argued that the most obvious cause of war is war itself—or, rather, the expectation of war. Since states live in an environment of anarchy, and since wars have frequently occurred in the past, each state must consider the possibility that another war may occur in the future. Hence, it must take steps to protect itself against such an eventuality. In taking these steps (bases, armaments, alliances, etc.) international insecu-

---

[1] J. Glenn Gray, *The Warriors: Reflections on Men in Battle* (New York: Harcourt, Brace & Co., 1959).

[2] Emery Reves, *The Anatomy of Peace* (New York: Harper and Brothers, Publishers, 1945).

rity may thereby be increased, and tension may reach a point of open hostility.

Whichever explanation or combination of explanations one prefers, war is a fact of international life. There are few states in the world which have not engaged in it at one time or another. Nor is resort to violence specific to international relations. It occurs within states and other groups as well, albeit less frequently and on a smaller scale. Indeed, the continuum from total amity to unrestrained violence exists within any community, except that here the situation will be more often toward the amity end of the scale than in international relations.

Within the relatively brief history of the Western state system (the system of independent sovereign states), there have been profound changes in the conduct of warfare. (See the article by Herz in Chapter II.) During the 16th and 17th centuries, warfare was usually conducted by hired mercenaries or small professional armies, not particularly anxious on taking undue chances. It was only in the 18th and 19th centuries that wars began to involve large portions of the population. Frederick II of Prussia and particularly Napoleon I of France relied on mass armies. To motivate conscripts, wars needed a "cause" other than mere selfish or dynastic gain. This trend has continued to our own day. According to Professor Morgenthau, war has become total in at least four respects: 1) it involves total populations emotionally; 2) it involves total populations actively and physically; 3) it is conducted *against* total populations (i.e., saturation bombings during World War II, during which conflict more civilians than members of the armed forces were killed); and 4) it is fought for total stakes, e.g., unconditional surrender.[3] This means that total resistance, and recourse to any and all means of fighting the war have become essential.

With the advent of weapons of total destructive capacity, recent years have witnessed attempts to re-evaluate the role of war as a means of policy. War is, after all, a means to an end; not an end in itself. The objective of war is not victory alone (even though that may be a necessary pre-condition), but the establishment of conditions after the war which are more congenial than those which existed prior to it. Thus to say that "in war there is no substitute for victory" is to posit merely an intermediate goal. The real question is what is to come after the victory has been achieved: will it be possible to establish (or re-establish) a world environment in which the "victorious" state can function?

The availability of new weapons of destruction has cast grave doubts on the answer to this question, because—as Bernard Brodie points out in his article printed in this chapter—it is dubious whether "victory" in a nuclear exchange can provide meaningful possibilities for a new and better world order. Because this is so, more and more thought is being devoted to alter-

---

[3] Hans J. Morgenthau, *Politics Among Nations* (New York: Alfred A. Knopf, Inc., 1954), Chapter 20.

natives to total nuclear warfare: non-military contests (competitive coexistence), and limited or localized wars. The first of these alternatives has been discussed in preceding chapters on the use of psychological methods and economic policies in international relations. The second and third alternatives are the subject of discussion by Admiral Buzzard and Air Marshal Slessor, also printed in this chapter. To their discussion one might merely add the new interest which has been shown in the subject of so-called "guerilla warfare," as practiced in Malaya, Indo-China, and North Africa.[4]

Unfortunately it would be puerile optimism to assume that, since total war has become irrational, it has therefore automatically become impossible. This conclusion (the counterpart of the idealist notion that whatever is necessary is also possible) would assume, in the first place that men always act rationally and that pathological behavior-patterns, such as those of Hitler, will never recur in international relations. But there are other reasons, too, why wars—even major nuclear wars—may still be possible. In the first place, one side or the other may miscalculate the likely effects of an aggressive action. It may believe that it can "get away with it," or it may believe that the other side is about to launch such action and that it is therefore essential to "get there fustest with the mostest," so as to at least minimize the effects of the enemy's action when it comes. This is the doctrine of pre-emptive war. The first blow in a nuclear exchange may not be decisive, but it is still important. Secondly, a war may break out not because of a miscalculation arrived at by deliberation (however faulty), but simply by accident; by a push of the wrong button. This possibility would seem to be enhanced by the advent of new methods of weapons delivery. An airplane can presumably be recalled in flight; an ICBM presumably can not. Thirdly, one side or the other may achieve a genuine technological breakthrough, in weapons, delivery systems, or defense capacities. Either of such breakthroughs might drastically shift the present uneasy balance,[5] and might make war once again seem to be (or possibly actually be) a rational policy choice. Fourthly, just as the American monopoly of nuclear weapons soon gave way to an American-Soviet duopoly, and as the two states have since been joined by Great Britain and France as nuclear powers, other states may soon join the "nuclear club." With the spread of nuclear weapons availability, the control problem will become constantly more difficult and quite possibly altogether insoluble. This relates to the fifth and final reason why one cannot be confident that another major war is totally impossible: local, limited conflicts may grow in area and scope until they embrace the major powers which have nuclear capabilities. Even if one can imagine that nuclear weapons may not be used at the outset of a war, it stretches imagination to assume that a country will prefer losing a war to using its full arsenal.

---

[4] See Raymond Aron, *On War* (New York: Doubleday Anchor, 1959), pp. 70–71.
[5] Albert Wohlstetter, "The Delicate Balance of Terror," *Foreign Affairs*, XXXVII (1959), 211–34.

There is, then, no assurance that the use of war as a method of international relations has forever ended. But one is left with the inescapable judgment that wars—whatever utility they may have possessed in the past —are not functioning well in the present era and will not function well in the foreseeable future, for they bear no relationship to realistic goals of policy. The task of statesmanship, and of informed citizenship, therefore would seem to be that of creating alternatives to a method of international relations which has become outdated.

1 • Strategy Hits a Dead End *

Bernard Brodie

The author, former Professor of International Relations at Yale University, is Senior Staff Member of the RAND Corporation. He is the author of A Layman's Guide to Naval Strategy *(1943),* Strategy in the Missile Age *(1959) and co-author of* The Absolute Weapon *(1946). The present article appeared under the general heading "How War Becomes Absurd" in* Harper's.

One of the commonest slogans in strategic literature is the one inherited from Monini, that "methods change but principles are unchanging." Until yesterday that thesis had much to justify it, since methods changed on the whole not too abruptly and always within definite limits. Among the most important limits was the fact that the costs of a war, even a lost one, were somehow supportable. At worst only a minor portion, literally speaking, of a nation's population and wealth would be destroyed. Even the two world wars did not go beyond this limit, despite their horrendous magnitude.

There could therefore be a reasonable choice between war and peace. There could also be a reasonable choice among methods of fighting a war, or "strategies." However unrestricted they were intended to be, wars were inevitably limited by the limited capabilities (as we now see it) of each belligerent for heaping destruction on the other. Indeed, there were even slogans insisting that the application of force in war *must* be unrestricted.

If the time has not already arrived for saying good-bye to all that, it will inevitably come soon—depending only on when the Soviets achieve an air-atomic capability comparable to the one we already have. (That time has now arrived, according to many experts— Ed.) For unless we can really count on using ours first and, what is more, count on our prior use eliminating the enemy's ability to retaliate in kind—and surely

---

* *Harper's,* CCXI (1955), 33–37. Reprinted by permission of Dr. Brodie.

the combination would deserve long betting odds—we can be quite certain that a major unrestricted war would begin with a disaster for us, as well as for them, of absolutely unprecedented and therefore unimaginable proportions.

There are impelling psychological reasons why strategists have in the past found it almost impossibly difficult to adjust their war plans to the possibility of national disaster at the outset. If not now, then soon, no other assumption for an unlimited major war will be realistically possible. Because we face a situation unique in history, most of our descriptions of it are understatements. For example, people speak bravely of atomic explosives being the most portentous military invention "since gunpowder." In doing so they only prove how hard it is to believe that something which has happened in one's own day—before one's very eyes, as it were—makes every other comparable development of the entire five or six thousand years of recorded time pale in importance.

Since we have recently passed the end of the first atomic decade, this is an appropriate time to observe how much has changed in these ten years. Though it was immediately apparent in 1945 that something of tremendous military importance had happened, we can see now how many of the interpretations then offered were too conservative. In retrospect it is clear that many of them were wedded to presumptions soon to be disproved—for example, that the bomb was fated to remain scarce, extremely costly, bulky and therefore difficult to deliver, and limited to about the same power and spatial effectiveness as the Nagasaki bomb.

The first decade of the atomic age has seen the collapse of the American monopoly, of the myth of inevitable scarcity, and of reasonable hopes for international atomic disarmament; it has seen also the development in both major camps of a thermonuclear weapon of vastly greater destructiveness. Since we have been living with the fission type of atomic bomb for a decade, it might appear to some that the fusion type introduces nothing essentially new other than a greater economy of force. That unfortunately is not the case.

No doubt the implications of the first atomic bombs were radical in the extreme, and it was right at the time they appeared to stress the drastic nature of the change. The utility of strategic bombing could no longer be questioned. At once it became incontrovertibly the dominant form of war, especially since it could be entirely carried through with air forces existing at the onset of war and at speeds which were phenomenally fast by any previous standard. Also, it could be carried out successfully over any distances that might separate the various great powers on this globe. This was change enough from the conditions of World War II.

Nevertheless, the bomb yields were still sufficiently limited to make the delivery of a substantial number of bombs necessary in order to achieve decisive results. That in turn made it possible to visualize a meaningful air defense, even if not a satisfactory one. It was therefore still necessary to think in terms of a real struggle for "command of the air." It was also still necessary to apply, though in much modified form, the lore so painfully acquired in World War II concerning "target selection" for a strategic bombing campaign. And the functions of ground and naval forces, though clearly affected by the new weapons, still appeared vital even in the "all-out" type of war.

These ties with the past, tenuous enough at best, were immediately threatened by the appearance of the modern type of thermonuclear bomb. Among the questions that thereupon became obsolete were most of those concerning the selection of strategic targets. Since a thermonuclear bomb could not be used on an industrial concentration in or near a city without destroying that city—and since one such bomb will effectively eliminate all the industry associated with that city—there is not much point in asking which industries should be hit or in what order. Whether we like it or not, the thermonuclear bomb used strategically is a "city-buster."

The same is of course true if we hit air fields near cities. We cannot talk about strategies being aimed against the enemy air force as distinct from the enemy economy or population, unless we actually intend taking deliberate measures to refrain from hitting cities. It cannot matter greatly whether the destruction of cities is a by-product of the destruction of air fields or vice versa.

The number of cities that account for the bulk of the so-called economic war potential of either the U.S. or the U.S.S.R. is small—possibly fifty or less, and certainly not over two hundred (the range depends on the weighting one gives to certain factors, such as industrial interdependence). Most of these cities, moreover, are concentrated in the eastern part of the United States, and especially the northeastern part, where urban and nonurban populations alike are subject to overlapping patterns of radioactive fallout. The concentration of industry in Russian cities, and the concentration of cities and populations in the western part of the country, makes the Soviet Union comparable as a target to the United States.

It seems likely, in the event of an all-out thermonuclear war, that the survival of people and industries will be far more important in determining the recovery of the nation following hostilities than in controlling the subsequent course of those hostilities. The reason for this is simply that the minimum of destruction one can reasonably expect from any *unrestricted* strategic attack will inevitably be too high to permit further meaningful mobilization of resources, perhaps too high even to permit the effective use of surviving military units.

So far as the population is concerned, the uninjured survivors may be many, though it is also conceivable that they may be relatively few—that is, down to a quarter or less of the original figure. In either case they are unlikely to be much concerned with the further pursuit of political-military objectives. We learned something about that from the apathy of the German and Japanese peoples in the latter stages of World War II.

The idea that prolonged hostilities might be carried on with conventional weapons following the initial massive exchange of nuclear ones has fortunately been abandoned, at least on the level of official pronouncement, both by us and by the British (as their *Defense White Paper for 1955* makes clear). Everything is now stacked on deterrence, and on the measures and attitudes that will make deterrence work.

Sir Winston Churchill has even derived some comfort from the phenomenon of fallout, because (he said) it tends to equalize in degree of vulnerability a small country like Britain with a large one like the Soviet Union. And in a sense he is right, because the difference is only one of numbers of bombs required to achieve comparable results, and whatever the larger number may be it will very likely be within easily deliverable limits.

Most of what I have so far said implies the judgment that the prospects for significant improvement of defenses against strategic bombing in the next decade or so are not bright. There are several reasons for this assumption. First, since the coming of the A-bomb, and largely as a result of a steady increase in the bomb's power, developments in the strategic bombing offense have outpaced to a fantastic degree those of the defense—and this movement has by no means run its course. Second, the growth of national nuclear stockpiles is irrepressible, and while delivery capabilities do not normally expand with the same exuberance, it is nevertheless likely to be far easier and less costly for one side to double the number of bombs on targets than for the other to double, by dispersing them, the number of targets that the enemy must hit.

Finally let us note the fact that there are enormous impediments—psychological, political, economic and, let us admit it, doctrinal—to the adoption of really drastic measures for defense. The proof of that lies in all we have conspicuously failed to do after ten years of living with the atomic bomb, especially in the field of "passive" defense. Our industry is not noticeably less concentrated than before, and existing measures of civil defense are almost universally regarded as ludicrous. New and effective stimuli to action may yet turn up, but some exceedingly powerful ones have so far failed to move us.

From all this it would seem that at least one conclusion can be drawn: barring revolutionary advances in air defense, an unrestricted strategic air campaign in a war in which the U.S. is engaged is bound to be decisive. On the other hand, when I say "decisive," I am not using the term in its traditional sense—that is, in the sense that implies a clear victory for one side or the other. I mean instead that if strategic bombing occurs on the grand scale, other kinds of military operations will prove either unfeasible or superfluous and most likely both.

I have thus far been discussing nuclear weapons strictly in terms of what is usually called strategic use—that is, against the enemy homeland. There also must be considered a prospective tactical use—that is, on the battlefield.

Whether or not we can relinquish strategic bombing as a way of war, it appears that we cannot afford to abjure the tactical use of nuclear weapons without dooming ourselves and allies to a permanent inferiority to the Soviet and satellite armies, at least in Europe. But the problems involved in the tactical use of atomic weapons seem to have peculiarly forbidding difficulties. It is all very well to say that the general development of troops must combine low spatial density with the capacity for instantaneous concentration, but how to accomplish it is another story. The few who are attempting to grapple with the problem in published books and articles seem always to assume—tacitly and perhaps also unconsciously—various restraints or restrictions on the size and availability of tactical nuclear weapons. And they also show a general predilection for small bombs.

In fact, one sees an increasing tendency to distinguish between tactical and strategic nuclear weapons according to size of weapons, the big ones being reserved strictly for the strategic function. Before this particular habit becomes too firmly established, we might ask whether there is any basis for it other than the obvious one—that it is easier to imagine ground forces operating in not too unaccustomed a fashion if the nuclear weapons they use and contend with are small and relatively few in number. But the enemy may not be so accommodating.

A justification one sometimes hears for using the smaller bomb is that one must be able to exploit through immediate advance of one's own troops the advantage gained. Here again we discern tacit assumptions—this time from thinking only in terms of the offensive. But if the French high command had possessed the thermonuclear weapon when the German forces were pouring through the Ardennes gap in May of 1940, they would surely not have withheld it because of a craze for exploitation.

The growing abundance of nuclear weapons on both sides may, however, force us to the ultimate conclusion that under their unrestricted use tactically no substantial forces will be able to live in the field at all. If organized bodies of troops cannot exist above ground in the field—or at any rate, cannot operate effectively there—it would seem that they must be either under ground or in the air. In either case we must think in terms of greatly reduced numbers; and, as for airborne forces, we must remember that in nuclear war usable air fields will become quickly scarce, and that small combat aircraft competing for the use of surviving fields can carry nuclear bombs.

Thus we tend in the end to get the same result in considering unrestricted tactical war in the future that we get in unrestricted strategic war. In each case the conclusion tends toward the nihilistic. The only distinction would seem to be that the strategic interchange must have prior consideration in our thoughts, because whatever else it is that an army is fighting for, it must be fighting for a nation that is healthy enough to have national interests.

If what I have said thus far makes any sense at all, it means at the very least that for any war among the major powers we cannot henceforward consider air strategy, naval strategy, and land strategy (or the political objectives they are supposed to secure) in separate categories—*unless* there is some form of deliberate restriction on the use of nuclear weapons.

There is a stark simplicity about an unrestricted nuclear war that almost en-

ables it to be summed up in one short statement: be quick on the draw and the trigger squeeze, and aim for the heart. One then has to add: but even if you shoot first, you will probably die too! This brings us a long way from the subtleties of a Clausewitz, a Jomini, or a Mahan. It brings us even a long way from Douhet, the prophetic theorist of strategic air power. It brings us, in short, to the end of strategy as we have known it.

And it requires us also to face one of the most disturbing of all the implications of nuclear weapons. With the speed and magnitude of destruction available through their use, any unrestricted war between the major powers must have a character and a conclusion that are fully predetermined at the outset. This is not to say that the relevant war plans will, in complete contrast to those of the past, prove themselves wholly "realistic"; it is only to say that they will govern the commitments made at the outset, and the results of those commitments will prevent any recovery from the errors exposed in the process of executing them.

A refusal to look plain facts in the face, on the grounds that to do so leads one to be too pessimistic, leads straight to dangerous nonsense. On the other hand, the fact that an inherited strategy tends toward the nihilistic, which is to say suicidal, indicates that it is wrong—that it reflects a tragically mistaken national policy. Let us be careful to distinguish between what is impossible and what is merely wrong. A future war resulting in mutual annihilation is far from being impossible. But surely it needs no argument to say that a policy that has such an end is a mistaken one.

There are those who believe they have found the answer in deterrence, which is hardly a new conception; but even the British in their *Defense White Paper* make allowance for peripheral challenges which do not call for total reactions. So far they seem to be stanchly refusing to consider the many conceivable borderline cases, but soon they will have to. Do not let me imply that we as a nation are in advance of them in this respect. Their planners have merely exposed their ideas in organized fashion in an official paper, while we leave that sort of communication to the conflicting, off-the-cuff remarks of high officialdom.

The key to the dilemma, if there is one, must be found in discovering the true sense for modern times of the old axiom of Clausewitz that "war is a continuation of policy." War is rational, he argued, only insofar as it safeguards or carries forward the political interests of the state. Certainly no one can dispute that, but it also seems at times that no idea could be further from the minds of people who presume to discuss national policy and strategy. One trouble is that even ordinary politicians and journalists feel impelled to utter resounding though meaningless platitudes when the phrase "national objectives" is mentioned, so that almost everything said on the subject is likely to be unrepresentative of what really lies in the minds and hearts of the people at large.

An unrestricted thermonuclear war is to the national interest of no nation. In view of the direction in which we are moving and the speed at which we are going, it seems absolutely beyond dispute that we and our opponents will have to adapt ourselves mutually to ways of using military power which are not orgiastic. The Great Deterrent will have to remain as the Constant Monitor, and its efficiency in that role should never be subject to doubt. But to argue that its efficiency requires it always to be straining at the leash is to uphold an argument today which—if we are actually intent on preserving the peace —we are bound to abandon tomorrow.

At a time when the opponent will be able to do to our cities and countryside whatever we might threaten to do to his, the whole concept of "massive retaliation"—and all that it stands for in both military and political behavior—will have to be openly recognized as obsolete. [This time has obviously arrived.] It is not enough to let a strategic idea die a lingering death from occasional verbal rebukes, leaving behind only confusion in public and professional opinion—including confusion about whether or not it is really dead. It is not enough to say that an unrestricted thermonuclear war cannot happen anyway because both sides will recognize its folly. There are various positive steps we must take to prevent its occurring even when military force is resorted to in disputes between nations.

In a world still unprepared to relinquish the use of military power, we must learn to effect that use through methods that are something other than self-destroying. The task will be bafflingly difficult at best, but it can only begin with the clear recognition that most of the military ideas and axioms of the past are now or soon will be inapplicable. The old concepts of strategy,... have come to a dead end. What we now must initiate is the comprehensive pursuit of the new ideas and procedures necessary to carry us through the next two or three dangerous decades.

2 • The H-Bomb: Massive Retaliation or Graduated Deterrence? *

Rear Admiral Sir Anthony Buzzard
Marshal of the RAF Sir John Slessor

Rear Admiral Sir Anthony Buzzard was Director of Naval Intelligence, 1951–54 and is presently Armaments Director, Vickers-Armstrong Ltd.

Sir John Slessor began his military career in 1915 as a pilot in France and rose to a number of command posts during World War II. He was Commandant of the Imperial Defence College, 1948–49, Air A.D.C. to King George VI from 1945–50. In 1950 he was appointed Marshal of the Royal Air Force and Chief of the Air Staff. Among his recent publications are Strategy for the West *(1954),* The Central Blue *(1956) and* The Great Deterrent *(1957).*

REAR ADMIRAL SIR ANTHONY BUZZARD:

One of the ugly facts of life which we now have to face fairly and squarely since the failure of the high-level discussions at Geneva in July and October 1955 is that nuclear disarmament is still a long way off, ... [This seems as true in 1960 as it did in 1956.]

Specifically, our defence policy must, I suggest, aim at three main objectives: to prevent all wars, small, medium, and large, and above all to ensure that the H-bomb is never used; to strengthen our hand in negotiations and in blocking Communist power politics, particularly in Germany but also all round the Communist perimeter; to pave the way for nuclear disarmament, and meanwhile to bring about and exploit any conventional disarmament that is practicable.

Our present defence policy, which Mr. Dulles has labelled 'massive retaliation',

seems to be becoming much too drastic and inflexible for these objectives. Increasingly we are getting into a position where, in effect, we shall be forced to threaten, and if necessary initiate, the destruction of civilization in the event of any measure of aggression too powerful for our small conventional forces to combat. For, except in the most restricted areas, our conventional forces are unable to withstand the vast Communist conventional forces without the tactical use of atomic weapons, and there seems at present to be no distinction between the tactical use of atomic weapons and the unlimited strategic use of the H-bomb.

The proposition which I want to put forward is, that we should, in fact,

* *International Affairs,* the Journal of the Royal Institute of International Affairs, London, XXXII (1956), 148–62. Reprinted by permission.

establish a clear distinction between the tactical and strategic use of nuclear weapons, so that we can use our atomic weapons tactically without provoking the strategic use of hydrogen weapons.[1]

I suggest that we work out and declare in peace, without waiting for Communist agreement, some such distinctions as these: we regard the tactical use of nuclear weapons as confined to atomic weapons only, and we exclude the use of even these against towns and cities; strategic use of nuclear weapons would refer to the use of hydrogen weapons and to the mass destruction of towns and cities, even by atomic weapons. We might also add that, to conform to the moral principle of limiting the use of force as much as possible, we would never resort to the strategic use of nuclear weapons unless absolutely essential.

Thus, without committing ourselves in advance or showing our hand too clearly, if we were ever threatened with aggression which, though limited, was too powerful for our conventional forces to combat, we should have the option of saying to the aggressor:

If you use aggression, we will, if necessary, use atomic and chemical weapons against your armed forces. But we will not, on this particular issue, use hydrogen or bacteriological weapons at all, unless you do, and we will not use mass destruction weapons against centres of population—regardless of the targets they contain—unless you do so deliberately.

To this we might specify certain exceptions to the definition of centres of population, such as cities in the front line of the land fighting and those with airfields adjoining them. Thus, with three graduated courses of action from which to choose we should be modifying

our present inflexible policy of massive retaliation to one aptly named 'graduated deterrence'.

Clearly there would be difficulties and disadvantages in such a policy, but when scrutinized in the light of the real menaces to peace, and the real needs of our defence policy, are they any worse than the many dangers and shortcomings of massive retaliation? Let us compare the alternative policies in the light of our three main objectives.

To Prevent War. In the first objective of preventing war, the real menace to peace (and this is often misunderstood) is not deliberate major aggression, which can be virtually ruled out, but local aggression on a minor or medium scale which, if not nipped in the bud, might well lead unintentionally to major war. Thus we require a policy which, while continuing to maintain the present deterrent against deliberate major aggression, would enable us to deter and, if necessary, to repel any medium or minor aggression by the Communists, to make unintentional war as unlikely as possible, and to deal firmly with any aggressive action by third parties.

In the unlikely event of intentional major aggression, our deterrent, and the results if it failed, would be the same with either policy—total war. But the crux of the problem lies in the much more likely event of medium aggression, i.e. any aggression too powerful for our small conventional forces but not so vital as to warrant the strategic use of nuclear weapons. With our present policy, we have only two extreme courses of action open to us—our small conventional forces at one end of the scale, and all our nuclear weapons, however used, at the other.

But since the Russians are now developing the power to strike back massively at America, massive retaliation is in danger of being interpreted as bluff in the case of medium aggression, for the

---

[1] In this paper the word 'tactical' refers to the use of weapons against armed forces and 'strategical' to use against centres of population.

Communists might well expect the United States to shrink from action which is becoming increasingly akin to suicide—and indeed, on the limited issues likely to be at stake in medium aggression, they might well be right. Thus massive retaliation leaves much room for Communist exploitation and misunderstanding in the event of any form of aggression between a major and a very minor one.

Graduated deterrence seeks to fill this gap by enabling us to take, if desired, limited tactical action with atomic and chemical weapons, and to exploit three great assets which we possess; our superiority in atomic weapons suitable for tactical use on land, sea, and in the air; the potentialities of atomic and chemical weapons used in defence, as opposed to offence, which favours us in our task of repelling Communist invasion; our technical superiority in making precision attacks with high explosive weapons, which could still be used against key pinpoint targets (such as bridges) within centres of population. Graduated deterrence seeks also to make use of our fourth great asset, namely, strategic hydrogen air power, as a means of compelling an aggressor to accept our distinctions in the use of nuclear weapons.

At the same time, we should be obviating, or at least mitigating, the effects of our two great weaknesses; Communist numerical superiority in men and conventional weapons, which are highly vulnerable to atomic and chemical weapons, particularly when open to mass attack; our relatively much greater dependence than the Communists upon ports to reinforce the threatened area—ports being the communication bottlenecks most vulnerable to attack by mass destruction weapons, which would be barred from such attacks by the distinctions I propose.

Before we feel confident to choose the intermediate course of action to counter medium aggression in all areas, some increase in our tactical strength may be necessary. But such tactical strength as we possess would at once be immeasurably enhanced by the establishment of our distinction between the tactical and strategic use of nuclear weapons; and this would greatly help to redress the tactical balance of power.

In the case of the most likely menace of all—minor aggression—whether by the Communists or other parties, our ability to use conventional forces would be the same under both policies. But with graduated deterrence we would have (and the Communists would know that we had) our intermediate limited course of action to fall back on, instead of the unlimited and much too drastic action of massive retaliation. We would therefore be less likely to shrink from the prompt and firm action required to prevent small wars spreading, and so be less likely to get into a position in which a series of Communist nibbles ultimately forced us to take drastic action leading to major war.

In the very real danger of war developing or spreading unintentionally, a policy of massive retaliation leaves much scope for misunderstanding such as an intended minor aggression being mistaken for and treated as major aggression. But with graduated deterrence our intermediate action would be clearly available, so that misunderstandings would be much less likely, and if they did occur we should be able to deal with the situation with far less risk of precipitating total war.

Finally, let us consider the distinct possibility of arriving at a complete impasse or deadlock with the Communists on some crucial, but limited, issue. With a policy of massive retaliation the stakes would be so high that it is doubtful whether the morale and unity of the friendly Powers concerned would stand the strain, for Communist propaganda would be emphasizing the effect of a hydrogen war on the cities of our Allies in the area, few of which are likely to have any appreciable air or civil defences. Under a policy of graduated deterrence our Allies would be far more likely to stand firm.

Moreover, since neither city destruction nor the use of H-weapons would seem inevitable to the Communists, they would be less tempted to forestall us with a surprise hydrogen attack on our ports and cities in the Pearl Harbour style. Indeed, on both sides the urgency of getting in the first blow would be reduced, and thus more time would be given for good sense and diplomacy to prevail.

The conclusion must surely be that a policy of graduated deterrence must, particularly in the light of the real menaces of minor aggression, medium aggression, and miscalculation, increasingly improve our chances of preventing war and of ensuring that the H-bomb is never used. The only proviso is that we should not disclose in advance—before an actual threat arises—the circumstances in which we would use our conventional, our intermediate, or our strategic course of action.

Strength In Negotiations. In the second main objective of strengthening our hand in negotiations and in blocking Communist power politics, a policy of massive retaliation becomes bluff and unreal as, with growing Russian strategic air power, strategic stalemate approaches. Our outstanding requirement for negotiations is, therefore, becoming increasingly that of redressing our present tactical inferiority in conventional forces by greater local tactical strength. Graduated deterrence would greatly enhance our tactical and local strength by making possible the tactical use of atomic and chemical weapons.

But apart from this direct and immediate strengthening of the West's hand in the conduct of its foreign policy, graduated deterrence, by demonstrating our determination and ability to redress the tactical balance of power, would assist our cause indirectly in two other ways: it would show the uncommitted countries of Asia and Africa (where Communist propaganda is so actively exploiting our massive retaliation policy) that we are doing all we can to limit the use of nuclear weapons, pending disarmament; it would show the Allied public, many of whom have mistaken the strategic stalemate for a general military stalemate, that we still have to continue building our tactical strength. And it would disillusion them of the growing feeling that it is pointless to continue supplying NATO and other forces with costly tactical atomic weapons when our policy is to blow the world to pieces in the event of any substantial aggression. In particular, it would convince the Germans, who are becoming increasingly impatient for reunification (and liable to compromise with the Russians), of the need to press on with their twelve divisions, wherein lies the best hope of the Russians agreeing to withdraw from East Germany on just terms. And it would convince the United States, who alone can still afford substantially increased defence expenditure, of the need to continue building tactical strength in the exposed areas around the Communist perimeter.

Thus, the establishment of our distinctions in the tactical and strategic use of nuclear weapons, while itself not necessarily requiring agreement with the Communists, might do much to pave the way for negotiating agreements with them. But if this proved optimistic, at least we would be better placed to block any expansionist designs they may have.

Disarmament. The factors concerning negotiation generally apply equally to disarmament negotiations, but disarmament requires special treatment in addition.

Our present policy of massive retaliation almost certainly engenders in Communist hearts a genuine fear of the vast United States strategic air potential, poised on advance bases (on land and at sea) so much closer to Russia and China than Communist bases are to America; and they may genuinely fear what might happen if the more antagonistic American personalities should gain a real following in the United States. Graduated deterrence might reduce this tension and gradually nourish the mutual trust necessary for disarmament.

At least it would afford some assurance to the Communists, and to the uncommitted countries, of our sincerity, showing that we genuinely wish to limit all possible use of nuclear weapons until their disarmament can be agreed. Conversely, it would be a test—for all to see—of Communist sincerity in the disarmament negotiations, for their denouncement of it would demonstrate their intention to continue exploiting our present tactical weakness in conventional forces, and their own vast superiority in manpower.

Graduated deterrence might also help to bring about disarmament in the following ways which, though individually far from decisive, might be a useful contribution collectively:

(1) The Communists are unlikely to give up force as an instrument of policy until we provide deterrents which will effectively block each and every form of aggression. Only graduated deterrence will do this.

(2) We are unlikely to get fully controlled disarmament until an effective collective force (perhaps under world government) is available to enforce it. Massive retaliation is too drastic for this, but the strong tactical forces envisaged under graduated deterrence might possibly form the nucleus of such a police force.

(3) We are unlikely to get the trust and confidence essential for agreements in the limited possession of nuclear armaments without a period of experience in which their use is limited by tacit understanding —if not by actual agreement. Only graduated deterrence can provide this.

(4) With the Communists' fundamental dependence on tactical rather than strategic strength for their security, the continued reliance by us on our strategic strength of massive retaliation is likely to make fair and balanced reduction in armaments difficult. Graduated deterrence, on the other hand, by converting our requirements for security into terms more tactical and therefore comparable with those of the Communists, would facilitate fair and balanced reduction, stage by stage.

(5) Finally, the establishment cf our distinctions in the tactical and strategic use of nuclear weapons would provide a natural corollary to our recent proposals for ground and air inspection, which in themselves are, of course, also measures designed to limit the use of armaments (i.e. the use of surprise) as well as pilot schemes for disarmament inspection. Now that the Communists have for the moment refused these proposals, the announcement of our distinction would enable us to retain the initiative by further positive action in our continuing efforts to face the Communists with arguments for making virtue of necessity.

The surest path to disarmament, therefore, probably leads through graduated deterrence. Certainly the responsibility for making the first move in reducing the threat of nuclear weapons rests upon our shoulders, just as that of making the first move in reducing conventional forces rests upon the Communists' shoulders.

Two other important considerations need to be examined—the Economic and the Moral Aspects.

Economic Aspect. At first sight massive retaliation might seem to be the cheapest way of keeping the peace. But if the Communists are to be convinced that we will retaliate massively, even for medium aggression, and that we are not bluffing, clearly a full scale of air and civil defence for the ports and cities of the Allies (and of friendly Powers liable to be threatened with aggression) is essential against every form of mass destruction. And for our deterrent to be effective the Communists must be fully aware that such defences have been provided. They are also essential if the morale of the Allied public in a crisis is to stand firm in support of a policy of massive retaliation. But air and civil defences on this scale are becoming increasingly impracticable economically (except perhaps for the United States), and they are certainly quite beyond the means of the more exposed and less prosperous friendly Powers. With graduated deterrence, on the other hand, the meagre scales of air and civil defences, which are all that we and most of our Allies can afford, would be more justifiable, on the grounds that this policy makes the destruction of cities a far more remote possibility.

Furthermore, with massive retaliation the fullest provision of offensive strategic weapons and means of their delivery is essential to deal not only with all the enemy's airfields and armed forces, but also with many of his important cities and ports, always in the strongest competition with the Communist offensive strategic potential. With graduated deterrence, on the other hand, we might gradually afford to take some risks and effect some economies in this matter, on the grounds that a saturation point, and therefore a stalemate, will soon be reached in our ability to destroy each other's cities, and that such destruction therefore becomes an increasingly remote possibility.

The only other alternative under our present policy of massive retaliation is to go to the other extreme and rely more on conventional (and perhaps chemical) tactical strength to deal with the various scales of medium aggression, in which case we should have to face the heavy cost, in manpower as well as material, of large conventional forces. That, too, would compare unfavourably with graduated deterrence, in which the tactical strength to deal with the medium scales of aggression is much more economically provided by being able to exploit the use of tactical atomic and chemical weapons.

In fact, rather illogically, the West seems to be expending considerable sums on tactical atomic weapons under our present policy of massive retaliation. Surely, under this policy, the money would have been better spent on more conventional forces or on improved civil and air defence measures. From whatever angle this problem is approached one concludes that, although graduated deterrence would not for some time provide any financial savings, it would certainly give us better security for our money. Moreover, some of the vast sums being spent by the United States on civil and air defence of their cities might become available for increasing the tactical strength so urgently required in Europe and other exposed areas.

Moral Aspect. Morally, we should not cause or threaten to cause more destruction than is necessary. All our fighting should therefore be limited (in weapons, targets, area, and time) to the minimum force necessary to deter and repel aggression, prevent its unnecessary extension, and return to negotiation at the earliest opportunity—without seeking total victory or unconditional surrender.

The moral standards which we profess to defend demand not only this action in the event of aggression, but the pursuance of long-term policies which will enable us to conform to these standards to the best of our ability in the future. Massive retaliation hardly passes this test, nor indeed does it square with the moral standards we professed to uphold at the Nuremburg trials. Graduated deterrence, on the other hand, at least aspires to pursue these principles so far as is possible, and it seeks to restore moderation and the rule of law in the future conduct of war, without which we will surely never succeed in abolishing it.

Would the Communists Conform? An obvious question which arises is: would the Communists conform to our limitation in the use of nuclear weapons if we chose to impose them on the threat of medium aggression or unintentional local war?

In peace the Communists would probably refuse at first to agree to our distinction between the tactical and strategic use of nuclear weapons, arguing, as they do now, that nuclear weapons must be abolished altogether, and knowing that this would leave the Red armies supreme. But if a war of limited aims should come and we elected to impose our limitations, it seems almost certain that the Communists would do their utmost to conform to them. They must appreciate the vast American superiority in nuclear weapons, American skill in delivering them strategically, and the extremely advantageous geographical location of American advanced air bases. In weighing the relative advantages, the Communists might well conclude, as we have, that our proposed limitations in the use of nuclear weapons would often favour us in the problem of holding territory, but the absolute disadvantage of having their cities pounded by hydrogen bombs would far outweigh such considerations from their point of view in a war of limited aims. As hydrogen weapons increase in power and numbers, this absolute consideration would weigh more and more heavily with the Communists. But, even if this estimate should prove wrong in war, we would have gained immeasurably in the unity and morale of the Allied people concerned by having placed the onus for initiating the mass slaughter of civilians on the enemy. Moreover, we would risk little since if the Communists did not conform, to be a few hours after them in city destruction would make no difference.

It is true that the Communists could, if they dared to disregard our limitations, forestall us by a few hours with hydrogen weapons against, say, our airfields while we were still attacking theirs with atomic weapons. But they would be unlikely to accept the consequences of this. If they did, we would probably be no worse off than with a policy of massive retaliation, in which the Communists would have every incentive, and probably the opportunity, to forestall us with hydrogen weapons.

The Only Real Difficulty. The only real difficulty in graduated deterrence is that of establishing a distinction between the tactical and strategic use of nuclear weapons which would have a reasonable chance of holding in a limited and local war. The problems of distinguishing hydrogen from atomic weapons, and of defining centres of population and their geographical limits, are certainly difficult, but provided they are thoroughly studied beforehand, there seems no reason to suppose they are insuperable.

The weapons to be classed as strategic, instead of being defined as hydrogen, might be more appropriately defined as those with major fallout effects, or those exceeding in power a certain number of kilotons. Similarly, centres of population could be defined in a number of ways. But there seems much to be said for excluding for tactical use the mass destruction of all towns and cities over a certain size, regardless of the targets they contain, excepting only those actually in the front line of the land fighting; those from which offensive missiles are launched; and those which, having adjoining airfields, launch offensive aircraft from them, when the airfields would become liable to atomic attack.

The front line of the land fighting might be defined as extending so many miles beyond the most advanced land units of each side. And any towns or cities in the front line could be declared 'open' if desired—provided they were proved to be so.

With some such distinction established well in advance the problem seems far from hopeless. For the difference between a bombing policy intentionally designed to knock out cities with hydrogen bombs, and one designed to strike other targets with atomic bombs which may occasionally hit a city by mistake, would be obvious. Moreover, the Communists would, like us, be desperately anxious that cities should be spared and that the war should not spread, so that both sides would be anxious—not reluctant—to overlook the occasional accidental breach of the rule, and to avoid giving the other any opportunity of putting the worst interpretation on its actions.

Thus, we should probably succeed in maintaining our limitations for at least a few weeks, which is what really matters; for, by that time, even a limited atomic war would probably have convinced one side or the other—if not both —of the need to return to negotiations.

But if, despite all this, our proposed limitations should break down, would anything have been lost by making the attempt? Little or nothing, I suggest, when compared with the alternative of massive retaliation, provided that we never lose sight of the risk of breakdown occurring, and become 'trigger happy' with our tactical atomic weapons.

The conclusion is, surely, that we probably can devise distinctions which are likely to hold in wars of limited aims. These are the only types we are considering for our intermediate grade of action, and if they are dealt with faithfully, all possibility of major war would be virtually ruled out.

The overall conclusion is, I suggest, this. By adopting a policy of graduated deterrence, and implementing our intermediate course of action if the occasion arose for it, we should risk only two things: that the enemy might ignore our proposed limitations in the use of nuclear weapons and forestall us by a few hours in the use of hydrogen weapons against airfields, etc., a risk which is probably at least as great in our present policy; and that either side might become 'trigger happy' with their tactical atomic weapons, a risk which could be mitigated by advertising the danger of their tactical use spreading. These risks might never materialize, and the first could not do so unless war actually breaks out.

On the other hand, many of the formidable advantages in favour of adopting graduated deterrence are positive ones which would materialize now, whether or not war breaks out, and which would help to make war itself less likely, particularly the most likely types of wars. Indeed, graduated deterrence would arrest the present dangerous policy of drift and constitute a definite step towards our objectives of preventing war, strengthening our hand in negotiations, and paving the way for nuclear disarmament.

Time Factor. One might ask whether it is not better to delay introducing distinctions between the tactical and strategic use of nuclear weapons until the eleventh hour before the outbreak of local war. Such a delay would surely be a great mistake, for the following reasons:

(1) In the cold war, unless the Western public are convinced that reasonable distinctions can be drawn, they will be unlikely to make the necessary economic sacrifices

to go on providing tactical atomic weapons, since they will feel that any use of such weapons would lead to total hydrogen war and therefore be of little value.

(2) In the event of a Communist threat arising, unless the country threatened is convinced that our distinctions are reasonably clear, it may well shrink from accepting any reinforcement in the form of tactical atomic weapons for fear that such use might lead to H-bombing of its cities. Similarly, the public of the Western Powers wishing to reinforce the threatened country may shrink from doing so on such terms. The Communists would not be slow to exploit such doubts and hesitations.

(3) In the event of local war breaking out, unless distinctions have been thoroughly engrained in the minds and plans of both sides for a considerable period beforehand, the prospects of their holding—a difficult matter in any case—would be greatly reduced.

(4) Only by announcing our distinctions at least sufficiently clearly for the world to believe that they are real and sincere, would we be able to reap the many benefits which graduated deterrence could contribute towards our second and third objectives of achieving successful negotiations with the Communists and of paving the way for disarmament and the abolition of war.

If not at the eleventh hour, when, then, should our distinction between the tactical and strategic use of nuclear weapons be established? There seems every reason for establishing it as soon as it can be worked out and agreed with the United States and NATO. Thereafter it would still take time for both sides to adjust themselves to the possibility of limited atomic war. Indeed, the longer the delay, the more difficult will such adjustments become. Moreover, since the Geneva deadlock, we are now in dire need of some positive action with which to retain the initiative with the Communists, to discourage any relaxation by the Allied public, and to spur

on the tactical rearmament of the disappointed Western Germans.

Here is a step—perhaps the only one open to us—which can do this, without having to obtain agreement from the Communists.

Let us therefore assemble the strongest team of Service representatives and international jurists to work out the best possible distinctions between the tactical and strategic use of nuclear weapons, and let them be supervised by two or three determined politicians, imbued with the urgent political need of these distinctions. If, as I feel confident, reasonably clear distinctions emerge, let us then announce them to the Communists on a take it or leave it basis. We should thus have taken a sizeable step towards our objectives, and towards sanity, moderation, and morality.

In due course this vital first step might lead to improved relations with the Communists, and perhaps a measure of conventional disarmament by which the disproportionate Communist conventional strength may be reduced. We might then conceivably feel that, with the help of German divisions and further improved tactical atomic weapons, we could keep the peace in all circumstances and areas without ever having to be the first to use the H-bomb. We might thus be able to take a second important step by renouncing in advance all use of this terrible menace to civilization, unless the aggressor uses it. And if this in turn should lead to further improvements of the same nature, we might then be able to renounce in advance all intention of being the first to use atomic and chemical weapons against centres of population, and so finally ban all strategic use of mass destruction weapons.

In this way we may learn to live a little more happily with the H-bomb. And together with the present pilot schemes for inspection and control, we might gradually move step by step towards our ultimate goal of nuclear disarmament.

Sir John Slessor:

The real object in my view is to abolish war. I do not believe that we do much good by trying to abolish or limit the use of any particular weapon of war, anyway in the context of world war between two great Powers. I feel that, in fact, total war has already been abolished by the fact of the existence of the hydrogen bomb in the armouries of the world. And so, very briefly, my view is first that, in a world war when the existence of great nations is at stake—and still more in the interest of preventing such a war, which is the real point—it is very doubtful whether graduated deterrence is either desirable or practicable; secondly that in periphery wars, the Koreas of the future which we may still see, adventures by the Red army or by the Chinese Communists, limitation in the use of nuclear weapons is worth very careful examination, because it might be possible. In other words we should differentiate between total war and minor war or police action; just as the heavy bomber of yesterday becomes the light bomber of today, so a quite serious war of fifty years ago would now be a relatively minor incident, while the real war of today was undreamt of when we were children.

Some general propositions are I think relevant to this subject. What has been described as the 'classic theory', i.e. that the object in war is the destruction of the enemy's armed forces, was finally disposed of with the advent of the atomic and the hydrogen bombs. The advocates of the classic theory always seem to me to confuse the means with the end, or the method with the object in war. The object in war has always been to impose your will on the enemy

and, in the old days, in order to impose your will on the enemy you had to start off by destroying his armed forces. Today, perhaps unfortunately, that can be done without destroying his armed forces. I do not say that there will not be a measure of attack on the enemy's armed forces in order to achieve that end, but it is not the object. We must be very clear about what this great deterrent is designed to deter. Advocates of the deterrent policy have never claimed more for it than the prevention of a potential aggressor from undertaking total war as an instrument of policy, as Hitler did in 1939, or from embarking on or developing a course of international action which involves a serious chance of total war. It is not claimed that it will prevent minor aggressions, such as the North Koreans walking across the 38th parallel in 1950.

An important weakness of Admiral Buzzard's case is his belief in our ability to provide with atomic weapons the tactical strength with which to match Communist tactical strength—the 'tactical balance of power'. I agree that modern weapons, not only the atomic and the hydrogen weapons but other modern weapons such as the proximity fuse and the recoilless anti-tank gun, have lent more strength to the defence in land-air warfare than they have to the offence. But that is not so at sea. Modern developments at sea have unfortunately given much more power to offence, especially by the U-boat, and we must remember that before we throw away our right to deal with U-boat bases with the atomic weapon. Although it has given added strength to defence on land, I still do not think it has tipped the scales to the extent that NATO, even with the addition of twelve German divisions, would be able to hold up 175 or so Soviet divisions (who will also have tactical and atomic weapons) and prevent them reaching the Channel coast before very long.

Bertrand Russell, for whom I have a great admiration and respect, makes a substantial point in a contribution to *The Bomb* (1955) in which he visualizes the rulers of the world saying: 'We ...only value the bomb because it prevents war, but there is a much cheaper way of preventing war, and that is mutual admission that war can no longer further the policy of either party...' (p. 51). That is perfectly true. But surely he overlooks the fact that that is only true because of the existence of the H-bomb. If, as Admiral Buzzard suggests, we now say that Russian U-boat bases and centres of communication leading to the Red Armies would be immune, and all towns and cities over a certain size, regardless of the targets they contain (except those actually in the front line of the land fighting, which would be defined by so many miles each side of the forward troops) then surely the effect would be that Russia herself would be virtually immune from nuclear attack, which would suit the Kremlin very well. Destruction would be confined to NATO soil, particularly to Germany, and possibly also to satellites like Poland and Czechoslovakia. That is a dangerous policy to advocate, especially in relation to the Germans. Those present at the Deutsch-Englische Gesellschaft's Conference at Königswinter in the spring of 1955 will remember that that was just what many Germans were saying: 'If there is another war the only people who are going to get it in the neck with atomic weapons are the Germans'. Incidentally, that is one of the great safeguards against Germany ever being a menace to her neighbours again, because I believe thinking Germans realize that whatever the issue of any war and whoever ultimately won it (if anybody wins modern wars) Germany would finish up as a radio-active desert.

If we say that atomic weapons may be used only in the area of the front line, or the towns in the battle zone, it will not ring a very cordial bell with our new NATO allies, and Russia herself would be immune except possibly for towns in the immediate neighbourhood of airfields. That seems to be a good bargain for the Russians who would surely rather capture places like Paris and the Channel ports intact than as masses of radio-active rubble. M. Paul-Henri Spaak said in an excellent article 'The Atom Bomb and NATO' in the American *Foreign Affairs* of April 1955 (p. 353), 'the plain fact is that war no longer pays', and for that reason he favours the policy of nuclear deterrence. So let us be very careful before we restore war as a paying proposition. An article 'Graduated Deterrence' in *The Economist* of 5 November 1955 (p. 458) says: 'Would a graduation of deterrence lead a would-be aggressor to believe that the game might conceivably be worth the candle? To be quite specific, would it diminish the Western Powers' ability to deter a Russian aggression, the only likely cause of major war in the near future? If the answer to either question is in the affirmative then it is a very dangerous proposal', and it goes on to say, 'To give the Russians the power to decide whether or not hydrogen bombs would be used would surely be, as things stand now, to restore to them the power to overrun Western Europe while keeping their bomb base intact'. That is my view also. Admiral Buzzard has rightly said: 'The absolute disadvantage of having their cities pounded by H-bombs would far outweigh such considerations' as whether graduated deterrence would pay them or pay us best. I think they would be prepared to take a chance on that, and the absolute disadvantage of having their cities pounded would outweigh all considerations.

This is not all simple and straightforward. It would present the most frightful dilemma that any statesman has ever had to face. Anybody who, like myself, was on the Air Staff in 1939–40 when we were worrying about the few hundred tons of high explosives of those days, knows that it would face us with an appalling difficult decision. But Lord Attlee put the point well when he said in a broadcast on the European Service (10 June 1954) that in a real war when the existence of nations is at stake '...any weapon will be used in the last resort'. The point which immediately arises is—what is the last resort? No one suggests that we should immediately drop a hydrogen bomb on Moscow the moment there is a frontier incident, for instance, on the border of the Soviet zone. That is one of the reasons why we must have conventional forces in Germany—the primary case in my opinion for a German army. We must have something between the hydrogen bomb and the frontier policeman in order to reduce the chances of having to use the bomb. We must have some force to deal with the tactics of infiltration without calling in the ultimate sanction. We cannot afford suddenly to wake up one fine morning to find that a lot of 'peace-loving democratic partisans' have 'liberated' Hamburg with the support of patriots of the so-called 'People's Police' or Eastern German army on the other side of the frontier. We must be able to deal with the tactics of the *fait accompli,* like Hitler's reoccupation of the Rhineland, which was effected with approximately one division. And I think the answer to the question 'When is the last resort?' is when it becomes absolutely clear that the Kremlin has decided on the gamble of total war.

Would this graduated deterrence policy be practicable in a major war? It might last for more than the few hours which have been suggested—it might last long enough to give the Red army a fatally good start into Europe. But I cannot visualize it lasting for any length of time. Can we really suppose that, if the Russians thought that the Allied armies were any serious obstacle to them, they would really refrain from bombing the ports and main rail centres through which we would be bringing our reinforcements and supplies? Would they—or for that matter would we—really be able to refrain from bombing towns? I cannot help remembering the example of Florence in 1944. Early that year, we in the Air Force were subjected to heavy pressure, I think perfectly justifiable pressure, from the army to bomb Florence, which was a crucially important centre in the German line of communication. We tried very hard to avoid having to do so, and tried all sorts of other ways of achieving the same effect. In that we were unsuccessful owing to bad weather and one thing and another, and the time came when we were hard pressed in the Anzio beachhead and the photographic aircraft brought back photographs showing the marshalling yards in Florence full of flat cars loaded with tanks and guns and so on, and eventually we had to give way and bomb—fortunately without doing any substantial damage to anything except the marshalling yards. That is the sort of thing that makes me feel that in practice in a great war when our very survival would be at stake, this graduated policy is not really practicable, and would soon break down. Moreover, surely in the last resort no nation is going to accept defeat with the hydrogen weapon still in its armoury unused? I cannot convince myself that, if it comes to major war—to a third world war—the hydrogen weapon will not inevitably be used sooner or later; and my own feeling is that, ghastly though it would be, it would be less awful for us in the long run if it were used sooner than if it were used later.

I think that in minor wars, such as Korea, where the very existence of great nations is not at stake, the conditions may be different, and that it may be possible to apply this idea in some form. That may sound selfish, because after all the existence of some small Allied nation may be at stake. But surely we must be realistic about this and accept the fact that in practice we will not, as the Americans would say, trade New York or London for some small town in a remote country. Nor will the Russians. Do not imagine that in a war of this sort Moscow or Peking would be just waiting for a pretext to blow it up into global thermo-nuclear war—they would be just as anxious to avoid that as we should.

But that means we must be able and willing in these circumstances to deal with limited aggression by limited means —in other words by land forces with air cover and support. That is an unwelcome idea, particularly in the United States, but it is one we must face if we are to meet our obligations to our smaller and more remote Allies. Unwillingness to do that would result in what Vice-President Nixon has called being 'nibbled to death'.

If we had to fight in, say, Asian conditions, however, we should have to use atomic weapons to help offset the inevitable numerical superiority of the enemy—the tactical atomic weapon, not the fission-fusion-fission bomb. And it is in these conditions that we might apply some form of graduated or limited use of weapons. Korea proved that in this sort of war it is possible to arrive at a curious sort of unwritten agreement between belligerents to limit the use of military force, if it suits both sides to do so. The reason why we did not bomb across the Yalu River—which of course suited the Chinese—was that on balance we thought that it also suited us best, in spite of its obvious disadvantages.

I do not pretend to have thought the subject out in detail, but it seems to me it should be very carefully examined, the object being, of course, to spare innocent civilians and centres of population the worst horrors of modern war. We might take a tip from the RAF method known as 'Air Control' which we used with effect against tribal enemies between the wars. Two features of that system which might be applicable were, first, ample warnings before any bombs were dropped on villages so as to enable non-combatants to get away to a place of safety; and, secondly, 'prescribed areas', notified in advance to the enemy, in which any movement was liable to attack without further warning but outside which people were safe. Something on those lines might be found to suit both sides in a minor war, where it is much more likely to be practicable than in a great war in Europe.

PART V   THE REDUCTION OF TENSION: UNDERSTANDING AND COLLABORATION

XVIII • Theories of Peaceful Change

Assuming that a static world is impossible and that attempts to rigidify any given distribution of power among nations can lead only to frustration or perhaps even catastrophe, statesmen and specialists in international relations are challenged to find methods of permitting existing relationships to change without loss of core values on the part of the participants and without resort to violence. The possible consequences of violence have become so horrible in an age when weapons are capable of being projected across vast oceans and continents to inflict mass destruction, that serious interest in the whole concept of "peaceful change" has been revived.[1]

Changes in the prevailing distribution of values within societies are fairly easily brought about through normal legislative and judicial institutions and procedures, but such institutions and procedures on the international scene are crude, inadequate, and all too often untried. Therefore new methods and new techniques must be found if cooperation is to replace tension, understanding to replace conflict, and collaboration to replace violence in the pattern of world politics.

There are many approaches to peaceful change, but few can be taken seriously by the sophisticated student of international relations. Several approaches are suggested here, not as representing a comprehensive catalog of the problem and its proposed solutions, but as being among the more promising avenues deserving of further experimentation and exploration. The first of these focusses upon a term used frequently in contemporary discourse in a purely propagandistic context, as an instrument of power politics in disguise, but used also in its more direct and open sense: reducing international tensions. Obviously, even the aggressive state seeks to reduce ten-

---

[1] For an interesting comparison of thought on the subject of peaceful change in two periods, see the analyses by Frederick S. Dunn, Director of the Center for International Studies at Princeton University, *Peaceful Change* (New York: Council on Foreign Relations, 1937), and "Peaceful Change Today," *World Politics,* XI (1959), 278–85.

sion, in its case by making less powerful entities submit meekly to its will. When the proposed "victim" resists, "tension" occurs. In the other sense, however, tension exists not because of intentions to control and responses of resistance, but because of stereotypes, "images" and assumptions which, when fully and dispassionately examined, prove to be exaggerated, inaccurate or unwarranted. Paul Kecskemeti of The Rand Corporation warns that merely to talk about reducing tensions does not reduce them. Since they exist because of fundamental differences of value and policy between powers, it is illusory to regard tension-reducing schemes as productive of any promising solution. If the policy differences were resolved, the tension they create would disappear of its own accord, but "we cannot make it vanish by incantation." Despite such scepticism, the interest of sociologists, psychologists, and political scientists in the phenomena of the effects of tensions upon politics (and vice versa) continues to produce a growing literature on this approach to peaceful change. The distinguished French sociologist, Georges Gurvitch, analyzes the sources of world tension and offers a number of techniques and methods whereby such tensions might be reduced.

A related theory, sometimes referred to as the "minds-of-men" approach, holds that tensions and crises occur because of a lack of understanding between states but even more basically, between peoples. When the words of Archibald MacLeish, "since it is in the minds of men that wars begin, it is in the minds of men that the defenses of peace must be constructed," were incorporated into the Constitution of UNESCO, only a few tentative and modest steps had been taken to implement so noble a concept. The hard-headed realist, needless to say, rejects the assumptions implicit in this approach, and contends that wars begin, if not in men's stomachs or their hearts, in the incompatible objectives of protagonists in the power struggle in a world devoid of legal and moral restraints. From this viewpoint, "understanding" may produce *more* rather than *less* hostility, as in the case of the later responses of the Western democracies to Hitlerism as they came to understand its implications for their own security, and the more recent "hardening" of free-world attitudes toward international Communism as its aims have become thoroughly comprehended. (For an explanation of this view, see Chapter XIV.) Yet it is not so much in the sense of "knowledge" about the intentions of others that the idealist utilizes the term "understanding"; it is rather in the sense of sympathy for others' situations, their attitudes, their fears and hopes, the values they share in common with people everywhere. The "minds-of-men" theory of international tension and its resolution is masterfully examined by Professor Dunn in the selection reprinted in this chapter.

A third theory of peaceful change is the institutional, the essence of which is that in order for states and men to cooperate, methods and techniques, developed within the framework of organization, must be instituted to promote and expand their mutual interests and enterprises. This approach is formalized, among other places, in Article 14 of the United Nations Charter, which provides for the "peaceful adjustment of any situation, regardless of origin, including situations likely to impair the general welfare or friendly relations among nations...." The approach finds expression in the multiple regional and functional international organizations which form the subject matter of Chapter XXIII.

Two other theories of peaceful change should be noted, one enjoying powerful influence and the other held only by a devoted few. The Marxist contention is that tension, conflict and violence are but manifestations of the class struggle, taking the form on the international scene of "a series of terrible wars" between the capitalist states themselves and then between them and the socialist states. The pacifist, on the other hand, pleads for love as the basis of all human relationships and practices non-violence at every level of life, including international relations, where war is rejected even if this rejection means submission to aggression. Reinhold Niebuhr's commentary on the pacifist position and the excerpts from a Quaker pamphlet, reprinted in this chapter, will clarify this position.

All of these theories of peaceful change merit close consideration, especially in a period when the preconditions for change are themselves rapidly changing. Professor Dunn, in the article cited earlier, distinguished between two implications of the development of nuclear weapons on problems of peaceful change. First of all, the major powers have been limited in their ability to use force to bring about or to prevent changes in the *status quo*. Secondly, the strategic importance of certain areas has changed, and with this change has come a transformation in the viewpoints of the powers in terms of altering the status of these territories. In some ways, the smaller powers have actually increased rather than decreased their influence as a result of the concentration on nuclear weapons by their larger neighbors.[2]

---

2 "Peaceful Change Today," *op. cit.*, pp. 284–85.

1 • Reducing International Tension *

Paul Kecskemeti

A graduate of Paxmany Peter University in Budapest, Dr. Kecskemeti has served as propaganda analyst and regional specialist for Germany with the O.W.I. from 1942–46, as editor in the Civil Affairs Division of the War Department from 1946 to 1948, and since that time as Senior Scientist, Rand Corporation. A frequent contributor to such journals as the Public Opinion Quarterly, World Politics, *and the* Journal of Social Psychology, *he is the author of* Meaning, Communication and Value *(1952), and* Strategic Surrender *(1959), which created a storm of controversy when it appeared.*

It is interesting to notice how the language of politics changes. When people nowadays talk about "international tension" and the need for "reducing" it, they use these words in a sense different from that current before the First World War. At that time, the word "tension" usually referred to a state of acute and dangerous irritation over some specific issue. When a state of tension was noted, it meant, more often than not, that the question of war or peace was raised in acute form. For example, one power made moves to establish itself in an area where another had vested interests. As the former was pushing its plans, the latter threatened to hinder them by force if necessary. The question was then whether the controversy could be settled by compromise before either power did something that made war inevitable.

Tension of this sort, when it became acute, called for immediate action and regularly touched off intense diplomatic activity. There were feverish consultations behind closed doors, and at the same time threatening gestures, naval demonstrations, and clamor in the streets. It was a race against time, for war could not be avoided once the prestige of any power was irrevocably committed. Such acute tension could not last long. Either it was speedily resolved, or it erupted into war.

It is clear that the "tension" being discussed in our own day is not of this acute sort. It is *chronic* tension, but of great intensity, so great, in fact, that it is called "cold war." How does such chronic tension compare with the violent, dangerous, and transitory periods of acute tensions before 1914?

For one thing, chronic tension of the cold war type expresses a deeper, more total antagonism than the older type of acute tension ever did. In acute tension, one power objected to what another was doing or was about to do in some disputed area—as when France pushed into the Sudan in 1898, or prepared to set up

---

* *Commentary,* XX (December, 1955), 517–21. Copyright held by the American Jewish Committee. Reprinted by permission.

a protectorate in Morocco in 1905, or when the Austro-Hungarian monarchy insisted upon punitive measures against Serbia in 1914. Acute controversies of this sort may usually have been symptoms of some deep-seated chronic antagonism, but never of total mutual rejection. This, however, is what characterizes our present chronic tension. The opposing powers not only have conflicting interests; they stand for antithetical basic principles. One power objects not only to what the other *does* but also to what it *is*. The existence of the one is viewed as offering a total challenge to the other.

One might assume, therefore, that chronic tension of the cold war type points to total war as its logical consummation, unlike acute tension which leaves room for compromise and threatens limited conflict at most. Paradoxically, however, the acute tension of 1914 did result in total war, while our present chronic tension has involved a kind of enduring equilibrium between the United States and the Soviet Union. Thus, while such tension is deeper and more fundamental than international tension used to be, it is less dynamic in its direct manifestations and can persist without explosive consequences.

In trying to explain this paradox, we have to remember that a power is readier to start a war when expecting it to remain limited than when sure beforehand that it will be total. Before 1914 the rules of international relations prescribed war under certain circumstances: once "irreparable" things had happened (e.g. once a power decreed general mobilization), all mediation was considered useless. Presumably, the rules of international conduct would have been different if people had then known how destructive modern war could be. But the point is that they did not know. Pre-1914 Europe it seems, was betrayed into a kind of fatalistic

light-heartedness about war because all European wars since Napoleon (the Crimean, Franco-Austrian, Austro-Prussian, and Franco-Prussian) had been short and far from ruinous for the participants, including the losers. In 1914, both government and public in all the European countries involved expected a short war: a long conflict was considered "unthinkable" because it unavoidably meant total ruin. As it turned out, however, war had a mechanism of its own. Once it got under way it could not be stopped short of the total exhaustion of one side or the other.

By 1918 most people had been thoroughly disabused of the idea that war under modern conditions could be a normal regulator of international affairs, an *ultima ratio* that could be resorted to without courting disaster. But the tragedy was that the democratic West drew wishful conclusions from this sobering thought: since war had turned out to be irrational, one could act as if it had become an impossibility. This set the stage for World War II. With the West disarmed, Hitler thought that a return to the old pre-1914 pattern of the short, relatively painless, and victorious war was possible. He started war over a local issue; it became a general conflict and, again, ran its course until one side —again the German—was totally prostrate.

With the advent of atomic weapons, the last excuse for such a wishful illusion as Hitler labored under when he attacked Poland has evaporated. It has become all too plain that a war between great powers must now be a totally destructive one. But at the same time political antagonisms have arisen between the great powers of the postwar world that are unprecedentedly radical in their nature. This has done away with the other illusion, namely, that the very irrationality of war would render it an impossibility.

But what are we left with after shedding both these illusions? Since unilateral disarmament is just as suicidal as resorting to arms, survival has become possible only in a state of tense, armed equilibrium. We face an opponent intent upon changing the face of the world; if he has his way, we are doomed. Nevertheless, it does not follow that we must fight him. It is enough to make sure that he *cannot* have his way. If we have enough ready military potential, he will be deterred from aggression. Our military potential is not meant for use, but for insurance.

This is the formula of chronic tension. Unlike acute tension, which represents a dangerous disturbance of the existing state of equilibrium, chronic tension serves to maintain equilibrium. It is a kind of adjustment to a totally threatening situation.

But the question is, how well can this kind of adjustment work in the long run? Can peace and security be preserved indefinitely on such a basis?

Theoretically, the mechanism of chronic tension works in the following way: one power seeks to upset the status quo and another is determined to prevent this. While they pursue diametrically opposed aims, each knows that overt conflict would be ruinous. Hence, as long as one power can convince the other that any attempt to change the status quo by force would be met by force, the status quo will be respected.

How well the status quo can be preserved on such terms depends on two crucial conditions: first, that the more aggressive power prefer the status quo to overt conflict; second, that no change be brought about without overt conflict. When the first condition no longer holds good, the equilibrium breaks down, tension becomes acute, and the less aggressive power must either yield or go to war. When the second condition goes unsatisfied, the more "dynamic" power will attack the status quo by means short of war or by purely local military action with which the defender of the status quo will not interfere.

Now the second rather than the first condition represents the weak point of the cold war arrangement, since it is much more difficult to satisfy than the first. With modern arms being what they are, it is not too difficult to deter an aggressive power from doing things which could only result in all-out war. But this category of offensives is limited. There are plenty of changes that a resolutely aggressive power can bring about by means short of war or by local, peripheral operations. In chronic tension, when all-out conflict is ruled out, the policies of the aggressive side will be increasingly concentrated upon gains that it can achieve without employing the bulk of its armed forces.

This puts the defending side in an increasingly uncomfortable and precarious position. Its prime political weapon is the threat of massive armed retaliation, but this threat cannot be effective where the conflict seems too circumscribed to justify its being carried out. In this way the status quo can be gradually undermined. It is essential for the defending side to halt the undermining, but this requires instruments other than the threat of massive retaliation.

Another difficulty the defender faces in a situation of chronic tension like the cold war is psychological. The attacker need not talk about war explicitly until he is good and ready for it; until then he can profess absolute and unconditional pacifism. The defender, however, must constantly maintain that he cannot, and will not, keep the peace if certain things happen. While many people understand that these conditional threats of war imply no actual intention of fighting—just as the aggressor's protestations of his hatred of war do not exclude such an intention on his part—

it is all too easy to confuse explicit references to war as a *possibility* with a *really* warlike attitude. The formula intended for deterrent effect, which tries to exclude the *actuality* of war by asserting its *possibility*, is far too subtle for most people to grasp. As soon as they hear a reference to war as a possibility under certain circumstances, they jump to the conclusion that the speaker has actual war in mind, and they imagine atomic bombs being dropped everywhere.

Such reactions are fairly widespread, particularly among European intellectuals and opinion-makers. Instead of criticizing the *real* weaknesses inherent in the deterrent policy, they meet it with lofty moral condemnation. Including the possibility of war in one's political calculations, if only as something to avoid, is, according to them, the archcrime, the first step towards perdition. Salvation can lie only in envisaging no alternative whatsoever to peace.

The prevalence of such an attitude explains the success of the cry for "reducing tension." Instead of threatening each other with retribution in case of attack, it is said, let the opponents assure each other of their heartfelt desire to avoid conflict. This will clear the air and lead in time to the abatement of chronic tension itself. In fact, the *détente* is already with us today; the cold war is a thing of the past, consigned to limbo by the Spirit of Geneva. Admittedly, none of the political differences between East and West has been resolved, but is this really important? Now there is a school of thought, popular in the United States and indeed in the whole Western world, which holds that political issues are, after all, only secondary. Human feelings of friendliness and hostility are the things that really count, and such feelings can be shaped and manipulated by public-relations techniques. If we cultivate the

Spirit of Geneva and multiply cordial get-togethers between representatives of East and West, politics will follow suit.

Now we may readily admit that the introduction of a more urbane tone and demeanor into international intercourse is a desirable thing. But it is courting catastrophe to believe that the underlying political tension itself is bound to be relaxed once it is made clear that neither side really wants to fight. After all, it was plain even at the height of the cold war that both we and the Russians were anxious not to go to war; the desire for peace is an essential feature of chronic tension as such. But to make this explicit does not change the situation. The issues that have been controversial remain controversial: the determination to handle these issues by methods short of war, however, is no dramatic new departure—it has existed all along....

...The Russians' immediate objective ...is the dismantling of the Western defensive alliance. Why keep such an alliance in being if everybody agrees that no attack is to be feared? As long as the world remains divided into "hostile blocs" we shall have tension, strife, the danger of war. If we want to do away with tension, we must get rid of the blocs; the Spirit of Geneva cannot tolerate alliances explicitly directed against any one power, or group of powers, that is designated as a prospective aggressor.

It would be wonderful if tension could be eliminated by such simple means, but would the dismantling of the Western alliance really eliminate tension, or even significantly reduce it? Let us look at the probable consequences of such a move. It would, first and foremost, weaken those forces which tend to defend the status quo and strengthen those which favor the expansion of the Soviet bloc. In a world without "hostile blocs," acceptance of changes brought about by force rather than the cowing of would be aggressors would become dominant.

The advent of such an era of uninhibited dynamism would certainly be welcome from the Communist point of view, but it would be disastrous for the West. And whether or not such unbridled "dynamism" would provoke a major war, one thing is certain: it would not reduce tension. Tension as such declines only if the situation becomes more acceptable to everybody concerned. If it becomes more satisfactory to one side and less satisfactory to the other, then it is their relative power position that changes, rather than the fact that tension prevails between them. In fact, such one-sided changes are likely to result either in increased tension and eventual conflict, or in the complete collapse of the power against whose interests they tend to harm.

If we dispense with conditional threats and absolutely exclude any alternative other than complete non-interference, we do not reduce tension; we merely enable our adversary to undermine our position to such an extent that in the end our only choice will be between a suicidal conflict and an equally suicidal surrender. This does not mean that our present policy of conditional threats is adequate. We must recognize that our position can be quite effectively undermined by action against which the conditional threats of nuclear devastation are of no avail. The problem this poses for us is far from being solved; it is not even sufficiently understood.

How to deal with this difficulty is, however, outside the scope of the present article. We are concerned here only with the problem of reducing international tension. So far we have pointed out only how chronic tension could not be reduced. We have seen that neither the protestation of peaceful intentions nor the abandonment of conditional threats and defensive preparations is a suitable means for eliminating or even substantially lessening tension. But what other means could one recommend then? Or is it best not to try to reduce chronic tension at all, and trust that it will continue to preserve stability without a conflict?

The answer is that chronic international tension can neither be maintained nor reduced by design. The extent and degree of such tension is not an independent datum that one can control by direct methods. It is what results when interests and wills are at odds. Tension may abate when interests and aims change, but this is not a matter of free choice. We have some choice as to the way in which we pursue our goals and interests, but not as to what these goals and interests are. And the existence and the degree of chronic tension are determined by ends rather than by means. If conflict of goals and interests leads to tension, it makes little difference whether we like the fact or not; we cannot make it vanish by incantation. It is not the desire to get rid of tension that causes it to be reduced.

2 • A Sociological Analysis of International Tension *

Georges Gurvitch

The author is Professor of Sociology at the Sorbonne, and head of the Center of Sociological Studies in Paris.

The present international tensions appear to me not as the auguries of a coming war but as the painful birth pangs of the coming international society. Such a society has not yet seen the light of day; but willy-nilly the nations are drawn together by common economic needs and by the feeling that they are linked together "for better or for worse." They know that they cannot avoid "One World," but they have no constructive plans for a satisfactory organization acceptable for all nations. The result is that nations accuse each other of bad faith or evil intention as an escape from responsibility or a guilty conscience. International tension has long been due mainly to traditional or artificially created misunderstandings, skillfully exploited for different reasons by warmongers and military castes. This situation has, however, never been so obvious as today, when international tension increases with every new effort to reach an understanding.

Comparing international tensions with ... other types of social tensions ... we reach the following conclusions:

(1) International tensions show a very paradoxical character: they seem to be the least real and for this reason the most artificial of all social tensions. Thus they should be the most easily settled and the least deep-seated. In-deed they are mostly founded on misunderstandings, unscrupulous propaganda, false information, and crude myths. However, (2) they are the most dangerous of all social tensions since they can lead to war, the destruction of millions of human lives and to cultural and social backsliding.

This tragic paradox may also be formulated as follows: the more nearly international tensions become real social tensions the more pacific will they become since they will be absorbed progressively into other types of social tensions.

FACTORS MAKING FOR INTERNATIONAL TENSION

Before undertaking an analysis of the means of reducing contemporary international tensions, let us set forth briefly the factors making for international tensions.

(1) Because of their all-inclusive and suprafunctional character, nations are not very intensive social units. But this does not prevent their members from having very definite, if remote, ideas regarding other nations. These other nations are generally believed to be

* *Tensions that Cause Wars* (Urbana: University of Illinois Press, 1950), pp. 248–53. Reprinted by permission.

morally "far away" or "much inferior"; they are considered suitable objects on which to exercise *national pride* ("there is no better country than ours"), *national hate* ("our enemy is always the same") or occasionally *national hopes* (e.g., the hopes of the Slav nations with regard to Russia, or those which the French nation placed during the last two wars in the United States). These are all aspects of national egocentrism and egotism. Other nations are thought of only in relation to one's own country. This precludes any possibility of mutual understanding.

(2) National egotism and egocentrism create a very favorable atmosphere for developing emotionally charged and standardized symbols and myths which seriously distort the real face and character of other nations. This traditional abuse of symbolical and mythological images—which may be seen for instance in high school history textbooks and in the international information of almost any national newspaper—has become particularly grave at the present time, when new tensions arise daily from the discussions in the Security Council and in the General Assembly of the United Nations. Compelled to face each other as close neighbors without any real understanding, nations take refuge in the further development of emotional mythology; and more and more distort the truth by oversimplifying very complex problems and situations.

(3) We are now living in an age of rationalized propaganda backed by such powerful technical media as the radio, movies, etc. Men are for the first time consciously manipulating symbols and myths, even elaborating them in a manner calculated to suit their by no means always honorable ends. This is a new and directly observable factor intensifying international tensions. Very high international tensions can be whipped up with astonishing rapidity at the dictate of controlling groups. And with no less rapidity they can be slowed down. Illusions and delusions can be imposed deliberately on large masses on an international scale, often in order to conceal the real social conflicts of greater significance.

(4) Finally, certain factors making for international tension are based on already long-standing conflicting interests between nations. These are the conflicts of geographic, colonial, commercial, and economic interests (unequal distribution of natural wealth or of raw materials for industrial products; e.g., coal and metallic ores); differences in population density; unequal numbers of unemployed; areas of traditional dispute; military castes supporting warmongering parties and interfering in civilian affairs; and also ideological conflicts, whether religious, political or social. All these factors, however, have been more important in the past than they are at the present time where the interdependence between nations has become so close that conflicts of real interests can be more easily settled by discussion and conciliation than by totally destructive war.

MEANS OF REDUCING INTERNATIONAL TENSION

Due to the highly artificial character of most international tensions and more especially to their rise and fall at the present time, deliberate intervention is likely to be more successful in this field than in that of any other type of social strain. Nevertheless, at the same time the risks of raising the existing tension and fostering new tensions through inappropriate action are far greater than in any other sphere. International relations are dominated by misunderstandings, misinterpretations, and the inability to view other nations in a non-egocentric manner. Consequently, emotionally charged national symbols and myths often become magnified and intensified through unskilled attacks against them or through inappropriate efforts to compromise with them.

At the same time, it is clear that the means of reducing international tensions will vary according to historical periods, types of society and social structure. It is hardly possible to discuss these means in general terms. We shall therefore concentrate exclusively on those methods applicable in present circumstances:

(1) Nations must be compelled to abandon their ignorance of each other by a better organization of mutual information regarding their real way of life, their ideals, aspirations, and achievements.

(2) All forms of disloyal propaganda directed against any nation by distortions of the truth, false rumors, false representation of national characters, etc. must be eliminated from the radio, movies, press, and textbooks of all nations through the aid of some international action possibly concerted by UNESCO.

(3) In order to compel each nation to know how it is viewed by other nations and how these other nations see themselves, large scale cultural exchanges will be necessary. Large numbers of professors and students should be exchanged every year between nations. Permanent international information centers showing the economic, political, intellectual, artistic, and religious life of each nation should be instituted. These centers should be able to utilize on the largest possible scale means of mass communication, such as the radio, television, newsreels, and the press. These instruments, which now mainly serve various propagandist ends, would thus counteract propaganda by true mass information.

(4) The same aim would be served by the organization of a permanent and stable international university. This body would move annually from one national capital to another. Professors and students would be delegated annually by national universities under UNESCO control. The social science faculty would specialize in the comparison and analysis of present-day social, economic, and political structures, as well as in the study of the conditions under which an international society and international institutions might best develop.

(5) Economic agreements and international economic planning could very much help to reduce international tensions. Both could in due time bring about a redistribution of natural wealth, and could help to foster national production and the rational exchange of goods. However, only world-wide economic agreements and world-wide economic planning can have any marked success in reducing international tensions. Regional agreements not integrated into a general world-wide system may very well only heighten the tension between powerful blocs, and thus become a factor making for war. *A world-wide International Economic Planning Board,* with direct representation of national economic organizations and labor unions, is badly needed. It would perhaps have much greater success than existing organizations, including the Economic and Social Council of the United Nations organization.

However, before international economic planning in the common interest can be brought into effect, fundamental changes in national economic and social structures will be necessary. The reduction of international tensions through the institution of a *world-wide International Economic Planning Board,* therefore, belongs more to the future than to the present.

3 • Politics, Culture, and Peace *

Frederick S. Dunn

Most government documents make deplorably dull reading and only on rare occasions are they illumined by new ideas or a fresh turn of phrase. An exception is to be found in the opening lines of the Constitution of the United Nations Educational, Scientific and Cultural Organization (UNESCO). With disarming candor and an easy poetic rhythm, the preamble discusses the eternal problem of war and peace in terms somewhat different from those which governments normally use in their relations with each other. It suggests that the origin of wars is to be found not, as had generally been supposed, in the formal acts of sovereign states, but rather in the minds of the masses of men, and it is accordingly in the minds of men that the defenses of peace must be constructed. The preamble further argues that ignorance among nations of each other's ways and lives leads to suspicion and mistrust which in turn lead to war, and hence the way to peace is to remove such ignorance. On the whole, it takes a distinctly skeptical view of the durability of a peace based principally upon the usual political and economic arrangements of governments, and places its faith instead on the removal from men's minds of the attitudes and predispositions that lead them to entertain the idea of war with each other.

The deceptive simplicity of this statement might give the impression that it is intended merely as melodious preamble music, to be repeated on solemn public occasions but not to be taken seriously as an expression of empirical truth about the source of political conflicts. There is in fact some reason to suppose that the drafters themselves were not in full agreement as to the precise significance of the theory they were offering as the basis for the operations of UNESCO. But whatever may have been the original intention, there can be no doubt that the phrase about the "minds of men" has caught hold of the imagination of a great many people in a number of countries and has come to symbolize a distinctive and somewhat optimistic approach to the whole problem of how to lessen the threat of war in the present age.

1. PEACE BY CHANGING MEN'S ATTITUDES

There are some obvious reasons why this idea of constructing the defenses of peace in the minds of men should have attracted so much attention.

In the first place, it is quite clear that there has been a general loss of confidence in existing notions about how to avoid war in the current world crisis. While most governments are proceeding on traditional assumptions about the sources of war and are endeavoring to construct the defenses of peace in an

---

* *War and the Minds of Men* (New York: Harper & Brothers, for the Council on Foreign Relations, 1950), Chapter 1.

expanded national strength and in useful alliances, there is a strong undercurrent of despair arising from the belief that in the end this method is just not going to work. The ancient dilemma of trying to achieve security in a world of sovereign states seems to have become vastly more baffling in an atomic age. The prospect of maintaining a lasting equilibrium in a bipolar world appears more doubtful than ever.

Now the threat of the hydrogen bomb, with its fantastic capacity for destruction, has come along to sharpen the dilemma a hundredfold. At the moment, it does not appear that armed forces of any size could insure the great industrial centers from instant incineration at the hands of a determined enemy possessing even a small supply of these bombs. Mighty ships and well-equipped divisions can no longer provide even a minimum of that comfortable feeling of safety which they used to be able to give. A trial by battle involving the use of all the newest weapons of mass destruction can appear only as the final madness of men. Hence great numbers of people have anxiously turned to this doctrine which seems to open up a whole new method of attack on the problem of war and peace.

A second reason why the minds-of-men theory has attracted so much attention is the realization that the masses of men are now exerting a great and apparently expanding influence on the making of policy decisions in international affairs. As the interests of people have spread outward, a greater concern with the way in which those interests are fostered has likewise begun to penetrate the international level. Everywhere outside the Soviet orbit there has been a definite tendency toward wider popular control of foreign policy. In the colonial empires of the world, the native populations have surged forward to enforce their demands for a direct voice in the determination of their status in the international community. In all save the dictator countries, legislative bodies seem to have won an increased share in the making of foreign policy. Hence, a theory which proposes to construct the defenses of peace in the minds of men appears to make much more sense today than it would have made when the management of foreign affairs was the exclusive province of a small group of officials.

A third reason why the minds-of-men doctrine has seemed to offer a ray of hope in the current crisis is the growing belief that we are at last coming into the possession of knowledge and techniques that will enable us to influence men's political behavior in desired directions and so exercise a greater control over international events. We seem to be traveling along the edge of a new and engrossing experience in the long and difficult enterprise of learning about the forces that influence social action. There is excitement in the air and a feeling that we are breaking out into new and fertile territory in the understanding of social behavior. Spectacular improvements in the technical means of communication with the masses of men have added to the hope that we are acquiring new power as well as new insights in the control of international events.

For these reasons, there has been a ready audience for the theory that the conflicts of nations arise in the minds of men and might be controlled by changing men's attitudes. On the surface there seems to be much in favor of the idea. It is easy enough to see that widespread feelings of hostility and misunderstanding provide fertile soil for the seeds of war. It is also obvious that conflicts among nations can grow fat on a diet of ignorance and bias. Presumably a state of peace and order is what nearly everybody wants, and if its achievement is really a matter of influencing men's minds, one would be hard pressed to say why massive efforts should not be made in this field.

2. LARGE HOPES AND SMALL RESULTS

However, when it comes to the actual effort to put this doctrine into effect, the difficulties seem mountainous.

. . . .

Everyone knows in general what is meant by "mutual understanding" and everyone approves of it as a sentiment, but little effort seems to have been made to translate it into categories of observable data about which hypotheses can be made and tested by objective methods. The result is that no two people who use the term can ever be sure that they are talking about the same thing or that what they say has any basis in reality. The language and the conceptual systems used in the halls of UNESCO are for the most part of a traditional character, and reveal little appreciation of what has been taking place recently in the way of systematic analysis of social action.

Some people who are genuinely convinced of the essential validity of the minds-of-men doctrine have nevertheless raised serious questions about the premises on which this doctrine is being put into effect. Thus the belief that men go to war because they are ignorant of each other's ways of life or have incorrect views of each other's motives has been strongly challenged on the basis of past history. It is pointed out that the nations which go to war most frequently are not those in which ignorance of other people is most common, but are instead the more advanced nations with the highest educational standards. For example, the people of France and Germany have had abundant opportunity to get to know each other well; yet this has not prevented them from engaging in wars of spectacular dimensions.

Even in everyday human affairs, the connection between knowledge of others and peaceful relations with them is not always evident. Thus on the family level the bitterest of controversies frequently take place between the closest of relatives. Civil wars, which are between peoples of the same civilization who presumably possess a good understanding of each other, are notoriously sharp and cruel. On the other hand, isolated nations have managed to live both in ignorance of, and in harmony with, other nations for long periods of time.

It is persistently asked whether the differences between Soviet Russia and the United States today are really due to a lack of understanding of their respective positions, or whether these differences do not in fact arise out of a clear realization that the two countries have fundamental goals which are to a large extent incompatible. One recalls the case of the European monarch who, when urged by his advisers to settle a boundary war with a neighboring sovereign, replied that there was really no dispute at all between them—they both wanted the same thing. Their mutual understanding was perfect.

Will full knowledge of what nations want in fact bring peace among them, or is it not more likely that, under certain circumstances, such knowledge might even increase the tendency to go to war? Those who raise this question are quite ready to concede that, where means can be found for giving both contestants substantially what they desire, a full exploration of the possible alternatives would undoubtedly contribute to the avoidance of hostilities. But when such inquiry reveals that the goals of the two sides are incompatible and there is no way in which they can be harmonized, it is a serious question whether public revelation of that fact would increase the chances for peace.

Past experience affords some ground for skepticism as to whether extensive cultural interchange has had much effect upon the underlying causes of wars. Does freedom of communication across national boundaries necessarily lead to the development of common conceptions of justice among nations? Is it even true that nations possessing similar conceptions of justice will therefore refrain from going to war against each other? Cultural interchange is freely conceded to be a good thing in itself. But some scholars have asked whether, in the light of historical instances, one can expect such interchange to have much effect in preventing wars.[1]

Finally, there is little reason, it is said, for supposing that governments are really serious in wanting to take action that would reduce the nationalistic attitudes of their citizens. Such attitudes may be a useful source of support for a government that is engaged in a power competition with a rival nation. Under such circumstances, it would be too much to expect that any government would seriously want its own citizens to become more internationally minded. Thus in the present contest between the Soviet Union and the United States, a program of education for international understanding on one side of the line but not on the other would merely strengthen the side that relies on the fostering of nationalistic attitudes among its people.

The upshot of all these criticisms is that a good many people who would normally be well disposed toward the idea that the defenses of peace should be built in the minds of men nevertheless feel that the doctrine really has no particular relevancy to the present world crisis. They believe that UNESCO's activities in improving standards of education, science and culture in various countries may be excellent in themselves, but that aside from the infinitely slow building up of the tissues of a world community, there is little that UNESCO can contribute to the maintenance of peace in the years ahead.

It would be difficult to deny the strength of many of the points made above. However, they could all be admitted, and it might still be a perfectly good working proposition that wars begin in the minds of men and that the defenses of peace must be constructed there. What is valid in these criticisms is directed not so much at the idea itself as at the way in which people have sought to apply it.

Where else, one might ask, could wars begin save in the minds of men? Even the greenest tyro in the halls of world politics is now aware that, although we talk about states acting and making decisions, only human beings can act. The state, being an abstraction of thought, cannot have a will of its own apart from human wills. It is in one sense just a name to describe the process whereby politically organized people arrive at decisions and take action which is accepted as the action of the collectivity.

But having said this, one is still a long way from knowing what to do about it, or even whether anything can be done about it at all. Having identified the source of our troubles, it is still a highly perplexing business to discover reliable ways of freeing men's minds from the impulses and attitudes that lead to wars. Yet it is obvious that, if there is a grain of truth in the minds-of-men doctrine, one must examine it with sympathetic care to see what guidance it can offer for more intelligent policy-making in the future.

In order to do this with any hope of success, it will be necessary to break

---

[1] See Hans J. Morgenthau, *Politics Among Nations*, New York, Alfred A. Knopf, 1948, pp. 407–412; also Reinhold Niebuhr, "The Theory and Practice of UNESCO," *International Organization*, February 1950, pp. 3–11.

out of the traditional framework of thinking about foreign affairs and to use a new focus for our analysis. This is always a difficult thing to do, but there is no other way of getting a fresh view of the problem and of arriving at an objective evaluation of the steps that are being taken to solve it.

At any rate it is time that the case for approaching the problem of war and peace through the minds-of-men doctrine should be placed on some other ground than that of stirring appeals to the sentiments. If the phrase has any useful meaning as a signpost to effective action, that meaning will be discovered only by a realistic analysis that will reveal its connection with the actual world of events and suggest hypotheses which can be tested by observation and concrete experience.

To a crusader in a cause, a realistic appraisal of the premises on which his beliefs are founded can appear only as rank heresy. Many people today have a sacred-cow attitude toward UNESCO that prevents them from looking at it with a detached eye. But if a movement or doctrine cannot stand up under a realistic examination, then it does not deserve the support of intelligent men; if it can, it is doubly strong.

3. A Problem of Communication

The most important thing to be observed about the minds-of-men theory is that it is primarily a theory of communication and learning. It asserts that, if only the right things are communicated by some people to some other people, a change can be effected in the attitudes of nations toward each other that will make a durable peace possible. This is a technical proposition which rests upon our knowledge of the processes of using ideas or symbols to modify the behavior of men.

. . . .

In the present state of the world, this is a very complicated business indeed. Because of the prodigious revolutionary changes taking place in various parts of the world, it is no easy matter to identify either the proper communicators or the appropriate audiences, or even the correct aims of communication policies. One cannot simply say that the purpose of such policies is to avoid open warfare, since that kind of peace might be purchased, at least temporarily, by making men submissive to tyrants. One would have to assume that the purpose is to achieve a peace based on those attitudes which make for the full development of the capacities of free men in a free society. Instead of merely seeking to deprive men of the will to resist those whose aim is to enslave them, the goal of the minds-of-men theory might even be to strengthen their resistance in the face of threats of violence. Certainly a peace of subservience based on the deterioration of human society and the breakdown of individual personality is not what is desired by those who embrace the theory. Such a peace could end finally only in the jungle warfare of barbarians. In the complex society of today, no enduring peace is possible that is not based on the continuing development of human potentialities.

. . . .

4 • A Quaker Search for an Alternative to Violence *

American Friends Service Committee

NOTE: *In earlier sections of the pamphlet from which the present extracts are taken, the authors describe the salient characteristics of the contemporary world in terms of violence, totalitarianism, and social revolution. The response of democratic countries to the totalitarian threat—described as a "commitment to violence" has, they claim, been wholly inadequate. As evidence for this judgment, the following considerations are adduced: 1) The influence of the Soviet Union, and the appeal of its communist doctrines, have grown steadily since the end of World War II; 2) Our policy has confirmed Marxist doctrine and hardened attitudes within communist countries; 3) The principles for which the United States stands have been seriously undermined at home and abroad; 4) Far from making us more secure, our policy is increasing the insecurity of the United States and of the rest of the world; and 5) Our moral standards have been debased.*

We cannot follow constructive policies because of the commitment to violence to meet the communist threat. In place of reliance on armaments, the authors suggest application of non-violent methods to reduce tensions. They point to successful experiences with non-violence in such areas as the treatment of prisoners, treatment of the mentally ill, liberation of slaves, achievement of equal rights for women, and attainment of political independence by India. Then the recommended policy and its expected results are described in some detail.

Our world is a dynamic world, with men and nations altering their habits, their attitudes, and their responses as the international climate shifts and changes. The pacifist wants to recognize this fact, and build policy around its existence. He suggests, therefore, that the more a minority could succeed in modifying belligerency and encouraging restraint, the more striking and unpredictable would be the resulting mutation in international relations.... We suggest that the more a nation focused on reconciling differences, the more creative would be the power and the life that would flow from it. A whole new dimension would be introduced into the world community just as elementary experiments have sometimes introduced whole new dimensions into the scientific community. Who could have predicted, for example, that Benjamin Franklin's early experiments with electricity would end by revolutionizing man's whole way of life? It is a long jump from Franklin's kite to television, too long for the human imagination to have fully encompassed. Similarly, it is a long jump from our present expressions of international good will, such as the Fulbright program for student exchange, to its fullest possible expression in world affairs. Is this, also, too difficult for the imagination of our generation to encompass? We are certain only that its impact on the world

* *Speak Truth to Power; A Quaker Search for an Alternative to Violence;* American Friends Service Committee, 1955. Reprinted by permission.

would be fully as profound in the sphere of human relations as the impact of electricity has been in the sphere of science. Beyond that is speculation, but we can venture suggestions of the broad outlines of such a full policy of international good will.

. . . .

1. There would be revolutionary changes within the United States itself. Since the non-violent insight underlines the necessity of first attacking our own evils, it is clear that the American people would be obligated to move farther in overcoming racial discrimination and religious intolerance. We would insist on maximum freedom of thought and expression. . . . We would discover again the wisdom of Jefferson that error may be tolerated, as long as truth remains free to combat it. Any nation which, in this fear-ridden age, had the courage to trust the democratic process instead of bartering democracy for the illusory security of an atomic stockpile would speak with undreamed power to enslaved men the world over.

2. *The United States would give its support to the great social revolutions, which are both a major problem and a major hope of our time.* Regardless of whether men strive to overthrow domination from without or outworn feudalism from within, their determination is to achieve new dignity and status as human beings and to banish the physical poverty that has so long condemned them to misery. They deserve the support of every democratic society, and they would receive the support of this country if it were freed from its preoccupation with defense and the military power struggle. If this took place, men who seek freedom would no longer conclude, as many already have, that the only source of support is from communist nations, and they would cease to be available for communist armies. American support, moreover, would make it more possible for these revolutions themselves to be non-violent.

3. The United States would devote its skills and resources to great programs of technical and economic assistance, carried on under United Nations auspices and with full participation in planning and administration by the receiving peoples. The resources needed for these operations are so large that our own standard of living might be seriously affected, but the dividends would also be large. The mere fact of reducing the great economic imbalance between the United States and the poverty-stricken masses of Asia, Africa, and Latin America, would itself remove one of the major sources of embitterment and strife. Our willingness to share our material blessings, without ulterior motives and to an extent well beyond our unused surpluses, would bring men to us as friends and cooperators, rather than alienate them as does present policy.

4. The United States would get rid of its military establishment. Various avenues might be taken to achieve this result. Many suggest that the most probable and most practical approach would be through the simple transfer of the security function to a world organization. The United Nations would assume the responsibility for defense, and might well be converted in the process into a federal instrument in much the same manner as the thirteen American colonies substituted a federal government for the unsatisfactory Articles of Confederation.

Others, less insistent on the importance of world federation suggest that disarmament would occur as the result of multilateral agreement: universal in character, enforceable in practice, and complete down to the level needed for internal policing. Both of these approaches are valid, and both could be supported by the United States in the era about which we speculate, but in the last analysis a pacifist policy would require unilateral action if agreement could not be achieved. There is no escaping the necessity to be willing to act first ourselves if we are to have solid ground for getting others to act with us.

It will be said that for a nation to consider disarming alone in an armed world is madness; but the fact that obviously stares men in the face today is that *an armed world in this age is itself madness*. To refuse any longer to labor under the delusion that it is anything else is the beginning of common sense, as it is the counsel of divine wisdom. Moreover, it is quite possible that the Soviet Union, confronted with such a change in American behavior, might startle us with a new response. At the very least, the example of a people living without the burden of militarism and offering friendship to all, would call forth the impulses to freedom that exist in all men. What might have happened, for example, if the remarkable East German uprising of June 1953 had had as its inspiration a United States free from involvement in the effort to rearm Western Germany and in the tragic perpetuation of an impossible division? As it was, the United States' position was a discouraging one. We welcomed the revolt, but could only stand idly by, unwilling to risk unleashing war, and yet unable to offer any other kind of encouragement. (Editors' Note: the same comment might, of course be made about the Hungarian Revolt of 1956.) Moreover, we were so preoccupied with power concepts that one of the most striking aspects of the uprising was largely overlooked: *the fact that a group of Russian soldiers refused to fire on the unarmed and non-violent demonstrators*. Not only were the demonstrators spared violence, but a number of their grievances were recognized and corrected. How can this outcome be squared with the familiar argument that only naked power is respected by the Russians?

Nor must it be forgotten how this whole non-violent era, about which we are speculating, would be brought about. Under our democratic philosophy, as we have already pointed out, it would not be created by fiat, but as the result of insistence on reconciling measures by a gradually growing pacifist minority. The writers are convinced that this process in itself would so change the climate of world opinion that no power on earth could oppose it effectively. The influence of growing programs of economic assistance, freed from the compulsions of strategy and carried forward by dedicated men and women through the operating agencies of the United Nations, would lift the heart of the world. Increasing support of the United Nations itself, as a world forum for peaceful settlement, universal in membership and inviolate of selfish national pressure, would create a new basis for an emerging world community of law. The earnest desire to negotiate differences, backed by a gradually increasing willingness to abandon our military posture, could open the way for the relaxation of tension and the achievement of disarmament. Nations which are at present hostile and threatening, would be relieved of any reason for being hostile and threatening, and would face a world opinion so warmly approving of the United States that continued hostility would be difficult to maintain.

NON-VIOLENT RESISTANCE

We must, however, face the possibility that hatred has gone so far, and injustice penetrated so deeply, that even a revolutionary policy of peace could not prevent international aggression. A nation which had disarmed would not in that event abjectly surrender and let an invader run over and enslave it as is often alleged. On the contrary, it would have open to it possibilities of non-violent resistance that offer more prospects of a creative and genuinely victorious outcome than is the case with violent resistance under modern conditions. It is the nation whose reliance is upon arms that now faces the bleakest prospect in the event of international aggression; for victory in any ensuing holocaust is clearly impossible for anyone. Both "victor" and "vanquished" would dwell together in a brutalized and devastated world in which the values of democratic civilization would have been largely swept away.

Non-violent resistance, as has been demonstrated on a large scale in India, and on a smaller scale in many other places, offers greater promise of confounding and overcoming an enemy without destroying our values or our world. While there are limits to the extent to which a program of non-violent resistance can be spelled out for a nation which is quite unready to adopt it, and for a future situation on whose character cannot be predicted, it is nevertheless possible to suggest the broad pattern that it would follow. The first necessity is *non-cooperation*. The population must resolutely refuse to carry out the orders of the invader. They would not run trains to transport troops. They would not operate factories to provide the invader with military supplies. They would not unload his ships. They would perform no services of any kind for him. At the same time, they would try through their words and their lives to show the meaning of a free and democratic society. Second, the population must maintain

good will toward the individual soldier of the invading forces. However difficult this is in practice, it is clear that the effective use of non-violent resistance has always demanded that a clear distinction be drawn between hatred of an evil policy and respect for the human instrument who is caught up in its execution. Good will is the spiritual weapon of non-violence just as civil disobedience is its physical weapon. Finally, the population must be well enough disciplined to *refrain from individual acts of violence* no matter what the provocation. . . .

All of this is not to suggest that everything would proceed in idyllic fashion and that no suffering would occur in a non-violent resistance campaign. We have tried to make it clear that readiness to accept suffering—rather than inflict it on others—is the essence of the non-violent life, and that we must be prepared if called upon to pay the ultimate price. Obviously, if men are willing to spend billions of treasure and countless lives in war, they cannot dismiss the case for non-violence by saying that in a non-violent struggle people might be killed! . . .

Such is the program we chart for the individual and for the state of which he is a part. We have not denied that it involves risk, but no policy can be formulated that does not involve risk. We have not suggested it will be easy, but only that no policy that aims at achieving peace can be easy. Finally, we have made no sweeping claims that it would work, but only that it appears to us more workable and more relevant than the barren doctrines of violence that now enslave us. We believe that it merits the consideration of thoughtful men.

5 • A Quaker Search for an Alternative to Violence *

Reinhold Niebuhr

The author, Professor of Applied Christianity at Union Theological Seminary, is the author of several books, including The Children of Light and the Children of Darkness *(1944);* Christianity and Power Politics *(1940);* Moral Man and Immoral Society *(1932); and* Christian Realism and Political Problems *(1953). Throughout his writings, he has attempted to reconcile questions of morality with the complexities of political action. He is one of America's outstanding theologians.*

There are many parts of the Quaker approach to world problems with which I personally agree....

One—Insistence that the contest with Communism, particularly in Asia and Africa, is conducted against the background of previous "imperialism" by the white nations and that our cause is gravely imperiled by residual resentments against "colonialism" and against the white man's arrogance toward the colored people. Any policy which corrects and expiates past evils is both morally and politically correct and better than undue reliance on military force....

Two—Our negative attitude toward our problems with Communism, our preoccupation with its evils and our frantic ferreting out of "subversives" with little discrimination between genuine disloyalty and mere dissent, has lowered our prestige in the world and not aided us in the real contest....

Three—Any undue reliance on military weapons in general, and atomic weapons in particular, and the concomitant neglect of all political, economic, and moral policies which strengthen the unity and health of the non-Communist world, is a grave error against which all democratic forces must marshal all their strength.

We can not, however, allow our knowledge of the limits of military forces in the world community to persuade us to adopt the pacifist disavowal of force as an end in itself. Force is merely the *ultima ratio* of political life. It cannot be disavowed even though every effort must be made to keep it in its proper place....

(My) points of agreement with the Quaker proposals, particularly on policies which do not raise the ultimate issue of the disavowal of force, cannot obscure the basic distinction between pacifist and non-pacifist policies. This distinction would seem to be on the absolute disavowal of force by the pacifists.

But the difference between pacifism and non-pacifism actually is more profound than the question of the use of force or "violence." The document makes

---

* *The Progressive*, October 1955, 11–12. Reprinted by permission.

this profounder distinction quite clear. The Quaker attitude toward political questions puts "power" and "love" in contradiction to each other. This contradiction leaves out the whole problem of the attainment of justice. Justice may be the servant of love, and power may be the servant of justice. Every historic form of justice has been attained by some equilibrium of power. Force in the narrow sense may be an element in the arsenal of power, but power is wider than force. It includes all the vitalities of life by which men seek to accomplish their ends.

Power is not evil. It may be put in the service of good ends. When the ends of men or nations conflict, the conflict may, of course, issue in violence. All sensible people will seek to avoid these violent conflicts whether on the national or international level. But only if one adopts the principle that it is better to suffer injustice than to resort to force can one wholly disavow the use of force. It is possible, though not always advisable, for individuals to suffer injustice rather than let the dispute come to an ultimate issue. But statesmen, responsible for values beyond their own life, do not have this option. They must seek for justice by an accommodation of interests and they must protect precious values by force if necessary. Even the terrors of possible atomic conflict cannot disengage them from such responsibilities, though it must naturally make them very hesitant to use a form of force which might spell mutual annihilation.

Every emphasis on the new dimension of destructiveness in war does not seriously alter the problem of the statesman's responsibility. It may persuade him, in the words of President Eisenhower, that "in an atomic age there is no alternative to peace," but it cannot persuade him to accept injustice or submission as the price of peace, particularly when the alternative is not between peace and war but between submission and the risk of war. We want our statesmen to be careful about that risk. But no nation will choose present submission as the alternative for a future risk. That is why pacifism remains an irrelevance even in an atomic age. But this need not prompt us to disrespect for the Quaker witness. That witness is most impressive in the Quaker works of mercy, and least impressive in all the problems of the political order where power must be placed in the service of justice, and where on occasion force may be legitimate in the arsenal of power and justice.

XIX • Problems of Disarmament and Disengagement in the Nuclear Age

Among the most persistent diplomatic issues since the Hague Conferences at the turn of the century is one of the most difficult practical problems in contemporary international relations: disarmament. Naive observers of war and threats to the peace argue that, if opponents in the political arena had no means with which to attack one another, there obviously could be no conflict. It is only slightly less naive to regard the problem as one of controlling exclusively "offensive" weapons, as if so-called "defensive" weapons could never be used by one nation to attack another.

Idealist and realist alike take fundamental positions on the issue, the one arguing that to prepare for war enhances the probability that weapons will be used and that their very existence creates tension; the other arguing that arms are merely the means used (actually or potentially) to gain political ends, and that their existence may even prevent war. Both agree, however, that *intent* is basic to the problem: whether it is a state's intention to use weapons, merely to threaten their use, or to hold them in reserve for defense against attack. That disarmament is still being discussed, after more than sixty years of almost continual frustration and disillusionment, reflects the ever-increasing danger of the arms race as technology perfects "better" weapons for killing more people more quickly.

The dilemma facing anyone attempting to bring about any degree of disarmament as phrased by Anthony Nutting, British Minister of State before resigning over his government's Suez policies: "You cannot have confidence without disarmament and you cannot have disarmament without confidence." He calls for a new Western approach to an old problem, involving an "act of faith" in the form of concessions which might inhibit the powers without actually undermining their security positions. Note that while he talks about the *cessation* of nuclear tests and production, his discussion is limited to the *reduction* of conventional forces and armaments. Determining which weapons are "conventional" and which are not becomes another complicating factor in the controversy, especially since tactical atomic weapons for limited objectives and not for mass destruction are already being incorporated into the armories systems of the military forces of various nations and coalitions. Actually, what is at issue is not "disarmament" at all, but a reversal of the trend toward increased and intensified production; in other words, arms reduction and arms limitation. It is only in this limited sense that the term "disarmament" has meaning in any serious contemporary discussion of the problem, at least among policy-makers! [1]

In considering choices open to responsible diplomatic, political, and military leaders concerned with the current arms race, Leo Gross considers its continuation as one of the most likely alternatives, paradoxical though this may appear, since to permit continuation may be in the interest of neither side in the "cold war." Because of the increasing difficulties of detection and with the prospect of unpredictable third parties acquiring atomic capability, other alternatives need to be considered. Of those he suggests, three (world government, limited world government, and a more adequate "organization of peace") all assume a degree of mutual trust and confidence which does not exist. A ban on weapons tests would of necessity require international inspection and control. Thus Gross concludes that it is better to "think in terms of a minimum program rather than in terms of an optimum program." Limited success is preferable to massive failure.

Unwilling to accept such a limited view, Albert Schweitzer has stressed one of the basic new dimensions of world politics, the involvement of all mankind in the consequences of all-out nuclear war and even in the preparation for such a war. Air raids and primitive V-bombs brought war to civilian populations in belligerent countries in the last war. In the next war, non-belligerent populations throughout the world will be affected. Because of their ultimate concern, the interest of men everywhere in seeking and proposing solutions to the leaders of the nuclear powers is legitimate and necessary. Atomic war would be "the most unimaginably senseless and cruel way of endangering the existence of mankind." Schweitzer sees but two alternatives: either the present "mad atomic race" will continue, or America and Russia must cooperate in the renunciation of nuclear arms. [2]

The concept of disengagement deserves attention because it represents a concrete attempt to arrive at a method of reducing tensions, and because it is directly linked to the question of armed forces and their weapons. As the Canadian political scientist, H. I. MacDonald, observes, the controversy raging over this formula has "revolved in full circle from containment to disengagement, then disenchantment with disengagement, and back again to containment." Containment of the Soviet Union, until internal changes would make her less threatening to the outside world, was

---

[1] To the pacifist, of course, the term has no meaning except in the total sense, but it is a perhaps unfortunate feature of contemporary world society that pacifists seldom become political leaders.

[2] Albert Schweitzer, "The Present Nuclear Crisis in the World," Statement made in the spring of 1958, distributed in the United States by the Committee for a Sane Nuclear Policy.

earlier advanced as a means of preventing (or at least limiting) conflict by resisting Communist advances at every point. Acknowledged as the author of this policy,[3] George Kennan later came to be identified with the new perspective, based on the proposition that an outbreak between the two protagonists would be less likely if their respective military forces were to be separated, no longer to face one another in close and potentially dangerous proximity in Europe. The Kennan proposals are given careful scrutiny in MacDonald's study, as are those of the Polish foreign minister Rapacki and some of the major critics of the idea such as Dean Acheson and Professor G. F. Hudson of St. Antony's College, Oxford.

1 • Memorandum on Disarmament *

Anthony Nutting

The Rt. Hon. Anthony Nutting was a Member of Parliament (1945–1956). From 1951 to 1954 he served as Parliamentary Under Secretary of State for Foreign Affairs, and between 1954 and 1956 he served as Minister of State. He resigned his posts in the Government and the House of Commons in connection with his opposition to Prime Minister Eden's handling of the Suez crisis of 1956. He has published widely, including a report of a world tour he made after his resignation, entitled I Saw for Myself: The Aftermath of Suez *(1958).*

You cannot have confidence without disarmament and you cannot have disarmament without confidence. This has long been the dilemma of all those who have sought agreement upon this most delicate and difficult of international issues. This is no new issue born of this turbulent twentieth century.

At the Congress of Vienna in 1816 Russia proposed a general reduction of armed forces by the Powers at a time when she was the only country in Europe which was still keeping its army on a war footing. Metternich commenting on this to Castlereagh said, "To take the initiative here, uncertain of a reciprocity of confidence, would be impossible (because of) the difficulty always of obtaining any true data from Russia".

Again at a conference in The Hague in 1899, the United Kingdom government "pointed out that the (disarmament) prohibitions could only be of serious value if some organization were called into existence which could secure that they be obeyed—. In fact the whole scheme depended on the action and ef-

---

[3] "The Sources of Soviet Conduct," *Foreign Affairs*, XXV (1947), 566–82.

* *Steps Toward Peace* (Bern: World Brotherhood, 1958), pp. 36–42. Reprinted by permission.

ficacy of the inspecting and restraining organization".

These quotations taken from the last century recur in almost every page of the copious records of the disarmament debates of the League of Nations and of the United Nations, showing that the basic issues of the disarmament question remain unchanged and unchangeable. What is new about the problem is the imperative and urgent need for a solution which arises from the vastly changed nature of the weapons which another major war would unleash.

It may be said by cynics that because no general disarmament agreement has been achieved and executed, therefore, no such agreement is possible. No one has endured more futile or frustrating hours of discussion of these issues than myself. Yet I say with deep conviction that the world may well be committing global suicide if it heeds this defeatist counsel.

Equally we cannot afford to fold our arms and say even with such a distinguished witness as Sir Winston Churchill that the atomic stalemate should be allowed to ride and that safety may prove to be "the sturdy child of terror". Such complacency ignores the very real danger of nuclear weapons falling into the hands of unscrupulous and irresponsible nations. And as with every day that passes scientific know-how spreads, so does this danger become more acute and the need for its elimination more urgent.

Yet the irony of the situation is that the very danger which creates the urgency of a solution also gives rise to unprecedented difficulties. For the more devastating the weapons that are to be controlled or eliminated under a disarmament program, the more essential it is for the control and inspection machinery to be fully effective. In the days of bows and arrows it would not have mattered much if a few weapons had gone unnoticed by the international inspectors. But it is a very different story with atomic bombs.

For this type of weapon, the control organ must have absolute powers of inspection and investigation and the United Nations must have adequate powers of enforcement. And it is here when dealing with inspection and enforcement that the disarmament discussions have so far always foundered upon a rock of Russian intransigence. Whether this reluctance to accept effective control is a hang-over from the Stalinist policy of letting nobody into (or out of) Soviet Russia or, as is more likely, part of traditional Russian policy dating back to the Congress of Vienna and beyond, the fact is no Soviet negotiator has yet conceded those essential provisions for inspection without which there can be no real confidence between the parties to any disarmament agreement.

If this attitude is to be broken down there must be a new approach to the disarmament question. In the course of the next six sections of this paper I propose to show how this might be done.

II

In the past few years the Western Powers have tried three different approaches to the disarmament problem. First, there was the Anglo-French plan of 1954 setting out all the disarmament that was desirable including the elimination of all nuclear weapons. Then there was the Anglo-French plan of 1956 setting out all the disarmament that was practicable, i.e. excluding the elimination of nuclear weapons on account of the impossibility of checking all stocks already accumulated. Finally there have been the various Western plans for partial disarmament or for such disarmament as might be immediately practicable notwithstanding the absence of political settlements.

Russia has finally rejected these plans as having either too much control or too little disarmament, or both. At the same time she has adopted those sections and provisions relating especially to reductions of conventional arms and armed forces as have suited her book.

Rather than dismissing these Soviet responses as pure propaganda, we should do better to examine how much policy and what kind of policy lies behind them. Such an examination will reveal two bases of Soviet thought and action: suspicion and aggressiveness.

If we are ever to overcome these two obstacles, we must put forward a plan which the Russians cannot reject or legitimately suspect. In the present conditions of Russia's newly acquired lead in the scientific race, it will not be easy to find a plan which it would be against their interests to reject and which would at the same time safeguard Western interests. The Russians when faced with a choice between policy and propaganda nearly always choose policy—as events in Hungary showed in 1956. And their policy today is to hold on to the lead that they have and to increase it in every way possible. Hence their refusal to agree to a cut-off of nuclear weapons production save in conditions which they know are quite unacceptable to the West.

The Soviets suspect—and perhaps with some justification—that the Western aim is to call a halt in the nuclear arms race while the U.S. still holds the largest quantities of stocks. Therefore, all that they have effectively offered or performed in the way of actual or immediate disarmament has been to stop tests which they have anyhow completed and to disband part of their vast military manpower which they need to step up agricultural and other productive efforts.

Yet it is not impossible to turn the Soviets away from rigid positions whether for policy or propaganda reasons, or more likely for both. It has been done before as the West found out on May 10, 1955 when the Soviet delegate in the Disarmament Conference at last abandoned the Russian insistence on a one-third reduction of all forces and an immediate abolition of all atomic weapons and accepted a number of the basic disarmament measures which the West had been insisting upon from the beginning.

It may also be possible to assuage some of the suspicions harbored by the Soviets against the West and incidentally hardened, so it appears, by the long debate in the Disarmament Sub-Committee.

III

How is the deadlock to be resolved? And who can help to resolve it?

On any impartial review of the rival disarmament proposals of the Great Powers there is a prima facie case for taking the Western position as a basis for negotiation. Yet the Soviets will seldom, if ever, accept a Western draft of any agreement, least of all of a disarmament agreement. If and when they accept Western ideas or proposals, they have nearly always done so by embodying these proposals in a document of their own with, of course, their own additions and subtractions.

In the atmosphere of suspicion which has pervaded the disarmament problem, this Soviet technique has proved no more acceptable to the West than Western proposals have been to the Soviets. Yet, when a similar situation arose during the Korean armistice talks in 1952–53, the deadlock was resolved by the intervention of a neutral party. In the event the Chinese and North Koreans were brought to accept proposals from India regarding the repatriation of prisoners of war—the main point at issue—which were almost identical to those which they had firmly rejected when put forward by the U.N. armistice negotiators.

Undoubtedly the issues of disarmament are far greater and graver than any that were discussed at Panmunjon. Yet the principle is very much the same. The Soviets, like the Chinese, are holding out against the U.N. which, they say, is a packed jury. Is it not possible that they too might respond to an Indian, or other neutral, initiative where they have refused to accept "dictation" from a U.N. majority? It is certainly worth trying out.

But if this method of working on the Soviets to break down their suspicions and to reduce their haughtiness is to work, the Western powers must agree unanimously upon several vital decisions. First, they must agree to make an act of faith. In other words, they must accept the need for concessions which, whilst not compromising their security, may inhibit their absolute superiority in the weapons field. Second, they must decide on what are the most essential and urgent requirements of a disarmament program and put forward complete, detailed and specific proposals for such a program. Having put these forward, there must be no back-pedalling such as has marred the Sub-Committee's discussions in the past.

Under this second heading there seem to be three urgent and imperative requirements. They are these: (a) nuclear disarmament designed to prevent the spread of nuclear weapons, (b) regional disengagement, coupled with conventional disarmament to reduce the danger of incidental war and (c) limitation of arms deliveries to areas of tension.

If a package deal could be worked out which would achieve these three essentials and were to be presented by India to the Soviets, the latter would find it hard to reject outright by insisting upon their own proposals. Apart from the fact that it tackles and removes the three greatest dangers facing a divided world, this program could be put into operation immediately. It would fulfill all the security requirements of the Western partial disarmament plan, and at the same time it would remove all legitimate Soviet and East European fears of a rearmed Germany and all legitimate Western and Israeli fears of a clash in the Middle East.

In a word, it would be a real start in disarmament. Unlike the restricted first-stage plans of the West or the Soviet Union, which leave all the political loose ends untied and a partially disarmed world in the same state of tension as before, such a package program would, if honorably carried out, bring with it at one and the same time a reduction of armaments and a reduction of tension. The world would be half way to those political settlements which are an essential prerequisite of the state of confidence without which no disarmament can proceed.

IV

What are the principles upon which this new approach should be drawn? Taking the disarmament measures first, the plan should be in two parts—immediate and future steps.

Among the immediate steps would be (a) cessation of nuclear tests, (b) cessation of nuclear weapons production, (c) reduction of conventional forces and armaments to the levels agreed between the powers at the Disarmament Commission in July 1956, (d) establishment of an International Control Organ with powers adequate to supervise such initial disarmament measures. The reductions in conventional forces would be global in the disarmament agreement but the global figures would have to be related to the regional reductions to be agreed under the disengagement program.

Future disarmament measures, which

would be carried out once the package program was in operation and pari passu with the conclusion of political settlements, would include the following: (a) unconditional ban on the use of nuclear weapons, (b) final reductions of conventional forces and armaments to figures agreed in principle by the Sub-Committee since May 1955 and (c), if scientifically possible, to control elimination of nuclear stocks.

The fact that several of these proposals have been submitted to the Soviets and rejected hitherto need not deter us from putting them forward again. Indeed, one of the Soviets' legitimate grievances in the Sub-Committee has been against the repeated inconsistencies of the West and the vagueness of their proposals for actual disarmament as distinct from inspection.

If the West is to meet these criticisms, the program they put forward must set out:

(1) The exact amount of disarmament, conventional and nuclear to be carried out at each stage.

(2) The precise requirements, functions and powers of the International Control Organ at each stage.

(3) A fixed maximum time limit for the fulfillment of each stage.

Various attempts have been made especially by the British and French delegations to the U.N. Disarmament Sub-Committee to work out such a detailed and specific program. But they have always fallen short of requirements, especially in regard to the question of the time limit.

It is very natural for a nation that is building up its nuclear armory to shy at specific time limits for say a cut-off of production of fissile material for weapons. But the time problem raises more Russian suspicions than any other issue, especially when we say that political settlements must also take effect as disarmament proceeds by stages. The Russians immediately conclude that the West wants to build up an international corps of inspectors to spy in the Soviet Union whilst retaining the power and the right to spin out the process of actual disarmament by refusing to make the political settlements required at each phase and by rejecting any time limit for the operation of the whole disarmament process.

Time and again I have had to answer Soviet speeches to this effect, pointing out that the need for political settlements to accompany disarmament makes fixed time limits impossible. But never have any words of reassurance proved convincing. Yet given the addition to the first phase of such tension-reducing exercises as disengagement in Central Europe and dissipation of the sinews of war in the Middle East, the prospects of broader settlements would be immensely strengthened and the practicability of operating to a fixed time limit in disarmament would be consequentially increased.

V

Passing now to the European disengagement aspects of the "package", it must be frankly admitted that here lies the most difficult and dangerous problem for the West. For one of the prime purposes of Soviet policy since 1948 has been to destroy NATO and to secure the withdrawal of American (and British) forces from continental Europe. How then can any disengagement plan which involves withdrawal of foreign forces from German territory not result in the complete achievement of Soviet aims in the West, whilst granting the Soviets a position of unchallenged supremacy?

The answer lies in the degree of great power disengagement that we are to aim at, and in the feasibility of a balanced reduction of forces and armaments in the disengaged zone. The most recent

Soviet proposals (made through the voice of Poland's Foreign Minister, Mr. Rapacki) provide only for a ban on stationing atomic weapons in Germany, Poland or Czechoslovakia. Conventional reductions are left to be dealt with later. Yet at previous stages in the disarmaments talks (May 1955 for example) the Soviets have offered "limitation and inspection of armaments in both parts of Germany and states adjacent to them". Furthermore, it is known that Poland at least among the East European states would welcome reductions in conventional as well as nuclear forces on both sides of the European divide, and has even tried to persuade the Soviet Union to agree.

There would be no difficulty in showing that a nuclear-only disengagement scheme would leave the Soviets with their overwhelming conventional forces in unrivaled mastery in Central Europe. Thus it would be only fair and reasonable for the package to insist on a scaling down of conventional forces so as to leave a balance of reduced strength on both sides.

Such an arrangement would be both safer and more practicable than one which either removes long-range rockets from shorter range firing positions or creates a demilitarized vacuum which, as recent history has taught us, immediately becomes an area of suspicion rather than confidence and an irresistible magnet for a potential aggressor.

The problem in the Middle East is in many respects similar to that of Europe. Vital Western interests are involved and the Soviets are constantly at work to undermine them and to stir up strife between Jew and Arab. A Palestine settlement would, of course, remove the Soviets' most powerful weapon. But we must assume that this is out of the question for the time being at least.

Yet without some pacification in the Middle East and without some agree-ment between the powers regarding arms supplies to this tinder-box area, no disarmament agreement would be much of a reality. It would be too much like the fire-brigade putting out the flames on the main and upper floors but leaving smouldering ashes in the basement. Britain has made it clear to Russia that she would fight to preserve her oil lifeline in the Persian Gulf. But left as it is the tension of the Middle East could flare up and the situation get beyond the control of Russia, Britain or anyone else....

I will not attempt to define the precise nature of an arms supplies agreement for the Middle East. But there should be two guiding principles. First, there should be an absolute prohibition upon the supply of atomic or nuclear weapons to any country in the Middle East. (This might even be extended to cover any country which has not at the time of signature of the package deal become a member of the nuclear club.) Second, the agreement should adopt the principle underlying the Tripartite Declaration of 1950 which laid down that the three powers (U.S., Britain and France) should observe a balance of arms supplies to Israel and her Arab neighbors and that arms delivered should not exceed quantities required for self-defense.

VI

I have, of course, assumed throughout the previous sections of this paper that all agreements included in the package and all measures of disarmament, disengagement and arms limitations shall be fully and effectively policed.

One point should be stressed. No control system could work effectively unless its officials had power to insist on the execution of the agreed disarmament measures and to order the cessation of any malpractice. Apart from this, it goes without saying that the control officials must have right of unrestricted movement and communication and the right to inspect without notice any installation producing or processing materials which could be used for war purposes.

All this demands, of course, the acceptance by the signatories of a degree of supra-national control such as has never yet been practiced between states. Yet this need not mean that, provided the Soviets could be brought to accept it (Russian reactions are considered in the next section), other states would fail to see that anything short of this would be ineffective.

The only insuperable difficulty lies in the fact that the final court for trying any wrong-doer must inevitably be the Security Council with all the frustrations of the veto that this involves. Yet, until some form of World Government can supersede the present form of world organization, there is no way out of this.

The only sanctions, therefore, which can be realistically prescribed for breaches of the disarmament agreement are (a) exposure of the culprit and (b) suspension of the disarmament measures being or about to be undertaken by the other parties until the culprit agrees to mend his ways and right the wrong he has committed.

VII

Will the Great Powers accept this new approach to disarmament?

For obvious reasons it is not possible to find any package or project which does not contain elements that one side or another finds objectionable. The Soviets will not like the disarmament proposals and the West will not like the disengagement plan and both may find, for varying reasons, undesirable features in the proposals for arms limitations in the Middle East.

But very often in international discussions the project which both sides dislike the most is the best and becomes, not infrequently and after tough bargaining, the adopted solution. The Trieste settlement of 1954 was a recent example of this.

Undoubtedly the toughest nut to crack is the Soviet attitude to international control. Even if, as Russia becomes progressively stronger in the military field, she may get less hostile to international inspectors roaming around her military establishments, she may be more than ever opposed to these same inspectors having access to atomic installations engaged on commercial development of energy. If, as seems to be the case, Russia is switching her offensive from the military to the economic field, she may fear commercial even more than military espionage. Yet no control system could be effective without the right to inspect atomic installations of all kinds whether labelled for military or peaceful purposes.

Again even if Russia one day decides she has achieved a quantitive balance of weapon stockpiles with the U.S. will she accept a cut-off of weapons production without imposing unacceptable conditions? If she does so, she must accept the type and degree of control just mentioned, and will she accept it?

There is only one answer to these questions. Try it and see. The Soviets have come a little way on paper in regard to control. Prior to 1955 they rejected the whole concept. Since then they have cautiously edged an inch or so in the right direction, by proposing control posts at certain specific points of military value and significance. Besides this, there have lately been some small but perceptible signs of a general easement and opening up of the Soviet mainland to foreigners. To push the Russians along the requisite distance to close the still yawning divide on these issues, the West must make it worth their while to overcome their traditional suspicion and frozen isolation. A package offer, designed to assuage the Russian frontier complex and to guarantee them on two very important sides of their borders peace by agreement rather than by enslavement, might seem to that archrealist, Mr. Khrushchev, good policy to accept and bad policy as well as bad propaganda to turn down. At the same time, it could prove a balance beneficial to Western interests.

One thing I know from my experience of these disarmament negotiations. With the Korean armistice, the Indo-China settlement and the Austrian Treaty, the Great Powers settled the outstanding "fringe issues". Since then they have been confronted with the "core issues" of disarmament, German reunification and European security—and now most recently the Middle East. The one-by-one approach that worked successfully at the periphery between 1951 and 1954 will not serve to obtain solutions of these issues at the center. They cannot be tackled separately and independently. For they are inseparable and indivisible. You cannot have a disarmed world until Germany is reunited, Europe made secure and the Middle East stable.

Yet to postpone any action on disarmament until solutions for all the other "core issues" have been found will not only confound an eventual disarmament agreement and compound its complexities, but will also frankly endanger world security by allowing time and opportunity for a spread of the most dangerous weapons ever devised. Hence the attempts to obtain partial disarmament by a "first-stage only" approach.

I am certain that this attempt has foundered largely because it has sought to separate disarmament from the other "core issues". Whether it be partial or full-scale disarmament it cannot be executed out of the context of the related issues of Germany, Europe and the Middle East. There must be a package deal whichever way the problem is approached.

You cannot have confidence without disarmament and you cannot have disarmament without confidence. There can be no confidence until a beginning has been made with settling all the issues which lie so heavily upon the consciences of a divided, suspicious and frightened world.

2 • Alternatives to the Arms Race *

Leo Gross

The author is Professor of International Law and Organization at the Fletcher School of Law and Diplomacy. He has served as consultant to the Legal Department of the United Nations and has written extensively on problems of international relations, with particular reference to the Security Council, the veto, and membership in the UN.

. . . .

1. CONTINUATION OF THE ARMS RACE

It may be paradoxical to include among the alternatives to the arms race its continuation. This is done for two reasons: First, the analysis of other alternatives may lead to the conclusion that none of them has any real chance of being accepted and that therefore it may be the better part of wisdom to get used to living for some time to come, at any rate, in a condition of arms race. Acceptance of this condition may require a more rational planning and the exploitation of what opportunities may arise for improving our position. Second, "peace by mutual deterrence" actually has been considered a possibility of ensuring coexistence between the free world and the Soviet bloc. Thus Sir Winston Churchill declared on March 1, 1955, that "it may well be that we shall, by a process of sublime irony, have reached a stage in this story where safety will be the sturdy child of terror, and survival the twin brother of annihilation."[1] The proposition was stated in even clearer terms on December 8, 1955, by our Secretary of State, Mr. John Foster Dulles: "The two elements I have described—on the one hand, a political warning system and, on the other hand, selective retaliatory power—constitute in combination a firm foundation for peace. If we want peace to continue, we must preserve that foundation intact."[2]

The "world-wide political warning system" consists of the multilateral and bilateral defense agreements to which the United States is a party or with which it is closely aligned.[3] As a "warning system" it seems to have failed completely in the recent Middle East outbreak of hostilies. Whether the "foundation for peace" is today as "firm" or "intact" as it appeared to be to Mr. Dulles a year ago is open to question

---

[1] *Disarmament and Security.* A Collection of Documents, 1919–1955. Subcommittee on Disarmament. 84th Congress, 2nd Session, Senate (Committee Print) 1956, p. 233.

[2] *Ibid.,* p. 236.

[3] The multilateral arrangements are: NATO, ANZUS Pact, Southeast Asia Collective Defense Treaty, the Balkan Alliance (Yugoslavia, Greece and Turkey), and the Bagdad Pact (Turkey, Iraq, Iran, and Pakistan). The bilateral arrangements are with the Philippines, Japan, the Republic of Korea, and the Republic of China on Taiwan. *Ibid.,* p. 235.

* *Proceedings of the Institute of World Affairs,* XXXII (1956), 211–23. Reprinted by permission.

in view of the rift produced by the Anglo-French action in Egypt.

In any event, it would seem that a "peace by terror" based upon a continued arms race can be at best a precarious peace. The tensions generated generally and the brush-fire wars breaking out here and there may well and perhaps unexpectedly erupt in a major conflagration. In other words, continuation of the arms race may bring about the war which it is hoped it will prevent.

But the arms race as a way to peace is also considered desirable on the ground that if it is possible to maintain the arms race for some years, there may occur in Russia a change in leadership which will make a genuine agreement possible. According to this view, we should be prepared to go "to the brink" of a disarmament agreement but avoid getting caught in one. This view, assuming as it does that time is on our side, is based upon these assumptions: "If we are prepared to continue to block off, at whatever cost, every avenue for Communist military adventure; if we can demonstrate over the next decade that the free societies and their economies can grow more rapidly than their Communist counterparts; if we can demonstrate that the national aspirations for dignity and independence can be progressively satisfied in a free world led by the United States—then the successors of the present generation of Soviet leaders may decide by the end of the coming decade that a true peace abroad and a true devotion to the welfare of the Russian peoples at home is the most attractive realist course." [4]

It would be useful to explore the validity of these assumptions. However,

apart from this and assuming for the sake of argument their validity, it is seriously doubted whether time is indeed on our side and whether at the end of a decade an effective control system can be established. The most impressive argument is that in the meantime the arms race will continue and that new weapons, particularly the ICBM (Intercontinental Ballistic Missile) will be perfected and produced in quantity. Simultaneously there will be developed and perfected installations for the delivery of such missiles. An expert opinion is to the effect that "well-camouflaged installations, conceivably for the most part underground, when completed will present the problem of detection of extremely small object sizes." The conclusion has therefore been presented that "if air reconnaissance is to prove effective as a tool for inspection, the inspection system must be in operation before intercontinental ballistic missiles are included in the Soviet inventory of weapons systems." [5] Once produced, such weapons can be "operationally deployed in such a way that we can not inspect for the weapon reliably." [6] This unfavorable situation would have to be faced until invention catches up and provides methods of detection which at the mo-

---

[4] Statement by Professor W. W. Rostow before the Subcommittee of the Committee on Foreign Relations. *Control and Reduction of Armaments*, 84th Congress, 2nd Session, p. 269.

[5] Statement by Walter J. Levison, Assistant Director of the Boston University Physics Research Laboratory, before the Subcommittee of the Committee on Foreign Relations, *Control and Reduction of Armaments*, 84th Congress, 2nd Session, p. 206. This view was endorsed by Professor Duncan E. Macdonald, member of the Scientific Advisory Board to the Chief of Staff of the United States Air Force in the field of reconnaissance and consultant to the Rand Corporation in Santa Monica. Macdonald declared that "as a physicist, I come to a conclusion based on technical arguments, which is diametrically opposed to Dr. Rostow." *Ibid.*, p. 286.

[6] Statement by Colonel Richard S. Leghorn, *ibid.*, pp. 99, 111, 116. See also statements by the Chairman of the Subcommittee, Senator Hubert H. Humphrey, *ibid.*, p. 116.

ment are presumably not yet available.[7] The conclusion then appears inevitable that time is not necessarily on our side and that the recommended continuation of the current arms race for another decade may indeed make it difficult or even impossible to devise a reliable inspection system.

Other factors creating new problems which will have to be faced in the decade ahead have been formulated as follows:

First, because of short reaction time for decision, the sense of responsibility, the degree of intelligence, the extent of counsel, and the number of checks and balances required for thoughtful decision must continually degenerate.

Second, because with time, technological advances of any nation become also accomplished by many other nations, irresponsibility within third parties must become of ever-increasing concern.

Third, the size of the total force base complex becomes ever smaller. With underground missile installations, the problem of search may well become analogous to the location of manhole covers, camouflaged at that. The problem, I daresay, is exceedingly difficult, even if restricted to a limited area.[8]

These are weighty arguments deserving of intense thought. Whatever the outcome of analysis and evaluation may be, it appears from the various arguments presented above that "peace by deterrence" rests indeed on very precarious foundations and that, moreover, a policy of walking to the brink of an agreement for control and reduction of

armaments may well cause us to miss the opportunity for establishing such control in the future. Therefore, other alternatives to the current arms race must be considered.

2. World Government or Limited World Government

One of the current proposals to stop the arms race and generally to establish conditions of stable peace comes from the World Federalists and their sympathizers. According to this view, no substantial progress toward world peace can be made except through a radical transformation of the existing system of international relations, based upon the coexistence and competition of a large number of states. It is in this respect that this alternative differs from all others which seek means of establishing a security, or at least a "no-war," community within the present state system. There is not merely a difference in degree, but a qualitative difference. Under almost any scheme of world government the constituent members would be deprived at once or gradually of all their armaments not needed for internal police purposes. At the same time, a monopoly of arms would be vested in the central world authority. Whether or not this arms monopoly would include nuclear or thermonuclear weapons would be of secondary importance since a monopoly would bring to an end the competition between constituent members. A world authority would not necessarily prevent all outbreaks of hostilities, which would be in the nature of revolutions against the central authority. As long as the arms monopoly were preserved such revolutions would be fought with conventional weapons. In other words, political integration even in the form of a world state would not necessarily create a dependable security community. It would, however, come

---

[7] See statement by Admiral Lewis L. Strauss, Chairman, United States Atomic Energy Commission, *ibid.*, p. 131. Admiral Strauss declared: "None of the physical principles we now know lead to that hope, but with so many people engaged on it, with so great an incentive, it would certainly be folly to say that it will not happen." *Ibid.*, p. 119.

[8] Statement by Professor Duncan E. Macdonald, before the Subcommittee of the Committee on Foreign Relations, *Control and Reduction of Armaments*, 84th Congress, 2nd Session, p. 287.

very close to this ideal the more it developed the techniques and the will to anticipate revolution by promoting necessary adjustments.

There is no need to dwell longer on the desirability of this alternative since obviously it is very attractive, but it is submitted that it is not realistic. In estimating realistically the feasibilty of world government schemes, it is necessary to consider the following facts:

(1) The low level of integration of the international community.
(2) The consequential absence of an international legal order even approximating the strength of most municipal orders.
(3) The limited area of general consensus as distinct from the area of conflict and misunderstanding between peoples.
(4) The vast unevenness of development among them as regards standards of life, cultural inheritance, internal political structure, and external power.[9]

In the light of these factors, it is difficult not to agree with the proposition that "the political realities of present international life rule out" any such far-reaching scheme. It has been noted that "the un-integrated, conflict-dominated international community, with its weak law and starkly unequal membership, gravitating around the poles of the two hostile great powers most advanced in the atomic fields, is the worst possible setting for any such plan."[10] ...

3. ORGANIZATION OF PEACE

During the interwar period the French government proposed to solve the problem of the limitation and reduction of armaments by the "organization of peace." This involved, in the first place, a guarantee against aggression and a foolproof system for the obligatory settlement of all disputes. In a system of security and arbitration, disarmament becomes both possible and necessary.

This approach still has some validity. In addition to security and peaceful settlement of disputes, there is proposed today the development of underdeveloped areas. It is also urged that for the functioning of the security scheme, the United Nations needs to be strengthened and that this could be achieved by the implementation of Article 43 of the Charter of the United Nations. It is perhaps useful to recall that under Article 43 the Members of the United Nations "undertake to make available to the Security Council, on its call and in accordance with a special agreement or agreements, armed forces, assistance, and facilities, including the rights of passage, necessary for the purpose of maintaining international peace and security." Article 45 extends this obligation to national air-force contingents to be used for combined international enforcement action. It may be noted in passing that the emergency force which has recently been constituted by the United Nations for service in Egypt was not constituted in fulfillment of this obligation as laid down in the Charter.

A comprehensive agreement for control, limitation, and reduction of armaments and armed forces would be an essential component part of the "organization of peace" indicated above. It has been proposed, though not necessarily as part of the above scheme, that outstanding political conflicts would require settlement either prior to or contemporaneously with a plan for disarmament. Thus, the United States memorandum, submitted to the subcommittee of the Disarmament Commission on May 3, 1956, contains the following paragraph:

"Comprehensive disarmament and drastic reductions can only be carried out safely as parallel progress is made in the solution of important political issues in the world,

---

[9] Julius Stone, *Legal Controls of International Conflict* (1954), p. 345.

[10] *Ibid.*, p. 346.

as otherwise the dangers of war would be increased." [11]

Among the political issues are Korea, Indo-China, Malaya, Asia, Austria, a broader European community, a free and united Germany, and full independence for the Eastern European nations.[12] Since President Eisenhower listed these eight issues on April 16, 1953, the Austrian question has been settled, and so has, in some measure at least, the question of Indo-China. The list has thus been reduced from eight to six, but little progress, if any, has been achieved since 1953 in the solution of any of these pending problems.

The "organization of peace" outlined above would, no doubt, strengthen the international community. That it has not yet been achieved is probably due to the reluctance of most states to accept the obligations implied in the scheme. Less than half of the total membership of the United Nations has accepted the compulsory jurisdiction of the International Court of Justice. And those who did accept it attached to their acceptance far-reaching and crippling reservations. The United States is one of these states. It seems rather obvious that if governments are to renounce the use of force for the settlement of disputes, reliable alternative measures must be accepted without any mental or other reservation. As the ... crisis over the Suez Canal demonstrates, it is simply intolerable to allow unilateral changes affecting vital interests of other states. The simple method of diplomatic negotiations is a useful but not a dependable tool of diplomacy. Some other means must be found, such as arbitration or adjudication, in order to assure a settlement of international disputes on the basis of law and justice.

It is also useful to recall that the United Nations Charter does not guarantee the security of its members. Again, the present conflict in the Middle East is largely due to the refusal of the Arab states to accept the fact of Israel's existence and the unwillingness or inability of the United Nations to bring about a change in this attitude.

The United Nations has realized the importance of economic assistance to underdeveloped countries. This matter is deemed so important that it has been offered by some as an alternative to an agreement on disarmament.[13] The governments of the United States, France, and Great Britain have indicated from time to time that as a limitation and reduction of armaments is achieved, the resultant economies could and would be devoted to a massive attack on poverty and disease and low standards of living.

On the whole, the "organization of peace" method offers an alternative to the arms race, but it too much presupposes a degree of mutual trust and cooperation, the absence of which is the cause of the arms race itself.

4. Ban on Testing of Weapons

As a means of strengthening mutual trust, various governments proposed the discontinuation of the testing of H-bombs and other weapons of mass destruction. It has also been urged that the fall-out and other by-products of testing might conceivably be injurious to human health in one form or another.

It would seem arguable that agreement on banning further tests would be tantamount to a standstill agreement on the development of certain new nuclear devices. It has therefore to be related to what has been said initially about the characteristics of the current arms

---

[11] U.N. Doc. DC/SC, 1/45.

[12] U.N. Doc. DC/SC, 1/48, p. 12.

[13] Barton Leach, Statement before the Subcommittee of the Committee on Foreign Relations, *Control and Reduction of Armaments,* 84th Congress, 2nd Session, p. 25.

race. One of these characteristics has been described as "invention, development, and production." Inasmuch as testing is an essential stage in the development and production of new weapons and weapons systems, the decision to stop testing would be virtually a decision to arrest the development of weapons and weapons systems at their present stage.

The point has also been made that even a ban on tests would require a control and inspection. Therefore it would run into the same sort of difficulties which have so far prevented agreement on control and inspection with respect to proposals for the reduction of armaments and armed forces.

Of particular significance would be an agreement to discontinue tests of intercontinental ballistic missiles or not to undertake such tests at all if they have not already been started. In view of the peculiar difficulties which this particular type of missile provides at an advanced stage of perfection, it would seem to be imperative to consider this particular weapon as a matter of great urgency. On the other hand, it may be extremely difficult to single out this weapon for such agreement in view of the fact that it is considered by certain of the powers as essential to their defense against other forms of attack.

. . . .

It would seem obvious that no step along disarmament lines can ever be taken without some risks. It would also seem idle to expect that advantages or disadvantages resulting from any one step will be equally distributed among the participating states. The essential point is that no state should be placed at a serious disadvantage. While the discussion on the banning of tests has not yet furnished clear evidence that it would be disadvantageous to the major powers, it is probably too early to consider taking such a step in isolation from other parts of a disarmament program. It may very well contribute to building up confidence and thus pave the way toward further progress. But this depends upon the more fundamental decision which the major powers would have to take, namely, whether and on what foundation they intend to pursue the wider program of disarmament. In the meantime, all the interested states run the risk that in this secret race one of them will achieve a substantial advance that will put the rest of them at a disadvantage. This, in turn, will impede progress until those nations have caught up with the advance of the other.

5. OPEN SKIES AND EXCHANGE OF MILITARY BLUEPRINTS

At the Geneva Conference of the heads of governments, President Eisenhower proposed on July 21, 1955, two steps toward development of mutual confidence. One step has come to be known as the "open skies" proposal, and the other was concerned with the exchange of "complete blueprints of our military establishment, from beginning to end, from one end of our countries to the other." As subsequently expounded, the term "blueprint of military establishments" was to be understood as "consisting of the identification, strength, command structure, and disposition of personnel, units and equipment of all major land, sea, and air forces, including organized reserves and para-military; and a complete list of military plans, facilities, and installations with their locations." The exchange of blueprints would take place in phases and each phase would have to be completely verified by each side before progressing to a subsequent phase. To meet a Soviet objection, the United States was prepared to include in this exchange of blueprints military installations maintained in the United States' bases abroad.

The means for verification of blueprints of military establishments are to include ground observers originally proposed by the Soviet Union at the Geneva Conference. The U. S. proposed that on-the-spot observers are to be posted "with operating land, sea, and air forces, at their supporting installations, and at key locations as necessary for the verification, continued observation, and the reporting of each category of information. The number and location of observers will be as mutually agreed upon prior to the exchange of information, and provisions will be made of changes in the location should the initial arrangements prove to be inadequate." The open skies proposal was defined as air reconnaissance to be "conducted by each inspecting country on an unrestricted, but monitored, basis to augment the efforts of the posted observers. Each inspecting country will utilize its own aircraft and related equipment. Liaison personnel of the country being inspected will be aboard each reconnaissance aircraft during allover flights." [14]

So far no agreement has been reached on either the open skies proposal or the exchange of military blueprints, or on the ground observers....

6. REDUCTION OF ARMED FORCES AND ARMAMENTS AND PROHIBITION OF THE USE OF NUCLEAR WEAPONS

During the past few years various proposals were made and agreed to in principle for a "balanced reduction" of armed forces of the major powers. There also seems to be agreement that at some stage the use of atomic weapons should

[14] Outlined plan for the implementation of the July 21, 1955, presidential proposal at Geneva regarding disarmament, August 13, 1955. Disarmament and Security, *op. cit.,* pp. 341, 342.

be prohibited and perhaps even stocks of such weapons destroyed.

Agreement on any one or all of these major programs would effectively reduce tension and limit the arms race. The reason no agreement has been reached lies largely in the realm of the extent and stringency of control measures rather than in disagreement on figures or amounts. There always seems to exist a rather basic disagreement as to the phasing of the different parts of the program. One need not search far for the reasons for failure. It is the absence of mutual confidence and certainly the absence of conviction that any plan advanced by one group of states is equally beneficial to the other. Neither side dares take the risks, and without taking risks, the deadlock can not be broken. One need not go so far as to say that if there were mutual trust and confidence there would be no need for the limitation and reduction of armaments. On the other hand, without some preliminary trust and confidence, it has been impossible to move ahead. Recent events in the Middle East and in Hungary may well cause a major setback in the efforts to stop the arms race. On the other hand, these events, and particularly those in the Middle East, have demonstrated the precariousness of the existing condition. It will be interesting to watch what conclusions are drawn by the major powers from these events.

The question may well be asked whether there is any merit at all in continuing discussions on ways and means to stop the arms race. One compelling reason on both sides seems to be the desire to demonstrate one's devotion to peace, and disarmament has come to be accepted as a road to peace. From a cynical point of view it might appear that both East and West have walked to the brink of disarmament, and that they have acquired a certain technique in this exercise. Certainly the discussions held over the last ten years have clarified a good many points and have dispelled a good many illusions. It may well be that in the second decade of these negotiations there will be greater realism, less brinkmanship, and a keener desire to think in terms of a possibly obtainable minimum rather than in terms of an unobtainable maximum. It may also be helpful to realize that not all problems of international relations are soluble. Some problems lend themselves best to being left alone for the time while more fruitful avenues of cooperation are explored. It may yet be impossible to reach an agreement on the unification of Germany, but it is surely not beyond the realm of the possible to achieve an acceptable settlement, if not a solution, in the Middle East. If the general overall distribution of power in terms of territorial influence among the great powers can not be changed in the foreseeable future, it may be both wise and realistic to accept the existing distribution as a fact.

3 • Disengagement Reconsidered *

H. I. MacDonald

The author is Lecturer in the Department of Political Economy and Dean of Men, University College, University of Toronto. He is a member of the Candian Institute for International Affairs and chairman of the Toronto Men's Branch study group on Canadian-American relations.

The recent crisis in Berlin has raised once more the central problem of "disengagement" in Europe and has suggested that perhaps some such plan will provide the only permanent solution in that danger zone. My purpose in this article is to explore the earlier suggestions and to consider their possibilities.

As the Soviet Sputnik bleeped its way about the earth in the autumn of 1957, the BBC was transmitting a Western reply to the Russian diplomatic challenge in the form of the Reith Lectures, delivered by George F. Kennan in November and December, 1957, and later published as a book entitled *Russia, the Atom, and the West*. His proposal was simple in essence but complicated in form: there should be a measure of disengagement in central Europe as a first step in easing the world tension created by a lasting "cold war."

"Disengagement" was in no sense the child of Kennan for it has long been advocated by both Sir Anthony Eden and Mr. Hugh Gaitskell; however, it now became a convenient label for a possible reversal in the Western policy of "containment." In recent months, the controversy has revolved in full circle from containment to disengagement, then disenchantment with disengagement, and back again to containment. The more primitive terms such as "buffer state," "cordon sanitaire," "no man's

* *International Journal*, XIV (1958/59), 21–32. Reprinted by permission.

land," and "neutral zone" have become mere linear forbearers of the more sophisticated terminology now in popular currency.

An unusual conjunction of circumstances conspired in late 1957 to produce this spirited controversy. In the first place, students of international affairs were surprised, perhaps even stunned, to hear Kennan propose the withdrawal of forces that disengagement would involve, for he, as "Mr. X," had produced that significant article in *Foreign Affairs,* July, 1947, "The Sources of Soviet Conduct" advocating "containment," and was considered the main author of the Truman Administration's foreign policy. Secondly, the Russians were riding the crest of a great propaganda triumph with the launching of the Sputnik and the ICBM which at once appeared to dwarf the relative importance of conventional weapons and to undo the strategic advantage of "massive retaliation" by the West. Thirdly, the Kennan doctrine immediately preceded the meeting last December of the NATO heads of government who could scarcely ignore the implied challenge of disengagement in Europe to the whole institution of NATO. And finally, the wide audience that any Reith Lectures command assured much public attention and pressure for full consideration of Kennan's proposals.

That they are simple in essence but complicated in form is apparent in the Reith Lectures but not without a twofold justification. Kennan was not at all concerned to recommend his "reflections to government as a finished programme for action." To use his own words, "What I have tried to suggest here is not what governments should do, but what they should think about." Moreover, his perspective is wider than Europe alone for he has attempted to pinpoint our place in the evolution of world history and to ask fundamental

questions about our future course. Revealing his burning concern, he asks:

"Are we to flee like haunted creatures from one defensive device to another, each more costly and humiliating than the one before, cowering underground one day, breaking up our cities the next, attempting to surround ourselves with elaborate electronic shields the third, concerned only to prolong the length of our lives while sacrificing all the values for which it might be worthwhile to live at all?"

Lord Keynes reminded us that in the long-run, we are all dead; George Kennan is more concerned to ensure that in the long-run some of us may still be alive. To be concerned with new vistas for guaranteeing peace is vastly different from being a pacifist, or even an isolationist. Such accusations against Kennan are clearly unwarranted. Kennan himself insists that "force is, and always will be, an indispensable ingredient in human affairs."

However, for Kennan the conditions have changed under which the threat of force is reasonable in an age where the Damocles' sword of thermonuclear destruction hangs over the world. This becomes clear if we recall Kennan's attitude in his July, 1947, article where he stated:

"...it will be clearly seen that the Soviet pressure against the free institutions of the Western world is something that can be contained by the adroit and vigilant application of counterforces at a series of constantly shifting geographical and political points, corresponding to the shifts and manoeuvres of Soviet policy but which cannot be charmed or talked out of existence. The Russians look forward to a duel of infinite duration, and they see that already they have scored great successes."

Now, we cannot exaggerate the changes since 1947 which have contributed to Kennan's own reversal of opinion. Stalin is dead: Khrushchev has become the master planner of Soviet strategy and diplomacy. Russian policy in turn has become more a game of chess than checkers and the stakes have broadened to include the whole Afro-Asian community of "uncommitted nations." Of even greater importance, the basic assumptions underlying the policy of "containment" have radically altered.

The West had assumed quite readily that danger of war existed almost entirely in the form of Soviet military aggression. However, the uprising in Hungary in 1956 more than disproved this notion as it became apparent that a real threat of warfare was latent in areas of intense nationalist pressure. This threat has become strikingly evident even more recently in Iraq, Jordan, Lebanon and the entire Middle East Area.

Secondly, the equalizing of thermonuclear power between the United States and the U.S.S.R., and the Soviet ability to employ "massive retaliation" on its own part, meant that the United States might not necessarily resort to massive retaliation if confronted by an act of aggression. In fact, the United States was now compelled to recognize a real possibility of being involved in limited war with or without resort to nuclear weapons. Moreover the more nations with access to nuclear weapons, particularly in the danger areas, the greater the danger of war.

These changes drove Kennan to focus his attention on the danger zones with the inevitable conclusion, for him, that the problem was no longer how to contain but how to withdraw. For us, however, the criterion of the validity of his judgment must be: will withdrawal hasten or deter military aggression that might lead to wider conflict, particularly in Germany? If the greatest danger of general war comes from the uncontrollable extension of a local conflict (whether that conflict arises by design or accident) will disengagement reduce the possibility of conflict between the United States and U.S.S.R. by separating their forces, or invite certain participation by opening the door for war between or within European nations?

These questions are hard to answer. The outcome will depend entirely on the extent and form of disengagement. Any conclusion cannot be considered apart from the results that will be produced in terms of nationalist sentiment in the nations of the disengaged zone. Also disengagement is considered by most of its authors and critics alike as part and parcel of wider agreements on disarmament that might follow but which would contribute to an alteration of the very assumptions upon which disengagement relied. Under certain strict conditions, then, disengagement might answer all the objections of the critics: under other conditions it might invite certain disaster. For example on the assumption that a Soviet military attack would invite limited nuclear reprisal from the West, might this not act as a starting point or catalyst for wider nuclear conflict?

Finally, much confusion, and even some of the misunderstanding between opposing nations, is produced by the dubious jargon that has become characteristic of international affairs: "massive retaliation," "graduated deterrents," "limited war," "tactical and strategic nuclear weapons," mean many things to many men. As Hugh Gaitskell has commented in a brilliant and subtle analysis in *Foreign Affairs,* the disengagement which he and Eden advocated for Europe was a different fish from the disengagement of Kennan or Rapacki. All plans call for disengagement but some suggest more than others.

I

Of the various disengagement proposals, the Kennan plan is the most far-reaching. On the assumption that the

Communist danger in Europe is more political than military, Kennan has advocated mutual withdrawal of American, British, and Canadian as well as Russian forces from a defined area of central Europe, an area which he alternately defines as East and West Germany, "the heart of Europe," and even the Continent. His plan presupposes that the countries involved, and certainly Germany, will be obliged to remain neutral and be limited to non-nuclear weapons, but will remain free politically, and be entitled to enter non-military arrangements internationally. Continuing frontier problems would be settled by treaty with the frontiers guaranteed by both sides. The result would be a militarily neutral, but politically free zone across Europe instead of the present Elbe frontier.

There would be local forces—a form of Home Guard—for defence which Kennan suggests might better be "paramilitary ones, of a territorial militia type, somewhat on the Swiss example, rather than the regular military units on the pattern of the second World War. Their functions should be primarily internal rather than external."

Kennan is careful to emphasize that the nuclear deterrent is not to be given up unilaterally nor is NATO to be abandoned. In fact, the military dispositions of NATO would be used as a bargaining device toward the wider goal of disarmament. In his own words,

"... the piecemeal removal, by negotiation and compromise, of the major sources of the military danger, particularly the abnormal situation now prevailing in Central and Eastern Europe, and the gradual achievement of a state of affairs in which the political competition could take its course without the constant threat of a general war ... should be the true end of NATO."

Of course, the immediate removal of Germany from NATO would raise some doubt about the future of the organization. Largely, this depends upon the extent and location of missile bases, a problem which we must consider shortly. At least, the whole basis of the western alliance would undoubtedly undergo fundamental alteration, even without the demise of NATO. Long ago Edmund Burke warned: "When bad men combine, the good must associate"; certainly, NATO has always stood for Western solidarity in opposition to the Soviet threat. Yet Kennan insists that the association would still exist; the form and purpose would perhaps be altered.

The problem of Germany stands out like a Cleopatra's Needle in the Kennan disengagement proposal. Kennan firmly favours the neutralization of Germany as a preliminary step to German reunification not only for its intrinsic merits but also for the prestige of the entire West. Present-day Germany is more, however, than a house divided; it has become virtually a pair of semi-detached houses. How the reunification and reconstruction into one house is to proceed without the danger of civil war is a vexed question but one which by its very nature demands prior consideration. Regrettably, Kennan and other exponents of disengagement have avoided this challenge.

Certainly, the West has had no monopoly on disengagement proposals. It was a welcome sign when the Polish Foreign Minister, Mr. Rapacki, set forth his plan to prohibit the stationing or production of all nuclear weapons on the territory of East and West Germany, Poland, and Czechoslovakia combined with limitation of conventional weapons in the same area. His plan had the twin merits of greater specificity and wider geographical application, but from the Western point of view it was hopelessly inadequate for NATO would be obliged to withdraw its nuclear weapons and still meet the conventional forces of the Soviet Union in Eastern Europe. Then it was clear that West Germany, although forbidden the possession of or access to nuclear weapons, would have made no further progress toward re-unification. Furthermore, such a plan was immediately beset by all the difficulties inherent in any general plan of nuclear disarmament—the problem of international inspection and guarantee. The great feature, on the other hand, for the Western viewer was the progress that would have been made toward eventual withdrawal of Soviet forces and influence from Eastern Europe.

If the Rapacki plan was doomed from the beginning as a serious proposition for Western consideration, the more general proposal for disengagement has attracted serious attention. Now it is difficult to assess whether the proposal is even more timely or actually *passé*. And although Mr. Gaitskell fairly protests that all degrees of disengagement have become targets for "Mr. Acheson's blunderbuss," certainly the Kennan thesis is the principal target for the critics.

II

True to his colours, Mr. Acheson has been Kennan's counterfoil as the spokesman of continued realpolitik. Yet much of their dispute appears to turn on the question of timing. We have noted Kennan's constant concern for the long-run, that his disengagement proposal is merely a portion of a wider programme leading to disarmament, and his concern for other aspects of American foreign policy such as the attitude to the new Afro-Asian nations. Kennan staunchly believes that the West must show positive initiative in defrosting the cold war, even although his guarantee of success is often no stronger than his now famous "personal assurance" that

any country which is in a position to make such a proposal to Moscow "... will have little need of foreign garrisons to assure its immunity from Soviet attack."

For Acheson, on the other hand, until the U.S.S.R. displays some significant change in outlook, disengagement can only be a concept and never a reality. He clearly sees no change in attitude at this time. In *Foreign Affairs*, April, 1958, Mr. Acheson may appear to have closed the door irrevocably on disengagement when he gloomily insists (and here we can almost hear the intonation): "For us, there is only one disengagement possible—the final one, the disengagement from life, which is death." His readiness, however, to consider disengagement as a possible eventual alternative becomes evident in his recent book, *Power and Diplomacy*, where he concludes:

"A further process of evolution is necessary both within the Soviet Union and Eastern Europe, before a change to more complete national identity in the latter can take place without erupting into a violence which might engulf the world. When that evolution occurs, Russian and American troop withdrawals may be possible without destroying the basis of American association in the security of Europe."

On the assumption then that little has changed, and where there have been changes, they have not been for the better, Mr. Acheson asks how can we possibly disengage when there is still the DEW Line and immediate thermonuclear contact throughout the world? "There is confrontation in every part of the world where the area of the open and free world system may be reduced by Soviet military, economic, and political penetration." Whether we accept the optimistic view that such nuclear confrontation or the "balance of terror" in Churchill's phrase will render a general conflict unlikely, or the unpleasant prospect that such confrontation will inevitably lead to a thermonuclear war, we cannot, in the opinion of Mr. Acheson, disengage from such a situation.

To what advantage then a disengagement in Europe? Mr. Acheson feels that we could not expect a Soviet withdrawal from Eastern Europe. Indeed it is difficult to accept the logic of Kennan's conclusion that the communist danger in Europe is political and not military considering the tragedy of Hungary. Furthermore, he [Acheson] feels that after the withdrawal we could not impose on Germany the conditions that we would consider necessary for the success of the plan. In fact, once out of NATO, Germany would soon drift into the Soviet sphere of influence. This would be a double disaster for Mr. Acheson considers that Europe is far from losing its vital significance in international diplomacy. In fact, it is crucial that the West should retain Europe as a sphere of influence just as it must retain its foothold in the Middle East. After a decade of struggle, Mr. Acheson feels that America is about to see a return of Western European power as "a common currency and political community are on the way."

Such strength would exercise a great pull on Eastern Europe and provide real vigour for a negotiated reduction in forces throughout the world. There is his persistent refrain that once this supremacy is attained, then will the time have arrived to force the hand of the Soviet Union—a doctrine of the diplomacy of power at the bargaining table. Mr. Acheson describes his goal in the following words: "The longer-range purpose would be to develop adequate conventional forces in Europe, with British and American participation, to make mutually desirable a real reduction and equalization of both Soviet and NATO forces, and a controlled elimination of nuclear material for military use." Presumably at that future time Acheson would agree to a beginning of disengagement, for then the power to state the terms of agreement would lie with the West while the advantage of survival would oblige the Russians to accept. For Acheson, conclusive bargaining must only take place from a position of Western superiority but never in a situation of equality.

Meanwhile, the sheer confrontation of the two leviathans in the centre of Europe will forestall any decisive move. Unlike those who regard critical zones as more likely to produce wars, Mr. Acheson feels that the danger cannot possibly be worse since the United States and U.S.S.R. can never be totally separate. "Geography has been annihilated by science." And since official American policy, if Mr. Dulles' remarks in his article of October, 1957, in *Foreign Affairs* are symptomatic, is to accept the possibility of limited war, even limited nuclear war, in such an area, then conflict might actually be confined to local areas instead of being waged on a global scale. Mr. Dulles suggests: "In the future it may thus be possible to place less reliance upon deterrence of vast retaliatory power. It may be possible to defend countries by nuclear weapons so mobile, or so placed, as to make military invasion with conventional forces a hazardous attempt."

Such bluntness, of course, was cold comfort to European opinion. Was America then prepared to transfer the risk of nuclear war from her own continent to Europe so readily? In fact, this point of view was not confined to American opinion alone for Professor George Hudson of Oxford University was appalled at the thought of American withdrawal across a three-thousand-mile ocean compared with an overnight train journey for the Soviet Union. On the other hand, Mr. Kennan would protest in his own words that "armaments are important not just for what could be done with them in time of war, but for the psychological shadows they cast in time of peace." And for Kennan, the only psychological shadows cast by NATO military forces in time of peace are the shadows of the thermonuclear war. And so, long-range missiles and the threat of their use would still be as effective if based in America as in Europe.

Here, Professor Hudson counters that the real possibility that missiles would indeed be called into use is gravely enhanced by withdrawal from Europe for we need only recall Korea. Hudson reminds us: "Within a year of this disengagement (in Korea), North Korea attacked South Korea: the sequel was a three-year war involving eighteen nations, costing more than a million casualties and ending in a military stalemate along a battlefront close to the original zone boundary."

Against this view, Mr. Denis Healey, British Labour MP, has commented in the *New Republic*: "What invited Communist aggression in Korea was not the withdrawal of troops in itself, but America's failure to make it clear that she would intervene if aggression did take place." And it is true that both General MacArthur and Secretary Acheson had stated publicly in early 1950 that America had no strategic interest in Korea.

For this reason Mr. Healey in his plan for disengagement insists that NATO must keep a military foothold in Europe both as a political pledge of its concern for the integrity of the disengaged zone and as a base for military sanctions short of global war if that integrity is challenged. This would entail military neutralization of the countries from which forces were withdrawn but military bases and tactical nuclear weapons would still be maintained in France and the Low Countries, or at least in the United Kingdom.

Mr. Healey was reinforced by Mr. Richard Lowenthal in his insistence that the presence, within range, of Anglo-American bombers or missile bases pledged and equipped to retaliate against any serious Russian aggression must be a necessary feature of any disengagement plan. Further, he adds, the signficant point toward which the West has too often adopted an ostrich-like attitude [is] that Russia is already the dominant land power in Europe, and no foreseeable efforts on the part of NATO can change that. Provided that local conventional forces capable of temporary resistance are maintained in the neutral countries, then the danger to those countries is no greater.

If this is true, then, at this point the Hudson and Healey arguments come very closely together indeed. In fact, it is all too apparent by what slim threads most of these disputes hang provided there is general agreement about basic assumptions. That there is such agreement between exponents and critics of disengagement alike is the view of Mr. Gaitskell. Both sides acknowledge the need to preserve some deterrent, agree that the maintenance of NATO is essential, accept the necessity for American and British forces remaining upon the continent of Europe, and insist upon the deterrent value of thermonuclear weapons.

III

Now that we have brought the planners and the critics face to face, what remains of the disengagement proposals and what will be their role in future negotiations? This is largely a question of the emphasis that is placed on the conflicting opinions. On the one hand, the threat of nuclear war (even on a limited basis) is increased by disengagement because the only alternative would be use of nuclear weapons by the West should the Russians violate the neutral zone in the manner of Korea.

On the other hand, any form of disarmament to reduce the threat of global conflict can only start in Healey's words "by a pilot scheme in the limitation, inspection and control of armaments in an area where Russia and America have a common interest in co-operation rather than conflict." And as Kennan has suggested the ideal case would appear to be central Europe because the development of long-range striking power has removed the indispensability of central Europe to the security of either Russia or America. It is, moreover, crucial that we find some method leading to wider disarmament for Mr. Acheson himself has demonstrated that the wide degree of confrontation that already exists on a global basis implies a daily danger of a thermonuclear war. In fact, we have come to accept that war will assume this form. If this were not the case, then it is curious that we have neglected the obvious remedy of building up NATO's local military forces, particularly in their capacity for a conventional defence. In terms of conventional weapons, however, we have scarcely provided a strong "container" in Western Europe.

Under such conditions, Mr. Kennan has urged us to consider NATO's real strength which

"does not lie in the paper undertakings which underpin it: it lies—and will continue in any circumstances to lie—in the appreciation of the member nations for the identity of their real interests, as members of the Western spiritual and cultural community. If this appreciation is there, NATO will not be weaker as a political reality, because it may be supplemented or replaced by other arrangements so far as Germany is concerned."

Kennan's real hope is that all who have a concern with Western policy and diplomacy are not so numbed by the cold war that they have lost all imagination.

Any future plans for disengagement must, however, recognize that if the stumbling block to the present proposals has been a lack of imagination, flexibility and foresight in Western thinking and an adherence to negative and anachronistic doctrine, there is good reason for such behaviour. It is no easy task to be decisive about the real sources of disagreement—the question of the proper timing of the proposals, methods for avoiding civil war or nationalist upheaval in the neutral zone, estimations of Soviet intentions, and the assumptions that can be made about massive retaliation and deterrence. If we are truly in a nuclear stalemate, then it is certainly time to devise new rules for the game, or even to start a new game. If we are not in a stalemate, and there is a genuine possibility that the next move might lead to thermonuclear war, then there is ample reason for caution. The difficulty is that the status quo itself is only a short-run concept constantly subject to alteration, and our attempt to match policy to the status quo is much like a dog chasing its tail; for example, the Middle East crisis threw much of the disengagement debate out of focus. The nerve-wracking element of the status quo being a moving concept appears when we attempt to guess what it may be when the new policy comes into effect.

We would perhaps all agree after a thorough examination of the arguments that the outcome of disagreement in terms of our criterion—will it increase or decrease the threat of war?—is largely indeterminate. Far more important, on the other hand, is the hope that an attempt at disengagement would indicate Western initiative in terms of disarmament and a new, non-military approach, to the U.S.S.R. This most certainly weighs more heavily in Kennan's balance than any number of actual disengagement proposals, for it might be a way of avoiding Denis Healey's warning that "the discovery of atomic power may prove to be not a milestone, but a gravestone."

XX · Collective Security

Few serious and widely-acclaimed theories of international relations have proved as difficult to translate into actual practice as that of "collective security." In simplest terms, this concept of achieving peace by cooperative means is as clear as it is appealing: all for one, and one for all. Proponents argue that the best—and, indeed, in an age of blitzkrieg and mass destruction warfare the *only*—way in which independent peace-loving nations can achieve any degree of real security is by pooling their strength with that of others, so as to be able to put down any disturber of the peace who may attack one of them. Indeed, the theory maintains, any potential aggressor will desist from his evil plan when confronted with the certainty of a strong coalition against him.

Without some such arrangement, there is nothing to prevent a well-prepared aggressor from picking off his victims one by one until it is too late for the remaining peaceful states to save themselves. It was in this way that Hitler was able to conquer most of Europe, and Japan much of the Far East, before Britain, Russia, China, and the United States pieced together the alliance which eventually won the war. Out of this experience came the most elaborate collective security system yet devised—the United Nations. The Charter, as Henri Bonnet points out, represents recognition by most statesmen of the postwar world of the necessity of a collective approach to the problems of international peace and security.

Although it is one of the predominant contemporary theories of international relations, the concept of collective security is not a new one. In ancient Greece, the Amphyctionic League was based on the principle, just as was the abortive "Grand Design" prepared by the Duc de Sully for Henry IV of France. It underlay the Holy Alliance and the Concert of Europe in their efforts to preserve the status quo in continental and world politics. In this century, it has been incorporated into the League of Nations Covenant (to which Hitler did not adhere), in several articles carefully defined at the heart of the Charter of the United Nations, and in vital provisions of regional pacts such as SEATO, NATO, OAS, and CENTO.

In theory, collective security has three characteristics:

a) it should be *universal* in scope, i.e., everybody (at least the Great Powers) must be in the system;

b) it should be essentially *automatic* in its operation, so that prescribed enforcement measures may be put into effect immediately;

c) there should be no exceptions, i.e. it should be *absolute* in its demands that every participant come at once to the assistance of any member under attack.

The theory also rests upon a number of assumptions, the chief of which are that all the members of the system share the same or at least compatible values, and that a threat to the peace will be instantly and universally recognized. In practice, however, the assumption that all the participants have compatible values (and can therefore agree on the application of their mutually-accepted principles) often does not accord with the facts of life. Recently, there has even been failure in a United Nations committee to find agreement on the term "aggression," the definition of which is the very basis for action under a collective security arrangement. Furthermore, instead of being *required* to act in specified circumstances, the Great Powers are empowered by the veto provision to *prevent* action.

Establishment of any universal system has had, therefore, to give way in practice to less ambitious regional systems for implementing collective security principles. The phraseology of Article 5, the key section of the North Atlantic Treaty, appears to constitute the definition of the ideal of regional collective security:

> "The Parties agree that an armed attack against one or more of them in Europe or North America shall be considered an attack against them all; and consequently they agree that, if such an attack occurs, each of them, in exercise of the right of collective self-defense recognized in Article 51 of the Charter of the United Nations, will assist the Party or Parties so attacked by taking forthwith, individually and in concert with the other parties, such action as it deems necessary, including the use of armed force, to restore and maintain the security of the North Atlantic area."

Yet, here again, certain requirements of a true collective security system are not met. It is not absolute, for each party can decide for itself what to do in case a neighbor is attacked, including, presumably, doing nothing at all. Nor is it really automatic, for the same reason. More fundamentally, NATO is not "universal," even in a geographically limited sense, for it is not directed against any of the participants within the system which might become disturbers of the status quo (no one thinks for a moment that the Treaty would ever be used against Portugal or the United States). Instead, it is directed against a possible attack by an outsider—in this case obviously the Soviet Union or one of her satellites. Despite the careful allusion to the Charter of the United Nations, the North Atlantic Treaty is thus really one alliance pitted against another, and not a collective security system at all.

This is what practice sometimes does to theory, especially when theory precedes reality rather than growing out of it. In Thompson's words, the U.N. Charter may be said to present "an anomalous picture of a system created to defend a status quo which has not yet been brought into being." One may add the further anomaly that change is the law of all life, and that a collective security system, unless accompanied by a system which makes peaceful change possible, is doomed to failure. Yet, the very presence of a system which prevents change by violent means detracts from the chance that states will agree to change by peaceful means—thus rounding a vicious circular arrangement of which a collective security system is both creator and victim.

The practicing diplomatist would perhaps be less demanding in his desire to have reality conform to theory. For example, M. Bonnet supports the utility of the United Nations as a means whereby security can be achieved. Numerous other statesmen, including such varied spokesmen as Comrade Litvinov of the USSR, Secretary Byrnes of the United States, and Chancellor Adenauer of the Federal Republic of Germany, have expressed their belief in the collective security principle. So its failure of achievement can hardly be said to be for lack of official advocacy. The reasons for the collective insecurity of our time are more fundamental.

To recognize that the basic purposes of a collective security system are first, to maintain peace, and second, to preserve the status quo is to realize that these objectives are often incompatible. While a state may wish fervently to avoid war and is therefore willing to enter into agreements with other states with the same objective, the very commitment involved may require that it go to war to resist aggression in order to maintain the status quo. Domestic pressures may tie a statesman's hands, especially when the emergency represents confusion and ambiguity. When does "aggression" actually occur? Must soldiers actually cross a neighboring country's borders? What about provocation or alleged provocation which may be said to justify attack? If intense provocation is mutual, who is the aggressor? How can enforcement measures be applied when supersonic warfare with mass destruction weapons may bring resistance to a sudden end?

Faced with the obstacles which the cold realities of world politics place in the way of smooth and predictable operation of what may be a theoretically foolproof system, the student of international relations may despair of collective security and be tempted to abandon it as a practicable approach to the problem of peace and security. But he must then consider the alternatives, which bring forth the familiar pattern of the fear, the uncertainty and the even greater insecurity which accompany the absence of international controls and the dependence of each state upon its own limited resources. It may be that, to paraphrase Churchill's famous backhanded defense of democracy, collective security is the worst system of international relations yet devised, except for every other that has been tried.

1 • Security Through the United Nations *

Henri Bonnet

The author was French Ambassador to the United States in the immediate postwar period. He also represented France on the United Nations Security Council. He had been a member of the Secretariat of the League of Nations for 11 years, and is the author of several books published in America on the subject of foreign policy and international relations.

The longing for security is undoubtedly the predominant desire among all the peoples of the world. Having gone through the hardship, destruction and hatred of the last war, they want, above all, to be sure that such a cataclysm cannot happen again. But they have good reason to know that it is not an easy task to establish a firm and durable peace, even though it seems incredible that, in our era of robots and atomic bombs, men can still think of war as a possibility.

To measure the difficulty of the undertaking, we have only to recall our own experience. Those of us who are old enough to remember it think of the period which preceded the outbreak of the First World War as a golden age we will never see again. If we consider that material and moral progress, as well as intellectual achievement, had never been greater, we may be surprised to see that the nations accepted the risk of destroying such wonderful results and did not compel their governments to settle their difficulties without recourse to war. The first successes obtained in the settlement of international disputes by conciliation and arbitration were wiped out when, on August 2,

1914, Germany crossed the frontiers of peaceful Belgium.

A System of Security

After the bloodiest of all wars, in which ten million people died on the battlefield, the nations of the world, patiently and stubbornly, tried again to build a system of security and co-operation in order to forestall a new catastrophe. For years, the League of Nations tried to define those legal and moral rules which should regulate international relations. At the same time, it established a very elaborate network of co-operation between our various peoples in every field: economic, financial, social, and intellectual.

Although this co-operation yielded very important results, all of them were wiped out when, in September 1939, war broke out, for the second time in a generation.

From this series of events the people of the world have concluded that the first and most important duty of the new international organization must be

* *Annals of the American Academy of Political and Social Science*, CCXLVI (1946), 13–18. Reprinted by permission.

to ensure security and prevent war. It is imperative for the U.N. to succeed where the League failed. It can easily find a powerful support among the nations and the peoples. It can be more strongly built than the League was.

There is one point on which there exists unanimous agreement today: peace is indivisible. Nations are so near each other, their interdependence is so great in every field of human activity that there are no longer national problems having no international aspects. But, although man, through his genius, and material achievement, has created the conditions for world unity, the world is not organized to cope with the consequences of that unity. If we are to avoid the return of tragedies such as the war we have just won, the world must be one. However, such a unity does not exist.

Man's material achievements have brought about changes in the conditions of all international relations, and, at the same time, created new and wonderful opportunities for the progress and welfare of mankind. Through international understanding and co-operation, the wealth of the natural resources at the disposal of man can be fully exploited to his advantage. By improving the way of life of large masses of people throughout the world, new and immense possibilities will be opened up —even to the most civilized and highly developed countries. Creations due to the inventive genius of the human mind would increase and increase again, both in the material and spiritual fields. Incredible progress would be in sight.

Having demonstrated an almost supernatural capacity for creations of all sorts, the human mind must prove that it is able to display the same gifts in the organization of international life, a sphere in which no striking progress has been made during the contemporary period.

THE PRACTICE OF PRINCIPLE

Unfortunately, it is not enough to define the moral principles by which men and societies must abide. There is no doubt that, if they were to live up to the moral values proclaimed long ago, and to apply the rules which were set up to protect and ensure the freedom and dignity of men and women in our democratic societies, war would be banished from this earth. There is no doubt either that hundreds of millions of human beings all over the world, whatever may be their faith or their way of life, are longing for the universal recognition of those principles and rules. But, there remains the problem of translating such convictions into an effective force, able to impose the will of the people devoted to peace.

It is comparatively easy to agree on the ultimate goal: that the peoples and the authorities responsible for their security and welfare should recognize that the general interest transcends special interests and must, therefore, dictate decisions to be followed by all. But today we have to cope with a situation worse than the situation that existed after the last war. It is very often said that we have just come out of a thirty-years war which began in 1914 and ended a few months ago. There is some truth in that concept, but one must realize, nevertheless, that profound differences existed between the two World Wars. When peace was re-established in 1919, too many statesmen thought that the world would quickly return to the happy and prosperous days of the early 1900's.

The destruction and losses of every kind had been greater than in any preceding war. In fact, the peaceful evolution of human society which was developing gradually, in Europe especially and also in Asia, had been completely upset. New aspirations and new problems arose which were very soon to lead to the division of the world into two camps. I need not recall how the people of the free countries reacted against the deadly danger of the Nazi-Fascist ideology and finally crushed the desperate attempt of those who wanted to impose a kind of slavery upon all men. But one should not forget that, although the Second World War presented itself to many countries as a struggle for their independence in the classical form, it was, in reality, a crisis of humanity. We must remember also that now the sufferings and hardships are much greater than after the last war. International problems are of such magnitude and complexity that there is little hope of establishing a new and better form of world organization, guaranteeing peace forever, without a prolonged and arduous effort.

However strong may be our desire to advance quickly from the present form of the U.N. to a more complete and powerful form of international organization, truly possessing the authority to decide on all those issues on which peace depends, we must first of all bend all our efforts toward the creation of those conditions which will allow such a happy development.

THE CREATION OF CONFIDENCE

Today, the first task of statesmen is undoubtedly to reassure the people of the world, to create confidence once again, to foster new understanding between the peoples and to make the United Nations live in a propitious atmosphere of trust and friendship.

To realize such aims completely, I know that results must be obtained in every field open to the U.N.; that is, in every field of international activity. For example, no one could underestimate the importance of restoring international trade, of improving the economic situation of the devastated lands. Certainly the prospects for mutual understanding would not be encouraging if the world were to remain divided into two economic spheres: one of prosperity and one of misery, the latter engulfing, for the time being, practically the whole of Europe and Asia. Neither should one underestimate the activities to be conducted through the U.N. in the fields of social welfare, public health, transportation, agriculture, and the like. Perhaps more important still in the task of dispelling ignorance and distrust, which are still poisoning the world's atmosphere, is the education of public opinion as a whole and youth in particular—a great mission in which the educators of the entire world have the sacred duty to participate.

But here I should like to dwell especially on the problems of international security properly speaking, and to emphasize first of all that at Dumbarton Oaks and San Francisco a step was taken, in principle, at least, with regard to international procedures, which represents great progress as compared with those adopted after the First World War. What some international experts and statesmen tried in vain to do after the establishment of the League—namely, to prevent war or crush aggression, if necessary, through a network of security—has now been made possible. The French security policy of the years 1920 to 1930 has now been practically accepted and put into effect. The formation of the United Nations, in January 1942, was in itself an application of the principle of collective security—too late, for war had already spread all over the world. The same determination and the same solidarity between peace-loving peoples, shown some years earlier, would have spared us the catastrophe of a global war.

The very fact that the United Nations did not dissolve, that even before the final defeat of Germany and Japan they created machinery for permanent co-operation, and that all of them, through their authorized leaders have proclaimed over and over their devotion to international co-operation through the U.N., leads us to hope that the organization will be able, during the months and years to come, to fulfill its primary duty: namely, the maintenance of peace.

It is clearly established in the Charter that the U.N. must, first of all, deal, at any time, with situations or disputes which may threaten peace. Its main body, the Security Council, is almost exclusively concerned with that task. We all wish to see it supported by an Assembly whose moral authority and power will grow constantly. However, the Council has to stand guard, like an alert sentinel, over the peace of the world. It will be equipped to deal, at any time, with any difficulty that may arise. Let me recall that it has at its disposal a Military Staff Committee responsible to it for the strategic disposition of the armed forces placed under the direction of the Security Council. The latter is, therefore, enabled, not only to ensure the pacific settlement of disputes, but, if necessary, to take action with respect to "any threat to the peace, breach of the peace, or act of aggression." It should be able to create that network of security which could give the various nations the satisfying feeling that they are protected against war.

THE PROBLEMS INVOLVED

The fact that the system adopted is satisfactory in many respects, at least to cope with the most pressing needs, should not make us forget, however, that the task of re-creating confidence and a feeling of security among peoples is not an easy one. It is not easy for two reasons: first, there are difficulties which are outside the scope of the U.N. and must remain so; second, there are difficulties in putting the machinery of the U.N. to work.

With respect to the first difficulties, they are largely the legacy of the past, of the many feuds and quarrels which divided the world during the truce between the two World Wars. They are directly related to the establishment of peace. They must be settled promptly in order to allow the nations, of Europe, especially, to embark on the construction of a better world. For many nations, to get rid of the possibility of war on their own frontiers is a kind of preliminary condition to the construction of peace. There are many examples of this situation on the old Continent. I shall cite only one, briefly, one which refers to France, that is, the desire of my countrymen to be sure that war will not be launched against them once more by a militaristic Germany.

In their opinion, the easiest and surest way to be protected against this eventuality is to deprive the Germans of the possibility of diverting the production of their industrial regions to the manufacture of armaments. No modern war can be waged without a great industrial potential. That is why the French Government proposes to set up an international authority to govern and control the industrial regions of Western Germany, the Ruhr Basin. This does not mean that Germany would not receive a share in the output of the Ruhr coal mines and of the production of the Ruhr plants and steel mills. This share should not exceed the needs of a peaceful German economy. The balance, instead of being used as before by the Germans to build up their military strength, would be divided between the many countries of Europe which need it for the development of their own economies.

Unfortunately, even if many problems of that category are settled through peace treaties and various agreements the U.N. will have to cope with other disputes which still divide a world not yet freed from the burden of national rivalries, inequalities in economic development and standards of living, and feuds and suspicions inherited from the past. I know that, in the face of such a situation, it is tempting to draw the blueprint of an international system which would drastically reform the relations between peoples, establish the reign of law definitely and immediately, and permit the constitution of a federal government of the world. Although such an ideal is good and stimulating for the mind, we must not forget that our most pressing task must be to pave the way for that gradual strengthening of the U.N., for its transformation—which we desire to be as rapid as possible—into a more nearly perfect and more powerful body.

Gradual Progress

The fact that its first steps seem difficult should not discourage us. We must remember that, in addition to the obstacles the Security Council has to overcome and which derive from the present situation of the world, it has also to face the most intricate problems of organization. It must be recalled that the U.N. did not have the benefit of an easy childhood. It did not have the opportunity to mature gradually. It could not acquire its experience through the handling of easy problems while its organization was becoming stronger and smoother. Right at the start, during its session in London, the Security Council was confronted with various difficult political questions.

Moreover, tackling them would have been much easier if the Council could have followed a well set pattern of rules and procedures tested by experience. But it was not so. Those who man the ship must sail her through uncharted waters. While discussions were going on at the beginning of last week in New York, a committee of experts was hard at work in an adjoining room setting down basic rules or procedure according to which future debates will be conducted. In the meantime, the Council had to go along and settle questions of procedure by itself as they came up.

Neither must we forget that some of the provisions of the United Nations Charter sprang from concepts entirely new in the field of international diplomacy. For example, the Council has to be in continuous session, to be at any time in a position to deal with matters pertaining to international security. Representatives of the eleven members of the Council will remain permanently in New York, each of them assisted by a group of experts. They will, by their very presence, constitute an international body endowed with the highest authority.

Next to them will function a powerful secretariat, composed, not of national delegations, but of international officials under the direction of the Secretary General of the U.N. I am sure that the most complete co-operation will exist, as it must, between these two important bodies of the new international setup, that together they will form an impressive combination for the preservation of harmony between peoples. But one must realize that the beneficial results of these new arrangements will not be immediately apparent, and that it will be some time before the U.N. machinery can function with complete efficiency.

The Method of Development

Once the new league of the free peoples has all its tools well in hand, it should be able to increase and develop its powers continuously. It should obtain this result in the following ways:

(a) By settling disputes and causes of dispute, by dealing with situations which might develop into threats to the peace. That will undoubtedly require negotiations, discussions, and studies in order to overcome the obstacles which lack of confidence and concern about the protection of national interests put on the road to peace. In this way, it will be possible to prevent the use of the veto granted at San Francisco to the powers which have the greatest responsibilities in the maintenance and protection of peace. In this way, the peoples will feel that peace is once more firmly established and that the habit of peace will be re-created.

(b) By obtaining more and more power to ensure international security. It would be impossible to overestimate, in that respect, the possibilities presented by the report on international control of atomic energy recently published. I consider that the suggestion to create an Atomic Development Authority points out the way to the future concentration in the U.N., of the real powers to make, and, therefore, to prevent, war.

(c) By developing, with the help of its Military Staff Committee, definite plans for mutual guarantees and assistance against aggression, and by supplementing them with pre-established agreements setting up a network of military security throughout the world. This could be achieved by putting at the disposal of the Council an international force and enabling it to protect at any time those routes across the skies, oceans and continents over which this force must move freely, if necessary, in order to discourage aggression before it takes place by ensuring that it would be defeated.

. . . .

2 • Collective Security Re-examined *

Kenneth W. Thompson

. . . .

It is important that we ask at the outset . . . : What is collective security in theory? What are its precepts and main tenets? What, in simplest terms, is the philosophy of collective security? The rock bottom principle upon which collective security is founded provides that an attack on any one state will be regarded as an attack on all states. It finds its measure in the simple doctrine of one for all and all for one. War any-

where, in the context of Article 11 of the League of Nations, is the concern of every state.

Self-help and neutrality, it should be obvious, are the exact antithesis of such a theory. States under an order of neutrality are impartial when conflict breaks out, give their blessings to combatants to fight it out, and defer judg-

* The American Political Science Review, XLVII (1953), 753–72. Reprinted by permission.

ment regarding the justice or injustice of the cause involved. Self-help in the past was often "help yourself" so far as the great powers were concerned; they enforced their own rights and more besides. In the eighteenth and nineteenth centuries this system was fashionable and wars, although not eliminated, were localized whenever possible. In a more integrated world environment, a conflict anywhere has some effect on conditions of peace everywhere. A disturbance at one point upsets the equilibrium at all other points, and the adjustment of a single conflict restores the foundations of harmony at other points throughout the world.

This idea of collective security is simple, challenging and novel. It would do for the international society what police action does for the domestic community. If the individual is threatened or endangered in municipal society, he turns to the legitimate agents of law enforcement, the police. The comparatively successful operation of this system has meant relative peace and tolerable harmony for most local communities. Through the action of police or "fire brigades" on a world scale, collective security has as its goal two comparable objectives. It would *prevent* war by providing a deterrent to aggression. It would *defend* the interests of peace-loving states in war if it came, by concentrating a preponderance of power against the aggressor. These two ends have been the goals of both the League and the United Nations. Through power and persuasion, a collective system would seek to deter aggression, as in the case of the Soviet imperialist threat to Titoist Yugoslavia. A potential aggressor must know that Yugoslavia and other United Nations powers stand together under the same protective umbrella. If war comes, the security system by pooling resources defends its inter-

ests against any nation which threatens to undermine it by swallowing up one of its members....

This simple picture of the idea of collective security hardly furnishes a useful and realistic perspective on the way such a system operates in practice today. Nor are we helped by comparing the structure of the two historic experiments in collective security. The formal agencies for collective security after World War I were in several important respects unimpressive. Article 16 of the Covenant provided that any member resorting to war contrary to the Covenant had committed *ipso facto* an act of aggression against all other members. It was intended that first economic measures and then overt force should be applied against any offender. But although the international obligations of members were less ambiguous than in the Charter, there was no clear provision for their implementation or organization by a central enforcement agency. Each nation had full freedom to provide what troops it saw fit. The Council could then advise on additional measures. In contrast, Article 39 of the Charter of the United Nations commissions the Security Council to determine the existence of a threat to the peace or act of aggression and Articles 43–47 obligate the members, upon the completion of agreements, to supply troops to the Military Staff Committee. The agencies for partial collective security, as found in the constitutional provisions of the North Atlantic Pact and the practical steps undertaken under NATO, are even more impressive and formidable today.

From the beginning, however, the real issue concerning collective security has had little to do with charters or compacts. The real issue has been the question of why the implementation of a system logically so flawless, and enjoying such impressive official devotion and popular support, should have been accompanied by a period of virtually unprecedented collective insecurity. It is a sobering fact that the nineteenth century was perhaps the most peaceful of modern centuries; the twentieth, by contrast, has been an epoch of unparalleled bloodshed. From 1815 to 1914 a system of old-fashioned balance of power contributed to the achievement of nearly a full century of uninterrupted peace. The past forty years have witnessed in rapid succession two great wars which the historian Arnold J. Toynbee compares to the double wars of the Romans and the Carthaginians and the two struggles of the Peloponnesian War which wrecked Hellenic Civilization. He has observed that quite possibly we have dealt ourselves the same "knockout blows" that these wars represented for the older civilizations. There were only eighteen months in the nineteenth century when France, Russia, Austria, Prussia, England and Spain found themselves at war with one another (excluding the Crimean War as a colonial struggle). By contrast, our experience thus far with the novel machinery of collective security has hardly warranted the unqualified postwar optimism of men like Mr. Hull that, with the new international organization, power politics and war were being left far behind in our progress toward utopia.

Instead the recent decades have been years of unceasing war or threats of war. What are the causes of this state of affairs? What are the reasons for the enormous gap between the theory and practice, the promise and performance of collective security? The most popular and reassuring answer has been that the radical doctrines of National Socialism and Communism have undermined the ideal system, and that modern technology has shattered the earlier limitations on conflict. Yet an equally dynamic creed challenged peace and order in the nineteenth century and provided a fighting faith for imperialist France.

The serious observer must look more deeply at the substance of political reality. In so doing he will find that collective security yesterday and today has been viewed unrealistically, and that its executors have been asked to perform tasks which could be performed with complete success only if certain objective conditions were realized. The most vital questions regarding collective security have seldom been asked; the real problems have often been evaded. The fundamental issues and problems which should have been boldly and realistically confronted have been concealed and obscured in constitutional verbiage and formal legalistic arguments. The four basic problems responsible for the tragic predicament of collective security include the problem of its basic preconditions, the political problem, the psychological problem and the problem of peaceful change. The first is from one standpoint most basic, for the preconditions of collective security, being frequently misunderstood, have presented the most stubborn obstacle to the maintenance of international peace.

Preconditions of Collective Security. Manifestly, collective enforcement is unattainable in the absence of appropriate international machinery and binding obligations clearly set forth in recognized legal instruments. Yet every informed citizen knows from experience that a legal arrangement imposed upon political and social conditions incompatible with its fulfillment makes successful political action difficult. Therefore it is essential in considering the reality of collective security that we understand fully its assumptions and requirements.

First, collective enforcement assumes a status quo, or situation of peace, on which the nations with predominant strength agree. In practical terms the peace which a collective system must defend is the territorial status quo existing at the time the system is brought into being. There is nothing in past experience to indicate that all nations, or even a combination sufficiently powerful to defy the rest, will agree on the meaning of a particular status quo. Following every war, the defeated powers who feel they have suffered most by the terms of peace come to oppose the established status quo. In the aftermath of World War II, however, the question of satisfaction or dissatisfaction with the status quo has largely been superseded by an earlier and prior question.

Up to the present time, no practical arrangement has been worked out acceptable to the major powers, who in this case are primarily the Soviet Union and the United States, on which the postwar status quo could be founded. The unresolved conflict between East and West has prevented the establishment of peace. Consequently, the latest experiment in collective security presents us with the anomalous picture of a system created to defend a status quo which has not yet been brought into being....

Second, collective security demands that nations subscribing to the status quo be willing and able at all times to muster overwhelming strength for collective defense at successive points of conflict. In theory, the supporters of the status quo might be capable in particular emergencies of mobilizing effective and decisive power against the single aggressor who sought to defy them. Or, by pooling the resources of all the nations in a permanently organized international force, collective enforcement could be made automatic, instantaneous, and preponderant. The former condition, however, is practically impossible of ful-

fillment, inasmuch as the threat to the status quo comes historically from more than one dissatisfied power or aggressor. The second condition would call for the unprecedented practice of international contingents operating under an international agency empowered to decide conclusively when and how they should be used.

The United Nations Charter seems to take a long step toward this objective by providing that all members are "to make available to the Security Council, on its call and in accordance with a special agreement or agreements, armed forces, assistance and facilities...." (Article 43, Paragraph 1.) Through this provision, the incurable weakness of decentralized enforcement by which past international systems have been rendered impotent is ostensibly rectified. For the Achilles' heel of the earlier experiments was the decentralized character of the enforcement process; separate nations retained the right to determine whether or not military forces would be made available to meet particular crises. In 1942, Cordell Hull had urged that "some international agency must be created which can—by force, if necessary—keep the peace...."[1] Yet Mr. Hull's proposition and Articles 43ff of the Charter, by which this historic difficulty apparently had been surmounted, in practice have remained a dead letter. No special agreements have been concluded by Members with the Security Council; talks in the Military Staff Committee soon reached an impasse. The Soviet Union has opposed proportionate contributions to an international air and naval force, which would leave it particularly vulnerable to forces overwhelmingly more powerful than its own. The United States has been concerned to make the United Na-

---

[1] 7 Department of State *Bulletin* (1942), p. 645.

tions Armed Force as strong as possible against the military preponderance of the Soviet Army in Europe and Asia, while the Russians have sought to keep it as weak as possible.[2] The stalemate in the Military Staff Committee is fundamentally a symptom of the struggle between the two great powers and between supporters and opponents of the undefined status quo. In practice, the realization of the second condition of overwhelming strength for collective enforcement has constantly run afoul of special national demands for military security and supremacy.

There is a *third* and final prerequisite of collective security, however, to which we now turn, that was widely assumed to be in existence at the time preparations for the United Nations were first being made. It is essential to collective security in a world of unequal powers that at least the major powers enjoy a minimum of political solidarity and moral community. On October 13, 1944, Premier Stalin asked himself, in an article appearing in the Soviet *Information Bulletin,* if the world organization could be effective. He predicted that it would "be effective if the Great Powers, which have borne the brunt of the war against Hitler-Germany continue to act in a spirit of unanimity and accord." [3]

The effectiveness of the United Nations and of the Security Council in particular was predicated upon the unanimity of the five great powers. It was an article of political faith in the Roosevelt Administration that trustworthiness and good will on the part of Americans would inspire the same qualities among the Russians. In a particularly revealing memorandum for President Harry S. Truman dated September 11, 1945, Mr. Stimson explained: "The chief lesson I have learned in a long life is that the only way you can make a man trustworthy is to trust him; and the surest way to make him untrustworthy is to distrust him and show your distrust." [4] Unanimity among the great powers which alien ideologies and conflicting interests might otherwise undermine would be secured through the application of a code of social ethics that had in general been effective within the United States.[5]

• • • •

The Political Problem. The chief practical obstacle to collective security is the political problem deriving from the conflict of independent foreign poli-

---

[2] It should be noted that the Russians have no monopoly on opposition to a powerful world police force. Senator Vandenberg declares in his Memoirs: "I am opposed to what is generally understood by the term 'international police force.' So, I believe, are the President, Secretary Hull and most realistic students of this problem. To be adequate, an international police force would have to be larger than the regular army and navy of any other power on earth. I think it is fantastic to believe that the people would long consent to the maintenance of any such enormous concentration of power in the postwar peace; and I also think that the temptation to reach for its ultimate control could become the greatest possible threat to peace in years to come." Arthur H. Vandenberg, *Private Papers of Senator Vandenberg* (Boston: Houghton Mifflin, 1952), pp. 120–21.

[3] USSR *Information Bulletin,* Oct. 13, 1944.

[4] Stimson, *On Active Service,* p. 644.

[5] It remained, however, for Premier Stalin in conversation with Harry Hopkins to furnish unwittingly the key to the success or failure of this endeavor. He declared that trust and confidence in international as in national relations is dependent upon the existence of "...a minimum moral standard between all nations and without such a minimum moral standard nations could not exist." Premier Stalin continued that the leaders of Nazi Germany "knew no such minimum moral standard [but] ... without a second's thought would sign a treaty today, break it tomorrow and sign a second one the following day. Nations must fulfill their treaty obligations," he said, "or international society could not exist." Nor, it might be added, could collective security survive. Sherwood, *Roosevelt and Hopkins,* Vol. 1, pp. 399–400.

cies. The loyalties and interests of nations participating in international organizations and collective security systems are of a different order from those of individuals taking part in the more intimate communities of the family and nation.[6] Both individuals and nations pursue their own interests, but in some areas and on certain occasions the individual may forsake his egotistic motives for loyalty to some higher institution or nobler cause. There are institutions in integrated societies which provide common standards under which the individual can realize his aspirations. There need be no inherent conflict between an individual's private interests and his national loyalties, and when the projected policy of an international organization conflicts with that of a particular nation, at all times and in all places the national interest prevails....

The Psychological Problem. Collective security founders on other shoals. It sometimes breaks down because of collective resentments or hatreds and reactions which express certain features of a particular national character. In 1931, the Japanese spilled over into Manchuria. Why was it that more positive action was not taken? To be sure there were legal, economic, and political obstacles existing. "War" in international relations is a weaselword, and debates which surround it easily become legal quagmires. Japan said it had not

declared war, China had not done so, and therefore the bombs were a mere illusion. Behind this legal smokescreen the struggle went on and men were as dead as if they had fought in a legally more respectable war. Economically, the world was deep in a painful depression; politically, Manchuria seemed far away and of little immediate interest to Western nations. There was in addition, however, a psychological factor. Certain groups in the West harbored deep resentments against the victims of Japanese imperialism. In particular, certain elements within the British trading community remembered private scores that had not been settled and the recent ingratitude of the Chinese toward the West. This sector of Western public opinion took a kind of vicarious pleasure in the punishment the Japanese were inflicting upon China which, with India, became a symbol of the heavy toll being taken economically and psychologically in Europe by Asia's revolt. The Japanese action was unconsciously viewed as a retaliation against the whole antiforeign movement that was sweeping Asia.

. . . .

In 1950–51, a new psychological obstacle appeared to block effective universal collective security. The British have had a Far Eastern policy for nearly a century-and-a-half. To them the policy of the United Nations, as influenced by the United States and especially by its spectacular and outspoken general, was from the first based on false assumptions. When General MacArthur's abortive thrust toward the Yalu River was turned back and the one action which all Western policy had sought to forestall—the intervention of the Chinese Communists—followed, the British reaction, however restrained, was clearly inevitable. Given the policy, the outcome was inescapable.

Peaceful Change. Collective security,

---

[6] Some years ago Monsieur Paul Henri Spaak in an address before the Foreign Press Union declared: "There must be a hierarchy in international obligations. The nations of the continent cannot be asked to consider with the same realism and sincerity of judgment affairs which directly concern them and events which are taking place thousands of kilometres away in regions where they have neither interests nor influence. Indivisible peace, mutual assistance, and even collective security are general ideas whose practical effect must be clearly explained and clearly limited." Quoted in *Survey of International Affairs, 1936* (London, 1937), pp. 354–55.

as we have seen, depends upon agreed concepts of justice in international society shared by all or most of its members. In domestic societies this consensus is arrived at by public opinion's availing itself of the instruments of government in registering the majority will. If societies were characterized by ideal justice and perfect equilibrium among contending social groups, the problems of social change would perhaps disappear. Since the demands for social change are continuously asserted in the market place and resolved in legislative and electoral debates, the pursuit of abstract justice assumes less urgency than the claims for justice of particular social groups.

In every society two social forces inevitably exist in basic tension with one another. The one force comprises the groups supporting the status quo as stabilized and perpetuated in the political and legal order of the day. Another force made up of the groups sharing common opposition to the status quo seeks to change or overturn it. In the light of this conflict, the basic problem of government is to provide ways by which continuity is achieved and social change not prevented. Within organized and integrated societies, the courts historically have contributed continuity whereas legislatures have been the faithful agents of change. As Congress was the forum in which the claims and grievances of distressed groups were alleviated by New Deal laws and decrees in the 1930's, the British Parliament in the nineteenth century was the agency in which the middle-class revolt against feudalism was expressed and achieved.

It should be apparent, however, that the process of change in society is made possible by other agencies as well. The executive has provided an instrument through which opinion can be channeled and transformed into effective policy. Peaceful change thus involves the whole of society with its orderly machinery

through which social groups seek support for their claims elevated into principles of justice that must be compatible with the society's fundamental values. It is the whole of domestic society, therefore, and not the legislature in isolation that brings about social change. For while the making of new laws is the formal act of social change, the role of legislatures is essentially the ratification of the choices at which unorganized society has already arrived. This is made possible by the generally accepted framework of justice within which dispute can be settled.

It is obvious that the conditions and institutions which exist within domestic societies are absent or greatly weakened in international society. Legislative bodies with law-making powers capable of fulfilling the functions that Congress or any other legislature performs are conspicuously absent on the international scene. The General Assembly has the power to "make recommendations" on matters prescribed in the Charter; the Security Council may "decide" on measures to be taken and "call upon" members to act. While these powers appear to mark an advance, in practice they have hardly resulted in any especially decisive step toward international law-making. The basic defects in the structure of international society are nowhere more apparent than in connection with peaceful change....

THE UNREALITY OF TWO APPROACHES TO COLLECTIVE SECURITY

In the face of the problems we have outlined and discussed, two approaches to the idea and reality of collective security have vied with one another in recent years. The one demands in the name of a principle that all nations at all times resist aggression. Its adherents maintain that only in this way can the national interests of independent states be protected and served. This approach takes its stand on the abstract and uncorruptible ideal of collective security.

Another approach, based primarily on what we have denoted the reality of collective security, reaches other conclusions on the basis of opposing concepts and principles. In the present state of world affairs, we are told, a policy of collective security leads inevitably down the road of general war and universal catastrophe. The Founding Fathers of this Republic knew more clearly than their present day heirs the futility of seeking to coerce sovereign states. At the Constitutional Convention of 1787, it was argued that unless states were united in one sovereign government (which both approaches agree is absent from the international scene today), they could be coerced only through civil war. Alexander Hamilton declared to the New York State Convention, met to ratify the new Constitution: "to coerce the states is one of the maddest projects that was ever devised. A failure of compliance will never be confined to a single state. This being the case can we suppose it wise to hazard a civil war." Uniting in the same tradition, Hans J. Morganthau has maintained: "Under a system of collective security operating under less than ideal conditions, war between A and B or between any other two nations anywhere in the world is of necessity tantamount to war among all or at best most nations of the world." Since ideal conditions are not presently in sight, collective security is tantamount to war.

Thus the West is presented, in theory at least, with a choice between almost equally hopeless and catastrophic alternatives. Through the fact of membership in the United Nations, Western nations are committed to a system of collective security embodied in the Charter. Confronted with reality, however, the staunchest champions of collective security are driven to invoke a dual standard as a guide for action. On the one hand, they must firmly resolve on principle to intervene to arrest aggression at its source. On the other hand, while unable to disavow the principle, in concrete actions they are required to apply it judiciously with immense self-restraint.

The gulf between principles and actions in 1935–36 and again in 1950 illustrates the irony of collective security in the real world for, under its dispensation, Mussolini's aggression in Ethiopia and the North Korean invasion of South Korea made intervention a foregone conclusion. Once aggression is identified, the duty of the nations espousing collective security is unequivocal. Yet since Britain and France were unprepared in 1935, it was doubtful that more could be accomplished than to drive Italy into the camp of Germany. Notwithstanding, the viewpoint prevailed that if the champions of collective security did nothing, other more dangerous acts of aggression would follow.

The perils in pursuing the idea of collective security to its logical conclusion are matched only by the hazards involved in abandoning it. It is tempting to say that since collective security against a great power is unworkable, since psychological and political obstacles exist, and since the requirements for peaceful change are quite frequently at odds with enforcement, the system should be scrapped and replaced. Yet the coalition of the Western nations has been aroused to the threat confronting it by the resolute stand that was taken in Korea, and the whole free world has been animated and inspired by our boldness, courage and, lately, our patience and restraint. In the struggle against Soviet imperialism, it is vital that we have firm friends and willing allies who recognize mutual interests. We can best assure their cooperation by preserving and strengthening the tenuous ties by which all are bound together within the United Nations.

Perhaps the supreme paradox of American foreign policy today is the necessity placed upon us to seize and employ the essentially utopian instruments of collective security in a brutally realistic power struggle. Its agencies furnish a political framework through which the broad coalition of the free world can be strengthened and a more stable equilibrium of world power be restored. Britain and France and the free powers of Asia are more likely to play their part and contribute to the restoration of a balance of power in Europe and Asia if we assure them of support through mutual guarantees and create confidence by discussions in the halls and anterooms of the United Nations.

Collective security, with its present foundations weakened and enfeebled, can contribute to peace and order if wisely and moderately employed. It has become clear in Korea that policies undertaken in the name of collective security are not necessarily tantamount to world war. Localized struggles are still possible if major powers are not confounded by the ideal or mislead by a too absolute interpretation of the meaning of collective enforcement. Moreover, the influence of other nations more skilled in historic diplomacy has served within the United Nations as a kind of built-in restraint on the impulses of American foreign policy. Our partners in utopia have nudged us in the direction of what would appear to be a more realistic foreign policy. Beyond this, with the recent breakup of the simple bi-polar balance of power in the world, the practical uses for collective agencies may be multiplied indefinitely as the prospect of action by coalitions of members against independent if minor centers of power becomes a reality.

The uses of collective security are more modest and limited than its more ardent advocates appreciate. Yet if participants base their policies on enduring political principles and judge and measure each action by the interests and power involved, it need not be an inevitable blind alley. Between the scylla of blind acceptance and the charybdis of logical rejection we must aim to establish the intellectual foundations required for an empirical and pragmatic approach to the modern concept of collective security.

PART VI • ORGANIZING INTERNATIONAL SOCIETY

XXI • The Utility and Limitations of International Law

The formalization of international collaboration should be thought of as serving and advancing the respective national interests of the participants, and as a supplement rather than as an alternative to conventional diplomacy on their part.

Thus, the first thing to recognize about international law is that it is law *among* states, not law *over* states. This is a world of sovereign states, and international law cannot be conceived as something which is either apart from the existing state system or which might in some way replace it.

Public international law consists of a great many conventional and customary rules presumably accepted by civilized states as binding upon them in their relations with each other. Customarily divided into the law of war (including the law of neutrality) and the law of peace, its sources, as indicated in Article 38 of the Statute of the International Court of Justice, are:

> international conventions which establish rules which are recognized by contesting states in the case of disputes between them; international custom as being evidence of general practices which are accepted as law;
>
> the general principles of law which civilized nations recognize; judicial decisions and teachings of "the most highly qualified publicists of the various nations" as indicating the means whereby customs and legal principles may be determined.

International law has been traditionally regarded as applying only to sovereign states. Professor Jessup of Columbia, however, has argued the view that, in "a modern law of nations," the individual should have more of a place, in terms of his relations both with states and with other individuals.[1] Interesting and potentially significant though this novel approach may be, the real issue is not the place of the individual in international law but the impact of law upon the conduct of foreign policy. Some have expressed doubt

---

[1] Philip C. Jessup, *A Modern Law of Nations* (New York: Macmillan, 1948), pp. 15–16.

that international law is really *law* at all, since it does not restrain or even affect the states in the actual pursuit of their respective national interests.

Before the outbreak of the First World War there was much more stress upon the efficacy of international law than there is today. The reason is clear: before the holocaust shattered the illusion, it was widely believed that there existed among the leadership of the Great Powers a consensus of values which could underlie the development of a rule of law. After the war, interest tended to concentrate upon the development of international institutions such as the League of Nations, until that body proved incapable of meeting the challenge of totalitarianism. The years following the Second World War have seen the emergence of not just two, but several competing value systems in the wake of what Hajo Holborn has called "the political collapse of Europe," whose values can no longer prevail. Thus to speak of a world rule of law today assumes that among the several systems of value, particularly but not only between the main protagonists of the "cold war," there is some degree of consensus upon which a universal legal structure could be built. Such a consensus is difficult to locate in a situation in which each side in the "cold war" tends to define error and illegality by whatever the other side does.

Thus many observers of the international scene contend that international law does not exist. Their principal argument is that since one bloc rejects the values of another bloc, it would hardly allow itself to be placed in a position of having to accept decisions of a tribunal whose values were not its own. In other words, international law is not law because there is no way in which it could be enforced when it is violated.

Others, however, contend that international law does represent reality. Enforceability may be lacking, but as long as states, or even some states, obey the law—for whatever reason—then it is perfectly proper and indeed essential to speak of the existence of an international legal system. In Ambassador van Kleffens' words, "...we feel in our heart and conscience it is right and useful that the law be observed.... We had the natural desire to see law respected precisely because it is law." As a spokesman for one of the smallest of states, he urges that this "powerful weapon of defense" no longer be neglected, arguing that an appeal to international law will be "understood and admitted by all decent people, and evil-doers without hesitation branded as such." The obligatory force of international law, like all law, is fundamentally based upon a sense of right and wrong.

As a spokesman for one of the most powerful states, Vice-President Nixon has stated that the "primary problem today is not the creation of new international institutions but the fuller and more fruitful use of the institutions we already possess." [2] Several weeks before his death, Secretary Dulles expressed similar determination to make more use of law in the kind of framework within which it could be expected to work. States with common stand-

---

[2] "Developing the Rule of Law for the Settlement of International Disputes," *Dept. of State Bulletin* (May 4, 1959), p. 624.

ards should advance the rule of law by submitting their disputes to the International Court or some other tribunal. Of the three methods Dulles outlined for the maintenance of peace, he firmly rejected tyrannical world rule and the balance of power. With a system of law and justice in the world, the renunciation of force would imply not the maintenance of the status quo but a peaceful change. But such a system is beyond our reach, according to Dulles, because the Communists have made observance of a rule of law impossible.

While the Soviet Union has so far "displayed nothing but contempt for international legal institutions as conceived in the Western tradition," Professor Bloomfield points out that: "it would be a mistake to assume that if the Soviet Union were not a factor in world politics, obstacles to the development of international law would disappear. Man will be ineffective in ending the battle between legalistic theory and political reality until he recognizes the respective places of law and politics in world society. Before a world system ruled by law could be established, something which could be called a community would have to exist, but such a community is lacking today. To create it will be a slow process, and caution must be exercised to avoid impatience which leads to trying to wish away the obstacles or to being overcome by disillusionment."

The article by Dr. Hambro gives some indication of the present status of international institutions in the legal field. But it is important to say that the problems involved in the application of law to the conduct of international relations cannot be solved exclusively by the elaboration of attractive organizational and legal formulae. Until the Great Powers agree to accept the limitations which a rule of law would impose upon their own actions and people everywhere agree to obey such a system, international law cannot play a decisive role in world affairs.

1 • The Place of Law in International Relations *

Eelco N. van Kleffens

Dr. van Kleffens has served as Foreign Minister of The Netherlands and President of the Ninth Session of the General Assembly of the United Nations.

I should like to speak to you about the place of Law in international relations, and, more especially, of the need there is for putting into the conduct of international relations a much greater emphasis on Law than has been done these last few years. And when I say "Law," I mean, by the nature of the thing, international law.

I believe that this would be to the advantage of all nations. Partaking of the majesty and authority characteristic of all Law, international law is the only objective and impartial yardstick in international relations; a solid basis for any international policy worthy of that name; a sure touchstone for the settlement of international disputes; and an effective reducing-agent of mere statecraft, cleverness, and opportunism. It sets up "a standard to which the good and the just can repair." International optimism, confidence and tranquility are in direct proportion to its strength and advancement.

All this is of special importance to nations who are in a defensive position. "In a diplomatic debate," said the former President of the International Court of Justice, Prof. Basdevant, "a State feels particularly strong when it is in a position to invoke a rule of positive international law."

I should like very much to explore with you why this is so true. For I believe that there is every reason for such an exploration. It seems to me that, without the slightest doubt, there has been a striking and highly undesirable neglect of international law in the conduct of international relations ever since the outbreak of the Second World War. . . .

It is clear that at this time international law has been relegated into the background; the general public does not seem to know very well what it is, and is not interested. Can it be that the nations have come to the conclusion that, inasmuch as international law has not prevented the outbreak of the Second World War, it is a useless instrument which therefore may be discarded?

No conclusion could be more rash or wrong. It is of course quite true that international law did not prevent the war. But neither did diplomacy, or anything else. The point is not whether international law can prevent a war, but whether it can make a contribution to preventing a war, and whether a well-founded appeal to international law can

---

* Text of an address delivered at Princeton University, reprinted in *United Nations Review*, I (1955), 20–23. Reprinted by permission.

perceptibly strengthen the case of who-ever appeals to it. And *that* it can.

There is much vague and confused thinking on this subject, and it seems to me that the time is overdue for these things to be clearly stated. Here is a strong shield, giving those who possess it better morale, a consideration un-doubtedly of special importance to the armed forces. A shield is a weapon of defense, not offense. No weapon can be more legitimate.

Fortunately, there are a few signs that a better understanding in this re-spect is at hand. Let me mention only the remarkable address given by the Secretary of State of the United States, Mr. John Foster Dulles, to the Ameri-can Bar Association at its Boston meet-ing of August 26, 1953, in which Mr. Dulles said that one of the inadequacies of the United Nations Charter "came out of disregard for the fact that world order, in the long run, depends, not on men, but upon law, law which embodies eternal principles of justice and moral-ity." And the Secretary of State quoted on that occasion from the late Senator Taft's book "A Foreign Policy for Americans," in which he said, speaking of the United Nations Charter: "The fundamental difficulty is that it is not based primarily on an underlying law and an administration of justice under that law."

Now why is it that an appeal to inter-national law has that power of strength-ening our position?

The answer is to be found in that quality, inherent in and typical for all law, which requires rights to be re-spected and the law upheld. If, as pri-vate persons, we have a right not to be attacked, damaged or insulted, then that means that this right is to be respected by all, that those who infringe it are wrong, and that those in charge of up-holding the law will if necessary make sure that it *is* upheld. A well-founded ap-peal to law will be understood and ad-mitted by all decent people. Similarly, if a state is wronged or about to be wronged, an appeal to international law will be understood and admitted by all decent people, and evil-doers without hesitation branded as such, with even less hesitation than in the case of an appeal to purely moral considerations (which after all have a strongly individ-ualistic tinge), and with very much less hesitation than in the case of an appeal to force.

Where does that peculiar quality of international law, and indeed of all law, come from? That is the basic ques-tion we must try to answer.

There are several countries where the constitution or some other enactment proclaims the binding force of interna-tional law. There are others where the judiciary has declared international law to be binding. You all know that in the United States a mixed system prevails: the constitution states that treaties are part of the supreme law of the land, whilst the Supreme Court has ruled that not only treaties, but international law in its entirety, rules based on custom included, are part of American law. All this, however, gives no final explanation of the binding force of law; it merely shifts the issue, for the question imme-diately arises: what, ultimately, gives the constitution, or an act of Congress or of Parliament, or a judicial precedent its binding force? Besides, in the law of many countries there is no such pro-vision as here referred to, and yet no-body has ever contended that interna-tional law is not binding there.

The answer to our question, therefore, must be sought outside of national con-stitution, laws or judicial precedents.

It would, of course, be quite wrong to say that law is binding because if you infringe it, the police come to fetch you. That simply would amount to confusing the foundation of the obligatory force of law with the fact that often (not always, and not necessarily) law has a sanction to restrain transgressors.

Also, there is no answer to be found in saying that all law, and international law with which we are concerned here in particular, is binding because the People want it to be binding. For immediately there arises the question: *why* do people want it to be binding? What is there in law, and in international law, that makes people want it to be binding? You see, we are all the time confronted with the same question. It is obvious that we must look for an answer elsewhere.

Much, in the course of the centuries, has been written on the subject.

Let us first listen to Cicero who, having observed that it is against nature to seek one's own advantage at the expense of others, clinched this by saying: "If everyone did that, human society would of necessity destroy itself." Grotius, who quoted him, added: "All that is unjust is against the nature of a society of reasonable beings." Before him, Celsus, quoted in the Digest (I, 1), had called law "the art of what is good and fair."

These pronouncements are worthy of note, particularly because they show very clearly that Cicero, Celsus, and Grotius (and they were far from being the only ones) consider that the foundation of the respect due to law belongs to the domain of sociology and morality, not to the realm of law. Disregard of law disregards what is good and fair, and destroys society; to destroy society is against the interest and nature of mankind, and therefore inadmissible for practical as well as for moral reasons.

The ultimate basis of the respect due to law, accordingly, is extra-legal, i.e. outside the realm of law. As a command of a social and moral nature, the obligatory force of law is enjoined directly on the individual through his own sense of

what is right or wrong, and not, as in the case of a command founded on law, through the medium of a fundamental legal rule he must obey whether or not he thinks that rule to be just. There simply is no such legal rule. I believe this explanation to be correct; it applies to the binding force of all law, not excluding international law.

From the 18th century on, however, attempts have been made to leave this safe ground indicated amongst others by Cicero, Celsus and Grotius, and to give the respect due to international law a *legal* basis. Christian Wolff, a remarkable German lawyer who lived from 1679–1754, was the first to advance a theory which for a long period of time found a numerous following, especially in France. It was based on the idea of there being certain fundamental rights of states, as permanent as the state itself, absolute and inalienable, of which the state cannot be deprived without ceasing to be a state. The catalogue of these rights varies from author to author, but it may be said with the late professor Antoine Pillet that there are five of them which have found general recognition: the rights to preservation, to independence, to equality, to respect, and to international commerce.

The assimilation of states to individuals is obvious; states as well as individuals are considered equal and autonomous. Although autonomous, the state, like the individual, respects the equal rights of his peers. In particular, agreements must be kept because, if they are not, one or more fundamental rights of the other partner or partners are infringed.

In the course of the present century, this theory has been under effective attack.

It was pointed out, amongst other things, that it is inconsistent with reality. If independence is an inalienable right of a state, how is it then that there are several states (take ... Andorra, or the Sheikdoms in the Persian Gulf) that are *not* wholly independent, without thereby ceasing to be states? Moreover, all states are becoming more and more inter-dependent instead of independent.

. . . .

This theory therefore has to be rejected.

Quite another attempt to show that respect due to intenational law has an ultimate basis of a legal nature was the theory that all international law rests on consent, given either expressly (as in the case of treaties), or tacitly (as with custom). In this way, there always is a contractual obligation, and *pacta sunt servanda*. Of this maxim, as eminent an authority as the late Professor Anzilotti has made the keystone of his theory of international law. I am none the less of the opinion that it cannot be left floating in the air; we must ask ourselves *why* pacta sunt servanda, for whilst nobody doubts that consent can create a legal obligation, this does not mean that the ultimate basis of the *validity* of that obligation is consent. So this consent theory really means little or nothing. Why, moreover, should a mere fiction of tacit consent be given so large a place? And can consent, express or tacit, perhaps be withdrawn with the same liberty with which it is supposed to have been given?

Other attempts of the same nature have been made, but time does not allow me to go into them. So far as I can see,

they are all intrinsically defective. I firmly believe that Cicero, Celsus, Grotius and all who thought and think like them are right: sooner or later one is driven to the conclusion, however one tries to look at it, that the ultimate basis of the respect due to international law (and to *all* law, for that matter) lies outside the realm of law—it is of a moral and sociological order. We respect law and its enforcement because we feel in our heart and conscience it is right and useful that the law be observed, and not because there is any fundamental rule of law commanding us that we *must* accept it as right, whether we agree to accept it or not.

This natural urge has nothing to do with the content or substance of law. In the same matter, that substance may differ from country to country, just as in one and the same country it may be different at different times. The appreciation of the *substance* of a given legal rule is the task of our sense of justice; as soon and as long as that sense of justice is satisfied, we have the natural desire to see law respected precisely *because it is law*. The alternative is anarchy, and from that we instinctively shrink.

Therefore, let us give international law a much greater place in our defensive preoccupations than we have been doing since the end of the war. We have neglected it too long. A powerful weapon of defense has been left unused. Let us then make full use of it. ...

. . . .

2 • The Role of Law in Peace *

John Foster Dulles

Long prominent in organizations dealing with problems of international relations, John Foster Dulles served as special assistant to Secretary of State Acheson and as Secretary of State from 1953 to 1959.

· · · ·

We in the United States have from the very beginning of our history insisted that there is a rule of law which is above the rule of man. That concept we derived from our English forebears. But we, as well as they, played a part in its acceptance.

As Commager and Morris have pointed out in their *The Spirit of '76* (volume 1, page viii):

"...the War for Independence was distinguished by its concern for an emphasis upon legality. The Americans fought for the rights of Englishmen, as they believed them to be guaranteed by the British Constitution, and for the rights of man as they understood them to be guaranteed by Nature and Nature's God."

and as John Marshall put it:

"There are principles of abstract justice which the Creator of all things has impressed on the mind of His creature man."

Thus our Nation since its inception has been dedicated to the principle that man in his relationship with other men should be governed by moral, or natural, law. It was believed that this was something that all could comprehend. So great responsibilities were placed upon a jury, and the "conscience" of the chancellor was relied upon to temper legal rigors with equity. And legislatures annually change our statute laws in the hope of thereby making these laws more conformable to justice.

Now we carry these concepts into the international field. We believe that the results thus obtainable, though not perfect, are nevertheless generally fair and that they are preferable to any other human order that can be devised.

A most significant development of our time is the fact that for the first time, under the Charter of the United Nations, there has been a determined effort to establish law and justice as the decisive and essential substitutes for force.

PEACEFUL CHANGE

What is vital here is to recognize that the renunciation of force under these conditions implies not the maintenance of the *status quo* but peaceful change. World order cannot be assured merely by the elimination of violence. There must also be processes of peaceful change whereby justice manifests itself.

This new and constructive approach was the distinctive contribution of the San Francisco Conference in 1945.

---

* *Department of State Bulletin*, Series S., No. 79 (January 31, 1959), pp. 1-7.

The covenant of the League of Nations had involved a dedication to the principle that the *status quo* should be preserved by the authority of the "great" powers. This concept, as Elihu Root pointed out, "would not only be futile; it would be mischievous. Change and growth are the law of life."

Yet, as drafted by the so-called "great" powers at Dumbarton Oaks, the United Nations Charter would have reflected that same principle. Behind it was the premise that, since the United States, the United Kingdom, and the U.S.S.R. had won peace by their combined military power, world order should be maintained—policed—by that same authority and power.

The Dumbarton Oaks proposals, as they went to San Francisco for adoption by the so-called "small" powers, contained pledges not to attack and undertakings to seek peaceful settlements. And provision was made for a Security Council, which was designed to prevent aggression. But they contained no reference whatever to "justice" as the alternative to force. Nor did they open the door to any processes for peaceful change.

LAW AND JUSTICE IN PLACE OF VIOLENCE

What came out of San Francisco was vastly different. The twin concepts of "international law" and "justice" were interwoven throughout the Charter as the counterpart of the renunciation of force.

The preamble expresses not only the determination of the peoples of the United Nations to save succeeding generations from the scourge of war but also:

"to establish conditions under which justice and respect for the obligations arising from treaties and other sources of international law can be maintained...."

The first subdivision of article 1 called for peaceful settlement of disputes "in conformity with the principles of justice and international law."

By article 2, members were admonished to settle their international disputes "by peaceful means in such a manner that international peace and security, and justice, are not endangered."

The Security Council was required to follow these principles in the discharge of its duties (article 24(2)). And a "peaceful change" article (article 14) was incorporated, permitting the General Assembly to recommend "the peaceful adjustment of any situation, regardless of origin, which it deems likely to impair the general welfare."

Of special significance is the conference statement on withdrawal which said:

"...withdrawals or some other forms of dissolution of the Organization would become inevitable if, deceiving the hopes of humanity, the Organization was revealed to be unable to maintain peace or could do so only at the expense of law and justice." [Underscoring supplied.]

These examples, among others, demonstrate that in the United Nations Charter we have on the one hand a renunciation of force as an instrument of policy and on the other hand the necessary balancing concept of a rule of justice and law.

. . . .

It is easy to support a principle when those who violate it are those who proclaim themselves enemies. It is hard to do so when the issue is raised by friends. Nevertheless it seemed to us, in the fall of 1956, that the entire peace concept of the United Nations was at stake and that if the article of the Charter involving the renunciation of the use of force were to become a dead letter, the world would revert to chaos.

As I stated in the General Assembly of the United Nations on November 1, the threatened course of action seemed:

"inconsistent with the principles and purposes of the Charter and one which if persisted in would gravely undermine our Charter and undermine this organization."

But I also referred to the provisions of the Charter requiring the settlement of disputes "in accordance with the principles of justice and of international law." And I pointed out that the Charter "calls not merely for a peaceful solution, but a just solution." I added, "The United Nations may have been somewhat laggard, somewhat impotent in dealing with many injustices which are inherent in this Middle East situation."

The overwhelming verdict of the United Nations was in support of the principle of nonuse of force to which we had given our support. The United Kingdom, France, and Israel responded. The invading forces were withdrawn. Tolerable solutions were found through peaceful means.

It is premature to say that the Suez affair marks a decisive historical turning point; it may so prove. What can be said at this time is that, if the Charter pledge to renounce the use of force had been interpreted by the members of the United Nations so loosely as to permit the Suez action, or if the United Kingdom, France, and Israel had shown toward the United Nations the same contempt that the U.S.S.R. showed the United Nations in relation to Hungary, then the whole peace effort represented by the United Nations would have collapsed, ending the present effort of mankind to organize the peace along rational lines.

Justice, Law, and Peaceful Change

We have through collective security arrangements largely deterred the Communist bloc from using force. But we have found no effective means of persuading or inducing the countries of that bloc to accept the principles of justice and law and peaceful change.

This is not true as respects the nations of the free world. There the twin concepts of the renunciation of force and the affirmative role of justice and international law have, generally speaking, prevailed. The reasons for this are not difficult to understand. The peoples of the free world have respect for religion; they recognize moral law; and they have a decent regard for the opinions of mankind. As a result, the nations of the free world have not only evidenced a healthy respect for the principles of justice and international law but they have also promoted a remarkable amount of "peaceful change" to conform to concepts of justice and morality.

Since January 1, 1943, for example, 21 new nations have come into existence in countries formerly ruled by other free-world countries and these new nations have been accepted into the community of nations. Others are scheduled to gain their independence and sovereignty in the near future. As another illustration I cite the meeting (in 1958) of 86 nations in Geneva to review the principles governing the law of the sea. While a number of the established rules of law in this field were reconfirmed by the conference, it is equally important to note that significant changes—responsive to the requirements of new conditions—were agreed upon.

Stability vs. Change

Peaceful change and development are, therefore, significant among the nations of the free world. Perhaps, indeed, the pendulum is swinging too far in the direction of change. Law serves not merely to settle specific disputes but to provide a sense of security in daily living. A measure of stability is an essential ingredient of peace and order.

Change—even political and social change—should not be so impetuous as to paralyze forward planning or to wreak unnecessary injury upon established rights. While law should be and is subject to an orderly process of change, as required by justice, law does have a role as a shield and a protector of those who rely in good faith on international engagements.

. . . .

3 • The International Court of Justice *

Edvard Hambro

The author became Registrar of the International Court of Justice at The Hague in 1946. He was co-author of The Charter of the United Nations: Commentary and Documents *(1949), an indispensable study of the meaning and development of the organization. He is presently connected with the Norges Handelshoyskole in Bergen, Norway.*

. . . .

I shall endeavour to examine the International Court of Justice in the general framework of present-day international relations, not as a jurist, but as a student of international affairs. It is, however, impossible to give an impression of the true position of such an institution without some understanding of international law and the place of law in the international community. The first fact which leaps to the mind is that some kind of international law has existed since early history, and international tribunals are known as far back as written records exist: some 5,000 years.

King Mesilim of Kish adjudicated between the States of Umma and Lovgash. Arbitrations often occurred among the City States of ancient Greece and were used frequently during the Middle Ages and onwards. This method of settlement was adopted even before international law, as we understand it, began at about the time of the Peace of Westphalia in 1648, and before the epoch-making work of Hugo Grotius, first published in 1625. In 1794 the Jay Treaties between the United States and Great Britain inaugurated the modern period of arbitration between States. From that time until today more than 400 cases between nations have been thus settled as well as literally thousands of minor cases involving governments, corporations, and individuals.

International law consists of written and unwritten rules which States habitually apply in their mutual relationships because it is convenient and because unpleasant consequences might follow if they did not apply them. A violation of a rule of international law may be

* *International Affairs,* the Journal of The Royal Institute of International Affairs, London, XXX (1954), 31–39. Reprinted by permission.

followed by demands for compensation, reprisals, and even war. States act in accordance with this law of nations on the assumption that they are under an obligation so to do. Since this is now generally accepted and since the evidence to this effect is quite overwhelming, there seems little point in engaging in a philosophical discussion about the legal or non-legal character of what we are accustomed to call international law. There is a universal tendency among human beings to develop behaviour patterns, and among organized communities these patterns take the form of law. It follows that there is today hardly a government department without its legal adviser; there is not a foreign office in the world without international law experts, and they are frequently on the staff of embassies and legations, international organizations, and conferences. International constitutional or institutional law has grown apace with international organization, and international tribunals have played an increasing part in organized international life, and the principal tribunal is the International Court of Justice in The Hague. Its chief task is to settle disputes between States. For the peaceful settlement of disputes there are, naturally, many procedures other than reference to the Hague Court, but the Court is pre-eminent for the settlement of disputes apart from the ordinary channels of diplomacy.

The fight against war involves a struggle for ever more perfected means for the peaceful settlement of international disputes. In 1899 and 1907 the two Peace Conferences in The Hague created the Permanent Court of Arbitration. This so-called Permanent Court of Arbitration did undoubtedly constitute a step in advance when it was created in 1899. But it was not a real Court and it was not permanent. It consisted of a panel of judges prepared to adjudicate when called upon; it had an administrative Council and a Secretary General as well as a code of procedure. But each time a case was brought before it, the Court had to be established anew, the judges had to be elected and a special agreement had to be concluded. There was, therefore, in reality a separate Court for each case and no corporate existence.

In 1920 the Members of the League of Nations accepted certain obligations not to resort to war and created the Permanent Court of International Justice. Twenty-five years later the Charter of the United Nations forbade not only war, but any resort to and even the threat of force. The International Court of Justice created by the Charter is to all intents and purposes a continuation of the League's Permanent Court.

This Court which is entrusted with the great task of effecting binding settlements in disputes between States on the basis of international law consists of fifteen independent judges, elected regardless of their nationality from among persons of high moral character, who possess the qualifications required in their respective countries for appointment to high judicial office, or who are jurisconsults of recognized competence in international law. This provision should guarantee that the best persons become judges; but it may to some extent be contradicted—though not necessarily so—by the further provision that the electors shall bear in mind not only that the persons to be elected should individually possess the qualifications required, but also that in the body as a whole the representation of the main forms of civilization and the principal legal systems of the world should be assured.

This last provision is not entirely satisfactory. The Court is an international court applying public international law; and there is of course only one such law. Another danger inherent in this provision is that it might seem to give expression to the theory of a kind of geographical distribution of the seats on the Bench. For psychological reasons it is necessary that the Court should to some extent appear wholly international in its composition even if personal ability and integrity must be the foremost consideration, and so far the Court in its composition has answered to these criteria. There is on the Bench at the present time one judge from each of the Powers with a permanent seat on the Security Council. There is also a judge from Canada, and four from Latin America; there are two judges from Eastern Europe and one from Western Europe, one from the Islamic countries, and one from India. Among these judges there are former university professors, ambassadors, foreign ministers and legal advisers to foreign offices, as well as barristers and those who have held judicial office in their own country. Together they have great insight into, and practical experience of, international law, statecraft, and diplomacy.

The Court is now in the fullest sense in being. It is permanent and it is in continual session. This is of capital importance because it means that States may at any time have recourse to it. No delay arises in forming an *ad hoc* tribunal each time a case arises. All members of the United Nations are *ipso facto* parties to the Statute of the Court, and Switzerland and Liechtenstein have been admitted on the same terms as the Members of the United Nations. The Court is also under certain circumstances open to other States. But no State is obliged to appear before the Court against its will.

The rule that no State can be forced to appear before an international tribunal is, so far, axiomatic in the field of international adjudication and is one of the expressions of the dogma of absolute sovereignty. This is, of course, the negation of an international legal system which, to be effective, must be binding. However, a complete compulsory jurisdiction does not exist, but there are many hundreds of treaties of one sort or another which confer jurisdiction on the Court for limited classes of disputes. All the efforts of jurists and statesmen before the creation of the League of Nations did not succeed in creating a really compulsory jurisdiction. The League did not succeed either. But a compromise solution was found whereby States were given the opportunity of signing a declaration whereby they recognize as compulsory, *ipso facto* and without special agreement, in relation to any other State accepting the same obligation, the jurisdiction of the Court in all legal disputes concerning certain specified matters. In the years between the two world wars some forty-two States accepted this obligation. In spite of this, however, even the San Francisco Conference of 1945 did not attempt to introduce compulsory jurisdiction. It was decided to retain the old system, and today thirty-six States are bound by the acceptance of this obligation.[1]

However, many of the States who have accepted this obligation have done so with so many reservations that the Declarations lose much of their value. The most usual of the reservations stipulate that only subsequent conflicts can be submitted to the Court in this way; that exceptions are made for treaties which provide for other means of settlement, or that matters of domestic jurisdiction are exempted. These reservations are not in themselves very serious, except the last one in the form it has taken in recent years, namely, reserving for the State in question to decide itself which matters fall under the domestic jurisdiction clause. Such a reservation can be potentially very dan-

---

[1] See *Yearbook* of the Court, 1952–3, p. 170.

gerous. It is also in contradiction with the recognized principle of law that a tribunal decides its own jurisdiction.

It is regrettable that the States have not yet found it possible to accept compulsory jurisdiction, but in the present-day political atmosphere it would probably be unwise to force the pace and try to introduce it. Such a procedure might endanger the Court instead of helping it. Another weakness in the jurisdiction of the Court is that international organizations cannot be parties before it—not even the United Nations. But the United Nations and the Specialized Agencies can request advisory opinions of the Court and thereby use it to settle legal disputes between them or within the framework of one organization. In both these fields—contentious cases and advisory opinions—the Court has rendered great service and done most useful work.

The old Permanent Court of International Justice created by the League of Nations gave thirty-two judgments in disputes between States, and the present Court in its short life has already given eleven judgments. The old Court gave twenty-seven advisory opinions and the present Court seven opinions.

Now, it may be claimed that these decisions are not of the first importance and that the Court could never prevent a war. It is frequently maintained that if the international atmosphere is such that States really want to go to war, they will do so irrespective of any tribunal; and if they want to keep the peace, they will find some way of solving their conflicts without appeal to arms whether tribunals exist or not. Plausible though such an argument may seem, it is not altogether convincing. First of all the conflicts settled by the Court have often been very important indeed as, for instance, the Greenland case between Denmark and Norway, the Corfu Chanell case between the United Kingdom and Albania, and the Fisheries

case between the United Kingdom and Norway. Lawsuits have not always involved only small States, but often a small State against a great Power, as in the instances mentioned above, or two great Powers, as in the recent Morocco case between France and the United States or the Channel islands case between the United Kingdom and France. Even several great Powers have been involved, as in the *Wimbledon* case (in which the applicants were France, Great Britain, Italy, and Japan, and the respondent was Germany), which was the first to come before the Permanent Court of International Justice. All cases between States are potentially important. It is submitted that all cases which come before the International Court of Justice are important. States do not easily go to the trouble and expense of international litigation for frivolous cases; and the importance of a case may be far greater than the actual conflict would indicate. As an example, the case concerning the nationality decrees in Tunis and Morocco settled not only a disputed point between two States but made very important contributions to the theory and practice of domestic jurisdiction, while the Fisheries case settled a dispute of forty years' standing between two friendly States and at the same time laid down rules about territorial waters; the Corfu Channel case not only brought to an end—in the legal sense—a conflict between two States, but laid down important rules concerning the right of innocent passage in international straits, rules on intervention, and on State responsibility.

Naturally, it must remain a matter of conjecture whether the disputes in some cases might have led to bloodshed if the Court had not existed. What is certain, however, is that peaceful settlement is immensely facilitated by the existence of tribunals. It might indeed be difficult in certain situations to find a way out of an impasse where the interests of States and even their honour may be involved were it not for the existence of the Court. If such a tribunal exists it may be made a point of honour on the part of States to appeal to it and to fulfil the award in good faith where a compromise solution on the political plane might have been well nigh impossible and where a retreat from the position taken might have been too painful. There is no doubt that the 'law habit' among nations has been growing in spite of serious set-backs.

. . . .

In deciding the matters brought to it, the Court must to some extent create new rules of international law. This function needs some explanation: international law is in certain respects a primitive law and because it is essentially a law without a legislature, its growth is slow and its content may be uncertain. This unsettled condition has often in the past proved a stumbling block. For, it has been asked, if the law does not exist, how can it be applied? The chief reason why the international prize court was not brought into existence was just that too great an uncertainty existed about the law to be applied. Now, however, the International Court is in process of creating a very important jurisprudence. Because it is permanent, it tends to follow a legal tradition which can now to some extent be foreseen by States and they are consequently more inclined to use it than to use *ad hoc* tribunals with untried judges. On the other hand, just because States do trust it and respect its decisions, it has a freer hand in the creation of new law. . . .

This cursory examination of the International Court of Justice seems to give some ground for confidence in the future both of international law and of the Court which is its organ.

There can be little doubt that the Court was intended to play a prominent role in the United Nations. The place of the Court was stronger in the Charter than it had been in the Dumbarton Oaks proposals. The very Preamble lays down that the Peoples of the United Nations are determined 'to establish conditions under which justice and respect for the obligations arising from treaties and other sources of international law can be maintained', and one of the purposes of the organization is to 'maintain international peace and security and to that end ... bring about by peaceful means, and in conformity with the principles of justice and international law, adjustment or settlement of international disputes or situations which might lead to a breach of the peace'; and the Members shall 'settle their international disputes by peaceful means in such a manner that international peace and security, and justice, are not endangered'. In order to give effect to some of these provisions the International Court of Justice was established as 'the principal judicial organ of the United Nations'. The link thereby created between the Court and the other organs of the United Nations expresses the importance attached to law in the organization, but does not in any way indicate that the Court is not completely free and independent in exercising its judicial functions.

It is, of course, too early yet to give an accurate estimate of the importance of the Court in these first seven years. The old Court contributed more towards the development of international law than any other body, and gained enormous prestige. The new Court has continued this tradition. As far as the importance of the cases is concerned, the new Court has certainly had to deal with cases of equal difficulty; in this connexion it is enough to mention the Corfu Channel case and the Fisheries case. It should also be underlined on the credit side that the United States has been party to a dispute before the Court and that two Republics from Latin America have brought their disputes before the Court. This never happened during the time of the League of Nations.

It should also not be overlooked that the other organs of the United Nations have done more than merely pay lip service to the Court. It was the Security Council which recommended that Albania and the United Kingdom should bring the Corfu Channel case before the Court. And both parties appeared, although Albania is not a Member of the United Nations or a Party to the Statute of the Court. In the Anglo-Iranian conflict the Security Council postponed discussion of the case until the Court decided the point of its jurisdiction. Again both States appeared before the Court even though Iran did so only to challenge—and challenge successfully—the jurisdiction of the Court. Furthermore, the General Assembly requested advisory opinions on seven occasions. However, the actual number of cases is not decisive. The very existence of the Court may often have led to a peaceful settlement which might not otherwise have been effected.

Still, in spite of the obviously important and useful contributions of the Court, it would not be wise to be overoptimistic. The Court, important though it is, cannot of itself prevent war. And if the world should become finally and definitely divided into two blocs, the Court can have little to contribute. It is, it is submitted, unlikely that any important questions between States on different sides of the border line will in the near future be submitted to the Court. On the other hand, it is possible that conflicts between States on the same side of the dividing line may still be solved by appeal to law. The role of the Court in the realm of politics is, and must be, limited. Where there is no basic unity and no real confidence, law will be of no avail and courts will be of secondary importance at best.

Seen in historical perspective the Court has still a great task to fulfil. Law can be created and developed and even in times of stress and danger will be applied to some extent. There has in the last thirty years been no agency more important and more useful in this respect than the Court at The Hague. If it is true that the Court is powerless in a divided society it is also true that by creating international law it helps to cement international society and to engender the necessary feelings of solidarity and confidence.

If we believe that the tendency of the modern world must be greater integration as an alternative to destruction, and if we believe that the only alternative to chaos is world organization, then we must strive towards the rule of law in the life of nations. If that aspiration is to be fulfilled the International Court of Justice must of necessity have a very great part to play.

4 • Law, Politics and International Disputes *

Lincoln P. Bloomfield

The author, a Harvard graduate, was a Naval officer in World War II. He served in the State Department for eleven years, most recently as Special Assistant, for policy planning, to the Assistant Secretary for International Organization Affairs. At the present time, Dr. Bloomfield is a senior staff member of the Center for International Studies, Massachusetts Institute of Technology. He has written extensively on problems of international relations, specifically in the area of international organization.

Arnold Toynbee once wrote: "Life and law must be kept closely in touch, and as you can't adjust life to law, you must adjust law to life. The only point in having law is to make life work. Otherwise there will be explosions."[1] Men have worked hard in this century to adjust life to law, and it has not seemed to work. There has been no want of good motives behind the effort, and the extra incentive, if one were needed, has been the increasing unattractiveness of international life.

Some of the jurists stuck to their guns and proclaimed a universal, all-embracing legal order into theoretical existence, pausing only to minimize the political world about them as a superfluous irritant. Other writers were so carried away by the sometimes brutal and irrational behavior of men in political groupings, that they dismissed for all time the possibility that law could ever rule the international jungle, governed then, now, and forever by the "iron laws of politics."

But some spokesmen perceived the subtle grays in the web of civilized life, where ideals and passions, reason and unreason, and law and politics, are linked together, incessantly clashing, struggling for mastery but intimate and inseparable. This continuous process produces a rough equilibrium, and while it denies a "pure" role for the law, it is still an odd fact, as Pascal pointed out, "that there are people in the world who, having renounced all the laws of God and nature, have themselves made laws which they rigorously obey."

There can be little argument that the kind of consensus needed in order for law to play a fuller role in international affairs is profoundly lacking today, just as it has been in the past. As early as 1899, at the first Hague Conference, the delegate of Imperial Russia made the following statement setting forth a rigid concept of national sovereignty and reservation of unilateral national rights that has never really been

---

[1] "The Lessons of History," in *Peaceful Change—An International Problem*, C. A. W. Manning, ed. (New York, Macmillan, 1937), p. 36.

* *International Conciliation*, No. 516, January 1958. Reprinted by permission.

departed from since by any major power:

There is no Government which would consent *in advance* to assume the obligation to submit to the decision of an arbitral tribunal every dispute which might arise in the international domain if it concerned the national honor of a State, or its highest interests, or its inalienable possessions.[2]

Fifty-seven years later the Soviet delegate to the United Nations General Assembly in an identical mood expressed the identical position, asserting that the decision to submit a matter to the world Court is part of a nation's "sovereign prerogative, and no State could be required to indicate such willingness in advance." [3]

It is both tempting and justifiable to cite the specter of the Soviet Union to support the conclusion that legal methods cannot work in today's world. The Soviet Union is a symbol of the sort of force—hostile, expansionist, sporadically revolutionary—that always seems to frustrate hopes for a legal world. The Soviet Union has so far displayed nothing but contempt for international legal institutions as conceived in the Western tradition, and efforts such as that of the United States to have the International Court of Justice adjudicate claims arising out of damages to United States aircraft and personnel at the hands of the Soviet bloc have been flatly rejected.

But it would be delusory to assume that, without the Soviet Union, the problem would disappear. There has also been a noticeable lack of effort on the part of the Western nations to translate into juridical deeds their verbal aspirations for a rule of law in the world. It is not at all clear that France, for example, would be willing to put at stake its legal position in Algeria. And undoubtedly, in the present political environment, the United States would simply have to defy a Court decision that Formosa legally belongs to Communist China. The United States has only recently refused the request of the Swiss government that the claim of the Swiss firm Interhandel to stock of the General Aniline and Film Company be arbitrated. According to the State Department, the matter is exclusively a United States affair. In 1957, Switzerland instituted proceedings before the International Court of Justice against the United States.

On the other hand, ... Communist Albania, albeit reluctantly, did accept the Court's jurisdiction in the *Corfu Channel Case*. Colombia and Peru could be heard breathing a sigh of relief when, after two tries, the Court unhooked them from the dilemma of the protracted asylum of Haya de la Torre. And the United States did swallow the pill of the Advisory Opinion upholding the United Nations Administrative Tribunal awards to suspected Communists among Secretariat employees who were United States citizens. One can hope that Egypt's alleged right to exclude Israel shipping from the Suez Canal, as well as other legal aspects of the Arab-Israel situation such as international status of the Straits of Tiran, will be submitted to the Court for adjudication. But as a general rule of thumb, it seems depressingly true, at least in recent practice, that a government "may not subject itself to those supreme laws of renunciation and self-sacrifice that represent the culmination of individual moral growth." [4]

[2] *The Proceedings of the Hague Peace Conferences: Conference of 1899* (New York, Oxford University Press for Carnegie Endowment for International Peace, 1920), pp. 173–74.

[3] United Nations General Assembly, Official Records: 11th Sess., 6th Cmte., 488th Mtg., 3 Dec. 1956, para. 25.

[4] George F. Kennan, *Realities of American Foreign Policy* (Princeton, Princeton University Press, 1954), p. 48.

The process has been a regressive one in recent years. The United Nations Secretary-General in his report to the twelfth General Assembly noted regretfully that in the previous two years the number of acceptances of compulsory jurisdiction of the Court had declined to a figure of 32 out of the 84 nominal parties to the Statute.

Some sober reflections on this score based on his experience as a judge in the International Court of Justice were recently set down by the distinguished Belgian jurist Charles De Visscher. They bear on the major themes explored in this inquiry. Regarding the distinction between legal and political disputes, he wrote:

Recourse, to an international court implies that, and is only completely effective when, the dispute is completely separated from politics. . . . Ever-present politics blocked the effort of doctrine to give what it called a rational definition to the political dispute or to classify political and juridical disputes in sharply distinct categories.

Arbitral agreements, he wrote, "depend, on one hand, on a sufficient moral community between the contracting parties, and, on the other hand, on the condition of general political relations between them." Reservations in the arbitration treaties had a valid purpose: "Experience has shown that agreements accompanied by maturely thoughtful reservations are often those which are the most carefully observed." He concluded:

There is no doubt . . . that a part of the present disappointment with regard to international justice is due to the survival of a state of mind which has exaggerated the possibilities of recourse to courts for the maintenance of peace.[5]

---

[5] "Reflections on the Present Prospect of International Adjudication," *American Journal of International Law,* Vol. 50, No. 3 (July 1956), pp. 468–71.

All history suggests that willingness to abide by law is the end product of a whole chain of social and political events, not the starting point. For nations consistently to act lawfully requires a generalized confidence—now lacking—that any losses they may suffer in one particular proceeding will be balanced out in the long run, as in any going legal order, by advantages based on the over-all protection and satisfactions a community would continuously furnish them.

If this is so, there is little sense in trying to "force" nations to submit disputes of vital political interest to judicial settlement as a general rule. This is not to argue that states cannot sometimes be persuaded to submit certain issues to adjudication. This is sometimes brought about by exploiting their vulnerability to public opinion, their sense of guilt, or their desire to "see the machinery used more frequently," or more concretely, by invoking the existing network of legal obligations in the United Nations Charter and other treaties. Perhaps such a development is the only practicable path to a more lawful world. Certainly its lack of lofty motivation only mirrors the pessimism that colors any analysis of recent experience.

Furthermore, if the limits of international law are not immutable, it does not necessarily follow that the axioms of politics are subject to drastic change. The experience of the past decades has shown that international problems of peaceful change more often than not involve factors no legal system could or should try to encompass. Even in domestic societies one does not legitimately expect municipal law ever to embrace completely those great areas of national life in which interests representing the plural power centers in the nation argue it out according to laboriously developed ground rules, generally without bloodshed, and ultimately through the process of legislation. Law must not be expected to do internationally what law cannot do at home.

Domestic society, in order to keep change within peaceful bounds, requires the seamless web of mutual confidence and purposeful centralized strength without which no community could long endure. In this setting, we have long since recognized the existence of an effective and, in this sense, constitutional relationship between law, politics, and community. The great hope for international society is that men will learn to apply with perception such a constitutional conception. But the *sine qua non* is some form of consensus that can legitimately be called community. For if a true community, however modest, rather than an abstract and purely postulated community, comes alive, the judicial process can concomitantly grow and bear fruit. Such community could emerge as a mutual interest in reducing the threat of a surprise attack, or it could appear as a function of evolution in the structure of the Communist world, or in other ways.

Characteristically unwilling to wait for this necessarily slow development, we tend to become frantic, wishing away the obstacles, or conversely, be-traying the disillusionment of the ex-Puritan who "has nothing left but a cynicism that clatters like invisible handcuffs tying his hands forever from any deep commitment or great purpose." [6]

While working to assist history in the creation of constitutionalism and community among the nations, we must be ever alert to the "backdoor" approaches to world law, and to their potential for growth and development. But nothing would be more fatal to the development of world community, or to the world law that will accompany its development, than to pretend that the process of politics has been, or can be, or even should be eliminated. For all our experience teaches us to assume that in that far-off world order under law, there will still be disputes that are predominantly legal and those that are political. It is only by accommodating itself to these verities of political life that law can be used to help make life work. The alternative is for the theorems of law and the facts of politics to remain locked in a meaningless and futile battle. In this battle, man is the loser.

---

[6] Margaret Mead, *And Keep Your Powder Dry: An Anthropologist Looks at America* (New York, William Morrow, 1943), p. 204.

XXII • The United Nations: One Body, Many Roles

While international law may lack general acceptance as an important element in world politics, international organization becomes ever more active. In any attempt to assess the value of the United Nations, it is essential to understand what the organization is and what it is not. Much of the criticism blames it for not doing what it was never empowered by its founders to do. To be sure, their *hopes* can be found in the Charter, whose first Article sets forth the purposes of the organization as being:

1. to maintain international peace and security;
2. to develop friendly relations among nations based on respect for the principle of equal rights and self-determination of peoples;
3. to solve international problems of an economic, social, cultural, or humanitarian character, and to develop respect for fundamental human rights and freedoms for all persons;
4. to be a center for harmonizing the actions of nations in the attainment of these common ends.

Yet two other basic strictures of the Charter must be understood in order to comprehend the role and the limitations of the United Nations in world affairs: that the organization is "based on the principle of the sovereign equality of all its members," and that nothing in the Charter authorizes intervention in matters "essentially within the domestic jurisdiction of any State." (Article 2, paragraphs 1 and 7.) Thus the United Nations as such can do little, if anything; only through its independent members or by their authority can it act.

Six organs make up the organization: the General Assembly, charged with considering general principles of cooperation in the maintenance of international peace and security; the Security Council, originally given primary responsibility for acting to preserve peace and security; the Economic and Social Council, which deals with health, educational, cultural, social and economic matters; the Trusteeship Council, which gives its attention to the advancement of people in the territories held by certain countries in trust

440

under the international trusteeship system; the International Court of Justice, the judicial organ (discussed in the preceding chapter); and the Secretariat, whose international civil servants act for the organization and may not act on behalf of any particular government.

The security function of the United Nations has already been discussed in Chapter XX, which dealt with the problems of collective security, the principle upon which this aspect of United Nations work is based. Because of the Soviets' extensive use of the veto, the functions of the Security Council have been to some degree assumed by the General Assembly. This was largely accomplished through the passage of the "Uniting for Peace" resolution passed as a result of the Korean crisis of 1950. The analysis by Professor Soward of the political forces at work in the Assembly explains how the United Nations reflects some of the realities of world politics. Certain observers in the West have viewed recent and probable future additions of members to the UN, which give more weight to the Asian-Arab-African bloc in the Assembly, as endangering the position of the Western powers in the United Nations. Actually, predictions of patterns of voting hostile or revengeful toward the Western powers (growing out of anti-colonialism) have not come true.[1] This has also been the case with the alarms sounded often, particularly in the United States, that the UN would come to be dominated by Communist countries. The nine Soviet-controlled votes have generally stood alone or merely followed the lead of other nations and blocs.

What seems to have happened is that the basic intention of the leaders of the Big Five at San Francisco to control UN action in the crucial area of international security has gradually given way to assumption of this role by the General Assembly with its majority-vote rule. Whether or not these gradual transformations will mean lessened use of the UN by the Great Powers, in favor of the more traditional methods of diplomacy and of stronger regional arrangements, only the future can tell. However, one authoritative American source has recently indicated that "if the nations of the world had been without a place to air their grievances and adjust their differences under a code of international behavior, our civilization might well have been destroyed in a nuclear war." [2] The United Nations *has* been useful in the political field, even if it has fallen short of the expectations of 1945.

Many feel that, in the long run, the organization will prove most effective through the extensive but usually unspectacular programs of the non-political agencies in solving economic and social problems which might otherwise lead to war. Coordinated through the Economic and Social Council of 18 members, these functions are performed mainly by Economic Commissions on four continents (Europe, Asia and the Far East, Latin America, and Africa), and by the eleven specialized agencies, each with its own membership, budget,

---

[1] Inis J. Claude, *Swords Into Plowshares* (New York: Random House, 1958), 2nd ed., pp. 454–57.

[2] Francis O. Wilcox, "The United Nations: The Road Ahead," *Department of State Publication* 6712 (October 1958), p. 20.

and set of operating principles. These agencies include: the International Labor Organization, World Health Organization, Food and Agriculture Organization, Universal Postal Union, International Bank for Reconstruction and Development, International Monetary Fund, International Civil Aviation Organization, United Nations Educational, Scientific and Cultural Organization, International Telecommunication Union, World Meteorological Organization, and the new International Atomic Energy Agency. Programs of these bodies are supplemented by an increasing number of agencies created by and working directly under the General Assembly, such as the Korean Reconstruction Agency, the Relief and Works Agency for Palestine, and the Committee on Information from Non-Self-Governing Territories. The activities of these bodies seldom make headlines, but they may promote peace in a manner never imagined by practitioners of the older diplomacy.

Those frustrated by the failures of the security system of the UN may take solace also in considering the avenues of contact and understanding between peoples which are provided by the organization and its facilities. Yet it is not only the idealist internationalists who find hope here; such scholars as Otto Klineberg, Professor of Psychology at Columbia University, see in the work of such agencies as UNESCO the first breakthrough in drawing into decision-making the findings and advice of specialists in the sciences of human relations. We have seen how realists like Kecskemeti tend to disparage efforts to reduce tension, but Klineberg takes the position that the reduction of tension can be approached directly, that tension itself creates further tension, and that it is therefore a political problem whose solution can have a significant impact upon political reality.

1 • The Role of International Organization: Limits and Possibilities *

Stanley Hoffman

A former officer of the French Political Science Association, the author is Associate Professor of Government at Harvard University. His writings include Organisations Internationales et Pouvoirs des Etats *(1954)*, Le Mouvement Poujade *(1956), and* Contemporary Theory in International Relations *(1960)*. He has contributed to France Defeats EDC *(1957) and* Area and Power *(1959)*. At present he is working on a study of the theory of international relations and has published a brilliant article "International Relations: The Long Road to Theory" in World Politics *(1959)*.

No field of study is more slippery than international relations. The student of government has a clear frame of reference: the state within which occur the developments which he examines. The student of international relations, unhappily, oscillates between the assumption of a world community which does not exist, except as an ideal, and the various units whose decisions and connections form the pattern of world politics—mainly, the nation-states. International organizations therefore tend to be considered either as the first institutions of a world in search of its constitution or as instruments of foreign policies. The scholar who follows the first approach usually blames, correctly enough, the nation-states for the failures of the organization; but he rarely indicates the means which could be used to bring the realities of world society into line with his ideal. The scholar who takes the second approach stresses, accurately enough, how limited the autonomy of international organizations has been and how little they have contributed to the achievement of their objectives; but because he does not discuss his fundamental assumption—the permanence of the nation-state's driving role in world politics—he reaches somewhat too easily the conclusion that the only prospect in international affairs is more of the same.

It may well be that this conclusion, too, is justified, but it should not be arrived at through a shortcut. The approach which seems the most satisfactory, though not the simplest, should be the following one. First, the objectives defined by the Charter of the United Nations are to be considered as the best moral goals statesmen can pursue; that is, the maintenance of peace and security, the promotion of economic, social and cultural cooperation, respect for human rights, and the establishment of procedures for peaceful change. (Implicit in this assumption is, of course, another one: it is legitimate that statesmen should assign moral ends to their

---

* *International Organization*, X (1956), pp. 357–72. Reprinted by permission.

policies, and that states' activities should be submitted to moral judgments, the absence of a single, supranational system of values notwithstanding.) Secondly, the means through which these objectives are to be sought are necessarily international agreements; no conquest of the world by one nation, or even by an alliance of nations, could bring them about; consent is indispensable, even if it means that they can only be reached gradually and partially. Thirdly, it cannot be assumed at the outset that the present structure of international society *must* be the permanent framework of action, for it may well be that the objectives cannot be reached within such a framework, as, for instance, the World Federalists have argued. Changes in the structure may thus appear necessary. But one has to avoid utopias; if it is unwise to postulate the perpetuation of the present system, it is equally unwise to advocate ways which an analysis of world politics reveals to be blocked.

The problem which we want to discuss briefly can thus be phrased in the following terms: given the present structure of world society, what *should* and what *can* international organizations do to promote the objectives which we have mentioned?

I

A short analysis of present world society reveals a number of paradoxes and contradictions.

In the first place, the scene is dominated by two opposite developments. On the one hand, there is the phenomenon usually described as bipolarity of power. On the other hand, at the same time that military and economic strength has become centered, temporarily perhaps, in only two superpowers, there has been a trend toward further political disintegration of the world. As the process of "social mobilisation" of hitherto "passive" peoples progresses, the number of sovereign states has increased, and the continuing break-up of former empires will undoubtedly add new ones. Both developments, contradictory as they appear, make the return to a concert of the great powers impossible; the necessary solidarity and fluidity of power are both gone. And yet, the technological gap between the advanced and the backward nations is greater than ever before.

In the second place, the process of interlocking interests and activities, which internationalists once hopefully described as leading inevitably to a world community, has indeed continued. The distinction between internal and international affairs is now ruled out; it has therefore become impossible to prevent one nation from influencing and intervening in the policies of another. The superb autonomy and specialization of diplomacy is over, and nearly the whole world has become a "Turkish question." At the same time, however, the psychological effect of this development has been rebellion and seeking refuge in a conception made for, and reminiscent of, a more idyllic age: the concept of national sovereignty and independence. The contradiction is nowhere more apparent than in the UN itself. The organization has contributed immeasurably to an internationalization of all problems, and to a kind of equalization of diplomatic standards and practices for all members; but at the same time its operations are based on the principle of equality and the myth of sovereignty. The smaller states use sovereignty as a fortress, and the superpowers as a safeguard of their own freedom of action against friendly or hostile restraints.

In the third place, the two sets of factors previously mentioned have produced a fundamental change in the politics of the two leading powers. The great powers of the nineteenth century used limited means for limited objectives. The relations between these powers could easily be described in equations, or at least in mechanistic terms—balancing process, equilibrium, etc. The superpowers of today have transnational objectives; each one stands both for a certain organization of the world, and for a certain distribution of social forces and political power in each nation. The means they use, with one important exception (the resort to general war), are also much broader. Their emphasis, in the choice of means, is far less on *national* power, far more on gaining allies. As some theorists have shown, this "multiple equilibrium" opens new channels of influence for the two superpowers and creates, at the expense of both, new procedures of restraint quite different from the restraints imposed on the big powers by the European concert. No big power can "go it alone" and define its interests to the exclusion of other nations' interests; the only, though very real and important, choice it has is between more and less broad international definitions of ends and means, depending on the kind and amount of international power it wants to mobilize.

In the fourth place, the smaller nations are torn between two modes of behavior in which they usually try to indulge simultaneously, as well as between two attitudes toward both the nation-state and the UN. The two modes of behavior represent two levels of world politics. On the one hand, the smaller states try to protect themselves, *collectively,* against the rivalries of the two superpowers. Individually, they would be the victims of the great conflict; together, they have the best chance of restraining the big powers and of gaining a number of advantages in return. Some seek such a common escape in a broad alliance with the United States (Rio Treaty, NATO, SEATO), others in a neutral belt. But in either case, thus protected against the "nationalistic universalism" of the superpowers, they practice traditional nationalism quietly. The smaller nations live in two ages at the same time. As for the two attitudes toward the nation-state and the UN, each one is taken by a different group of states. The new nations focus on the nation-state their highest ambitions of international power, economic development, and social unity. Furthermore, their attachment to the nation-state is proportional to the intensity of their will not to get involved in the big-power conflict: a feeling that neutralists in Europe have echoed and expressed sometimes in impressive theoretical arguments. These nations, at the same time, look on the UN with great enthusiasm; they see in it an instrument for the advancement of the smaller nations (in number and in power), and a mechanism for restraining the superpowers. On the contrary, the older nation-states of continental western Europe are more disabused of the nation-state, even though it retains the citizens' basic loyalty; and they look at the UN with greater misgivings, both because they have been out-voted so often in the UN on colonial issues, and because they contest the wisdom of spreading all over the world the disease of nationalism which they, too, contracted once, and from which they have suffered grievously.

This brief description leads to a few remarks concerning the scholar's or the politician's usual approaches to the understanding of world politics. First, it shows the fallacy of simple models or categories of analysis. The assumption of a Hobbesian state of nature among states is misleading. It exaggerates the degree of opposition between loyalty to the nation and cooperation among nations, as well as the degree to which the more unmitigated forms of "power politics" are being used by nations; it leads to the presently hopeless solution of world government as the only alternative to a world of militarized, anti-liberal, indeed carnivorous nations. Now, this is not at all the way in which many people think of the nation-state. It over-simplifies the reasons for the rise of anti-liberal forces which are not engendered only by the clash of sovereignties and nationalism; it leaves out all the restraints which, in the 19th century, made the state of nature a rather Lockian one, and, in recent years, shaped a system so new and complex that no theorist has anticipated it. The model of Hobbes is not more accurate than the model of the world community—which may explain why it is so easy to jump from the first to the second.

In the second place, the analysis of foreign policies in terms of power, or of power and purpose, is also insufficient. The concept of national power is no guide in a century where ideas are the most powerful weapons, if it does not include the strength of ideological appeals. Even if it does, it fails to explain the differences between the ends and means of foreign policy in periods of limited conflicts and relative stability, and in revolutionary periods.

Thirdly, the usefulness of reasoning on the basis of internal or even international precedents appears very limited. Those who show, not without truth, the distorting effects of the nation-state on the thinking of the citizens, are sometimes the first to use examples drawn from the development of constitutionalism. Those who deplore the forces which have destroyed the simple and autonomous mechanisms of nineteenth century diplomacy are too easily inclined to use it as a standard and as a still attainable ideal.

Finally, the statesmen's view of world politics is sometimes equally over-simplified. Western statesmen have tended to assume too readily that there are two completely separate spheres of world politics today: the conflicts with the communist bloc, all around the iron curtain, and the relations with the rest of the world, where all the objectives of the UN may be gradually reached, where anti-Soviet collective security and solid, supranational communities can be organized without any Soviet leap over the barriers of containment. The Soviets have tended, and still tend, to assume too easily that, in the non-Soviet world, all is tension and conflict, as if the alignments established as buffers against the cold war did not dampen minor antagonisms.

II

Before examining what international organization should and could do in such a world, let us see what its recent role in international politics *has been*.

The UN was built on two assumptions; both have proved to be unjustified. The first was, of course, the survival of a concert of great powers. The second was what one might call the Kant-Wilson hypothesis. The organization was supposed to harmonize the interests of sovereign states, conceived as nineteenth century nations. Their international policies would therefore be distinguishable from their internal problems. Their usual antagonisms would be limited in scope, or at least seldom involve their national existence. This was the assumption of a world squarely based on the nation-state—the hypothesis of inter-state cooperation for and with peace and security. There was nothing revolutionary about it; historically, it was rather reactionary, in so far as it tried to revive conditions whose disappearance had brought about two world wars. Both assumptions implicitly envisaged the establishment of a widely acceptable *status quo,* on the basis of which the organization would operate. The tragedy has been the conflict between these underlying hypotheses and the two major realities of world politics: the bipolarity of power and the further disintegration of the world.

The consequence of the conflict between the first postulate and bipolarity has been the failure of the collective security mechanisms of the Charter. The conflict between the second postulate and the multiplication of nation-states, due to the anti-colonial revolution has led the UN to use as channels of peaceful change the procedures created for the settlement of ordinary disputes. It was hoped that the UN might thus harness that revolution. However, change has taken place, not as the consequence of, but either outside of or before the decisions of the UN, and it has been violent and often savage. The UN has given the impression of merely smoothing some of the edges and of running after the revolution so as not to be left too far behind.

In order to avoid complete paralysis on cold war issues because of the first conflict, and to transcend the procedural limitations which have made it difficult to cope with the second, the organization has escaped from its original Charter and changed into a "new United Nations." However, the new, unofficial charter is based upon an assumption which conflicts not only with the old ones, but also again with the reality. Both the "Uniting-for-Peace" resolution, charter of the "cold war" role of the UN, and the more fragmentary code of practices adopted by the UN in dealing with the anti-colonial revolution were obviously necessary in order to keep the UN in line with the main currents of international politics. But the policy of collective assertion, parliamentary debates and majority votes assumes the existence of a sort of world community, where decisions similar to those reached in the framework of a constitutional system would make sense —a far cry from both the hierarchical big-power rule and from the inter-state league of the Wilsonians. All these contradictions have engaged the UN in a series of vicious circles.

On the cold war front, bipolarity has made the resurrection of a concert of power against the one threatening big state fairly ineffective. The fear many small nations have of becoming engulfed in the cold war has, of course, undermined the whole argument behind the Uniting-for-Peace Resolution. Furthermore, the impossibility of tracing a clear line between internal and international affairs has obscured the idea of aggression; when aggression is easily disguised as social liberation, it is not astonishing to see the very nation which advocates a clear-cut definition of aggression suggest that civil or national-liberation wars be left out of the organization's reach. Finally, the fact that recommendations have to be made by a $\frac{2}{3}$ majority increases the small nations' power to destroy the new system either by refusing to make it work or by irresponsible recommendations which not they, but the big states, will have to carry out; the balance between proclamation and performance is a difficult one. Both the difficulties and the dangers of putting into effect the "Uniting-for-Peace" machinery show that the primary emphasis in the UN cannot be put on collective security.

The attempts to cope with the nationalist revolutions and the problem of change are not much more satisfactory. Conditions are so revolutionary that the UN has been unable to use effectively conciliatory procedures tailored only for conflicts between stabilized sovereign states. But world politics remain so strongly based on the sovereign state that the UN cannot get its assertions of competence and declarations of policy accepted by those of its members whose sovereignty is thereby infringed. If the members of the majorities point out that sovereignty means little in an era when internal tensions become matters of international concern, the outvoted members can always argue that the majorities policies lead not to greater integration of the world, but to an increase in the number of sovereign units eager to shield their own activities behind Article 2, paragraph 7. The issues between states, in an era where conflicts do indeed involve the very existence of nations, the birth of some, the dismantling of others, cannot be settled by resort to a world court: hence the constant refusal of the Assembly to submit such questions to it. But precisely because the issue is the life and death of the basic units in world politics, it is useless to expect the more threatened ones to submit to majority votes.

The result, not unexpectedly, is frequently deadlock followed by a retreat of the UN. The policies advocated by it are not carried out, and after a decent resistance the UN ceases to recommend them. The committees established for the implementation of these policies fail to obtain the cooperation of the other party, and when the walls of Jericho refuse to collapse, it is the committee which is broken up. At the same time the more modest task which the original Charter did allow the UN to perform—what we called the smoothing of edges, the curbing of the worst forms of unavoidable violence—becomes more difficult for two reasons. The decision of the UN to take a substantive stand reduces the chances of conciliation by increasing the opposing party's resistance and distrust. Furthermore the two main trends of present world politics have interacted. The cold war has first thrown a shadow over, then a monkey wrench into, UN attempts at securing peaceful change. The break-up of the original concert of powers in these matters has increased the chances of change through violence; it has emancipated the anti-colonial nations from a possible big-power tutelage; in so far as the Soviets support them, while the US is allied to the colonial powers in such institutions as NATO and SEATO, it has become far more difficult for the UN to oblige the antagonists or the reluctant side in a colonial conflict to renounce violence.

It may have been vain to expect, in a world where the two main trends create for existing states a good deal of trouble, that an international organization established for coping with the irrepressible, minimum degree of insecurity that persists during stabilized periods could do much to eliminate the glaring insecurities of today. Maybe the organization could, indeed, be nothing but a "gentle civilizer." But the civilizer has not always been gentle. It has rather tended to increase the degree of insecurity, while both the cold war and the peculiar voting system which gives the loudest notes to sing to the weakest voices have prevented it from harnessing the forces it helped to set in motion. The reliance on, and exploitation of, the vague, broad and yet-to-be achieved principles and purposes of the Charter have combined the maximum of ambiguity with the maximum of resistance from the members. The result has been a somewhat disturbing division of labor between the world body and the regional organizations; the problems that could be solved were quite legitimately dealt with by the latter, but the UN has become the recipient of those problems which just cannot be solved diplomatically, *a fortiori* by parliamentary votes in the Assembly. This was particularly apparent in the case of all the cold war conflicts which were submitted to the UN by both parties for propaganda purposes; on these issues, and on most of the colonial problems as well, Mr. Kennan's rather cruel description of the Assembly's votes as a series of "tableaux morts" is an apt one.

Self-restraint or resignation to very limited and superficial soothing tasks might have killed the organization. But taking worthy stands and cheering itself up until it gets hoarse, has not really saved it as a force in world affairs—though such attitudes might have made it useful as an instrument serving a number of widely different foreign policies. The rules of the "new UN," like the rules of the original Charter, create both too rigid and too big-meshed a net of obligations for member nations. It is too rigid, in so far as compliance with these rules has proved to be impossible. It is too big-meshed, because in order to be applicable to so many different states, these obligations inevitably had to be few and vague. Thus, the rather obvious and recognized solidarity of interests among smaller groups of states is not sanctioned by any set of norms and institutions common to them. These great gaps increase insecurity, the chances of conflicts, and uncushioned power politics.

III

The following considerations on what the role of international organization *should be* in the present world are based on the following postulates. *a*) The nation-state, conceived as a legally sovereign unit in a tenuous net of breakable obligations, is not the framework in which the ideals we have defined at the outset can *all* be realized or approximated. It can hardly be maintained that it affords the greatest possibilities of economic advance, and even, in many areas, of orderly political and social change. *b*) Experience to date has shown that political organization on a world scale cannot, by itself, advance beyond the stage of the nation-state: its fate is linked to the nation-state. Three consequences flow from these postulates.

The first consequence concerns the role of the political organs of the UN. If they cannot shape new forces, they should at least prevent the nation-states from getting even further away from the distant objectives which the UN proclaims. The two tests—rather negative ones, one may fear—which each decision or recommendation should meet are, first, a test of responsibility: will it decrease, increase, or leave unchanged the state of tension with which it is supposed to deal? If it will not contribute to decreasing tensions, it should not be made, except if inaction is clearly bound to produce even worse consequences than intervention. This test is particularly necessary in colonial affairs. ...Secondly, a test of efficiency: is the measure advocated, sound as it may be, backed by a sufficient combination of interests and forces? Otherwise, it will be an empty gesture.

The second consequence suggests the need for building new institutions which will help the nation to go beyond the stage of the nation-state. A case can be made—and has often been made—against excessive and premature attempts at establishing "rigid legal norms" and institutions; it has been said that the process of integrating nations must be left to the free interplay of political, economic and social forces within them. Undoubtedly, no organization can be effective if there are no such favorable forces; it can not create them. But where they do exist, a network of legal obligations and institutions can consolidate the common interests at the expense of the divergent ones, and act as the indispensable catalyst of an emergent community; otherwise there would be no opportunity to select, seize, save and stress the unifying forces.

The reason why the nations tend to organize themselves as states and why the highest allegiance of the citizens usually belongs to the state is that this form of political organization affords them protection, security, justice, gratifications and services. Therefore, the only way to transfer loyalty to another set of institutions is to create new agencies which will provide the citizens with some of these advantages and help in gradually building communities larger than nations.

But these new agencies will be solid and effective only if they are accepted freely by the peoples they are supposed to link. This means, in the first place, that the peoples will have to reach the "national stage" first. Recognition of the insufficiency of the nation as framework of social organization can only come *after* the nation has achieved a large measure of self-government. Consequently, in areas where no nation-state has yet been established, the national stage cannot, in all probability, be skipped. However, independence might be accompanied by an agreement on "interdependence" with other countries for clearly defined and accepted functions.

In the second place, wherever the nations, new or old, have all the attributes, blessings and curses of the sovereign state, a difficult task of incitement and negotiations will have to be performed. Political federation is probably ruled out in the early stages. Except perhaps in the limited European area where disillusionment with the nation-state is strongest (but how far does it go?). One cannot expect, even under the stress created by necessities of defense or economic development, that nation-states will agree to the kind of wholesale transfer of powers which political federation requires. Suicide, so to speak, if it takes place at all, will have to be piecemeal. Political power cannot be expected to

be abandoned first. Nor is it sure that political federation is always a desirable goal. The main enemy of international stability and individual liberty, in those countries where the nation-state has ceased to be a refuge and become a prison, is not the nation, but the state; it is the concentration of political, economic, military power, etc.... in one set of institutions. The creation, by amalgamation of existing nation-states, of a new state similar in its essence to the previous ones and even larger in area can hardly be called an improvement. A federation strong enough to survive the strains of birth and youth might soon develop into a super-nation; the trend toward centralization, observed in all federations, could lead to such a result. A decrease in the number of leviathans is no gain if it is compensated by an increase in their respective power. Thus, the only practical way to reach the aim— a decentralization of allegiance—seems to be the establishment of functional institutions based on trans-national interests. In order to be effective, these agencies would have to be geographically limited. Or, if in certain cases a regional limitation makes little sense economically, they should possess some ideological, historical or technical justification. They would therefore, as a rule, not be universal institutions like the UN and its specialized agencies, but, for instance, organizations in which certain underdeveloped countries sharing one common economic problem would cooperate with more advanced nations which have solved or faced the same problem at home or in their colonies. The nation-state would thus be caught in a variety of nets. Gradually, unobtrusively perhaps, a large measure of economic power would be transferred to the new agencies. They would for a long time to come leave to the state a kind of negative power to destroy the net; nevertheless, they could reach and provide the individuals with tangible services. They would not constitute an immediate rival for the states and would therefore expect more consent or at least less violent resistance. The most effective attack on sovereignty is not a frontal one—it is one which slowly but clearly deprives sovereignty of its substance, and consequently of its prestige. The build-up of interlocking functional communities is required both by the presently strong attachment to formal sovereignty and by the actual interlocking interests which can become a positive force in world politics only if they are institutionalized.

As a third consequence of our two postulates, the UN should concentrate on, and develop, its role as a "center for harmonizing the actions of nations in the attainment of (the) common ends" which these joint interests suggest. Indeed the UN should either take the initiative or at least assume responsibility for the establishment and coordination of the regional or functional communities we have advocated. Two reasons militate for such a policy. In the first place, it is necessary to provide the UN, checkmated on political issues, with a new area of activities in its own interest. Secondly, the west, increasingly unable in political matters to get its views accepted by others through a process of "collectivization of interests," but unable also to discard the world body, must find constructive ways of seizing the initiative. In the inevitable clash of ideas between east and west, the west cannot merely offer to the nations the ideal of internal democracy; it must also present the image of a more satisfactory world order. The Soviet Union, which wants to prevent a consolidation of the non-communist world, plays upon the strong attachment which is still felt to the nation-state and to nationalism, sovereignty and independence. The west cannot fight back on this ground; it would mean giving up the objectives we have mentioned. Nor can the west propose such revolutionary changes that the Soviets might successfully exploit this continuing attachment to the shelter of sovereignty, as well as charge the west with hypocrisy, since none of the leading western states is ready to sacrifice large areas of its own sovereignty.

Again, a progressive middle road seems to be the right one. This is precisely where the UN can operate. Militarily, the role of the UN, as we indicated, can only be a very limited one; it is therefore normal that initiatives for collective defense be taken outside of it. But initiatives for economic action should be made within the UN. This would be politically advantageous. The suggested regional or functional institutions can hardly function without western economic assistance. Now, the new nations have shown a distrust of purely western initiatives, interpreted as cold war moves, and a respect for the UN, which suggest that the UN should be selected as the channel for such assistance. It is also wise technically; there is a need for coordination of the present and future technical institutions, which can best be exercised by the UN. As the French Foreign Minister, M. Christian Pineau, has recently suggested, an agency for world economic development should be created within the framework of the UN. This agency would coordinate and control specialized agencies such as the International Monetary Fund and the International Bank for Reconstruction and Development, as well as the UN technical assistance activities and more recently created or proposed UN institutions such as the International Finance Corporation and the Special United Nations Fund for Economic Development. It should give its aid, gifts, loans, technical assistance, raw materials or energy, etc., to the regional or functional organizations we have recommended, rather than to states directly. These organizations would be sponsored by the UN agency and established among the under-developed nations (with or without direct participation of the industralized ones). They would be the pioneers of supra-national development. The UN agency, being international by virtue of the Charter, would play the more modest but essential role of an instigator.

IV

The last question we have to discuss is obviously the most difficult one: *can* international organizations play the role we have tried to assign to them?

First, as for limiting the political organs of the UN to the rather limited tasks we have suggested, there is little doubt about the answer. On colonial and self-determination issues, the small powers, which are indispensable in the decision-making process, cannot be led to abandon the policy they have promoted in recent years; the Soviet bloc may be expected to fan the flames, and the United States cannot easily try to stop the movement—the more so, since it needs the small powers in case of a return to acute cold war tension. The answer here is: no. However, on the issue of collective security and also in the settlement of ordinary disputes, the organization might be condemned not just to violate the two tests we have indicated, but not even to reach the stage where proposals would be submitted to the tests. Both the reluctance of a majority of members to face the cold war and the neutralization of UN procedures by the conflicting maneuvers of the big powers could lead to such a paralysis. Writers who have shown how useful an instrument of American foreign policy the UN is have attached too much importance to the Korean miracle

and the mechanical "50 to 5" votes and underestimated the eventuality of Russian exploitation of UN procedures. However, any American attempt at penalizing the small powers either by direct pressure or by de-emphasizing the importance of the UN would leave the field wide open to the Soviet Union. The Soviets, who adopted in the worst years of the cold war an attitude of disdain for the UN, have now realized what possibilities of counterattack they have neglected; nor can the United States afford to abandon the UN in favor of pure bilateralism or regionalism. Each of the superpowers is, in a way, caught in the UN. In spite of the partial excesses and the partial paralysis, the political organs must be preserved. By promoting diplomatic intercourse among all nations, they allow the more underdeveloped ones to use their participation as both a compensation for and as a weapon against the gap that separates them from the more advanced states. Also, if the world should return to multipolarity and stabilization, the UN must be there to perform at last the services that had been prematurely expected in the days of euphoria.

Secondly, could the UN play the new economic and social role which we have suggested? The obstacle here seems to be the reluctance of the United States and Great Britain to allow the UN to play such a role, and to transfer a major part of their foreign aid funds to the UN. It has been suggested that the west might lose its freedom of movement on the economic front of the "cold war" if it accepted a system in which the smaller powers, and the USSR itself, could control the use of western resources. This argument is debatable on two counts. It is better to risk providing the nations concerned with a sort of right of veto or a brake on the activities of a UN economic agency than to sow the seeds of grave economic rivalries, misallocation of resources, and social and international tensions by taking no intiative at all. Such would undoubtedly be the effects of the uncoordinated policies of nations which may all want to industrialize themselves without regard for the regional distribution of opportunities and the scarcity of investment funds. To resort to purely western initiatives made outside of the UN is to court failure, as the new nations fear colonialism in disguise and western "cold war" intentions. To wait for local initiatives is not very wise either. A study of existing economic agencies shows that with the significant exception of the European Coal and Steel Community and new continental European projects, American or British initiatives have been decisive. The institution we suggest, which could be an irritating check on western policies, would also provide the west with a big and subtle channel for getting the main points of its policies across far better than through direct aid to a few selected allies; the dose of economic medicine administered to the peoples of underdeveloped areas through such an institution may be excessively sweetened in consequence of their objections, but it will still be administered to more.

Furthermore, the opportunities that a UN agency might give to Soviet maneuvering are not greater than the opportunities the Soviets already have for exploiting nationalism and driving wedges between those nations closer to the west and the uncommitted ones. If the main western powers carry their hostility against the restraint exercised at their expense by the small nations so far that the more traditional emphasis on bilateral diplomacy and "self-interest," narrowly defined, is preferred, then indeed Soviet strategy will have won. Bilateralism breeds separation, and further opportunities for political and economic conflicts. It allows the Soviets to outbid the west, or at least to drag the west into an endless bidding game. On the contrary, if the west did take the initiative in proposing a world agency on the lines we suggest, and if the Soviets refused to join in order to "go it alone," their own unilateral offers of aid would then become as politically suspect as western offers have sometimes become. The example of SUNFFD should be kept in mind. The Soviets, in the beginning, were as cool to the Fund as were the western industrial nations. Strengthening an important area of the non-communist world could hardly have been welcome to the Soviets; but in 1954 and 1955 they saw that they could exploit western reluctance at no cost to themselves, and they rallied to the under-developed nations' claim for a rapid establishment of a Fund. Western reticence and insistence on priority for bilateral aid may prove to be a serious mistake. American opposition, at first, to close bonds between the proposed Atoms-for-Peace organization and the UN, and the shift, between 1953 and 1954, from a revolutionary and truly supra-national institution to a mere clearing house, can also be criticized on these grounds. The more rapidly the world moves out of the situation of bipolarity, the more useful it will be for the west to deal with the under-developed, uncommitted members of the "third force" through a world organization, where their moves and maneuvers can be more easily controlled than if they too enjoyed total freedom from international restraints.

Finally, it remains necessary to dis-cuss the chances of success of regional or functional institutions sponsored by a UN agency of the kind we have suggested. The record of existing regional and functional organizations such as NATO, the Colombo plan, the OEEC, the European Coal and Steel Community, and the OAS, does not really answer the question, because most of them have not been launched for the purposes and in the conditions we have advocated. However, the main conclusions have to be taken into consideration. In the first place, outside of the Soviet bloc in which regionalism is an instrument of Soviet hegemony, there has been no political integration. In political matters, interstate cooperation remains the most one can expect. Secondly, the greatest measure of effective supranational integration has been achieved, ironically enough, in military alliances. This is an ominous sign indeed, whose meaning can best be seen in connection with a third conclusion. The most successful non-military organizations are those which are squarely based on their members' calculations that the common agencies will bring benefits to them as nations; the framework of expectations remains the nation-state, not the larger area served by the agencies. States are more willing to confess their military insufficiency than their economic and social weaknesses. When it is a question of welfare, not of survival, the urgency seems smaller. This explains why NATO has never been able to play the same role in economic and political matters as in military affairs. The only relative exception to the last conclusion is western Europe, for the reasons which were indicated above. It is no accident that the only area in which individuals may appeal, in case of a violation of their rights, to a supranational body is part of the territory covered by the Council of Europe; and even there the process is a slow and limited one.

Thus, the precedents show a need for caution and realism. Many serious objections must be contemplated. First, there are obstacles to the very establishment of the institutions we have advocated. The most obvious one is, again, the cold war. How will it be possible even for a UN agency to convince the new uncommitted nations to harmonize their development plans and, as it may appear necessary, to "de-nationalize" a part of their economic resources and policies, when they are encouraged to stick to the nation-state by Soviet strategy and may even receive Soviet help if they refuse to join western-inspired arrangements? There is no doubt about the crippling effect Soviet policy could have; but this is not a reason to give up trying, since this is precisely what the Soviet Union would like to force the west into. Furthermore the Atoms-for-Peace case shows that the west disposes here of such a powerful lever that even the Soviet Union cannot afford to remain aloof and hostile—or else, as in the Marshall Plan precedent, in spite of all her threats and baits the nations which see the advantages of such common enterprises will join at great cost to Soviet prestige.

A second obstacle can be called the vicious circle. The new institutions can not be created without the consent of and, especially in case of UN sponsorship, without a controlling role for the recipient nations. Will they not therefore be able to veto, for nationalistic reasons, more ambitious plans of supranational development, and end up with nothing more than the more timid and traditional inter-governmental cooperation schemes, loaded with safeguards and rights of veto? This may well be. But even modest schemes are better than unbridled competitions, and additionally, in so far as most of the functional plans would depend on support from the industrialized nations of the west, the bargaining power of the latter should not be underrated. The needs of the under-developed nations are such that if they had to choose between the discomforts of isolation and the sacrifice of sovereignty involved in joint development projects, it should not be lightly assumed that they would prefer the first—unless the west couched its appeal too much in cold war terms, or asked at the outset for too many sacrifices of sovereignty. The possible advent of a "third industrial revolution" should give to the western nations, who have such an advance in atomic energy experience, a very powerful counter. The debates in the 1955 General Assembly on Atoms-for-Peace have shown that the under-developed nations are willing to accept and even to promote joint undertakings as an alternative to the western tactics of bilateral agreements, which they resent.

A third obstacle could prevent either the establishment or the efficient functioning of the suggested institutions. Will not the basic political antagonisms between states paralyze these agencies? Will not, for instance, the fear that the members might have of each other's ambitions or power prevent any joint undertaking? Or will not the nation which has the greatest resources and skills, or whose economic development will appear to be the most necessary for the whole area's advance, seize these advantages and impose gradually its domination over the other members under the cloak of supra-national arrangements? Here again, one must recognize that the risk does exist and that such fears may either play a deterrent role or saddle the institutions with crippling provisions for balancing purposes. It would indeed be naïve to expect these institutions to put an end to "power politics." They would provide new channels, new restraints and new fields of action for it. But it would be equally naïve to expect, in the absence of any joint undertaking, that the effects of uneven distribution of power would not be felt. They cannot be eliminated; but they can be softened and used for the common good if adequate common mechanisms are established. Thus, this objection is, and should be, a cause for great caution in the establishment of new institutions, but definitely not for inaction.

The last objections bear upon the effects such mechanisms, if they are successfully established, might be expected to produce. On the one hand, it is suggested that the decentralization of allegiance to which we have referred will not take place because the various states will still act as a screen between the individuals and the supra-national bodies. State borders might lose their political significance, but their psychological effects will be preserved, and the states will have a vested interest in not allowing too big a transfer of loyalty to the new units. On the other hand, one might say that even if the states did not insist on keeping their subjects' full allegiance, the transfer of loyalty to utilitarian, technocratic bureaucracies deprived of any contact with the peoples they work for is very unlikely indeed. There really is no easy refutation of this argument; the dreams of rational internationalists have been shattered more than once; there is little doubt that the splitting of loyalties can only be the result of a very long process, and that it will require a period of peace in which the state's prestige and resistance to encroachment on its powers can be eroded. Common economic interests have not prevented nationalist explosions; nor can the institutionalization of these interests be expected to suppress them. In most parts of the world, on the most elemental and vital problems, the nation-state will keep the final say. But this is not an argument against trying both to remove the greatest possible number of questions from the sacred zone of nationalism and sovereignty to the unglamorous sphere of international cooperation and to create such patterns that even when the last word remains with the state, this word will be in no small way conditioned by the state's commitments and by the growing habit of common action.

V

If we state, then, what can be done, and compare it with what should be done, the prospects appear both modest and not at all hopeless. Far less can be done than the most ardent internationalists desire or sometimes expect. But somewhat more can be done than the spokesmen for reliance on "wise statesmanship" or on the manifestation of "perennial forces" seem to believe, and certainly quite a lot more should be tried.

The defenders and promoters of international organizations would have a much stronger case if they recognized frankly the two following limitations. First, there is no sudden mutation in world politics, and the forces that may some day break the crust of the nation-state can only be helped, not created, by international organization. This is why the basis of action remains the state, why the chances of truly supranational institutions, even limited to certain functions, are far smaller, in most parts of the world, than those of organs of international cooperation, why even ambitious supra-national schemes might not operate very differently from these, and finally why in the new bodies "power politics" will continue. But this is not what matters. Power politics also survive in the internal affairs of any nation. What counts is the framework and the general direction of the process.

Secondly, the mushrooming of international institutions will not solve the fundamental issue of security. They can be created on all sides of the big abysses that separate the nations and threaten world peace—the cold war, the colonial revolution; they cannot bridge the gaps. Here the balance of power between the superpowers, and between the crumbling empires and the rising new nations, are the decisive factors. The most international organization can do is to provide restraints on the superpowers and centers of cooperation between old and new nations after the colonial issue has been decided by force or by local agreements.

Once these limitations are accepted, the role of international organization should appear in its true light. Even if it were not much more than that of an "amiable civilizer," it would still be a far bigger one than many challengers seem to suggest. They usually leave this role to traditional diplomacy. International organization as a fragile but still badly explored diplomatic method can, within its own limits, help the nations to transcend the limits of the nation-state.

2 • The Changing Balance of Power in the United Nations *

F. H. Soward

The author is Associate Dean of Graduate Studies, Head of the Department of History, and Director of International Studies at the University of British Columbia. He is a Fellow of the Royal Society of Canada and the author and contributor of several books in the field of Canadian external policy and international relations. He was a member of the Canadian delegation to the United Nations General Assembly for the year 1956/57 and was Rapporteur of the Fourth Committee at that session.

An American scholar who has made a special study of regionalism commented recently that "clearly, an uneasy and unstable equilibrium among contending and overlapping blocs has arisen at the United Nations which is defining the limits of international action and also imposing distinct reins on the freedom of multilateral and regional action."[1] This verdict by Professor Haas can be illustrated by a study of the pattern of voting at the Eleventh Session of the General Assembly. However, for reasons that will be indicated later, the writer would prefer to use the word "group" rather than "bloc" for all but one of the electoral combinations which were manifest in Assembly proceedings.

THE EFFECT OF NEW ADMISSIONS

What seems to be emerging in the United Nations is a kind of group veto in the General Assembly which, although not as obvious as the individual veto possessed by the Great Powers in the Security Council, may seriously detract from its effective working. Basically, such a development arises from the decision when the Charter was drafted that it should recognise, in the words of Article 2, "the principle of the sovereign equality of all its Members." Much indignation and sarcasm has been expended upon the resulting parity in voting strength of the United States and Luxemburg, the U.S.S.R. and Panama or India and Libya, but such unreal equations of power must be accepted as among the facts of international life. The sole concession made in the Charter to those who dislike this principle was the stipulation that decisions in the General Assembly upon important matters should require a two-thirds majority of those present and voting but not unanimity as in the League of Nations Assembly. The second factor which has produced the present difficulties has been the one-third increase in U.N.

---

[1] Ernst B. Haas, "Regional Integration and National Policy," *International Conciliation,* May 1957.

* *The Political Quarterly,* XXVIII (October/December 1957), 316–27. Reprinted by permission.

membership, which has taken place since December, 1955.

. . . .

As a consequence, the United Nations now...with the exception of Outer Mongolia, *persona non grata* to the United States, Switzerland,...and the divided states of Germany, Korea, and Viet-Nam...contains all political states (this phrase is used because of Vatican City) of any substance. As compared to the early Fifties, the result has been to increase European representation in the United Nations by ten, including four "Iron Curtain" countries, Asian by six, and African by five. If all member states are present and vote upon some important question, twenty-eight adverse votes can prevent adoption of the recommendation. Gone are what may seem to some American diplomats the "good old days" when the Latin Americans and the United States with a total of twenty-one votes could block action, if they so desired....

...the search for the necessary... votes led to some involved bargaining and dubious compromises. Fortunately, it was not quite as bad as it seemed at first glance, since there has not yet appeared in the Assembly a bloc of... (votes) which can be depended upon to vote with mathematical monotony as their leader dictates. Only one voting combination is monolithic in character: the Soviet bloc. As for the rest, there are three clearly recognisable groups, the Afro-Asian, the Latin American, and the Commonwealth, while a fourth composed of the European states outside the Iron Curtain is beginning to take shape. Not included in these groups are four states: China, Israel, the United States, and Yugoslavia which do not attend any caucus.

The Monolithic Soviet Bloc

The Soviet bloc of nine, if Hungary is included, consists of the U.S.S.R., two of its components, the Ukrainian S.S.R. and Byelorussian S.S.R., and the six satellites. Whether they caucus or not is unknown, but there is no question that all major decisions on policy are made in Moscow. On one occasion only during the Eleventh Session Poland abstained on a resolution concerning the Hungarian question and its action caused a flurry of excitement in the corridors. The offence was not repeated, but thereafter delegates listened carefully to see if they could detect, as occasionally happened, slight Polish variations on the themes enunciated by the Soviet spokesmen. Otherwise it was axiomatic that all Soviet bloc speeches were the same speech. Jaded delegates left it to their advisers to adjust their earphones and listen while an Albanian, Bulgarian, Czech, or Roumanian dutifully read his script. On many occasions a Yugoslav would vote with the other communist delegates, but it was obvious that both he and they realised that his support was not automatic. On some issues, such as Hungary, the Soviet bloc would be almost isolated. On others, particularly of an anti-colonial nature, it could have support from many who were not fellow travellers in an ideological sense, but who distrusted Western "imperialism" more than Soviet communism. The Indian ex-communist who once remarked that in Asia communism is simply nationalism painted red would have perfectly understood their position. The appeal of the Russians to this powerful sentiment of anti-colonialism was all the more effective in the Eleventh Assembly because of the intensified distrust of Britain and France which had been created by their attitude in the Suez crisis.

The Afro-Asian Group

The most significant group emerging in the United Nations is the Afro-Asian, which now numbers twenty-eight with the admission of Ghana. It may justifiably count upon further recruits in the near future as Malaya, Nigeria, and Somaliland, to list those at or closest to statehood, secure admission to the U.N. In a sense, this group has grown out of the early Arab one, largely as a result of the Bandoeng conference of 1955, which helped to define its membership and gave it a sense of common purpose in striving to secure freedom for all Asian and African peoples. Afro-Asian caucuses at the U.N. were regularly announced over the loud-speakers in the delegate's lounges. They were chaired in monthly rotation by the leader of the various delegations,... Their discussions were held in English, the language which the great majority preferred to use in the Assembly debates.

Although these states will vote in bloc fashion upon anti-colonial issues, they are by no means a disciplined bloc with an unchallenged leader. In fact, they do not refer to themselves as a bloc. The main reason for this absence of constant unwavering solidarity, which is the real proof of a bloc's identity, is to be found in the fact that a careful scrutiny of the Afro-Asian group will reveal the existence of no less than four groups within the larger one. Their composition is not hard and fast as attitudes change and new issues appear, but they are capable of identification. The first group consists of eight states which are linked with Western powers in regional associations or bilateral defence arrangements, established to combat Soviet or Chinese imperialism. The eight states in this category are Turkey, Iran, Iraq, Japan, Laos, Pakistan, the Philippines, and Thailand. They are associated with the United States, the United Kingdom, France, Australia, and New Zealand in such groupings as NATO, SEATO, and the Baghdad Pact or, as is true of Japan and Laos, are closely associated with the

United States or France.[2] From their ranks come such well-known figures in the U.N. as Prince Wan of Thailand, president of the Eleventh General Assembly, General Romulo of the Philippines, and Mr. Entezam of Iran, a former president of the Assembly, who speaks little, but is said to exert a strong influence among his colleagues. Although this group will side with the West on many anti-communist issues or at least abstain, they will vote against the West on most anti-colonial issues and they will normally support their Arab colleagues over any issue involving Israel.

There are three African states: Ethiopia, Liberia, and Ghana, which share the anti-colonial views of the whole group, but on many issues are well disposed towards some of the Western powers, particularly the United States or the United Kingdom. Although anti-communist, they do not belong to any regional defence arrangement. On the other hand, they are less vocal than many of their confreres about their "non-alignment" with either the Soviet Union or the West.

THE UNCOMMITTED STATES

The largest "inner group" among the Afro-Asians consists of Burma, Cambodia, Ceylon, India, Indonesia, Lebanon, Libya, Morocco, Nepal, and Tunisia. They may be best described as the uncommitted states, to use Adlai Stevenson's phrase, who like to insist upon their independence between East and West and distrust armed alliances as widening the danger of war. They vary in their attitude towards the West from a genuine sympathy with it, such as Mr. Charles Malik, the Foreign Minister of Lebanon, displays and which is shared on many matters by Mr. Habib

---

2 (Iraq has since withdrawn from the Baghdad Pact.—Ed.)

Borguiba, the President of Tunisia [3] to the annoying combination of a wide knowledge of Western manners and institutions and waspish censure which characterises Mr. Krishna Menon of India, the most influential member of the group and the ablest debater among the Afro-Asians. The states in this group are much less disposed to combine with Western states on anti-communist issues than such countries as Iraq or the Philippines.

The fourth and bitterest group among the Afro-Asians is largely drawn from the Middle East, including as it does Egypt, Jordan, Saudi Arabia, Syria, and Yemen. But it also contains Afghanistan and Sudan. All of these states were vociferous in their denunciations of the West over the Suez crisis during the Eleventh Assembly and were frequently to be found voting on other issues with the Soviet bloc, Afghanistan probably holding the record in that respect. Their ablest spokesman was Dr. Mahmoud Fawzi, Egyptian Minister of Foreign Affairs. This group has already begun to disintegrate as the breach between Jordan and Egypt widens and . . . Iraq, Saudi Arabia, and Jordan draw much more closely together than seemed possible at the end of 1956.

THE LATIN AMERICAN NATIONS

The senior group in the United Nations in point of continuity is composed of the twenty Latin American countries who have maintained their habit of association which was nurtured in the League of Nations, the Pan American Union and its successor, the Organisation of American States. During each Assembly, these states caucus regularly

[3] According to the *Manchester Guardian Weekly*, April 25, 1957, their correspondent lately in Tunisia described it as "perhaps the only Arab country in which common sense pervades the whole body politic."

under the chairmanship of whichever Latin American delegate has been elected as one of the Vice-Presidents of the General Assembly. . . . They are pro-Western and anti-communist, normally responsive to American leadership if tactfully exercised, but also anti-colonial. The last-mentioned attitude arises from their romantic tradition of rebellion against European supremacy which all share, except Brazil, whose peaceful separation from Portugal was affectionately recalled when that country ran into severe criticism in the United Nations. The Latinos, as their more irreverend colleagues describe them, cannot be accurately described as a bloc, since they are jealous of authority and acknowledge no unchallenged leader. Like the Afro-Asians they would reject such a description. But they do act like a bloc whenever the time comes to secure representation from their region on committees, councils, or commissions.

THE COMMONWEALTH COUNTRIES

That the Commonwealth countries would never speak of themselves as a bloc is probably far more obvious to themselves than to others, but even the latter could not but have noticed how the Commonwealth was split on the Suez issue. With the addition of Ghana there are now nine Commonwealth countries in the U.N. During the Eleventh Assembly they normally met each Thursday morning for an informal discussion, attended by only the senior representatives from each country and a minimum of advisers. Such meetings were largely expositions of points of view on the issues before the Assembly and from the very nature of the Commonwealth could not result in a decision to have one state speak for the whole Commonwealth on any particular question. There might be occasionally a Commonwealth chorus in the U.N., but there was no possibility of a Commonwealth solo! But it can be safely claimed that in no group could differences of opinion be more frankly stated or more sincerely accepted. Membership in the Commonwealth did not of course preclude the participation of Ceylon, India, Pakistan, and now Ghana in the Afro-Asian group and would not prevent the United Kingdom from participating in a European group. The Commonwealth countries are all anti-communist, but differ widely on how best to combat communism. The "Old Commonwealth," as the term is occasionally used, is instinctively pro-Western while the Asian members are equally firmly anti-colonial. For the reasons already given there could not be Commonwealth leadership in the United Nations, but from within the Commonwealth there came during the Eleventh Assembly far less leadership from the United Kingdom than in the past and a greater influence upon U.N. policy, for quite different reasons, by Canada and India....

A EUROPEAN GROUP?

Outside the Iron Curtain there are now seventeen European states represented in the United Nations. Two of them, Turkey and the United Kingdom, are already in other groups. As yet there is no formal organisation of a European group, but towards the end of the Eleventh Assembly there were signs of an embryo caucus, chiefly of NATO states. But it was noticeable that the European countries were becoming more conscious of themselves as a potential group, a feeling which was intensified by their common indignation at the tragedy of Hungary and the failure of the U.N. to achieve any effective action. Among the European states there are twelve already closely linked together by NATO and correspondingly inclined to vote as a group on many U.N. issues,

including colonial ones but not Suez.... The other five European states present individual problems: Spain because of the legacy of feeling left by the Spanish civil war and Franco's attitude during the second world war, Finland acutely aware of its geographical and political position *vis-à-vis* the Soviet Union, Austria, whose neutrality is the price of its freedom, Sweden with a tradition of neutrality that is over a century old, and Ireland with its own peculiar grievance over partition which left her out of NATO. All of these states are anti-communists in feeling and none can be classed as anti-colonial.

Of the four states which belong to no caucus the United States is, of course, by far the most significant and the one state which does not *need* a caucus. China is allied to the United States, but because of its government's confinement to Formosa is not regarded as a suitable member of the Afro-Asian group. The same was true at the Bandoeng Conference. Israel is barred by the Arab veto from the same group and was probably the most isolated state in the last Assembly. Yugoslavia stands alone as a "national" communist state and while disclaiming the description seems defiantly proud of its position.

THE PATTERN OF VOTING

With this description of the groups in the United Nations in mind it is interesting to analyse the character of some of the votes on important questions. Where the issues arising from the challenge and machinations of communism are clear-cut, it is not difficult to get a satisfactory majority based upon the European states, the Western Hemisphere and some of the Commonwealth and Afro-Asian countries. Thus, a resolution urging the establishment of a "unified, independent and democratic" Korea was carried by a vote of fifty-seven to eight (the Soviet bloc, of course, with Hungary absent) and with nine abstentions, mainly Afro-Asian.

All of the Afro-Asians voted for a resolution proposing the prompt dispatch of aid to the Hungarian people in the form of medical supplies, foodstuffs, and clothing. On December 8, 1956, by a vote of fifty-six to eight with thirteen abstentions, including India, the Assembly condemned the Soviet Union for its intervention in Hungary. On that occasion such states as Burma, Ceylon, Iraq, Libya, and Nepal were to be found among the majority. A third resolution to set up the special committee to take evidence on what happened in Hungary, a committee which has since produced so impressive a report, was sponsored by the United States, six Latin American countries, nine European countries, including the United Kingdom, two other Commonwealth countries, and six Afro-Asian states. Only ten states, including India, abstained on the resolution which was carried fifty-nine to eight. But there were other resolutions involving communism in which the issues were less clear-cut. One of the best examples was the vote on a resolution proposed by the United States "not to consider ... any proposals (as had come from India) to exclude the representative of the Government of the Republic of China or to seat representatives of the Central People's Republic of China." The issue was not a new one and the United States, well aware of the feeling among many of its own people, was eager to poll as large a vote as possible on the resolution. Despite assiduous canvassing, the best it could do was to secure a vote of 47-24-8. The Soviet bloc was joined in opposition by the Scandinavian countries, Finland, Yugoslavia, and ten Afro-Asians. Ten Afro-Asian countries voted with the United States while seven ab-

stained or were absent. Clearly, the United States cannot afford many more victories of that kind....

Anti-Colonialism in the Assembly

On colonial matters the massive strength of anti-colonial feeling and the anxiety of both the Soviet Union and the Western Powers to win friends and to influence former subject peoples is reflected in the votes cast. Here, too, a clear-cut issue easily won indorsement. Thus, no state opposed the admission of Ghana to the U.N.... But in the colonial field as elsewhere there are few simple issues. The future of French Togoland, which has become by plebiscite "The Autonomous Republic of French Togoland" and has chosen to remain in the French Union, provoked a sharp three weeks' debate in the Fourth Committee before a resolution was finally hammered out for presentation to the General Assembly. The French wanted the trust territory freed from U.N. supervision. In the plebiscite which they had conducted without U.N. co-operation they had linked the establishment of the autonomous republic with freedom from Trusteeship, but had not permitted a vote on its independence outside the French Union. Some of the Afro-Asian group regarded the plebiscite as a fraudulent one and were contemptuous of the degree of self-government which French Togoland had acquired. After intricate negotiations a group of powers, including the United States, Canada, Thailand, Denmark, and the Dominican Republic secured the adoption of a resolution in the Committee calling for a Commission of six to visit French Togoland and study on the spot the degree of progress achieved and report to the next Assembly. In the Assembly this resolution was carried by 53-16-7. The Afro-Asians were badly split, ten supporting, eleven opposing and six abstaining.

The Russians scored their first success in the Fourth Committee at securing adoption of a resolution sponsored by themselves on a colonial issue. But their triumph was achieved only by watering down their original resolution calling for complete independence of five African trust territories and New Guinea within five years so as to omit New Guinea and the five-year time limit and substituting the requirement in the African trust territories that self-government or independence should be granted "at an early date." This resolution carried in the Assembly by 45-14-16 with the only Afro-Asian states not voting for it being Turkey and Laos. The one occasion upon which the Western Powers succeeded in blocking adoption of an anti-colonial resolution arose when one was presented to the Assembly calling upon the recently elected members to review their statements in reply to a letter from the Secretary-General, inquiring as to their possession of non-self-governing territories, and establishing a committee to "... study the application of the provisions of chapter XI of the Charter in the case of members newly admitted." The resolution was obviously aimed at Portugal, which stated that it had listed no non-self-governing territories, since under its constitution all parts of the national domain ranked as "provinces." When what began as an attempt to force Portugal to alter its position developed into what appeared to many as an unwarranted trespass upon national sovereignty there were many who regarded the issue as far more than a colonial one. As a result the vote in the Assembly was 35-35-5 to the chagrin of states like Iraq, India, and Sudan, which threatened to raise the issue at the next Session.

The Countervailing Power of Groups

In the light of these developments it appears that the Afro-Asians, when united, can block the adoption of any resolution. Similarly, the United States, Latin America, Western Europe, and the Old Commonwealth can defeat resolutions sponsored by the Afro-Asian group and supported by the Soviet bloc. Contrariwise, neither the United States nor the Soviet Union can hope to secure the adoption of an important resolution without winning support from the uncommitted states. Mr. Walter Lippman has gone so far as to declare in his column of February 7, 1957, that "... the United States working loyally through the U.N. can on the crucial issues take no positive or affirmative position to which Mr. Menon is seriously opposed." Most observers would regard this assertion as somewhat exaggerated, but it does point to a dilemma which is likely to be with us for some time. It certainly means that the Great Powers must develop even more effectively than in the past a technique of "getting out the vote" by using what might be described as national whips which can be exasperating and almost humiliating. It also means that corridor conversations in New York or diplomatic overtures in Washington will be required to create "assumptions" or "assurances" to make palatable a U.N. resolution. . . .

In their annoyance at the current trend in the U.N. there have been suggestions in both British and American circles that it is time to get away from the one-state one-vote absurdity and establish a system of weighted voting such as exists at the meetings of the International Bank or Fund. But no such change can take place without the Charter being amended. Amendments require the concurrence of all the Great Powers. Can anyone imagine the Russians losing an opportunity of demonstrating their concern for the rights of the smaller nations? Even if the Soviet Union did consent, the proposed amendment would require the concurrence of two-thirds of the members. How many small states can be expected to surrender their right of sovereign equality? It is significant that when the Committee established by the General Assembly in 1955 to recommend a time and place for a Charter Review Conference met for the first and only time on June 3 this year, it decided without a single dissenting vote to postpone making any recommendation for such a conference until 1959. The conclusion seems inevitable, therefore, that we may expect in the United Nations a period of uncertainty and uneasy balance which will test to the utmost the adroitness and patience of world's leaders.

3 • The United Nations *

Otto Klineberg

The author is Professor of Psychology at Columbia University; former Director of the UNESCO Project on Tensions Affecting International Understanding; Past President of the Society for the Psychological Study of Social Issues; author of Tensions Affecting International Understanding (1950).

It is not an easy matter to describe in brief compass the role played by the United Nations in the solution of international tensions. In a very real sense nothing that the United Nations does is irrelevant in this context. Tensions, and the solution of tensions, are its business, its reason for existence. Directly or indirectly, that is the meaning and purpose of all the activities of the United Nations, as well as of the specialized agencies such as UNESCO (the United Nations Educational, Scientific and Cultural Organization) and W.H.O. (the World Health Organization). There are differences in method and to a certain extent in underlying philosophy, but the final goal is one and the same.

It has become fashionable in recent months to ridicule the United Nations; to dismiss it as a debating society or as a forum for propaganda; to predict for it an early burial alongside the League of Nations. It is true that there has been understandable disillusionment among those who viewed it as a promise of permanent peace, and acute disappointment at its failure to prevent the present crisis. Especially at this particular moment of history, reaffirmation of one's faith in the United Nations must impress many as the blindest optimism. It should not be forgotten, however, that the United Nations has a

---

* *World Tension,* George W. Kisker, ed. (New York: Prentice-Hall, Inc., 1951), pp. 276–82. Reprinted by permission.

number of important successes to its credit, and that the world situation would be considerably worse than it is if no such international organization existed.

This last statement is not difficult to document. The armistice which marked the cessation of hostilities in Palestine was certainly due to the conciliation machinery of the United Nations; so was the solution of the Indonesian crisis and the establishment of a new national entity, the United States of Indonesia. The quarrel between India and Pakistan over Kashmir has not yet been settled, but the fact that the United Nations is studying the question has certainly reduced, at least for the time being, the threat of overt conflict. It is true that aggression in Korea has not been prevented, but the policing action of the United Nations, though costly in human lives and resources, may be expected to have the salutary effect of demonstrating to the world that aggression no longer will go unpunished. Even the danger of war between the Soviet Union and the United States has been rendered less likely because of the existence of an international platform from which grievances may be aired. We are all justifiably impatient at the slow pace of action, but there is hope as long as the representatives of different nations continue to talk together, and take advantage of the international machinery which makes such talk possible.

It is important that the successes of the United Nations should be more widely realized and understood, because that would contribute to our hope and faith that a third World War may still be averted. Such hope and faith are badly needed, since the belief that war is inevitable is itself one of the causes of war. Professor Gordon W. Allport of Harvard University has stressed the role of "expectancy" in his contribution to the volume on *Tensions That Cause Wars*, published for UNESCO under the editorship of Professor Hadley Cantril of Princeton University. Allport speaks of the development of a state of cynicism "wherein men despair of ever achieving their desire for peace. They expect war—and this expectancy itself brings war." He goes on to suggest that "only by changing the expectation in both leaders and followers, in parents and children, shall we eliminate war." International organizations, including the United Nations and its specialized agencies, represent the possibility of a change in our attitudes so that we will expect not war but peace; such a possibility will be realized, however, only if we believe in these organizations, if we substitute faith and cooperation for skepticism. "The success of the United Nations," says Allport, "will be guaranteed as soon as the people and their leaders really *expect* it to succeed."

One may summarize the possible contributions of the United Nations to the solution of international tensions, therefore, by pointing to three specific functions; first, the direct handling of an international conflict through conciliation or mediation; second, the provision of a forum for discussion; third, the creation of an expectancy of peace instead of an expectancy of war.

There are obvious difficulties in the way of developing this expectancy of peace. People of one nation are suspicious of another, or they have false notions of what other nations are like, or they have aggressive attitudes which prepare the way for war. These aspects of international tensions are not fully understood, but the attempt is being made, notably by UNESCO, and specifically by the UNESCO Project on Tensions Affecting International Understanding, to investigate their nature in greater detail.

This Project was initiated by the General Conference of UNESCO in Mexico City in 1947, and modified slightly the following year in Beirut. The resolutions passed at Beirut in 1948 read as follows:

The Director-General is instructed to promote enquiries into:

the distinctive character of the various national cultures, ideals, and legal systems;
the ideas which the people of one nation hold concerning their own and other nations;
modern methods developed in education, political science, philosophy and psychology for changing mental attitudes, and into the social and political circumstances that favour the employment of particular techniques;
the influences which make for international understanding or for aggressive nationalism;
population problems affecting international understanding, including the cultural assimilation of immigrants;
the influence of modern technology upon the attitudes and mutual relationships of peoples.

The Project made a definite start in the early months of 1948, and since then a number of activities have been initiated, and in some cases carried to completion. A critical account of previous studies relevant to this whole area has been published by the Social Science Research Council under the title *Tensions Affecting International Understanding: A Survey of Research*. Early publication is planned for a bookshelf of monographs on the "Way of Life" of a number of different nations; a study of individual communities in four countries, with special reference to attitudes toward the "stranger" or "foreigner"; a series of booklets presenting the scientific facts concerning race and racial differences; a survey, of the public opinion type, referring to the "stereotypes" held by members of one nation concerning others; an analysis of the effect of technological change on mental and so-

cial adjustment; an account of what happens in connection with the cultural assimilation of immigrants; a study of inter-group tensions in India, of race relations in Brazil, etc. This list could be considerably expanded, but it gives at least a partial picture of the scope and variety of the activities which constitute the UNESCO Tensions Project. Through the cooperation of social scientists in many countries, there is gradually being accumulated a body of information which will help in the understanding—and, it is hoped, in the control—of international tensions. This is a long-term project, and one from which practical results are not to be expected in the immediate future. At the same time it represents an important application of scientific techniques to a complex area of human relations. As such, it, too, holds out some hope for a future "expectancy of peace."

The United Nations and UNESCO may perhaps best be considered as agreeing in their aims, but differing in their methods of approach to international tensions. The United Nations acts at the political level; UNESCO makes use of education, science and culture in order to bring people of different nations closer together. For this purpose it has engaged upon a series of undertakings which may seem to be unconnected, but which have the common aim of increasing international understanding. So, for example, UNESCO has aided in the founding of international organizations in the field of the natural and the social sciences, as well as in humanities and the arts. It has arranged for international fellowships so that students from one country may study in another. It has facilitated the purchase of books from other countries, and has encouraged the translation of important books into other languages. It has conducted seminars on educational problems in the field of international relations, and has given special attention to the development of an educational program relating to the United Nations. It has undertaken an active campaign of publicity and exposition, through the use of mass media, of the most important aspects of the Universal Declaration on Human Rights. It has aided in the educational reconstruction of countries devastated by the war. It has helped to set up international "villages" where children of many nations can live and work together. It has prepared, and made widely available, factual material concerning various national cultures so that international cooperation may be based on knowledge and understanding. Once again this is only a partial list, but it is by no means an unimpressive one. Though its approach is somewhat more indirect than that of the United Nations, UNESCO has a very real part to play in connection with international tensions. Whereas the United Nations deals with situations of tension as they arise, UNESCO is attempting to create, through education, science, and culture, an atmosphere of cooperation and friendliness which will reduce the likelihood that tensions will develop.

The approach of other specialized agencies to international tensions is still more indirect, but their possible contribution should not be minimized or lightly dismissed. The World Health Organization, for example, in addition to its program of prevention of epidemic diseases and its attempts to improve sanitation, maternal and child health, conditions of work, etc., also describes its task as including the fostering of "activities in the field of mental health, especially those affecting *the harmony of human relations*" (italics ours). It states further that: "Health is a state of complete physical, mental, and social well-being. The health of all peoples is fundamental to the attainment of peace and security." It is clear that for the

World Health Organization health is not only of value in itself, but also as a means to the end of reducing international tension. Mentally healthy people are better prepared for cooperation with others, and less likely to welcome the opportunity to express aggression against an "enemy." This view has been stated most explicitly in the phrase: "No peace without mental health," in an early memorandum published by the World Federation for Mental Health, an international non-governmental body working in close cooperation with both the World Health Organization and UNESCO. W.H.O., in line with the general viewpoint expressed above, has worked closely with UNESCO on the Tensions Project, particularly on that aspect of the Project which raises the question as to "the influences which make for international understanding or for aggressive nationalism." Certainly it would be dangerous, in any attempt to understand these influences, to overlook the part played by the varying degrees of mental and social adjustment of the individuals concerned. It is not far-fetched to state that any contribution to mental health is a contribution to peace.

Similarly, any contribution to physical and economic well-being, other things being equal, is also a contribution to peace. Satisfied people are less likely to become aggressive (again it must be stressed, *other things being equal*) than those who are dissatisfied. In this sense many of the other specialized agencies of the United Nations also have a part to play in the reduction of international tensions. The Food and Agriculture Organization lists among its goals: "raising levels of nutrition and standards of living," and "bettering the condition of rural populations." The International Labor Organization states explicitly that "Poverty anywhere constitutes a danger to prosperity everywhere." The International Monetary Fund has as one of its purposes "to contribute to the development of the productive resources of all members." These organizations, if they succeed even in part, will be helping in the establishment of a more stable international economic situation in which states of tension will be less likely to arise.

This account, brief though it is, of what the United Nations and its specialized agencies are doing to reduce friction among nations and to create conditions conducive to better understanding, should give us some basis for hope. It is a striking fact, revealed by a careful investigation of public opinion on world affairs (reported in *American Opinion on World Affairs in the Atomic Age,* by L. S. Cottrell, Jr., and Sylvia Eberhart) that those who are well-informed are on the whole more optimistic. This is an encouraging sign, and one which justifies a program of the widest possible dissemination of relevant information on the international situation. In such a program, increased knowledge regarding the United Nations, UNESCO, W.H.O., and other related agencies must occupy a position of fundamental importance.

For specialists in the psychological sciences there is another encouraging sign. Psychiatrists and/or psychologists are serving on the secretariats of the Economic and Social Council of the United Nations, of UNESCO, and of W.H.O.; they have been included in national delegations to the General Conferences of both of the latter two organizations; they have been called in frequently as advisers and consultants. There is hope in the fact that those who have specialized in the scientific study of human relations are beginning to have a voice in international affairs.

XXIII • Regionalism and Functionalism

Concurrent with—and to a large extent because of—disappointment and even disillusionment about the ability of universal international organization to deal effectively with the security problem, there has been a striking development of two other types of organization in the postwar world. We have witnessed the creation or strengthening of a number of regional associations and groupings, and—often coincident with the new regionalism—the emergence of functionalism. Both regional and functional agencies exist within the framework of the United Nations, but they also exist and flourish outside the UN system. This relatively successful substitution of viable regional and functional arrangements for unwieldy universalism constitutes the most noteworthy advance in recent international organization, although much needs yet to be done before the "region-state" becomes a force in world politics.

In his analysis of the general problem of regionalism, Professor Haas emphasizes the necessity of a real community of interest as the *sine qua non* of success. This is what is lacking on a world scale. Within each system there are factors of conflict as well as factors of cohesion. It is the process of adjustment of these forces which determines the viability of each system. Contrasting the voluntary groupings of the West with the Soviet system of states, Haas stresses the high degree of "congruence" within the Eastern European Communist bloc. (Whether as high a level of cohesiveness exists in the Russo-Chinese alliance is open to doubt.) An alliance need not necessarily reflect a region, and it certainly cannot create a region where essential geographic, economic and political conditions do not prevail.

The very term "region" is imprecise. As recently as a generation ago, one would hardly have thought of the North Atlantic as a "region," or if he had, he would hardly have placed Turkey and Greece in it. Yet perhaps the strongest regional arrangement extant today is the North Atlantic Treaty Organization. It regards itself as implementing Article 52 of the United Nations Charter, which specifically recognizes "regional arrangements or agencies," but it grew out of a realization in the West that Soviet threats to international peace and security could not be dealt with through the UN as long as the USSR had and intended to use its veto power. Mutual dependence of Europe and America for security against Russia has made NATO into a substantial military force, and may, according to some, provide a nucleus for a political union of the Atlantic countries. In retaliation, the Soviet Union has created the Warsaw Pact, and thus two regional military associations face one another across the heart of Europe. One of the great spokesmen of regional integration, militarily in NATO, and politically in Western Europe, Paul Henri-Spaak, has decried skepticism about the need for NATO induced by new developments in military technology and made a frank appeal for closer integration of the nations which comprise the Atlantic alliance. His appraisal indicates that NATO's real weakness is still a lack of sufficient unity to achieve full development. The regional concept has yet to mature in the Atlantic world.

On the opposite side of the globe, the conception of "region" is even more anomalous. In the ANZUS Pact are provided coordinated defense plans between this country and Australia and New Zealand, several thousand miles distant. While the United States has bilateral military agreements with others in the Pacific, Japan and Taiwan (Republic of China), there has been no conclusive effort to create a defense pact for the entire Pacific region. Nor have efforts to create regional security organizations in Southeast Asia and the Middle East met with the expected success. While SEATO is a going concern, as Counselor Reinhardt demonstrates, the broad geographical gaps made up of the states in the area which have declined to go along with the organization seem more impressive than the organizational and security viability which has been achieved. Pakistan, the Philippines, and Thailand are the only *Asian* members of a group which excludes the largest regional countries, India and Indonesia. Efforts to create another body analogous to NATO, a "Middle East Treaty Organization," proved abortive because it was identified with essentially Americo-European interests. Even the more exclusively regional grouping known as the Arab League has lost a great deal of its vitality. The Baghdad Pact collapsed when the country from whose capital it derived its name withdrew. On the other hand, the project known as the Colombo Plan has done effective work in providing technical assistance to Commonwealth countries of South and Southeast Asia; the contrast between this example of functionalism and the apparently less attainable security objectives of other regional agencies is an instructive one.

Functionalism involves organization to facilitate the performance and coordination of special kinds of activity, usually economic. Experience indicates that through the efficient operation of practical functional programs and their agencies, the unity of Europe has been brought nearer to reality than it ever could have been through elaborate blueprints and theoretical planning. Mr. Hurtig describes the work of the Organization for European Economic Cooperation, which developed during the Marshall Plan period, the European Coal and Steel Community, and the more recent emergence of the Common Market or Economic Community, showing how their creation helped to meet the urgent practical necessities of industrial and commercial life on the continent. Both within the United Nations—through its specialized agencies and the quartet of Economic Commissions—and within the regional associations themselves, such as the Organization of American States, the functional approach is enjoying what one writer has termed an "exuberant growth."

Adoption of supranational institutions of a regional and/or functional character offers a striking contrast to the hesitating steps, with all the attendant pitfalls and obstacles, which have reluctantly been taken toward universal international organization. This serves to demonstrate that while the age of nationalism may be passing, in much of the world at least, the age of globalism is not yet on the horizon. What may characterize the political framework of the next phase in the development of international relations is the "age of functional regionalism." It may prove to be the most satisfactory way to meet the insistent demands of the "revolution of rising expectations" in regions no longer content to be regarded as "backward."

1 • Alliances and National Objectives *

Ernst Haas

There are eighty-one states members of the United Nations—all in principle devoted to universal collective security and the peaceful settlement of disputes under United Nations auspices—58 of these are also members of at least one of the nine multipartite military alliances now in existence. Seventeen of them belong to more than one such grouping, while an additional eight maintain bilateral military ties with one of the major powers.

Certainly the mere formation of military alliances is hardly a novelty. Nor is the coexistence of such pacts with the obligations of universal collective security arrangements at all an unprecedented development. What is an inno-vation is the transformation of military groupings into systematic, permanently functioning, regional "treaty organizations."

Justifications for this development have not been lacking. Some commentators argue that if world unity is impossible, closer regional ties may lead to federations or confederations on a regional basis, thus at least supplanting the nation-state as the dominant unit of international relations. The great majority of defenders of regionalism, however, merely contend that the development is justified as an *ad hoc* device to gain mili-

* *Regional Integration and National Policy,* *International Conciliation* #513, May 1957, 381–94. Reprinted by permission.

tary strength against an overwhelming external threat, made necessary by the alleged inability of the United Nations to maintain peace in the face of aggression by a superpower. These defenders —and there are many governmental leaders among them—freely grant that the development of regional military strength begets the need for common economic and political planning, thus in fact creating a large body of interdependencies among nations far transcending the military realm.

Yet doubts concerning the advent of regionalism have been equally common. Despite the fact that it is sometimes difficult to define the geographic extent of a given "region," especially in terms of the commitments governments are willing to assume, regional measures, it is argued, are irresponsibly held out as panaceas.

Does the Near East suffer from Big Bear jitters? One dose of MEDO should calm the nerves—if the Arab League would only stand still long enough for the dose to be administered. Does South East Asia suffer from Creeping Maoism? Doctor Dulles will shake up a soothing syrup of SEATO.[1]

The resulting pact systems overlap and create confusion. Some nations may be located in the "region" but not be members of the pact, thus producing intraregional friction and division. Some nations not in the region may be members and may, in fact, dominate the actions of the group. Preoccupation with military build-ups and rearmament is held to interfere with more urgent needs of economic development and social reconstruction, adding to external tensions rather than solving internal ones. Conversely, preoccupation with purely regional questions of internal development is held to lead to neglect of universal needs and interrelations at the expense of the United Nations. Finally, it is argued, if modern war is to be fought primarily with intercontinental missiles in the hands of the Great Powers and long-range bombers carrying nuclear weapons, why aren't organizations such as the North Atlantic Treaty Organization (NATO) already obsolete?

Neither the defense for nor the attacks on regional pacts pose the true issue. Regionalism is a patent fact of our era and it is likely to remain with us in any case as long as the superpowers do not disarm. For the dispassionate study of national policy and world order the true questions are these: How do military pacts serve as instruments of national policy, and can pacts serve as stepping stones to larger political communities? If so, how?

The attempt to answer the first question compels us to study the convergence of separate national policies which led to the conclusion of a given pact, or the definition of the objective to be achieved by joint action. Changing international conditions, however, inevitably lead to a revision in the definition, thus bringing about the need for almost continuous consultation among the governments concerned and giving rise to a pattern of joint decision-making. This may lead to the institutionalization of decision-making procedures, ignoring the traditional centers of national policy in favor of those of the "treaty organization." Separate national aspirations may thus be converted into joint regional objectives, resting on a process of continuous multilateral compromise.

Our two questions, therefore, are strongly interrelated. Alliances have in fact become more than military agreements: they are centers of continuous coalition diplomacy, possessing economic, political, and propaganda, as well as purely military functions. NATO, for example, has even acquired a permanent

---

[1] Edgar S. Furniss, Jr., "A Re-examination of Regional Arrangements," *Journal of International Affairs,* vol. IX, no. 2 (1955), p. 82.

staff, procedures, codes of conduct, and symbols.

At the beginning of each pact, the relevant national policy aspirations must be pinpointed. Periodically thereafter they must be examined in order to detect changes in aspiration or emphasis. Did shifts in national policy bring about changes in the pact? Or, conversely, did the impact of collective decisions bring about changes in national policy?

Certain earmarks of the development toward collective thinking and action can be identified and their presence established in the institutions and events analyzed. What is the nature of the system's central institutions? Does decision-making require a unanimous or a majority vote? Are decisions made by instructed delegates of governments, by uninstructed delegates, or by independent experts? Are decisions merely recommendations or are they binding?

Certain characteristics of resistance to collective thinking and action must also be looked for in the practice of regional systems. Do national governments insist on using the regional machinery *exclusively* for the realization of their own immediate and narrowly-viewed policy objectives? Do governments refuse to change their policies after a regional consultation or decision contrary to their aims? Do governments fail to carry out centrally made decisions? Do governments pursue policies outside the pact framework inconsistent with regional decisions? And finally, is there a growth or a decline in the importance and the scope of the decisions made jointly? If the formal structure remains intact but is rarely used, or applied only to situations of little importance in the minds of the member governments, no development toward a political community transcending the nation-state is likely. The evolution of regional military pacts toward a larger political community may be said to take place only if constantly changing conditions result in consistently broadened powers of the central structure, rather than in resistance to such development.

STRESS ON INTERNAL SECURITY

In the efforts of governments to ally for military purposes, two fundamental aims have become plain: the establishment of security *within* a given region, including the protection of the independence of its members against other members, or the organization of collective self-defense against an *external* threat. If the first set of aims predominates, the system is likely to be equipped with firm rules and standing machinery for the peaceful solution of disputes among members. If external security is the major aim, joint military arrangements and assurances of mutual support will take first place in the organization's objectives. Although the majority of pacts do not fall tidily into one or the other of these categories, many of them bear the hallmark of a greater concern with one or the other.

The years from 1945 to 1948 saw the negotiation of a series of treaties among 21 states of the Western Hemisphere which established a self-conscious system of collective security, pacific settlement, and continental solidarity against outsiders. This eventually became the Organization of American States (OAS). The disparity in power and influence between the huge and industrialized "Colossus of the North" and the 20 underdeveloped and agricultural Latin American countries was one of the motives for creating the organization. Latin American governments, notoriously weak and unstable, were anxious to tie Washington to a legally firm system of non-intervention and protection for the territorial *status quo,* under which established governments could claim the protection of the Inter-American System in defending themselves against revolutionaries and threats originating on the territories of their neighbors. They were also interested in minimizing extra-continental influences in the Americas. This double motivation received ideological support from a strong legalistic intellectual tradition, despite constant violations of legal procedures in fact, as well as from an historical body of doctrine alleging an institutional and spiritual unity and uniqueness as contrasted with "corrupt" European influences. As for the United States, few Latin Americans associated it with their unique traditions, but for reasons of self-protection nevertheless sought to tie Washington to their aspirations. . . .

Under the system all inter-American disputes must be submitted to OAS peaceful settlement procedures and any settlement voted by a two-thirds majority is binding upon the states concerned. In the case of extra-continental threats, the machinery for consultation comes into play and collective measures may be decided upon to meet an attack —"an armed attack by any State against an American State shall be considered as an attack against all the American States." However, no state is required to use armed force unless it wishes to do so.

The movement for Arab unity, resulting in the formation of the Arab League in March 1945 owed much to British influence.

. . . .

Symptomatic of a preoccupation with the protection of the internal *status quo* was the stress given to the pacific settlement of inter-Arab disputes. When disputes not involving the "independence of a State, its sovereignty or its territorial integrity" have been referred to the League by the parties concerned, a simple majority vote of the League's Council suffices to hand down a binding decision. A unanimous decision is re-

quired to determine collective measures in the event of aggression either by a member state or by a non-member. If unanimity cannot be obtained, only the governments voting for common measures are bound to act.

STRESS ON EXTERNAL SECURITY

The growing preoccupation of the Arab League with Israel and anti-colonialism, and its manifest unwillingness to fulfill the objectives originally sought by the British, led late in 1951 to another outside effort to organize the area and to strengthen it as a bulwark against communism. This was the abortive Middle East defense system sponsored by the United States which incurred the implacable suspicion and hostility of the Arab states. Having learned its lesson the United States then tried to encourage the Arab states themselves to take the initiative. This finally bore fruit in 1955 as the Baghdad Pact.

Initially it was a bilateral agreement between Iraq and Turkey and became a multipartite alliance with the accession of the United Kingdom in April, Pakistan in September, and Iran in October 1955, thus forming the "northern tier" defense system against the Soviet Union. It contains no firm obligations and is little more than a mutual agreement to consult: its purpose and aims are ambiguous and the only specific commitment assumed by the members is to "cooperate" for mutual defense. Pakistan is primarily concerned with the threat which India poses, Iraq with that of Egypt and Saudi Arabia, while the United Kingdom seems less afraid of the USSR than anxious to retain a diplomatic and institutional toehold in the Middle East. Preoccupation with anti-colonialism and with economic development equals, if it does not override, military considerations.

. . . .

Another link in the world wide network of alliances was forged in 1951 when the ANZUS Pact was signed by Australia, New Zealand, and the United States. Such a small membership would seem to facilitate an easy identity of national aims. This, however, was not the case. The treaty obligation to meet outside threats by common military measures is very weakly worded. The only obligation assumed by the members is to "meet the common danger in accordance with [their] constitutional processes." The most important reason for this is that the primary enemy identified in Washington differed from that feared in Canberra. For the United States, Communist aggression in general and Peiping in particular was the danger; for Australia and New Zealand a resurgent and rearmed Japan appeared to be an equally great danger. These latter countries were willing to agree to a peace treaty with Japan which imposed "no restrictions upon Japanese rearmament, only if the United States would formally express concern for their security and agree to stand with them in the event of an attack." [2] The ANZUS Pact, as drawn, covers both contingencies and therefore represents once more a basic convergence of separate national policy aims.

In 1954 the Southeast Asian Defense Treaty (SEATO), largely superseded ANZUS by adding France, Pakistan, the Philippines, Thailand, and the United Kingdom to the three countries already committed to opposing aggression in that region. However, the increase in numbers was matched by a dilution of purpose. Again the parties pledged themselves merely "to meet the common danger in accordance with [their] constitutional processes" and the United States was exempt from even this commitment unless there were Communist aggression. At the same time, unlike the ANZUS Pact, SEATO excluded from the "treaty area" South Korea and Formosa, the most likely seats of trouble from Communist sources. Cambodia, Laos, and Vietnam were included in the area covered by the Treaty, although it was not anticipated they would join.

But the parties differed on defining the target. France, which had just lost its Indo-Chinese empire, was primarily interested in maintaining some influence in that area. Pakistan was anxious to strengthen its defenses against India. The Philippines was mainly interested in curbing the danger of Chinese military expansion. Thailand was preoccupied with the problem of internal subversion, fomented by Communist infiltration, particularly from Malaya and Vietnam. The United Kingdom was preoccupied with the future of Malaya and Singapore and the possibility of maintaining them within the Commonwealth. And the United States hoped for greatly stepped up military preparations by all members against communism in general.

The divergence in fundamental objectives was also reflected in the means to be utilized. The United Kingdom tended to stress the need for economic development to stem subversion as contrasted with Washington's military emphasis. And the three Asian nations insisted on giving the Pact a firm anti-colonial tone despite Australian, British, and French participation. This emphasis was reflected in the drafting of a Pacific Charter in which the parties proclaimed their willingness "to promote self-government and to secure the independence of all countries whose people desire it and are able to undertake its responsibilities."

By far the most important regional alliance in terms of its development since its inception in 1949 is the North Atlantic Treaty Organization (NATO).

---

[2] R. G. Casey, *Friends and Neighbors* (Melbourne: F. W. Cheshire, 1954), p. 73.

Under the terms of this Treaty, if one party is attacked, every other party will come to its assistance "by taking forthwith, individually and in concert with other Parties, such action as it deems necessary, including the use of armed force." Certainly the minimum common denominator among the twelve original members was the fear of Soviet attack in Europe and the need to find a deterrent to that danger. Yet national policy also dictated a series of differences in emphasis and aspiration which, in the long run, were as important as the points of convergence. Thus Denmark and Norway hoped that legal deterrence would suffice, that is, that no military operations would ever take place and they therefore considered the commitment to fight more important than preparations for battle. France and the Benelux countries hoped that if fighting were necessary it would take place on German soil, while the United States and United Kingdom foresaw the possibility of a mobile campaign across the European Continent. Canadian opinion tended to see the need as more than a narrowly military one. Many Canadian statesmen urged

that if NATO were to serve more than the immediate crisis, and were to be a success militarily, a sense of Atlantic community must be fostered and habits of cooperation established in the economic, political and cultural fields as well as in the military realm.[3]

Initial United States opinion, however, was the opposite. Secretary of State Dean Acheson denied any obligation to act collectively along these lines although he acknowledged the "ethical essence of the treaty...tolerance, restraint, freedom, and well-being."[4] Key members of Congress, indeed, feared that emphasis on non-military matters and on large-scale political and economic consultations would undermine United States trade policy, freedom of action, and support for the United Nations. Hence they opposed a wide interpretation of the Treaty.

Militarily speaking, Western European Union (WEU) is the continental European sector of NATO and, as far as operational jurisdiction is concerned, it is subject to NATO orders. The main purpose of the WEU Agreement was to facilitate German rearmament after the defeat by France of the European Defence Community (EDC) treaty, and to pave the way for Germany's entry into NATO with appropriate safeguards. France had refused to ratify EDC because the United Kingdom had declined to participate and without British participation the French were afraid of German hegemony once Germany was rearmed. WEU thus represented the minimum common denominator: it met the German government's desire for rearmament, which was supported by the United Kingdom and the United States, and it also met the French demand for special guarantees against the resurgence of German militarism.

The WEU Treaty fixes troop and armament ceilings for the member states, including Germany. These can be lifted only by unanimous vote of the WEU Council. Further, certain types of weapons are forbidden to Germany, a prohibition which can be lifted only with the consent of the WEU Council. The Council has at its disposal an Armaments Control Agency to inspect and report on levels of troops and armaments maintained by the members. Under WEU the United Kingdom is pledged to maintain a minimum force on the Continent which can be withdrawn or reduced only with the consent

[3] Norman J. Padelford, "Political Cooperation in the North Atlantic Community," *International Organization*, vol. IX, no. 3 (August 1955), p. 357.

[4] *Ibid.*, p. 356.

of the other members. Within the frank context of the political and military integration of Europe, then, WEU permits the rearmament of the member—West Germany—most distrusted by the other members while reassuring the remaining countries of their safety.

Formally speaking, the Soviet-sponsored multipartite Warsaw Pact is a latecomer to the field of regional systems. In 1955 it took the place of a series of earlier bilateral treaties between the Soviet Union and the Eastern European Communist nations. But the close ties and mutual commitments of the governments in question probably owed little to formal treaties and more to such factors as ideological identities among Communist leaders, Soviet military occupation, and policy "coordination," as well as satellite economic dependence on the Soviet Union. Whatever the causes, the effective military coordination of Eastern European forces and policies with those of Moscow was so complete as to have resulted in common tables of organization, standardized armaments and uniforms and, in the case of Poland until 1956, a Soviet marshal actually commanding a satellite army.

Following eight years of rigidity in Communist relations with the European powers and the United States, the Pact coincided with a strong offensive to undermine the will of the NATO partners to continue the alliance. It was, in effect, a negotiating device to induce the West to withdraw from Germany or to limit NATO commitments without making any real reciprocal concession. Realizing that countervailing or dominant military power was not sufficient to deter NATO defensive efforts, the Soviet leaders apparently tried a diplomatic gambit in the German *impasse* by creating a multipartite alliance superficially resembling NATO. This interpretation is strengthened by the fact that the active steps taken by the Warsaw Treaty Organization have been confined to underlining Soviet diplomatic and propaganda moves with regard to Germany, NATO, and "European collective security."

The Pact promised its own abolition if a general system of disarmament or a general European collective security treaty—implying the scrapping of NATO—came into being. As such it appealed to neutralist groups in France and was beamed at anti-militarist and anti-NATO circles in a West Germany which was just about to begin its rearmament program under WEU. Diplomatically, therefore, the initial purpose of the Pact was to provide merely another device for keeping West Germany out of the Western military structure. However, an additional common incentive may have been the desire to give a semblance of national equality to the satellites, by a multilateral relationship instead of a mere bilateral dependence upon Moscow.

2 • What SEATO Means to the United States *

G. Frederick Reinhardt

*A graduate of California and Cornell Universities, the author has been a
Foreign Service Officer since 1937, serving in Vienna, Tallinn, Riga, Moscow, Algiers, Naples, Paris, Frankfurt, and at the Department of State. He
became Chief of the Division of European Affairs in 1950, Counselor of
Embassy at Paris in 1951, Ambassador to Viet-Nam in 1955, and Counselor
of the Department of State in 1957.*

. . . .

(In the early 1950's) things looked
rosy indeed for the Communists, who in
a few short years had absorbed eastern
Europe and the great heartland of eastern Asia. In 1953 the fighting stopped in
Korea, with the Communists' aggression
halted at about the point where it had
begun. But in the following year they
were at it again. They intervened massively in Indochina and put a hand on
the rich resources of that Southeast
Asian peninsula. The Geneva conference
in 1954 confirmed their retention of half
of Viet-Nam and compromised the
future of two provinces in Laos. Individual countries standing alone seemed
powerless to resist this pressure.

FORMATION OF SEATO

By this time, however, wider awareness of the long-range dangers had developed. Threatened nations of the free
world decided it was imperative to take
a determined stand.

And so it came about that against this
menacing background of Communist
pressure in Southeast Asia and aware
of the effectiveness of NATO in its first

5 years, representatives of three Asian
nations—Thailand, the Philippines, and
Pakistan—joined by those of Australia,
New Zealand, France, Great Britain,
and the United States met in Manila in
September 1954. There they negotiated
and signed the Southeast Asia Collective
Defense Treaty and created an alliance
for their mutual safety and the protection of the area.

Communist propaganda still trumpets
charges that SEATO is "an aggressive
instrument of warmongering imperialists." The fact, of course, is that it is
strictly a defensive alliance which stands
as a barrier against aggression in Southeast Asia. And collective security arrangements such as SEATO are a major
feature of the United Nations peace system. They are specifically authorized in
article 51 of the charter, which recognizes the inherent right of nations' individual and collective self-defense. Fortunately most people remember the actual
circumstances of threatening crisis under

---

* Address made before the International
Relations Club at the University of South
Carolina, Columbia, S.C. on March 5, 1959.
Department of State Bulletin, March 23,
1959.

which SEATO was born and are thoroughly aware of its purely defensive character. It is not directed against any government, any nation, or any people. It is directed only against Communist aggression. The fact that the Communists find it so objectionable reveals that they recognize it for what it is—an obstacle to their own aggressive plans.

What Has SEATO Accomplished?

Now, what has SEATO accomplished? To put it briefly: SEATO has interrupted the Communists' march in the Far East. Although the organization, unlike NATO, has no combat forces assigned to it, it has brought confidence to its members and, despite the continuing struggle against Communist subversion in Southeast Asia, general tranquillity has returned to the area. Quiet conditions have prevailed, and the Southeast Asian nations, relieved of the threat of imminent Communist invasion, have been able to make appreciable progress in programs for social and economic betterment.

With no armed forces of its own and no peacetime military headquarters, SEATO relies upon the mobile striking forces of its members for its defense. Yet SEATO's mere existence has served as an effective deterrent.

And SEATO has other positive attributes. The preamble of the treaty contains a reaffirmation of the principle of equal rights and self-determination, and in the treaty the signatories declare their intention to strive by every peaceful means to promote self-government. The non-aggressive nature of SEATO is further emphasized by a passage of the treaty under which members solemnly undertake to settle by peaceful means any international disputes in which they may be involved and to refrain from the threat or use of force inconsistent with the purposes of the United Nations.

SEATO's Military Planning Office devises the methods to resist possible armed aggression. It plans joint military exercises to give the combat forces of member countries training in joint operations and in the coordination of methods, personnel, and equipment so that in case of need they will be able to fight effectively together.

SEATO's civil activities are concentrated in three fields. First, its Security Experts Committee distributes among member states information on Communist methods of infiltration, and it holds conferences within the treaty area to exchange views and information on methods of combating subversion.

The Committee on Information, Culture, Education, and Labor stimulates an active exchange of information, talents, and skills in order to knit more closely together the diverse peoples represented in the alliance. There is a developing program of fellowships, scholarships, professorships, and traveling lectureships.

Finally, SEATO's Committee of Economic Experts meets periodically to consider special economic questions arising out of the treaty commitments of the member countries. United States economic aid is extended to the Asian member countries primarily on a bilateral basis, but we have supported two special SEATO projects. In Bangkok American professors have made studies preliminary to the establishment at a Thai university of a SEATO graduate school of engineering which will be organized to serve students from the treaty area. Another SEATO project will establish vocational training programs in the three Asian member countries.

3 • Europe Moves Toward Integration *

Serge Hurtig

The author was trained in Economics and Political Science at Georgetown University and the University of Paris, from which he was graduated in 1950. He is Assistant Director of Documentation Services at the Foundation Nationale des Sciences Politique and teaches at the Institut d'Etudes Politiques in Paris.

· · · ·

...six Western European countries have tried for several years to strengthen the bonds, both economic and political, that link them. The six countries which have collaborated with varying degrees of success are Belgium, France, the German Federal Republic, Italy, Luxembourg, and the Netherlands.

The first of these efforts involved Belgium, Luxembourg, and the Netherlands. Belgium and Luxembourg had had an economic union since 1921. Negotiations between them and the Netherlands, which began in 1943 while they were all still under German occupation, resulted in 1944 in a customs union agreement. Since then the implementation of Benelux, slow at first, has become increasingly rapid. Unification of the national economies is far from being achieved, but already goods, persons, and capital can circulate with relative ease. Successive agreements have made it possible to overcome problems as they arise, and if the results of the policy adopted have seldom been spectacular, they have satisfied the three countries concerned.

A very different fate met the Franco-Italian customs union which was pro-

vided for in the 1949 Treaty of Paris. In this case the products of the two countries are similar, while in Benelux the industrial economies of Belgium and Luxembourg are complementary to the agricultural economy of the Netherlands. Employers in both France and Italy opposed implementation of the Treaty and their opposition was reinforced by French labor unions frightened by the prospect of an influx of unemployed Italians. In consequence the Treaty has remained a dead letter.

The idea of a common market limited to coal and steel was advanced in May 1950 by Robert Schuman, French Foreign Minister, and was brought into being in record time. The purpose of the Schuman Plan was primarily political. It was designed to effect a Franco-German reconciliation by pooling a vital sector of their economies. In addition to France and Germany, four other countries— Italy and the three members of Benelux —signed the Treaty setting up the European Coal and Steel Community (ECSC) in April 1952.

---

* *The European Common Market, International Conciliation,* #517, March 1958, 321–43. Reprinted by permission.

The Coal and Steel Community is a highly original venture. It has created among its six members a common market limited to coal and steel production and this production has been removed from the controls of national governments. A collegial High Authority, not subject to governmental veto, has been charged with the task of eliminating progressively, during a five-year transitional period ending in 1958, all barriers and obstacles to trade in coal and steel. The High Authority has direct authority over the industries and citizens of the six countries and has the right of levying taxes. It is responsible to a special parliamentary assembly and subject to a court of justice.

Although the High Authority has exercised great restraint in using its broad powers, particularly in regard to coordinating the flow of investments into industrial development, ECSC has made possible considerable economic progress. The elimination of national barriers on coal and steel has led to a more rational flow of trade and to its increase, as well as to a lowering of transport prices. Thanks to the precautions that have been taken, dislocations involved in readapting enterprises adversely affected by the abandonment of protective tariffs have been remarkably slight. Unquestionably, the fact that between 1954 and 1957 European economies have been expanding has contributed to the success of the venture.

On the political level, however, the supranational character of the institution has created some problems. ECSC has entailed the abandonment of a fairly substantial degree of sovereignty, and large sectors of French public opinion have not become reconciled to this. It has also meant the exclusion of the United Kingdom, which is strongly opposed to supranational bodies and is willing to cooperate only within an intergovernmental framework. The limitations on sovereignty and the absence of the United Kingdom have been the two principal arguments advanced by the French opponents of "little Europe."

. . . .

NEW IMPETUS TOWARD INTEGRATION

Three years after ratification of the Treaty creating the European Coal and Steel Community and one year after rejection of EDC, the governments of the six countries of "little Europe"—Belgium, France, Germany, Italy, Luxembourg, and the Netherlands—made a new effort to achieve European integration. This was the formal purpose of the conference of the six Foreign Ministers in Messina in June 1955. Remembering the failure to achieve military integration and believing that the lack of progress in the negotiations to pool resources in specific fields was due to the very narrowness of the objectives, the six Ministers decided to study the creation of a common market among their countries. They accepted with enthusiasm a proposal put forward by the Benelux countries to "pursue the establishment of a United Europe by developing common institutions, by the progressive fusion of national economies, by creating a common market, and by the progressive harmonization of social policies." The resolution they adopted provided for the creation of a preparatory committee of governmental delegates, assisted by experts, under the chairmanship of some well-known political figure.

The individual chosen to head this committee was the Belgian Foreign Minister Paul-Henri Spaak, a man well known for his energy and his devotion to the cause of European unification. Under his supervision, the experts made rapid progress and the report of the heads of delegations was submitted on 21 April 1956. It was divided into three sections: the first dealt with the Common Market; the second with an Atomic Energy Community; and the third with "areas requiring immediate attention"—sources of energy other than nuclear, air transport, postal services, and telecommunications. Progress with respect to "areas requiring immediate attention" has been negligible. The Treaty establishing the European Atomic Energy Agency (Euratom) came into effect concurrently with the Treaty creating the Common Market. Euratom is intended to provide extensive cooperation in a very limited field. Institutionally, it is closely linked with the Common Market.

Regarding the Common Market, the Spaak Report laid down a whole series of principles and rules. The Common Market was to be a real customs union and not merely a free trade area; that is to say, there would be a common external tariff. It was to be brought into being according to a definite timetable, with a maximum delay of fifteen years; its supranational powers were to be limited and questions of general policy would remain within the jurisdiction of governments. The Spaak Report was adopted at the Venice Conference which met on 29 and 30 May 1956.

· · · ·

The Common Market Treaty was signed in Rome, together with the Euratom Treaty, on 25 March 1957 and was speedily submitted to the national parliaments for ratification. The other countries, anxious to avoid a repetition of the EDC experience, deferred action until the French National Assembly had pronounced itself. In that body, a lively debate was held on the remarkable report made by Alain Savary on behalf of the Foreign Affairs Committee. M. Savary did not hide the dangers to the French economy but he emphasized that the Common Market would open up opportunities and that the efforts it would require would have salutary ef-

fects. France would be obliged to forego the protection of anachronistic enterprises that were acting as a brake on its development.

Pierre Mendès-France, however, maintained that the Rhine Valley, the industrial center of "little Europe," would certainly be the principal beneficiary and declared that the French economy should modernize itself before participating in the Common Market. He argued that political morality, the dignity of France, and its real interests required that no obligations be undertaken that could not be fulfilled.

Despite this opposition, the Assembly on 9 July 1957 approved the Treaty by a vote of 342 to 234. This opened the way for action by the other countries and, in turn, Germany, Italy, Belgium, the Netherlands, and Luxembourg all ratified the two Rome Treaties. The only significant opposition came from the Communists. The Common Market Treaty came into effect on 1 January 1958, and on 8 January, the members of the Commission, headed by Walter Hallstein of Germany, were appointed....

STRUCTURE OF THE COMMUNITY

The European Economic Community, unlike OEEC or the General Agreement on Tariffs and Trade (GATT), is not a body lacking in decision-making powers and totally dependent for its functioning upon agreement among its member states; nor are its organs essentially technical in character. Although its structure is very similar to that of the Coal and Steel Community, EEC has fewer supranational powers than the ECSC High Authority. The evolutionary trends it is designed to set in motion should, in the view of its supporters, be irreversible....

· · · ·

THE COUNCIL

The Council, responsible for ensuring coordination of the general economic policies of the Treaty signatories and exercising powers of decision (Article 145),[1] is composed of one member from each government. The chairmanship is assumed in rotation (Article 146). Normally the Council acts only on a proposal by the Commission, which it may not amend except by unanimous vote (Article 149). In regard to questions of major importance or those that pose political problems, however, the authority of the Council is supreme. These include progression to the second stage of the Common Market, adherence of third states, and decisions to suspend emergency measures taken by a state. In addition, the Council may act without formal concurrence of the Commission on such matters as its own rules of procedure, remuneration of members of the various organs of the Community, and adoption of the Statute of the Court. In those few cases where, for reasons of urgency, the Commission has the power of decision (as, for example, the invocation of emergency measures), its acts may subsequently be revoked by the Council.

"Except where otherwise provided ... conclusions of the Council shall be reached by a majority vote of its members" (Article 148). However, the exceptions are so numerous that a simple majority—four out of six—applies only in rare instances, principally as regards the development of the Community's organs.

---

[1] References in parentheses are to Articles of the *Treaty Establishing the European Economic Community*. No official English text exists. Citations in this study are from the unofficial translation published, with connected documents, by the Secretariat of the Interim Committee for the Common Market and Euratom, Brussels.

In most other instances decisions require unanimity, a "qualified" majority, or *ad hoc* majorities.

Unanimity is required for a wide range of Council decisions during the twelve to fifteen year transitional period provided for implementation of the Treaty. Even after this period, the unanimity rule will obtain for acts sufficiently important to require the compliance of all member states (for example, the harmonization of legislation and the coordination of policies), for acts that implement the Treaty (as, for example, the institution of programs provided for in the Treaty), and for certain acts that constitute modifications of the Treaty (such as an increase in the number of judges of the Court or adherence of third states). Thus in every field member states retain full sovereignty and the decisions of the Council must in each case be consonant with the position of the most conservative state. Nevertheless, abstentions cannot block the adoption of measures requiring unanimity.

. . . .

THE COMMISSION

The Commission is composed of nine nationals of member states, selected for their "general competence" and "indisputable independence" (Article 157). The Commission, which no longer bears the ambitious title of "European Commission" given to it in the Spaak Report, is a collegial organ which acts by a simple majority. Elected for four-year terms by agreement among the governments, the members are re-eligible for an indefinite period (Article 158). They are independent of governments and serve the general interest of the Community (Article 157).

The Commission is the permanent organ of the Community. It submits annually to the Assembly a general report on the work of the Community (Article 156), replies to questions put to it by the Assembly or its members (Article 140), and is responsible to the Assembly. If a motion censuring the activities of the Commission is adopted by two thirds of those voting, representing a majority of the members of the Assembly, the members of the Commission shall resign their office in a body (Article 144).

The Commission is specifically charged with supervising the application of the provisions of the Treaty and measures adopted by the organs of the Community created by the Treaty. To these ends, it can formulate recommendations or opinions which, however, merely suggest action and have no binding force (Article 189). It can also assemble and verify information (Article 213). Its right to address to the Council precise proposals for action, which the Council may not amend except by unanimous vote, makes the Commission the normal source of Council decisions. The permanent body is therefore far more than a secretariat.

Moreover, the Commission is empowered to make its own decisions either to carry out measures specifically provided for by the Treaty, or to examine and authorize safeguard measures by member states in cases of emergency (Article 108), such as a balance of payments crisis. It is the Commission that administers the finances of the Community and represents it in legal matters and in relations with international organizations and with third countries.

However, power is in fact concentrated in the hands of the Council; the influence of the Commission will doubtless depend upon the personal authority of its members and the conception that they hold of their functions, as well as upon the extent of the difficulties encountered in bringing the Common Market into being. The High Authority of ECSC has much more extensive powers than the Commission of EEC: it can act without preliminary authorization from governments and can take decisions that are binding not only on governments but also on the coal and steel industries of the six countries; in thus acting it is subject to no right of veto.

THE ASSEMBLY

As in the case of ECSC, the Treaty envisages for the European Economic Community parliamentary control over the executive. The EEC is to have an Assembly of 142 members appointed by the national parliaments in accordance with the quota allotted to each state (Article 138). The Spaak Report, as was pointed out above, had recommended that this function be assumed by the Common Assembly of ECSC enlarged for the purpose. This recommendation was supported by the negotiators. Effect was not given to it in the text of the Treaty itself; but, by virtue of the Convention Relating to Certain Institutions Common to the European Communities, the Assembly of EEC is the same as that of ECSC and Euratom.[2] Article 21 of the Treaty establishing ECSC has accordingly been modified and the new Assembly will assume from the beginning the duties of the Common Assembly of ECSC.

This re-organization of European institutions is a praiseworthy response to a desire for simplicity and efficiency; however, it creates the unprecedented situation of three international executive bodies with different statutes, operating in the same area together with six national governments, all three bodies responsible to a single parliamentary Assembly appointed by the six national

---

[2] *Convention Relating to Certain Institutions Common to the European Communities,* Articles 1 and 2.

parliaments. Even the appointment by the national parliaments is not a certainty. The Treaty provides that "the Assembly shall draw up proposals for elections by direct universal suffrage in accordance with a uniform procedure in all Member States" (Article 138). Should there be a direct election, a true European parliament would be brought into being that might command greater authority....

The Assembly now has in regard to EEC and Euratom considerably greater powers than it has over ECSC. As far as this last body is concerned, the Assembly can exercise its right of censure only once a year—when the High Authority submits its annual report—while with respect to EEC and Euratom, the Assembly may be seized of a motion of censure at any time. The adoption of such a motion by a two-thirds majority requires, as has been seen, the resignation of the members of the Commission in a body.

· · · ·

COURT OF JUSTICE

For the judicial organ of the Community, the same solution has been adopted as for the Assembly: the duties of the Court are prescribed in the Treaty, and the convention on common institutions provides that the Court shall replace that of ECSC. Its terms of reference in regard to Euratom are identical with those for EEC.

The single Court is composed of seven judges who may form Chambers of three or five judges (Article 165). It is assisted by two advocates-general whose duty is to present publicly "reasoned conclusions" on cases submitted to the Court (Article 166). The judges and the advocates-general are appointed by agreement among the member governments for six-year terms, the terms overlapping to ensure continuity of juris-

prudence. The President of the Court is appointed by the judges for three years but may be re-elected (Article 167). A protocol on the Statute of the Court of Justice outlines the functions and organization; the Court will prepare its own rules of procedure which must be approved unanimously by the Council.

· · · ·

ADVISORY ORGANS

In addition to the four major organs responsible for the achievement of the Community's tasks, the Treaty provides for an Economic and Social Committee to advise the Council and the Commission, and for several other specialized committees.

· · · ·

EUROPEAN INSTITUTIONAL FRAMEWORK

It was the task of ECSC to create a common market for coal and steel products pending, and in fact opening the way for, a wider common market. It would have been possible in theory to envisage a single institution responsible for the economic unification of the six countries, but in practice certain countries, particularly France, are not very happy about surrendering certain of their sovereign powers to an international organization, even if the organization makes only the most circumspect use of its supranational authority. Since it was impossible, in the case of coal and steel, to undo what had been done, the idea of a single organic whole was abandoned; hence the complexity of the system adopted and the difference, already mentioned, in the powers of the Assembly and the Court, in respect of the various institutions. Coal and steel will therefore continue to constitute an enclave governed by a special statute and free from the authority of governments: the decisions of the High Authority are directly executory. In EEC, on the contrary, the organs can act in many cases only through government channels, that is, with the agreement of the states concerned. The decisions of the Community as they affect states are only broad policy directives—and significantly this point was stressed in the report submitted to the French National Assembly.

Thus two additional institutions—EEC and Euratom—have been added to those already existing in Western Europe—ECSC, OEEC, Council of Europe, and Western European Union. All of them function with an almost complete absence of coordination. This situation has been a matter of concern to some governments and several recent proposals for streamlining have been advanced. The United Kingdom, for example, suggested the amalgamation of all European institutions in order not to accentuate the growing gulf between "little Europe" and "big Europe." France proposed the creation of a European General Assembly that would serve as a bridge connecting all the institutions and to which members of the various Assemblies now in existence would belong automatically: each of these Assemblies would then become a kind of specialized standing committee of the General Assembly. These ideas are interesting, but any marked progress in such a direction will be very difficult to achieve in the near future.

Under these conditions, only "the six" will be called upon to take real decisions, and European integration, if it is achieved, will be comprehended within this narrow framework....

PART VII NATION AND WORLD IN THE SPACE AGE: A PROBLEM IN FAITH AND RATIONALITY

XXIV • The Responsibility of Statesmanship

It is from two different, yet related, perspectives that the authors wish to conclude this study of international relations. In both, the wisdom of certain perceptive spokesmen and analysts of foreign policy and international relations is brought to bear upon the deep problems of faith and rationality. The first perspective is the internal—that of the state: the world as it looks from the vantage point of the policy-maker and commentator within the state. These men contemplate the future course of their nation's policies in a period of human destiny which promises the greatest hopes and, at the same time, forebodes the ghastliest dangers for an ignominious, if spectacular, end for man. The second perspective is the external: the world as a whole as it looks from the vantage point of the more detached commentator and the philosophical observer of the human scene, who endeavors to discover a basis for world order and cooperation toward the end of the threat of mutual destruction.

Only one of the principal changes confronting both the American states-man and his counterpart at the beginning of the century involves the *geographical* dimensions of his concern. No longer is it sufficient to negotiate through the chancellories of the Old World exclusively in order to deal with the totality of world diplomacy. Indeed, Europe presents one of the main obstacles to an efficacious foreign policy in those parts of the world which have either just overcome their colonial status or are still under the control of America's friends and allies. Dr. Thompson sets forth six principles upon which a solution of or, at least, an approach to this awkward and crucial problem may be based, warning that "it may be necessary for the United States to choose sides." But this is only one obstacle imposed by the new dimensions of statesmanship. Another is posed by the moral problem. Shall an action be called "good" if it serves the group of primary loyalty, i.e. the state, only; or must it serve a more inclusive purpose in order to deserve the label? There is an "indefiniteness" in political morality created by many and often contradictory values. Thompson's critique notes that spokesmen for the American republic "talk a great deal more about promoting the impact of morality than about determining its content."

It is difficult to escape the tendency on the part of any state to provide its own ethic. Nothing transcends it, even though the state may make use of universally appealing symbols to buttress its case before world public opinion. One of the ironies of the increasingly close interaction of foreign policies is the fact that the only people in a position to make important decisions are, by virtue of their position and their immediate responsibilities, prevented from going beyond the state's own ethical standard.

Since his retirement from the office of Secretary of State, Dean Acheson has been a frequent critic of imprecise thinking and action in the conduct of foreign affairs. In his treatment of the moral dimension in foreign affairs, he comes to grips with some crucial distinctions, which focus light upon the confusions and complexities of this dimension of the foreign policy process, which is complicated enough even without the infusion of the moral question. His comments are directed against what he sees as a tendency to equate superficial "moralism" with true morality in the conduct of a nation's external policies. Moral principles are a guide to action, but not a substitute for action. In international relations there is unfortunately "no consensus of opinion or monopoly of force to create and enforce standards." Therefore the statesman has an even greater responsibility to endeavor, in the methods he chooses, to "aim high."

Professor Wolfers places the problem into an even broader context in his attempt to view—not without charity—the behavior of states and statesmen in the light of the environment in which they must act. His attempt takes the form of fashioning a statement of a non-perfectionist view of international morality which deserves the most careful analysis of any student of international relations.

The American people—no doubt like most others—suffer from certain illusions about the outside world and America's relationship to it. May we suggest that one such illusion has been that of moral superiority? It has, in part, been the consequence of confusing the natural benefits of geographic isolation with aloofness from sordid political practices. This attitude has been found wanting as the American people have themselves been drawn into the power struggle. The realization that they are not "different," "immune" or "better" has been painful. The adjustment is far from complete, but what is noteworthy about some recent statements by policy-makers, as well as analyses of detached observers, is the new recognition of the relevance and the significance of the concept of moral responsibility of the United States in world affairs. Such is the source of an ethical posture in international relations. In a world where the number of sovereign nation-states is nearing a hundred, the state itself must attempt to find such a posture—at least until some other order of power comes to transcend the state in governing international relationships.

1 • The Mood of Foreign Policy and the Cold War *

Kenneth W. Thompson

. . . .

Both the Soviet Union and the United States have been blessed with the most favorable of geographic situations. The United States is surrounded in the north and south by friendly and weaker states and bounded and safeguarded in the east and west by two great ocean moats. The geographic area of the Soviet Union, constituting about one-seventh of the earth's surface, has historically swallowed up any would-be invader, although its western boundaries are exposed by the open terrain of the European plains. The natural resources of both powers are immense, and their technology is far advanced. In conventional military weapons Russian strength probably exceeds American, but in the production of new weapons—first of an offensive type but more recently of a defensive kind—the Russians despite their progress with satellites have lagged behind. Russia's population is greater than America's although their per capita technical skill is probably less. American political institutions should in the long run prove superior, but the Russians may temporarily enjoy the advantages that flow from a system in which instantaneous decision-making and kaleidoscopic initiative are possible. National morale, particularly in the hydrogen age, is difficult to measure before a crisis. The quality of diplomacy on both sides is subject to the broader tendencies and probems that have been described.

Americans live by the faith that other peoples will come to embrace a political creed involving a decent respect for the dignity of mankind, and that an international order may be founded on respect for the rights and interests of other sovereign states. However, there are three obstacles that confound American policy-makers and that must at least be mitigated if the struggle is to be won.

The first obstacle is inherent in the problem of marshalling support domestically for American policies while at the same time putting America's best foot forward in the eyes of the rest of the world. To mobilize support for policies, Americans say things to themselves that from the standpoint of other peoples might better be left unsaid. (In this the United States is of course not unique.) America is a vast sprawling continent of great diversity of political and religious beliefs; in its constitutional system power and responsibility are broadly diffused, although less so in foreign affairs than in the conduct of domestic affairs. Thus Americans speak in many voices, some raucous and strident, as they seek to persuade one another of the right course to follow. The language of domestic politics is not the language of political theory. It aims to unite as many as will join to support policies or programs. It looks to a common denominator that can more often be found in

* "Theories and Problems of Foreign Policy" in Roy C. Macridis, ed., Foreign Policy in World Politics (Englewood Cliffs, N.J.: Prentice-Hall, Inc., 1958), pp. 372–77. Reprinted by permission.

broad principles and moral generalities than in specific directives of strategy, which like military policies must be cast in practical alternatives to meet circumstances. It prefers militant slogans to qualified truths and a crusade to public conversations on a problem.

Above all, it is a permanent part of the landscape of international relations that American foreign policy must draw its support from a union of the experts, the public, and friends and allies abroad. History demonstrates that no American statesman can ignore any point on the triangle without courting disaster. Before World War II, the public ostensibly lagged behind the thinking on foreign affairs of experts and allies. Following World War II and up to 1950, American policy—especially for Europe—was acceptable alike to the authoritative views of the experts, to the public, and to the members of the postwar grand alliance. This day has passed; and demands of the three groups have tended increasingly to go their separate ways. America's allies have more and more viewed their national interests as not necessarily identical with the United States', and ironically, at the time when American policies are vulnerable to criticism by experts at home and abroad, they enjoy broad endorsement at all levels of American life to the point of becoming virtually untouchable. By stressing one side of the triangle and striving above all for harmonious domestic political relations, the Eisenhower administration created difficulties for itself at the other points on the triangle. In this way it illustrated a perennial problem in the conduct of foreign relations.

Another obstacle stems from the colonial dilemma, which reaches beyond America's national life and touches conflicting interests at work throughout the rest of the world. We know that the colonial problem stands at the top of every agenda for discussion of American foreign policy. Responsible officials are encouraged to issue proclamations and to throw America's weight behind popular revolutions. In this setting it is tempting to take general and sweeping positions and to express an American doctrine on the rights of peoples everywhere to independence and self-government. This is particularly true because Americans' own experience is so rich in its lessons and apparently pregnant with meaning. The fruits of attempts thus far made to propound a dogma should serve, however, to give us pause, for the record of America's efforts to align itself squarely with either colonial or anticolonial powers is sprinkled with as many failures as successes.

Nevertheless, Americans face new situations today and demands crowd in upon them for new and more vigorous policies. We are reminded that Senator Vandenberg with his emphasis on Europe and Western unity never disparaged the rights of colonial or former colonial peoples. Nationalism is on the march in Asia, the Middle East, and Africa, and Americans implore one another to identify their country with these movements rather than appearing to stand in their pathway. Unhappily, the colonial problem is less tractable than those exhortations suggest. For at the same time as the fight is waged to end old imperialisms, a new and more demoniac expansionism threatens. To meet it, some feel that America must cleave to its trusted friends and allies with whom it has interest and military bases in common, striving to preserve a more stable world balance of power. Yet, in itself, this is not likely to be enough. The present equilibrium of power will be upset unless America can join with new forces in the so-called underdeveloped areas. We may say, therefore, that the United States faces the triple challenge of stemming the tide of Russian imperialism and world Communism, uniting the other Western states, and drawing closer to non-Western peoples only recently emerging as independent states. In a manner of speaking, policy-makers must keep three balls in the air. This is the unenviable task of American statesmanship.

· · · ·

Perceiving these problems can we say anything about this perplexing picture that will offer some guidance to the juggler or policy-maker of whom we have spoken? Are there guidelines or principles we can enunciate to spotlight a few of the darker corners of this colonial problem? Perhaps there are. First, we must start with the presumption that the colonial problem is fraught with dilemmas with which America must learn to live. Nor will dogmas for or against colonialism waft them away. Solutions must be worked out case by case; and as, for example, Tunisia is not identical with Algeria, policies must be shaped to meet individual needs. Second, timing is of the essence.... Third, if any general solution can be found it rests in the coordinating of mutual interests, not in the wholesale sacrifice of one set of interests to another.... The goal should be the harmonizing of interests. This calls for a judicious balancing of claims. Fourth, it is one of the ironies of history that force may be necessary to preserve colonial arrangements not in order to perpetuate them but that their orderly liquidation may be achieved. Fifth, it will not do to call every conflict of view between America and its European allies a colonial issue. On October 2, 1956, in what one commentator called a Freudian slip that betrayed the main lines of American thinking, Mr. Dulles noted that Britain and America were at odds over Suez on the question of the "shift from colonialism to independence." He treated Suez as an issue between the "colonial powers" and "the powers which are primarily and uniquely

concerned with the problem of getting their independence as rapidly as possible." Walter Lippmann was prompt to point out that Egypt could hardly be considered a colony, especially as it sought to expand its national power. A British journal observed: "The American desire to keep the goodwill of the Arab states is good sense ... but it will defeat itself in the end if, in pursuing it, the Americans think in anti-colonial conventions which are current.... In that way they will merely seek to please everybody, committing their strength to the support of local weak men, and overlooking that the conflicts which trouble the region, being real conflicts, require solutions of substance which are bound to give offense to some." [1] Finally, conflicts of interest—as in the past between Britain and India or the Dutch and the Indonesians—may be swept along by powerful historical movements until one side emerges supreme. Here it may be necessary for American policy-makers to choose sides and in this way inevitably give offense. These facts need not preclude prudence and restraint.

A final obstacle has roots in the moral problem. The question of right and wrong is continuously raised in international relations as in all the other social orders. Nations as individuals either seek to do, or claim to have done, what is right. The nature of Western values as embodied in American culture assures that far from being an exception, America persistently aspires to justice and to the goal of international order. We are pained when we are told that some aspect or another of national conduct cannot be justified in broader international terms, yet we can take comfort from the fact that historically this has been among the most baffling philosophical problems. The question is whether

---

[1] *The Economist* (London), December 8, 1956, p. 853.

an action shall be called good if it serves the group of primary loyalty or whether it must serve a more inclusive purpose. Political morality as distinct from pure law or justice answers this question in terms that give it a unique flavor. It looks for the point of concurrence between the particular and the general value or interest, rather than calling for the sacrifice of the part to the whole. Politics can count on a residual egotism or self-interest which represents the creative potential of individuals and groups. The nascent international community must guard against extreme forms of parochial loyalty that claim too much and reserve to themselves the right to suppress and overwhelm weaker neighbors. Short of this, however, the larger community is able to harness, beguile, and deflect the more limited national purposes even though it cannot easily transcend them. In Reinhold Niebuhr's words: "The individual or the group may feel called upon to sacrifice an immediate value for the sake of the more ultimate or general interest. But the community cannot demand this sacrifice as its right." Nor, one might add, can another sovereign state.

The American credo of political morality, especially in recent years, has been more pretentious and less modest than this. It has oftentimes called upon others to sacrifice local advantage to some nobler and higher cause. Some of the statements we have had from French, Israeli, Egyptian, and British leaders on the Suez crisis have thrown a dash of political realism on the standards that the United States sought to impose. Justice and international order are properly considered the broad framework of political morality, but their relative emphasis in any decision and the particular content they should receive can never be determined in advance. The values of community and order are frequently in tension with the principles of justice,

which are liberty and equality. In the fall of 1956, the international order suffered a threat to the peace. At the same time three of the nations invoked the principle of justice, which in equality calls for giving each man his due, including his right to survival. If the national community cannot assure a tolerable measure of justice, even though as a despotism it maintains order, in the long run its authority tends to erode. Similarly, if the international order lacks the power and prestige to safeguard all its members, they will be tempted to seek justice in other ways. There is an indefiniteness in political morality resulting because "various and frequently contradictory values are involved in political decisions and the preference which is given one value and end over another, must be determined by historical contingencies rather than fixed principles. There are fixed principles and norms in the political realm, but there is no fixed principle for relating the norms to each other. It is possible to define as 'bad' only those situations in which one or more norms are completely wanting...."[2]

America's policy-makers by contrast look for shortcuts to the moral problem. They talk a great deal more about promoting the impact of morality than about determining its content. They seize on the most readily available expressions congenial to their tastes and interests, like "majority rule" and "the will of the United Nations." The workings of political machinery are invested with all the trappings of a religious exercise and political pronouncements are equated with the glorification of God. Repelled by all the talk of "missions" and "crusades," one of our most sensitive critics has said: "I would rather *be* moral than claim to be it; and to the extent we succeed in lending moral de-

[2] Reinhold Niebuhr, unpublished manuscript on "Theory of International Politics," p. 11.

struction to the conduct of our affairs, I would rather let others discover it for themselves." The deep pathos of the moral problem calls more for Christian humility than for a moralistic self-righteousness, which can win few friends abroad and serves only to lower the currency of moral principles.

2 • Morality, Moralism, and Diplomacy *

Dean Acheson

A graduate of Yale University and Harvard Law School, the author served as Private Secretary to Justice Brandeis, 1919–1921. He was a member of a prominent Washington law firm until 1941, briefly interrupted by a half year as Under Secretary of the Treasury in 1933. In 1941 he was appointed Assistant Secretary of State, and from 1945 to 1947 served as Under Secretary of State. He became Secretary of State in 1949, serving until 1953. Since that time, he has published frequent articles and several books, including A Citizen Looks at Congress *(1957),* A Democrat Looks at His Party *(1955) and* Power and Diplomacy *(1958).*

In the course of a book published a few months ago I observed that, in discussing certain questions of foreign policy, I would not "for the most part, use the language of moral discourse or invoke moral authority," but would "state principles in terms of their purpose and effect without characterizing them as moral or immoral." I explained that it was "not because moral principles can, or should be, excluded from the relations of states to one another.... It is rather because to characterize conduct between nations as moral or immoral will involve us in confusions of vocabulary and of thought with which, despite their importance, we need not struggle. ... The language of moral discourse— colored as it is apt to be at one end with fervor, and, at the other, with self-righteousness—is more likely to obscure than clarify our discussion. And the substance of moral discussion, which concerns the conduct of individuals within a society toward one another, is more likely than not to be misleading if applied to the relations of one society to another. Undoubtedly the problems have something in common. Morality in individual life has to do with those restraints upon conduct which are adopted or imposed because there are others upon whom one's conduct impinges with more or less directness and effect. So, too, restraints upon the conduct of a society as a whole may be adopted or imposed because of the effect of one society upon others. But they are not the same restraints. They deal with different situations."

This brought me letters from writers disappointed that one brought up in a clerical family, under the very guns, so

* *The Yale Review,* XLVII (1958), 481–93. Reprinted by permission.

to speak, of morality and religion, and having shown no previous signs of apostasy, should have disclosed an attitude so callous to virtue. Perhaps the course of wisdom is not to go further with a subject so full of pitfalls, but the temptation is too great to be resisted.

We Americans are, for the most part, a pretty moral people, as these things go; certainly we set great store by morality. Our traditions are deeply rooted in the Puritan theocratic state of the seventeenth century and in the evangelical revival of the nineteenth. They are both Cromwellian and Wesleyan. It is true that we fall from grace often and far, not the least in our treatment of our fellow men whose skins differ from the prevailing color, or whose religion differs from that locally accepted. This, and some of our other actions, lead people, viewing us from afar, to suspect us of hypocrisy. But they are wrong about this. We are only more like them than they had realized. We are all—as the Book of Common Prayer says—"miserable offenders," and our professions are beyond our practice; both we and our critics have erred and strayed from true ways "like lost sheep"; the remembrance of our misdoings should be "grievous unto us," though it seldom is. All of this should not—and happily does not—make us any less determined to be guided by moral light; but it should lead us to take a modest view of our capacity to generate a beam pure and strong enough to be convincing to others.

Those who advocate what they refer to as a moral or idealistic foreign policy usually contrast this with what seems to them opportunism, or pure expediency. These terms are very slippery ones, and often elude a firm grasp. If we think about it, what is moral is characterized by what is excellent in conduct, and this is not explained much better by saying that excellence means what is right and proper, as against what is wrong, by established standards. At any rate morality would seem to be a branch of idealism, which affirms the preëminence of the product of mind and spirit in determining reality.

All of this seems a long way from what we usually hear discussed by people who call for moral or idealistic foreign policy. What they discuss seems more nearly moralism, the reduction of morals to maxims. These can easily be corrupted into slogans.

For instance, how seldom those who demand a moral policy appeal to the principles, the primacy of which is rarely denied, at least publicly—such principles as that to deal truthfully, honorably, and courageously is better than to practice duplicity, conspiracy, and treachery. Far more often the principles espoused are more complicated, and often closely related to the holder's most deep-seated prejudices and the limitations of his experience.

Let us think for a moment of a principle which is often put forward as a highly moral and idealistic one. This is that not only do communities which wish to break off existing political connections and become independent national states have a moral right to do so, but that a moral foreign policy on the part of the United States requires that we go to considerable lengths to help them, including the use of force, as President Wilson's Fourteen Points will recall to those who remember them. In that enumeration this principle was called the right of self-determination.

It was first applied against our enemies, whose resultant difficulties we could contemplate with commendable detachment, if not with enthusiasm. Its embodiment began with the dismemberment of the Austro-Hungarian and Ottoman Empires. As one looks back upon the results in Eastern Europe and the Middle East, one has more difficulty in seeing the moral or ideal achievement than in recognizing the immediate and, perhaps, irrevocable disaster.

Recently, however, to avoid complications, the principle has chiefly been invoked against our friends. Indeed, the more distant our relations with a state, the more restrained we appear to be in urging the moral imperative of self-determination. With India, for instance, a particularly touchy, if not prickly friend, we are most reticent about mentioning the United Nations' call for a plebiscite in Kashmir, which India (for highly moral reasons, it insists) has alternately ignored and defied for the past eight years. Hungary is no longer what we lawyers call an active case. And need I speak of the Baltic states?

If this passion to free all men, everywhere, under all circumstances, and at once, is, indeed, a moral principle, it seems, as Mr. Louis Halle has pointed out (in THE YALE REVIEW, Autumn 1956), to partake more of the morality of John Brown than of Abraham Lincoln. Lincoln's moral attitude—excoriated as immorality by abolitionists and secessionists alike—disclosed what we might call a strategic, as against an ideological, approach to great and complicated problems: "...my paramount object in this struggle," he wrote to Horace Greeley on August 22, 1862 (almost as the armies locked in the crisis of the second Manassas), "is to save the Union, and is not either to save or destroy slavery. If I could save the Union without freeing any slave, I would do it; and if I could save it by freeing all the slaves, I would do it; and if I could do it by freeing some and leaving others alone, I would also do that. What I do about slavery and the colored race, I do because I believe it helps to save this Union; and what I forbear, I forbear because I do not believe it would help to save the Union. I shall do less whenever

I shall believe what I am doing hurts the cause, and I shall do more whenever I shall believe doing more will help the cause."

As I read these words and ponder them, I am comforted by the belief that Mr. Lincoln would have understood and approved stating "principles in terms of their purpose and effect without characterizing them as moral or immoral."

To those who have any appreciation of the perils which surround us, of the lightning speed with which relative (indeed, absolute) positions can change, of the effect which popular attitudes, so easily and often unworthily stimulated, can have in forcing governments to foolish action or restraining them from wise action, a moralistic approach to foreign relations—and by this I mean one which attempts to apply the maxims or ideology of moral teaching—seems ill-adapted to the complexity of the task.

The moralistic-ideological approach to the conduct of foreign affairs consists in finding in one theme both a central evil, which is thought to dominate our time, and also the clue to its eradication. With the goal thus established and the weapon chosen, the ensuing operation can easily become a crusade. So to Senator Kennedy, "the challenge of imperialism" is the "single most important test of American foreign policy." But President Eisenhower, in his State of the Union Message, puts it differently. "Now, the threat to our safety and to the hope of a peaceful world, is simply stated. It is Communist imperialism." Note that the danger is not the power, military and otherwise, of the Soviet Union, which would be simpler still to understand, but "Communist imperialism." To Senator McCarthy the threat was Communists in government. His crusade had the advantage of not tackling the difficult and dangerous task of countering a powerful and armed state, but only of browbeating frightened and defenseless minor employees of the government.

Among the more serious traps of this approach is the delusive simplicity it offers in choosing those whose purposes and efforts are helpful to our own, and those whose acts are hostile. If, for example, the central theme is that Communism is the threat and evil, then those who most loudly assert their enmity to Communism must, by this simple test, be our most assured co-workers in establishing an environment in which free societies can exist and flourish. So, in the past, both Hitler and Mussolini have been presented to us as dyed-in-the-wool anti-Communists, who not only made the trains run on time, but also represented the "wave of the future." So, also, more recently Generalissimo Franco has been hailed as a bulwark against Communism.

Others are put off by Mr. Nehru. He does not seem to them wholly true blue. He is critical of Western policy and apt to fall into enthusiastic applause at a good skit by Messrs. Bulganin and Khrushchev. Does he really belong to the team? The problem is, of course, quite different and wholly unrelated to considerations of this sort. Indeed, I have ventured to suggest that despite his "unusual gifts of causing annoyance," "if Mr. Nehru did not exist, our greatest hope for India would lie in inventing him; for he, alone, seems to have a fair chance of holding India together while economic development lays a foundation for social and political stability."

The lesson is, of course, that, in determining those whom it is wise to support, the test is not what they say they oppose, but in the purpose and effect of what they are doing.

One could go on to point out the plethora of moralistic maxims which we have adopted. Forty years ago a principle was put forward as a sure foundation of the conduct of international rela-tions which, since then, has had quite a vogue. This is the principle of "open covenants, openly arrived at." But today no less an authority than the Secretary General of the United Nations is not so sure. " 'Open agreements' represent the response to a sound demand," Mr. Hammarskjold said at Ohio University. "How and to what extent they should be 'openly arrived at,' on the other hand, is a principle which requires serious consideration in the light of the very aims which the public procedures are intended to serve." And he added: "The legislative process in the United Nations is not a substitute for diplomacy. It serves its purpose only when it helps diplomacy to arrive at agreements between the national states concerned. It is diplomacy, not speeches and votes, that continues to have the last word in the process of peace-making."

Again, toward the other end of the spectrum from the anti-Communist school are those who believe that the purpose and content of foreign policy must be to have "talks with the Russians." Where, when, by whom, about what, and to what effect seem comparatively unimportant. Here is a case, not of the end justifying the means, but apparently of the means justifying—or, at least, probably producing—a most unpredictable end.

Another approach, with which one can sympathize, if not approve, springs from the vast urge to do anything to lessen the horror of nuclear war and diminish its possibility. The terrible difficulty is that "anything" will not do this. The possibility of accomplishment by negotiation under present circumstances is small. The most promising courses are hard ones. The best chance is not along lines of moralistic maxims, but along the Lincolnian approach— what I have called the strategic approach. If you ask me what I mean by a strategic approach, I could say a good deal but probably would not improve on Bret Harte's description of "Tennessee's Partner." "In fact, he was a grave man, with a steady application to practical detail which was unpleasant in a difficulty." The real task is to negotiate by action, sustained, wise, and disciplined action, by ourselves and our allies. Here lies, I believe, the best chance to convince the Russians that they cannot win by default, that in the end they must come to an understanding, and to assure that the understanding, whenever it comes—and it will not be soon—is one with which we, as well as they, can live.

What I have said thus far is, first, that many of the moralistic maxims adapted to the conduct of foreign affairs are apt to reflect personal prejudice or sententious sentiment. Secondly, I have suggested that, even if these utterances were generally of a higher quality and more detached, one cannot find in ethics and aesthetics, alone, a complement of tools for dealing with the relations between states. Into these relationships enter factors governed by forces which operate in the physical rather than the metaphysical world. There also enters human conduct, which all too often is neither moral nor ethical nor controllable by exhortation. Those who, so rightly, admire the Gettysburg Address, should remember that it dedicated a field of action and was not a substitute for action. The conduct of foreign affairs must achieve its purpose by causes and effects of a varied and complicated nature upon a wide assortment of human, geographical, and physical material. From this activity moral factors are by no means absent.

As one probes further into the moral aspects of relations between states, additional causes for treading warily appear. A little reflection will convince us that the same conduct is not moral under all circumstances. Its moral propri-

ety seems to depend, certainly in many cases, upon the relationship of those concerned with the conduct. For instance, parents have the moral right, indeed duty, to instill moral and religious ideas in their children and punish error. Ministers, priests, rabbis, and mullahs have much the same duties to their flocks, including that of correcting heresy, when they can make up their minds what it is.

But these same acts on the part of public officials in the United States would be both immoral and a denial of the fundamental rights of the citizen. . . .

So, acts, moral in one human relationship, may become quite the reverse in another. Generally speaking, morality often imposes upon those who exercise the powers of government standards of conduct quite different from what might seem right to them as private citizens. . . .

When we come . . . to relations between states, rather than within a state, we find no consensus of opinion or monopoly of force to create and enforce standards. A great and powerful bloc of states rejects with contempt almost all in which we believe; and says so quite frankly. The experience and condition of peoples of some other states differ so from our own that many of our most cherished beliefs—such, for instance, as the worth of the individual and all that flows from this—seem to them unreal and shadowy.

But, one may reply, at least some moral standards of right and wrong seem pretty well agreed upon. Surely, the opinion of the world has condemned the use and the threat of force by one state against another, as the United Nations Charter bears witness. Does this not give us firm ground on which to stand? Well, does it? Ever since the Charter was signed, those whose interests are opposed to ours have used force, or the threat of it, whenever it seemed to them advisable and safe—in Greece, Czechoslovakia, Palestine, Berlin, Korea, Indochina, and Hungary. Both sides used it in regard to Suez. Is it moral to deny ourselves the use of force in all circumstances, when our adversaries employ it, under handy excuses, whenever it seems useful to tip the scales of power against every value we think of as moral and as making life worth living? It seems to me not only a bad bargain, but a stupid one. I would almost say an immoral one. For the very conception of morality seems to me to involve a duty to preserve values outside the contour of our own skins, and at the expense of forgoing much that is desired and pleasant, including—it may be—our own fortunes and lives.

This leads me to suggest an area in our foreign relations where guidance from what is excellent in conduct may more confidently be sought than in some others. This is in the methods by which foreign relations are conducted. There is pretty general agreement in some parts of the non-Communist world, as has been suggested, that it is better to act straightforwardly, candidly, honorably, and courageously than by means of duplicity, conspiracy, and treachery. For us to act on this principle will not reform our opponents, who will continue to use such methods whenever they suit their purposes. But it might do much to give them, as well as our own people, a much clearer idea of our intentions. This, in itself, would inspire confidence and increase stability. If this standard included a considerably greater insistence on truth than at present—not necessarily the whole truth, but, perhaps, nothing but the truth; not the conception of truth which enters the techniques of advertising, which is the gilding without the lily—the effect on policy might be great. For one thing, it would diminish the tendency to regard the art of diplomacy as the stratagem of going to the verge of war to accomplish a purpose.

I stress the application of this standard to the methods we use because I believe—although I am doubtless in the minority on this—that ends of action are not, for the most part, determined by ideals, but the other way around. It has been said that "Man . . . is born to act. To act is to affirm the worth of an end, and to persist in affirming the worth of an end is to make an ideal." And again, "Philosophy does not furnish motives, but it shows men that they are not fools for doing what they already want to do."

Even though you find this doctrine unpalatable, you may still, as a practical matter, go with me to my conclusion. Not long ago, before a university audience, I was talking about the substance of desirable foreign policy. A student expressed the view that in stressing factors of power, of the capabilities of our own nation and others, I had left no place, as he put it, for moral or idealistic conceptions. I ventured to disagree, pointing out that the results of the policies I advocated would—and I knew of no others which could—stand a good chance of preserving not only our own nation, our allies, and I hoped, peace in the world, but also the whole civilization which had given us the values by which we lived, or tried to live.

Out of this Graeco-Roman-Judaic civilization, with some of its roots in other cultures, came the idea, and the often-faltering recognition, of the worth of the individual, in whose mind and spirit all values must be tested. From this sprang freedom in all its forms—of mind and person and of communities of persons. From this civilization, too, came unsurpassed teachings, in the dialogues of Socrates, the writings of Marcus Aurelius, and the Sermon on the

Mount, of life committed to goodness and virtue. Among them is the teaching that strength is not itself a virtue— "blessed are the meek."

I pointed out to the young man that I found it hard to believe that to oppose a powerful and brutal state which was threatening the independence of others and, indeed, the existence of our civilization, was less admirable because it preserved our own nation as well. Nor did it seem to me less good to help peoples to improve their conditions because this was essential to keep the free world free and to strengthen it. Furthermore, the idea of sacrifice for interests beyond one's own is not a materialistic conception. The policies I advocated required us to pay for them with our taxes. This young man and others would have to give a part of that time in their lives when they are eager to push on to the experience and responsibility of manhood to military service, often irksome and wasteful. Surely in all of this the highest and best ideas which our prophets and teachers have given us played a vast part.

To return, in a closing word, to the methods we use. Here we can and should aim high. There should be no bullying, no advantage taken of the hardship of others to drive political bargains, no lying or boasting in our propaganda or our dealings with others, no sanctimonious lecturing of others on their faults, no consciousness of our own effortless righteousness, or the thanking of God that we are not as other men. I have ventured to sum this up somewhere else.

"Perhaps what we do is less important than how we do it. 'What one lives for may be uncertain,' writes Lord David Cecil of Conrad's view of life, 'How one lives is not.... Man should live nobly though he does not see any practical reason for it, simply because in the mysterious inexplicable mixture of beauty and ugliness, virtue and baseness in which he finds himself he must want to be on the side of the beautiful and the virtuous.' "

3 • Statesmanship and Moral Choice *

Arnold Wolfers

Throughout the ages moralists have expressed horror at the way princes and sovereign states behave toward each other. Behavior which would be considered immoral by any standard can obviously be detected in all realms of life; but nowhere does the contradiction between professed ethical principles and actual behavior appear so patent and universal as in the conduct of foreign relations. Governments spy on each other and lie to each other; they violate pledges and conduct wars, often at the

* World Politics, I (1949), 175–95. Reprinted by permission.

cost of millions of lives and untold misery. No wonder, then, that in western democracies if not elsewhere indignation over such practices should be voiced with vehemence. In our day it frequently expresses itself in wholesale denunciations of the multi-state system on the ground that sovereign states cannot deal with each other except by the use of immoral means, derogatorily called power politics. Some draw the cynical conclusion that morality has no place in international politics, while others would have men fulfill their moral duty by substituting world government for the present immoral political system.

This sweeping moral condemnation of foreign policy as pursued by all nations points to a striking and disturbing contradiction in our public life. Most of our statesmen claim to be pursuing policies of peace and enunciate high moral principles upon which their policy is supposed to be based; they and many publicists praise the democracies for the moral superiority of their conduct of foreign affairs over that of aggressive and ruthless dictators. Yet at the same time many respected students in the field of international relations insist that all sovereign states alike are compelled by the "system" to play the evil game of power politics. The two positions would seem to be incompatible. Either our statesmen and their supporters are deceiving themselves and others or those who without discrimination condemn all power politics as immoral are overstating the case. In a country like the United States where moral passion tends to run high and where the question of morality in politics is a matter of genuine and wide concern, it is important to try to resolve this contradiction.

The idea that power politics are beyond the pale of morality is not new. Down through the centuries Machiavelli and Machiavellianism have stood for a doctrine which places princes and sovereign states under the rule not of ordinary morality but of the "reason of state," considered an amoral principle peculiar to the realm of politics.[1] German writers have been particularly insistent that ethical standards which apply to private individuals cannot measure the behavior of states which are said to be guided by necessity if not by a *höhere Sittlichkeit*.[2]

The English-speaking world, not seldom accused of comfortably ignoring or hypocritically denying the contradictions between ethics and international politics, has been unwilling on the whole to admit of any peculiar ethics of state behavior. Because states are abstractions, or at best fictitious personalities, it is not the state that decides and acts but always individuals, though they be statesmen. Should their behavior be

---

[1] One might question whether Machiavelli meant to draw a sharp distinction between the ethics of state behavior, the behavior of "princes," which was his main concern, and the ethics of individual behavior. In the same Chapter XV of *The Prince,* in which he advises the sovereign to learn "how not to be good," he also speaks generally of the condition of man, saying that "whoever abandons what is done for what ought to be done will rather learn to bring about his own ruin than his preservation." He goes on to say that such a man "must necessarily come to grief among so many who are not good."

[2] Friedrich Meinecke's *Die Idee der Staatsräson,* Munich and Berlin, 1925, is a classic study of the relations between ethics and power politics as seen by Machiavelli and his continental disciples down to Treitschke. No similar study has been written on the views of their Anglo-Saxon contemporaries, though Gerhard Ritter, in *Machtstaat und Utopie,* Munich and Berlin, 1914, makes a suggestive beginning to such a study. He contrasts Machiavelli, "pioneer of the continental power state," with Thomas More, "ideological father of the English insular welfare state"—the former setting power above morality (p. 31), the latter seeking the "Ethisierung und Entdämonisierung der Macht" (p. 89).

judged differently from that of other individuals merely because they act for the state? To answer in the affirmative would mean accepting the hardly more palatable idea of a double standard of morality, according to which individuals when acting for themselves shall follow one set of moral principles while the same individuals when conducting their nation's foreign policy shall be bound by another and presumably less stringent code of behavior.[3]

At first sight the facts seem to bear this out. Do we not condemn and punish citizens for committing the very acts of violence, treaty violation or untruthfulness which we condone in international politics? Are we not constantly struck by the gulf that separates the relatively peaceful and humane life within the national borders of states from the events occurring on the international scene? It is this contrast—more apparent than true, as we shall see—that has led some to demand that statesmen be made to give up their sinful ways and to conform to the rules of behavior expected from individuals in an orderly community. Unfortunately, advice of this kind often proves so patently impractical that instead of inducing statesmen to mend their ways it provokes in them a sense of moral cynicism. What is the use of

listening to moral advice, they ask, if statesmanship, capable of mastering the problems which present themselves in practice, is apparently incompatible with morality?

The fundamental discrepancy which seems to exist between the morality of "state" and private behavior would disappear only if it could be shown that politics conducted in a multi-state system is not necessarily any more immoral than average private behavior, or that the chief difference pertains not to the degree of immorality prevailing in the two spheres of human action but to the circumstances under which men are required to act. Much of what strikes people as immoral practices of governments may prove to be morally justified by the peculiar and unhappy circumstances which the statesman has to face and which, moreover, he may often be unable to change.

Any ethical perfectionist will be shocked at such a suggestion. He will deny that any action that would be evil under one set of conditions could be morally justified under another. If men are held to be morally bound to act in accordance with an absolute ethic of love such as the Sermon on the Mount, obviously no set of circumstances, even circumstances in which the survival of a nation were at stake, could justify acts such as a resort to violence, untruthfulness, or treaty violation. The concern for self-preservation and power in itself would have to be condemned as evil. This being the case, the ethical perfectionist can offer no advice to statesmen other than that they give up public office and turn their backs on politics. As a matter of fact, in order to be consistent, the perfectionist, as some have pointed out, must give the same advice to private citizens, requiring of them that they abandon their concern for their own welfare, for family or business. If, as Hans

---

[3] While Hans J. Morgenthau in *Scientific Man vs. Power Politics,* (Chicago, University of Chicago Press, 1946), declares that "No civilization can be satisfied with...a dual morality" (p. 179), William Ernest Hocking, *The Spirit of World Politics,* (New York, Macmillan, 1932), writes that statesmen distrust public opinion in international affairs because the public "takes for granted that the codes (for individuals and for states) are the same." E. H. Carr, *The Twenty Years' Crisis,* (London, Macmillan, 1940), in contrast to these authors asserts that most people, while believing that states ought to act morally, do not expect of them the same kind of moral behavior which they expect of themselves and of one another (p. 199).

Morganthau holds, "the very act of acting destroys our moral integrity," only a life of saintliness could come close to satisfying perfectionist moral commands.[4]

We must address ourselves exclusively then to the non-perfectionist who demands of man, not that he follow an absolute code of ethical rules—what Max Weber calls the "natural law of absolute imperatives"—but that he make the best moral choice which the circumstances permit.[5]

But surely, it will be objected, no moralist, at least in our culture, could deviate so far from perfectionist standards as to condone even in wartime such inhuman practices as the torture of enemy soldiers or the shooting of hostages. One would wish that this objection would always be valid, but the fact is that the non-perfectionist cannot escape the conclusion that circumstances may justify what superficially appear to be the most despicable kinds of human conduct. Or would he condemn without careful prior investigation all the members of the French Resistance movement who, in the face of brutal Nazi tactics, are said to have answered their enemy in kind. What if they were unable to discover any other alternatives but either to stop in this repulsive fashion the horrors committed by the Nazis or else to leave their friends and their cause unprotected? This does not imply that circumstances morally justify every act of power politics from the violation of the pledged word to aggression and concentration camps; the chances are that in most instances they will not, whether because the cause is unworthy of such extreme sacrifices or

because other means are available which will assure morally preferable over-all results. Nor does it mean that where circumstances do justify such acts men may not be guilty of having brought about these circumstances or of having failed to remove them.

There is nothing peculiar to international politics in this impact of circumstance. Our conscience revolts at the idea of men putting other men to death. Yet non-perfectionist moralists throughout the western world agree in condoning the acts of those who kill in self-defense, in obedience to an order to execute a criminal, in war, or possibly in the case of tyrannicide. In other cultures it has been considered morally proper, if not a moral duty, to put the first born, aging parents, or widows to death. One and the same act, then, will be judged differently depending on the context within which it is performed and depending also, of course, on the ethical standards by which behavior in general is judged.

This is not the place to enter upon the age-old discussion of what the standards of a non-perfectionist ethic should be, nor is such a discussion necessary for our purpose. However much non-perfectionists may disagree on ethical standards and thus on the nature and hierarchy of values, they hold in common the process by which they reach their moral judgments. They start with the conviction that there can be no escape from sacrifices of value whether, as theologians maintain, because of man's original sin and essential corruption, or because of the dilemmas of a world in which man is faced with incompatible moral claims. With this as a basis they hold that men, statesmen and private individuals alike, are morally required to choose among the roads open to them the one which under the circumstances promises to produce the least over-all destruction of value or, posi-

---

[4] Hans J. Morgenthau, *op. cit.*, p. 189.

[5] See Max Weber's "Politics as a Vocation," in *From Max Weber: Essays in Sociology,* (New York, Oxford University Press, 1946), pp. 120 ff.

tively speaking, points toward the maximization of value.[6]

Moral condemnation, according to non-perfectionist ethics, rests not on the fact that values have been destroyed, however deplorable or downright evil such destruction may be judged. Instead it is based on the conviction either that the action in question rested on false ethical standards or that in terms of agreed ethical standards a less destructive choice could and should have been made.[7]

Thus a private citizen who breaks family ties in order to serve what he considers a higher cause may find himself condemned because his cause is not considered worth the sacrifice or because there were other less costly ways of attaining his end. Similarly a statesman who decides to break off diplomatic negotiations rather than to accept the terms of the opposing side may be judged wrong because he placed undue value on an increment of national prestige which was at stake or because he failed to appreciate properly the dangers involved in his choice of action. There is no difference either in the method of evaluation or in the ethical standards, whether the case be one of political or private behavior. In that sense the ethic of politics is but a part of general ethics. The question which remains to be answered, however, is why the sacrifices of value in international politics should be as widespread, continuous, and shocking in extent as they so obviously are. Is it because the circumstances under which foreign policy is conducted are so different and so unalterably different from those under which private citizens make their choices?

German writers on international politics have emphasized what they consider a unique and all-pervasive circumstance characteristic of inter-state relations. Writing in the heyday of German *Realpolitik* Ratzenhofer declared categorically that the relations between sovereign states are unalterably relations of enmity.[8] His assertion reminds one of the no less dogmatic Marxist proposition according to which the relations between capital and labor in a capitalist economy are relations of enemies engaged in a class war.[9]

If one looks at the facts of history and

---

[6] Max Weber's "ethic of responsibility," (*op. cit.*, pp. 118 ff.) comes closer to what is here described as a non-perfectionist ethic of maximization of value than it might appear from some of his statements. Weber, it is true, declares that "from no ethics in the world can it be concluded when and to what extent the ethically good purpose 'justifies' the ethically dangerous means and ramification" (p. 121). He is here taking issue with the revolutionary fanatic who from the point of view of an "ethic of ultimate ends" considers every act of violence justified so long as it serves his ultimate end. But when Weber goes on to demand of men that they hold themselves responsible for the consequences of their acts, especially their acts of violence, he does not refute their moral right to "contract with the diabolic powers of violence" which as political men they must do, but implicitly calls on them to choose the road which will minimize the evil consequences for which they bear responsibility.

[7] Hans J. Morgenthau, *op. cit.*, following in the footsteps of Max Weber, also emphasizes the "ethical paradoxes" of politics. "Political ethics," he says, "is indeed the ethics of doing evil" (p. 202). Yet he too concludes that "it is moral judgment," meaning presumably the best a man can morally do "to choose among several expedient actions the least evil one" (p. 203).

[8] See Gustav Ratzenhofer, *Wesen und Zweck der Politik*, (Leipzig, 1893).

[9] Carl Schmitt, in *Der Begriff des Politischen*, (Munich, 1932), modifies Ratzenhofer's thesis by declaring that inter-state and, in fact, all truly political relations are in the nature of "friend-foe" relations. While he does not claim that relations between all states at all times are inevitably hostile, he maintains that nations always group themselves as friends and foes and that, there could be no such thing as statehood or politics if it were not for the existence of potential enmity, by which he means the possibility of deadly physical combat.

of the contemporary world, one cannot subscribe to this German view. Instead it seems as if the relations between sovereign states no less than the relations between other groups or individuals run the whole gamut from almost complete amity—take Canadian-American or Anglo-Canadian relations—to almost unmitigated enmity, as in the days of war. Amity and enmity appear as the two extreme poles of a wide scale of human relationships. It remains true, however, and a matter of great political and moral consequence, that the multi-state system, for reasons which cannot be analyzed here, has a tendency to push relations between at least some states in the direction of enmity—and, for that matter, more so in our century than in the last. The Nazis certainly saw to it that this would be so. As faithful disciples of Gustav Ratzenhofer, Carl Schmitt and others, they not only believed in the inevitability of international enmity but true to their theoretical assumption conducted German policy in such a way as to arouse the fiercest kind of enmity in most parts of the world.

The concepts of amity and enmity can be usefully employed to shed light on the context within which statesmen are forced to make their choices. They stand for the two opposite and marginal extremes of human relationships. Behavior changes as the relationship approximates one or the other of these poles. The causes of enmity in inter-state relations are significant to the moral problem only to the extent to which statesmen may be responsible for bringing about or for not eliminating enmity, and thus become responsible for the consequences of such enmity.

One can imagine a condition of complete enmity between states. There would be no trace of community between them, no sense of commonly held values or of common interest. Each individual state would have to be looked upon as an entirely separate entity operating in the social vacuum of absolute anarchy. There would exist a state of latent if not actual war all the time, turning diplomacy into warfare with other means. With good reason nations could consider themselves in a constant state of emergency with all the things gravely endangered to which they attached value. It would be a situation, as we know it from the experience of total war, in which the sheer quest for survival would justify almost any course of action. "Out-group morality" of the most extreme type would prevail.

Take the other extreme, that of amity or the "friend-to-friend" relationship. While there would be no complete identification, a sense of community would exist sufficient to eliminate mutual fear and suspicion. There would be no expectation of violence and therefore no need for preparations with which to meet the dangers of conflict. Despite the fact that each state would be sovereign, or rather because each state would be free to handle its own affairs, such friendly nations could behave toward each other according to the codes of "in-group morality" and live in peace with each other.

The more relations between states degenerate toward enmity the more nations are justified in fearing for the things they cherish and the more reason they have to make and require sacrifices by which inimical claims can be defeated. Greater enmity therefore increases the likelihood that Machiavellian practices will become necessary and morally justified. The degree of amity or enmity thus appears as a morally portentous circumstance. While in a state of amity statesmen are likely to be able to choose between different avenues toward cooperation, compromise and conciliation. Enmity, however, may preclude such choices and place before the statesman a different set of alternatives. He may be able to take steps which will promise to mitigate if not to eliminate existing enmity. Often, however, he will have to choose between efforts to deter his opponent, thereby neutralizing the effects of enmity, and efforts to defeat him.

This cannot be said to be a peculiarity of international politics or of the multistate system. The same phenomenon can be found in the relationship between father and son, employer and employee, white and colored man. There may be complete amity between them with no trace of distrust, no shadow of fear, no concern for self-protection, no awareness of conflicting demands or expectations. But here, too, relations may degenerate into fierce hostility for reasons too numerous to detail. Behavior then may change beyond recognition.

. . . .

It will be objected, and rightly so, that intra-state relations are less likely than inter-state relations to reach a degree of hostility that would call for the use of violence and other Machiavellian devices.[10] The state protects many of the values to which people are attached. The state can also prohibit the use of means to which society is opposed and can enforce its prohibition—though only by the very means which the components of that society have renounced for themselves. This holds true, however, only for well organized states where the government can marshal sufficient authority and police power to prevent family feuds and social or racial conflicts from breaking into the open and degenerating into violence and the use of other Machiavellian means. But while the pacifying influence of such a state and its influence on human behavior should not be minimized, exponents of world statehood tend to exaggerate the case for government.[11] The kind of government and therefore the kind of internal peace which this country enjoys at this time represents the exception rather than the rule. Our government operates under conditions, not wholly state-made, of widespread amity between most of the groups that are powerful enough to influence the course of domestic events. It is recognized as legitimate by practically everyone and is ordinarily obeyed not because it has the force of coercion but because its authority is freely accepted. If one looks at the performance of other governments either in the contemporary world or in past periods of history, one finds no lack of examples of governments operating under quite different conditions and with quite different results.

Some governments are strong and ruthless enough to suppress the hostilities that would otherwise break out between warring factions, ethnic, social, or

---

[10] Some writers while agreeing that the ethical problems of political and private life are basically the same nevertheless stress the difference, if only quantitative, which makes international power politics the domain of evil *par excellence*. In his earlier works Reinhold Niebuhr stresses the peculiar selfishness and immorality of human communities including the state, as indicated by the title of his book, *Moral Man and Immortal Society,* (New York, Charles Scribner's Sons, 1936). Later, however, he places more emphasis on the fact that all life is a "contest of power" and that international war and conflict are but a revelation of the general character of human existence and human sinfulness. (See his *Christianity and Power Politics,* (New York, Charles Scribner's Sons, 1940), especially pages 11, 12, and 103.)

[11] Mortimer Adler, *How To Think About War And Peace,* (New York, Simon and Schuster, 1944), declares anarchy to be the only cause of war and defines anarchy as "the condition of those who try to live without government" (p. 69).

religious, but they do so by means of suppression, often tyrannical or terroristic. Rather than eliminate Machiavellian practices, such governments merely monopolize them. To what extremes of behavior this may lead has been drastically demonstrated by the way modern totalitarian regimes have persecuted the "enemies of the people." Other governments are too weak to control the forces of internal enmity; then there are bloody revolts or civil wars. When that happens enmity often reaches a degree of fierceness which relations between states rarely approximate. Machiavellian practices of the most extreme kind become the order of the day.

Government or statehood, whether national or world-wide, is therefore no panacea against those aspects of power politics which are morally deplorable. The real evil is enmity and its threat to values to which people are devoted.

However, the moralist needs to be reminded of the fact that there is not only no sure way to eliminate the fateful circumstance of enmity but that at a given time there may be no way at all. Certainly the elimination of the multi-state system itself, whether within a region such as Europe or on a world-wide scale is not one of the objectives statesmen are free to choose and therefore morally obliged to choose under all circumstances. Even if a radical change in the existing order were morally desirable because there was reason to suppose that a regional federation or a world government would create circumstances of greater amity than exist today, the psychological prerequisites for a concerted move of major nations toward such a goal are beyond the control of governments.

If it be true that statesmen cannot at all times choose to work for conditions of world-wide amity under world government, is it not their moral duty at least to promote amity at all times and at all costs? Once it is conceded that enmity requires and justifies sacrifices of value often of the most shocking kind, it would seem as if no price paid for amity could be considered too high. Yet statesmen would be rendered incapable of maximizing value if, without respect for the context in which they were forced to operate in a given instance, the quest for amity were taken as the sole measure of their actions. Amity is a condition passionately to be desired; but there are times when efforts to bring it about will lead to disaster. It takes two to make friends. An attempt to establish bonds of friendship may be interpreted as a sign of weakness; the result may be aggression. Again the demands of the opponent may call for sacrifices of value greater than those connected with continued enmity. Firmness and even resort to force may under certain circumstances require less loss of life, less human suffering, less destruction of faith and principle than the most sincere attempt to eliminate the causes of hostility by concessions.

This is not the same as saying that power politics generally preclude the opportunity for persistent and active pursuit of amity—or of justice for that matter. There are many occasions when disputes can be settled peacefully and when enmity can be eliminated or avoided, provided one side at least has enough courage, imagination and initiative. Sometimes a spirit of conciliation or even of generosity can do wonders in evoking a ready and sincere response. Whenever the lines of enmity are not irreparably drawn, there may remain room for moderation and self-restraint, for better understanding of each other's true designs and for fair compromise. While it is true that in the end it needs two to make friends, it is not always the other side which must take the first step.[12]

Only those who extol the value of national "virility" which is supposed to express itself in obstinate resistance to compromise, or those who are afraid of being the suckers will insist that the "necessity of state" is always on the side of toughness and unrelenting assertion of national claims. Harold Nicolson castigates Napoleon for being able to ascribe Castlereagh's "splendid moderation" only to treachery or corruption, ignorance or folly.[13] Whether moderation is politically practical or suicidal depends on the circumstances. Those who feel called upon to give moral advice to statesmen must be realists if they are to be true to the tenets of non-perfectionist ethics to demand restraint of power, charity and forgiveness in our situation, as when feelings of revenge and war passions run high, but to insist on a break with an opponent, if not on the use of violence, when weakness or procrastination threatens to bring on greater evils. If world government were not only practical but would, if established, temper enmities and help nations protect or attain what they rightly value most highly, it would be the moral duty

of statesmen to seek to bring it about. As things stand today, however, lack of consensus among the major nations about the desirability of world government, as well as about the kind of world government they would accept is so obvious that any attempt to establish such a government today would be more likely to lead to war than to reduce enmity.

To the extent that enmity exists and cannot be eliminated at a given moment it would appear to dictate to the statesman a course of action that will often run counter to his moral preferences. Does this not mean that those exponents of *Realpolitik* are right who claim that the statesman, instead of being able to make moral choices, is left with virtually no leeway, having to bow to the dictates of the "necessity of state?"

It confuses the moral issue to state the case in this way. The "necessities" in international politics and for that matter in all spheres of life do not push decision and action beyond the realm of moral judgment; they rest on moral choice themselves. If a statesman decides that the dangers to the security of his country are so great that a course of action which must lead to war is necessary, he has placed an exceedingly high value on an increment of national security.

Necessities of a similar kind are known to private citizens. Parents may decide that in order to save the family business they must try to get their son to enter the family firm. Although they know that they are asking him to choose a career he abhors, they are ready to sacrifice his happiness to the "necessity of family." A trade union leader who calls a strike which he knows to be ruinous to patrons to whom he is devoted makes and requires a painful sacrifice for the "necessities" of the labor movement. In every such case conflict-

---

[12] Winston Churchill, *The Gathering Storm*, (Boston, Houghton Mifflin, 1948), p. 320, testifies admirably to these opportunities for statesmanship. He says "those who are prone by temperament and character to seek sharp and clear-cut solutions of difficult and obscure problems, who are ready to fight whenever some challenge comes from a foreign Power, have not always been right. On the other hand, those whose inclination is to bow their heads, to seek patiently and faithfully for peaceful compromise, are not always wrong. On the contrary, in the majority of instances they may be right, not only morally but from a practical standpoint. How many wars have been averted by patience and persisting good will!"

[13] Harold Nicolson, *The Congress of Vienna*, (London, Constable, 1946), p. 236.

ing values, interests and loyalties call for choices in which what is deemed to be the higher cause or value calls for submission to its necessities.

It is no play on words to say that the necessity or reason of state is but another of these necessities of life which become compelling only as a particular pattern of values is accepted. If the position of the statesman differs from that of private citizens it is because he must take upon himself the responsibility for sacrifices of value in order that others, as a nation, may protect or attain the things which they treasure. He may feel in duty bound to do so even though in a given instance he may disagree with the moral judgment of those to whom he is responsible. In that sense if in no other it may be justifiable to speak of the peculiar "demonic" quality of politics and public office, as Max Weber and other writers frequently do.

There is good reason why the controversy about the relationship between necessity of state and ethical standards should be rife in our culture. It points to a clash between two sets of ethical standards, one Christian or humanistic, the other nationalistic. Nationalistic ethics place what are called vital national interests—and not national survival only—at the very pinnacle of the hierarchy of values. The preservation or attainment of these values—territorial integrity, colonial possessions, *Lebensraum*, treaty rights or economic interests —are therefore assumed to justify the sacrifice of almost every other value whether it be life, generosity, humane treatment of others, truthfulness or obedience to the law. Especially, the interests of other nations count for little, if anything, on a nationalistic scale of values.

While those who adhere to non-perfectionist Christian or humanistic ethical views accept the fact that sacrifices of value are inescapable, as non-nation-

alists they may nevertheless, in the case of any policy decision, question whether a particular national interest is worth the sacrifices required or could not be protected by a less costly method. This may not seem to hold true when national survival itself is unquestionably at stake. It could properly be said that the multi-state system, since it rests on the co-existence of a multitude of independent states, is incompatible with any ethic which would forbid sacrifices necessary for national survival. Moral advice not to submit to the necessities of survival would not only be advice to commit national suicide but would tend to wreck the multi-state system itself.[14]

As a matter of fact, the controversy between exponents of nationalistic and non-nationalistic ethical standards in our culture is not over the moral right to pay the price of survival. None but the perfectionists or absolute pacifists deny a nation which is engaged in a life and

---

[14] It is not surprising that authors who believe that international politics is essentially a struggle for national survival should reach very pessimistic ethical conclusions. Thus, Nicholas J. Spykman, *America's Strategy in World Politics,* (New York, Harcourt Brace, 1942), bases his case on the proposition that "the struggle for power is identical with the struggle for survival" and that states can survive only by constant devotion to power politics. Although the use of power "should be constantly subjected to moral judgments" (p. 12), Spykman concludes that the "statesman can concern himself with values of justice, fairness and tolerance only to the extent that they contribute to or do not interfere with the power objective," meaning the quest for survival. In his further statement that the quest for power is not made for "the achievement of moral values" he is taking issue with those exponents of nationalistic ethics who place supreme moral value on national survival. See also in this connection Mortimer Adler's statement that "so long as national self-preservation remains the dominant end for which prudence must choose means, the principles of morality cannot be reconciled with the counsels of prudence" (*op. cit.,* p. 78).

death struggle the right to make and demand every sacrifice necessary for victory.

But this is not the same as saying that the non-perfectionist must capitulate before every alleged "necessity of state." Nations engaged in international politics are faced with the problem of survival only on rare occasions. How otherwise could it be explained that most of the nations which have attained independence in recent centuries have survived when surely most of them most of the time have been devoted to anything but an unrestrained quest for power? If ever any country did employ Machiavellian principles consciously and methodically it was Hitler's Germany, but with the result that she lost her independence as conclusively as few great nations have done.

As a rule, not survival but other "national interests" are at stake, such as the preservation of outlying bases and possessions, the protection of treaty rights, the restoration of national honor, or the maintenance of economic advantages. While it is a prerequisite of the system that nations attach a high if not the highest value to their survival, the same cannot be said of these other national interests. As a matter of fact, the moral dilemmas with which statesmen and their critics are constantly faced revolve around the question of whether in a given instance the defense or satisfaction of interests other than survival justify the costs in other values. Does the expropriation of American investments abroad, for instance, justify the choice of military intervention rather than of unpromising negotiation? Is it morally preferable to risk a loss of prestige with its possible dangerous consequences for the safety of the country rather than to insist on maintaining a position which threatens to provoke hostilities? In every case the interpretation of what constitutes a vital national interest and how much value should be attached to it is a moral question. It cannot be answered by reference to alleged amoral necessities inherent in international politics; it rests on value judgments.

Even national survival itself, it should be added, is a morally compelling necessity only as long as people attach supreme value to it. In that sense the multi-state system itself depends on a value pattern in which there is an element of nationalism. If at any time those who have the power to decide over the foreign policies of the major countries should come to attach higher value to the attainment of world government than to the preservation of independence, the psychological, though not necessarily all other practical, obstacles to world government would be removed.[15] Until that happens nations are likely to consent to all kinds of Machiavellian practices, however much they may abhor them, whenever they are convinced that their independence can be saved in no other way.

International politics offer some opportunities and temptations for immoral action on a vast and destructive scale; they tend to present themselves in the guise of "necessity of state." Statesmen in command of the machinery by which

[15] R. M. MacIver, *The Web of Government*, (New York, Macmillan, 1947), suggests that these basic value judgments may change as the old myths of national sovereignty and national interests lose their grip on people, while Arnold Toynbee, *A Study of History*, (New York and London, Oxford University Press, 1947), p. 299, passing moral judgment, denounces the "pagan worship of sovereign nation-states" calling it a monstrous product of the impact of parochialism on the Western Christian Church." See, in this connection, also Harold Lasswell, *World Politics and Personal Insecurity*, (New York and London, McGraw-Hill, 1935), who devotes Chapter XI, "In Quest of a Myth: The Problem of World Unity," to the problem of how, by the use of symbols, myths, and other practices, human value judgments might be changed in favor of world unity.

public opinion can be manipulated may make it appear as if they were acting for the sake of objectives to which the people attach high value when in fact they are out to serve material personal interests or to satisfy personal ambitions for power. Where men wield as much power as they do in international politics there is room for an infinite variety of abuses for which the "necessity of state" can serve as a convenient cloak. Then again, statesmen may sincerely believe that a particular course of action is dictated by vital national interests; but judged by non-nationalistic standards of ethics they may be placing undue value on certain interests of their people or underestimating the value of things not pertaining to their nation which their policy would sacrifice.

While this makes moral criticism and self-criticism imperative, the difficulties which stand in the way of their proper use in international politics need to be emphasized. If it is hard for statesmen to make proper moral choices, it is not any easier for others to do justice to their conduct of foreign policy.

It is a baffling task, almost exceeding human capacity, to compare the value of an increment of national security with the value of human lives, or the value of a continued period of peace with the risks of a more destructive war in the future. Yet the statesman is faced with even more exacting and truly terrifying problems. Forced to make his choices whenever a decision is called for, he may have to compare the value of an uncertain chance of greater security with only roughly predictable risks of conflict and destruction. It may be easy with hindsight, and years after the event, to condemn a statesman for having failed to maximize value; but it also becomes increasingly difficult as time goes on to do justice to the inevitable lack of knowledge and foresight under which the decision-maker labored at the time.

Yalta is a good example to illustrate this moral problem.[16]

The trouble about much of the moral condemnation of foreign policies and with much of the moral advice tendered to statesmen goes back to a lack of appreciation of the kind of knowledge required for proper and useful moral criticism in international affairs. From a non-perfectionist point of view the circumstances, however technical, have to be taken into consideration; moral conviction and high ideals, much as they are needed to guide moral judgment, cannot by themselves offer an answer. Nor is this true in international politics only. It needs some knowledge of economics to judge whether an industrialist is exploiting his workers; he may be paying the highest wages the traffic will bear. It needs psychological understanding to decide whether in a particular situation divorce represents morally the least evil choice.

Similarly, in international politics where the circumstances are no less involved and technical, moral convictions cannot tell what roads are open to a statesman under the specific conditions under which he is forced to act, nor can they reveal what the political consequences and therefore the relative costs in terms of value of any one of several courses of action are likely to be. Will an alliance provoke war or will the failure to make a commitment tempt an aggressor? Will an appeal to the United Nations in a given case help bring about a peaceful settlement or instead create graver tension, perhaps even going so far as to destroy the organization? Disarmament may be morally the best choice under one set of circumstances; it may be downright evil in another in which it would place a nation—and small na-

---

[16] See Rudolph A. Winnacker, "Yalta—Another Munich?" in *The Virginia Quarterly Review*, Vol. 24, No. 4 (Autumn, 1948), pp. 521–37.

tions dependent upon it for their security—at the mercy of an ambitious conqueror. The same holds true for all the other panaceas or devices so dear to the heart of those who are most quickly ready to give moral advice to policy-makers or to condemn them for their actions. In one context it may be right to offer concessions whereas in another it may constitute "appeasement" with all of its evil consequences.

There might seem to be one exception to the rule that no general principle can guide non-perfectionist moral judgment on all occasions. It might seem proper to assume that the "defensive" side is always right and that every action is justified and justified only if necessary for the protection and preservation of values already possessed. Unfortunately, while individuals can disprove their guilt if they can rightly claim to have acted in self-defense, the case of nations is far more complex. Neither the nation's self nor its possessions are clearly circumscribed. May a nation defend as its self and its possessions only its territorial integrity and independence, or does the right of self-defense cover a way of life, national honor, living space, prestige, colonial possessions and economic rights abroad? *Status quo* powers whose main concern is the preservation of the values they possess and therefore the defense of the established order are prone to blame all Machiavellianism on those nations that seek to bring about change, whether it be revison of treaties, revolution of the social order or liberation from foreign domination. Yet, the "offensive" side may have a valid case for insisting that it has a vital need for things withheld from it and may rightly value them to a point where any means of attaining them become morally justified. Those who refuse to make the sacrifices of change or who, having brought about an unjust distribution of possessions and power are unwilling to correct

it, may be guilty of provoking enmity and aggression. If the Moslems in India or the Zionists in Palestine resorted to violence, they were not defending an existing order but were seeking to establish new and independent national homes through changes in the existing order. They were not necessarily at fault merely because they wanted these changes so urgently or because they despaired of any means short of violence. The *beati possidentes* may be more peaceful and less inclined to initiate open hostility, but their guilt may lie in their self-righteous and blind devotion to the *status quo* or in the resentment which they evoke in others.

Despite the difficulties of doing justice to the statesman and of avoiding the pitfalls of politically dangerous as well as morally untenable condemnations, men who have non-perfectionist and non-nationalistic moral convictions dare not evade the task of moral judgment whether of their own political acts or of the acts of others. Where there is so much room for moral choices as there is in international politics and where the destiny of entire nations depends on these choices, attempts to evade, silence or ignore moral judgment merely play into the hands of those who relish the uncriticized use or abuse of their power. The Nazi leaders were helped by the climate of moral cynicism which prevailed in Germany. It made it easy for them to justify even the most brutal acts on the grounds of necessity of state or to glorify their freedom from any "decadent" moral inhibitions.

The world will not fail to suffer from the immoral acts of statesmen as of other men in the future as it has in the past, nor does it look as though nations would soon be freed from the bitter consequences of international enmity, or from the appalling sacrifices inflicted and justified in the name of national interest and survival. A single powerful government, engaged for whatever reasons, in a policy of aggression and aggrandizement may force all others into line with its Machiavellian practices, provided these others have the will to survive. In such cases moral exhortations and intentions will serve little unless the causes of such aggression and the dangers inherent in it are removed.

Yet international politics are not beyond the pale of non-nationalistic, non-perfectionist morality. Statesmen need not be fooling either themselves or others if they contend, as they frequently do, that in specific instances they have restrained their nation's quest for power; nor need they apologize if, on occasion they choose a conciliatory or even a generous course of action, though a more egotistical policy would promise more tangible national benefits. Despite the continued strength of nationalist sentiment in all parts of the world, there is no reason to assume that people value national benefits only. They often attach a great deal of value to a good record of international collaboration and at times applaud a leader who takes risks for the good will, the amity or the interests of other nations —or seeks to keep his own conscience and that of his people clear.

This explains why under certain circumstances a national government might receive the backing of its people even in sacrificing national independence itself, particularly if it were done for the purpose of establishing a better international order, perhaps a world-wide federation. From the point of view of non-nationalistic ethics such national self-sacrifice for world government might appear morally justified if there was assurance of enough amity and all-round consent to permit the establishment and functioning of an orderly and humane government of the world; it might be condemned if it led to world tyranny or world anarchy. There are historical instances when such sacrifice of independence has justified itself in the eyes of almost everybody, as when the thirteen American states federated successfully.

Under the circumstances usually prevailing in a multi-state system painful limitations are set on policies of self-negation, generosity or restraint of power. It would be utopian to expect drastic changes in this respect. But to say that the field of international politics is reserved for selfishness, brutality, self-righteousness or unrestrained ambition for power is not only cynical but manifestly unrealistic.

XXV · Ethics and International Relations

The ethical problem in international relations demands a larger focus: the world as a whole rather than a composite of states. Yet, what is most essential is often most elusive. While specific details of governmental policy-making procedures or complex organizational charts of international agencies may be difficult to master, they at least *can* be mastered and a great deal of "expertise" can be developed about them. Elaborate, awesome blueprints of incredibly complicated new weapons-systems may defy comprehension, but they no longer defy imagination, for they form part of the reality of the new military technology. The present age may best be thought of as the age of technique, when man learned more about *how* to do things than he had ever known before; there is more question about whether man yet knows *why* he does things. This epoch, which prides itself upon its rationality, is unfortunately characterized by profound confusion about the normative basis for the relations between men and nations.

Should the nation-state system prove to be an anachronism, as some believe, what would replace it? Mere realization of its inadequacy does not produce an acceptable or an adaptable alternative. Some evidence seems to point to the next phase as being one dominated by larger and larger units, first by the great multinational Super-Powers which with their allies and satellites are presently engaged in the "cold war," but later on by emerging regional groupings which, as they develop centers for decision-making, may become the new gargantua of world politics. Yet just as much evidence would seem to demonstrate that such new "region-states" would prove in many respects almost as unable to cope with overriding issues on a universal level as is the nation-state. Thus the fundamental problem facing 20th-century man lies beyond the realm of diplomacy based on states of any size or shape or composition; it lies in the discovery of a basis for world collaboration less sterile than fear and more substantive than hope; focused less on the prevention of a military holocaust and more on the creation of world order; less responsive to the demands of *Realpolitik* and more responsive to the satisfaction of human needs. The basic unit in international relations is not the state, but man. Whether the traditionalist likes it or not, the narrow restrictions of Victorian diplomacy have been broken, and whether the militarist likes it or not, there is more to diplomacy than von Clausewitz thought there was.

One of the leading Protestant theologians of the day, Emil Brunner, endeavors to discover the basis for the "moral postulates which might serve as a norm to govern international relations and international law." Social ethics differ from personal ethics because of the legitimate organizational demands of society and its multiplied agencies, and thus the policy-maker is bound by the values and goals of the state, a point already introduced by Wolfers in the preceding chapter. Since these involve the monopolization of the use and means of force, anyone who fails to recognize this "takes upon himself the consequences of anarchy." The norms Brunner suggests as the basis for an international ethos are the creation of an order of peace through law, abolition of war through the establishment of a lawful order "standing above the individual nations," surrender of national sovereignty to a higher unity which would limit both people and nation, and the combination of the negative quality of counteracting national egocentricity and the positive quality embodied in the idea of a community of people and states. In arguing that the formation of international relations should be recognized as a common task, Brunner rejects the competition of separately-determined foreign policies as the basis of world policy. Since they would probably not be followed, such principles would have no "direct practical significance," but "even if people and nation cynically ignore the principles they have accepted, or, what is worse, just mouth them hypocritically, the fact that they know them and have once professed acceptance of them has great importance in the long run." The first task, needless to say, would be to reach at least the stage where such a profession of acceptance could take place.

An entirely different approach to universal acceptance of a given norm is to convert men everywhere to a way of life for which this or that nation has preference, an ideological crusade on a world scale. Thus by self-extension or cultural imperialism an international ethos may presumably be created by the simple expedient of making one state's ethic the ethic of all. As Ernest Lefever explains, the dangers implicit in such a crusade are profound; it misunderstands the fundamental nature of the "cold war," which is a political, economic, diplomatic, and military struggle, and not merely an ideological one. Winning wars by converting millions to one state's point of view is beyond the competence of any government. It is because of what Lefever calls the "morally ambiguous nature of man" that international conflict cannot be removed by educational means. While it may not be true that one nation is just as good as another, the zeal of crusading tends to place one's own country in the role of the "good guy" against the "bad guys." Thus instead of promoting the development of an international ethos, such a program seems more likely to produce holy wars of a characteristically unlimited nature. Establishing a world Empire is not the same as establishing an internationally-determined standard for state behavior. Capitalist, Christians, and Communists have their separate convictions and none seems likely to prevail over the other.

A fairly similar perspective underlies the address by the Secretary-General of the United Nations before the combined Houses of Parliament in London. Pleading for reconciliation between the two protagonists in particular but other states as well, Dag Hammerskjold makes a case for private or "quiet" diplomacy through the facilities of international organization. The United Nations represents the natural and logical development from lines of thought and aspiration ever since "men first began to think about the decency and dignity of other men. Now the lines between national and international policy have begun to blur," the Swedish financier-statesman concludes, and "what is in the national interest, when truly seen, merges naturally into the international interest." Herein may lie the ultimate meaning of a "diplomacy of reconciliation," bearing within it the seeds of a viable international ethic and the foundations for world order.

Yet no world order can grow out of the present political climate, according to one of the most highly respected of American specialists on international relations, President Grayson Kirk of Columbia University. Expressing no interest in the "mechanics" of world order (for schemes for international federation provide only an outlet for missionary zeal and intellectual exercise), Kirk believes that there must be some sort of understanding among nations on the terms at least of coexistence with one another. The world must learn the lesson of the Sermon on the Mount, which this distinguished political scientist regards as being not "a pious exhortation but a categorical imperative."

While the spokesman for the state is bound to confine his approach, at least officially, to an essentially national ethic which limits his ability (and perhaps his capacity) to think in truly international terms, the student of international relations enjoys the unique, if perhaps somewhat unrealistic, position of the neutral, dispassionate observer. This is not to say that he should abandon his own love of country in his search for international understanding. All the authors would plead for, in concluding their study, is an outlook which—while based upon the realities of the often sordid and invariably selfish interaction of national policies—keeps the vision of a better world always before it. Mere analysis is not enough. But, as many would-be reformers of the world fail to perceive, sound analysis must precede and undergird any effort to improve world conditions.

1 • In Search of an International Ethos *

Emil Brunner

> *One of the most prominent theologians and Christian ethicists of our time, Emil Brunner is the author of numerous works. Among his books which have been published in America are* Christianity and Civilization *(1948–49),* The Divine Imperative *(1947), and* Justice and the Social Order *(1945).*

1. By an international ethos we mean moral postulates which might serve as a norm to govern international relations and international law. Thus we enter the sphere of a problem ... of social ethics. Social ethics differ from personal ethics inasmuch as they apply to collective groups and institutions and not to individual persons. Such collective groups and institutions are, of course, always represented and directed by individual persons, but these individuals are not free in their actions, but are bound by the goal of their respective institutions, and by the task they have undertaken within them. Thus the leader of a project, a school, a community or a state cannot do simply that which seems right to him, but he is bound by the task entrusted to him by his employers, or which he has received and undertaken according to the statute or law of the organization to which he belongs. It should not be said, however, that his own, personal will has been eliminated, and that his will becomes completely dependent upon the organization which gives him his particular task, but rather that the collective will essentially determines his. If a conflict arises between his own will and the will of the organization which has hired him, after vainly trying to persuade them that his own choice is the right one, he must choose either to resign, handing back the task to those who have given it to him, or else to act against his own personal judgment. As long as he remains in office, the will of those who have placed him there remains authoritative. It is precisely this point which distinguishes personal ethics from social ethics. First of all, therefore, a moral code should exist for organizations as such. In this connection we must above all be aware that institutions and organizations are determined by the respective goals and common wills which constitute the reason for their collective existence; the school is determined by the school's purpose, the community, the state by the state's purpose. It is evident that the ethical direction means something quite different here than it does in the sphere of individual persons.

Unfortunately most theological moralists are not clear about this fundamental distinction. The result is large-scale

* *Cross-Currents,* VIII (1958), 1-8. Reprinted by permission. The present article appeared in the monthly *Reformatio* (Zurich, Switzerland), August 1957.

confusion in which as a rule the real overall aims of a given institution or organization are not recognized, although this recognition is decisive. An undertaking must above all proceed so that it can attain the results desired; the school must conduct itself so as to correspond to the aims of the school, and the state so as to correspond to the aims of a nation. The question may well be asked: is this particular goal ethically justified? And under certain circumstances one may become convinced that the goal of a particular organization or institution cannot stand up against any ethical norm. Once one has, however, conceded the value of any particular goal, he is then obliged to give assent to other things which such a goal presupposes.

2. This is particularly true of the state and its end. Only anarchy denies the value of the goal of a state and with it of the state itself. Anyone who sees the state as a necessity, however, must see all things necessary for the state as equally necessary. Whatever else the state may be, it is first and foremost an organisation of coercive force. It can even be said that the fundamental aim of the state is to monopolize the use and the means of force, taking it out of the hands of individuals and substituting instead a primarily peaceful order. No state exists or can exist without coercive power. Anyone who does not recognize this fact must take upon himself the consequences of anarchy.

3. We ask now: what norms does Christian belief offer to collective groups? If we consult the bible, it is immediately apparent that it says very little on this problem. On the contrary it is almost entirely oriented to personal ethics. There are commandments relating to the head of the house as such, to the nobleman, to the knight, to the king, to the servant, the master and to slaves. But these ethical commands relating to social roles by no means constitute a social ethics.

4. Only one significant exception occurs in the New Testament, *Romans 13*, 1–7, where Paul speaks on the power of authority and on the duty of subjects. Because it is the one great exception, this section of the letter to the Romans takes an added importance.

a. The first line distinguishes clearly and unmistakably between personal and social ethics. Paul has spoken in the 12th chapter about love as the fundamental commandment for the members of the community. The chapter ends with the inculcation that the Christian should not offer resistance to evil nor seek to revenge himself. The teaching on authority follows directly after—we believe the authority he refers to is that of the state—and the duty to obey it. While the individual Christian is commanded to forego revenge and resistance as a self-evident expression of love, it is now expressly stated that in carrying out the command of God the state must offer resistance and take revenge. One may say indeed that *because* the state has taken over these activities, and indeed monopolized them, that the individual Christian is able to renounce resistance and revenge.

. . . .

d. Thus . . . Paul's social ethics—he uses the state as his example—differ from his personal ethics. While the entire ethics of the person can be summed up in the one word "love," principles of an entirely different sort determine social ethics which can be summed up in the phrase "aim of the thing." Indeed it is evident that it would be madness to command the state to love. "The state knows nothing of love" (Karl Barth). Love which does not repay or revenge would dissolve the state. The application of the commandment of love to the state is identical with anarchy.

e. These conclusions might make it appear that a dualism exists which threatens the unity of the person. One thing is asked of the Christian in his personal life and another is demanded of him as a subject in relation to the citizens of his state. Above both commandments, however, stands the will of God. The dualism is not the metaphysical dualism of the religion of Zarathustra, but it is the duality of *Aion hutos* and *Aion melloön*, of the preservation of the world and the salvation of the world. It is the same God who saves the world in Jesus Christ who preserves the world through others, through the state. Behind this duality, which is truly present for ethics and hence for the action of Christians, there stands a unity which ultimately removes the duality. It is the unity of the will of God in His desire to create and preserve and His will to save which has been revealed to us by Christ. This victory over dualism, which a Christian gains by indirectly subordinating the work of the state and his obedience to the state to the will of God, corresponds on the human side to the thought that the state must work for "the good." This is also the way in which Christian ethics must harmonize personal ethics and ethical forms for institutions and organizations. The Christian as citizen of a state, whether subject or statesman, must always keep in sight the end of the state, remembering that love which neither resists nor revenges is demanded of him as a person. At the same time, however, he knows that his obedience to this state must ultimately, if indirectly, serve love. The Christian then *always* stands under the command of God, but when it concerns his position in the state or his political activity, he knows that he is not to follow the command of love directly—if he did, the state would collapse—but he must keep in mind the end of the state, and then carry on politics which embody justice

in the order of reality. He may understand this task as a service to people and to all peoples, and finally even as (although indirect) obedience to the commandment of love.

f. It is evident that from this point, from the kingdom of God as it is understood in faith, even the end of the state takes on a breadth and a profundity in its expression of love. It is true in the sense of the words by Pestalozzi that instead of nationalizing humanity, it humanizes the state. The idea of the welfare state as an improvement over the mere constitutional state has its origin in the Christian idea of love as the highest goal.

At last we have found some ground on which, without illusion, we can pose the question of an international ethics. This freedom from illusion in posing the question is a prerequisite for having the voice of the church taken seriously by the world. Surely there are enough men who would improve the world, along the lines of our theme, who hand their phantastic-idealistic plans to those who must deal with them and who understandably ignore them. Our earlier conclusions show that we may not expect to find direct answers to our question in holy scripture. If the social-ethical problem of the state is treated directly as a theme in only one place in the bible, we cannot be surprised that the problem of international relations lies beyond the horizon of prophets and apostles. We must of necessity, then, take the indirect path of "extrapolations" and conclusions after the fact.

1. The first thing we must become aware of is the fact that the problem of regulating peoples as a whole is as far away as possible from the center of biblical revelation. His relation to civil force is always a practical question pressing upon every Christian because he must seek a way to unify his role as a subject or a citizen of a national state

with his Christian faith, and his obedience to his Lord Jesus Christ with his obedience to the civil power, and he must also decide just what he must hold back from the latter. (This is the problem of *Romans* 13, 1 ff.) The question of regulating populations is much farther removed from his own responsibility. On the other hand the Christian, like every man in his natural existence, is so directly threatened by chaos, that the absence of a real *order* among nations seems to him like a constant threat of war. He is, therefore, interested in order among nations at least and above all through a desire for peace. As a Christian, however, he has beyond this desire an especially serious moral concern, for he knows that war is the maximal contrast to the love which has been revealed to him by Jesus Christ as the essence of true life.

2. The basic essence of the state lies in its creation of a peaceful order through the monopolization of force. This thought is implicit in *Romans* 13. Killing and brutal force have been by-passed because the state has to some extent succeeded in seizing and maintaining a monopoly of coercive force, and also because it bound this force to the law. It succeeded, however, only in the course of struggles which lasted hundreds and even thousands of years. This point must be made clear, so that we may know what peace has cost and what it still costs. It is understandable, therefore, that hopes for world peace, when they are not simply vague sentimentalities, most frequently take on this form: hope for a world organization through which the use of force among nations could be bound by law, and which would in similar fashion by the monopolization of force establish an order of peace, even if it were imperfect peace. Instead of anarchic force it would substitute force bound to the law. Since this view corresponds to the logic of *Romans* 13, we

may say that this idea agrees with Christian thought. At the same time it can be understood independently of Christian faith. All peoples—whatever may be their religion—have understood and enthusiastically advocated the idea of a union of all nations; the creation of an order of peace through the law, abolition of war through the establishment of a lawful order standing above individual nations. This would be a first ethical postulate which, proceeding from the Christian west, could become a postulate of an international moral code.

3. This poses a second problem: the state as a servant of God cannot be its own end. No state, no people exist for their own sake. A supra-national order presupposes the self-limitation of the sovereignty of individual states. Surrender of the absolute value of the individual nation or state not only contradicts national egoism and the egocentrism of all peoples but it also opposes the ethics of those nations which have gone so far as to divinize their own state and people (cf. the Japanese state religion). The demand for the surrender of sovereignty of individual nations and states, therefore, can only be accomplished in a struggle with such a national or popular ethos. Despite this fact it is already clear today that this idea of a higher unity limiting both nation and people could already gain some footing not only among Christian nations but among all peoples, as it is a reversal of the facts of their experience, which even among the Christian peoples of the west is with difficulty set against their national egoism and egocentricity. The idea as a moral postulate is one that is not bound to any religion but can be grasped by human reason as an evident postulate. It belongs to an international ethos.

4. This limitation of sovereignty calls at the same time for the recognition of law in the supra-national realm. The

idea of international *law* not only corresponds to the natural wish for peace, it is an idea which is customary as well. Just as the individual in a particular state is bound by the law of his state and knows that he is so bound, so too are all people bound by the idea of international law and know themselves to be so bound even if such a law does not yet exist in fact.

The Christian, in his relation to the Christian Church, knows the basis of this bond. It lies precisely where the boundary of sovereignty lies: in the will of God whose servant the state is. This idea of universal law is one that can be grasped and accepted independently of Christian belief. It is the task of the Church to free this idea from its origin in faith, and make it valid as a moral idea conforming to the principle of cooperation with other believers and non-believers.

5. This limitation of national sovereignty has however a positive hypothesis: a community of people and states. This principle may not of course be grasped in the sense of a community that is final and perfect, for *such* a community can only exist "in Christ," and hence only under the hypothesis of Christian knowledge and Christian faith. On the other hand the idea of a family of nations is at least useful for people everywhere in its analogical resemblance to a natural family. If this idea strongly held also presupposed the Christian faith in creation—God, the creator of all men and peoples, God, the father of all mankind—whom man, split up into many religions and in part into an entirely unbelieving world, cannot claim as an actual possession of knowledge, then this idea of a community of nations, although it surely springs from biblical faith, can also be understood and affirmed by people all over the world who do not share this faith.

The idea of community which is cen-

tral to Christian belief and directly bound to the center of belief means that the individual parts of a whole are bound by destiny (for better or for worse) and solidly (so that the welfare of one involves that of the other, and the guilt of the other is also one's own). Applied to the problem of nations and states, this would mean a positive complement to the idea of limiting sovereignty. But its significance extends even further. It would mean for example, that even the guilt of any one nation, which in recent times has played such an enormous role, would never be seen merely as the guilt of an individual nation, but would be recognized as the common guilt of the others as well. Similarly the need of one would be made the need of the others. Above all, it would mean that the formation of international relations would be recognized as a *common task*. Thus would the idea of community lead on beyond the sterility of the legal point of view, without allowing itself to be labeled utopian.

These are, it seems to me, the principles which have historically and materially arisen from Christian faith, but which, once found, present universal rational evidence and hence are clear to non-believers and to those of different beliefs. There are, however, other moral postulates, equally rooted in Christian faith, and equally valid independently of that faith, which are of only indirect international significance. Besides, many of these postulates have already become the subject of international conversation and have even become a part of international *law*. They do not relate directly to the international conduct of nations and states, but they are of such a universal nature that they form the basis for a relation between the single individual and the single state as well for the interrelations of all people.

1. The idea of the dignity of the person, as someone to be respected for himself, regardless of the race, culture or social group to which he belongs. This idea has a double origin historically, in late Greek philosophy among the Stoics and in Judaeo-Christian belief. The reasons for human dignity are not the same in these two cases, but historically they have united into one stream which formed a foundation for the humanism of the West. The idea of the dignity of the person gained an entry into Asia and Africa in the nineteenth century with followers of the most diverse religions.

2. Even more significant historically is an idea derived from the previous one —that of human rights—which has been largely understood as rights of freedom independent of the law or the religion of any people, rights which should be recognized by states as "fundamental," unconditional and inalienable.

3. Further derived from human rights are the ideas of equality and freedom as moral postulates (not as metaphysical theories). These ideas, which stand in irreconcilable opposition to certain religions and national ideologies (e.g. caste systems) have nevertheless penetrated all nations and create everywhere the ferment of revolution to the extent that they are not rigidly defined or limited. The idea of freedom understood as *absolute* freedom necessarily leads to anarchy and consequently to self-destruction. It is therefore necessary to understand these ideas in the relative, limited meaning which they have in their Christian context. The Christian concepts of freedom and equality contain their limitation: man is free and all men are equal "in Christ." This explanation and this limitation is understandable only to faith, and so it cannot be made a constituent part of an international moral code. Understood as a universal moral principle, it must be stated: man is destined to freedom which is at the same time limited by the freedom of others— men are equal in their ultimate destiny, but unequal in respect to the different amount and different kind of ability they have to serve all the others.

The ideas of freedom and equality have both found entry today into all nations and act as dynamic forces for reorganization. One can say indeed that they are destructive ferments of revolution everywhere where they are not limited, and, on the other hand, constructive when their limitations have been clearly grasped: free for service, free from despotism and tyranny, equal *for* service, but not equal *in* service.

4. There is one idea, however, which has recently become a political slogan and has even been included in certain international legal documents which we must avoid as an extension of the idea of freedom which cannot be sanctioned by the Christian Church: self-determination of nations, which means that the idea of freedom in its unlimited form is carried over to collective groups instead of individuals. This principle ought rather to mean: self-determination of that nation which does not contradict the freedom of others, in other words a freedom which has a boundary determined by the freedom of others. Without this restriction and limitation the postulate of self-determination is nothing other than an invitation to world anarchy.

5. This last point has already indicated the danger that ethical postulates may take on the form of political principles and become ideologies of great power yet possessing doubtful ethical value. Slogans like "colonialism," "imperialism," even the idea of democracy, unless they are exactly defined and carefully circumscribed become slogans whose popularity and frequent usage stand in inverse proportion to their ethical clarity. The Church should refrain

from proposing them as postulates of an international moral code.

6. Let us conclude with a few thoughts of a general nature. The over-all agreement with the idea of human rights gives us two such ideas: First of all it proves how strong, one may even say how universal is the resonance which such ideas find with members of other religions and even with people who officially declare atheism to be the basis of their national system, despite the fact that these ideas unquestionably grew on Christian soil. On the other hand, history since the acceptance of human rights as the preamble of international law shows how little such agreement means when it touches upon the actions of peoples and nations.

Nothing could be more mistaken than to attribute a direct practical significance to the drawing up of an international ethos. But it would be disastrous to conclude that non-observance of such solemn principles would make them worthless and unworkable. Even if people and nations cynically ignore the principles they have accepted, or, what is worse, just mouth them hypocritically, the fact that they know them and have once professed acceptance of them has great importance in the long run. Ideas have power reaching out even over generations and over the group of leaders who have hypocritically or more or less superficially accepted them.

. . . .

2 • The Dangers of an Ideological Crusade *

Ernest Lefever

The author has been associated with the National Council of Churches and the Political Science Department of the University of Maryland. His interest in the moral and ethical aspects of foreign policy is reflected in his publications, which include Protestants and United States Foreign Policy: 1925–1954 *and the book from which the present excerpt is taken. At the present time, he is Foreign Relations Consultant to Senator Humphrey.*

. . . .

...proposals for launching a global psychological and ideological crusade have never been accepted by the State Department, the Congress, or the general public. This is a tribute to the good sense of the American people and their leaders. There are certain inescapable dangers in any aggressive national ide-

ology, especially for a nation such as the United States which believes in and practices government by popular consent.

Advocates of an officially-sponsored ideological offensive tend to overlook the

* *Ethics and United States Foreign Policy* (New York: Meridian Books, 1957), pp. 158–61. Reprinted by permission.

fact that ideology is but one element in the struggle between Soviet Communism and the free world and, what is more important, ideology is precisely the element which governments are least capable of dealing with. The Cold War, as far as foreign policy is concerned, is primarily a political, diplomatic, military, and economic struggle. Certainly ideas and loyalties are involved at every level of this struggle. But the objectives of a democratic foreign policy are and must be more modest than the objectives of national political religions such as Nazism and Communism. The central foreign policy goal of the United States today can be said to be the maintenance of our national independence, without war if possible, and the creation of an international climate where government by consent can flourish. In a vital conflict we would have to sacrifice the more inclusive values of this objective for the less inclusive values, because governments of nations have a primary moral responsibility for the security of their own people. "Winning the war in the minds of men" and "converting millions of people to our point of view" are lofty goals beyond the competence of any government. Dealing with the ultimate loyalty of men is essentially a religious and not a political question.

Proposals for a democratic ideology to counteract Communism embrace the rational-idealist illusion that to know the truth is to accept it. Religiously it can be said that the knowledge and acceptance of the Truth will make one free. Politically this is not true. We can preach the democratic gospel throughout the world, but it may have little impact on the ultimate loyalties of men, or even on their contingent political loyalties. Political loyalties are a product of many non-rational factors. Knowledge of the "democratic truth" alone will not insure that the possessor of that truth will become a democrat, much less a politically

effective one. Political allegiance is the product of one's economic status, one's political environment, and one's total culture as well as one's religious values. Furthermore, the proclamation of political truth does not insure that it will be enthroned; to prevail in the political world truth must be backed by power. Education, even democratic education, will not remove international conflict, because conflict is rooted in the morally ambiguous nature of man. Does this mean that we should stop extolling the virtues of democracy? Hardly. It means only that we should not expect too much from preaching democracy and should turn our major attention to practicing it, and to the pursuit of foreign policies which respect the legitimate interests of all nations even though some of them may be undemocratic.

Crusading national ideologies with sweeping objectives tend to be expressions of national self-righteousness, or at least of the self-righteousness of the ruling elite. As such they fail to acknowledge the partiality and one-sidedness of the "truth" they proclaim. No man or nation can know, much less proclaim, the whole truth. Every man and nation is a mixture of truth and falsehood, vice and virtue. The crusading nation, in order to combat the half truth of another, is tempted to absolutize its own partial truth, making the nation into a god and demanding that contingent political loyalties become absolute religious loyalties. To recognize the contingent and relative character of men and nations is not to fall into the trap of saying that one man or one nation is just as good as the other. There are significant moral differences between the Communist world and the free world which dare not be overlooked. But the enemy's vices and our virtues may not be so exaggerated that the struggle becomes a simple crusade of the "good guys" against the "bad guys."

The temptation to moral and political oversimplification in any crusading ideology tends to lead to "holy" and unlimited wars. We tend to adopt the mood and psychology of the relatively simple shooting war to the vastly more complex Cold War. In a shooting war the overwhelming tangible objective is military victory, which calls for the military surrender of the enemy. In the Cold War the black-and-white contrasts of a shooting war give way to the subtle grays of a complex and many-sided struggle in which good and evil cannot be so absolutely identified. In 1934 William Graham Sumner said: "If you want a war, nourish a doctrine. Doctrines are the most frightful tyrants to which men ever are subject, because doctrines get inside of a man's own reason and betray him against himself." One need not accept Sumner's moral distinction between doctrine and reason to acknowledge the basic political truth of his statement, made just after Hitler had come to power. National political religions tend to lead to unlimited wars; they oversimplify the political and moral differences between the opposing camps and inspire in the faithful a religious zeal, a determination to give their all in the holy crusade to enthrone Truth over Error, Good over Evil, "Christian democracy" over "atheistic Communism." Ideological wars become total struggles between politically organized systems of self-righteousness. Compromise, adjustment, and negotiation, which are the very heart of diplomacy, become treason. "Unconditional surrender" of the enemy becomes the only acceptable objective.

The United States entered World War I to "make the world safe for democracy," and fought it with crusading zeal. There was less of the crusading mood in World War II and more of the "mournful warrior" mood, although we still insisted upon "unconditional surrender." The Korean War, like World War II, saw a mixture of moods among the American people. The temptation to adopt a crusading attitude toward the Soviet Union and World Communism is still disquietingly alive in the United States. We have our advocates of a "holy war," ideological or military, or both. And there is always a minority of our people ready to rally to a crusade for a "Free World ideology." Under certain conditions this minority could become the decisive majority.

3 • The Vital Role of the United Nations in a Diplomacy of Reconciliation *

Dag Hammerskjold

The author was a Swedish civil servant and diplomat and in 1953 became Secretary-General of the United Nations, a post in which he has served with great effectiveness.

The pioneering work upon which the United Nations is engaged in international life owes much to those who, in these precincts of Westminster, generation after generation, sought to establish and apply the principles of orderly government in the life of the British nation.

Over the centuries your ancestors pioneered in the development of the parliamentary system, in the defence of human rights and in the techniques of peaceful adjustment of your institutions to the changing needs of peoples. In that process your kingdoms became united: borders within this island ceased to divide, and the individual interests of your different peoples were left to express themselves individually within a common framework. And then the principles which your nation had learned to apply were exported and transplanted throughout an empire, carrying with them the seeds of self-government and of the structure for a commonwealth of nations that is a unique achievement in the history of man.

Now that the cycle of growth can be seen within its perspective of several centuries, it is easier to see that it had to be a slow process, that a pragmatic development served your interests best, and that periods of conflict did not stop the process of growth. It is more difficult to study the conditions of growth for the United Nations in the same perspective and with the same detachment. As contemporaries we are apt to be too much swayed by the immediacy of danger and conflict and to lose sight of the positive responses that are also evoked by the underlying need for more effective world organization.

These developments come at a time when we are still far from being prepared for world community. It is because world community does not exist at a time when world interdependence has become a reality, that world organization has become a necessity as a bridge, which may help us to pass safely over this period of transition.

The United Nations, despite some formal resemblances, has none of the powers of a world government or parliament. It is a framework for diplomatic operations. The power of decision remains, in almost all cases, with the Member governments. Beset as we are

---

* The address from which these comments are excerpted was delivered at a meeting of both Houses of Parliament of the United Kingdom of Great Britain and Northern Ireland. *United Nations Review*, IV (1958), 6–10. Reprinted by permission.

with what often seem to us to be the truly desperate anxieties of our age, it is easy to be impatient with both the evident weaknesses of world organization as thus constituted and the new complexities of international relations which it reflects.

Some are tempted to seek a solution in constitutional reform which would turn the United Nations into a world authority enforcing the law upon the nations. While respecting the goal of those who advocate such a course, most of us would agree that the political realities with which we live, rooted as they are deep in the disparate histories and cultures of many peoples, make this course impracticable in the foreseeable future.

Others are tempted to go in the other direction. World organization sometimes seems to be more of an added complication than an agent helping to resolve the procession of harassing problems with which they are faced. So there is a natural temptation to direct policies and programs through familiar channels that avoid the interposition of world institutions and, in the short term, seem to be more manageable or to be more in accord with what are thought to be realistic politics. Such a course, if it were to be persisted in, would consign the United Nations to the fate suffered by the League of Nations.

AN INDISPENSABLE INSTRUMENT

I think most of us agree that between these two extremes lies the sensible and truly realistic course. We should recognize the United Nations for what it is —an admittedly imperfect but indispensable instrument of nations in working for a peaceful evolution toward a more just and secure world order. At this stage of human history, world organization has become necessary. The forces at work have also set the limits within which the power of world organization can develop at each step and beyond which progress, when the balance of forces so permits, will be possible only by processes of organic growth in the system of custom and law prevailing in the society of nations.

Since a universal collective security system which can enforce peace is not yet within reach, since the nations in the meantime are maintaining systems of alliance for collective self-defence against armed attack—as they are authorized to do under Article 51 of the Charter—what is the role the United Nations can and should play today and in the immediate future as a contribution to the national security and well-being of its Member States?

It seems to me that the Organization has a unique and vital role to play in this respect.

The present systems of alliance, reflecting as they do the prevailing balance of forces in the world, are, in the opinion of many, necessary expedients for a period of transition. But they do not lead directly toward solutions. To move toward solutions which will make the future of the nations more secure than it is today, we need to take whatever steps we can toward reducing the tensions and toward blunting the sharp edges of conflict.

I believe,...that, "if properly used, the United Nations can serve a diplomacy of reconciliation better than other instruments available to the Member States. All the varied interests and aspirations of the world meet in its precincts upon the common ground of the Charter. Conflicts may persist for long periods without an agreed solution, and groups of states may actively defend special and regional interests. Nevertheless, and in spite of temporary developments in the opposite direction under the influence of acute tension, the tendency in the United Nations is to wear away, or break down, differences, thus helping toward solutions which approach the common interest and application of the principles of the Charter."

It is quite true that the United Nations cannot assure even-handed justice in the settlement of disputes, mainly because it does not have power to enforce its recommendations. But what the United Nations can do, if wisely used, is to help us to move forward in the direction of that goal. A diplomacy of reconciliation—I use the term of the Charter—practiced under the Charter, must be guided toward the goal of justice, and it is not only a pious phrase. On the contrary, whatever success can be achieved in this direction would be the greatest contribution that could be made to the reality of national security for the Member States.

It is sometimes said that the system of one vote for one nation in the United Nations, and the consequent preponderance of votes by the middle and smaller powers, damages the usefulness of the United Nations for the purposes to which I have just referred. It is certainly not a perfect system, but is there any proposal for weighted voting that would not have even greater defects?

In any case, this criticism seems to reflect in part the illusion that the United Nations, because the form of its legislative process resembles a national government, is in fact like a government. Of course it is not. The General Assembly, for example, is not a parliament of elected members but a diplomatic meeting of delegates of Member States who represent governmental policies. These policies are subject to all the influences that would prevail in any case in international life, where all nations are sovereign but the minority of greater powers obviously exerts more influence than the majority of smaller powers.

It is also sometimes said that the representation in the United Nations of the nations of Asia and Africa, many of them newly independent, is out of proportion to their power and tends to exacerbate the many problems of transition in the relationship of these continents to the West, especially to Europe.

I believe a careful appraisal of the realities of our time would lead most of us to the opposite conclusion in both respects. In the United Nations we see reflected the political rebirth of Asia and the awakening of Africa. But the United Nations, of course, is in no sense a cause of these great changes. Indeed, the conscious policy of the United Kingdom has played a very large part indeed in the appearance upon the world scene of so many newly independent states. And I believe that the role of the United Nations, like the policy of your Government, in the evolution that has occurred over the past twelve years, has tended, on balance, to ameliorate rather than to exacerbate conflicts that would have occurred in any case.

THE USE OF PRIVATE DIPLOMACY

As to the future, a more effective and increasing use of the United Nations as a diplomatic instrument, in which the functions of debate and vote are used more frequently to further a diplomacy of reconciliation in the sense of the Charter rather than merely to score propaganda points, or to defend against them, offers the best hope, I believe, for a peaceful evolution in the relationship of Asia and Africa with the West, just as it should do in the relationships of the West with the communist countries.

Criticism has been directed against the great emphasis which I have in recent years put upon the adaptation of private diplomacy to the multilateral framework of the world organization in pursuit of the goals of the Charter. But whether you call it private diplomacy, or quiet diplomacy or something else, I believe it is in the interests of the Member States that we move in this direction.

I would not for a moment suggest that the functions of debate and vote do not have their essential place in world affairs today. Nor would I suggest that any step be taken that would retard the development of an increasingly influential role for a well-informed public opinion in the making of foreign policy. But the United Nations is subject to the same principles that apply to diplomacy in all its forms. Long experience has shown that negotiation in public alone does not produce results. If the United Nations is to serve as an increasingly effective instrument of negotiation, the principles and methods of traditional diplomacy need to be applied more fully alongside its public procedures.

. . . .

I believe that a greater use of private diplomacy in the work of the Security Council might also yield fruitful results. There is an unused paragraph in the United Nations Charter, Article 28, paragraph 2, which reads: "The Security Council shall hold periodic meetings at which each of its members may, if it so desires, be represented by a member of the government or by some other specially designated representative." In his commentary to Parliament at the time the Charter was being considered, the then Secretary of State for Foreign Affairs of the United Kingdom said of this paragraph, "It is by these meetings in particular that governments would be able to carry out the fourth purpose of the Organization." This fourth purpose is "to be a centre for harmonizing the actions of nations in the attainment of these common ends."

I do not suggest any move at this time to give formal effect to this paragraph, but I do think that its application from time to time to the negotiation of appropriate questions might contribute not only to the processes of conciliation but also toward developing in a new direction the important role that the Security Council is intended by the Charter to play in the task of peacemaking....

Those who fought here in these precincts in past centuries for the rights of men belonged to the world and not only to England. Across the earth many lands can fairly boast of such champions of freedom through the centuries. In this sense, the United Nations is not a new idea. It is here because of centuries of past struggle. It is the logical and natural development from lines of thought and aspiration going far back into all corners of the earth since a few men first began to think about the decency and dignity of other men.

Now the lines between national and international policy have begun to blur. What is in the national interest, when truly seen, merges naturally into the international interest.

I am reminded of a memorandum written in 1907 by Mr. Eyre Crowe for the British Foreign Office. He advised then that Britain's best safeguard for the future would be a national policy that is "so directed as to harmonize with the general desires and ideals common to all mankind, and more particularly that ... is closely identified with the primary and vital interests of a majority, or as many as possible, of the other nations."

This seems to me to be a policy—and a principle—which it would be both right and wise for all nations to seek to follow. It is, in effect, the policy and the principle of the United Nations Charter.

4 • Problems of World Order *

Grayson Kirk

A graduate of the University of Wisconsin, the author taught first at that University and moved to Columbia University in 1940. He has served with distinction in the Department of State, at the Dumbarton Oaks Conference, and at the San Francisco Conference to frame the United Nations Charter. He is the co-author of Contemporary International Relations *(1940) and the author of* The Study of International Relations *(1947). He is a frequent contributor to such journals as* Foreign Affairs, Political Science Quarterly, Yale Law Review, *and* The American Political Science Review. *Since 1953 he has been President of Columbia University.*

Let me say at the outset that I am not greatly interested in the mechanics of a world order. Schemes for international federation will continue to be hatched so long as there are men whose idealism is untarnished by familiarity with the lessons of history. Such schemes provide interesting intellectual exercise and a modern outlet for missionary zeal, but that is all. At our stage in the history of the state system, confronted by ... great changes in international affairs, changes brought on by the effects of the new technology, the new clash of warring ideologies, and the new level of mass aspirations, the only proper concern of sensible men is with the study of conditions that must be precedent to an improvement in international relations. We ought to be concerned, not with the requirements of a world order, but with the circumstances that will bring a *détente,* a relaxation of tension, a lessening of fear. No world order can grow in our present climate. If we have a more favorable climate, the problem of a world order will take care of itself.

Obviously, the first, and an ideal, requirement would be that all peoples live under governments that are freely of their own choosing, and that all governments refrain from ideological crusades or from the use of ideologies as a means of imperialist expansion. To say this is about as revealing as to hear a candidate for political office say that he stands on a platform of honesty and prosperity.

Ultimately, however, there must be some kind of mutual understanding among the nations on the terms of coexistence. It may be implicit and unrecognized in any document that can be filed in the archives, but the sense of it must be mutually understood. Undoubtedly, it will not be wholly to our liking because our first preference would be for the disappearance of communism, and our second preference would be for a Soviet Union restricted to its prewar

---

* From "Mass Aspirations and International Relations" in *The Changing Environment of International Relations* (Washington: The Brookings Institution, 1956), pp. 15–18. Reprinted by permission.

frontiers. Undoubtedly, it will not be to the full liking of the Soviet leaders because their ideological creed is based on the world-wide triumph of communism. But we must assume that both sides will shrink from a gigantic test of strength in order to make their most cherished aims prevail. Therefore, unless they drift into such a major conflict as a result of Soviet probing techniques in uncommitted countries, there must gradually develop some kind of mutual understanding between the Eastern and the Western worlds.

Any such trend has been greatly impeded by the legacies of the last war, notably the division of Germany, the dangerous tension in the Middle East, and the Southern Asian ferment among the masses, which could not fail to invite Soviet attention. Progress toward such an understanding has been aided by the stabilization of Western Europe, the continued prosperity of the United States, and a developing military situation that has reduced the likelihood of direct conflict. On balance, therefore, there seems little prospect of much mutual understanding between the two great clusters of opponents in the near future. Indeed, it will never come so long as the social and political instability in Asia and Africa remain such a lodestone for Soviet imperialism. But until it does come, it is futile to talk of world order.

The second requisite is better mutual understanding between the West and the non-Western peoples outside the Iron Curtain. We must learn to understand and accept the principle of Asian neutralism and, instead of trying to coerce or persuade these peoples into close association with us, we must do what we can to strengthen them in their chosen position so that they will not be drawn gradually into the Soviet orbit.

We shall succeed in accomplishing this objective only if we can build a more satisfactory cultural relationship with the peoples concerned. We must come to understand that there is no room in the modern world for Western feelings of superiority over the East or for Eastern superiority over the West. We must come to have a man-to-man and a nation-to-nation relationship as equals, laboring together in the endless task of enabling all men to gain for themselves the best life that human society is capable of providing. Brought up as we are in the traditions of education oriented toward Western Europe and our cultural heritage from Europe, we must now learn more of the East and its ancient culture. We know so little of these lands where men lived and wrote and built temples and speculated about the universe at a time when our lands were still savage and primitive.

It is my own feeling that we can do more to stem the Soviet advance in Asia through cultural collaboration and the fostering of mutual understanding than through economic and technical assistance. The one can be reciprocal and it builds a sense of mutuality and obligation. The other becomes too easily a donor-recipient relationship.

This is another way of saying that the foundations of any future world order are to be found in the minds of men, not merely the minds of their leaders but of the masses as well. These foundations will not be laid down by force because today the weaker nations are in some ways stronger than their strong neighbors. They can be courted by both antagonists, and their charms do not diminish with the passage of time. The foundations will not be laid down by money except in so far as its intelligent use will cause men to be more rational and less desperate in their choices. The foundations will begin to appear when, and only when, the men of different nations learn what the men of great democratic societies have already learned about each other, which is that their differences must be made less meaningful than their similarities, and that none can be safe or prosper except as all are safe and prosperous. This is the lesson of the shrunken globe. It is the lesson of the Sermon on the Mount. It is not a pious exhortation but a categorical imperative. It is the price not of contentment but of survival.

Index